THE
DARK SIDE
OF
THE EARTH

ALSO BY MIKHAIL ZYGAR

*War and Punishment: The Story of Russian Oppression
and Ukrainian Resistance*

The Empire Must Die: Russia's Revolutionary Collapse, 1900–1917

All the Kremlin's Men: Inside the Court of Vladimir Putin

THE
DARK SIDE
OF
THE EARTH

HOW THE SOVIET UNION COLLAPSED
BUT REMAINED

MIKHAIL ZYGAR

WEIDENFELD & NICOLSON

First published in the United States in 2025 by Scribner,
First published in Great Britain in 2025 by Weidenfeld & Nicolson,
an imprint of The Orion Publishing Group Ltd
Carmelite House, 50 Victoria Embankment
London EC4Y 0DZ

An Hachette UK Company

The authorised representative in the EEA is Hachette Ireland,
8 Castlecourt Centre, Dublin 15, D15 XTP3, Ireland (email: info@hbgi.ie)

1 3 5 7 9 10 8 6 4 2

A CIP catalogue record for this book is
available from the British Library.

ISBN (Hardback) 978 1 3996 0905 0
ISBN (Export Trade Paperback) 978 1 3987 1403 8
ISBN (eBook) 978 1 3996 0907 4
ISBN (Audio) 978 1 3996 0908 1

Interior design by Silverglass

Typeset by Input Data Services Ltd, Bridgwater, Somerset

Printed in Great Britain by Clays Ltd, Elcograf S.p.A.

www.weidenfeldandnicolson.co.uk
www.orionbooks.co.uk

CONTENTS

★

8

9

INTRODUCTION

1

Who won the Cold War?

All my life, I thought I knew the answer: The people who believed. Believed in democracy.

At the time, I was living in the Soviet Union and saw it from the inside—most Soviet citizens didn't believe in anything anymore. They had lost faith in the ideals of communism. And yet, there were those who truly believed that democracy was possible—even in the USSR. They fought for it, convinced that their struggle and their sacrifices were not in vain.

Now, thirty years later, I find myself asking the same question again. These days, I often hear a different theory: that the United States will eventually collapse just like the Soviet Union did—because people have lost faith in the "American religion" of liberal democracy.

The Soviet Union fell when belief in communism ran dry. The state no longer had the money or strength to continue spreading its ideology—either into the minds of its own children or across the world.

Has the same thing begun to happen to liberal democracy? Has a new ideology emerged in its place—this time from Russia—cynicism?

Thirty years ago, many Russians lost faith in anything at all and concluded that the simplest solution was not to believe in anything. If nothing matters, everything is allowed, and nothing is truly frightening.

Russian cynics love to suggest that the United States is destined to meet the same fate as the Soviet Union because even many Americans—especially their new leaders—seem more drawn to pragmatic cynicism than to liberal democracy.

This book is about the collapse of an empire that lost its values. And about those who still believe in democracy and fight to change the world.

The events described in this book mirror much of what's happening now in the United States and across the world—only in reverse.

And so, once again, I find myself asking: *Who really won the Cold War?*

2

The collapse of the Soviet Union was probably the first major story of my life. It played a huge role in shaping who I am.

I was a Soviet child. The USSR, with its culture and mythology, was my entire universe. I was four years old when perestroika began and ten when the Soviet Union fell apart. I believe that, during those years, I learned how the world worked and what people were truly like.

The dissolution of the USSR wasn't a painful experience for me—but I felt, with great sensitivity, all the transformations my country was going through.

"My country is the most beautiful because it's mine." That's what many children around the world think. But do people need to let go of that belief as they grow older? All my life, I've watched people who refuse to think otherwise—those who fight for the right to declare their country the greatest of all.

But for me, letting go of this myth was easy. Because even as a child, I heard the opposite: that my country was the worst, the embodiment of evil. First, I was astonished to discover that there were countless people on this planet who believed I lived on the dark side of the Earth while they lived on the light. That realization alone was enough for me to understand just how wrong both myths were.

Strangely enough, my values haven't changed a lot since I was six. I am still convinced that there are no great or lesser nations, no lands of either light or darkness. Nothing is flawless and pure simply because it is yours.

Even as a child, I understood that things were far more complicated. That humanity isn't split into just two halves, each considering itself good and the other evil. It is divided into countless small pieces. And within each of those societies, the number of myths and delusions is limitless.

Some people genuinely believe that certain nations are superior to others. Others think that nations have destinies or even distinct national characters.

I was six when, in school, I was told that the Russian people would lead the whole world toward a bright future and communism—because that's what Lenin had said. By the time I was ten, I had also heard that the Russian people were a "God-bearing nation," as Dostoevsky once wrote.

But doesn't every nation consider itself special, chosen, and superior to others? I asked myself.

I was surrounded by Armenians and Azerbaijanis—some of whom hated each other, while others, on the contrary, loved each other. There were Russians and Jews. Ukrainians. Lithuanians. By the time I turned ten, I hadn't yet met a single American or Chinese person—but I suspected they, too, believed they were the best.

By the age of ten, I had already figured out that all national stereotypes were nonsense.

At the same time, I was reading books that claimed Russia was a country meant to show the whole world how not to live—as the Russian philosopher Pyotr Chaadayev wrote in the nineteenth century. I also read in newspapers that Russians were supposedly a nation of slaves, destined to serve a tsar and doomed to live under dictatorship.

If every nation has its own destiny and predisposition for either freedom or tyranny, then what's wrong with the Koreans? ten-year-old me wondered. Do North Koreans really love dictatorship while South Koreans love democracy? Did God divide them along the 38th parallel? No, people did that.

But the most important realization for me as a child was this: the question "What is the meaning of life?"—and how a person answers it—defines everything.

In the USSR, the official answer was clear: the meaning of life was to serve—serve the state, the Communist Party, and the bright future ahead. "The public above the personal" was the motto of Soviet Young Pioneers. We, as children, were constantly given the same examples of Young Pioneer heroes who had "given their lives for the motherland." Dying in war—that was the highest ideal, the true meaning of life.

But before I even became a Young Pioneer, I learned that there was another world, where human life itself was the highest value. In that world, a person wasn't obligated to serve their government (or their homeland, or their people). There, the state existed for the individual, not the other way around.

"If each person did everything they could on their own little patch of land, how beautiful our Earth would be."—this quote from Chekhov was printed on every Soviet school diary when I started first grade. I wasn't sure what exactly Chekhov meant, but it seemed to me that this thought clearly contradicted the idea of duty, service, and self-sacrifice.

As a schoolboy, I became fascinated by the different meanings of life humanity had invented throughout history. The Christian Church, for instance, taught for centuries that the purpose of life was to prepare for death—because this life had nothing good to offer, and all the interesting things awaited in the afterlife.

It's a fairly standard formula that has appeared in many countries across many centuries: to live for the sake of one day dying for something. The only variation was the object of devotion—whether it was faith, the leader, or the fatherland.

During the Enlightenment, humanity came up with a different meaning of life: to live for the sake of living. Thomas Jefferson even coined a formula for it—"life, liberty, and the pursuit of happiness."

I was a teenager when this question seriously troubled me: What should one truly strive for—happiness or death?

It seemed to me that at that moment, the entire Soviet Union was intoxicated by the same question. After seventy years of living for death, Soviet society suddenly discovered the possibility of another path. And it caused a psychological revolution. The sense of duty was forgotten—people wanted to live for the present, to enjoy the moment, to experience happiness.

In childhood, perhaps it's easiest to ask the most difficult questions. And so I asked myself, *Is it even right to live for happiness?*

"Life is given to us only once, and it must be lived in such a way that there will be no tormenting regrets for wasted years"—this quote was memorized by every Soviet schoolchild. Its author, Nikolai Ostrovsky, was a boy who joined the front lines of the Russian Civil War at fourteen, was seriously wounded by sixteen, paralyzed by eighteen, and dead by thirty-two. His novel *How the Steel Was Tempered* was mandatory reading for all Soviet children—and was promptly forgotten after 1991.

Was it immoral to pursue happiness? Would such a life be nothing more than "wasted years"? I kept asking myself.

3

I wrote this book to clarify for myself the story of how the Soviet Union fell apart—to make sure that it all really happened, that it wasn't just something I dreamed up in childhood. To understand why the values that triumphed back then are now facing defeat.

It took me six years to write this book—just as long as perestroika lasted. The Soviet Union unraveled over those same years, and so did my own coming of age. For this book, I conducted several hundred interviews with people from vastly different generations.

I also wanted to be sure of something else: that many of the myths people believe today—whether they're Russian, Ukrainian, European, American, or Chinese—didn't exist since the dawn of time. Most of them emerged only a few decades ago, though they now seem eternal and unshakable.

While I was writing this book, the world changed all over again. The history of the Soviet collapse itself has been transformed: winners and losers have swapped places. From today's perspective, it seems the victors weren't the democrats after all, Gorbachev didn't manage to prevent a bloody civil war, and the Soviet conservatives now appear to be the true triumphalists.

But it's not just Russia or the former Soviet republics that look different now—the whole world has changed. Not long ago, it seemed the Cold War had ended. And yet, humanity hasn't been able to let it go. We never truly believed it was over. It turns out living under the shadow of a cold war is much easier.

But this book is not about politics. It is about people—villains and victims, heroes and bureaucrats, poets and soldiers. It is about the psychology of those living through turning points in history—about those who believe in living for death and those who live for happiness. About those who think the world is divided into two sides, light and dark. And about those who know that is not true at all.

SOVIET UNION
FROM 1961 TO 1991

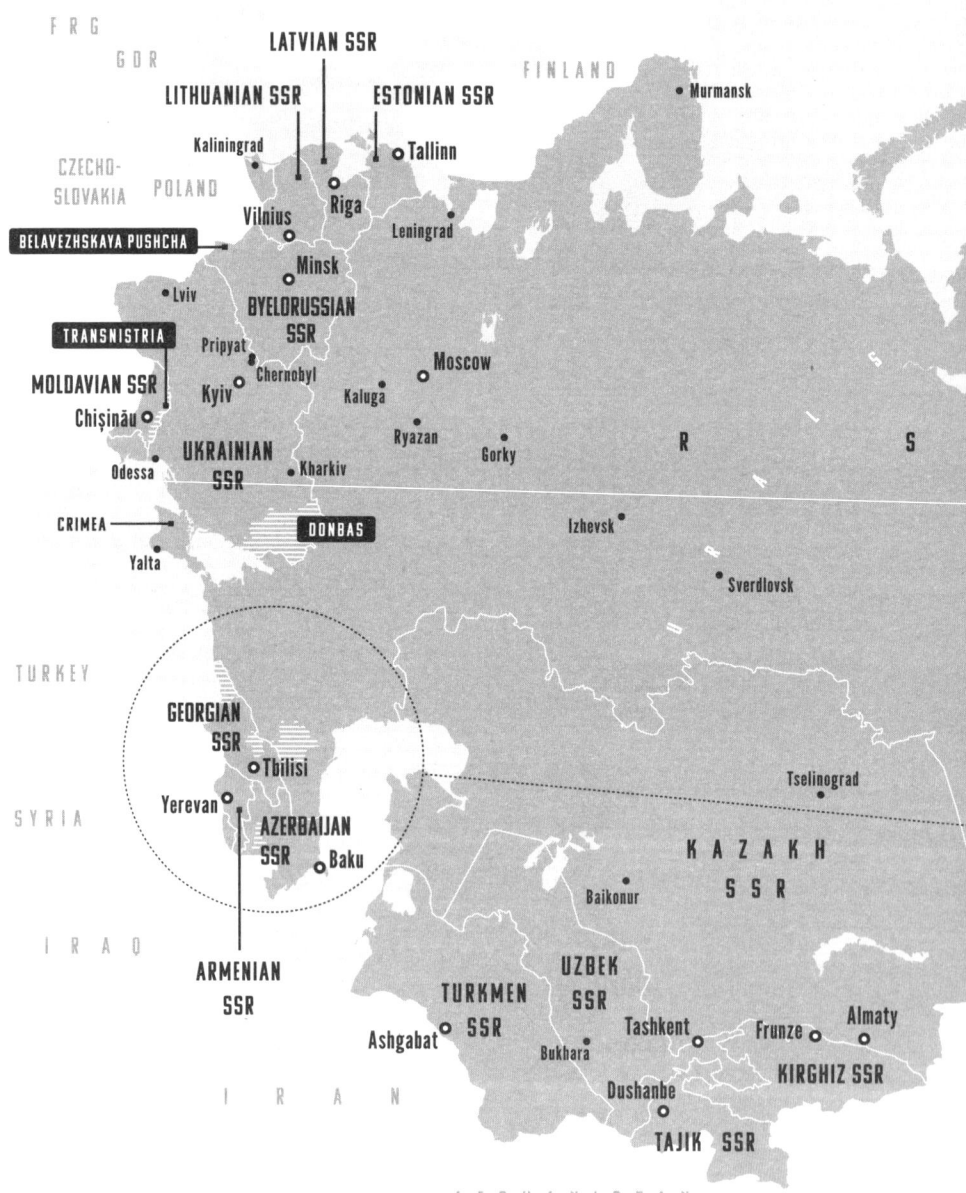

FRG

GDR

LATVIAN SSR

FINLAND

Murmansk

LITHUANIAN SSR

ESTONIAN SSR

CZECHO-
SLOVAKIA

POLAND

Kaliningrad

Tallinn

Vilnius

Riga

Leningrad

BELAVEZHSKAYA PUSHCHA

Minsk

Lviv

BYELORUSSIAN
SSR

TRANSNISTRIA

Pripyat

Moscow

Chernobyl

MOLDAVIAN SSR

Kyiv

Kaluga

Chişinău

Ryazan

UKRAINIAN
SSR

Gorky

R

S

Odessa

Kharkiv

CRIMEA

DONBAS

Izhevsk

Yalta

Sverdlovsk

TURKEY

GEORGIAN
SSR

Tbilisi

Tselinograd

SYRIA

Yerevan

AZERBAIJAN
SSR

Baku

K A Z A K H
S S R

Baikonur

I R A Q

ARMENIAN
SSR

UZBEK
SSR

Almaty

TURKMEN
SSR

Tashkent

Frunze

Ashgabat

Bukhara

KIRGHIZ SSR

I R A N

Dushanbe

TAJIK SSR

A F G H A N I S T A N

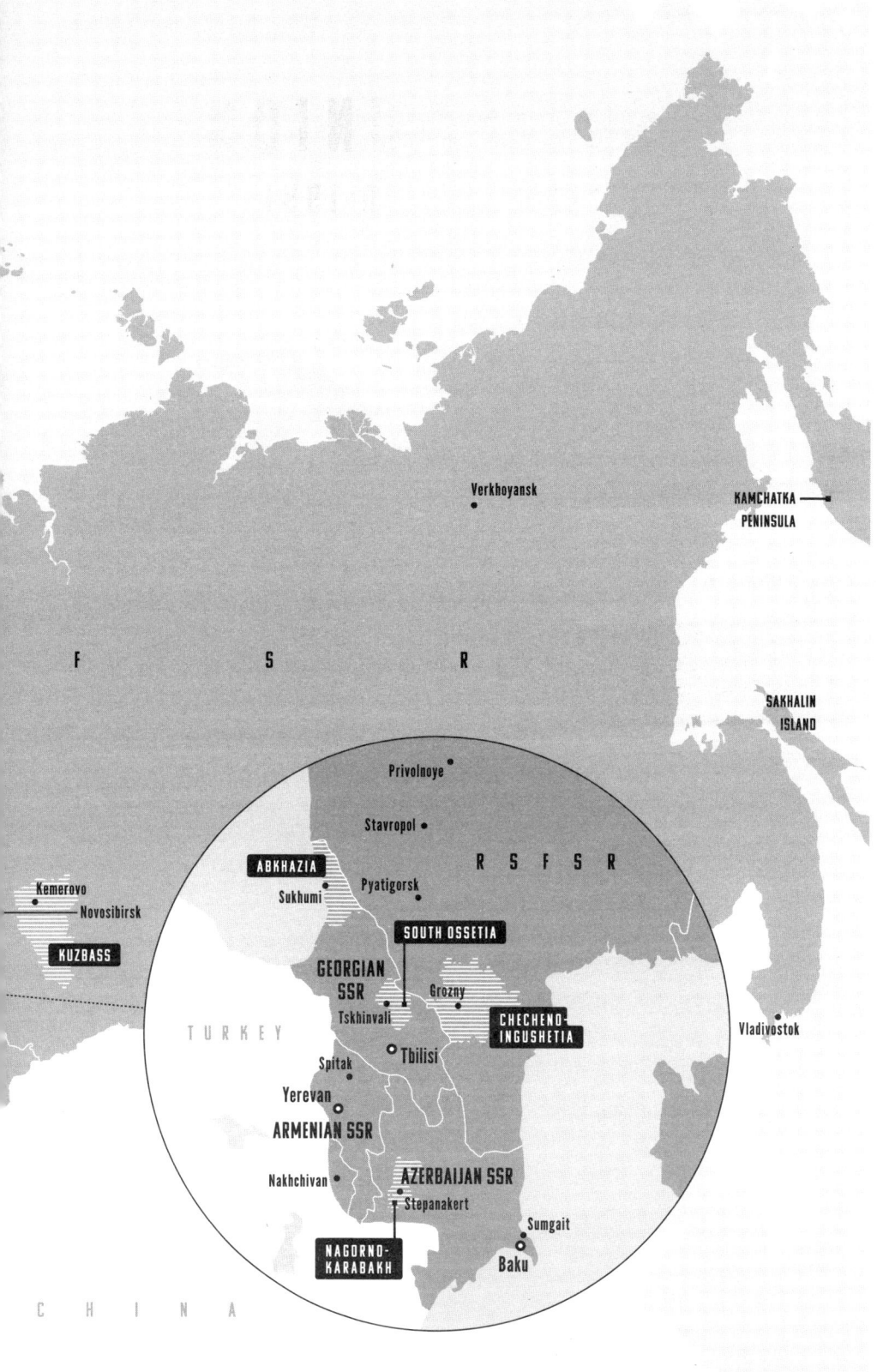

Verkhoyansk

KAMCHATKA
PENINSULA

SAKHALIN
ISLAND

F   S   R

Privolnoye

Stavropol

ABKHAZIA   R S F S R

Pyatigorsk

Sukhumi

SOUTH OSSETIA

Kemerovo   GEORGIAN
Novosibirsk   SSR   Grozny

KUZBASS   Tskhinvali   CHECHENO-
                                     INGUSHETIA   Vladivostok

TURKEY

Spitak   Tbilisi

Yerevan

ARMENIAN SSR

Nakhchivan   AZERBAIJAN SSR

                    Stepanakert

                              Sumgait

NAGORNO-
KARABAKH   Baku

C H I N A

UNFULFILLED HEROES

My father was born on the same day as Putin, in the same city—Leningrad. He also joined a judo club. Perhaps he was the quintessential teenager of his time.

But he never spoke to me about his childhood. And I think I understand why.

Many of his relatives died during the siege of Leningrad—like all the siblings of his father, my grandfather. What happened in Leningrad when the war ended? How did people feel when peace finally came? They don't write about that in books. But I have a sense that they drank. A lot. In the Soviet Union, drinking was a way to drown any kind of soul-crushing pain—but in Leningrad, it seemed especially so.

As a child, my father was often ill—he suffered from rheumatism. But he excelled at school, and one day, his math teacher brought him home with her. I can only guess what his parents, my grandparents, were doing at the time. But my father spent entire days solving math problems. And he kept going to his judo club, eventually earning the title of Master of Sport.

In high school, he won first the city math olympiad and then the all-Union one. His teacher, Eleonora Emilevna, was so proud of him. She said he had a brilliant future in science. Then, one day, recruiters from the security services came to the school. They told my father he could become a cryptographer— guaranteed admission to the KGB Higher School, no exams required. They might have said "like Alan Turing," but of course none of them had ever heard that name.

He agonized over the decision: on one hand, the dream of becoming a great scientist; on the other, an easy path, a stable future, no extra effort. In the end, he chose the simpler option. No need to strain, no need to prepare for university entrance exams.

I don't know how Eleonora Emilevna reacted. He never told me.

COUNTDOWN

On April 12, 1961, the Soviet Union begins its countdown: "Ten, nine, eight, seven . . ." On this day, from the steppes of Kazakhstan, the first human in history—the Soviet cosmonaut Yuri Gagarin—launches into space.*

Yet another countdown begins as well—only thirty years remain until the dissolution of the Soviet Union. Who could have imagined that just three decades would separate these two moments: the peak of the Soviet empire's greatest achievement and its collapse? Both events unfolded within the lifetime of a single generation.

Gagarin is twenty-seven years old. He spends less than two hours in orbit. The Soviet authorities do not announce the flight until he safely lands back on Earth.

After returning, Gagarin is taken to the nearest air-base command center where he waits for several hours—far longer than he spent in space—for a chance to speak with Soviet leader Nikita Khrushchev. Meanwhile, in Moscow, spontaneous and grand celebrations erupt around Red Square. The crowd refuses to disperse, and anyone named Yuri is hoisted up and cheered as if he were the hero.

For many of the characters in this book—and for millions of Soviet citizens—the first human flight into space will become one of the brightest and happiest memories of their lives. "Oh, how we rejoiced!" Raisa Gorbacheva would later recall. She is twenty-nine years old at the time, living in Stavropol and working on her dissertation.

"What was happening in the streets of Moscow. . . . An unorganized sea of people, feeling like it was the first day of victory in '45—standing tall, proud, and grand," wrote poet Yevgeny Yevtushenko, who is twenty-seven

---

* At the time, Kazakhstan was one of the fifteen republics of the Soviet Union—in terms of territory, slightly smaller than Alaska, Texas, and California combined; in terms of population, about the size of two Virginias.

at the time. For many in the USSR, it is the second truly joyous day of their lives—after the day the war ended.

Upon learning that the Russians had sent a man into space, Alan Shepard, who was set to become the first man in space, puts his head in his hands. He was ready to fly three weeks earlier, but chief engineer Wernher von Braun insisted on sending an unmanned ship first.

"The people of the United States share with the people of the Soviet Union their satisfaction for the safe flight of the astronaut in man's first venture into space," says President John F. Kennedy. Just a few months passed since his inauguration—when he delivered his famous "Ask not what your country can do for you, but what you can do for your country"—a phrase that any Soviet leader could have confidently said.

But in reality, not everyone in the Soviet Union is happy. Alexander Solzhenitsyn is forty-two years old, working as a physics and astronomy teacher at School No. 2 in the city of Ryazan. He has served time in the Gulag, been released and rehabilitated, and written several stories that he knows he will never be able to publish. He is far from proud of the space flight, seeing it as "pointless cosmic boasting amidst domestic ruin and poverty."

Gagarin, at twenty-seven, is perhaps the first hero of a new generation. He symbolizes a new, peaceful life.

When Gagarin goes into space, Mikhail Gorbachev is thirty years old. He heads the communist youth organization in his hometown of Stavropol in southern Russia. On that day, he leads a celebratory rally. He is married with a four-year-old daughter.

Andrei Sakharov is thirty-nine, already the inventor of the Soviet hydrogen bomb and an elected academician. He can even afford to publicly challenge Soviet leader Nikita Khrushchev, protesting against the arms race and confrontation with the United States.

Finally, eight-year-old Vladimir Putin goes to school and, in the evenings, fights bullies in his troubled neighborhood.

THE GIRL IN THE COAT

Twenty-nine-year-old Raisa Gorbacheva learns about Gagarin's flight into space while at work—she is teaching philosophy at the Stavropol Agricultural

Institute. After work, she rushes to pick up her four-year-old daughter from kindergarten, feeling so overjoyed, as if she has flown into space herself that day.

As a child, Raisa dreamed of becoming a sea captain, an explorer. She spent her days searching for treasure like the characters of her favorite book, Robert Louis Stevenson's *Treasure Island*, convinced she would find it.

Raisa Titarenko was born in Siberia to a family of politically repressed Ukrainians. Her grandfather, a peasant, was accused of being a Trotskyist—after that, he disappeared, and no one ever saw him again. Her grandmother died, according to Raisa, "from grief and hunger." No one in the family ever learned who Trotsky was or what her grandfather's crime had been, but all their property was confiscated.

Raisa always believed she had to excel in school to help her family, and she graduated with a gold medal, which allowed her to enter any Soviet university without exams. At seventeen, she decided to go to Moscow to study at the School of Philosophy at Moscow State University.

Her family was very poor. When she finished school, her father was able to buy her a coat for the first time—at the time, clothing in the USSR was a rare commodity. Raisa went to Moscow filled with absolute joy—she was traveling by train for the first time in her life, heading to the capital, with a coat, and the philosophy school ahead of her.

In Moscow, Raisa lived in a dormitory, sharing a room with nine other girls. They were often visited by boys: her roommates were courted by their fellow students Merab Mamardashvili and Yuri Levada. Decades later, Mamardashvili would become a renowned philosopher, and Levada would be known as the founder of Russian sociology. But at the time, none of the students could foresee this—just as they didn't know what Raisa Titarenko would become.

Soon Raisa caught the attention of a law student, twenty-year-old Mikhail Gorbachev—known as "Misha with the Order" among his friends. Back home in the Stavropol region, Gorbachev had worked as a combine operator while still in school. In the post-war Soviet Union, this was common—many men had died or were maimed on the fronts of World War II, so women and children often did all kinds of work in the post-war years. For his hard work, the teenage Misha received a state award—the Order of the Red Banner of Labor. This award, along with his silver medal for school, helped him get into university.

THE BOY AND THE BOMB

On the day the first human flies into space, Andrei Sakharov is thirty-nine years old. He is older than Gagarin. Yet he looks much younger—like a lanky youth in glasses, what we would now call a nerd.

He is a physics prodigy. At twenty-eight, he invented the hydrogen bomb—almost simultaneously with Americans Stanislaw Ulam and Edward Teller, but independently of them. At thirty-two, Sakharov was elected an academician. He instantly became the pride of Soviet science, a darling of the government, the highest-paid young scientist in the country, and a frequent guest at the Kremlin. An additional reason the authorities adore him is that he is Russian, whereas most of the star Soviet physicists are Jewish.

Sakharov is so absorbed in his work that he has yet to consider how many lives his creation might take.

In July 1961, Sakharov is once again invited to the Kremlin for a meeting between scientists and the head of the Soviet government, Nikita Khrushchev. During this session, the sixty-seven-year-old Soviet leader mentions that he has decided to resume nuclear weapons testing, which had been halted three years earlier. Sakharov is surprised and even writes a note to Khrushchev expressing his doubts—he believes that relations with the new American president, John F. Kennedy, are improving; after Gagarin's launch, the world already respects the USSR's scientific prowess, and further nuclear tests seem unnecessary.

Khrushchev reads the note and flies into a rage. He raises his glass—but instead of offering a toast, he launches into an angry tirade directed at the young Sakharov.

"Leave the politics to us; you just make your bombs, and we won't interfere—we'll even help. We have to conduct policy from a position of strength. There can be no other policy; our enemies understand no other language. We helped get Kennedy elected. You could say we put him in office last year. After that, I met Kennedy in Vienna. That meeting could have been a turning point. But what does Kennedy say? 'Don't put too many demands on me; don't put me in a vulnerable position. If I make too many concessions, they'll topple me!' Some boy! What the hell do we need him for? Why waste time talking to him? Sakharov, don't try to dictate to us politicians what we should do!"

The room falls silent. Sakharov does not dare to argue.

A few months later, the USSR and the United States move even closer to war. On Khrushchev's orders, the Berlin Wall is erected, and near the North Pole the USSR tests the Tsar Bomba—the most powerful explosive device in human history.

Physicist Sakharov forgets that reprimand and enthusiastically continues his research. He becomes concerned that in a nuclear war, a bomber carrying this bomb would not reach the United States. He proposes an alternative: delivering the massive nuclear charge to the US coast by submarine. In this scenario, coastal cities would be wiped out by a giant tsunami.

Sakharov shares his idea with a professional military man, a veteran of World War II, Rear Admiral Pyotr Fomin. Fomin is horrified by the "cannibalistic project" and replies that naval officers are accustomed to fighting armed enemies in open battle and that the very thought of mass murder is repugnant to him. Sakharov feels ashamed. He never discusses this project with anyone again.

SOVIET FAITH

At that moment, the Soviet Union is a country with a blurred memory. The approximately 216 million people living in the USSR hardly remember the past. A few historical myths are maintained at the state level, but, overall, there is little discussion of the nation's history. The Soviet Union is an invented, synthetic country that denies nearly everything that existed before its founding, and it has yet to reach its fortieth anniversary. Everyone knows that the Soviet Union is not only the greatest but also the most just country in the world.

Soviet ideology is more akin to a state religion. Soviet citizens are meant to believe not in heaven but in communism, to fear not hell but capitalism. The founder of the Soviet state, Vladimir Lenin, is revered as a prophet, and the Communist Party fulfills all the functions of a church. Lenin's Mausoleum on Red Square in Moscow looks almost like an Egyptian pyramid, and this is no coincidence.

The central, sacred event in Soviet history is the so-called Great October Socialist Revolution of 1917. The entire Soviet canon is built around veneration of this event, much like Christmas in Christianity or the Hijra in Islam.

November 7 (the day the revolution occurred according to the Gregorian calendar) is the most important holiday in the USSR.

However, how exactly the October Revolution happened is something Soviet textbooks typically gloss over—the revolution's real organizer, Leon Trotsky, is rarely mentioned, and all credit is mythically attributed to Lenin.

As for what came before the revolution, previous centuries have been almost entirely erased by Soviet authorities. In textbooks, this era is summed up by the ominous term "tsarism." The foundation of Soviet ideology is simple: under tsarism, life was terrible, and every Soviet citizen owes everything to the October Revolution.

Literature is perhaps the only remaining source of information about what Russia looked like in the nineteenth century and earlier. Few other traces remain: nearly all pre-Soviet traditions, cultural phenomena, holidays, and even national cuisine were obliterated in the first half of the twentieth century. Religion, which contradicted communist ideology, is almost entirely forgotten.

In the decades following the 1917 revolution, the Bolsheviks were guided by the principle of class struggle, which meant exterminating those populations deemed "hostile elements." This included nearly everyone with any form of education: urban intelligentsia, the clergy, and prosperous peasants.

Constant terror continued for the first twenty years of the Soviet Union's existence, peaking in 1937. Then came the Second World War. In 1939, Stalin and Hitler signed a nonaggression pact and divided Eastern Europe between them. Thus, for the first two years of World War II, the USSR was an ally of Nazi Germany. But in June 1941, the Third Reich invaded the Soviet Union—a moment that Soviet mythology marks as the start of the "Great Patriotic War." The first two years of the war were consistently omitted from Soviet history, as if they never happened.

In May 1945, Soviet troops captured Berlin. Victory in the war would become one of the main pillars of Soviet (and post-Soviet) history. The central mantra: Soviet soldiers saved the world from fascism (i.e., from death), and the world owes them eternal gratitude.

After the war, in 1945, at a meeting in Crimea, Soviet leader Joseph Stalin, British prime minister Winston Churchill, and American president Franklin Roosevelt divided the world—granting the Soviet Union its share: Eastern Europe, where pro-communist governments were installed. Soon after, the Cold War began—a global contest over whose system, Soviet or American, would prevail. Repression in the USSR resumed, this time targeting anyone suspected of sympathizing with the West.

The persistent terror led to a widespread silence within Soviet families—parents had long since stopped sharing their personal histories with their children to protect them. The connection between generations was often severed. "Regrettably, I know very little about my parents and other relatives," physicist Andrei Sakharov would later write in his memoir. Such mysteries, silences, and a lack of knowledge about one's parents were common for Soviet citizens of the twentieth century. And this applied not only to the intelligentsia. "They were silent about their lives," Vladimir Putin would similarly say of his own parents.

The Soviet Union of the 1960s is a genuinely new country, with little connection to previous Russian culture. The first generation of Soviet people, out of fear for their lives, repressed memories not only of their families but even of their own pasts. Lead designer of the Soviet space program Sergei Korolev, the man who would send Gagarin into space in 1961, had himself been arrested, interrogated, and tortured in 1938. In prison, his jaw was broken, and he nearly died of starvation in Kolyma, East Siberia. He was released in 1944 and rehabilitated in 1955 after Stalin's death.

Korolev's story is not unique—arrests, repression, torture, and executions touched many, though few speak of it. While Stalin's successor, Nikita Khrushchev, began the rehabilitation of the victims of Stalinist repression, much of it remained unspoken. Most Soviet citizens believe that their history must be something to be proud of, and they prefer not to recall the horrors. Gagarin, like the other young cosmonauts, knows nothing of the dark past of his mentor Korolev. The "Gagarin generation" has no idea on what kind of soil the new Soviet life is blooming.

HAPPY SOVIET FAMILY

For Misha Gorbachev and Raisa Titarenko, Moscow seemed to be a magical city, but Misha's classmate Zdeněk Mlynář, who came to study law from Czechoslovakia, felt differently.

"Moscow appeared to us as a huge village with wooden houses," Zdeněk would later recall. "There was a shortage of food. Five years after the war, people were still wearing old military uniforms, and most families crowded into a single room; pockets were picked in crowds; drunkards lay in the streets, and passersby stepped over them calmly and indifferently, not even checking if they were alive. But all this was understandable. We knew we were not coming to a consumer paradise. Five years after the war, no European country was materially prosperous. We explained Russia's poverty as war devastation. In the ability of the population to endure material hardship, we saw proof of the strength of the 'new Soviet man.'"

Two years after they met, in 1953, Mikhail and Raisa decided to marry. To save money for the wedding, Gorbachev went back to Stavropol in the summer to work as a combine operator. He managed to buy a dress for his bride—but he didn't have enough for shoes, so Raisa borrowed them from a friend.

The bride often fell ill—the scholarship money lasted only the first ten days of the month; she had no warm clothes, and no money for transport, so she often had to walk across the city to get to her classes. Raisa developed rheumatism, and frequent bouts of tonsillitis caused complications with her heart. After the wedding, she found out she was pregnant, but doctors warned her that she had little chance of surviving childbirth. The Gorbachevs had already decided to name their son Sergei but reluctantly agreed to have an abortion.

It was the first tragedy of their lives. After graduation, Mikhail was given a choice: either go to Siberia or return to his hometown of Stavropol in southern Russia to work in the prosecutor's office. Gorbachev chose to return home to care for his wife. Raisa, disheartened, agreed.

Stavropol was a relatively small town, and it soon became clear that there was no work for philosophy graduate Raisa. The top student who had graduated from school with a gold medal and university with honors struggled to accept that she was not needed.

In 1957, she gave birth to a daughter, and soon after, she was offered a teaching position at the agricultural institute, an offer she accepted without hesitation. This meant putting her daughter in day care, but the young mother could no longer bear staying at home; she was eager to work.

At the same time, she was accepted into a postgraduate program—another long-held dream. Raisa began working on her dissertation on the changing psychology of Soviet peasants. This required field research: wearing rubber boots, often wading knee-deep in mud, she walked from one neighboring village to another to interview local residents.

"When I went to the villages, and every fourth or fifth house turned out to be the home of a lonely woman, I saw with my own eyes these houses and these women," Raisa would later recall. "Women who had never known the joy of love or the happiness of motherhood. Women living out their days alone in old, crumbling homes that were also on their last legs."

During one of the interviews, according to Raisa, the conversation goes something like this:

"Sweetheart, why are you so thin?"
"Oh, no, I'm fine. . . ."
"You must not have a husband?"
"I do. . . ."
"He drinks, doesn't he?"
"No. . . ."
"Beats you?"
"What? No, of course not."
"Sweetheart, don't lie to me. I've lived a long life, and I know—
people don't wander door-to-door when everything's fine at home."

THE WRITER AND THE NOBEL PRIZE

In 1961, Alexander Solzhenitsyn is living in Ryazan, where he teaches physics and astronomy at a local school. However, this job is merely a cover; in reality, he is an underground writer. He writes books that he can only share with a handful of friends, as they are too dangerous for wider circulation.

For years, Solzhenitsyn has been convinced of his higher purpose: to tell the unvarnished truth about Stalin's labor camps. He is prepared to suffer for his art. The story Solzhenitsyn wants to tell the world is also his personal story. In 1945, while he was serving as an officer at the front, military censors intercepted a letter he had written to a fellow soldier. In it, the two of them critically discussed the Soviet system and referred to Stalin as "the kingpin."

Solzhenitsyn was taken straight from the front to Moscow's Lubyanka prison and sentenced to eight years for anti-state activities. There, he discovered the unimaginable scale of political imprisonment in the USSR and the hellish conditions in which prisoners lived—a hidden world he would later call the Gulag Archipelago, making it his mission to tell its story to the world.

In 1952, Solzhenitsyn was diagnosed with cancer. He underwent surgery in the camp. He then received news that his wife, Natasha Reshetovskaya, had divorced him.

In February 1953, Solzhenitsyn completed his eight-year sentence, but this did not mean freedom. After his release, he was sent into perpetual exile in a remote part of the USSR—Southern Kazakhstan, not far from where Gagarin would later launch into space. In March 1953, news came of Stalin's death. Solzhenitsyn was jubilant inside but knew he had to hide his feelings.

By the end of that year, Solzhenitsyn's health had deteriorated sharply. He was diagnosed with terminal cancer and given no chance of survival. "It was a terrifying moment in my life: death at the threshold of freedom and the loss of everything I had written, the very meaning of my life up to that point," he would later recall. His greatest concern was that there was no one to whom he could entrust his manuscripts: his mother had died, and his wife had remarried.

Solzhenitsyn was sent to spend his final days in a hospital in Tashkent. But somehow, he didn't die. This miraculous recovery solidified his belief that he had a higher purpose: God had saved him so that he could write all his books.

What followed was a series of miracles. Solzhenitsyn was rehabilitated, he moved to Ryazan, and his wife, Natasha, returned to him. He worked as a teacher but wrote passionately day and night.

Meanwhile, change was brewing in the USSR—the so-called Thaw. In 1956, Nikita Khrushchev delivered a speech at the 20th Party Congress condemning Stalin. Yet Solzhenitsyn still didn't believe it was safe for him to emerge from hiding.

In 1958, when legendary Russian poet and writer Boris Pasternak won the Nobel Prize in Literature, Solzhenitsyn, who had not yet published a single word, already knew: "I need that prize!" He needed it to fight against the USSR—to strengthen his position and make his voice heard worldwide.

However, Pasternak's life changed drastically after receiving the award. He was vilified by the entire Soviet propaganda machine. "Even a pig doesn't defile the place it eats, unlike Pasternak," said Soviet leader Nikita Khrushchev about his novel *Doctor Zhivago*. Pasternak was expelled from the Union of

Writers and threatened with criminal charges for treason. He was offered the chance to leave the USSR but chose to stay, rejecting the Nobel Prize.

Solzhenitsyn was baffled: Why did Pasternak yield to Soviet pressure? "I cringed with shame for him as if it were my own: how could he be frightened by mere newspaper scolding, how could he weaken before the threat of expulsion?" Solzhenitsyn would later reflect. "If called to battle, and in such excellent circumstances, one must go and serve Russia!" At this moment, he is certain that serving Russia means speaking the harsh truth about it.

Solzhenitsyn's plan was always simple: win the prize, go abroad, and, from the Nobel podium, tell the whole truth: "Hold out until the Nobel pulpit—and thunder!" For the young Solzhenitsyn, the fight against a criminal regime was the ultimate act of service to his homeland.

A year after Pasternak received the Nobel Prize, the seventy-year-old author was diagnosed with lung cancer. A few months later, in May 1960, Pasternak died.

BREAKING THE SILENCE

That very spring of 1961, as Gagarin flies into space, forty-two-year-old Solzhenitsyn falls into depression. He begins to doubt—what if his books are never published? What if a fire breaks out in his tiny apartment and all his manuscripts simply burn to ashes? "I became despondent: my carefully devised, silent, and invisible literary venture was hitting a dead end."

But at the end of the year, everything changes: the 22nd Party Congress convenes, where Khrushchev more boldly attacks Stalin. Moreover, the party leadership makes a symbolic decision: to rebury the dictator who lies alongside Lenin in the Mausoleum on Red Square. The congress participants vote for this unanimously. Most are in shock, but everyone understands that this is Khrushchev's idea, and they are not used to arguing with their superiors.

On the evening of October 31, Stalin is removed from the Mausoleum, where he had lain next to Lenin. As the coffin is sealed, some members of the government commission overseeing the reburial cannot hold back their sobs. Stalin is buried behind the Mausoleum, at the Kremlin Wall, among other members of the Soviet government.

After this, Solzhenitsyn suddenly feels that he might try to publish something from his works. In early November, he travels to Moscow, where he manages to obtain a samizdat copy of Ernest Hemingway's *For Whom the Bell Tolls* for three days—an underground, hand-typed reproduction, as Soviet censorship banned the book's official publication. This is a rare stroke of luck—he sits in his hotel room, reading the novel, tormented by doubts. In the end, he dares to send one of his short stories about life in the camps, titled "Sh-854," albeit in a softened version, to the magazine *Novy Mir* (New World).

Immediately after he sends the text, panic seizes him: "What have I done!—he thinks—I am in their hands again. How could I, driven by nothing, denounce myself!" Terrified, he rushes back home to Ryazan.

THE WRITER AND SUICIDE

Solzhenitsyn is deeply fond of Hemingway—one of his favorite authors. When he locks himself in his hotel room, reading *For Whom the Bell Tolls*, he already knows that the author of this book has recently died, though without any details.

Hemingway, in fact, shot himself just four months ago, in his home in Ketchum, Idaho—a few months after the first man had flown into space. The last months of Hemingway's life were poisoned by paranoia—at least so his loved ones believed. The writer was convinced he was being watched, that FBI agents were tapping his phone calls, reading his mail, and sifting through his trash. Friends and family saw his depression and delusions of persecution as a mental illness, and he was subjected to harsh electroconvulsive therapy. But it wasn't paranoia at all—Hemingway was right. The FBI had been surveilling him; agents had planted bugs in his home and even in the psychiatric clinic where he was being treated with electroshock. FBI director J. Edgar Hoover believed Hemingway was a Soviet spy.

Perhaps Hoover wasn't entirely wrong—Soviet archives confirm that the great writer had collaborated with Soviet intelligence back in the 1930s during the Spanish Civil War. But now, in 1961, all that was long in the past. Yet surveillance, mistrust from those close to him, and their belief in his madness drove the Nobel laureate to suicide.

Solzhenitsyn is also constantly looking over his shoulder, fearing surveillance, searches, and arrests. Having survived the Soviet camps, he knows all too well that his suspicions are justified. His impoverished life in a barrack in Ryazan is a paradise compared to the slave existence in the Gulag. At sixty-one, Hemingway felt his life was over, lonely, with nothing left to write. At forty-three, Solzhenitsyn had yet to write or publish anything, but he lives with the belief that everything is still ahead of him.

Shortly after Solzhenitsyn's return from Moscow to Ryazan in November 1961, he receives a telegram from the editorial office of the magazine *Novy Mir*. His text had reached the hands of the editor in chief, poet Alexander Tvardovsky. Impressed, Tvardovsky tracks down the author, invites him to Moscow, promises to publish his story "Sh-854" under the title "One Day in the Life of Ivan Denisovich," signs a contract with Solzhenitsyn, and demands more works.

However, Tvardovsky understands the challenges of publishing such a story. While Soviet leader Nikita Khrushchev had already denounced Stalin and exposed his crimes, not a single literary work about the Great Terror had been published in the USSR. Everyone is still afraid.

Tvardovsky hesitates for almost a year before finally handing the manuscript to Khrushchev himself in July 1962. Khrushchev doesn't read books himself but enjoys having them read aloud to him. He likes the story.

In October 1962, Khrushchev summons Tvardovsky. At that exact moment, Soviet nuclear missiles are being deployed in Cuba, and Americans find out. The world is on the brink of nuclear war. Yet Khrushchev sits calmly in his Kremlin office discussing prose. He allows Tvardovsky to publish Solzhenitsyn's story, thereby sparking a revolution in Russian literature.

Solzhenitsyn is accepted into the Union of Writers, meaning he no longer has to work as a schoolteacher to make ends meet; he can earn a living from his writing. In 1963, he is even nominated for the Lenin Prize. A special committee debates the award. Among those given a say is the second Soviet cosmonaut and Gagarin's backup, Gherman Titov—who, for some reason, is also part of the committee that awards literary prizes.

"I don't know; maybe for the older generation, the memory of these injustices is so vivid and painful, but I'll say that for me personally and my peers, it doesn't hold the same significance," twenty-eight-year-old Titov says with an innocent smile during the discussion of the nominees. It turns out that Khrushchev's personal favor isn't enough; too many Stalinists remain among officials and writers. Solzhenitsyn is left without the prize.

THE OTHER SIDE OF THE IRON CURTAIN

In the 1960s, the Soviet Union's global reputation undergoes a dramatic transformation. Once seen as a terrifying, closed-off totalitarian state, it now appears in a completely new light. The new face of the USSR is Yuri Gagarin, who travels the world, dines at Buckingham Palace with the queen, gets hugs from Fidel Castro and Che Guevara in Cuba, and receives kisses from Italian diva Gina Lollobrigida at the Moscow Film Festival. He speaks at the United Nations, receives ovations from crowds in India, Brazil, Japan, Canada, France, and Egypt.

Following Gagarin's flight, the Soviet Union sets two more space records: in 1963, Valentina Tereshkova becomes the first woman in orbit, and in 1965, Alexei Leonov makes the first-ever spacewalk.

The world is also witnessing a wave of decolonization: in just a decade, nearly all African countries gain independence. The USSR actively supports these newly formed African states, being among the first to recognize their independence and send specialists.

The anti-colonial rhetoric dominating Soviet propaganda conveniently ignores the fact that the USSR itself is a colonial empire. According to Soviet ideology, however, the republics within the USSR are not colonies but supposedly voluntarily united territories. Meanwhile, the government pursues classic colonial policies: Russification and the persecution of local dissidents. Yet this fact remains almost entirely unknown in the West— where the USSR appears uniform and monolithic.

The Soviet Union has many admirers. One of them is Jean-Paul Sartre, arguably the most influential philosopher in the world. He first visits the USSR shortly after Stalin's death, in 1954. His first trip lasts a month—and it's a nightmare. He's made to drink vodka and Georgian wine daily, shuffled around various landmarks, and constantly surrounded by officials. By the end of the trip, Sartre collapses with a hypertensive crisis.

However, upon returning home, Sartre declares in interviews that there is complete freedom in the USSR and confidently predicts that in ten years the Soviet Union will economically surpass France: "I saw people who were brave and full of hope, driven to build a better world for themselves and their children—people against whom war is impossible, with whom only friendship is possible."

Moreover, Sartre fiercely argues with anyone who claims the USSR is a dictatorship marked by repression and violence. In 1964, Sartre is awarded the Nobel Prize in Literature, which he refuses. In his letter of explanation, he accuses the Nobel Committee of political bias, citing the award given to "anti-Soviet" Boris Pasternak rather than the USSR's top novelist, Mikhail Sholokhov.

Just a year later, shocked by Sartre's actions, the Nobel Committee awards the prize to Mikhail Sholokhov.

Sartre will visit the USSR eleven times. He meets with members of the writers' union and travels across Soviet republics, visiting Ukraine, Georgia, Armenia, Estonia, and Lithuania. At home, he passionately supports Algerian independence from France and is willing to criticize his homeland for colonialism but sees nothing similar in the USSR.

And Sartre is far from being unique. Western writers and intellectuals are frequent guests in Moscow. The Soviet system finds sympathizers in Bertrand Russell, Arthur Miller, John Steinbeck, and Heinrich Böll. At a time when the United States is waging an aggressive war in Vietnam while the Soviet Union attacks no one, supporting the Eastern Bloc is seen as fashionable.

A DRUNK THUG IN THE TRAIN CAR

In October 1964, something extraordinary happens in the Soviet Union. The ruling elite decides to challenge their leader, Nikita Khrushchev. This event is often called a coup in Soviet history, but in reality, it's probably the most democratic transfer of power in the USSR's entire existence.

Khrushchev returns from vacation, only to be met at the airport and driven straight to the Kremlin for a Politburo meeting. His colleagues, once sycophantic, are ready: one by one, they criticize Khrushchev for his impulsive and authoritarian management style and vote for his removal.

Khrushchev, who has won so many internal battles in his life, decides not to resist. He accepts his defeat and retreats to a dacha outside Moscow, where he will spend the next seven years.

The Soviet intelligentsia celebrates Khrushchev's fall. Yes, he fought against Stalin, but by the end of his rule, he had turned into a quarrelsome autocrat—so no one really mourns him. Instead, there is cautious hope for the new, younger leader, Leonid Brezhnev.

After Khrushchev's ousting, the honeymoon between Solzhenitsyn and the Soviet authorities ends. Most of Solzhenitsyn's works still cannot be published; they are not just anti-Stalinist but genuinely anti-Soviet. The writer doesn't forget his habits from the camps. For instance, he hides his archives, fearing searches, arrests, and the destruction of his work.

On the eve of New Year 1965, Solzhenitsyn is traveling by train, carrying his manuscripts in a suitcase—deciding it's inconvenient to store them in Ryazan and planning to re-hide them in Moscow. Suddenly, a drunken hooligan bursts into the carriage, mocking the passengers. "None of the men opposed him," Solzhenitsyn recalls, "some were too old, others too cautious. It was natural for me to jump up. . . . But the cherished suitcase with all the manuscripts lay at our feet, and I didn't dare: after the fight, I would inevitably be taken to the police, at least as a witness. . . . It would be a typically Russian story for my cunning threads to snap over such a lout. So, to fulfill my Russian duty, I had to have un-Russian restraint. I shamefully, cowardly sat there, eyes lowered at the women's reproach that we were not men."

It's worth noting that Solzhenitsyn, who has a knack for dividing everything in the world into "Russian" and "un-Russian," writes in a very peculiar language. He constantly invents words, stylizing them to resemble some ancient, original Old Russian speech. This nuance is often lost in translation, but in Russian, Solzhenitsyn sounds oddly off—his desperate attempts to be quintessentially Russian often come across as unintentionally comical.

After Khrushchev's fall, Stalinists in the Politburo gain strength, and in 1965, they ramp up arrests of dissidents. The first targets are two writers, Andrei Sinyavsky and Yuly Daniel, who smuggle their works abroad and publish them under pseudonyms. In the fall of 1965, they are exposed and put on trial.

Later poet Yevgeny Yevtushenko would tell a strange story: that during their meeting in New York, Robert Kennedy, hiding in the bathroom with the water running, confided to him that the CIA had deliberately tipped off the KGB about Sinyavsky and Daniel to divert world attention from Vietnam. Soviet dissidents would consider this theory nonsense, chalking it up to Yevtushenko's wild imagination.

The show trial of the two writers becomes a major scandal. Global literary stars like Arthur Miller, Graham Greene, Iris Murdoch, Heinrich Böll, and Günter Grass publicly defend them. Sartre doesn't react to the trial at all.

The newly minted Nobel laureate Mikhail Sholokhov delivers a savage speech about the accused writers at the Communist Party Congress: "Had these scoundrels with their black consciences been caught in those memorable 1920s, when justice wasn't bound by strictly defined criminal code articles but guided by revolutionary conscience . . ." (The hall applauds. . . .)

Everyone gets the point of Sholokhov's joke—he means that during the Red Terror, they would have been shot on the spot.

Solzhenitsyn remains free, but during a search at an acquaintance's apartment, his archive is seized, and part of his unpublished works fall into KGB hands. It's a crushing blow—worse than arrest:

"The main blow was that I had gone through the full camp school—and still ended up stupid and defenseless. . . . For 18 years, I had been weaving my underground literature, testing the strength of every thread; the plan seemed grand; another decade, and I'd be ready to present everything I'd written, and in the explosion of that literary bomb, it wouldn't matter if I burned up myself; but then one slip, one misstep, and the entire plan, the work of a lifetime, was wrecked."

Now Solzhenitsyn throws himself into his work on *The Gulag Archipelago* with doubled energy. It's not even a novel—it's a colossal nonfiction work at the intersection of journalism and literature. Hundreds of former inmates of Stalin's camps send him their stories, and he weaves them into a literary memorial to the victims. No one knows about this work except his wife and a few assistants who help type the pages. He now takes every precaution: multiple copies, each safely hidden in different locations.

Meanwhile, Sartre travels to the USSR and expresses a desire to meet Solzhenitsyn. The latter walks up to the restaurant doors, where the French writer is already seated, just to explain to his interpreter why he is refusing the meeting: "What kind of meeting between writers can there be when one of them has his mouth gagged and his hands tied behind his back?"

In 1967, Solzhenitsyn has important new acquaintance. He learns that the renowned Soviet cellist Mstislav Rostropovich is coming to Ryazan for a concert. Usually, the writer doesn't like to be distracted from his work, but this time he decides to buy a ticket.

Rostropovich is told that the now-disgraced writer is in the audience. Eager to meet the author of *One Day in the Life of Ivan Denisovich*, the next day the musician finds out his address in Ryazan and pays him a visit. Solzhenitsyn and Rostropovich talk all morning and agree to meet again in Moscow. This encounter will significantly impact the lives of both men.

SHADOWS OF FORGOTTEN ANCESTORS

On September 4, 1965, an important premiere takes place at the Ukraina movie theater in Kyiv—the film *Shadows of Forgotten Ancestors* by director Sergei Parajanov.

Before the screening, the filmmaker delivers a brief speech about the bureaucratic obstacles he had to overcome—an already unusual introduction for the Soviet Union. Afterward, the audience presents flowers to the film crew, and thirty-four-year-old journalist Ivan Dziuba, after handing his bouquet to the costume designer, suddenly steps up to the microphone.

"Right now, mass political arrests of Ukrainian intellectuals and young people are taking place in Kyiv, Lviv, and other cities. The youth must protest," he begins.

Of course, Ukrainian officials, eager not to lag behind Moscow, have begun cracking down on their own dissidents in the wake of the Sinyavsky-Daniel trial. Dziuba starts reading out names, but the cinema director snatches the microphone from him. Someone in the audience shouts, "Provocation!" Music starts playing.

Two young men jump to their feet—critic Vyacheslav Chornovil and poet Vasyl Stus, both twenty-seven years old. Chornovil shouts, "Whoever opposes political repression, stand up!" In the vast eight-hundred-seat hall, about fifty to sixty people rise.

At that moment, the lights go out, and the screening begins. The film—what Parajanov himself calls a "poetic drama"—is an adaptation of the novel by the legendary Ukrainian writer Mikhaylo Kotsyubynsky, a kind of *Romeo and Juliet* set in the Ukrainian Carpathians. It is in Ukrainian—an unusual choice in the USSR, where most films are released in Russian.

After the screening the audience quietly disperses. The KGB does not detain anyone. No one foresees the catastrophe to come.

The consequences come swiftly. Dziuba and Chornovil are fired from their jobs, and Stus is expelled from graduate school. Even Parajanov faces problems—his next film, *Kyiv Frescoes*, which is already in production, is shut down. This despite the fact that *Shadows of Forgotten Ancestors* is about to win numerous awards at international film festivals.

Sergei Parajanov is forty-one years old. An Armenian born and raised in Georgia, he studied in Moscow before being assigned to Kyiv after film school. He has lived in Ukraine for thirteen years, immersing himself in folk culture and forming close ties with local artists. His first films were mediocre Soviet socialist realism: formulaic Soviet heroes reeducating wayward comrades. But in 1964, he suddenly changed everything—creating a film that was defiantly aesthetic, poetic, and unlike anything typically Soviet.

Parajanov also has a secret. He is gay. In the Soviet Union, this is a criminal offense. In his youth, his sexuality had already caused him problems. In 1948, when anti-cosmopolitan purges swept the USSR, including Georgia, one of the victims was a state security officer—the head of Georgia's cultural exchange society, and Parajanov's former lover. The authorities opened a criminal case against everyone the accused named, including twenty-four-year-old Parajanov, who was still a student at the time. He was sentenced to five years in prison but was released after a few months following appeals from his professors in Moscow.

Parajanov is an incredibly open and sociable person. He believes that with the advent of the Thaw, the worst is behind him. He does not yet realize that the KGB has already begun watching him closely.

A GUEST FROM PRAGUE

In 1967, Raisa Gorbacheva defends her PhD thesis: "The Formation of New Features in the Life of Collective Farm Peasantry." It's essentially a sociology paper, but since sociology doesn't officially exist in the USSR at that time, Gorbacheva takes quite a risk by choosing such an unconventional topic. Instead of sticking to scientific Marxism-Leninism, she dares to analyze real life.

Meanwhile, her husband is climbing the career ladder. For seven years, he works in the Komsomol—the Communist Youth League, a training ground for future party cadres.

Since 1966, he's been heading the party organization in Stavropol, effectively becoming the city's mayor. The roles in the Gorbachev household are quite clear: Mikhail is the practical one, the breadwinner; Raisa is the intellectual, always reading books and interested in the theater. Whenever they argue, she half-jokingly reminds him, "Misha, you only got a silver medal in school."

In 1967, an old friend and former classmate of Mikhail's, the Czech Zdeněk Mlynář, visits the Gorbachevs in Stavropol.

When they first met in 1950, Zdeněk was a staunch Stalinist. For instance, he once terrified his law professor by insisting that in cases of anti-state crimes, the presumption of innocence didn't apply. The professor, though uneasy, disagreed with the zealous student—risking the possibility that someone present might report him, causing trouble.

But during his studies, Zdeněk began noticing things that shook his faith in Stalin and communism.

For example, Mlynář and his dorm mates, including Gorbachev, often drank together—just the sight of a vodka bottle was, as Zdeněk would later recall, reason enough to celebrate. The Czech student noticed that in such moments, their older friends would often flip the Stalin portrait on the wall to reveal an erotic picture from an early-twentieth-century prerevolutionary magazine glued to the back. "Only then did I understand the role vodka plays in Soviet life: it allows people to forget reality, even if just for a moment, creating the illusion of freedom. Normal, open human interaction only began under the influence of alcohol," Mlynář would write in his memoir.

Through these conversations, he realized how unhappy and unfree the citizens of the so-called most free country, the USSR, truly were—the very country his native Czechoslovakia was supposed to emulate.

When Stalin died in March 1953, Mlynář and Mikhail Gorbachev went together to pay their respects to the great leader—and were nearly crushed in the crowd. Zdeněk's coat was torn to shreds. But that wasn't what struck him most: "The crowd I spent hours with, moving toward Stalin's coffin, wasn't thinking about him. These weren't people overcome with grief. . . . Where the crowd had a little room, they joked and talked like people on their way to a football match. Some were stealing, some were groping women, some were drinking vodka straight from the bottle. It was a crowd united by the desire not to miss a spectacle."

Later, after the 20th Congress, came the exposure of Stalin's crimes. "The Soviet youth of that time often didn't even realize how deeply and tragically they were marked by Stalin's terror," Mlynář recalled. He and Gorbachev had a classmate, an active Komsomol member, one of the few who still hadn't lost his true faith in communism. During Marxism-Leninism seminars, he would passionately and convincingly recite clichés condemning Trotskyists, imperialist agents, and other enemies of the people. Then, during Khrushchev's Thaw, he was unexpectedly given documents rehabilitating his parents, who had been convicted as Trotskyists and died in the camps. The student hadn't even known he'd been adopted as a child by party officials and raised in a different family. These sudden revelations led to a serious mental breakdown.

What shocked Zdeněk most was how the Soviet state didn't match his idea of socialism: "The arrogance of Soviet bureaucrats, their disdain for petitioners standing in endless lines for some pitiful scraps of paper, their lack of culture, incompetence, and arrogance—we had never seen any of this in Czechoslovakia."

After his studies at Moscow State University, Zdeněk returned home with very different political beliefs. "We went to Moscow dreaming of seeing our future. And see it we did," he would write, and it scared him off Stalinism.

Back in Czechoslovakia, Mlynář joined the Academy of Sciences, where he began developing political reforms that he believed could change the country. He drafted a plan for transitioning from totalitarian dictatorship to pluralist democracy and separating the ruling party from direct control of the economy, which would, in turn, reduce the bloated party apparatus. The one thing Mlynář wasn't ready to embrace was a multiparty system.

He also believed that any change required the Kremlin's blessing—so, in the spring of 1967, he went to Moscow to test his program on Soviet officials of various levels. Most of them told him his ideas were "interesting" but didn't specify whether they meant that in a good or bad way.

After spending a few weeks in Moscow, Mlynář traveled south to Stavropol to visit his friend Mikhail Gorbachev.

In his memoir, Mlynář recounts two conversations with his classmates. One of them reacted to his project by saying, "What you're aiming for is impossible here; otherwise, they'll just slit our throats." "'We' meant the Soviet bureaucracy, and 'they' meant the Soviet people," the Czech commented.

But there was another opinion: another of Mlynář's interlocutors was deeply impressed and hoped the reforms in Czechoslovakia would succeed— paving the way for democratization in the USSR.

Mlynář doesn't specify which of these views belonged to the young Mikhail Gorbachev. But we can guess.

"I returned to Prague convinced that things weren't as hopeless as they seemed and that democratization was possible even in the Soviet Union," Mlynář would write.

WRITERS' REBELLION

Just before the New Year in 1967, Alexander Tvardovsky, the editor of *Novy Mir*, is stripped of his positions in the Central Committee of the Communist Party and the Supreme Soviet. It's clear that the new authorities are punishing Tvardovsky for his past daring, particularly for supporting Solzhenitsyn. Tvardovsky takes the fall hard, but Solzhenitsyn doesn't pity him at all—he thinks it's a noble sacrifice and that Tvardovsky should be proud: it's not punishment, but liberation. They end up arguing: Tvardovsky believes Solzhenitsyn should keep quiet to avoid harming others, while Solzhenitsyn insists he owes nothing to anyone.

At this point, Solzhenitsyn decides to stage an open revolt. He does the exact opposite of what his editor advises: in May 1967, Solzhenitsyn writes a letter to the writers' union and sends copies to almost every writer he knows.

This letter turns out to be one of the most unexpected political manifestos written in the Soviet Union. Solzhenitsyn demands the abolition of censorship, calling it "unconstitutional and therefore illegal." He begins his appeal not with his own problems but by listing all the great Russian writers and poets who have been banned in the Soviet Union—a lengthy list including Dostoevsky, Yesenin, Mayakovsky, Akhmatova, Tsvetaeva, Bunin, Bulgakov, Pasternak, et alia.

He also accuses the writers' union of never defending persecuted writers but instead acting as a punitive organ. Finally, he turns to his own troubles: he demands the return of his seized archive and reveals that two of his novels, *The First Circle* and *Cancer Ward*, have been rejected by every Soviet publisher.

Solzhenitsyn's letter is an explosion. But the most unexpected part isn't the uprising of a former convict, a loner who isn't published anywhere, but the fact that almost one hundred of the most prominent Soviet writers—people who had no plans of rebelling and weren't preparing for a mutiny—spontaneously voice their support. It's a spontaneous surge of solidarity. Even Tvardovsky is happy.

Solzhenitsyn is stunned. "Is this not astounding? I didn't even dare to hope for this! A writers' rebellion!! Here! After they've been steamrolled forward and backward, forward and backward by the Stalinist asphalt roller so many times! The unfortunate intelligentsia! And yet here you are, alive again! Growing in your unprotected, selfless, desperate way once more! It's you again, and not your prosperous brothers—the rocket scientists, the atomists, the physicists, and chemists with their steady salaries, modern apartments, and lulling lives!"

When Solzhenitsyn writes these words, he doesn't yet know that very soon the leader of this rebellious intelligentsia will be none other than nuclear physicist Andrei Sakharov.

FIREMEN'S BALL

Solzhenitsyn's letter is published in Western media and discussed around the world. His courage inspires writers from other countries too. At the end of June 1967, his letter is read aloud at the Congress of the Czechoslovak Writers' Union—they also demand the abolition of censorship. Suddenly, society begins to more openly demand change. In October 1967, student protests erupt. The police respond with tear gas and rubber bullets, and Czechoslovak students hold sit-ins, just like the American students protesting the Vietnam War at the same time.

In 1967, young Czech filmmaker Miloš Forman directs an absurd comedy about a village fire brigade whose chief is retiring, so his subordinates decide to throw him a party—a ball complete with a beauty contest. But as the event unfolds, all the prepared prizes are stolen, a fire breaks out in the village, and nobody cares; the ball continues.

The film, *Firemen's Ball*, comes across as a harsh satire of communist Czechoslovakia. Cultural officials are clearly unimpressed—they claim that Forman has insulted the working class. The head of Czechoslovakia, Antonín Novotný, is furious—he bans the film "forever."

But any "forever" has to end someday, Forman muses. He manages to convince French producers to get involved, the film is released worldwide, and it's even nominated for an Oscar. Banned in his home country, Miloš Forman finds himself suddenly famous in America. He's overjoyed—it's a once-in-a-lifetime chance to move to the United States and make movies there, an incredible stroke of luck for a filmmaker living behind the Iron Curtain.

In the USSR, Solzhenitsyn's battle with the writers' union continues: one of the union's secretaries, Nobel laureate Mikhail Sholokhov, demands that Solzhenitsyn be "kept away from the pen" and condemns the writers who supported him. Solzhenitsyn will never forgive Sholokhov for this stance—years later, he will argue that Sholokhov is a plagiarist and not the true author of his famous novel *And Quiet Flows the Don*.

What doesn't move in Moscow moves much faster in Prague. By the end of the year, the desire for change is palpable even within the Czechoslovak Politburo: half of its members vote for the removal of Antonín Novotný, the First Secretary of the Communist Party. He is ousted on the second attempt—in January 1968, following a secret ballot. Alexander Dubček is elected in his place.

On the surface, it resembles the recent ousting of Khrushchev. However, Czechoslovakia is a Soviet satellite, and such changes in leadership usually require Moscow's approval. But Brezhnev dislikes Novotný and decides not to intervene.

From January, Gorbachev's classmate Zdeněk Mlynář joins a working group tasked with drafting the official document "Action Program of the Communist Party of Czechoslovakia." He is no longer just a dreamer; he's now a party official implementing his visions of democratization.

New communist leader Dubček's popularity skyrockets. He appears close to the people: sitting with regular citizens in the stands of hockey stadiums, chatting casually, but most importantly, he symbolizes newfound freedom. Censorship is abolished in Czechoslovakia, Dubček describes his new policy as "socialism with a human face" in one of his speeches. "It turned out that it was enough to allow people to express their views freely—in meetings, in the press, on radio, and on television. This alone freed people from fear," Mlynář writes of the spring of 1968.

The changes in Czechoslovakia infuriate Soviet leaders and officials from other Eastern Bloc countries. What irks them most is that Dubček doesn't consult Moscow on his personnel decisions.

Dubček is regularly summoned for dressing-downs, which oddly resemble

Solzhenitsyn's meetings with the leadership of the writers' union. Interestingly, in both cases, the accusers see a conspiracy: they believe both Dubček's policies and Solzhenitsyn's writings are influenced by the West, American intelligence agencies, and foreign meddling.

Ultimately, both Solzhenitsyn and Dubček are fighting for freedom of speech and against censorship. However, there's a significant difference between them: Dubček is a sincere communist; he believes the people support him, and he's confident he can justify his actions to his comrades in Moscow, Warsaw, and Berlin. Solzhenitsyn harbors no such illusions. He genuinely despises his interlocutors and knows they despise him. Yet he tries to play the game.

Are they doomed? Both believe they have a shot at beating the bureaucrats on their own turf. Solzhenitsyn has the experienced Tvardovsky backing him, and Dubček is convinced that Brezhnev, who affectionately calls him Sasha, is on his side.

But soon the game spills beyond the boundaries set by the participants. Solzhenitsyn's manuscript of *Cancer Ward* is leaked to the West. The *Times Literary Supplement* begins publishing excerpts from the novel. This means there is no longer any hope of publishing it at home. But Solzhenitsyn is almost jubilant: the dam has burst. "A blow!—thunderous and joyous! I walk and walk along the trail under the spring snowstorm—it's begun! I had expected it—and hadn't."

Two Soviet leaders head to Czechoslovakia for inspection. First, Defense Minister Andrei Grechko tours military units. Then Soviet premier Alexei Kosygin goes on vacation to Karlovy Vary, where he meets with various officials. Grechko and Kosygin represent different factions in the Soviet leadership. The defense minister believes the situation in Czechoslovakia is dangerous and slipping out of control—possibly under Western influence. The only solution, he says, is to send in the troops.

Premier Kosygin, however, takes a different view. He believes military force is premature.

In Karlovy Vary, Kosygin is strolling through the park with a cup of healing mineral water when a Czechoslovak TV crew suddenly stops him. A persistent journalist starts asking him questions. The Soviet premier is shocked—he didn't know this was even possible; who gave them the right? He dismissively avoids the questions, thinking he's put the reporter in her place. But the next day, the interview airs on national television. This experience changes Kosygin's view of the situation in Czechoslovakia—he sees that the lack of censorship is a huge problem.

Upon returning, Kosygin and the Moscow Politburo revisit the Czechoslovak question and decide to send in the troops.

RUSSIAN OPPENHEIMER

In the spring of 1968, physicist Andrei Sakharov writes an article—not about science, but about freedom and the fight against dictatorship. He's inspired by the news, listening on the Western radio stations to reports of democratic reforms in Czechoslovakia, and begins dreaming of similar changes in the USSR. He is also fascinated by the theory of "convergence"—the idea that the opposing Western and Soviet systems will gradually merge and interact.

At first, none of his colleagues understand what the inventor of the hydrogen bomb is up to. Sakharov doesn't hide his work from anyone; he even hands over his handwritten pages to the typists working at the classified facility, just like he does with his scientific papers. "I fully expected the manuscript might end up in the hands of the KGB. But it was more important to me not to put myself in immediate jeopardy by engaging in secret activities—it would have been uncovered anyway, given my position."

Over the years, Sakharov had become increasingly disturbed by his own invention. He found inspiration in Robert Oppenheimer, the creator of the atomic bomb who came to despise his own creation. During the Cuban Missile Crisis in October 1962, Sakharov began to think that the world was on the brink of destruction—and partly because of him.

Sakharov starts by fighting for a ban on nuclear testing. He reads banned dissident publications more and more frequently. His wife, Klavdia, sees that he's involved in something dangerous—she's worried but can't stop him.

And so, in April 1968, Sakharov completes a text titled "Reflections on Progress, Peaceful Coexistence, and Intellectual Freedom."

He calls for an end to the Cold War and for closer ties with the West for the sake of survival: "Human society needs intellectual freedom—the freedom to receive and distribute information, the freedom of unbiased and fearless discussion, and the freedom from the pressure of authority and prejudice. Such a triple freedom of thought is the only guarantee against the infection of the people by mass myths that, in the hands of cunning hypocrites and demagogues, easily turn into bloody dictatorship."

Of course, Sakharov's article can't be published in the USSR—not only because the scientist's name is classified, along with everything related to nuclear weapons, but also because the text is blatantly anti-Soviet.

Once finished, he goes to tell his boss, academician Yuly Khariton. Khariton is horrified and pleads with Sakharov, "For God's sake, don't do this." Sakharov replies, "I'm afraid it's too late to change anything now." And indeed, copies of the article are already circulating in samizdat. At the end of May, the head of the KGB, Yuri Andropov, reads it. He summons the elderly academician Khariton and scolds him like a schoolboy, demanding that he immediately stop Sakharov from spreading this subversive text.

By June, the article reaches members of the Politburo. In July, the text makes its way abroad, published in the *New York Times*. Sakharov is thrilled—he feels he's done something significant. Most importantly, he has come out of hiding. No longer the USSR's most secretive scientist, he can now speak openly. He probably feels much like Solzhenitsyn did a few months earlier when he learned that his *Cancer Ward* was being published abroad.

In early August, Khariton summons Sakharov and informs him that his presence at the classified site in Arzamas-16 is no longer welcome—effectively, he's been removed from his work. He is to remain in Moscow. But Sakharov is not upset: he listens to Western radio news every day and senses that something is happening in the world—something unprecedented. He's not the only one rebelling against the system—the whole world is rising up.

YOUTH IN VOGUE

After he arrives in the USA, Miloš Forman plans to adapt Kafka's unfinished novel *Amerika*—a very dark and hopeless work. But he's so captivated by the lively atmosphere of Manhattan that he shifts his focus to making a film adaptation of the popular Broadway musical *Hair*. However, after failing to secure the rights, he turns his attention to writing a screenplay about teenagers running away from home because they can't stand living with their conservative parents.

Nineteen sixty-eight becomes the year when the new, postwar generation takes center stage globally. At first glance, it's hard to pinpoint what sparks the wave of unrest and why these protests cross borders so easily. People worldwide rise up under various slogans. American student pacifists rally against the Vietnam War with "Make Love, Not War," while French students riot in Paris with slogans like "Under the paving stones, the beach" and "Be realistic—demand the impossible." African-Americans fight for civil rights, followed by American feminists, then gay and lesbian activists. Amazingly, at the same time, on the other side of the world, the dissident movement is also beginning to emerge in the Soviet Union.

Forman decides he needs a quieter place than New York to write his screenplay and heads to Paris. But when he arrives, a student revolution breaks out, so Forman moves on to Prague, only to find the Prague Spring in full swing.

It's impossible not to notice that all the revolutions of 1968 are the result of technological revolutions that have destroyed previously sacred values and social institutions.

Television, entering every home, changes everything. For example, it challenged the previously unassailable value of war. In the past, people dreamed of dying for their country; war was considered the noblest pursuit for a man, and dying in battle was a high aspiration for many. But the generation that saw war on television for the first time viewed it not as a sacred fight but as a bloody mess. They understood that young people in war were just cannon fodder. As a result, the youth of the 1960s became the first pacifist generation in history.

Another significant consequence of television is the beginning of globalization. International stars start appearing, known everywhere. If, at the beginning of the twentieth century, two people from Brazil and Japan met, they would likely have nothing to talk about. But from the 1960s onward, things are different. They likely listen to the same music, watch the same movies, and root for the same athletes—they share a common cultural code. In 1966 John Lennon had just declared that the Beatles were more popular than Jesus Christ, and in 1968 the Beatles are at the peak of their popularity.

Space exploration also changes humanity's psychology. The ability to see Earth from a distance, to imagine it as a tiny sphere, completely alters how we view the world. In essence, this is where the global environmental movement begins. In 1966 *The Undersea World of Jacques Cousteau* launched, and in 1968 Stanley Kubrick's film *2001: A Space Odyssey* is released.

Technology also shatters another sacred institution—the family. In 1967, *Time* magazine put the birth control pill on its cover. The pill sparked a psychological revolution. The role of sex in human life changes. Once primarily a means of procreation, sex becomes a form of leisure, a way to spend time.

When French youth dance in the streets of Paris in May 1968, the conservative older generation is horrified—they are sure that degeneration is happening and that the new generation is in decline.

But from the 1960s onward, youth becomes fashionable. Until then, people tried to look older to be taken seriously in society; men didn't shy away from round bellies—age was a sign of status and respect. But in the 1960s, everything flips 180 degrees. Now, to be relevant, you have to be young. People start listening to the youth; men and women would strive to look younger, not older. The world that had always been oriented toward the past, valuing it as a source of wisdom and knowledge and relying on tradition, had come to an end. Now humanity turns to the future. If common sense once said, "The past was better," and, "The new generation isn't like it used to be," starting in the 1960s the world begins to get used to the idea that the future will be better and that the new generation knows best.

And of course, the older generation, grumbling indignantly in 1968, will turn out to be wrong—no degeneration will happen. We know this for sure today because the generation raised in the 1960s will give humanity the next technological revolution—for instance, they will invent the internet.

SOVIET ELVIS

In the spring of 1968, students all around the world carry portraits of Che Guevara, Mao, Lenin, and Karl Marx to rallies, denounce American capitalism, and accuse the United States of aggression in Vietnam. The press calls the protest leaders reds, and they don't even bother to argue. Jean-Paul Sartre is not only the Soviet Union's biggest fan in the West but also a hero to the rebellious Sorbonne students—he's the only "adult" allowed on the occupied university grounds. For protesting left-wing students the Soviet system seems fairer than Western societies.

Of course, their admiration is from afar—most have never been to the Soviet Union and have only a vague idea of what life is like there. But there's no doubt that in the spring of 1968 the Soviet Union is winning the battle for hearts and minds. American democracy's reputation is tarnished by Vietnam, while the popularity of the Soviet model has soared since Gagarin's space flight.

But 1968 will change everything.

Incidentally, Gagarin also believes that this year should change everything in his life. Since his historic flight, he's become a rock star and is tired of his own fame. In a sense, Gagarin is the Russian Elvis. He's toured the world, gained weight, and lost the sparkle in his eyes.

So in 1968, he decides to put his public life behind him, get back into the cockpit, and start flying again—with the ultimate goal of returning to space.

Gagarin and his comrades are deeply concerned that after the death of engineer Sergei Korolev the Soviet space program has stalled. They believe they'll soon be able to fly to the moon, but there's still no reliable rocket to get them there. Gagarin's name is absent from the list of cosmonauts vying for a lunar mission, but his friend Alexei Leonov, who was the first to walk in space three years ago, tops the list.

On March 19, Gagarin reads Joseph Heller's novel *Catch-22*, laughs heartily, and even leaves a note: "The novel is excellent. The guys should read it. Definitely."

On March 27, he has a training flight. The plane carrying the first cosmonaut completes all tasks and is on its way back to base when, suddenly, it stops responding. Communication cuts off at 10:30 a.m. The wreckage is found 4.5 hours later.

No official explanation for the crash is ever released. Gagarin's friend cosmonaut Leonov claims that supersonic jet fighters were being tested in the same area and one of them broke the rules, flying too close to Gagarin's plane, causing it to go into a spin and crash. However, numerous conspiracy theories would surface: some say he had a conflict with the authorities and was deliberately killed; others suggest his death was faked, and that the real Gagarin was sent to a psychiatric hospital, or that he survived and lived somewhere under an assumed name. The story of the Russian Elvis ended the same way the story of the American Elvis would end almost ten years later.

THE BIRDS ARE SINGING

At the end of June 1968, the Czechoslovak Politburo meets late into the night. They are alarmed by recent publications in the uncensored press and fear that

Brezhnev will be enraged, leading to a terrible Soviet response. (None of them realize that, in Moscow, the decision has already been more or less made.)

By morning, they still haven't found a way to fix the situation. The meeting room is thick with smoke. One Politburo member opens a window. Dawn is breaking. "People, stop this nonsense," he says. "The birds are already singing outside."

Meanwhile, Solzhenitsyn is also listening to the birds singing at his dacha. "No happier summer could have been imagined," he writes. Following *Cancer Ward*, another of his novels, *The First Circle*, is published in the West. He also manages to finish and smuggle *The Gulag Archipelago* abroad.

At 8:00 p.m. on August 3, 1968, Petro Shelest, the First Secretary of the Ukrainian Communist Party and a member of the Soviet Politburo, enters a public restroom in the Intourist Hotel in Bratislava, the second-largest city in Czechoslovakia. There, he is set to secretly meet with Vasil Bil'ak, the First Secretary of the Slovak Communist Party. It is one of the strangest—and most disgraceful—meetings between politicians in the twentieth century.

Bil'ak and Shelest are hiding for good reason—one is handing the other a letter signed by several members of the Czechoslovak Politburo. The letter is addressed to Brezhnev and contains a request to send troops into Czechoslovakia and put an end to the "counter-revolution"—as the authors call the democratization and "socialism with a human face."

Shelest delivers the letter to Brezhnev and is delighted. As the leader of Soviet Ukraine, Shelest is one of the hawks in the Politburo, fiercely advocating for sending tanks into Czechoslovakia to crush the reforms. He agrees with the leaders of Poland and East Germany, who believe that democratization in Czechoslovakia poses a great threat to them all. Shelest is among those who loudly accuse the Czechoslovak leadership of working for the CIA.

On the night of August 21, military units from Poland, Bulgaria, Hungary, East Germany, and the USSR head toward Prague. The Czechoslovak army offers no resistance.

At that moment, the Czechoslovak Politburo is in session. "I could physically feel the end of my life as a communist," Zdeněk Mlynář would later recall. "Everything suddenly seemed pointless—both the ideas and the actions. The same meeting room, the same people—but in just a few minutes, the world had become unrecognizable."

Protesters take to the streets of Prague, erecting barricades, and the first clashes begin. On the first day alone, fifty-eight Czechoslovak citizens and eleven Soviet soldiers are killed.

Soviet soldiers arrest Dubček and his closest allies and take them to Western Ukraine. The initial plan is to try them in a specially created "counter-revolutionary tribunal." The former Czechoslovak leaders prepare to face their deaths.

But in Prague, things do not go as planned. Most local officials and Communist Party members demonstrate not loyalty to Moscow but a willingness to resist. Facing this unexpected problem, Moscow changes its strategy. The arrested leaders are brought to Moscow for negotiations with Brezhnev and other Soviet Politburo members. They are required to sign guarantees that the previous course of reforms will be reversed.

Brezhnev openly states that his main grievance with Dubček is his appointments without consulting Moscow. "I trusted you; I defended you in front of others," the Soviet leader scolds him with wounded pride. "I said, 'Our Sasha is still a good comrade.' And you let us all down!" During these outbursts, Brezhnev's voice quivers with self-pity; he stammers as he speaks, Mlynář recalls.

According to Brezhnev, having won the Great Patriotic War, the USSR earned the right to consider Eastern Europe its own and would defend these borders. Moreover, he claims that before the invasion, he contacted US president Lyndon Johnson to confirm whether the United States would respect the agreements signed at Yalta. Johnson assured him that they would, regarding Czechoslovakia.

After Dubček signs everything required of him, Brezhnev relaxes and begins to speak candidly: "You thought that just because you had power, you could do as you pleased. Even I can't afford that; I manage to achieve about a third of my intentions. What would have happened if I hadn't raised my hand for military intervention during the Politburo vote? You certainly wouldn't be here now. But perhaps neither would I."

At this moment, Miloš Forman is back in Paris. This time, the city is quiet and deserted—everyone has left for their August vacations. He listens to the news on the radio and doesn't know what to do next. If he goes home, he'll never be allowed back to the West, and he'll lose his chance to make films in America. He asks his French friends to drive to Prague and bring his family back: his wife and two young sons. Vera, Forman's wife and one of the most popular Czech actresses at the time, is terrified—she doesn't speak French and has no idea what she'll do abroad, but she takes the children and leaves, even forgetting their passports at home.

ASHAMED TO BE SOVIET

The invasion of Czechoslovakia is a shock to many Soviet citizens, especially the Moscow intelligentsia.

Solzhenitsyn is working at his dacha, watching tanks, trucks, and special vehicles drive south along the highway. He's convinced that "ours are just bluffing, it's maneuvers." When news breaks of the invasion, Solzhenitsyn thinks of Alexander Herzen, the nineteenth-century Russian writer who, a hundred years earlier, during Russia's suppression of the Polish uprising, wrote that he was "ashamed to be Russian." Solzhenitsyn echoes this sentiment: "ashamed to be Soviet."

At first, he wants to go to Moscow to gather signatures from four or five celebrities, including Sakharov, for a public statement. But he decides against it, doubting they would sign. Mostly, though, he tells himself, "I need to save my voice for the main shout."

"A coward's excuse? Or reasonable thinking? I stayed silent. And from this moment—a new burden on my shoulders. . . . Even more shameful because I had a personal responsibility for Czechoslovakia: everyone agrees that it all began with the Writers' Congress, and that started with my letter," Solzhenitsyn reflects. "And I can only clear this stain from myself if something starts with me again someday at home."

Meanwhile, the loyal and state-favored poet Yevgeny Yevtushenko sends two protest telegrams—to Soviet leader Leonid Brezhnev and Premier Alexei Kosygin. Then he writes a piercing poem, "Tanks Roll into Prague," which will circulate widely in underground publications.

> Tanks roll into Prague,
> in the blood-red dawn of sunset.
> Tanks roll over truth,
> which is not a newspaper.*

---

* The official Soviet newspaper is called *Pravda*, which means "truth" in Russian.

Cellist Mstislav Rostropovich learns of the invasion while on tour in London. That evening, he's set to perform a concert of works by Antonín Dvořák, a nineteenth-century Czech composer. Protesters gather around the Royal Albert Hall, shouting, "Soviet fascists, go home!" But still the performance is a huge success. One London newspaper writes that even if Rostropovich had rolled into the Albert Hall in a tank, he would still have been greeted with applause.

At noon on August 25, eight people step onto Red Square. At first, they look like regular passersby—Red Square is always full of tourists. But then they approach the Lobnoye Mesto, a platform once used for public executions in the Middle Ages. Strangely, it's never been removed, even as Moscow's main square has transformed over the centuries.

Exactly at 12:00, the eight protesters sit next to the platform in a sit-in protest, much like the anti–Vietnam War demonstrations in America. One of them is Natalya Gorbanevskaya, a poet. She's thirty-two years old and had just given birth three months ago; she's on Red Square with a stroller, where her three-month-old son, Joseph, is lying. Hidden beneath him is a handwritten sign that reads: "For your freedom and ours."

Gorbanevskaya is a dissident who frequently participates in protests in Moscow and signs petitions defending arrested human rights activists. In February 1968, she was even sent to a psychiatric hospital directly from the maternity ward—a common tactic in the USSR against regime opponents. Dissenters often receive a diagnosis of "sluggish schizophrenia."

After her release, Gorbanevskaya started compiling the USSR's first underground journal documenting human rights violations—the *Chronicle of Current Events*. The Prague Spring and other global protests have a big impact on her and her friends. They feel compelled to step onto the Lobnoye Mesto and voice their protest against the invasion of Czechoslovakia, knowing it's like willingly going to the scaffold—no protests are allowed in the USSR.

As soon as Gorbanevskaya and her seven fellow activists unfurl their banners, KGB agents rush them, tearing away the signs and beating them. They seize Gorbanevskaya's stroller, and all eight are arrested. Cars pull up to the Lobnoye Mesto through the crowd, and the protesters are loaded in one by one.

Around the same time, eight protesters are being arrested on the other side of the world—in Chicago. There, mass protests are underway against the US invasion of Vietnam, coinciding with the Democratic National Convention, which is set to nominate a presidential candidate.

Thirty-year-old activist Jerry Rubin brings a pig named Pigasus to the rally, intending to symbolically nominate it for US president. As soon as Rubin begins his speech, he, along with seven other activists, is arrested by the police.

In Moscow, the interrogation of the Red Square demonstrators begins. The youngest dissident, twenty-one-year-old Tatyana Baeva, claims she ended up on the square by accident. She won't face charges but is expelled from her institute. Thus, the "Demonstration of Eight" will become the "Demonstration of Seven."

In Chicago, charges of inciting riots are brought against eight: Jerry Rubin, Abbie Hoffman, Tom Hayden, David Dellinger, Rennie Davis, John Froines, Lee Weiner, and Black Panther leader Bobby Seale. In court, Seale lashes out at the judge, prompting the judge to order a gag be placed in his mouth. Seale's case is soon separated, turning the "Chicago Eight" into the "Chicago Seven."

Just a hundred meters from the Lobnoye Mesto, Soviet leaders, led by Brezhnev, are pressuring Czechoslovak leaders.

And near the Chicago protesters, the Democratic National Convention continues. Delegates choose their presidential candidate—Hubert Humphrey, backed by President Lyndon Johnson. Many convention attendees demand that the attorney general prosecute the instigators of the Chicago riots.

News of the Red Square arrests spreads worldwide. Andrei Sakharov is horrified. He goes to the Kurchatov Institute—the center of Soviet nuclear research in Moscow. Years earlier, the institute's founder, Igor Kurchatov, had ordered that Sakharov always be allowed access to his office when needed. Though Kurchatov has passed away, the order remains in effect, allowing Sakharov to enter the director's office freely. He knows the room is equipped with all secure government communication lines.

The office's occupant isn't there, so Sakharov picks up the phone and demands to be connected immediately to KGB head Yuri Andropov. When connected, the academic pleads with Andropov for leniency toward the arrested protesters.

Andropov is shocked by the call, though he's already aware of Sakharov's new article and the profound internal transformation the scientist is undergoing. Andropov replies that he's very busy and hasn't slept much in the past week, adding that the protest is being handled by the prosecutor's office, not the KGB, though he thinks the sentences won't be severe.

Two of the Red Square protesters receive prison sentences. Another two, including Gorbanevskaya, are sent to psychiatric hospitals. The rest are sentenced to exile. The Soviet press only begins writing about them after the sentencing.

Five of the Chicago Seven are also sentenced to prison, but their sentences are soon overturned on appeal.

ONE DAY IN THE LIFE OF ALEXANDER ISAYEVICH

On August 28, 1968—just three days after the Red Square demonstration—one of the most important days in Alexander Solzhenitsyn's life unfolds. He arrives in Moscow for an interview with a woman who is willing to become his assistant and literary secretary; his wife, Natasha, is overwhelmed with the workload of retyping his manuscripts.

The candidate's name is also Natasha—or Natalya Svetlova—but Solzhenitsyn will call her Alya. She is twenty-nine years old and passionately shares the latest news from Moscow with the legendary writer, who knows little about the recent arrests on Red Square. Alya is closely acquainted with the protesters. "Her civic fervor appealed to me greatly; her character was like mine. She must be put to work!" Solzhenitsyn will later write. He assigns her to retype *The First Circle*.

Directly from Svetlova's apartment, Solzhenitsyn heads to another underground meeting: his first encounter with Andrei Sakharov. They have heard much about each other but have never met.

The physicist and the writer sit in the kitchen of a mutual friend's apartment and talk the entire evening, hardly leaving each other's side. Solzhenitsyn spends much of the time explaining to Sakharov why he disagrees with his article: "The West isn't interested in our democratization; it's tangled in its material progress and permissiveness, and socialism could be its undoing. Our leaders are soulless automatons clinging to their power and privileges, and they won't let go without a fist to their faces," Solzhenitsyn argues. "It's wrong to dream of a multiparty system; what we need is a no-party system. . . ."

Sakharov listens attentively and politely responds that the article reflects his own beliefs. "Alexander Isayevich, leaning on the table with one arm, was hammering his points into Andrei Dmitriyevich. Sakharov would utter a few slow phrases, listening more than speaking, as was his habit," recounts the apartment's host.

Solzhenitsyn returns home very late and falls asleep at his desk. It is his meeting with Natalya Svetlova, not Sakharov, that will completely change his life.

Around this time, Solzhenitsyn's fame explodes in the West. The publication of his novels in Britain and Germany becomes a triumph. Glowing reviews appear in the *New York Times*, the *Guardian*, and the *New York Review of Books*. In late September, *Time* magazine features Solzhenitsyn on its cover. The Soviet press, however, remains silent.

By late 1968, Solzhenitsyn suggests to his wife that they divorce. He is preparing to write a new novel about the 1917 revolution and insists that he needs solitude. "You don't need a wife; you don't need a family!" she cries. "Yes, I don't need a wife; I don't need a family. I need to write my novel," he replies. "Consider that you don't have a husband."

Meanwhile, Solzhenitsyn begins a relationship with Alya Svetlova, who takes over all work with his manuscripts. But Natasha Reshetovskaya refuses to grant him a divorce. She has already embraced the role of Sophia Tolstaya—Leo Tolstoy's long-suffering wife—and is unwilling to let go of it.

Solzhenitsyn often compares himself to Tolstoy. The latter was excommunicated by the church in 1901; Solzhenitsyn, in turn, is expelled from the writers' union in 1969 during a hastily convened meeting of the Ryazan branch, which lasts just ten minutes.

Meanwhile, despite his new protest lifestyle, Sakharov still enjoys his former privileges. In the fall of 1968, he even vacations at a government sanatorium in the North Caucasus. During his stay, he notices that conversations stop when he enters, and other guests avoid him. It doesn't bother him much, though—he is more concerned with his wife Klavdia's worsening health, though doctors insist she is perfectly well.

Only in December 1968, they accidentally discover that Klavdia, Sakharov's wife of twenty-five years, is in the terminal stages of cancer. She dies in March 1969, leaving Sakharov tormented with guilt for not paying her enough attention and for missing her illness. After Klavdia's death, Sakharov plunges into human rights activism: attending dissident trials, participating in pickets, and distributing leaflets become his new way of life.

THE SPY AND THE HOOLIGAN

What do ordinary Soviet citizens think about all this? Mostly, nothing. They typically don't delve into what the propaganda says. They know little about the Prague Spring and largely believe that Western intelligence agencies are waging a war against the Soviet Union.

On August 19, 1968, just before the Soviet invasion of Czechoslovakia, the film *Shield and Sword* hits Soviet theaters—a story about a Soviet spy who infiltrates the Nazi army and works undercover. The sequel comes out in September, just as Soviet propaganda continues to claim that Soviet tanks have saved Czechoslovakia from a Nazi resurgence.

At the end of the year, in December 1968, another patriotic blockbuster titled *The Dead Season* is released. This film tells the story of an evil scientist—a former Nazi now working for the American government—who tries to create a new psychotropic weapon to turn people into obedient slaves. Naturally, a Soviet spy uncovers the sinister plan and foils it. By this time, five James Bond films starring Sean Connery have already been released in the United States—Soviet spy films are a direct response.

Of course, the Bond movies aren't shown in the USSR, but *Shield and Sword* and *The Dead Season* are wildly successful. For sixteen-year-old Vladimir Putin, these films have a profound impact—they spark a transformation in him.

Before 1968, young Putin is a street tough in Leningrad. His parents have neither the time nor resources to raise him properly, so he grows up on the streets, part of one of many teenage gangs. He's even denied entry into the Young Pioneers (the Soviet equivalent of the Boy Scouts), usually mandatory for all schoolchildren; only the most notorious troublemakers and juvenile delinquents are rejected.

Putin's only passion is judo, which he takes up at the age of eleven—because on the streets, disputes are settled through fistfights; it's the only way to survive. Teenage Putin also strums on a guitar; his idol is Vladimir Vysotsky, the most popular underground singer in the USSR. His songs are sung with guitars by young people across the Soviet Union, mostly prison ballads. Vysotsky himself has never been to prison, but his lyrical persona is that of a man who's been through the Gulag and come out the other side. Putin, like many street kids in the USSR, knows Vysotsky's songs by heart.

In 1967, Vysotsky stars in the film *Vertical* about mountain climbers, in which several of his songs are featured. This cements his status as a youth idol, and fifteen-year-old Putin is no exception.

But 1968 changes everything, even for Putin. After watching *Shield and Sword* and *The Dead Season*, the sixteen-year-old hooligan becomes obsessed with the idea of becoming a spy. He even goes to the public reception office of the KGB in Leningrad. An indifferent duty officer tries to get rid of the pesky teenager, telling him that "self-starters" aren't accepted into the service. First, he must get a higher education, perhaps in law.

THE YEAR 1968 HAPPENED

Half a decade later, French philosopher Gilles Deleuze writes an essay titled "May 1968 Didn't Happen," arguing that the protests achieve nothing and change nothing in French society.

Looking from the twenty-first century, it's impossible to agree with this. Global culture, all the values that matter to humanity at the end of the twentieth and beginning of the twenty-first centuries—they all grow out of 1968. The enemy of French students Charles de Gaulle remains in power in 1968 but leaves in 1969. In the United States, Richard Nixon, hated by protesting youth, wins the presidential election, but it's he who eventually pulls troops out of Vietnam. The ideas of respecting human rights, women's rights, minority rights, and LGBT rights—all of this begins in 1968.

Finally, 1968 deals the first major blow to the Soviet Union. Leonid Brezhnev never grasps this, but it's the tanks in Prague that destroy the Soviet model's former popularity in the West. A system that recently seemed just and humane is now thoroughly discredited. Nineteen sixty-eight kills the belief in Soviet ideology.

2

TIMELESSNESS AND VODKA

I wish the atomic war would just start already, *thought the little girl sitting under the table.*

That little girl was my mother. She attended a good school, excelled in her studies, and spoke English fluently; her father was in the military, and her mother was a doctor. Her father drank. No—he was an alcoholic.

It was New Year's Eve. They had decorated the tree, set the table, and were waiting for her father to come home from work. He arrived drunk and, finding no vodka in the house, started a fight. He knocked over the tree. The ornaments shattered. He tore the tablecloth off the table—plates and cutlery crashed to the floor.

The little girl hid under the table.

"Let the atomic war start now," she whispered under the table. "Then everyone will feel as miserable as I do."

Her mother simply lay down on the bed and turned away—not to look at him, not to speak to him. He yelled and hit her with his fists, trying to make her respond. Then he cried, fell to his knees, and begged for forgiveness. But she was proud—she never turned to face him.

My mother told me this story a few times, always with a didactic smile. I thought she meant that the worst was behind us, and a bright future lay ahead.

Or maybe it was the opposite—a reminder that even when everything seems fine, we're always just a step away from the atomic war.

SLAVA AND GALINA

In October 1969, the cellist Mstislav Rostropovich—known to all his friends as Slava—meets an acquaintance who tells him that Solzhenitsyn is in trouble—living in a tiny, unheated summer cottage and possibly dying of cancer. Upon hearing this, Rostropovich immediately sets off for Ryazan to see Solzhenitsyn. The weather has already turned cold, and the cellist finds his friend in a small guardhouse, lying under "a pile of quilts, jackets, and blankets, like a cabbage."

"What's wrong with you?" Slava asks. "I think it's sciatica," Solzhenitsyn replies, as Rostropovich later recounts.

"I have a small house I built for special purposes, and I want you to move there. It's heated, it's warm. If it's sciatica, you'll recover, and if it's cancer, well, then it doesn't really matter where you die, does it?"

So, Solzhenitsyn moves into Rostropovich's dacha in Zhukovka. Solzhenitsyn's illness coincides with escalating repression against him—right in November 1969, he is expelled from the Union of Writers. In other words, Rostropovich is effectively housing an "enemy of the people."

Slava and his wife, opera diva Galina Vishnevskaya, are the epitome of Soviet high society. At just forty-two years old, they already have it all. Both are People's Artists of the USSR. She's a leading soprano at the Bolshoi Theatre; he's a professor at the Moscow Conservatory, a laureate of the Lenin and Stalin Prizes, and one of the world's most famous cellists. They tour the globe, own a luxurious apartment in central Moscow, and seem to be on top of the world.

Soviet officials are baffled—why would such a couple take on the kind of trouble that Solzhenitsyn represents? Slava gets calls from Minister of Culture Yekaterina Furtseva and Interior Minister Nikolai Shchelokov. Rostropovich tells them that if the ministers can find Solzhenitsyn a heated room in Moscow, he'll move. If not, he'll stay at the dacha. "A good owner wouldn't leave a dog out in the cold, let alone a person," Rostropovich insists.

By the 1960s, Zhukovka, located west of Moscow along the Rublyovka Highway, is already known as an elite dacha community, home to famous scientists, artists, and musicians. One of his neighbors is Andrei Sakharov. Thanks to Rostropovich, Solzhenitsyn and Sakharov end up as neighbors, meeting more often, sharing their thoughts, and even discussing joint actions.

However, finding common ground isn't easy. Sakharov urges Solzhenitsyn to speak out in defense of dissidents persecuted by the authorities. "No! These people have chosen their path; they've accepted their fate. Saving them is impossible. Any attempt might harm them and others," the writer firmly declines.

The dacha is constantly under KGB surveillance, and the pressure on Rostropovich intensifies. He warns friends and family that visiting him is now risky. The police demand that Solzhenitsyn leave. In response, he writes a statement: "Serfdom was abolished in our country in 1861. They say the October Revolution swept away its last remnants. So, as a citizen of this country, I am neither a serf nor a slave."

WHAT DO YOU WANT?

In 1969, Soviet writer Vsevolod Kochetov publishes his new novel in the magazine *Oktyabr* (October). It's titled *What Do You Want?* The work is astonishing—it reads like it is written by twenty-first-century Putinist propagandists.

Kochetov isn't just any writer—he's the editor in chief of *Oktyabr* and a leading figure among neo-Stalinists in Soviet society. His new novel is a remarkable phenomenon: a manifesto of Stalinism, calling for the immediate crackdown on the liberal intelligentsia in the USSR, especially those who sympathized with Czechoslovakia during the Prague Spring and dared to hope for democratization within the Soviet Union.

What is Stalinism, and how is it understood in 1969?

The cornerstone of Stalinist ideology is the victory in the Great Patriotic War (World War II). On May 24, 1945, at a Kremlin reception celebrating the defeat of Germany, Stalin makes a toast "to the Russian people," a speech that even gets printed in newspapers: "I drink, first and foremost, to the health of the Russian people because they are the most outstanding nation of all the nations that make up the Soviet Union."

This toast marks the starting point of a new Stalinist ideology. Before this, the rhetoric was all about internationalism and world revolution. But now everything changes: Stalin declares the superiority of the Russian people, ushering in a new era of Russian nationalism.

Previously, the Soviet high priests of the communist cult were obligated to preach ideas of equality, brotherhood, and the dictatorship of the proletariat, maintaining that the struggle between capitalist and communist worlds would eventually end with a communist victory, unifying the world under a single system. But after 1945, Stalin no longer needs this theory. In fact, it becomes dangerous because it implies a free exchange of ideas and competition. So Stalin effectively proclaims a return to the ideals of the Russian Empire—minus the Orthodox Church.

Thus, a split emerges among the true believers in communism (and there are still many in the 1940s). Some adhere strictly to the sacred texts: Lenin's works. But as Stalin shifts toward Russian nationalism, many follow him. Among the priests of communism, two factions emerge: dogmatic tradition-alists and Russian nationalists. Despite their differences, both groups equally despise the West and zealously participate in Stalin's 1950s campaign against "rootless cosmopolitans," targeting the country's best writers and composers suspected of Western sympathies. Both camps also share Stalin's anti-Semitism.

After Stalin's death, the new Soviet leader, Nikita Khrushchev, denounces the "cult of personality," initiating an investigation into crimes committed under Stalin, though it remains incomplete. For the first time, a public debate ignites in the Soviet Union, polarizing society. A new liberal flank, previously too scared to show its face, now speaks out loudly. The key issue that divides society is Stalin. Some see him as a murderer, while others regard him as a deity.

This ideological battle is symbolized by two rival magazines. The liberal standard-bearer is *Novy Mir* (New World), led by the poet Alexander Tvar-dovsky. The nationalist-Stalinist camp rallies around *Oktyabr* (October), edited by writer Vsevolod Kochetov.

The greatest achievement of *Novy Mir* is the discovery of Solzhenitsyn. But after 1968, the conservatives regain the upper hand, and one of the most fervent radicals, Vsevolod Kochetov, calls for a new Great Terror. In his novel *What Do You Want?*, he argues that liberals are nothing but traitors and spies.

Here's the gist: A group of Western spies—former Nazis—sneaks into the USSR to corrupt Soviet society. Liberal cultural figures immediately become enemy agents, but the true Stalinists expose the infiltrators.

Here's a snippet from the villain's monologue:

They, the communists, have always been ideologically strong, superior to us with their unwavering beliefs, their sense of being right in everything. . . . There was no way to shake them, no way to break in. Now, though, there's some hope. We skillfully exploited the denouncement of Stalin. . . . But it took the work of hundreds of radio stations, thousands of publications, thousands upon thousands of propagandists, millions and millions, hundreds of millions of dollars. . . . We're flooding their movie market with our products; we're sending our singers and dancers. In short, their strict communist aesthetics are being diluted.

The novel's publication terrifies many. The book is seen as a call for a cultural revolution similar to the one that just took place in China. A group of Soviet intellectuals—writers, scientists, and filmmakers—writes a letter to the Central Committee, accusing Kochetov of slandering Soviet society and insisting that no Western spies exist within it. Even the *New York Times* publishes a review, interpreting *What Do You Want?* as the start of a new conservative era in the USSR.

The reaction of the communist high priests is unexpected: the second-most powerful man in the USSR, Secretary of Ideology Mikhail Suslov, hates any sort of loud controversy, whether from the left or right. He bans not only the debate surrounding the novel but also the publication of *What Do You Want?* as a stand-alone book.

Silence falls, and soon after, the leaders of both ideological camps will die. Both Tvardovsky and Kochetov are diagnosed with cancer. Tvardovsky will die in 1971, while Kochetov will end his own life in 1973. In the end, history puts everything in its place: Tvardovsky will become a staple of school Russian literature curricula as a great poet, while Kochetov will fade into obscurity—forgotten even during Putin's era, despite his values becoming mainstream once again.

THE CARDINAL OF COMMUNISM

If the Communist Party of the Soviet Union is a church, then in the 1970s, it has its own cardinal: Mikhail Suslov, the second-most powerful man in the party and the overseer of ideology.

Subordinates love to tell this story about Suslov: The Central Committee secretary fears catching a cold, so he always tries to keep his feet dry. For this reason, almost year-round, he wears galoshes. However, as he grows older, he develops a peculiar ritual. In the morning, as he leaves his house, he puts on his galoshes. Then he walks to his official car, which is parked near his home on Kutuzovsky Prospekt. To avoid bringing dirt into the vehicle, he takes off his galoshes, gets into the car, and drives away, leaving them on the sidewalk. In the evening, after he finishes his workday, the car brings Suslov back to the exact same spot—he steps out, puts his galoshes back on, and calmly walks home. Do the galoshes really stay on the street all day without anyone taking them? Yes, because a patrol officer stands guard over them daily.

Suslov is a true conservative. His sacred mission is to preserve traditions (as he understands them), choke out anything new, and block any hint of reform. Suslov's most significant contribution to Soviet history (though he would never know it) comes on October 1, 1970, during a Politburo meeting. Brezhnev is away in Azerbaijan, and Prime Minister Kosygin is in Egypt.* Suslov presides over the meeting. The topic: the invention of the internet. Of course, it's not called that at the time. The head of the Kyiv Institute of Cybernetics, Viktor Glushkov, proposes an idea for the National Automated System for Management (OGAS)—a network of interconnected computers that could freely exchange information. The United States is known to be working on similar research. The Politburo must decide whether to invest heavily in this "Soviet internet" or not.

After hearing Glushkov's proposal and the objections of various Soviet bureaucrats, Suslov makes his decision: "Comrades, perhaps we are making a mistake by not fully accepting this project, but this transformation is so revolutionary that it's difficult for us to implement it right now." The Soviet Union, which had beaten the United States in the space race just a decade earlier, will fall behind technologically in the race for computers—it won't even get off the starting line.

Suslov despises debates and discussions. He believes, as Stalin taught, that the party must always maintain unity—any communist must side with the majority and sacrifice their personal opinion for the party. Therefore, Suslov systematically cuts down anything he deems abnormal or deviant. He punishes both Tvardovsky and Kochetov, showing that in his vision, there is no room for discord, only conformity.

In 1972, a major ideological scandal is unfolding in the party. Suslov's subordinate, acting head of the Propaganda Department Alexander N. Yakovlev, writes a lengthy article in *Literaturnaya Gazeta*. Titled "Against Anti-historicism," it is a bold and unexpected attack on the "Russian

---

* At the time, Azerbaijan was one of the fifteen republics of the USSR, with a population roughly equal to that of Massachusetts and an area comparable to Maine.

Party" in literature—nationalist writers—and a critique of the increasingly popular ideas about Russia's "special path."

On the one hand, Yakovlev is Suslov's right-hand man, and many see his article as an expression of a directive from above. But the "Russian Party" quickly mounts a counteroffensive. The Nobel laureate Sholokhov joins in, and nationalists from Brezhnev's inner circle complain to the General Secretary, warning that the article could play into the hands of Brezhnev's rivals.

According to Yakovlev's own recollections, however, it is another misstep that seals his fate. In the presence of several colleagues working on an article praising the "great Brezhnev," Yakovlev makes a reckless remark: "Why are you glorifying this mediocrity?" The very next day, this comment is relayed to Brezhnev, and it becomes the decisive blow.

At the Central Committee meeting, Yakovlev's article is harshly criticized. Suslov, wary of defending his protégé, steps aside. Yakovlev is punished with exile—he is sent off as ambassador to Canada.

ANDREI AND LYUSYA

In 1970, Sakharov travels to a trial in Kaluga, where two samizdat distributors are sentenced to five years in exile. During a break between hearings, the prosecutor approaches him:

"How do you like the trial? In my opinion, the court has very thoroughly and objectively considered all the circumstances of the case."

The prosecutor, clearly thinking that Sakharov is on his side—after all, he's an academician—expects some praise for his indictment speech. But Sakharov replies:

"In my opinion, the whole trial is a complete violation of the law."

After the sentencing, the wife of one of the convicted men approaches Sakharov and hands him a folder—she's managed to steal case materials, including the stenographic record of her husband's final statement. Sakharov skillfully hides the papers under his jacket, walks past the militiamen (who don't dare search the famous scientist), and heads to the station.

Just before the train departs, a woman rushes into the carriage—Sakharov recognizes her from the courtroom. Her name is Elena Bonner, and she is also a dissident. She emotionally tells him that the court noticed the missing folder and there's now a huge commotion. Sakharov admits that he has the stolen documents.

This spy-like incident is the beginning of a romance between Andrei and Lyusya, as he will affectionately call her. He is forty-nine, and she is forty-seven.

At first, they mostly meet in courts—or because of them. In 1970, Lyusya's relative is arrested, accused of attempting to hijack a plane to Sweden. The plan wasn't carried out—the suspect was detained on the ground, near the aircraft—but he is charged with high treason and sentenced to death.

The KGB agents sitting in the courtroom applaud. "Fascists! Only fascists applaud a death sentence!" shouts Lyusya from the audience, so loudly that they even stop clapping.

Sakharov begins to fight for a review of the case. He writes a double letter: to the Soviet authorities, urging them to soften the sentence for the would-be hijacker, and to President Nixon, asking for help in the case of Angela Davis, an African-American activist charged with complicity in a murder—a case considered politically motivated worldwide.

Sakharov receives no reply from the Soviet authorities, but a response from Nixon: the American president informs him that Davis's trial will be open and Sakharov is welcome to attend if he is in the United States.

In the end, the Soviet court commutes the death sentence for Lyusya's relative to fifteen years in prison. Angela Davis spends only eighteen months behind bars and is acquitted.

Sakharov and Bonner grow very close—she types and edits his texts, and they visit each other more frequently. A year after they meet, they confess their love for each other.

Bonner's life story is not an easy one: she is the daughter of "enemies of the people"—her parents were repressed in 1937. During the war, she served as a nurse and was severely shell-shocked. In 1953, at the height of the Doctors' Plot, she was expelled from medical school, but was reinstated after Stalin's death.

At the time she meets Sakharov, she is divorced, works as a pediatrician, and teaches at a medical college. Lyusya doesn't want to formalize their relationship, fearing that being married to a dissident would bring trouble to her children. But Andrei insists.

They marry in January 1972. Soon life for her family does indeed become complicated: her daughter, Tatyana, is expelled from her final year of journalism school, prevented from defending her thesis. Bonner herself is summoned to the city party organization, where she is threatened with sanctions for her regular participation in protest actions. In response, she coldly pulls out a pre-written statement from her bag, announcing her resignation from the Communist Party "due to my beliefs."

A colleague, horrified, whispers:

"What are you doing! You have children!"

"Leave me alone. What do children have to do with this?" Bonner retorts.

Many new acquaintances are convinced that it is Lyusya who pushes Andrei into dissident activities. But both Andrei and Lyusya are indignant at these assumptions.

SANYA AND ALYA

It's at Rostropovich's dacha in October 1970 that Solzhenitsyn learns he has been awarded the Nobel Prize in Literature. Previously, the prize had gone to Soviet writers considered living legends: Boris Pasternak in 1958 and Mikhail Sholokhov in 1965. But no one could have predicted that in 1970 it would be awarded to a former prisoner who had published only one novella in the USSR—*One Day in the Life of Ivan Denisovich*—and four short stories. Yet the Nobel Committee made just that decision.

The reaction among Soviet writers is outrage. Now forgotten in the twenty-first century, back then, they judged their works as great classics, each one expecting to win the Nobel Prize at some point. And now they've all been bypassed by some upstart who criticizes the government. Twelve years earlier, in 1958, the Soviet cultural elite had viciously attacked Boris Pasternak without even reading his novel *Doctor Zhivago*—because that was the order from above. Now, in 1970, they turn their fury on Solzhenitsyn, this time with sincere, heartfelt, and furious indignation.

Solzhenitsyn has been preparing for world recognition since 1958. Back then, he dreamed of winning, going abroad, and speaking at the Nobel lecture to "tell the whole truth: Get to the Nobel podium and let it rip!" But now, twelve years later, a new opponent to his plan has emerged—his new wife, Alya.

Alya insists that leaving is not an option. "We have to live and die at home, no matter what happens," she says. Solzhenitsyn argues back, "Let those who are fools die here; I want to be published while I'm alive." She counters, saying that whatever he says abroad won't be understood back home. "She thinks like that because she's never been in a Gulag," Solzhenitsyn comments in his memoir.

Gradually, under his wife's influence, Solzhenitsyn begins to change his perspective—not just on this but on other matters as well. Sometimes it seems as if he's slowly becoming a different person.

He decides it's far more important to influence the situation in the USSR rather than explain himself to the West. So he writes a letter to Suslov, whom he had met once in the distant Khrushchev era, offering to have all his books published in the USSR.

Suslov doesn't reply, but the Swedish Nobel Committee keeps sending invitations to the prize events. Solzhenitsyn begins to suspect a trap—he believes the plan is to let him leave the country and then strip him of his citizenship while he's abroad, preventing him from returning. So he decides not to travel to Stockholm to receive the award.

"HIDING TODAY'S NEWSPAPERS IN SHAME"

Slava is horrified by the smear campaign against Solzhenitsyn. He can't betray his friend, and the bitter memories of the campaign against Pasternak are still fresh. Back in 1958, the authorities had summoned Rostropovich to attend a party meeting at the conservatory and give a speech denouncing the writer. But he deliberately delayed his return from a concert tour in Ivanovo, coming back a day late with the perfect excuse—he had been performing for the local weavers.

After Solzhenitsyn is awarded the Nobel Prize, Rostropovich writes an open letter to the Soviet newspapers and shows it to his wife. Galina Vishnevskaya forbids him from sending it: "Do what you want with your life, but don't jeopardize the future of me and our children," she insists—they have two daughters. Rostropovich persists, even suggesting a fake divorce to shield Vishnevskaya from danger. According to his recollections, they argue for two days straight. In the end, Vishnevskaya relents, agreeing to edit the letter, realizing she can't dissuade him. Rostropovich sends the letter to the editors of *Izvestia*, *Literaturnaya Gazeta*, *Pravda*, and *Sovetskaya Kultura*.

Haven't the years taught us to be more cautious about destroying talented people? To refrain from speaking on behalf of the entire nation? I bring up the past not to complain but to prevent us from hiding today's newspapers in shame 20 years from now.*

The Soviet newspapers, of course, don't publish Rostropovich's letter, but it appears in the Western press. From this moment on, Rostropovich begins his slow transformation into an outcast. Many former friends cut ties with him. Nevertheless, he persists. In 1972, together with Andrei Sakharov, Elena Bonner, and other cultural figures, he signs two open letters: one calling for the amnesty of political prisoners and the other demanding the abolition of the death penalty.

Rostropovich's situation worsens: he is no longer invited to conduct at the Bolshoi Theatre. He goes to see the minister of culture, Yekaterina Furtseva, to discuss his predicament.

"Have you listened to *Eugene Onegin* and *War and Peace* conducted by me?"

"Yes, magnificent."

"So why am I being kicked out?"

"They don't want you."

"But many people don't want you as minister, and yet here you are."

The conversation goes nowhere, and Furtseva warns Rostropovich that he will be banned from performing abroad. "I didn't realize that performing at home was a punishment," the cellist retorts defiantly.

Rostropovich is neither jailed nor evicted, but he is left without work. All of his concerts are canceled, usually citing his "illness" as the official reason. The musician starts drinking more, which infuriates Galina. Her career, despite her fears, continues—she still sings at the Bolshoi Theatre, though she's no longer mentioned in the press.

IN KYIV, THEY CUT OFF FINGERS

At the end of December 1971, Ukrainian KGB officers send a series of reports to their superiors, warning that people in Kyiv and Lviv have been singing carols in

---

* Rostropovich's prediction is spot-on: in exactly twenty years, everything will change, and both he and Solzhenitsyn will become classics, legends, adored by the authorities.

a highly suspicious manner. To clarify: New Year's is an entirely secular holiday, introduced by the leadership of Soviet Ukraine in the 1930s and spread across the USSR in 1937. But carols—those are clearly a religious tradition associated with Christmas. Worse still, the reports note that the carols are being sung in Ukrainian—an obvious manifestation of "bourgeois nationalism."

Then, of course, a foreign spy enters the picture—because the KGB needs to prove that all dissidents are "puppets of the West." Just after New Year's, a student—a Belgian citizen of Ukrainian descent—is detained at the border after a tourist visit to his ancestral homeland. Under interrogation, they extract a confession: he is, supposedly, an agent of Western intelligence who came to give orders to the Soviet "fifth column." His forced confession is then broadcast on Soviet television.

By January 12, 1972, the KGB launches raids on the homes of those who had been caroling. In a single day, dozens of dissidents are arrested in Kyiv and Lviv, including the poet Vasyl Stus (who, after being expelled from graduate school, had been working first as a stoker and then as an engineer) and the journalist Vyacheslav Chornovil (previously imprisoned for anti-Soviet activities and now working as a railway laborer). This day will later be called the General Pogrom of Ukrainian culture—marking the start of a sweeping crackdown on Ukrainian dissidents.

During the January raids, the KGB finds a copy of *Internationalism or Russification?* at the home of journalist Ivan Dziuba. This isn't a new text—he wrote it back in 1965, shortly after his protest at the premiere of Parajanov's *Shadows of Forgotten Ancestors*. Dziuba hadn't tried to hide it; in fact, he had sent it as a letter to the Central Committee in Moscow, as well as to the First Secretary of the Ukrainian Communist Party, Petro Shelest, and the head of the republican government, Volodymyr Shcherbytsky.

In this pamphlet, Dziuba—writing as a faithful communist and citing Marxist classics extensively—argues that Stalin betrayed Lenin's principles of internationalism and embraced Russian great-power chauvinism instead. At the time, his argument was ignored. But now the political climate has shifted. The Ukrainian Communist Party forms a special commission, which declares the text to be a "libelous attack on Soviet reality."

The unfolding campaign is skillfully exploited by Volodymyr Shcherbytsky, the head of the Ukrainian government, who happens to be a longtime acquaintance and countryman of General Secretary Brezhnev. He convinces

Brezhnev and Suslov that the Ukrainian nationalists are being shielded by none other than Shelest himself. The maneuver works—Shelest is removed from office, and Shcherbytsky takes his place.

The arrested dissidents receive various prison sentences; some are sent to psychiatric hospitals. In pretrial detention, Vasyl Stus writes a collection of poems, which the KGB meticulously reviews: "From an artistic standpoint, Stus's poems are some sort of delirium, and from a social and political perspective, they are deliberate slander, a defamation of our reality." The poet is sentenced to five years in prison and three years of exile.

Chornovil, who had been publishing the underground journal *Ukrainian Herald* in Lviv, receives six years in prison and three years of exile.

Dziuba is sentenced to five years in prison and five years of exile, but he serves only a year before being pardoned. The dissidents will be convinced that this can mean only one thing—he has begun cooperating with the KGB.

At the same time, Shcherbytsky launches a large-scale campaign of Russification in Ukraine. Ukrainian-language instruction in universities is practically eradicated; professors are instructed to explain that "Lenin spoke Russian." All official documentation is now conducted exclusively in Russian, the number of Ukrainian-language media outlets and books is drastically reduced, and an extensive blacklist of Ukrainian authors is created.

This is not just a Ukrainian phenomenon but part of a broader trend. Back in 1971, at a Communist Party Congress, Leonid Brezhnev declared that a unified Soviet people had emerged, uniting all classes, social groups, nations, and ethnicities. The true architect of this concept is, of course, Suslov. And since the Soviet people, according to Suslov's definition, must speak Russian, the KGB begins intensifying its suppression of nationalist movements across all Soviet republics. But it is Shcherbytsky who wants to be the model student. Repression in Ukraine is felt in exaggerated, even grotesque proportions—giving rise to a saying: "When they trim nails in Moscow, they cut off fingers in Kyiv."

"ALL MERCHANTS ARE THIEVES!"

In late May 1972, the Kremlin witnesses an unusually heated discussion—something rarely seen in the Soviet Politburo, where debates are usually discouraged. Stalin himself had demanded that communists always align with the majority, maintaining party unity at all costs. But this time, the Politburo is deeply divided. Defense Minister Andrei Grechko, a recent proponent of the invasion of Czechoslovakia, demands the cancellation of US president Richard Nixon's upcoming visit to the USSR at the end of the month. American forces have begun bombing Hanoi, the capital of Vietnam, and opened fire on Soviet ships, killing several sailors. Marshal Grechko is outraged and insists on retracting Nixon's invitation.

General Secretary Leonid Brezhnev, on the other hand, believes the visit is crucial. Just a few months earlier, in February 1972, Nixon made a historic trip to China and met with Mao Zedong. The prospect of a US-China anti-Soviet alliance terrifies Brezhnev. He reminds the Politburo that the only American president ever to visit the USSR was Franklin Roosevelt, who stayed with Stalin during the Yalta Conference in 1945. Brezhnev wants to become the first Soviet leader to officially host a US president in the Kremlin.

Mikhail Suslov sides more with the defense minister. He presents Brezhnev with a stack of letters addressed to the Central Committee of the Communist Party—Soviet citizens protesting the visit of Nixon, whom Soviet television routinely brands as a "warmonger."

"So what?" Brezhnev chuckles. "We're just reaping the rewards of our own propaganda."

Ultimately, Brezhnev manages to persuade the Politburo.

Preparations for Nixon's visit resemble the frantic efforts of a remote Soviet town preparing for a visit from a high-ranking official. Repairs are made all over the city, and new asphalt is laid. Dilapidated buildings along the route from the airport to central Moscow are demolished, including entire historic neighborhoods in some places. A few structures near the Kremlin's entrance are razed, and a lawn is planted on the cleared ground. This area will be known among Muscovites as "Nixon's Lawn."*

The KGB spares no effort to prevent so-called provocations—a term used in the USSR for any anti-government demonstration. Dissident students at Moscow University are expelled and sent to the army. Phones

---

* Nixon's Lawn will stand empty until 2016—until Vladimir Putin orders a towering monument to Prince Vladimir of Kyiv to be installed there. At the unveiling, the guest of honor will be the widow of Alexander Solzhenitsyn, once known as Alya Svetlova.

of prominent human rights activists, including academician Sakharov, are cut off a week before the Americans arrive.

To the surprise of Soviet bureaucrats, the visit goes off without a hitch. Their American counterparts aren't so different from them after all. Brezhnev and Nixon sign a series of historic agreements on strategic arms limitation and anti-ballistic missile defense—acknowledging that both sides possess enough nuclear weapons to destroy the world multiple times over and agreeing not to do so. Both Brezhnev and Nixon love life too much to contemplate death. Thus begins the era known as détente, where the USSR and the USA promise to slow down the Cold War and avoid a nuclear confrontation.

The two leaders also agree on a joint space mission—previously, the USSR and the USA had been locked in a fierce space race, but now, for the first time, the concept of cooperation in space emerges. Brezhnev takes the Nixons to see *Swan Lake* at the Bolshoi Theatre, while First Lady Pat Nixon visits a fashion house and a watch factory. Brezhnev even gifts Nixon a hovercraft. The American president embarks on a grand tour of the USSR, visiting Leningrad and Kyiv, where he explores museums. Hardly any discussion of human rights, Vietnam, or Czechoslovakia occurs—only realpolitik.

Brezhnev is particularly taken with Nixon's National Security Advisor, Henry Kissinger. The Soviet side believes that it was Kissinger who set the constructive tone of the visit.[*]

On May 27, 1972, the Nixons fly from Moscow to Leningrad. Meanwhile, unemployed Leningrad poet Joseph Brodsky is packing his bags. On May 10, ten days before Nixon's arrival in the USSR, Brodsky is summoned to the passport office and given a choice: either leave the country immediately or face "some hot times ahead." Brodsky doesn't need an explanation—he has already endured a humiliating trial that refused to recognize him as a poet, spent three weeks in the notorious Pryazhka psychiatric hospital for evaluation, and was convicted of "parasitism" and sentenced to a five-year exile to northern Russia. Sensing that worse could follow, Brodsky offers no resistance. On June 4, just five days after Nixon departs from the USSR, Brodsky will be stripped of his citizenship and sent first to Vienna, and then he will go to the United States, where he will spend the next decade teaching at the University of Michigan.

---

[*] From this moment on, and for decades to come, the Kremlin will maintain the belief that Republicans are easier to deal with, thanks to pragmatists like Kissinger.

But Nixon and Kissinger, of course, don't discuss Russian poetry—or the everyday realities of Soviet life. Although perhaps they could. Nixon is no stranger to the USSR; this is not his first visit to Moscow. His previous trip was just as notable. In July 1959, Nixon visited Moscow as vice president under Eisenhower. Back then, the Soviet leader was Nikita Khrushchev, the country was in the midst of the Thaw, and relations with the USSR were improving. Nixon arrived to open an exhibition on American home appliances called the American National Exhibition.

It's unclear how such an exhibition was even possible in the USSR in the 1950s—after all, household appliances were practically nonexistent in the country at the time (and would remain so for years). There was no middle class, and most people didn't even have private apartments. The rural population was only beginning to move en masse to cities, and the majority lived in so-called communal apartments: crowded spaces resembling hostels, where each family occupied one room and entire floors shared a single bathroom. Such living conditions could last decades—or an entire lifetime. In short, household appliances were utterly foreign to the average Soviet citizen. Yet Khrushchev couldn't admit this, so he engaged Nixon in a conversation that would go down in history as the "Kitchen Debates."

Khrushchev looked at dishwashers, lawn mowers, and other everyday items common to an American household as if he were an alien—he simply didn't understand them. In the end, he concluded that they were all luxuries and unnecessary frills. "Do you have a machine that puts food in your mouth and pushes it down?" he quipped.

He went on to claim that American houses were flimsy, would fall apart within a few years, and cost an outrageous amount of money. According to him, the only freedom ordinary Americans could afford was "the freedom to sleep under a bridge." Nixon countered by sharing that he had once helped his father in his small shop, yet had risen to become vice president. Khrushchev had a clear, communist view of business: "All merchants are thieves!" he declared. This Soviet approach to commerce would persist in Soviet society for many decades.

Only thirteen years separated Nixon's two visits to the USSR, but the everyday life of Soviet citizens had changed very little in that time. Most people still didn't have private apartments and lived in communal housing. Nixon likely didn't think much about it—because in 1972, the Soviet side did everything possible to pull the wool over his eyes.

"I DON'T GIVE A SHIT ABOUT THE RUSSIAN PEOPLE"

In 1973, in the elite suburbs of Moscow near the Rublyovka Highway, Andrei Sakharov and his wife, Elena Bonner, head to see Alexander Solzhenitsyn. The writer isn't home—he's out on some errands, so they are greeted by his new wife, Alya Svetlova. She promptly starts lecturing the scientist on his recent actions.

Alya reprimands Sakharov for spreading himself too thin—defending minor dissidents, writing too many protest letters, and attending every court trial. As Solzhenitsyn would later summarize his grievances: "Defending not the entire 'humanity' or 'people' at once, but each individually oppressed person drains Sakharov's energy and health disproportionately compared to the results (which are nearly zero)." Alya goes on to criticize Sakharov's penchant for signing endless petitions and appeals, which have become so frequent that they lose impact, overshadowing his more significant works that deserve international attention.

What especially irks Solzhenitsyn is Sakharov's campaign for free emigration rights for those who wish to leave the USSR—a feat impossible without government permission. Alya insists that emigration is simply running away from responsibility and that there are far more pressing issues in the country: millions of collective farmers who are essentially serfs, denied the right to leave their farms, and millions of parents unable to provide education for their children.

"Infuriated by the didactic tone of Svetlova's 'lecture' directed at me," Sakharov recalls, "Lyusya exclaims: 'I don't give a shit about the Russian people! You cook porridge for your own children, not for the whole Russian people.'"

A heavy silence follows. Andrei and Lyusya leave, and Alya silently sees them out.

"Lyusya's words about the Russian people may have sounded blasphemous in that house. But in essence, and emotionally, she had the right to say them. By her entire life, Lyusya herself is the 'Russian people,' and she will sort things out in her own way," Sakharov later reflects. Solzhenitsyn, however, will never mention this conversation in his own memoir.

This is perhaps the most symbolic argument in Russia's post-war history: What matters more, the people or the individual? The collective or the personal? "We" or "I"?

After this encounter, Solzhenitsyn and Sakharov hardly speak again—not because of the porridge comment, of course, but because of broader circumstances. Solzhenitsyn married Alya and moved into her apartment in central Moscow. Solzhenitsyn also recognizes the trouble he's brought upon his friend Slava. "Rostropovich was growing weary and weak from the long, hopeless siege. . . . I had to ask: is it right for one artist to wither so that another can grow?" he writes. Still, the persecution of Rostropovich does not cease.

Within a few months, both Sakharov and Solzhenitsyn become the primary enemies of the Soviet Union, which draws them together. On August 21, 1973, Sakharov holds a major press conference for Western media, boldly declaring the USSR "a vast concentration camp." Solzhenitsyn celebrates: "Bravo! He voiced our prisoner's mindset even before I did!" Their speeches captivate the world's attention, and Solzhenitsyn gives several interviews as well.

The Soviet government responds by unleashing a media campaign against both men. First, a collective letter is penned by Soviet scientists; then the newspaper *Pravda* publishes a statement from the most prominent Soviet writers, signed by Nobel laureate Mikhail Sholokhov, Soviet anthem lyricist Sergei Mikhalkov, and others. The letter states: "The behavior of people like Sakharov and Solzhenitsyn, who slander our state and social system, attempt to sow distrust in the peace-loving policies of the Soviet state, and effectively call on the West to continue the Cold War, can evoke no other feelings but deep contempt and condemnation." Similar articles condemning "traitors of the motherland" are published in other Soviet newspapers.

However, the Soviet authorities do not dare to take direct action against Solzhenitsyn and Sakharov. At this point, relations with the West are crucial for the Soviet economy: the USSR buys grain from the United States and pipes from West Germany for gas pipelines. A Pepsi factory opens in the Soviet Union. Earlier in 1973, Soviet leader Leonid Brezhnev traveled to America and returned with a blue Lincoln gifted to him by President Richard Nixon. Moreover, the Conference on Security and Cooperation in Europe is scheduled for the summer of 1973—a major event the USSR cannot afford to jeopardize, as it is keen on maintaining favorable Western public opinion. Meanwhile, global support for Sakharov and Solzhenitsyn reaches unprecedented levels, prompting the Soviet government to make concessions, such as ceasing the jamming of Western radio broadcasts like those of the BBC, Voice of America, and Radio Free Europe.

But in October 1973, war breaks out in the Middle East as Egypt attacks Israel, diverting global attention away from the Soviet Union.

Solzhenitsyn attempts to keep the spotlight on him and Sakharov, writing a letter to the Nobel Committee urging them to award the Peace Prize to the scientist. However, his plea goes unanswered, as the prize has already been earmarked for US secretary of state Henry Kissinger and Vietnamese diplomat Le Duc Tho—a particularly controversial decision, given that the Vietnam War has not yet ended.

Meanwhile, Soviet authorities debate how to deal with the dissidents. KGB chief Yuri Andropov proposes secret negotiations with European countries, offering to have them take in Solzhenitsyn. As for Sakharov, KGB chief Andropov suggests threatening him with the revocation of his awards and salary as an academician unless he stops engaging with Western media, and relocating him to Novosibirsk, a restricted area for foreigners. Soviet premier Alexei Kosygin argues that these measures are too lenient—he insists that Solzhenitsyn should be put on trial and exiled to Verkhoyansk, the coldest place in the USSR: "No foreign journalists will go there; it's too cold."

Solzhenitsyn is determined to publish his monumental work, *The Gulag Archipelago*, abroad at any cost, but he is plagued by threatening letters and phone calls. He even fears that his sons might be kidnapped to force him to halt the book's release. He discusses this with Alya. "Our decision is super-human: our children are not worth more than the memory of the millions tortured; we will not stop the Book for anything," he will later write.

VOLODYA AND MARINA

A couple steps into a supermarket in West Berlin. They're both thirty-five. He's the most famous singer in Russia, and she's a French film star. As he glances around, staring at the sausages, cheeses, and fruits, he suddenly pales and starts vomiting. His wife leads him back to their hotel.

It's 1973. He is Vladimir Vysotsky, the childhood idol of Vladimir Putin. His wife is the famous French actress Marina Vlady.

"How can this be? They lost the war, and they have everything, while we won, and we have nothing!" Vysotsky whispers in their room. "In some cities, there hasn't been meat for years; there's a shortage of everything, everywhere, all the time!" He doesn't sleep all night.

This is his first trip to the West. Ordinary Soviet citizens aren't allowed to travel abroad, but he's lucky—his wife is a foreigner, so he was granted permission.

In 1976, the couple travels to the USA, where Vysotsky experiences an unexpected triumph. CBS requests an interview for *60 Minutes*. Soviet television had never interviewed Vysotsky. The host, Dan Rather, introduces him as the "Soviet Bob Dylan" and "an unyielding critic of Soviet society."

"You call yourself a protesting poet, but not a revolutionary poet. What's the difference?" Rather asks.

"I've never considered my songs as protest songs or revolutionary songs. . . . In revolutionary times, people write revolutionary songs. In ordinary, normal times, people write protest songs; they exist everywhere in the world. People simply want life to be better than it is now, for tomorrow to be better than today."

"It might not be the case, but I sense that some in the USSR are worried about whether you'll return. Am I wrong?" the host inquires.

"Well, why?! Come on! This is my fourth or fifth time abroad, and I always come back. It's ridiculous! If I were the kind of person they were afraid to let out of the country, this would be a completely different interview. I'm sitting here calmly, answering your questions peacefully. I love my country and don't want to harm it. And I never will."

Vysotsky's interview is flawless—there's nothing for the KGB or party officials to criticize. It's clear that if the poet had uttered even one careless word, he would have permanently lost the right to travel abroad.

In the USA, Vysotsky and Vlady visit Disneyland—he rides every amusement ride, eats ice cream, drinks Coca-Cola, and enjoys himself like a child. Later they fly to Los Angeles, where they meet Miloš Forman, the Czechoslovakian director who immigrated to the United States in 1968 after the Soviet invasion. At the time, Forman is at the height of his fame, having just won every possible award for *One Flew over the Cuckoo's Nest*. He warmly welcomes his guests from behind the Iron Curtain and even invites them to a Hollywood party at the house of his producer, Mike Medavoy, who is, like Vlady, also a descendant of Russian emigrants. At first, Vysotsky feels out of place among the American stars, so he sits quietly in a corner, strumming his guitar and humming. One by one, the guests gather around him to listen, including Liza Minnelli, Robert De Niro, and

Sylvester Stallone. Vysotsky stops singing, but they urge him to continue, and he performs his songs in Russian for nearly an hour. When he finishes, they applaud and shout, "Bravo!"

Vysotsky occupies a peculiar position in the Soviet Union. He's a countercultural star: he isn't shown on television, written about in newspapers, or played on the radio, yet the entire country knows his voice and face.

In 1967, twenty-nine-year-old Vysotsky starred in the mountaineering film *Vertical*, where he also performed several of his songs, instantly becoming famous across the nation. He performs at Moscow's most progressive venue, the Taganka Theatre, and writes songs sung with guitars all over the USSR. Initially, his work is largely prison themed. Although Vysotsky himself never spent time in jail, his lyrical persona is that of a man who has endured the Gulag. By the late 1960s, his themes broadened, and his songs included increasingly political satire.

For Vysotsky, as for many artists and intellectuals of the mid-twentieth century, 1968 was a turning point. Soviet authorities could no longer tolerate him. In 1968, a smear campaign began against him in the press. "Vysotsky sings on behalf of and for the sake of alcoholics, convicts, criminals, and morally and mentally deficient people," said the newspaper *Soviet Russia*. "These are unruly hooligans, boasting of their impunity. In pursuit of dubious fame, he does not hesitate to mock Soviet citizens and their patriotic pride."

Vysotsky was deeply affected by the backlash—at times, he plunged into heavy drinking bouts, leading to conflicts in the theater.

In that same fateful year, 1968, he met Marina. She was a European cinema star who recently won Best Actress at Cannes. Born in France to Russian émigré parents, she speaks Russian. Vlady arrived in Moscow for a film festival; her Moscow friends took her to the theater, where she saw Vysotsky onstage for the first time. Two years later, they married—though Soviet citizens are generally forbidden from marrying foreigners. To circumvent the obstacles, Marina joined the French Communist Party, allowing her to visit Moscow more frequently and helping ease Soviet resistance to their union.

They spent their honeymoon in Georgia, where their friend the eccentric director Sergei Parajanov staged a performance for them: he invited them to stay in his apartment and, in preparation for their arrival, covered the entire floor with fresh fruit.

JOHN AND YOKO

March 1973. While Vysotsky is still dreaming of his first trip to the West, a knock comes at the door of John Lennon's New York apartment. He doesn't answer, and the uninvited guest just slides an envelope under the door. It's a deportation order from the Immigration Service. The former Beatles front man must leave the United States within sixty days. For him and his wife, Yoko Ono, it's a shock—she has a green card and can stay.

The official reason for the deportation is that four years earlier, Lennon was arrested in London when the police found a joint in his home. Lennon insists it was planted by the officer, but no one is fooled; the minor offense in England is just a pretext. The real reason is Lennon's political sympathies.

In 1968, he underwent a moral transformation. He was so deeply moved by student protests around the world and the anti–Vietnam War movement in the United States that he completely abandoned his previous apolitical and somewhat carefree stance. Previously, Lennon had been an elevated poet, sometimes a self-absorbed Buddhist fascinated by Eastern spiritual practices. But in 1968, everything changed. He fell in love with Japanese artist Yoko Ono, and she profoundly influenced his world view. Together, they staged a series of highly unusual protests—not sit-ins, as was common among students at the time, but "bed-ins." John and Yoko lay in bed in their hotel rooms—first in Amsterdam, then in Montreal. During one of these protests, Lennon wrote "Give Peace a Chance," which became the anthem of the Western protest movement for the next decade.

Soon after, he connected with American revolutionaries and anti-government protest leaders Jerry Rubin and Abbie Hoffman. Moreover, in December 1971, Lennon and Ono participated in a concert supporting American dissident John Sinclair, who had been sentenced to ten years in prison for possessing two joints of marijuana. Lennon's involvement had such a powerful impact that, under public pressure, the court reconsidered the sentence and released Sinclair. This development deeply alarmed President Nixon's administration.

In 1972, Nixon was up for reelection, and his staunch opponents—Rubin, Hoffman, and others—were preparing to fight him with all their might. They planned a "political Woodstock" to coincide with the Republican National Convention that would officially nominate Nixon for president. The previous Democratic convention in Chicago in 1968 had erupted into massive riots, and this time the consequences could be even more severe—especially if Lennon joined the protesters.

In February 1972, Republican senator Strom Thurmond wrote to the White House, recommending the deportation of British citizen John Lennon as a "strategic countermeasure." Soon after, the US Immigration and Naturalization Service initiated deportation proceedings against the musician. At the same time, the FBI began overtly surveilling Lennon and Ono, wiretapping their phones.

This provoked an enormous backlash in American society. Bob Dylan wrote a letter in their defense:

> John and Yoko inspire, transcend, and stimulate, and in doing so, they help others see the pure light and thus put an end to this dull taste of petty commercialism imposed by the all-powerful mass media. Cheers to John and Yoko. Let them stay here, live, and breathe. There is plenty of room and space in this country.

From a political standpoint, the pressure on the couple was effective: John and Yoko withdrew from activism, emphasizing that they were merely musicians and artists with no political agenda. They did not attend the "political Woodstock" and stopped speaking out about the Vietnam War. Richard Nixon won reelection, but the legal battle against Lennon continued. His lawyers were convinced they had almost no chance of winning the case.

But as the immigration officer slips the deportation order under Lennon and Ono's door, the Watergate scandal is already unfolding. In August 1974, Nixon is forced to resign.

On October 8, 1975, Lennon wins his court case, and he will soon receive his green card. It's a triple celebration. On October 9, John turns thirty-five, and on the same day, Yoko gives birth to their son, Sean. After this, Lennon decides to quit not only politics but also music, dedicating himself entirely to raising his son, taking walks, playing games, cooking, and changing diapers.

"CONGRATULATE FOR A MISFORTUNE"

In August 1973, amid the vicious smear campaign against Sakharov and Solzhenitsyn, the KGB pays a visit to one of the writer's assistants—an elderly pensioner from Leningrad named Yelizaveta Voronyanskaya. They search her apartment, interrogate her for hours, and she eventually breaks, revealing where a copy of *The Gulag Archipelago* is buried. Upon returning home, overwhelmed by the betrayal of her idol, she hangs herself.

Solzhenitsyn doesn't learn of this immediately, but when he does, he decides the time has come to publish the book in the West. He's waited a long time for the right moment, and now he knows—it's time.

Shortly after, his first wife, Natasha, calls him and suggests they meet at an unusual spot—the platform of the Kazansky Railway Station in Moscow. From the first words, he realizes she's now an emissary of the KGB. She's agreed to collaborate with the authorities, given testimony against her ex-husband, and is now acting as a go-between:

"My world has really expanded. And the smart people I've met! You don't know anyone like them; you're surrounded by idiots. Why do you keep blaming Andropov? He's got nothing to do with it. It's others," Solzhenitsyn recalls her saying. "You're being deceived, provoked, horribly blackmailed."

The deal she presents on behalf of the KGB is straightforward: Solzhenitsyn must promise not to publish *The Gulag Archipelago* for twenty years, and in return, the authorities will allow the publication of *Cancer Ward* in the USSR. He pretends to agree.

Three months later, the first volume of *The Gulag Archipelago* is released in France. Solzhenitsyn learns of it while listening to the Western radio on December 28, 1974. From that moment, his family's life turns into a nightmare. Threatening letters had arrived before, but now the phone rings nonstop with men's and women's voices shouting threats and insults. His wife, Alya, has to answer the calls because Solzhenitsyn is mostly working at the dacha outside of Moscow. But Alya manages to respond with composure: "Are you done talking? Well, then tell Yuri Vladimirovich that with such dumbasses, he's in for a rough time," she says, referring to KGB chief Andropov.

All Soviet newspapers accuse Solzhenitsyn's new book of insulting the memory of those who died in the Great Patriotic War, labeling him a "literary Vlasovite," which means traitor—even though no one in the USSR has actually read the book yet.

On February 12, 1974, Solzhenitsyn decides to go for a walk with a stroller—his third son with Alya, Stepan, was just born. But soon he returns. The courtyard of their home is filled with plainclothes officers.

They come upstairs, take the writer away, and drive him to Lefortovo—the KGB's investigative detention center.

Friends rush to the Solzhenitsyns' apartment, including Sakharov. Later Sakharov and several others go to the Prosecutor General's Office to protest.

The next day, the Nobel laureate in literature is charged with treason—but within hours, he's whisked away to the airport and sent to Germany. Upon landing in Frankfurt, he is surrounded by journalists, but he offers no comment: "I spoke enough while I was in the Soviet Union. Now, I'll keep quiet."

Western radio stations announce that Solzhenitsyn is not in prison but has been exiled abroad, and friends begin congratulating Alya. "But why is everyone so joyful? This is a misfortune, it's a form of violence, no less than prison," Solzhenitsyn reflects on his wife's feelings. "It burns. They call, they congratulate us—for a misfortune? . . ."

"TRUE ANTI-LENIN"

Back in September 1973, when Solzhenitsyn makes the decision to publish *The Gulag Archipelago* abroad, he carefully considers the impact of its release. He is convinced it will be a monumental blow to the Soviet Union, one that will force the authorities to come to their senses and start negotiations with him. So he writes a "Letter to the Leaders of the Soviet Union" and sends it to General Secretary Leonid Brezhnev. It's a political manifesto. Solzhenitsyn positions himself as the new ideologue for the country, proposing that the USSR abandon communism and transform into an Orthodox national state.

There is evidence that the Politburo members read the letter. But they never discuss its contents. Instead, on February 12, 1974, Solzhenitsyn is arrested, stripped of his Soviet citizenship, and flown to Frankfurt, after which he heads to Switzerland.

"In moments of pride, I feel like the true anti-Lenin," he writes from Zurich. "I'll blow up his legacy, leave not a stone upon a stone. . . . But to do that, I must be as he was—a taut string, an arrow. . . . Isn't it symbolic: he from Zurich to Moscow, I from Moscow to Zurich. . . ." Solzhenitsyn means that in 1917 Lenin arrived in Russia specifically from Switzerland to prepare the revolution.

To many of Solzhenitsyn's admirers, both in the USSR and the West, his exile marks a surprising transformation. Once a freedom fighter and enemy of dictatorship, he suddenly appears to morph into a defender of empire and conservative values the moment he crosses the border. This dramatic metamorphosis is striking, but not unique in Russian history. A similar shift occurred a century earlier with Fyodor Dostoevsky, who, after narrowly escaping execution and spending nearly a decade in a Siberian penal colony, emerged more religious and conservative, trading his liberal ideals for imperial ones. Yet, unlike Dostoevsky's influence in the nineteenth century, Solzhenitsyn's ideological shift has a profound impact on Russia's future.

In early March 1974, British and American newspapers publish his "Letter to the Leaders of the Soviet Union." The *Sunday Times* releases a softened version that Solzhenitsyn edits in exile, followed by the original text in the *New York Times*—the original version sent to Brezhnev.

In his letter, Solzhenitsyn sharply criticizes the West, declaring that its culture is in decline, that Europe is kneeling before the USSR and its diplomatic victories. He dubs the Western political system a "rampant democracy," often powerless against "a handful of snotty terrorists," alluding to the 1972 Munich Olympics hostage crisis. He argues that technological progress and economic growth should be halted because they are destroying rural life, traditional ways, and those charming old towns. Instead, he urges the USSR to channel its resources into building new cities in Eastern Siberia and populating the "Russian Northeast." Yet he insists the Soviet system of government should remain authoritarian. Solzhenitsyn urges Brezhnev to allow freedom for religion, art, literature, and publishing—"but not for political books, God forbid, manifestos, or campaign leaflets."

He later explains that this letter reflects his "sobering up": "In the prison camps, we dreamed only of revolution, and for many years, I carried that same feeling by inertia—but now I see that our salvation lies in the regime's evolution, otherwise everything will fall apart."

The letter is met with bewilderment and heavy criticism in the West. Even Sakharov, who remains in the USSR, condemns it, calling Solzhenitsyn a "non-aggressive nationalist" and dismissing his program as more mythmaking than a viable plan. "Creating myths," he warns, "is not always harmless." Solzhenitsyn's claims that technical progress is harmful, and that Marxism is a Western idea that has led Russia astray, draw a wry smile from Sakharov: "I don't even understand the idea of dividing concepts into Western and Russian."

The conflict between Solzhenitsyn, Western media, and Soviet dissidents only deepens. Both those who have emigrated and those still in the USSR increasingly accuse Solzhenitsyn of nationalism and Great Russian chauvinism. He has no desire for Russia to become a democratic country; his ideals are entirely different.

FREEDOM AND OTHER DEBAUCHED ACTS

Russification and the fight against nationalism are intensifying in Ukraine. Yet only filmmaker Sergei Parajanov laughs, saying that he alone cannot be accused of Ukrainian nationalism—because he is Armenian. And he is not shy about loudly defending dissidents, protesting censorship, and signing open letters. Back in 1968, his name was the first on a petition by Ukrainian cultural figures against political persecution. In 1972, after the arrest of Dziuba, Parajanov began supporting his family.

Parajanov no longer lives in Kyiv—he works in Armenia, where he recently filmed *Sayat-Nova*, a stunning movie without words, as if a painting had come to life.* But the censors demand it be reedited and rename it *The Color of Pomegranates*.

Parajanov returns to Kyiv for a few days—his son is seriously ill and hospitalized. At that very moment, in December 1973, a denunciation lands on the desk of the Kyiv police:

> Comrade Chief! My civic duty compels me to report the debauched and pederastic activities of Sergei Parajanov. For many years, he has engaged in the corruption of minors, young men, and adult males. He has turned his home into a den of depravity. I urge you to put an end to these immoral acts.

The author of the denunciation is never found—most likely, it was written by KGB operatives. Nevertheless, a criminal case is opened against the filmmaker. All his acquaintances are interrogated. Many provide confessions, along with stories about the famous guests who have visited Parajanov's home:

---

* At the time, Armenia was one of the fifteen republics of the USSR, with a population roughly equal to that of Utah and an area comparable to Hawaii.

various dissidents, American writer John Updike, Italian screenwriter Tonino Guerra, and even Vladimir Vysotsky.

Parajanov denies any violence, but he is sentenced to five years of hard labor. "Finally, so-called poetic cinema is defeated," declares Ukraine's First Secretary Shcherbytsky at the party plenary session.

"He was guilty of being free," poet Bella Akhmadulina will later write.

DON'T LEAVE

After Solzhenitsyn's arrest and expulsion, on March 29, 1974, Rostropovich and Vishnevskaya write a letter to the head of the USSR, Leonid Brezhnev, asking for the permission to leave the country with their children for two years.

Leonard Bernstein, an American composer well acquainted with Rostropovich, tries to help. He learns that Senator Edward Kennedy is heading to Moscow and asks him to persuade Brezhnev to let Slava and Galina leave the country.

The matter is discussed in the Kremlin. KGB general Filipp Bobkov argues in favor of allowing Rostropovich to leave, claiming years later that he "saved" the cellist. According to Bobkov, if Rostropovich had been denied permission to leave, he would have succumbed to alcoholism. The authorities display uncharacteristic leniency: Rostropovich's request is granted.

Minister of Culture Yekaterina Furtseva insists that Rostropovich leave by June 11, before the start of the International Tchaikovsky Competition—an important event in the world of classical music—to avoid any scandal in front of foreign guests. On May 10, 1974, Rostropovich conducts his final concert at the Moscow Conservatory. Everyone knows this is a farewell: the audience stands in the aisles and sits on the floor. Many are in tears. After the performance, the crowd chants, "Don't leave!"

On May 26, 1974, Slava departs for London; Galina and their daughters join him two months later, after the girls finish the school year in the USSR.

Initially, Rostropovich refrains from making political statements. However, after two years, the question of returning to Moscow is never raised, and in 1977 Rostropovich accepts the role of chief conductor of the National Symphony Orchestra in Washington, D.C. In an interview, he says, "The Soviet Union is a country of dead souls where everything alive and progressive is destroyed." Asked how life in the West compares, the cellist responds, "I am very, very happy here."

In March 1978, Slava and Galina fly to Paris. They have recently applied to renew their expiring Soviet passports in Washington and are waiting for the new documents. On March 15, Soviet television announces that the government has decided to strip them of their citizenship.

The next day the newspaper *Izvestia* publishes an article titled "Ideological Renegades":

> They systematically provided material assistance to subversive
> anti-Soviet centers and other hostile organizations abroad. While
> formally remaining citizens of the Soviet Union, Rostropovich
> and Vishnevskaya have essentially become ideological renegades,
> conducting activities against the Soviet Union and the Soviet people.

The next day, outraged, Rostropovich and Vishnevskaya write to Brezhnev:

> We do not recognize your right to this act of violence against us
> unless specific charges are brought against us and we are given
> the opportunity for legal defense. We demand a trial anywhere in
> the USSR, anytime, with one condition: that the process be open
> to the public.

Stripping citizenship is a common punishment in Soviet times, though reserved for a select few—often famous writers, artists, and musicians. More commonly, dissidents are imprisoned under Article 70 of the Criminal Code for "anti-Soviet agitation and propaganda" or confined to psychiatric hospitals with diagnoses of "sluggish schizophrenia." In 1976, while in prison, Ukrainian poet Vasyl Stus writes a letter to the Supreme Soviet of the USSR, requesting to be stripped of his citizenship: "To be a Soviet citizen means to be a slave. . . ." But the authorities ignore his request.

Slava and Galina probably know about the dissidents left behind in the USSR—but they are focused on music. They become part of the global cultural elite, befriending Bernstein, Horowitz, Menuhin, and other stars of the classical music world. They collect art, porcelain, and antiques. As for the fate of those who remained in Russia—meaning "politics"—they never speak out.

THIRTY PIECES OF SILVER AS THE NOBEL PRIZE

In 1975, Lyusya develops glaucoma—a consequence of a wartime concussion—and needs surgery that's too complex to be performed in the USSR. But Sakharov knows his wife can be helped if she goes abroad for treatment. Bonner submits a request to leave the country, but she is soon denied.

So, just like in 1973, Sakharov holds a press conference with his wife and announces that during the thirtieth anniversary of the Soviet victory in World War II he will go on a hunger strike until she is allowed to travel for treatment. Many international organizations send letters urging the Soviet authorities to grant Bonner an exit visa. And in the end, it works—at the end of August, Lyusya leaves for Italy.

Then, on October 9, 1975, it is announced that Sakharov has been awarded the Nobel Peace Prize, for which Solzhenitsyn first nominated him in 1973. A new scandal erupts in the Soviet Union, with open letters in the press, fresh caricatures, and attacks. "The bribe was slipped in under the guise of the Nobel Peace Prize. Sakharov is promised over a hundred thousand dollars," says the newspaper *Trud*, insinuating that the Nobel is a reward for Sakharov's pro-Western stance. "It's hard to say exactly how that translates to the 30 pieces of silver from ancient Judea. Perhaps Mrs. Bonner, who is quite knowledgeable in these matters, could provide a qualified answer."*

There is, of course, no question of Sakharov going to collect the prize himself—after all, the inventor of the hydrogen bomb is a non-traveler, a keeper of military secrets. Instead, Lyusya goes to Oslo in his place and reads his speech, "Peace, Progress, Human Rights."

SPACE AND DEMENTIA

On July 17, 1975, a historic event occurs: the Soviet Soyuz and American Apollo spacecraft dock in space. Commanders of the two ships, Alexei Leonov and Tom Stafford, shake hands in zero gravity.

Several years of preparation lead up to this flight. Initially, Leonov is reluctant to participate in the project, as he still dreams of being the first

---

* The *Trud* journalist is implying that because Bonner is Jewish (and hence comparable to Judas), she should know the exchange rate of the thirty pieces of silver from ancient Judea, and how much that amount would be in US dollars.

Soviet man on the moon. But in 1974, the Soviet lunar program is canceled. "Flying to America is almost like flying to the moon," Leonov jokes.

The Soviet cosmonauts' first trip to the United States is, of course, a shock. They're overwhelmed by the variety of products in stores, the standard of living, and, just like Vladimir Vysotsky, they ask to be taken to Disneyland.

After one of the preparatory trips to NASA, Leonov's colleague, flight engineer Valery Kubasov, is summoned to a Communist Party meeting and reprimanded—someone reported that he brought back ten umbrellas from the United States. "Umbrellas are nothing!" Leonov interjects. "I know someone who brought back forty pairs of women's underwear! You know who that was? It was me! In America, they have these 'weekly' packs of underwear. I brought them back for my wife, my daughters, and even for Gagarin's widow and their daughters! Seven pairs each!"

Leonov's status as a hero shields him from any punishment. Party officials don't dare reprimand him for the underwear.

As the preparation for the mission progresses, Leonov's attitude toward the project changes dramatically—he comes to believe it's far more important than a lunar mission. After all, he would never have been the first man on the moon anyway, and what difference does it make who was first—Russian or American—when the point is that humanity overcame that frontier? The joint Soviet-American flight, he believes, could prevent a nuclear war if they can prove that the two superpowers can cooperate effectively.

As the first person to walk in open space, Leonov tends to view the world differently from his superiors: "I saw this Earth from the outside. It's a small, round ball. You'd have to be an idiot not to want to preserve it, but instead to divide it up."

During the mission's preparation, Leonov and Stafford quickly become friends. They have to endure constant bickering between their superiors, who argue and refuse to concede on anything. For both NASA leadership and Soviet mission control, it's crucial to be first in everything.

Stafford often tries to speak up, but Leonov stays silent and, glancing at his partner, places a finger to his lips—signaling that he, too, should stay out of the arguments. One day, Leonov pulls him aside and says, "Let them argue. In space, it'll just be you and me, and we'll do everything our way, not the way they demand." Stafford laughs and agrees: "You're wiser than me."

This project becomes the main symbol of "détente," the new thaw in relations between the USSR and the USA initiated by Brezhnev and Nixon. However, Nixon loses his presidency before the project is completed, resigning in 1974 in the wake of the Watergate scandal.

His successor, Gerald Ford, is also supportive of space collaboration. On September 7, 1975, he hosts the astronauts, their families, and the cosmonauts (along with the Soviet ambassador, Anatoly Dobrynin, and his granddaughter) at the White House. After the official ceremony, Ford invites everyone to fly by helicopter to a picnic in Alexandria, Virginia. The evening of the picnic completely wins Leonov over—they all sit together, as one big group, with the American president, drinking beer and eating crabs. Such warmth and informality with a national leader would have been unthinkable in the Soviet Union, Leonov would later recall.

Shortly after the crab picnic with the cosmonauts, Ford flies to the USSR for talks with Brezhnev. On November 23, they meet for the first time in Vladivostok. They drink tea with cognac in a train car. After the meeting, Brezhnev falls ill—he suffers a brain spasm. Doctors urge him to cancel further talks, but Brezhnev insists on continuing and demands that they conceal his illness from the rest of the delegation.

The next day, the US and Soviet leaders discuss reducing nuclear weapons. Brezhnev admits that not all members of the Politburo support disarmament and that if he makes too many concessions he might lose their backing and end up in a difficult position. The first day of discussions stretches past midnight.

After Vladivostok, Brezhnev travels by train to Mongolia. On the way, he suffers a stroke and falls into a confused, unresponsive state. It takes great effort for the doctors to stabilize him.

On July 15, 1975, the historic launch occurs: Apollo and Soyuz take off from Florida and Kazakhstan. The docking is a success. After the mission, the cosmonauts and astronauts are celebrated as heroes in Moscow. A reception is held in the Kremlin, and Stafford presents Brezhnev with a watch on behalf of the crew. Jokingly, Brezhnev asks if it's any good.

Leonov shows him his wrist, revealing the same watch, and taps the dial. This scene is broadcast on television, but the audio is removed. A scandal breaks out at the Ministry of Defense—the authorities think Leonov rudely cut off the General Secretary by pointing to the time and demand that he be punished, even calling for his expulsion from the party. It takes considerable effort to explain what really happened.

The cosmonauts and astronauts embark on a triumphant tour of the USSR and the USA together. A year later, Leonov meets Brezhnev again—only to find that the Soviet leader no longer recognizes him. Leonov is horrified to see the signs of dementia. In early 1976, Brezhnev had suffered clinical death, and his brain never fully recovered.

In August of the same year, another incident rocks the Soviet leadership. Prime Minister Alexei Kosygin, usually healthy and vigorous, is kayaking on the Moscow River. He deliberately leaves his security detail behind to enjoy some solitude. Suddenly, his kayak capsizes, and the seventy-two-year-old premier is stuck upside down in the water for several minutes, unable to free himself.

His security eventually rescues him, and he is rushed to the hospital, where doctors manage to revive him. Kosygin never fully recovers and is unable to work effectively, though he retains his position as prime minister for several more years. In the following years, the Soviet Union will be led by a number of gravely ill men.

COFFIN LIDS

On August 3, 1976, two Leningrad dissidents stage an unusual protest. Using white paint, they scrawl an enormous inscription on the wall of the Peter and Paul Fortress in the heart of Leningrad—a place that in Soviet times serves as a museum but in the nineteenth century was a prison for political prisoners. The message, directed not at the tsarist authorities but at the Soviet regime, reads: "You are crucifying freedom, but the human soul knows no shackles!"

The inscription spans 138 feet, with each letter standing four feet tall. The bold, defiant text is clearly visible from the other side of the river, including from some of the city's most iconic spots, like Palace Bridge and the Hermitage embankment.

KGB officers scramble to cover up the writing. In their haste, they grab about twenty coffin lids from a funeral bureau located on the fortress grounds and try to use them to obscure the letters.

A month later, the KGB tracks down the dissidents responsible for the inscription, artists Oleg Volkov and Yuliy Rybakov. Both are arrested. Among those conducting the search of their homes is a twenty-four-year-old KGB lieutenant named Vladimir Putin. It is quite possible that he was the one tasked with finding those coffin lids and attempting to cover up the rebellious message just a month earlier.

Volkov and Rybakov are charged with "malicious hooliganism" and damaging state property. Rybakov is sentenced to six years in a labor camp, while Volkov receives seven.

For Vladimir Putin, this case is one of the first in his budding KGB career. Just a year earlier, in 1975, he had graduated from the law school of Leningrad State University, and his dream had come true—he was assigned not to the prosecutor's office (like future Soviet leader Mikhail Gorbachev, a graduate of Moscow's law school), but to the KGB. However, his work is far from the glamorous spy operations he imagined. Nevertheless, he understands that to make it into foreign intelligence, he must first spend several years working in counterintelligence, catching spies—or perhaps not spies, but simply dissidents like Brodsky (who had been expelled from Leningrad when Putin was still a second-year student) or Volkov and Rybakov.

Putin enjoys working for the KGB, even finding amusement in how his colleagues creatively deal with dissidents.

"They had planned an event and invited diplomats and foreign journalists to draw the world's attention. What to do? We couldn't break it up—it wasn't allowed. So we organized our own wreath-laying ceremony at the exact spot where the foreign journalists were supposed to gather. We brought in the party committee, trade unions, and police, and cordoned off the area. We laid the wreaths ourselves to music. The journalists and diplomats stood there, yawned a couple of times, and left. Once they were gone, we lifted the cordon. Whoever wanted to come could, but by then no one was interested anymore," Putin would later recall with a laugh, describing one of his counterintelligence operations.

Such work indeed bore a resemblance to the spy games he had seen in the film *The Shield and the Sword*—playing a role, pretending to be someone else. Lying isn't shameful; on the contrary, it is honorable, as it means misleading the enemy.

Putin has no interest in understanding what the dissidents are actually fighting for. He has other passions. In 1976, he becomes the judo champion of Leningrad. And ever since his student years, he has moonlighted as a stunt man in films alongside his judo buddies. He is known to have appeared in several war-themed patriotic films.

By 1976, as a promising young KGB officer, Putin is sent for retraining courses, preparing him for a future career in foreign intelligence.

THE DIAMOND EATER

Parajanov's life in prison is unbearable: he writes to friends that he is swelling from hunger, that he is forced to work standing knee-deep in icy water. Still, he sees his imprisonment as a reenactment of Oscar Wilde's story and advises his friends to reread the biography of the English writer: "It's just terrifying—the parallels are everywhere. . . ." Indeed, Parajanov the prisoner remains an aesthete of the highest order. Here is how he describes a frozen prison latrine in a letter:

> Imagine a wooden outhouse in the corner of the yard, covered
> in colorful stalactites and stalagmites. The convicts pissed in the
> cold, everything froze, and everything is multicolored: those with
> nephritis—greenish urine, those with damaged kidneys—red,
> those who drink *chifir*—orange. . . . It all sparkles in the sunlight,
> an indescribable beauty—"Venus's Grotto"!*

Even in prison, he continues to create. On the foil lids of milk bottles, he engraves portraits with his fingernail: Pushkin, Gogol, Bohdan Khmelnytsky, Peter the Great. He makes collages from paper, foil, photographs, candy wrappers, and anything else he can find. "Bosch's world is astonishing. I don't know which circle of Dante's hell this is. But to everyone here, I'm just a crazy old man—preaching something and gluing things together," he writes.

Soviet and global icons keep fighting for his release, including Andrei Tarkovsky, Federico Fellini, François Truffaut, Jean-Luc Godard, Burt Lancaster, and Robert De Niro. But no one works harder than

---

* Chifir is an extremely strong and bitter prison-style tea, known for its almost narcotic effect.

eighty-five-year-old Lilya Brik, the legendary muse of the Soviet revolutionary poet Vladimir Mayakovsky.

Parajanov and Brik met shortly before his arrest and only saw each other twice. He amused her by claiming that he had never heard of Mayakovsky in his life—not even in school. Brik did not immediately realize that this was one of Parajanov's typical fabrications. After all, Mayakovsky was the poet whose verses every Soviet child was forced to memorize. But Parajanov kept going:

> I was a terrible student because I often skipped classes. Every night, the police would raid our home, and my parents would make me swallow diamonds, sapphires, emeralds, and corals—swallow, swallow . . . before the police could climb the stairs. And in the morning, they wouldn't let me go to school until the jewels came out of me—they'd sit me on a pot with a colander underneath. And so, I kept missing my lessons.

Parajanov completely won Brik over—and now she does everything in her power to get him out of prison. Her sister's husband is the renowned French poet Louis Aragon. A member of the French Communist Party, Aragon had become highly critical of the USSR after 1968, speaking out in defense of Solzhenitsyn, Sinyavsky, Daniel, and other dissidents. But Brik persuades her brother-in-law to travel to the USSR, meet with Brezhnev, accept an award from him, and, in exchange, demand Parajanov's release.

The plan works flawlessly—Brezhnev, of course, is completely baffled because he has never heard the name Parajanov before in his life (Parajanov was not well known in the Soviet Union). But the director is released a year before his sentence was supposed to end.

Upon his release, Parajanov immediately heads to his homeland in Tbilisi, initially forgetting even to thank Lilya Brik.

A few months later, when an Armenian radio journalist asks him in an interview to say a few words in his native language, Parajanov grabs the microphone and, in pure Russian, declares:

"Lilya Brik and Louis Aragon helped secure my release. In gratitude, I wish to join the French Communist Party!"

RESORT SECRETARY

On November 26, 1978, Raisa Gorbacheva comes home late—around ten o'clock. She's a philosophy professor at the local agricultural institute and could have easily avoided working, given her husband's position as de facto governor of the region, serving as the First Secretary of the regional party organization. But Raisa is determined to pursue her career, teaching and working on her post-doctoral dissertation.

The Gorbachevs live in an official residence. Their daughter, Irina, had entered medical school four years earlier and recently married a fellow student. Raisa is in no hurry to come home; her husband is away on a business trip in Moscow.

She arrives home, and soon the phone rings—it's her husband calling from Moscow. "You know, I've received an unexpected proposal," he begins intriguingly.

Raisa is unaware that her husband has long been considered a potential candidate for a promotion to Moscow. His name had even been floated for the position of prosecutor general, though some in the Politburo opposed the idea.

However, Gorbachev finds a unique way to win over Moscow's leadership. He manages the Stavropol region, home to popular spa resorts such as Pyatigorsk, Kislovodsk, and Yessentuki, where the Soviet elite, including aging leaders, regularly go to drink mineral water and take healing baths. This earns him the nickname Resort Secretary later in his career, as he skillfully hosts high-ranking officials, leaving them with a favorable impression of his administrative competence. One person particularly fond of Gorbachev is KGB chairman Yuri Andropov, who often visits the spas due to his kidney issues.

Just months before Raisa's late-night phone call, in September 1978, a fateful meeting occurred. General Secretary Leonid Brezhnev and his right-hand man Konstantin Chernenko were en route to Baku by train. The train stopped in Pyatigorsk, and Andropov, who was resting there, went to the station to greet the General Secretary, bringing along Gorbachev. Brezhnev and Chernenko walked the platform for about half an hour, accompanied by Andropov and Gorbachev. Little did any of them know that this would be a symbolic encounter: for the first and last time, all four of the last Soviet leaders were together in one place.

Shortly before that, party overseer of agriculture Central Committee Secretary Fyodor Kulakov dies in Moscow—or takes his own life, having despaired of convincing the leadership of the need for reforms, as cosmonaut Leonov recounts a rumor in an interview. Andropov suggests Gorbachev be appointed to fill Kulakov's position. Gorbachev later will recall that his "interview" with Brezhnev unfolds in a very strange manner: the elderly general secretary doesn't ask a single question or even glance in his direction. He merely says, "It's a shame about Kulakov; he was a good man." With Brezhnev mentally disengaged, Andropov and Chernenko agree that promoting the diligent "resort secretary" is a sound idea.

The next day, Mikhail calls his wife again. The Politburo has decided to appoint him as a Central Committee secretary overseeing agriculture, meaning the family would relocate to Moscow.

Raisa is thrilled. Even as the "First Lady" of the region, she has long been frustrated with life in provincial Stavropol, missing the opportunity to attend theaters, exhibitions, and concerts. Despite the fact that the Gorbachevs are extremely privileged compared to other Soviet citizens—they have traveled to the West twice in the past eight years, to Italy and France—Stavropol is still stifling for Raisa. But what weighs on her most is the chronic shortage of goods. It is nearly impossible to buy fashionable clothes, household appliances, or even basic groceries in Stavropol, and Gorbachev constantly has to pull strings to obtain items like shoes for his wife.

The entire family is overjoyed. "Finally, I've escaped the provinces," Raisa would later recall her feelings.

Once they are in Moscow, however, their lives change dramatically. They are given a state dacha and apartment, but Raisa can no longer work—wives of Central Committee secretaries and Politburo members are not expected to hold jobs. Making new friends is out of the question too; their neighbors are now her husband's colleagues, and socializing outside of work, especially as families, is frowned upon—it can raise suspicions of conspiracy.

Instead, as she recounts in her memoirs, Raisa finds herself obliged to participate in events alongside the other Kremlin wives.

"Even in private, personal gatherings, the same rules of 'political games' applied. Endless toasts to the health of higher-ups, gossip about those lower in the hierarchy, and endless talks about food." The only form of entertainment seems to be card games, which irritates Raisa. At one gathering, where several Politburo families, including their grandchildren, are present, Raisa warns the children to be careful: "Watch out; you'll break the chandelier!"

"Don't worry," the hostess of the house responds. "It's state property. They'll write it off."

"THE TEETH OF RUSSOHATERS"

In 1975, Solzhenitsyn visits America for the first time, speaking before Congress in support of the Vietnam War and calling for an end to any cooperation with the USSR. In March 1976, he travels to Spain, just four months after dictator Franco's death. And the former Gulag prisoner, who once celebrated Stalin's death, now suddenly praises Franco and warns Spain against "rushing too quickly toward democracy."

In April 1976, Solzhenitsyn and his family relocate to the United States, buying a property in Vermont, where the landscape resembles the Russian heartland. Two years later, he is invited to speak at Harvard's commencement ceremony, where he delivers a scathing critique of Western capitalist society and its obsession with freedom and human rights.

He begins by chastising the West for its "loss of courage" and excessive comfort: "Even biology knows that a creature accustomed to a high level of comfort is not at an advantage."

He argues that Western democracy has overindulged in protecting human rights to the detriment of society: "The defense of individual rights has reached such extremes as to make society defenseless against certain individuals—and in the West it's time now to defend not so much human rights but human obligations. . . . The West has finally defended human rights, even excessively—but at the expense of the sense of duty to God and society."

Solzhenitsyn sees the main flaw of democracy in its restraint of true leaders, favoring mediocrity instead: "A statesman who wants to carry out significant reforms for his country must move cautiously, even timidly. He is surrounded by thousands of hasty (and irresponsible) critics, constantly restrained by the press and parliament. He must prove the impeccable correctness of every step. As a result, an outstanding or great person, with bold, unexpected measures, cannot even emerge—they'll trip him up ten times at the start."

The sixty-year-old Solzhenitsyn is also unimpressed by Western culture, condemning it in terms reminiscent of Soviet ideologues: "Destructive freedom, irresponsible freedom, has taken the widest scope. Society is weakly protected from the abyss of human decay, such as the abuse of freedom for moral violence against youth, as seen in movies with pornography, crime, or devilry."

After his Harvard speech, Solzhenitsyn becomes a target of criticism from all sides: the Western press, Soviet émigrés, and dissidents in the USSR. And he continues to fiercely battle them all.*

The American press dubs him an Orthodox fascist. Solzhenitsyn counters, claiming he is caught between two millstones: the communist Soviet Union on one side and the liberal West on the other, both equally hostile to him: "One cannot ally with the communists, the executioners of our country, but neither can one ally with the enemies of our country."

Though Solzhenitsyn doesn't know the term "Russophobia," so popular in twenty-first-century Russia, he embraces the concept wholeheartedly: "The teeth of Russohaters are already tearing into the Russian name. What will happen when, in weakness and helplessness, we crawl out from under the ruins of the crazed Bolshevik empire? We won't even be allowed to rise."

TOTALITARIANISM AND US

Alexander Solzhenitsyn is far from alone. In the late 1970s, nationalist ideas are gaining increasing popularity in the Soviet Union. On December 21, 1977, in Moscow's Central House of Writers (CDL), a discussion titled Classics and Us unfolds. On the surface, it appears to be a routine gathering of literary critics convening to discuss nineteenth-century Russian literature. However, with real discussions on politics and ideology strictly prohibited, this literary debate turns into a major political scandal that, in many ways, foreshadows the ideological battles that would shape the USSR and, later, Russia.

One of the most provocative speeches comes from writer Stanislav

---

* There's no doubt that Solzhenitsyn is wrong in his assessments of the West. Liberalism proves far stronger; just months after his Harvard speech, the collapse of the Soviet Union begins. But it is along Solzhenitsyn's path that post-Soviet Russia eventually treads. It is Solzhenitsyn, not Sakharov, who becomes the spiritual father of Putin's Russia. Moreover, in the twenty-first century, Solzhenitsyn will become an icon for the American New Right.

Kunyaev. His talk seems innocent enough at first—an analysis of the works of Eduard Bagritsky, a Soviet poet from Odessa who was known for glorifying the Russian Revolution and Civil War during the 1920s and 1930s. Bagritsky, a Jew, was considered a Soviet classic. However, Kunyaev argues that Bagritsky was a "hater of mankind" who celebrated violence and murder in his poetry. Kunyaev attributes this, controversially, to Bagritsky's Jewish heritage, claiming that the poet's works reflected hatred for Russians and revenge for the suffering of his ancestors. Kunyaev points to a passage from Bagritsky's poem "February," which depicted a Jewish Chekist raping a Russian prostitute. For Kunyaev, this image symbolized the Jewish Bolsheviks' metaphorical rape of Russia.

The audience at the Central House of Writers is in shock. Such blatant anti-Semitism is rarely expressed publicly in the USSR. At the same time, Kunyaev, without stating it outright, delivers a speech that is both nationalist and oppositional, even anti-communist. According to the Soviet canon, the October Revolution is sacred, Lenin is a messiah, his comrades are apostles, and the Civil War of 1918–19 is a heroic struggle for the creation of the USSR and a bright future. But Kunyaev rejects this entire value system. For him, the Jewish revolutionaries and Jewish Chekists are villains, with Trotsky—Jewish himself—being the main symbol of evil. To him, the Civil War represents an act of violence against Russia and the Russian people.

In this world view, Lenin's declaration of the Red Terror and its execution by Jewish commissars was essentially genocide against the Russian nation. The avant-garde art of the 1920s—embodied in the works of Kandinsky, Malevich, Mayakovsky, and Meyerhold—was, to Kunyaev, an assault on classical Russian culture. Stalin, in this narrative, emerged as Russia's savior. His "Great Terror" of the 1930s is seen as just retribution for Russia's desecration, as Stalin purged the very Bolsheviks and revolutionaries who had brought him to power.

Kunyaev's remarks prompt opposition from poet Yevgeny Yevtushenko and theater director Anatoly Efros, known for his modern interpretations of Russian classics. Traditionalists in the audience, however, rally against them, accusing the latter of desecrating the Russian heritage. Many of the statements sound more like religious sermons: it's a cult of worshippers devoted to the sacred, mystical Russian culture.

Writer Yuri Seleznev, in a manner reminiscent of the novel *What Do You*

Want?, delivers a speech proclaiming a cultural war being waged against the USSR by unnamed evil forces:

"We say that today is a peaceful time, that we need to unite now, that we've had enough of fighting—yes, it's a peaceful time, bombs and missiles aren't falling on us today, but we must not forget that a war is still ongoing. . . . The Third World War has been going on for a long time, and we all know this well, and we must not turn a blind eye to it. . . . I want to say that classical literature, including Russian classical literature, is now becoming one of the main battlegrounds of this Third World Ideological War, and there can be no peace here. . . . This world war must become our Great Patriotic War—for our souls, for our conscience, for our future—until we win this war."

In his memoir, Kunyaev will proudly recall that these speeches—his and those of his like-minded colleagues—are the "first rebellion" of Russian nationalists. However, they are not rebelling against the authorities, of course, but against the pro-Western cultural establishment. He does not consider dissidents to be a persecuted part of society—quite the opposite. He points out that all notable Soviet celebrities sympathize with the dissidents. Kunyaev explains this simply: they are mostly Jews.

Brazenly flaunting his anti-Semitism, Kunyaev asserts: "Our main concern isn't who among the dissidents is Jewish and who isn't. . . . We view non-Jewish dissidents with the same distrust and alienation. Russian writers distance themselves from the dissidents and reject them because they sense that the will and efforts of these extraordinary people are destroying our state and our way of life. We fight, as best we can, against both voluntary and involuntary destroyers of it. It's not our fault that the vanguard of these destroyers mostly consists of Jews, calling themselves human rights activists, socialists with a human face, internationalists, democrats, liberals, and so on."

According to Kunyaev, none of the nationalists ever considers emigration and the idea of publishing their works abroad, as Solzhenitsyn does, seems unacceptable to them. At the same time, he acknowledges that he and his like-minded colleagues are entirely stifled by Soviet censorship, with no freedom and no opportunity to pursue creative work. Almost all of them are sick and drinking themselves into ruin.

Yet even in this situation, he does not blame the state. To him, it is not a group of incompetent people who have seized power, but an inviolable sacred entity that must not be challenged. He may resent certain officials—but never the system as a whole. He reserves his hatred for those who fight against the system.

In 1979, Kunyaev writes two letters to the Central Committee of the Communist Party of the Soviet Union addressed to Suslov, demanding action against the authors involved in the *Metropol* collection, which is published abroad, bypassing Soviet censorship. The collection includes both approved authors and semi-underground and underground figures, such as Vladimir Vysotsky (who takes this risky step to assert his right to be considered a poet). In his letters, Kunyaev demands action against these authors, whom he calls Russophobic Zionists, and calls for measures to be taken against them and the so-called Jewish mafia in the Central Committee that, according to him, enables their travel abroad. Kunyaev concludes, referring to the Prague Spring: "The Czechoslovak events must not be repeated in our country."

Kunyaev admits that he has sympathizers within the KGB who support his ideas. They warn him to be cautious. Even Suslov's subordinates are quite tolerant: the anti-Semitic poet is summoned to the Central Committee for a scolding and then let go. His position is bureaucratic—he is one of the secretaries of the Moscow Writers' Union—they don't fire him but simply send him on a six-month vacation.

Several years later, Kunyaev pens rather striking words praising totalitarianism:

Sometimes we, like parrots, repeat after professional provocateurs, "totalitarianism!" "totalitarianism!" without realizing that we are trapping ourselves. What is totalitarianism? It's the mobilization of all forces. It's the submission of personal will to the national-state necessity, a taboo on all excesses, options, variations, and experiments in material and cultural life. It's the restriction of rights in the name of duty. In general, all of Russian life is not a life of rights, but a life of duty.

MASTER OF TANKS

Perhaps the living symbol of Soviet totalitarian power is Dmitry F. Ustinov. A year before the Classics and Us debate, in 1976, Soviet defense minister Andrei Grechko died, and Ustinov took his place. Ustinov is not a military man—he has been a Central Committee secretary and longtime overseer of Soviet military industry. However, he soon awards himself the rank of Marshal of the Soviet Union and distributes general's epaulets to all his civilian advisors.

Ustinov's political career began just days before the outbreak of the Great Patriotic War when Stalin appointed the thirty-two-year-old as minister of armaments. In a way, Ustinov was lucky—more experienced specialists had already been purged, leaving Stalin with few options. Ustinov might have shared their fate, but the war saved him, making his role indispensable. (In fact, Stalin even reinstated Ustinov's predecessor, pulling him out of prison because the dictator realized that wasting specialists was no longer an option.)

Throughout the war, Ustinov oversaw weapon production. Even after the war, he retained Stalin's work style, boasting of sleeping only two or three hours a day and spending the rest of the time working. He demands the same from his subordinates. Since Stalin often worked at night, Ustinov keeps the habit throughout his life.

In the 1960s, during a meeting, one subordinate dared to tell Ustinov that there was no need to impose unrealistic deadlines, saying, "It's not war anymore." Ustinov immediately kicked him out. For Ustinov, the war never ended.

Ustinov believes that the military-industrial complex is the top priority, the one thing deserving all available funds. He remains its stubborn advocate throughout his life. According to one of his colleagues, former Moscow mayor Nikolai Yegorychev, "Ustinov was fixated on defense industries. He made significant contributions to defeating fascism, but I believe he also caused damage to our economy, as the Brezhnev leadership spared no expense on defense, even at the cost of the people's well-being."

Once he becomes minister of defense, Ustinov works tirelessly to modernize the Soviet military. In this sense, one could say that it is he, rather than Prime Minister Kosygin, who truly runs the Soviet economy: defense spending in the USSR accounts for more than half of the national budget.

Among his peers, Ustinov has a mixed reputation: everyone knows he is an excellent schemer and enjoys Brezhnev's unconditional trust. Ustinov's track record includes several dubious achievements. For years, he headed the Soviet side of the "moon race," pouring vast resources into the N1 rocket, which was supposed to deliver Soviet cosmonauts to the moon. All four attempts to launch the N1 failed—it never left the ground.

Learning that the United Kingdom and France were developing the

Concorde supersonic airliner, Ustinov insisted on creating a Soviet equivalent. And indeed, the first flight of the Soviet Tu-144 supersonic airliner took place in 1968—before the Concorde took to the skies. However, it soon became clear that the Soviet Union had no real need for such a plane. There were no wealthy individuals able to afford its costly tickets for fast flights. The Tu-144 began commercial operations in 1975 but ceased them by 1978.

Ustinov also pushes for the development of the Buran space shuttle program, a Soviet response to the US Space Shuttle. He believes the American shuttle was designed to carry nuclear warheads and bomb the USSR from space. He insists that the Soviet Union produce a similar system at all costs. The Buran will fly into space only once—after Ustinov's death. All these projects cost the USSR billions of rubles.

When Ustinov becomes defense minister, his previous position as Central Committee secretary responsible for military industry goes to Sverdlovsk party leader Yakov Ryabov. After examining the situation in the country, Ryabov discovers vast stockpiles of tanks from World War II stored in military warehouses. These tanks take up enormous amounts of space, guarded by military garrisons. In effect, these are enormous cemeteries of obsolete equipment, yet each warehouse has a military town nearby, complete with housing for officers and their families and barracks for soldiers guarding the tanks. Ryabov questions why the army needs such outdated equipment, which no country in the world wants to buy, or even take for free. Yet maintaining these warehouses drains colossal resources.

Ustinov is irritated: "Listen, Yakov, why do you care? These towns exist, they're not bothering anyone, so let them be."

Ryabov is soon reassigned to a different position, and no new Central Committee secretary responsible for the military-industrial complex will be appointed—Ustinov will oversee himself.

"Self-control is lost, and the person becomes incapable of objectively assessing their actions," Ryabov will write in his memoir. "D.F. [Ustinov] never considered the costs to the state for various military-industrial programs, even when their necessity had not been fully determined. He lived and acted as though it were wartime, stopping at nothing."*

---

* In the Putin era, Ustinov will become an icon, remembered with reverence as the man who "forged the nuclear shield of the motherland" and ensured Russia's status as a superpower.

THE COLDEST NIGHT

On the eve of the New Year in 1979, Moscow is gripped by a cold so fierce that boilers in several city heating plants burst. The temperature outside plunges to a bone-chilling minus forty degrees, where Fahrenheit and Celsius are the same, and inside many homes it approaches freezing.

In their apartment, even the most famous couple in the Soviet Union—poet Vladimir Vysotsky and his wife, the French actress Marina Vlady—cannot escape the chill. They trudge around their home in hats, winter coats, and fur-lined boots.

On the evening of December 30, 1978, Marina hears terrifying screams outside. Vladimir rushes out to the stairwell and quickly returns—there is an uprising in the courtyard; they must go and see what is happening.

Outside, a colossal bonfire blazes. Residents from the surrounding buildings are tearing down the fence of a nearby construction site, feeding its wooden planks to the flames. The crowd is in a frenzy: "We can't take this anymore! Monsters! Shame on you! Burn it all down!" This is a genuine revolt, a citizens' uprising, fueled by anger at the authorities' delay in repairing the heating system, which means that New Year's, the most cherished holiday for all Soviet citizens, is destined to be ruined.

Vysotsky and Vlady are stunned that such an event is even possible—that their neighbors are capable of such fiery passion. But soon the police arrive, and the crowd quickly disperses. The poet and the actress are left alone in the courtyard, with only the police shouting threateningly at them through a megaphone: "Clear the area immediately!"

They return home. By morning, the heat is restored. The night's rebellion has not been in vain.

In early January, Vysotsky begins his own revolt. Or rather, he dares to do something that no other Soviet citizen would even consider. He slips out of the USSR and makes his way to America—to perform there in secret.

He and Marina devise the perfect plan to ensure no one suspects the impending act of defiance. First, they fly to France, as Vlady is a French citizen, with her primary residence in Paris. Only after this do the announcements of Vysotsky's upcoming concerts appear in the Russian-language newspapers in America. Vysotsky deliberately avoids applying for a US visa in

Moscow so that the Soviet authorities don't know he is planning to go to the United States. Instead, he obtains his visa in Europe. And from there, the couple flies to New York.

ESCAPE TO AMERICA

A major scandal erupts at the Soviet embassy in the United States. The diplomats learn from newspapers about Vysotsky's upcoming concerts—concerts that had not been authorized by the Soviet authorities.

Anatoly Dobrynin, the Soviet ambassador to the United States, calls the consulate in New York from Washington, ordering them to locate Vysotsky immediately—the poet is clearly planning to "complicate Soviet-American relations." In the diplomatic language of the time, this means that Vysotsky is suspected of planning to defect from the Soviet Union and stay in America, and this must be prevented at all costs.

The ambassador has more pressing concerns, though: at the end of January, the new Chinese leader, Deng Xiaoping, is scheduled to visit Washington. It has already been announced that the United States will finally recognize the People's Republic of China and establish diplomatic relations with it. From now on, it is the Soviet Union, not America, that will be China's primary enemy. Deng Xiaoping publicly declares that the Russians and Chinese will soon go to war, which could escalate into World War III. He wants to secure American support.

But the Soviet diplomats are not yet preparing for a third world war. They are terrified of what will happen if the poet Vysotsky defects to America, as ballet dancer Mikhail Baryshnikov did five years earlier. They know that Vysotsky and Baryshnikov are friends, having met several times during the poet's previous trips to the United States. This is clear evidence of a conspiracy.

On January 17, Vysotsky gives his first concert in New York—at Brooklyn College—followed by a second one at Queens College. It is at this second performance that Soviet diplomats, led by Consul General Ivan Kuznetsov, manage to intrude. "Volodya, how did you end up here?" the diplomat asks. Without batting an eye, Vysotsky lies that these aren't concerts at all, just meetings with future philologists studying the Russian language (in reality, of course, the hall is packed with Soviet émigrés, not American students).

The singer reassures the diplomat that there is nothing to worry about; he will definitely return to the USSR.

But Vysotsky doesn't stop at just two New York concerts. He performs eight more: in New Jersey, Boston, Philadelphia, Detroit, Chicago, and Los Angeles. He works himself to the bone: on his birthday, January 25, he performs in two cities.

During the tour, he earns $34,000—later, he tells a friend that it's more than he's made in his entire previous life. The singer is, of course, exaggerating. He had decent earnings before—he even owns a gray-blue Mercedes, an unimaginable luxury in the USSR. According to popular myth, there are only three Mercedes cars in the entire Soviet Union: one belonging to General Secretary Leonid Brezhnev, another to world chess champion Anatoly Karpov, and the third to poet Vladimir Vysotsky. With the fees from his American tour, Vysotsky and Vlady buy a second Mercedes in Germany—a brown one. And they drive it back to Moscow.

On January 27, he is home and is immediately summoned to report to the KGB. The meeting with his "handlers" takes place at the Belgrade Hotel, across from the Soviet Foreign Ministry building. The KGB officers shout at Vysotsky, demanding to know how he dared to go on a concert tour in America without permission. Vysotsky calmly replies that he ended up there unexpectedly—just passing through. He explains that he went to visit his wife in France, but her children were vacationing on the island of Tahiti, in French Polynesia. So they had to fly to see the children—with a layover in the United States. And there, quite by chance, some students asked him to hold a few meetings.

The KGB officers shift the conversation to money—Vysotsky insists that he didn't receive any fees for the performances. He behaves so boldly and confidently that the KGB agents conclude that his tour must have been authorized—at the very top. Perhaps even by Brezhnev himself? After all, rumor has it that the General Secretary's daughter, Galina, is a fan of Vysotsky's songs and that he has performed at her home several times. So they let him go.

Once again, the poet has outwitted the system. But he increasingly wonders why he has to humiliate himself like this, why he can't legally tour, publish his poems, and record his songs. He increasingly returns to the idea that he wants to leave the USSR for good. His friend the writer Vasily Aksyonov later recalls that Vysotsky and Vlady came to his dacha for advice: Volodya complains that he can no longer stay in the USSR, that he's suffocating there. He wants to move to New York and open an artistic club. Aksyonov tries to dissuade him: it would be akin to the first cosmonaut Yuri Gagarin deciding to defect from the USSR and move to the West. (Aksyonov himself immigrates to the United States two years later.)

On February 12, the Taganka Theatre premieres *Crime and Punishment*, based on the novel by Fyodor Dostoevsky. Vysotsky plays a very peculiar role—Svidrigailov, a character who constantly talks about his intention to move to America. But what does America mean for Dostoevsky and his character?

"I'm going to foreign lands, brother. To America. . . . If they ask about me, just tell them I've gone to America," Svidrigailov says before he shoots himself.

"This man is already from there, an otherworldly gentleman," Vysotsky reflects on his character. "And even Dostoevsky himself wrote in his diaries that Svidrigailov should look like a ghost from the other side, especially since he's always talking about ghosts. So, I know what it's like over there, in the afterlife. That's why I'm in a very strong otherworldly mood right now."

THE END OF THE WORLD BEGINS

While Vysotsky and Vlady witnessed a spontaneous uprising in a Moscow suburb, far more significant events were unfolding in Iran.

Since January 1978, anti-government demonstrations have been sweeping through Iran. Each protest draws more participants than the last. By December, between 6 to 9 million people—nearly 10 percent of the population—are taking to the streets. Western journalists note the unprecedented scale of these protests, pointing out that previous revolutions, such as the French Revolution of 1789 or the Russian Revolution of 1917, were driven by roughly 1 percent of the population. The protests in Iran are thus labeled the largest in world history.

It all begins when the authorities opened fire on a student demonstration in the holy city of Qom in January. Forty days later, at the end of the mourning period, the parents of the slain students lead a new protest. This cycle repeats every month—with each new shooting, the number of protesters only grow.

The opposition is led by an Islamic preacher from Qom, Ayatollah Ruhollah Khomeini. He calls for the overthrow of the corrupt, decadent monarchy headed by Shah Mohammad Reza Pahlavi and the establishment of a just state based on Islamic law. Khomeini is exiled from the country, but he proves to be even more effective from Paris, where he records his sermons and has them distributed across Iran on audiocassettes. The technological revolution comes to the aid of the revolutionaries.

Khomeini becomes a hero in the Western media, portrayed as a mysterious "mystic from the East" or the "Iranian Gandhi," who dreams of ending the dictatorship and establishing true democracy in his country. Even the American government is sympathetic to Khomeini. In November 1978, the US ambassador to Tehran, William Sullivan, reports to President Jimmy Carter that saving the Shah is impossible—they should instead persuade him to abdicate and help Khomeini establish a new democratic order. President Carter's National Security Advisor, Zbigniew Brzezinski, disagrees. He believes the United States should support the Shah in retaining power, possibly even by sending troops to Iran. But President Carter, a deeply religious man and preacher himself, sees Khomeini as a relatable and respectable figure. The constant human rights violations in Iran disgust Carter, and he has no desire to support the bloody Shah.

On the eve of 1979, Mohammad Reza Pahlavi agrees to leave the country, appointing a new government composed of liberal opposition members. On January 16, he flies out, and President Carter refuses to grant him asylum in the United States.

The new government hopes the crisis has been resolved. They invite Ayatollah Khomeini to return to Iran and even announce that Qom will become something akin to an Islamic Vatican—a state within a state, governed by the ayatollah.

On February 1, Khomeini flies into Tehran from Paris. When a journalist on the plane asks him how he feels about returning to his homeland after years in exile, he replies, "Nothing." He is greeted by several million people chanting his name. The crowd is so massive that his car cannot even reach the airport—he has to be flown out by helicopter.

He goes to the cemetery and delivers a speech there. Khomeini refuses to support the interim government and vows to "knock out the teeth" of the current authorities. He then appoints his own government and orders all Muslims in Iran to obey only him. The dual power in the country lasts only ten days. By February 11, 1979, most state institutions have sided with the clergy.

If you read the diaries of Soviet or American citizens following the news in early 1979, a surprising theme emerges—anxiety over the approaching end of the world. The Iranian Revolution has caused a sharp spike in oil prices. In the United States, gasoline is in short supply, with long lines at gas stations. Wars and revolutions are breaking out one after another across the globe, and talk of World War III is becoming more frequent. The news is so terrifying that ordinary people on both sides of the planet see it as a sure sign of an impending apocalypse.

The world watches as jubilant crowds greet Khomeini in Tehran, a moment that mirrors, in a way, the visit of the new pope, John Paul II, to Mexico. Elected to the papacy just a few months earlier, in October 1978, the fifty-nine-year-old Pole Karol Wojtyla becomes a rock star pope, celebrating Mass at a stadium in Mexico City. Religion is on the rise worldwide, whether it's Islam or Christianity.

Meanwhile, Vietnamese troops enter Cambodia's capital, Phnom Penh, overthrowing the regime of Pol Pot—one of the most inhumane in the twentieth century. Up to 1.5 million people died during the dictatorship of the Khmer Rouge. Vietnam's invasion is not coordinated with the USSR, although Soviet military advisors are working in the country. Still, it provokes outrage in China.

Chinese leader Deng Xiaoping arrives in America just after Vysotsky's departure, on January 29, 1979. In his first meeting with US president Jimmy Carter, he states that for China, Vietnam is like Cuba is for the United States. He urges the Americans to unite against "Soviet hegemony."

Deng Xiaoping also warns that he plans to go to war with Vietnam to "teach them a lesson." He acknowledges that the USSR might retaliate by attacking China but claims he isn't afraid of war with the USSR because China also has nuclear weapons.

President Carter remains silent in response—he is about to meet with Soviet leader Brezhnev and isn't ready to support Deng Xiaoping's intention to wage war against the USSR. However, he does advocate for maximum cooperation with China.

On February 17, China attacks Vietnam. Soviet citizens believe this could be the start of World War III—matches, salt, oil, and grain quickly disappear from store shelves.

Meanwhile, Vysotsky writes a new satirical song, "A Lecture on the

International Situation." The song's protagonist, a Soviet prisoner, rejoices that the new pope is "one of ours, a Pole, a Slav," but laments that "we missed the Shah's spot"—suggesting that instead of Ayatollah Khomeini, the Iranian Revolution could have been led by someone from the Soviet Central Asian republics. It's, of course, irony—Vysotsky mocks Soviet "armchair analysts" and the USSR's desire to control the entire world.

In 1979, a new word emerges in the Russian language—"Khomeinism." Russian émigrés, in particular, use it, often to label writer Alexander Solzhenitsyn as the "Russian Khomeini." The Nobel laureate, living in Vermont, also advocates for Russia's spiritual revival, while criticizing the West and its values. Solzhenitsyn angrily rejects such comparisons, but he certainly sees himself as a formidable opponent of the Soviet regime, believing that he deals the USSR crushing blows from time to time.

However, the popularity of Khomeini in Iran and Solzhenitsyn in the USSR in 1979 is not comparable. The hidden strength of the ayatollah lies in the fact that the entire country listens to his sermons on audio-cassettes. Solzhenitsyn's works, primarily *The Gulag Archipelago*, are also distributed underground, through samizdat—in the form of handwritten books. But he is not an idol of the youth, and his voice is not heard on tapes. This niche in the Soviet Union is occupied by another persecuted talent—Vladimir Vysotsky.

THE RABBIT ATTACK

In April 1979, US president Jimmy Carter is fishing near his hometown of Plains, Georgia, when a swamp rabbit suddenly swims toward his boat—likely frightened by the barking dogs on the shore. Carter uses his paddle to shoo the rabbit away, and the animal retreats. Surprisingly, this seemingly trivial incident will play a significant role in American political life.

Jimmy Carter is a simple American man. Modest, deeply religious. He is the complete opposite of his predecessors, Republicans Nixon and Ford—in 1977, he even invites former outspoken critics of American policy musician John Lennon and boxer Muhammad Ali to his inauguration.

Carter is committed to promoting peace around the world and works tirelessly to achieve it. In 1978, he convinces the longtime enemies Israel and Egypt to sign a peace treaty. Israeli prime minister Menachem Begin and Egyptian president Anwar Sadat both receive the Nobel Peace Prize for this achievement.

Another of Carter's accomplishments is establishing relations with China. But the president's ambitions reach further—he aims to launch a new US foreign policy: one that is moral and value based. Carter is no longer willing to support dictators who are loyal to America. He does not help the Shah of Iran stay in power and watches indifferently as pro-American rulers in Latin America and Africa lose their grip on power—because he believes it is immoral to interfere in the internal affairs of other countries.

Franklin Roosevelt is credited with the phrase "Somoza may be a son of a bitch, but he's our son of a bitch," referring to the Nicaraguan dictator Anastasio Somoza. The Somoza family had ruled the country for more than half a century—but it is Carter who refuses to consider the latest Somoza "our son of a bitch." In July 1979, a revolution wins in Nicaragua; Anastasio Somoza Debayle flees the country with the national treasury in tow, and heads to Miami—but the United States does not grant him political asylum, forcing him to flee farther.

On June 18, 1979, US president Jimmy Carter arrives in Vienna. He is scheduled to meet with Soviet leader Leonid Brezhnev to sign the Strategic Arms Limitation Treaty (SALT II): the USSR and the United States plan to reduce the number of missile launchers and agree not to deploy nuclear weapons in space.

In fact, these negotiations were originally supposed to take place in America, but Brezhnev was already so old and so ill that his doctors forbade him from flying. As a result, Carter agrees to meet him halfway—in Austria—and Brezhnev travels by train.

"God will not forgive us if we fail," Brezhnev says during their first meeting. The religious Carter is struck by hearing such words from a communist atheist.

Later, the two leaders attend the Vienna Opera together (Brezhnev, exhausted, stays only until the intermission before leaving). Then, in the Hofburg Palace, in the very hall where peace in Europe was once established after the defeat of Napoleon's army, Brezhnev and Carter sign the treaty.

Carter returns home in a deeply philosophical mood. He senses that despite all his efforts, something is clearly going wrong. In July, he plans to address the nation regarding the energy crisis—gas station lines continue to grow. But then he feels the problem runs deeper. He decides to consult with the people, holding a series of meetings at the Camp David retreat with individuals representing various social and age groups. The result is his address on July 18, where he delivers what he himself calls the "Crisis of Confidence" speech.

This is one of the most unusual speeches ever given by an American president. Carter begins by recounting the criticisms he received from ordinary Americans with whom he spoke: "Mr. President, we are confronted with a moral and spiritual crisis."

Carter describes the crisis as follows: Americans have become a consumer society; piling up material goods cannot fill the emptiness of lives that have no confidence or purpose.

He notes that "there is a growing disrespect for government and for churches and for schools, the news media, and other institutions" and that "for the first time in the history of our country a majority of our people believe that the next five years will be worse than the past five years." He urges the nation to abandon "a mistaken idea of freedom, the right to grasp for ourselves some advantage over others," to abandon its "worship" or "self-indulgence and consumption" and to return to true American values.

This pastoral speech generally resonates with voters, and Carter's approval rating jumps by 11 percentage points—from 26 to 37. Inspired, the president gathers his cabinet members at the White House, informs them that he intends to lead a completely different lifestyle from now on, and even delivers a sermon to them. In response, one of those present asks if the government should resign so that Carter can replace those cabinet members he is dissatisfied with and appoint new ones in line with his revised moral principles. This is exactly what happens.

However, the cabinet's resignation has the opposite effect—newspapers increasingly write that Carter's administration is in chaos and that he himself doesn't know what he wants. The president presents no clear plan for addressing the energy crisis—or the "spiritual and moral" crisis.

In August, Carter's press secretary, Jody Powell, has drinks with a journalist friend at a bar and casually mentions the fishing incident: a crazed rabbit tried to climb into the president's boat, and Carter had to fend it off with a paddle. On August 29, the Associated Press reports the story, followed by the *Washington Post* running a front-page article titled "Rabbit Attacks President." For several weeks afterward, the media has a field day mocking the "killer rabbit" that attacked Jimmy Carter.

The preacher-president, who had just resolved the Middle East conflict and reconciled with China and the USSR, suddenly becomes a laughingstock. The press portrays him as weak and helpless, unable to tackle America's problems. Ten years later, the Soviet press will describe their own idealistic president, Mikhail Gorbachev, in much the same way.

A SYRINGE TO THE HEART

"Dear Warren. Excuse me my English, because I never speak in English. This first much I speak." Vladimir Vysotsky is visibly nervous in front of the camera, but he still tries to speak in broken English. "I will not speak English. I will speak Russian. Because you know, you understand Russian."

It's May 1979. Vysotsky knows that American director and actor Warren Beatty is planning to make a film about the Russian Revolution of 1917, an adaptation of John Reed's *Ten Days That Shook the World*. Vysotsky is eager to secure a role in this film, so he records a video message for Beatty.

He recites a few poems and sings two songs in front of the camera.

Interestingly, even for someone as popular as Vysotsky, it is nearly impossible to find a camera in the USSR to record an audition. His manager barely managed to arrange for Vysotsky to be allowed into a student TV studio at the Journalism Department of Moscow State University.

Vysotsky, of course, has his doubts: Will he be of any interest in America? He remembers how, once in Canada, he saw his idol, Charles Bronson, the star of *The Magnificent Seven*, and tried to strike up a conversation with him—only to be rudely dismissed. After that, Vysotsky often imagined Bronson accidentally attending one of his concerts in the United States, where Vysotsky would get his revenge by refusing to speak to him. But Bronson, of course, probably had no idea who Vysotsky was and never showed up at his concerts.

During another trip to the United States, dancer Mikhail Baryshnikov introduced Vysotsky to the poet Joseph Brodsky, who had emigrated from the USSR to the United States in 1972. According to Baryshnikov, Vysotsky idolized Brodsky. At their first meeting, Brodsky asked him, "Why do you keep running around, constantly touring?" Vysotsky looked puzzled, but

Brodsky continued, "You're a real poet." At that moment, tears welled up in Vysotsky's eyes. When they parted, Brodsky signed his book for Vysotsky: "To the best poet of Russia, both within and outside it." In the Soviet Union, however, Vysotsky isn't even recognized as a poet.

In June 1979, disregarding Brodsky's recent advice to stop wandering and focus on writing poetry, Vysotsky embarks on yet another tour—this time to Uzbekistan, one of the fifteen Soviet republics.* The concerts are organized by local mafia figures: they print counterfeit tickets, pocket all the proceeds instead of reporting them to the state (as required by law), and bribe officials to turn a blind eye.

Vysotsky performs for two weeks, giving about four concerts a day, and is utterly exhausted. The heat exceeds one hundred degrees Fahrenheit every day. On July 25, 1979, he performs in Bukhara, the ancient capital of the once-powerful Iranian state of the Samanids. That evening, back in his hotel room, he suddenly feels unwell. Staggering across the room, he wheezes, "I think I'm dying," and collapses.

The artist's friends rush to his side. His personal doctor notices that his heart has stopped beating and shouts that clinical death has occurred. He quickly pulls a syringe from his bag and injects caffeine directly into Vysotsky's heart.

Vysotsky regains consciousness and even starts to smile. His friends joke that there are only four concerts left on the tour, but one might have to be canceled. However, the doctor yells that all the concerts need to be canceled—it's time to return to Moscow.

They all know that Vysotsky is addicted to drugs. His attending physician is the one who procures morphine for him. The only one who remains unaware of this is his wife, Marina Vlady—she spends most of her time in Paris or on film sets, and Vysotsky has managed to hide his addiction for several years. For many years before that, Vysotsky struggled with alcoholism—he could stay sober for months, but then he would relapse and go on a binge. Marina would search for him, drag him out of friends' houses, strangers' apartments, and restaurants, and take him home. Now

---

* At the time, Uzbekistan was one of the fifteen republics of the Soviet Union, with a population roughly equal to that of Florida and a territory larger than Tennessee, Georgia, and Alabama combined.

she believes she has won—he hasn't touched alcohol for several years. But she has no idea what is really happening with her husband and how dangerous the situation has become.

Marina is also unaware that Vysotsky has a new girlfriend in Moscow—Oksana. She is with him on that trip to Central Asia and holds his hand when the doctor injects the caffeine into his heart.

SEIZING FOR FORTY-EIGHT HOURS

On October 22, 1979, Jimmy Carter finally permits the deposed Shah Mohammad Reza Pahlavi to enter the United States for medical treatment—he has been diagnosed with cancer. This news sparks a storm of outrage in Tehran—many see it as proof of a renewed conspiracy between the old regime and the Americans. They believe that Carter has essentially admitted that the Shah is his puppet and that a special operation to restore Pahlavi to the throne is about to begin. Iranians still remember how, in 1953, the United States orchestrated a coup in Iran that granted the Shah unlimited power.

Tehran students, active participants in the Islamic Revolution, are not just angry—they are eager for action. A twenty-four-year-old student at the University of Technology, Ibrahim Asgharzadeh, comes up with the idea: storm the American embassy and stage a sit-in, much like the protests often seen in America. He believes that occupying the embassy for forty-eight hours will be a powerful and symbolic gesture. His friends like the idea—but not all of them. Twenty-three-year-old Mahmoud Ahmadinejad suggests targeting the Soviet embassy instead, arguing that capitalist powers no longer pose a threat to Islamic Iran, but communists remain undefeated—and now is the time to confront them.

But this time, Ahmadinejad is in the minority; most students agree with Asgharzadeh's proposal.* On November 4, a massive demonstration gathers at the American embassy. Women pull out tools from under their hijabs, cut through the chain on the gate, and the crowd rushes inside.

---

* Years later, Ibrahim Asgharzadeh will regret his actions. He will call for reforms, openness, and improved relations with the United States. In response, he will be beaten with iron rods, imprisoned, and barred from participating in elections. His rival, Mahmoud Ahmadinejad, will take a different path: he will remain a staunch anti-Western radical and will become the president of Iran in 2005.

That evening, Imam Khomeini publicly approves the students' actions. "Today in Iran, a new revolution has taken place. It is even greater than the first. This is a revolution against the Great American Satan!" he declares.

The organizers are thrilled but soon realize they no longer control the situation. The idea of releasing the hostages within forty-eight hours is abandoned; everyone is waiting for orders from Imam Khomeini. Demonstrations with slogans like "Death to America" take place daily outside the embassy windows.

Khomeini uses the radicalization of society to its fullest—Iran's provisional government resigns, and all power falls into the hands of the clergy. Those who had recently called Khomeini the Iranian Gandhi now realize they were mistaken.

President Carter responds that the United States will not give in to blackmail. However, he is unable to help the American citizens taken hostage in Tehran. The embassy takeover becomes the defining tragedy of his presidency, a symbol of his weakness and inability to resolve the crisis. The hostages will remain in captivity for 444 days—until Carter loses the presidential election to Republican Ronald Reagan.

CARPETS SQUELCHING WITH BLOOD

On December 12, 1979, while the drama in Tehran is just beginning, a meeting takes place in the Kremlin that will shape world history for the next decade. Eleven people are present, ten of whom are members of the Politburo, the de facto highest authority in the USSR. The average age of those attending this Kremlin meeting is seventy-one. At first glance, this seems like a normal age for politicians today—just slightly above the average age of US Senate members. The Politburo is discussing the situation in Afghanistan and deciding whether the Soviet Union should embark on a new war.

They view global events as if on a chessboard, believing they are losing ground to the Americans in this game. The Islamic Revolution in Iran, the overthrow of dictators in Cambodia and Uganda, the reconciliation between Egypt and Israel, as well as between the United States and China—the Soviet leaders suspect there is an underlying logic to all of it. But what troubles them most is the latest news from Europe: on that very day, December 12, they receive word that NATO leaders in Brussels have voted to deploy American Pershing II missiles in Europe. In the USSR, this is seen as utterly unacceptable—a provocation that demands a response. But how? The Politburo opts for an asymmetrical response—by sending troops into Afghanistan.

Afghanistan is one of the USSR's allies, into which millions of dollars are poured annually. Back in 1978, a military coup brought Marxists to power in the country. The Soviet leaders were very pleased. However, the Marxists did not control the entire country; parts of the territory were held by various opposition groups supported by Pakistan. Civil war broke out in Afghanistan.

Pro-communist Afghan president Nur Muhammad Taraki had gained the trust of Leonid Brezhnev. Taraki requested that Soviet leaders send troops into Afghanistan. But Moscow was in no hurry to act on this.

The last time Brezhnev and Taraki met was in September 1979: the Afghan leader was flying to Kabul from Havana and made a stopover in Moscow. Brezhnev warned his comrade to beware of Defense Minister Hafizullah Amin, whom the KGB strongly disliked. Brezhnev believed Amin needed to be removed. Taraki also feared Amin, so a week after returning home, he summoned the defense minister with the intent to have him killed.

On September 14, Amin arrived at the presidential palace and was ambushed by the president's guards at the entrance. The defense minister's bodyguards returned fire—Amin himself escaped. Since the military was loyal to the defense minister, they quickly stormed the palace, killed the president's guards, and arrested Taraki. Amin declared himself the new president.

The next day, General Secretary Leonid Brezhnev and Premier Alexei Kosygin sent telegrams to Amin, congratulating him on becoming the new leader of Afghanistan.

But two weeks later, on October 10, news reached Moscow that the former president, Taraki, had been smothered with a pillow. Brezhnev was outraged—how could Amin dare to kill a man to whom the USSR had given security guarantees? The KGB was even more displeased: Amin began a campaign of repression against his opponents, including members of the ruling party who were closely allied with Soviet intelligence. The KGB suspected that Amin was systematically eliminating Soviet agents in Kabul for a reason—they believed he had likely been recruited by the Americans.

The situation in Afghanistan worsens, the civil war intensifies, and

Amin, even more persistently than Taraki before him, requests that the Soviet Union send troops to crush the mujahideen.

This is the request that the elderly Politburo members discuss in the Kremlin on December 12. None of them have any doubts. Traditionally, the head of government, Alexei Kosygin, has opposed the deployment of troops, but he is gravely ill and not present at the meeting. Most army generals, especially those with experience in Afghanistan, are also against sending troops, but they are not invited to the meeting, and Defense Minister Ustinov says nothing about their opposition during the Politburo session.

KGB head Yuri Andropov insists that Amin cannot be trusted—that he is a CIA agent who likely wants to invite the Americans into Afghanistan. The KGB has no concrete evidence. Their main "proof" is that Amin briefly studied at Columbia University in New York in his youth. He also had the misfortune of meeting with an American diplomat in Kabul. According to the diplomat's own recollections, Amin was extremely hostile during their meeting, expressing hatred for the time he spent in the United States (he was unable to finish his dissertation). But for the KGB, the fact of the meeting matters more than any proof of guilt. Years later, it will become clear that all their suspicions were baseless.

On December 12, 1979, the eleven members present at the meeting unanimously decide to deploy Soviet troops to Afghanistan.

On December 14, 1979, the operation to overthrow Amin begins. A KGB agent poisons the food of the Afghan president and his nephew, the head of intelligence. Special KGB units are prepared to take control of the presidential palace. Meanwhile, the man who is supposed to succeed Amin, Babrak Karmal, is smuggled to Bagram Air Base disguised as a Soviet officer. Karmal, a protégé of Andropov and the Afghan ambassador to Czechoslovakia, waits quietly with Soviet officers, expecting Amin to die from the poisoning. But something goes wrong—the poison doesn't work. The operation is called off.

In the meantime, Amin, unaware of the threat against him, continues to request that the Soviet Union send troops.

On December 25, the large-scale introduction of Soviet troops into Afghanistan begins. Amin is delighted, believing that with the help of the Soviet army, he can accomplish what his predecessors could not—defeat the mujahideen. On that same day, the first casualties of the war occur: a

Soviet Il-76 aircraft carrying paratroopers and military equipment to Bagram crashes into a mountain.

On December 27, a celebratory reception is held at Amin's palace. Suddenly, both the president and the guests begin to feel unwell—the chef, working for the KGB, has again laced the food with poison. Amin calls for a doctor—a Soviet one, of course, as he does not trust the Afghans. The doctor from the embassy, unaware of the poisoning, earnestly saves Amin's life.

But the Soviet command proceeds with the previously planned scenario: that evening, December 27, they order the storming of the presidential palace. Even the Soviet ambassador in Afghanistan is not informed of the operation.

Soviet special forces soldiers are briefed: Amin is a traitor who plans to hand the country over to the Americans. The soldiers are perplexed—why then was Amin so insistent on the USSR sending troops? No answer is given. But that evening, December 27, Soviet special forces begin the assault on the presidential residence.

Several groups of armed men approach the palace: these are KGB and GRU special forces in unmarked uniforms, as well as the so-called Muslim Battalion, a group of Soviet soldiers in Afghan uniforms—mostly Uzbeks, Tajiks, and Turkmen, who have been sent to Kabul, officially, to guard Amin.

The battle begins. Amin is killed, along with his children, the Soviet doctor who saved the president from poisoning, around two hundred guests and guards, and several Soviet soldiers in Afghan uniforms—mistakenly shot by their own comrades. According to one of the soldiers who participated in the assault, the carpets in the palace "squelched with blood."

However, this is only the beginning. On January 9, 1980, in the second week of the war, a mutiny breaks out in an Afghan artillery battalion in Baghlan Province—killing all Soviet advisors. In response, Soviet forces kill about one hundred people. This incident marks the beginning of a conflict that will last for ten years.

"THEY'RE FUCKING OUT OF THEIR MINDS"

The beginning of the war in Afghanistan is not reported on Soviet television, but many Soviet citizens learn the news from "enemy voices"—Radio Liberty, Voice of America, or the BBC, which, though frequently jammed, still manage to broadcast within the country.

Vladimir Vysotsky learns about the Soviet invasion of Afghanistan while in Paris. He returns to Moscow in a state of extreme outrage: "They're fucking out of their minds," is how he characterizes the Politburo's decision. His close friend Vadim Tumanov recalls that the poet is ready to go to Andrei Sakharov, to arrange joint actions, to give interviews to foreign journalists—he wanted to pour out everything that had been boiling inside him. "To tell the authorities: you are not human; I am against you!" Tumanov remembers.

But his friend dissuades Vysotsky: "Such a step would mean a complete break with the authorities and its inevitable consequences—arrest, exile, or, at best, unavoidable emigration."

"If you don't want to go, I'll go alone!" Vysotsky shouts.

But Tumanov insists: "Hundreds of thousands of people are waiting for your songs. They're being copied; many live by them. You don't understand what you mean to Russia today. You're doing no less than Sakharov and Solzhenitsyn!"

In the end, Tumanov manages to talk the poet out of it. But Vysotsky suffers deeply, regretting that he hadn't protested earlier. During these days, he writes one of his most tragic poems:

Budapest left no splinters in my soul,
And Prague did not tear my heart apart.

. . . .

We lived, unable to lift our eyes—
We too are children of Russia's terrible years,
When timelessness poured vodka into us.

During these days, Vysotsky is overwhelmed by a profound sense of disappointment. In early December, he travels again to America, spending several weeks in California, where he pitches his ideas to some Hollywood producers he knows. He dreams of making a film titled *A Vacation After the War*, about three friends escaping from a concentration camp. He envisions himself in one of the lead roles, alongside the Polish actor Daniel Olbrychski and the French actor Gérard Depardieu. But the Americans politely evade any commitments. There's no response from Warren Beatty either—he goes on to begin filming *Reds*, based on *Ten Days That Shook the World*, without Vysotsky.

In November 1979, Soviet television premiers the detective series *The Meeting Place Cannot Be Changed*, in which Vysotsky played the lead role. Yet even here, he feels slighted: the film is a huge success, but the actor isn't invited to any of the audience meetings or television shows—the director and other actors from the film attend instead.

Vysotsky's role in this film is quite ambiguous. On the one hand, he plays a positive hero, Captain Zheglov, a crime fighter. However, his methods are more than questionable—at one point, he plants a wallet on a suspect to frame him for theft and send him straight to prison. There's no doubt that Vysotsky's character is a former Stalinist executioner who regards human life as insignificant. Yet Vysotsky portrays him so charismatically that his Zheglov becomes the viewers' favorite—they don't even notice that the character himself breaks the law and easily imprisons the innocent.

Interestingly, it's right after this premiere that Vysotsky finds himself entangled in three criminal cases: the organizers of his recent concerts in Kharkiv, Minsk, and Izhevsk are accused of fraud, having concealed profits from the state. Vysotsky is summoned for questioning several times, with investigators threatening him with prison.

As the New Year approaches, Marina Vlady arrives in Moscow. The couple celebrates the holiday at their dacha with friends. On January 1, Vysotsky asks one of them to tell Marina that he urgently needs to go to Moscow. But this is just an excuse to leave—in reality, the poet is experiencing withdrawal and needs a new dose. He gets behind the wheel of his Mercedes, takes a few friends along, and races toward the city, ignoring traffic lights, at nearly 200 km/h. As he nears the center of Moscow, he crashes into a trolleybus. One passenger suffers a broken arm, another a concussion. Vysotsky himself is unharmed.

3

LAVISH FUNERALS

"Well, Galya, it's time to join the party," the boss said to my mother one day. The suggestion caught her completely off guard. "I can't," she blurted out quickly. "I'm pregnant."

She obviously lied. But strangely, her bizarre reply was enough to satisfy him—the boss didn't push further. But really, why couldn't a pregnant woman join the Communist Party? What exactly would stop her? He could have asked, but he didn't.

The real mystery, though, was why she had refused in such a panic. She had no particular prejudice against the party—there were no victims of repression in her family, she'd never read samizdat, and she didn't know any dissidents. It was simply a matter of time: she had absolutely no desire to waste endless hours at party meetings, listening to utterly meaningless speeches and reading absurd, convoluted texts. As the Soviet dissident Andrei Sinyavsky would say, my mother's disagreements with the Soviet regime were purely aesthetic.

A few days later, she found out she was, in fact, pregnant. Turned out, she hadn't even lied. And nine months later, I showed up.

EXILE TO GORKY

The Soviet invasion of Afghanistan immediately triggers reactions worldwide. By the end of December 1979, US president Jimmy Carter demands that the USSR withdraw its troops by February 20, threatening sanctions, such as a boycott of the Moscow Olympics scheduled for August 1980, if they fail to do so.

On January 3, 1980, the phone rings in the Moscow apartment of fifty-eight-year-old Andrei Sakharov, who lives on the Garden Ring near Kursky

Station. The caller is the wife of a correspondent for the German newspaper *Die Welt*, relaying her husband's question: What does Sakharov think about the Olympic boycott? "According to ancient Olympic tradition, wars cease during the Games," Sakharov replies. "I believe the USSR should withdraw its troops from Afghanistan. . . . Otherwise, the Olympic Committee should refuse to hold the Olympics in a country engaged in war."

Sakharov's statement is published in the German newspaper, and the next day a journalist from the *New York Times* visits him to record an interview on the same topic.

On January 8, the Politburo discusses Sakharov's behavior and decides to strip him of all his state awards. For Soviet leaders, awards are of immense importance. Sakharov, after all, is a three-time Hero of Socialist Labor, a recipient of the Order of Lenin, and a laureate of the Stalin and Lenin Prizes.

On January 22, he plans to attend a citywide seminar at the Lebedev Physical Institute (FIAN), and on the way, he intends to stop by the Academy of Sciences' special-order department to buy sour cream. Sour cream is a scarce commodity—good quality is not available in regular stores, but as an academician, Sakharov has privileges—he is entitled to shop at the Academy of Sciences' canteen.

On the morning of January 22, taking a glass jar for the sour cream, he leaves his home and gets into the official car. But they don't get far— just two minutes from his building, a traffic police car overtakes them and signals them to stop. Sakharov then notices that traffic has been blocked in both directions—there are no other cars on the bridge. His driver is ordered to follow the traffic police car to the USSR Prosecutor General's Office.

Sakharov is worried that he won't get the sour cream, so he hands his bag with the jar to the driver to bring it home to his wife. The scientist is led to the deputy prosecutor general, who reads out a decree: "A decision has been made to exile A. D. Sakharov from Moscow to a place that precludes his contact with foreign nationals. This place has been designated as the city of Gorky, closed to foreigners." Gorky—now Nizhny Novgorod—in 1980 is a restricted city due to its concentration of defense enterprises, and entry is only possible with special permits.

He is then taken to Domodedovo Airport, where his wife, Elena Bonner, is also brought, and both are sent to Gorky on a special flight. The flight is comfortable: the onboard meal is so good that Bonner, just in case, wraps some fish in a napkin to take with her, not knowing what lies ahead.

Thus, Academician Sakharov becomes the most famous Soviet exile. "A spiritual renegade, provocateur Sakharov, through all his subversive actions, has long placed himself in the position of a traitor to his people and state," writes the newspaper *Komsomolskaya Pravda*.

THE OTHERWORLDLY GENTLEMAN

At the beginning of January, Vysotsky goes to the Taganka Theatre and requests a leave of absence. He wants to make a change in his life. He has decided to become a director and plans to make his debut film. However, the theater's artistic director persuades him to continue performing his most iconic roles from time to time: Hamlet, Lopakhin in *The Cherry Orchard*, and Svidrigailov in *Crime and Punishment*.

In March, Vysotsky flies to Venice to visit his wife. There, they finally have a heart-to-heart conversation: he confesses his addiction to drugs. "Now I know everything. You dared to say the 'forbidden' words," she would later write about that trip in her memoir. Marina urges her husband to start treatment—one of her sons also struggled with drug addiction and spent a long time in a clinic where he was helped. She threatens to divorce her husband if he does not promise to overcome his illness. He swears.

The couple rides a gondola and makes plans for their future life in Paris: he will seek medical help and start writing a novel. Vysotsky fantasizes: "I'll pull myself together. As soon as I get to Paris, we'll start following a routine, we'll do gymnastics, and we still have our whole lives ahead of us." After all, they are both only forty-two years old.

However, Marina doubts that Vysotsky will be able to leave Russia permanently—she believes he won't be able to make such a decision. She recalls phrases he's said at different times: "I work with words, I need my roots, I'm a poet. Without Russia, I am nothing. . . . Without the people for whom I write, I don't exist. I can't live without the audience that adores me. I suffocate without their love. But without freedom, I die."

Vysotsky returns to Moscow, where Oksana is waiting for him. She is only twenty, but they have been seeing each other for over a year. In reality, Marina hasn't learned everything.

At the end of March, Vysotsky is summoned to Izhevsk to testify in a criminal case involving ticket fraud.

In May, he flies to Paris and, as promised to his wife, checks into a clinic to kick his drug habit. However, he is unable to complete the course of treatment—Lyubimov, the theater's director, asks him to come to Poland, where the theater is successfully touring and audiences are eager to see the legendary *Hamlet*. Vysotsky rushes to Warsaw.

From Poland, the poet returns to his wife. They travel to the south of France. "Silence, cold, bottles hidden in the garden, tranquilizer pills that don't calm anyone, and around—a vast emptiness," she would describe this vacation in her memoir. Both are exhausted after it. *Everything is futile, my willpower is wearing out like a rag, I'm overwhelmed by fatigue, and despair forces me to retreat*, she thinks, crying as she sees her husband off to Moscow on June 11. "Don't cry; it's not time yet," he says as he leaves.

In June 1980, John Lennon sets sail for Bermuda with his five-year-old son. On the way, their yacht gets caught in a storm, and the entire crew is stricken with severe seasickness—everyone except John. Alone, he takes control of the boat and navigates it to shore—or at least, that's how Lennon himself told the story of the journey.

The trip to Bermuda changes his life. For the first time in five years, he starts writing music again. It seems like he is a completely different Lennon now—he no longer uses drugs or abuses alcohol. He is ready to start anew, preparing to release a new album, with its first single aptly titled "(Just like) Starting Over."

FASCISTS

On July 19, the Olympic Games open in Moscow. Sixty-five countries, including the United States, China, and some Western European nations, boycott the Games in protest against Soviet aggression in Afghanistan.

The Olympics are inaugurated by the seventy-three-year-old Soviet leader Leonid Brezhnev, with the stands filled with party officials and guests from communist parties of friendly countries. Even for them, it is decided not to hold a formal reception—so as not to tire Brezhnev. The party officials understand that the General Secretary is weak and quickly exhausted by social interactions.

Moscow is closed off during the Games: residents from other Soviet cities are not allowed entry. Trains to the capital are nearly empty—those without a Moscow residence permit are simply not sold tickets. There are few foreign tourists in Moscow, and the competitions take place before half-empty stands.

On July 23, Vysotsky calls Marina and tells her that he has quit drugs—and has booked a ticket to Paris for the twenty-ninth. "You know, I always wait for you," she replies.

The next day, July 24, Vladimir is supposed to visit the Mission Control Center for a communication session with the cosmonauts in orbit. They are eager to talk to Vysotsky and listen to him sing. But he suddenly falls ill. "Vysotsky is delirious, shouting at the top of his lungs 24 hours a day, you can hear it for blocks. Witnesses say they've never seen him so bad. Doctors refuse to admit him, and if they do, it will be to a psychiatric ward; they're arguing among themselves," his friend actor Valeriy Zolotukhin records in his diary.

A doctor stays with Vysotsky in the apartment at all times, monitoring his condition and administering sedatives. Despite this, in the early hours of July 25, 1980, he dies—his heart stops in his sleep.

Marina Vlady flies to Moscow.

Vysotsky's death during the Olympics is a nightmare for the authorities. It is taboo—nothing should "spoil the celebration." Nevertheless, Soviet citizens hear the tragic news from the "enemy voices." This is enough for over a hundred thousand people to come to bid farewell to Vysotsky.

In the crowd during the farewell, people talk about the unfairness of losing the young, one after another—the best writers, filmmakers, and poets of the generation. Meanwhile, the old men in the Politburo continue to strangle the country.

All day on July 28, fans flock to the Taganka Theatre—the line stretches for many kilometers. The courtyards are packed; people hang from lampposts, and sit on the roofs of bus stop shelters and newspaper kiosks. There is a heavy police presence, but they can do nothing—they cannot disperse those who wish to say good-bye to their idol, especially during the Olympics, with so many foreigners in the city.

Vysotsky is buried in the black sweater he wore as Hamlet. At one point, street-cleaning machines appear near the theater and begin washing away the piles of flowers lying on the sidewalk. The mourning crowd starts chanting, "Fascists, fascists."

THE END OF AN ERA

On September 11, 1980, something strange happens to Alexander Solzhenitsyn: he is almost eaten by wolves. He's sitting and working on his estate in Vermont. His desk is set up right in the middle of the forest, far from the house—so no one can disturb him while he writes. Suddenly, he lifts his head and notices a wolf just a meter and a half away. He looks around and sees a pair of huge predators passing by.

"I had no time to think or prepare—there wasn't even a stick nearby," the writer will later recall. "Was it God who spared me? Or maybe they were just full? I sit there, coming to my senses: what an ending that would've been—eaten by wolves! Right at my desk on my own land. No Russian writer has ever died such a pathetic death. The joy and laughter of my enemies. . . . A life torn apart in its prime."

Meanwhile, in October, John Lennon releases his first single after a long silence, and in November, his new album, *Double Fantasy*. He and Yoko continue working on new songs.

By this time, Lennon is no longer an outcast in America. His troubles with the Nixon administration are behind him; in fact, he was a guest of honor who attended Jimmy Carter's inauguration. Lennon's song "Imagine" has become one of the major political anthems of the 1970s.

On November 4, 1980, the dreamer-president Jimmy Carter loses the presidential election to Ronald Reagan. Two weeks later, *Double Fantasy* is released.

And on December 8, 1980, John and Yoko are preparing for something big—they invite photographer Annie Leibovitz for a photoshoot for *Rolling Stone*. After five years of silence, John Lennon is set to reclaim his status as a figure more popular than Jesus Christ.

The photoshoot turns out to be quite paradoxical: Lennon, completely naked, lies in a fetal position, embracing Yoko Ono, who is dressed in black.

A few hours later, Lennon will be shot dead at the doorstep of his own home. One of his fans will first ask for an autograph on the *Double Fantasy* album, and later will shoot him four times in the back.

With Lennon's death in the United States, just as with Vysotsky's death in the USSR, an era comes to an end. Yet both Lennon and Vysotsky will have a profound impact on the main players of the next one.

A FREE MAN AND A MONSTER

On March 30, 1980, a Komsomol meeting takes place at Leningrad State University. Students, members of the communist youth organization, are there to judge one of their own, twenty-seven-year-old graduate Boris Grebenshchikov.

Out loud, they read a denunciation that arrived by mail. The accused remembers the text as something like this: "During his performance in Tbilisi, Grebenshchikov appeared onstage naked, shouted anti-Soviet slogans, threw leaflets around, called for the overthrow of the current government, and to top it all off, engaged in homosexual activity right there onstage." He says the letter was signed by the director of the Tbilisi Philharmonic.

Boris Grebenshchikov—his friends call him Bob or BG—denies all the accusations and asks them not to believe in "such harsh and baseless criticism." He knows that being expelled from the Komsomol in Soviet reality is almost like a death sentence. It automatically means getting fired from work and a lot of other problems. Fortunately, no one really believes the accusations. What does it even mean that a Soviet citizen "engaged in homosexual activity" onstage? Pure nonsense. And Grebenshchikov hopes that the Komsomol members will use their common sense.

But the attendees bring up every old grievance they have against the musician: for example, the chairperson notes that he never gave a single free concert at the university. In the end, they all support his expulsion—"for distancing himself from the collective life of the Komsomol." They, of course, envy Bob terribly and are offended that he considers himself cooler than any of them. Some even believe they have no choice—the letter came from above, so they need to make an example of him. Otherwise, they might have problems themselves.

The musician mutters that he'll file an appeal and leaves—utterly crushed and defeated. His life collapses in just one hour. In today's terms, he is canceled.

"In my youth, I thought we were three times lucky: we lived in the best country in the world, we had corn, and we had the Beatles and all that music. And the combination of all this filled me with absolute joy," Grebenshchikov will later recall about his life before his expulsion from the Komsomol.

Of course, the Beatles' songs were never officially released in the Soviet Union, and most people had never even heard of them. But Grebenshchikov had heard them at fifteen, on one of the Western radio stations officially banned in the USSR—and as he says, on that day, he realized why he was born. In short, Grebenshchikov was not your average Soviet young man—he even prefers John Lennon and Bob Dylan to Vladimir Vysotsky.

Rock music is banned in the Soviet Union. Moreover, for graduates like Grebenshchikov, from the Department of Applied Mathematics at Leningrad State University, becoming professional musicians is out of the question. In the USSR, there is a strict system of job placement for university graduates, which means only those who study music can become musicians. Since Grebenshchikov studied mathematics, he can only work as a mathematician. And no one can be a rock musician in the USSR because there are no schools that teach rock music.

"From the very beginning, when I started to understand the world a bit better, I realized that it's impossible to make any kind of deal with the monster that is the state. No matter what you say, the monster is always thinking just one thing: 'I'm going to eat him now,'" Grebenshchikov will later recall.

But he is far from thinking about fighting the system; instead, he hopes to simply remain unnoticed. "We're talking about eternal things. And a political system? It's like a bad spring day. Today it's here, tomorrow it's gone," he says.

Grebenshchikov graduated from the university and was assigned to a research lab at the Institute of Sociology, where his mother was already working. In the USSR, you can't just choose where you want to work; the system guarantees everyone a job after graduation, but it also means almost everyone is forced to work where they are assigned, not where they want to be. However, Grebenshchikov is privileged. He has a residence permit in Leningrad, and his mother has connections. So, instead of being sent to another city—a common practice—he was assigned to his mother's lab. After all, not working in the USSR is not an option; that could lead to criminal charges for parasitism, as happened to Brodsky.

But Bob's main focus is his music. He creates a band called Aquarium, and in March 1980 they are invited to participate in a music festival in Tbilisi, the capital of the Georgian SSR.

At this time, Georgia is considered one of the most liberal republics in the Soviet Union.* The Georgian Communist Party is led by a fifty-two-year-old First Secretary, Eduard Shevardnadze, and because of this, many things are allowed in Georgia that would be unthinkable in other Soviet republics. For example, the Beatles records in the USSR could be released at the Tbilisi

---

* At the time, Georgia was one of the fifteen republics of the USSR, with a population roughly equal to that of Minnesota and a territory slightly larger than West Virginia.

recording studio in 1974. In 1978, Georgia hosted the country's largest jazz festival, and in 1979, B. B. King performed there. Now Georgia is hosting the first-ever rock festival in the USSR, called Spring Rhythms.

Twenty-seven bands from various Soviet cities, all playing modern youth music quite different from official Soviet pop, are invited.

The performances are judged by a jury made up of members of the Komsomol, the Communist Party, the writers' union, and the composers' union. The musicians don't receive payment, but their travel and accommodation are covered.

After watching the early performances, Bob concludes that the other bands are dull and old-fashioned, and that Aquarium needs to show the audience real avant-garde and punk rock. The audience is shocked by everything: the Leningraders' appearance, their music, and their politically risky lyrics. At the end, the band stages a punk performance: Bob, playing his guitar, falls to the floor, and cellist Seva Gakkel jumps around him, gripping the cello between his legs.

The jury leaves the hall and disqualifies Aquarium for "inappropriate behavior." However, co-organizer critic Artemy Troitsky himself praises the performance. "If not for Aquarium, you might think this festival is happening in 1975, not 1980. Compared to them, all the other bands sound a bit archaic," he says in an interview with a Finnish journalist. "I really like how natural and free they are onstage. It's always a lot of fun and has never been typical of our bands."

At first, Grebenshchikov doesn't even realize that something has gone terribly wrong. Aquarium plays all their scheduled concerts in Tbilisi, and they are even invited to perform in Gori, Stalin's hometown. But when the musicians return home, the director of the Tbilisi Philharmonic writes a letter about the scandal to Leningrad. And since it's a national-level scandal, the Leningrad authorities decide to make an example of Grebenshchikov: the Komsomol cell of his university is ordered to expel him.

Grebenshchikov, who worked at the Institute of Sociology, is immediately fired. He has a wife, Natasha, and a two-year-old daughter, but Natasha's parents have never been too fond of their son-in-law. After he's kicked out of the Komsomol and loses his job, they push Natasha to leave her "no-good" husband.

For two days, Grebenshchikov says, he sinks into deep thought. "And on the third day, I suddenly realize they've given me the best gift ever. I don't owe anyone anything anymore, at all. They've completely freed me, cut all my ties with society. And with a totally clear conscience, I take a job as a night watchman. And becoming a watchman makes me a free man."

How he survives during this time isn't exactly clear: "It's a really interesting period. For about a year and a half, I basically live off collecting bottles. You walk around the usual spots in the neighborhood, see where people leave bottles, and pick them up. One bottle is worth ten kopecks. So you can easily make three to five rubles per day. But the most amazing thing—we drink every night. With what money? I still can't figure it out. But we drank and had snacks."

THE POPE'S DIAMONDS

On October 31, 1981, Sergei Parajanov arrives in Moscow from Tbilisi—he's been invited to a rehearsal of *Vladimir Vysotsky*, a play in memory of the late poet, at the Taganka Theatre. Everyone knows the production will never be approved, and friends warn him not to go, fearing he'll attract unwanted attention. But Parajanov, being Parajanov, ignores them. After the performance, he tries to cheer up the director, Yuri Lyubimov:

"Yuri Petrovich, I see you're popping pills—don't stress so much. If you have to leave the theater, you'll manage. Look at me; I haven't worked in years, and I'm still alive. The pope sends me diamonds—I sell them and live off the money!"

"Sergei, come on, what diamonds? The pope has never sent you anything!" a friend whispers.

"Well, he should have!" Parajanov retorts with mock indignation.

A few days later, he's back in Tbilisi, hosting his old friend filmmaker Andrei Tarkovsky. As always, Parajanov puts on a spectacle—lavish feasts, elaborate pranks, theatrical flourishes. One night at dinner, he suddenly declares, "Andrei, you are, of course, a brilliant director. Very talented . . . but not a genius!"

Tarkovsky looks stunned.

"Because you're not a faggot, and you've never been to prison!" Parajanov smirks.

Tarkovsky doesn't tell him the real reason for his visit—he's come to say good-bye. The censorship, the bureaucratic meddling, the endless battles with

Soviet officials, have worn him down. He's preparing to leave for Italy. As a farewell gift, he slips off his emerald ring and hands it to Parajanov.

"He has no work—maybe he can sell it. Sergei was deeply moved and said he'd cherish it," Tarkovsky later writes in his diary.

Barely a month later, in February 1982, Parajanov is arrested. Supposedly, four years earlier, he had given a bribe to help his nephew get into university. And right away, they hint to him that the case could be "settled" for a small sum.

Naively, Parajanov rushes to his sister, borrows 500 rubles, and tries to hand it over—and at that moment, he is caught red-handed. That same day, the police turn his house upside down in search of the mythical pope's diamonds.

The trial drags on for almost a year. Once again, global celebrities petition on Parajanov's behalf. Poet Bella Akhmadulina knows that the First Secretary of Soviet Georgia, Eduard Shevardnadze, admires her poetry, so she writes him a heartfelt letter. She understands that the Soviet justice system will never acquit Parajanov, but she begs for a suspended sentence.

And it works—Parajanov is sentenced to five years but conditionally released right there in the courtroom.

But at first, he refuses to leave.

"My cellmates are waiting for me. I promised to bring them the parcels—I can't let them down."

THE ROCK CLUB AND THE KGB

In the late 1980s, Boris Grebenshchikov will write a song in which he refers to his fellow musicians as the "generation of janitors and watchmen." The situation Grebenshchikov finds himself in is more the norm than the exception at that time: making big money in the USSR is impossible, and it's even harder to find something to spend it on. Many young people live in a kind of parallel world, one that has little in common with the everyday life of Soviet citizens. The young people briefly emerge from their underground existence to create the illusion of working somewhere, but they spend most of their lives in what they call "internal exile," surrounded by friends and family.

Since the late 1970s, underground rock music fans in Leningrad have been visiting various officials, asking for permission to let amateur rock bands gather occasionally and play for their friends. According to legend, in January 1981 the director of the Leningrad House of Amateur Culture (LMSDT) on Rubinstein Street, Anna Ivanova, says, "Fine, if I get fired, my husband will support me." She allows the rockers to gather, providing them with a permanent space for rehearsals and performances.

However, the creation of the rock club is not just Anna Ivanova's personal initiative—everything is done with the approval of the KGB. The Leningrad KGB believes it will be easier to control the youth's mood if they gather and sing their songs in an organized, rather than underground, setting.

This move is part of a broader strategy conceived by General Filipp Bobkov, the first deputy head of the KGB. Bobkov oversees culture and is responsible for combating ideological enemies and dissenters. His method is to "smother them with affection." He has long tried to befriend musicians and artists, convincing them that they owed him a debt and that thanks to the KGB's protection, they are allowed to perform and create. In 1981, Bobkov and his subordinates decide to apply this approach to rock music: after all, young people are already secretly listening to Western bands like the Beatles, Queen, Led Zeppelin, and Pink Floyd, and more and more young people in the USSR are forming amateur bands, imitating their Western idols. It is better to keep them under control and create the illusion of support and cooperation.

Soon all rock musicians have their run-ins with the KGB. Grebenshchikov will recall that one day, after a rehearsal, the director of the rock club asks him to step into a small room behind her office, where two plainclothesmen are waiting. They are KGB officers, and without preamble, they ask Grebenshchikov to sign a paper agreeing to cooperate with the authorities: "They always needed a piece of paper, so they could use it when necessary."

This encounter with the KGB is the first but far from the last. After the creation of the rock club, such meetings become regular. Grebenshchikov describes them like this: about once every two months, a handler summons him to a secret apartment—these are always the homes of ordinary citizens who cooperate with the KGB and provide their houses for their needs. Sometimes the handler changes, but they all have the same initials: "V.V." "It could be Vladimir Viktorovich or Vadim Vasilyevich."

THE RISKY COMPANION

Vladimir Vladimirovich Putin—his name and patronymic sounding as if they were tailor-made for a KGB officer in Leningrad—is already well on his way to transitioning into foreign intelligence. However, he keeps his place of work a strict secret from everyone.

In 1980, he meets a girl named Lyuda—a flight attendant from Kaliningrad, in Leningrad for just three days. During those three days, they go to the theater multiple times—Vova Putin, being a KGB officer, has privileges so he can get any tickets, even though they're unavailable at the box office.

A relationship begins between them, but Putin doesn't tell Lyuda where he works. His official story: "criminal investigation." He doesn't think that lying to his girlfriend is wrong—in fact, he believes a spy must always deceive to mislead enemies, just like the heroes of his favorite spy movies.

Throughout their relationship, he tests Lyuda several times. Once, he sends an agent to approach her, pretending to be a random admirer trying to get to know her.

"Miss, this is fate! How I'd love to get to know you!" the stranger shouts, chasing after Lyuda. "Please, I beg you, give me your number."

"I don't have a phone," she replies.

"Then take mine."

"I won't. I'm sorry, but this just isn't fate," she says firmly.

"But what if you change your mind? Write it down just in case," he persists.

"There's no chance," she says, passing the test with flying colors.

However, Putin is in no rush to propose. Later he would explain that he had grown used to bachelor life and might never have gotten married. But, according to Lyuda, she courted him for three and a half years.

One evening, Lyuda and Vova are sitting at his place—this is how she would recount the story twenty years later—when he suddenly says, "You know what I'm like now. I'm not exactly an easy person." He goes on to list his unpleasant traits: "I'm quiet, sometimes quite abrupt, and I can be hurtful at times—in short, I'm a risky companion."

"You've probably made up your mind over the last three and a half years?" Vova asks. Lyuda takes this as a clear sign—he's about to break up with her.

"I have," she says. But Putin isn't convinced. "Really?" he asks, his voice full of doubt. At that moment, Lyuda is even more sure it's over.

"Well, if that's the case, then I love you and propose we get married," he says unexpectedly.

The wedding takes place on July 28, 1983. Afterward, Vova, Lyuda, and their friends head on a road trip for their honeymoon—to Kyiv, in Putin's car.

After strolling around the city and going to the theater, they continue their journey—to Crimea. But this is where things go awry for the newlyweds. The car's radiator overheats, and their friends have to tow Putin's Zhiguli to the nearest town. After the repairs, they eventually make it to Yalta.

On the way back, Vova needs to stop in Moscow—arrangements are being made for his upcoming foreign assignment. However, even after the wedding, he says nothing to Lyuda about his real job—and she doesn't ask.

LIZA'S LOVE

Andrei Sakharov and Elena Bonner are living in Gorky in an apartment allocated to them by the KGB. A police officer sits at the entrance around the clock, letting almost no one inside. Sometimes those wishing to visit are detained and taken to the police station. Sakharov and Bonner are allowed to walk around the city and go to the movies. Initially, they even have a car, but in 1981, it is stolen—Sakharov is certain it is the work of the KGB.

Sakharov is forbidden to leave Gorky, but Elena Bonner periodically travels to Moscow. There, she holds press conferences to relay news about her husband's life to foreign journalists, visits her elderly mother, and collects letters from her children, who have immigrated to America. On her return trips, she brings groceries that are impossible to find in Gorky: cottage cheese, butter, meat, and more.

In Gorky, Sakharov never parts with his bag full of manuscripts. Still, it gets stolen. The first time is when he visits the dentist. Sakharov is deeply affected by the loss of his diaries and articles, making great efforts to rewrite them from memory. But a few months later, a new incident occurs. Sakharov drives his wife to the train station. While she stands in line for a ticket, he waits in the car. A stranger approaches, sprays gas in his face, smashes the window, and steals the bag with his manuscripts. Dazed, Sakharov stumbles out of the car, trying to gather his senses. When Bonner returns, she finds him swaying, looking as if he's drunk. He remembers nothing of the robbery.

These events initially shake Sakharov. "I won't write my memoir," he tells his wife. "Lyusenka, we can't beat them." Bonner shouts back, "No, you will!"

Elena Bonner has two adult children—Tanya and Alyosha. Sakharov cares about them and helps them immigrate to America. But before leaving for the

United States, Alyosha suddenly confesses that he has fallen out of love with his wife and wants to take his classmate Liza Alexeeva with him to America.

Leaving the Soviet Union isn't easy. The state must grant permission—an exit visa—and many are denied. Liza is not allowed to leave.

Then begins the long and painful struggle of these young people to be together. Once in America, Alyosha files for divorce and even marries Liza in absentia. But the Soviet state remains unyielding. That's when older lovers, Andrei Sakharov and Elena Bonner, step into the fight for the happiness of the young couple. Sakharov believes Liza's troubles are due to him—clearly, he is tormented by guilt. Bonner and Sakharov declare a hunger strike in Gorky, demanding that Liza be allowed to join Alyosha in America.

The hunger strike causes an uproar. The Soviet press falsely claims that Liza is a promiscuous woman and a drug addict, and that the hunger strike is part of a cunning plan by Elena Bonner, who dreams of getting rid of her aging husband so she can finally move to America. But dissidents are also upset: they write to Sakharov, arguing that he has no right to risk his life for something so trivial—he is too important to science, the human rights movement, and more.

Even those who oppose the Soviet state and have already emigrated are outraged, most of all Solzhenitsyn. He recently experienced a similar situation: his elderly aunt wanted to leave the USSR, but she was denied an exit visa. Solzhenitsyn felt the same as Sakharov—he believed the state was taking revenge on his aunt because of him. He wrote letters to Brezhnev's right-hand man Chernenko, pleading with them not to take it out on the old woman. He didn't respond. But Solzhenitsyn didn't make the situation public because, as he said, he was ashamed to cause a fuss over a family issue. He considers Sakharov's behavior equally unworthy, believing that one should not fight for specific people, especially relatives, but for the entire Russian people.

The general condemnation does not deter sixty-year-old Sakharov and fifty-eight-year-old Bonner. Their hunger strike quickly becomes one of the world's top stories: the US secretary of state, the Senate, twenty American Nobel laureates, and Western newspapers speak out in support of them.

For thirteen days, they hunger strike at home. Then they are forcibly taken to different hospitals, where they continue their hunger strike separately for another four days. Food is regularly brought to their rooms, but they place it outside the door. They also refuse any medical examinations until they are allowed to see each other.

On the eighteenth day of the hunger strike, December 8, 1981, Liza Alexeeva is granted permission to leave the country. The story has an unexpected happy ending. Sakharov and Bonner are allowed to return to their apartment in Gorky.

On the way back from the hospital, they ride in the same car with a KGB major, and Bonner asks him, "Why are these articles in the newspapers saying that Liza Alexeeva is a drug addict and other lies?" He replies, "Mrs. Bonner, that's not written for intelligent people like us. It's written for the rabble." Bonner, outraged, starts yelling at the driver and the nurse sitting in the front, "Listen, listen! It's for you, apparently, written for the rabble. You are the rabble!" The major, embarrassed, starts mumbling.

TWO MIRACULOUS ESCAPES

On March 30, 1981, the Academy Awards ceremony is set to take place in Los Angeles. Leading the nominations are David Lynch's *The Elephant Man* and Martin Scorsese's *Raging Bull*.

Twenty-six-year-old musician John Hinckley is eagerly awaiting the ceremony—he's obsessed with Scorsese's film *Taxi Driver*. After seeing it for the first time, he began to identify with the main character, played by Robert De Niro. He also became infatuated with the character played by Jodie Foster.

Hinckley has mental health issues: a doctor prescribed him antidepressants, but he doesn't take them. He invents an imaginary girlfriend, telling his parents about her to keep them off his back. What he doesn't tell them is that his true love is Jodie Foster.

In *Taxi Driver*, De Niro's character, in an attempt to save his love, tries to assassinate a presidential candidate. Hinckley decides that he must kill the US president to win Foster's attention. For months, he stalks Jimmy Carter, but in November 1980, Carter loses the election, so Hinckley shifts his focus to Reagan.

On March 30, 1981, Reagan gives a speech at the Hilton Hotel in Washington, D.C. He has been in office for just over a month. Outside the hotel, a crowd waits, and among them is Hinckley. As Reagan steps out, the crowd applauds, and Hinckley opens fire—six shots. The first bullet hits the president's press secretary, and others wound his bodyguards. One bullet ricochets off the limousine and lodges in Reagan's lung.

At first, seventy-year-old Reagan insists he doesn't need to go to the hospital, claiming he's fine—but doctors insist on examining him, and he undergoes surgery. If not for their persistence, he would have surely died. A bullet in the lung is far too dangerous for someone his age. Twelve days later, Reagan is discharged.

In Vermont, Alexsander Solzhenitsyn is deeply worried about Reagan: "How else, if not by a miracle of God, can you explain it: a bullet just a centimeter from the heart, and such a swift recovery for a 70-year-old man? Our sympathy for him only grew stronger. Yes!—we need this president, in his desperate attempt to strengthen peace in the face of communism's ambitions."

Hinckley is arrested. During his interrogation, his first question is whether the Academy Awards ceremony will be postponed. The Academy Awards ceremony is indeed postponed by one day. On March 31, De Niro wins the Oscar for *Raging Bull*. The second *Star Wars* film, *The Empire Strikes Back*, wins for special effects and sound. But the biggest surprise of the night comes in the Best Foreign Language Film category. Instead of films by legendary directors Akira Kurosawa or François Truffaut, the award goes to *Moscow Does Not Believe in Tears* by Vladimir Menshov from the Soviet Union—despite the tensions over Afghanistan and the Olympic boycott. The award is accepted by a representative of the Soviet embassy, as Menshov was not allowed to travel to Los Angeles for the ceremony.

Exactly one year after the attempt on Reagan's life, in March 1982, Soviet leader Leonid Brezhnev travels to Tashkent for an official visit to his dear friend the First Secretary of Soviet Uzbekistan and Politburo candidate, Sharof Rashidov.

Uzbekistan is famous in the Soviet Union for its cotton—called white gold in the USSR. Year after year, five-year plan after five-year plan, Uzbekistan's leadership promises to produce more cotton than the previous year.

The socialist system demands that enterprises, labor collectives, and even entire regions set production targets, then exceed them to earn rewards and bonuses. Failing to meet the plan is a disgrace, so it never officially happens—on paper, at least. Even if a plan isn't met, the numbers look good. This practice is known as "padding the numbers."

Rashidov is highly esteemed by the Soviet leadership: he is twice a Hero of Socialist Labor and holds ten Orders of Lenin—all for his republic's consistent overfulfillment of cotton production plans.

In 1976, on the eve of the 25th Party Congress, Rashidov visited Moscow and reported to Brezhnev that 4 million tons of cotton had been produced. He promised that by the next five-year plan, it would be 5 million tons annually. Suddenly, Brezhnev interrupted, asking, "Why not make it six million?" Rashidov replied, "We'll try."

From an agricultural standpoint, it's absolutely impossible—everyone understands that 6 million tons is pure madness. It's hard to say who was deceiving whom: Did Brezhnev, the Council of Ministers, Rashidov, or their subordinates know that the cotton production numbers were growing only on paper? At the very least, they must have had some suspicion, as the quantity of cotton products wasn't increasing at all, as if the raw material was vanishing somewhere between the fields and the store shelves. Trains often arrived empty at textile factories, but for a bribe, the factory managers would sign off on the delivery documents, pretending the trains were full of cotton. And every year, Uzbekistan would report that everything was fine. Brezhnev and the Moscow leadership were pleased, and Sharof Rashidov, the First Secretary of Uzbekistan, received more medals.

Now, in March 1982, Brezhnev flies in to present Uzbekistan with the Order of Lenin. It sounds absurd, but in the USSR it is common to give state awards not just to people but also to inanimate objects—organizations and even regions. A joke went around that the Order of Lenin itself should be awarded the Order of Lenin.

The schedule for Brezhnev's visit changes several times. At first, an aircraft factory is on the agenda, but it's later scratched. Then, suddenly, Brezhnev insists on visiting it. His security team protests, saying nothing has been prepared. Stubborn, Brezhnev gives them fifteen minutes to check it. At the factory, a crowd of workers rushes to the hangar where Brezhnev is arriving, eager to catch a glimpse of him. To get a better view, many climb onto scaffolding. Just as Brezhnev and Rashidov pass beneath, the structure collapses—right on top of them. A piece of metal scrapes Brezhnev's ear, but more importantly, his collarbone is broken.

The next day, high on painkillers, Brezhnev appears at a party event to give a speech. The audience is shocked: Brezhnev already has very poor diction, and now he looks completely dazed and is nearly incoherent.

At this point, Leonid Brezhnev is seventy-five years old and has led the Soviet Union for eighteen years. In recent years, the head of state has suffered several strokes, he can barely move, and he speaks slowly and indistinctly. At Politburo meetings, he has repeatedly broached the subject of his resignation, but his party comrades always respond in unison that it's impossible—no one could manage without him.

Brezhnev is just five years older than Reagan, but unlike the spry American president, he already appears half-dead.

News of the incident in Tashkent never leaks to the world press. Only years later does a conspiracy theory emerge in Russia, speculating that seventy-five-year-old Brezhnev was the target of an assassination attempt by rivals within the Politburo.

BREZHNEV AND THE VOID

On September 24, 1982, Leonid Brezhnev arrives in Baku. This time, the General Secretary is to present Azerbaijan with the Order of Lenin.

An extraordinary celebration is organized for the visit. The head of the republic, Heydar Aliyev, prepares for the event as if it were a grand spectacle—no less momentous than the opening of the Olympic Games. The city's entire workforce, college students, and schoolchildren line the streets along Brezhnev's route, some applauding, others waving flags—supposedly to show the state's leader how hard the harvesters are working.

Heydar Aliyev appoints Azerbaijan's most famous showman at the time, Yuli Gusman, as the director of the celebration. Gusman had already orchestrated several such events for Brezhnev's previous visits to Baku. The climax of the event is set for Lenin Square, the city's main square.* Twenty round stages are set up on the square, where folk and children's ensembles will perform continuously. "We knew that Leonid Ilyich loved children and anything national," Gusman will recall.

Gusman vividly remembers what happened on the day of Brezhnev's arrival: "The wind is rustling the flags, hundreds of thousands of people on the square are watching me. I am standing on the roof and have to signal them: I raise the checkered flag, and they clap. I raise the red flag, they wave their arms. I raise the striped one, and they look sad."

Brezhnev's motorcade enters the square: motorcyclists, followed by about

---

* Until 1957, it was called Stalin Square, and in 1991, it will be renamed Freedom Square.

30 ZiL limousines. The General Secretary steps out of the car. The crowd goes silent, dancers are poised to rush onto the stages, triumphant music plays from the loudspeakers, and Soviet television is already broadcasting live. Brezhnev looks toward the tribune—he must climb five steps to reach it.

He leans toward Heydar Aliyev and whispers, "I won't make it, Gaydar." (Brezhnev mispronounces Aliyev's name as "Gaydar.") "I'm tired. I'll go rest." He gets back in the car, and the entire motorcade drives away.

The event organizers stand in shock for a few seconds—but the cameras are already rolling, and there's no turning back. "We're holding a celebration in honor of Brezhnev without Brezhnev," says Gusman. "Folk ensembles are dancing in front of empty stands, and a saber is being presented to empty space." Meanwhile, Brezhnev's personal TV director, Kaleriya Kislova, expertly alternates between the fantastic concert on the main square and shots of the motorcade driving through the streets of Baku. The broadcast makes it look as if the entire city is one continuous celebration. Wherever the motorcade goes, there are flowers, more stages, and new performers.

Brezhnev arrives at his residence, has a hearty lunch, and goes to sleep. The show on Lenin Square concludes, and the organized columns of people disperse. "I take my flags and come down from the roof—my power is over," Gusman says. "The wind blows scraps of newspaper through the city. The cleaners have come out to sweep. Just recently, I had all of Azerbaijan's resources at my disposal, and now everyone's gone, and I'm walking home across the whole city on foot."

That evening, Brezhnev wakes up and watches *Vremya*, the main Soviet news program, which broadcasts footage of his reception in Baku. He's astonished. "Listen, I don't remember anything," he confesses to his aides. But he's extremely pleased—every organizer of the celebration receives awards and bonuses. Brezhnev has only seven weeks left to live. He will die on November 10, 1982.

"COMMUNISM IS INEVITABLE"

Around the same time that Vova Putin meets a girl named Lyuda and Bob Grebenshchikov is expelled from the Komsomol, their peer Grigory (Grisha) Yavlinsky finishes graduate school and is assigned to work in Eastern Siberia. He was born in Lviv, in Western Ukraine, but moved to Moscow to study at the Plekhanov Institute of National Economy. After graduating, he is assigned to work for the Ministry of Coal Industry in the small mining town of Leninsk-Kuznetsky in the Kemerovo region.

"It was there that I first saw how people really lived. I had simply never known before. And what a scene it was. It was scorching hot, about forty degrees, and I was walking down the street. There was a 'glass kiosk'—a little café where everyone drank vodka. And coming toward me along that same street was a funeral procession, people carrying a coffin. Dust everywhere. And across from that 'glass kiosk,' a huge banner hung: 'Communism is inevitable.' I will never forget it in my life."

Yavlinsky is a labor specialist. His job is to develop schedules for miners, foremen, and engineers, defining their qualifications and requirements. And he is horrified.

After completing his mandatory two years, he returns to Moscow, to the Research Institute of Labor. "The Communist leadership of the country is searching for a model that would make the economy function," he would later recall. "They come up with all sorts of economic incentive funds, bonus systems, and so on. But I saw that people didn't care in the slightest. Not at all. Their lives were completely programmed. They could work well or work poorly—it wouldn't change a thing. Life itself was a dead end."

Nevertheless, he does his job—he writes a study in which he concludes that the system cannot function. Either the country must return to the Stalinist model, where people work out of fear, or they must be given freedom: "In my report, I talked about the freedom of enterprises."

His work is published under the classification "for official use only," meaning the print run is extremely limited. A month later, he is summoned to the highest authorities.

"Did you write this?" the deputy minister interrogates him. "Yes."

"Only the CIA writes things like this. Who do you work for?"

"No one."

"This kind of thing cannot exist in our country, this kind of writing. Who do you work for?"

"I wrote what I saw," twenty-nine-year-old Yavlinsky insists.

He is threatened with expulsion from the party, but it turns out he is not a member. He is ordered to track down all printed copies and bring them to a KGB officer. He tries to find all six hundred copies. At one point, he goes to his former university professor, the well-known economist Leonid Abalkin, and pleads with him to return his copy.

"What kind of disgrace is this? I'll get to the bottom of it," Abalkin promises.

Eventually, Yavlinsky recovers all the copies—but from that moment on, he is summoned to the KGB about twice a week and subjected to the same monotonous interrogation: "Who put you up to this? There's no way you came up with this on your own. You have a good father, a good mother. Your mother is a university professor; your father is a decorated war veteran. You couldn't have written this by yourself."

Then they start suggesting possible answers: "Maybe it was your institute's director? Or the deputy director?"

"Who told me to do that? Marx and Engels!" he snaps when asked the same question for the hundredth time.

"One more joke like that, and you won't be walking out of here," the KGB officer calmly replies.

This goes on for six months, until one day that same KGB officer suddenly says, "Leave now. Forget everything that happened here. And if you ever tell anyone, you will deeply regret it."

Grisha is stunned. As he walks back to the institute, he overhears people talking in the streets. They are discussing the fact that Brezhnev has died.

Soon the deputy director calls him in: "Now listen—either you will become a very famous economist, or you will end up in prison. Be prepared for both."

THIEVES IN LAW

In 1982, an extraordinary event takes place in the capital of Soviet Georgia, Tbilisi—a gathering of the top gangsters of the Soviet Union, the leaders of all major criminal organizations, known as thieves in law. These men play a crucial role as the guardians of criminal traditions.

In the USSR, the underworld is a distinct subculture, with roots stretching back to Stalin's Gulag—a period when a significant portion of the population passed through prisons and labor camps. "Half the country are criminals. Half the country are guards," poet Robert Rozhdestvensky would later describe this phenomenon.

The Soviet criminal world follows its own unwritten laws—living by the code. This code demands absolute rejection of the Soviet system: true thieves must not serve in the army, must not work, must not own property, and must have no dealings with state institutions. The image of such a freedom-loving outlaw is highly romanticized in the USSR, aided by the immense popularity of *blatnye* (criminal) songs. One of the songwriters of the genre's classics, Vladimir Vysotsky, had never been to prison himself.

But in 1982, at the Tbilisi gathering, one of the most influential kings of the Soviet underworld proposes a radical shift. He argues that corruption has flourished across the country, many party officials have turned into mafiosi, and real gangsters must not ignore this process—they must take control of it.

The godfather pushing to turn Soviet criminals into tycoons of the shadow economy is named Jaba Ioseliani. His biography is remarkable—he was imprisoned under Stalin and genuinely despised the dictator, as any true Soviet convict was supposed to.

"In my youth, there was no other path—either prison or the Komsomol. I simply couldn't join the Komsomol; I saw all the scum flocking there," he would later recall. "Even a monastery wasn't an option—there were no monasteries. Where else was there to go? And then there was the street, the romance of it. I was 15, I needed someone to knock some sense into me, but instead, they gave me five years."

After serving several sentences, which he completed at the age of forty-eight, he finished high school, graduated from university, earned a PhD, and became a playwright and theater scholar—all while continuing his primary occupation, which was crime.

By the late 1970s, Ioseliani had built a trade network for Georgian fruits and vegetables across the USSR—a seemingly legal business, but since any trade outside the state's control, and indeed any entrepreneurial activity in general, was considered a crime in the Soviet Union, this made him a criminal in the eyes of the law.

Ioseliani is not merely a thief in law but the head of an underground corporation. He believes the criminal world must abandon its old principles and begin working with corrupt officials, with the police, and take control of the entire illegal economy.

But not everyone agrees. The most respected thief in law in the Soviet Union, Vasya Brilliant, is categorically opposed—he adheres to the old code, believing that collaborating with the state and its representatives is beneath them.

At this moment, the Soviet underworld fractures—Georgia, under Ioseliani's leadership, breaks away and adopts a new, commercial approach. This is a significant shift, as by this time nearly a third of all thieves in law in the USSR are based in Georgia.

Three years later, in 1985, Vasya Brilliant will die, and at the next thieves' gathering in 1986—again in Tbilisi—the previous decision will be overturned. Jaba Ioseliani will prevail. Essentially, he will become the Soviet Lucky Luciano—revolutionizing the USSR's criminal world and, more than that, paving the way for Soviet crime bosses to enter politics.

LAVISH FUNERALS

The first mention in the Soviet press that the country is at war doesn't appear until the summer of 1980.

Astonishingly, the first five years of the Soviet war in Afghanistan will go down in history as the "Five-Year Plan of Lavish Funerals"—but not because the country will ceremoniously honor its fallen soldiers. Quite the opposite: this statistic will be hidden. Instead, one after another, the members of the Politburo who made the decision to send in troops will die.

In 1980, 1,484 Soviet soldiers die in Afghanistan, while in the USSR seventy-six-year-old premier Alexei Kosygin, the only member of the Politburo who opposed the intervention and did not attend the fateful meeting, passes away.

In 1982, 1,948 soldiers perish, and the second-most powerful man in the USSR, seventy-nine-year-old Mikhail Suslov, dies, followed by the most powerful man—seventy-five-year-old General Secretary Leonid Brezhnev.

In 1983, 1,448 soldiers die, and the oldest member of the Politburo, eighty-four-year-old Arvid Pelshe, passes away.

In 1984, a grim record is set in Afghanistan—2,343 Soviet soldiers are killed. Meanwhile, in Moscow, two of the main architects of the war effort die peacefully in their beds: the new General Secretary and former head of the KGB, Yuri Andropov (age sixty-nine), and Defense Minister Dmitry Ustinov (age seventy-six).

In 1985, 1,868 Soviet servicemen are killed, and seventy-three-year-old General Secretary Konstantin Chernenko joins the ranks of the deceased.

Over ten years, according to official figures, 15,500 Soviet soldiers will die in Afghanistan. Thousands more will be wounded. Tens of thousands of young men will serve in Afghanistan, many of whom will be haunted by the war for the rest of their lives—Soviet doctors will call it the Afghan Syndrome.

And the frequent funerals of Soviet leaders will become a popular topic for jokes—people living in a state of internal emigration can afford to laugh at the government, though the idea of actually challenging it is far from their minds.

YOU'RE DISHONORING THE FAMILY

In 1981, at one of his home concerts, Boris Grebenshchikov meets a quiet nineteen-year-old with Asian features named Viktor (Vitya) Tsoi, who decides to form his own group.

That new band's rise ends before it even begins. In the fall of 1981, Tsoi learns that the group's drummer, Oleg Valinsky, has been drafted into the army. He's lucky—he's sent to serve in Cuba rather than Afghanistan, which is every Soviet conscript's worst nightmare.

Vitya searches for new bandmates and comes up with a new name—Kino (Cinema).

Soon, at a house party, nineteen-year-old Vitya meets twenty-three-year-old Maryana Rodovanskaya, who works in the circus. They start dating, and Maryana immediately decides that Tsoi has a great future ahead of him. At first, Maryana brings old costumes from the circus for the band. Then she becomes their manager. Tsoi takes a job as a boiler stoker to avoid accusations of being a parasite, allowing him to dedicate most of his time to music.

In the summer of 1983, Viktor Tsoi himself receives his draft notice for the army. The war in Afghanistan is ongoing, and while not everyone is sent there, it's widely believed that those with Asian features, like Tsoi, who is Korean, will definitely be deployed.

But that's not the only thing bothering Tsoi. He doesn't feel connected to the Soviet Union at all; he exists in his own world, where he writes songs with his friends and performs them at underground apartment concerts. Military service is an invasion by the hostile outside world into his life—a world Tsoi wants nothing to do with. He's determined to preserve his way of life, which means avoiding the draft at any cost. The only way out is to be declared unfit for military service due to health reasons.

Among Tsoi's friends, it's common knowledge that the easiest illness to fake is mental instability. Sure, you might have to spend a little time in a psychiatric hospital, but afterward, the authorities will leave you alone forever.

Tsoi's father, Robert, is extremely anxious. He calls his son, saying, "You're dishonoring the family. You need to go; you need to serve." Vitya laughs and reminds his father that he himself never served because he finished university.

Tsoi carefully asks his friends how to fake manic-depressive psychosis (MDP). The plan involves simulating a suicide attempt—slitting his wrists. But Vitya can't stand the sight of blood, so he asks his girlfriend, Maryana, to help. Together, they manage to scrape his wrists enough to summon an ambulance.

Friends told Vitya that the process would be simple: a few days in the hospital and then they would send him home with a certificate. But things don't go as planned. The authorities take Tsoi's case seriously. He's sent to Psychiatric Hospital No. 2, known colloquially as Pryazhka. It's a place with a history—in 1941, the writer Daniil Kharms was held there (he would die in a prison hospital a year later), and in 1964, the poet Joseph Brodsky underwent forced psychiatric evaluation there after being tried for parasitism. Just across the river from the hospital is the house where, in 1921, the poet Alexander Blok died.

In 1921, the gravely ill Blok had tried to escape Soviet power by fleeing abroad, but he wasn't allowed to leave. Tsoi doesn't need to escape—he's already living in internal exile. All he wants is for the government to leave him alone. But Tsoi's doctor at Psychiatric Hospital No. 2, seemingly unimpressed by the superficial cuts on his wrists, is determined to expose Tsoi's act. The singer is kept in the hospital for a month and a half.

"It was terrifying to look at Tsoi," Maryana would later recall. "When he was finally released, I barely managed to drag Vitya to the car and take him home—to yet another apartment we were renting at the time. I woke up around two in the morning, and Tsoi wasn't next to me. I went into the kitchen, and there, in the pitch-black darkness, he was scribbling something with a pencil on a torn matchbox." Under the weight of his experience in the psychiatric hospital, Tsoi was writing one of his most scary songs, called "Tranquilizer."

In May 1984, Grebenshchikov gives an apartment concert in Novosibirsk and tells the audience, "There's this Korean guy in Leningrad who works in a boiler room. He recorded an amazing concert all by himself. I'm sure he'll become really popular."

"A Korean? In Russia? That's unlikely . . . ," they reply.

Officially, there is no racism in the Soviet Union, and the friendship of peoples is said to reign supreme, but imagining a star with Asian features is utterly impossible.

THE NEW TIE

The election of a new General Secretary, sixty-eight-year-old Yuri Andropov, sparks a wave of enthusiasm. Members of the Central Committee burst into applause when they hear the name of Brezhnev's successor. From day one, Andropov shows that he intends to change everything: the stagnant old style is a thing of the past. The former head of the KGB believes it's time to bring order to the country.

Andropov builds a team of younger, loyal officials. His first move is to bring Heydar Aliyev into the Politburo. Then he sets his sights on Grigory Romanov, the head of Leningrad, transferring him to Moscow to serve as Secretary of the Central Committee for the Military-Industrial Complex.

Another of Andropov's protégés is Mikhail Gorbachev, Secretary of the Central Committee for Agriculture. To understand what this role means, I need to explain a bit about how the Soviet state functions under its strange, unwritten rules. On paper, the constitution sets up a division of powers: the highest body is the parliament, called the Supreme Soviet, and the head of the Presidium of the Supreme Soviet is the nominal head of state. But in reality, this is purely ceremonial.

The real supreme power in the USSR is the Politburo, an unofficial "board of directors" that governs the country. Although it isn't mentioned in the Soviet constitution, everyone knows that the Politburo holds the reins of authority.

For example, in the USSR, there is a minister of agriculture, but Gorbachev, as the party secretary for agriculture, is the one truly overseeing it. In 1979, 1980, and 1981, Gorbachev faced a series of failures—declines in agricultural production, drought, prolonged rains, record-low harvests, and an American economic embargo following the Soviet invasion of

Afghanistan. Yet, rather than punish Gorbachev, they promoted him. In 1979, Gorbachev was appointed as a candidate member of the Politburo, and in 1980, he became a full member.

As the youngest of the Soviet "cardinals," he initially kept a low profile, agreeing with his senior colleagues, refraining from arguments, and showering Brezhnev with praise—doing his best to appear as the "model student." He put in a great deal of effort. His then-assistant, Valery Boldin, recalls that Gorbachev ties a fresh tie every day rather than pulling an already-knotted one over his head.

And yet, even as he brings in energetic young talent, Andropov isn't in a hurry to dismiss the old Brezhnev-era patriarchs. The second-in-command, the so-called Second Secretary and official successor, becomes the elderly Konstantin Chernenko. He is the ultimate bureaucrat, whose main achievement is faithfully delivering papers to Brezhnev and controlling access to the leader, claiming that only he can properly explain things to the aging boss. Chernenko is significantly older than Andropov, so he likely has no illusions about one day leading the country himself.

CORRUPTION FIGHTERS

Andropov has some unique ideas on how to set things right. He's convinced that all Soviet citizens simply need to work more, and work better. His most notable innovation: law enforcement across the country starts rounding up people during work hours in stores, bathhouses, and movie theaters to check if anyone's skipping work. The new General Secretary believes this will boost discipline, productivity, and the economy.

It doesn't occur to Andropov or anyone around him that the Soviet economy just doesn't work, that no one believes in communist ideology anymore, or that the system is paralyzed. He's certain that if people just work harder and if speculators and corrupt officials are dealt with, things will improve. And the funny thing is, most citizens don't think the system is broken either. They assume that the reason for shortages, for the empty stores, is simply that everything's been stolen or saved for privileged party members. And so, Andropov's anti-corruption campaign actually resonates with the public.

Andropov kicks off a vigorous purge, gradually firing Brezhnev's favorites. First up in December 1982 is Nikolai Shchelokov, head of the Ministry of

Internal Affairs and Andropov's old nemesis. Shchelokov's wife, Svetlana, is devastated by her husband's disgrace and by how quickly former friends cut ties with them. In February 1983, she takes her own life.

Many Soviet citizens are skeptical about the suicide story; rumors circulate that she shot at Andropov, her next-door neighbor, but failed to kill him—so she shot herself instead. Opera singer Galina Vishnevskaya, now living in Washington, tells friends she doesn't believe the suicide story either. She's sure the real reason is the mutual hatred between Andropov and Shchelokov and suspects Svetlana was actually murdered.

General Secretary Andropov never uses the word "corruption" (he says "instances of abuse of official position for personal enrichment"), but in essence, he launches a showy anti-corruption campaign. The next target is Sharof Rashidov, head of Uzbekistan. In January 1983, Andropov gives Rashidov a personal scolding, expecting him to resign on the spot. But Rashidov refuses. So Andropov brings the matter before the Politburo and initiates a full-scale operation.

The case is assigned to two senior investigators, Telman Gdlyan and Nikolai Ivanov. They arrive in Tashkent and quickly expand the case to massive proportions.

In reality, Uzbekistan's agriculture is in crisis: excessive fertilizer use, chemicals, and reckless irrigation have depleted the soil, and the region's largest water source, the Aral Sea, is slowly being destroyed. In the 1960s, the Aral Sea was the world's fourth-largest lake, fed by the Amu Darya and Syr Darya rivers. But now nearly all the water from these rivers is diverted to irrigate cotton fields. Soviet scientists even promote the idea that the Aral Sea is a "mistake of nature" and would be better drained, using the lake bed for farming. They're also developing a plan to divert Siberian rivers, the Ob and Irtysh, southward to irrigate Central Asia's cotton plantations.

Investigators Gdlyan and Ivanov are sure that they are fighting against a system where everyone is complicit, from the lowest officials to the top. But the Moscow authorities demand results at any cost. So they use all means necessary: round-the-clock interrogations, handcuffs, threats, and, of course, no lawyers. The Moscow investigators believe they're doing what's right—otherwise, corrupt officials would escape justice.

By the summer of 1983, the investigation team finally obtains testimony against Uzbekistan's First Secretary, Rashidov. He receives an unpleasant phone call from Moscow and on October 31, 1983, Rashidov dies suddenly of a heart attack.

EMPIRES STRIKE BACK

On May 25, 1983, *Star Wars: Return of the Jedi* premieres in US theaters. It's the final installment of George Lucas's trilogy: good triumphs, the Galactic Empire is destroyed, its dictator, Palpatine, is dead, and the Death Star is blown to bits. For audiences worldwide, the battle between the "good Jedi" and the "bad Sith" naturally aligns with the Cold War. The Galactic Empire is, of course, the Soviet Union, and the villain Palpatine even resembles an elderly Politburo member—a blend of Brezhnev and Suslov. Incidentally, the second film in the series, *The Empire Strikes Back*, came out in 1980, shortly after the Soviet invasion of Afghanistan.

Since January 1981, the US president has been Ronald Reagan, a former Hollywood actor determined to prove he's a man of action, unlike his predecessors. In March 1983, he delivers a historic speech, clearly inspired by the Star Wars aesthetic—he calls the Soviet Union an "evil empire." A few weeks later, he gives another speech, this time announcing the "Strategic Defense Initiative," a missile shield to protect the United States from Soviet attacks with combat stations equipped with lasers to be deployed in space. The American media instantly dubs the program "Star Wars."

These speeches send psychological shock waves around the world. Brezhnev's friendly relations with previous American presidents reassured people that nuclear war was unthinkable. The general assumption was that it would wipe out the entire world, so no one would dare start it. But with cowboy Reagan on one side and KGB man Andropov on the other, everything suddenly changes: both sides start acting like a new nuclear world war is entirely possible. The USSR and the United States pull out of international treaties, develop new weapons, and visibly deploy them worldwide.

When Anatoly Dobrynin, the Soviet ambassador to the United States, is told to prepare for nuclear war, he can hardly believe it. Dobrynin has been in America for twenty years, raised his grandchildren there, witnessed the Cuban Missile Crisis and Watergate, and taken Brezhnev to Hollywood and cosmonaut Leonov to Disneyland—and now nuclear war, really?

On August 31, 1983, a Korean Air flight leaves New York for Seoul. Onboard are 269 people: South Koreans, Americans (including Congressman Larry McDonald), Taiwanese, Japanese, and Filipinos. After refueling in Alaska, the plane heads for Seoul. Somehow, the crew misconfigures the autopilot, causing the plane to veer off course into Soviet air space near Kamchatka. On this day, the USSR is conducting ballistic missile tests, and ground services mistake the passenger Boeing 747 for an American spy plane. Passengers sleep, the crew relies on autopilot, and no one checks the coordinates. Soviet ground services don't contact their Japanese or American counterparts for information—they fear the intruder will escape and don't want to lose time. Two Soviet interceptors are sent to meet the plane. They're ordered to destroy the target, and Captain Gennady Osipovich fires two missiles. The plane's wreckage falls into the La Perouse Strait southwest of Sakhalin.

The world learns within hours that a plane with nearly three hundred people onboard has disappeared over the Soviet Union. The Politburo is holding a routine meeting in the Kremlin. General Secretary Andropov is clearly unaware. Soviet chief of staff Nikolai Ogarkov insists the downed plane was a military aircraft. The Politburo decides to deny everything. Andropov is unwell and is due to leave for a vacation in Crimea the next day.

The next day, the Politburo meets again. Konstantin Chernenko, the Second Secretary, is in charge in Moscow. He orders officials to "minimize the anti-Soviet campaign." Defense Minister Dmitry Ustinov is firm: "Nobody can prove anything."

In reality, things spiral out of control for Soviet authorities. While Moscow denies everything, the United States accuses the USSR of deliberately downing the plane. "Two hundred and sixty-nine innocent men, women, and children were killed. This is a crime against humanity," declares President Reagan.

On September 26, three weeks after the Korean Air tragedy, an alarm goes off at the missile defense command center in Serpukhov. The system reports that the United States has launched a nuclear missile aimed at the USSR. The estimated flight time: about thirty minutes. Sirens wail. Lieutenant Colonel Stanislav Petrov is on duty. Amid the panic, Petrov orders his subordinates to stay in position. He reports to headquarters that it's a false alarm: if this were a real attack, missiles would be launched from multiple American bases, not just one. But then a signal of a second missile launch comes through, then a third.

Aides with the nuclear briefcase race to Andropov—who is in a government sanatorium in Crimea, undergoing dialysis. However, Petrov insists again that there's no need to take retaliatory action.

Within half an hour, the situation becomes clear: Petrov was right. There was no missile launch from the United States. Sunlight reflecting off high-altitude clouds caused the Soviet satellite's sensors to malfunction. September 26, 1983, could have marked the start of a nuclear war between the USSR and the United States, but Lieutenant Colonel Petrov canceled it.

A month and a half later, Soviet divers find the black boxes of the Korean airliner in the Sea of Japan, confirming the Americans' version: the plane wasn't a spy. Its crew simply made a mistake, and none of the pilots knew they were off course.

PERSON OF THE YEAR

November 7 is the main holiday in the Soviet Union: the anniversary of the October Revolution. On October 25, 1917 (according to the old Russian calendar, which corresponds to November 7 on the modern calendar), the Bolsheviks overthrew the Provisional Government and took power in Russia. In Moscow, this day is marked by a military parade: all the missiles and fearsome machinery roll across Red Square, while Politburo members line up on the Lenin Mausoleum's platform.

On November 7, 1983, observers are stunned—the General Secretary isn't on the platform. Everyone is left wondering, *Where is Andropov?* He's at the Central Clinical Hospital, still conscious but unable to walk.

Despite his absence from the November parade—or from any public appearance—Yuri Andropov is named *Time* magazine's Person of the Year in December 1983, alongside US president Ronald Reagan. The magazine dubs them the two most unyielding leaders who nearly brought the world to nuclear war.

On December 26, 1983, Moscow prepares for the next gathering of the ruling elite—the CPSU Central Committee Plenum, which takes place twice a year, in spring and fall. Traditionally, it opens with a speech from the General Secretary, but of course, Andropov is too ill to appear. Nevertheless, he instructs his speechwriters to draft a speech. He won't deliver it in person, but the text will be distributed to all Central Committee members and published in the newspapers, so Soviet citizens won't realize that the leader wasn't actually present at the Plenum.

On December 24, Andropov's assistant, Arkady Volsky, visits him at the hospital to review the speech prepared by his aides. Later Volsky will claim Andropov adds two paragraphs himself. The final one supposedly reads: "For reasons known to you, I cannot actively participate in managing the Politburo and the Central Committee Secretariat at this time. I therefore ask the Central Committee Plenum to consider assigning the responsibility of overseeing the Politburo and Secretariat to Comrade Mikhail Sergeyevich Gorbachev."

With this line, Andropov effectively names his successor. Volsky delivers the document to the Central Committee, where it is retyped. Two days later, Volsky reviews the text and suddenly finds the final sentence missing. He hesitates: Should he check with Andropov? On his way, he's intercepted by Chernenko's right-hand man, Klavdy Bogolyubov. "Go ahead and call—it'll be your last phone call," Bogolyubov warns. Volsky agrees, realizing his boss is not long for this world and that soon there'll be no one left to protect him—the Politburo elders have already settled everything among themselves. Volsky doesn't make the call. Later he overhears Premier Tikhonov whispering to Defense Minister Ustinov, "It'll be easier with Kostya [Chernenko] than with Misha [Gorbachev]."

The next day, Andropov learns that his final paragraph was cut. Does he confront the Politburo plotters, led by Chernenko? No, he takes it out on the fearful Volsky.

Later, party officials will claim that Andropov never wrote such a "will" and that Volsky invented the story.

After the Plenum, Andropov summons Gorbachev. Gorbachev arrives at the hospital, barely able to contain his shock: Andropov is so thin and altered that he's barely recognizable. On February 9, 1984, Andropov dies. The "Person of the Year" had been in power for only fifteen months. The Politburo elects seventy-two-year-old Konstantin Chernenko as the new leader.

JOANNA FROM CALIFORNIA

Nineteen eighty-four is the year of Orwell's dystopia. In the USSR, *1984* is considered anti-Soviet and therefore banned. But Soviet reality is, of course, nothing like the book. There's no total control, no universal fear, and no one demands love for "Big Brother." Apathy and disbelief in state ideology are what bind citizens across the country.

In Leningrad, rock musicians try, in their own ways, to maintain good relations with their "handlers" from the KGB. Grebenshchikov recalls, "Once, a gentleman who introduced himself as Vladimir Vladimirovich told me, 'You know, I could come to your house, and if I see Solzhenitsyn on your shelf, you might have to take a little trip to some distant place.' 'But I don't have Solzhenitsyn on my shelf!' I replied. 'Oh, really?' he said. 'Really, I'm just not interested.' But Vladimir Vladimirovich, in a friendly voice, continued, 'We could bring it for you.'"

But in reality, the KGB is primarily interested in Soviet citizens' contacts with foreigners. Meeting tourists and students from abroad is a dream for many Soviet citizens; they bring records of trendy Western music, books, and fresh Western press. They carry stylish clothing, including the prized jeans unavailable in the USSR, along with imported alcohol and cigarettes—everything that has value for Soviet youth. BG recalls that each year, a new group of American students would come to Leningrad, and the Leningrad underground crowd would immediately take them under their wing, introducing them to the city's cultural life. The Americans would leave, passing their friends' addresses to the next group.

In March 1984, two American sisters, Judy and Joanna Fields from California, arrive at Moscow's Sheremetyevo Airport. Joanna, twenty-four, tried her hand at being a rock singer, but it didn't work out. She's ready for a change of scenery and wouldn't mind annoying her anti-communist father. Plus, it's cheap: the Reagan administration encourages student exchanges between the USSR and the United States to show Soviets how much better life is in America. The trip to Moscow and Leningrad costs Joanna only $300. They're part of a tour group—traveling solo in the USSR is, of course, forbidden.

Before leaving California, Joanna had spoken to a Russian émigré acquaintance, who told her that the USSR has rock music too and that she should look up "the main star of the Russian rock underground" in Leningrad: Boris Grebenshchikov.

After three days in Moscow and leaning toward the idea that their father was right—the USSR really was a terrible place overrun with monsters—the sisters head to Leningrad. There are no phones in the hotel rooms, but

Joanna, gathering courage, asks the hostile floor attendant to call the number she'd been given in California. That evening, Joanna and Judy break away from their tour group, skip the excursion, and head to the nearest metro station to meet BG.

Joanna plays her songs for Grebenshchikov, and he plays his music for her. She realizes: "I'm no artist, just a silly girl with baseless ambitions. Boris has more talent in one song than in all my attempts combined." The next day, she goes to a secret concert.

Joanna is thrilled: the underground Leningrad she sees reminds her of the legendary Los Angeles of the sixties, which she heard about and read about in her childhood. "If Moscow was a bear's den, then Leningrad's underground scene was the storm's eye, pulsing with raw electricity and energy," Joanna would later recall.

Joanna asks Boris about life in the USSR, and he tries to explain the KGB's role in rock music: on the one hand, they allow performances, but on the other, they try to control everything. As she leaves, Joanna promises to return—and bring him a guitar. He asks for a white Fender Stratocaster, like David Bowie's.

HIT BY A TROLLEYBUS

At the very beginning of 1984, thirty-two-year-old economist Grigory Yavlinsky is unexpectedly summoned for a medical checkup. He is surprised—regular full medical examinations are typically reserved for much higher-ranking officials. But during the examination, the doctors make a startling discovery—Yavlinsky has tuberculosis, a diagnosis he had never even suspected.

Strangers show up at his home and workplace, confiscating all his personal belongings and documents, telling him that everything is contaminated and must be destroyed. Then, without further explanation, he is taken to a tuberculosis hospital.

In the USSR, tuberculosis is a common disease in prisons, so most of the patients are former convicts. The hospital rules reflect that reality.

Nine months later, the doctors inform Yavlinsky that his tuberculosis is not improving and that his lung must be removed. That would mean becoming disabled, permanently saying good-bye to his normal life. He calls his wife; they discuss it—what else can be done? If the doctors say it's necessary, there is no other option.

They begin preparing him for surgery. But the day before the operation, the professor overseeing his case suddenly leans in close and whispers in his ear, "You're healthy. Get out of here."

And so he decides to run.

Escaping from a tuberculosis hospital in the USSR is a criminal offense—it means deliberately spreading a disease among Soviet citizens. Grisha Yavlinsky has no documents, no proper clothes—but he manages to get home. His wife lets him in. Together, they come up with a plan.

She borrows clothes from a neighbor, and Yavlinsky sets off to various clinics. Each one offers fluorography scans, and in fact, Soviet citizens are constantly urged to get their lungs checked as part of the state's tuberculosis prevention efforts. Since he doesn't have a medical file ("I forgot it at home"), Grisha buys several Alenka chocolate bars. These simple bribes work like a charm, and he is admitted everywhere.

"I urgently need a certificate for work; please make one," he says, which is enough—everyone knows that in the USSR, even the most absurd paperwork is required at every step. In a single day, Yavlinsky undergoes four fluorography scans at four different clinics—and in each one, he receives a certificate stating that he is completely healthy.

Armed with the certificates, he returns to the hospital and goes straight to the chief doctor.

"Doctor, please understand, this is a mistake. I am healthy. Let me go," Grisha pleads. "I have a wife, two children. One of them is only two years old. My mother is a pensioner. I have to support my family—everything depends on me. Please, let me go."

The chief doctor stands up, locks the door, looks Yavlinsky straight in the eyes, and says:

"Can you imagine being hit by a trolleybus?"

"Why a trolleybus?" Grisha asks, confused.

"Well, if you prefer, a bus," the doctor replies hopelessly, pointing out the window at the trolleybus terminal. "It doesn't matter. The system ran over you. There's nothing you can do. It's like a trolleybus, a bus, a car— the system ran over you. So if you resist, we'll send you to a psychiatric hospital. It's a tuberculosis hospital too, but also for the insane. Don't fight it; it's useless. You'll get a pension. You'll be entitled to your own one-room apartment. What's so bad about that?"

"Listen to me—I'm thirty-two years old. A pension? What are you talking about?" Yavlinsky is nearly in tears. "What apartment? I don't need any of that!"

"Decide for yourself." The doctor shrugs. "But there is no other way out."

HAPPINESS IN GORKY

On May 2, 1984, Elena Bonner leaves Gorky for Moscow, carrying another batch of manuscripts from Andrei Sakharov. Since her husband's exile, she has become the go-between, the link between him and the outside world. She brings his letters to Western journalists and delivers his new articles to Moscow.

But this time, she's stopped right on the tarmac. Sakharov watches from the airport window, having just seen his wife off. That same day, Bonner is charged with "anti-Soviet agitation and propaganda" and "slander against the Soviet system." While she's being interrogated, Sakharov sends a telegram to the Kremlin, declaring a hunger strike. He demands that his wife be allowed to leave the country for medical treatment.

Bonner's health troubles began a year and a half earlier. In December 1982, she returned to Moscow from Gorky by train. At the Yaroslavsky station, KGB officers entered her compartment. Her husband's manuscripts were hidden under her blouse, wrapped in cellophane taped to her body. They searched Bonner for a long time, confiscated the papers, and then released her. By then, the train had been shunted to the depot—she walked back along the tracks but fainted on the bridge over the railway. The diagnosis: pre–heart attack.

Back in Gorky with her beloved husband, she felt fine again. Years later, she would recall that her life with Sakharov in exile was immensely happy—except for the times they were separated. They cherished each other's company, going for walks, and even to the movies. One summer, they snuck out to spend a night in the countryside in a haystack. To do this, they had to tiptoe barefoot out of the apartment, holding their shoes and stepping over the legs of the sleeping policeman stationed at their door before sneaking out of the building. At dawn, they climbed back into their apartment through the window. "It was a romantic escape, a secret tryst hidden from the world," Bonner would later remember.

But Bonner's trips to Moscow and back took a toll on her. "We must, Lyusenka, we must," Sakharov would encourage her each time.

In 1983, Bonner had a heart attack. Sakharov began demanding that she be allowed to go abroad for treatment. At that time, coronary artery bypass surgery was rarely performed in the USSR, so Sakharov insisted she should be treated in the United States, convinced that a Soviet hospital would be a death sentence for her.

After Bonner's arrest on the tarmac in May 1984, Sakharov resorts to a drastic measure: he goes on a hunger strike. She is released, and they're initially allowed to live together at home. Sakharov accompanies her to interrogations every day. But on May 7, he is forcibly taken to the hospital from his wife's interrogation session; he clings to Bonner, but they are pulled apart. They're denied visits: an investigator tells Bonner that any meeting could adversely affect Sakharov's health.

Sixty-two-year-old Sakharov attempts several escapes from the hospital, but each time he is brought back.

"The methods of forced feeding varied as they searched for the hardest one to break my will," Sakharov would recall. "They used intravenous nutrient infusions. They would throw me down on the bed and tie my arms and legs. When the needle was inserted, orderlies pinned down my shoulders. The first day, someone from the hospital staff sat on my legs. Before the nutrients were administered, they injected something into my vein with a small syringe. I lost consciousness (along with involuntary urination). When I regained consciousness, the orderlies were already standing back by the wall. Their figures seemed grotesquely distorted, twisted (like on a TV screen with heavy interference). I later learned that this visual illusion is typical of brain vessel spasms or a stroke."

"We won't let you die. . . . But we'll make you a helpless invalid," the head doctor tells Sakharov one day.

The Nobel laureate's hunger strike becomes headline news worldwide. On May 19, US president Reagan asks Soviet leader Chernenko to allow Bonner to leave. The Kremlin responds: "This lady and her associates are intentionally dramatizing the situation for anti-Soviet purposes. As for her actual health, she will outlive many of her contemporaries." By this point, Soviet propaganda has thoroughly demonized Elena Bonner. "In her youth, she was a promiscuous girl who nearly mastered the art of seducing and then exploiting elderly, well-positioned men," states *Smena*, a Soviet magazine. "And now, she's pushing this mentally unstable man to actions that betray the image of Sakharov, the scientist."

Sakharov's forced feeding continues for over two weeks, including on his birthday—he turns sixty-three on May 21. On May 27, he promises to eat voluntarily. Privately, he decides he'll resume the hunger strike as soon as he regains his strength—in July or August.

Meanwhile, Bonner is put on trial and sentenced to five years of exile in Gorky. While Sakharov was exiled there without a trial, his wife must remain in Gorky by court order. She can no longer travel to Moscow or deliver Sakharov's letters to foreign journalists.

Sakharov is released from the hospital on September 7, 1984—with a twitching lower jaw due to a ministroke suffered in the hospital.

They're together again, though now completely cut off from the world. Sakharov is in deep depression. He writes a letter to the Academy of Sciences, promising to cease all political activity if Bonner is allowed to leave for surgery.

"We must accept defeat," Bonner tells her husband. But he remains stubborn: "No, I will never accept defeat," he says. "It would be easier for me to die than to surrender." And he begins preparing for a new hunger strike.

CANDIDATES PREPARE TO TAKE OFF

The new General Secretary, Chernenko, is only seventy-three—a prime age for leadership, by today's standards (Vladimir Putin is the same age in 2025; Donald Trump is six years older). But Chernenko is ill, rarely attending Politburo meetings, and when he does, he's brought in with assistance, seated before the other participants enter. Chernenko's election has set off a new race for the leadership of the USSR.

The Chernenko Politburo has twelve members, who will soon decide on the next General Secretary. Most are conservative Brezhnev loyalists. There are five main contenders for the position after Chernenko's time ends: Brezhnev's favorites, leader of the Communist Party in Moscow Viktor Grishin and Ukraine's First Secretary, Volodymyr Shcherbytsky, as well as Andropov's protégés Grigory Romanov, Heydar Aliyev, and Mikhail Gorbachev. In a sense, one could even say that these are two parties: one made up of conservatives, the other of reformists.

Each contender has strengths and weaknesses.

The oldest, Grishin, is seventy and has led Moscow since 1967. He is closest to Chernenko and could be a compromise choice for the old guard.

Volodymyr Shcherbytsky, another Brezhnev favorite, is from the powerful "Dnipropetrovsk clan." Shcherbytsky grew up on the same street as Brezhnev. In 1982, Brezhnev told the Central Committee's head of personnel that he envisioned Shcherbytsky as his successor, not Andropov, and urged a succession plan accordingly.

Sixty-year-old Romanov led Leningrad from 1970 to 1983 and was also considered a likely successor during Brezhnev's tenure. Brezhnev frequently mentioned Romanov to foreign leaders, including Fidel Castro, as his choice to lead the USSR after him.

Romanov's reputation, however, is marred by an old rumor. Back in 1974, there was talk that when he married off his daughter in the former tsar's Tauride Palace, guests allegedly broke a borrowed set of imperial china from the Hermitage. The story was likely a fabrication, yet Romanov's rivals gave it traction. Chernenko, then just Brezhnev's secretary, circulated a note about the incident to the Politburo members. When Romanov went to KGB head Andropov to complain, Andropov advised him not to worry or respond publicly—it would blow over. Shortly after, the German magazine *Der Spiegel* published the story, likely with the KGB's help. The rumor about Romanov's daughter's wedding was soon retold everywhere.

Romanov wasn't chosen as Brezhnev's successor, but Andropov brought him to Moscow, making him Central Committee secretary in charge of the influential military-industrial complex lobby—an ideal position to become the next General Secretary. Under Chernenko, Romanov is effectively the second-in-command, seated to Chernenko's right at all meetings.

Gorbachev, on the other hand, is seen as a less significant player in this competition. For instance, Marshal Ustinov suggests that Gorbachev, as the youngest Politburo member, chair Central Committee meetings—mainly to annoy his rival Romanov. In addition, when Romanov is on vacation Chernenko offers Gorbachev the honorary seat to his right.

Gorbachev's work ethic makes him a favorite with Politburo members, especially since Chernenko can no longer function independently. Speaking, even reading from a script, is increasingly difficult for him. Politburo meetings take place on Thursdays, but it's always uncertain whether Chernenko will be able to lead them. Every Thursday, Gorbachev shows up prepared, just in case he needs to step in. Such decisions are announced last-minute, as news of Chernenko's deteriorating health is always kept under wraps. Gorbachev is a patient bureaucrat, always prepared, knowing that none of his colleagues would ever be so conscientious.

Each contender for the General Secretary's chair is building their own team. Romanov has the defense industry backing him. Grishin has Chernenko's administrative circle. Gorbachev has the "youth" around him—newcomers to Moscow. As the older Brezhnev-era generation dies off, regional leaders take their places, naturally aligning with the youngest Politburo member.

In 1983, Andropov brought the First Secretary from Tomsk, sixty-two-year-old Yegor Ligachev, to Moscow, making him head of party personnel. Gorbachev mentors Ligachev, understanding that personnel decisions are vital. On the surface, they seem to have a lot in common. Gorbachev is modest and diligent; Ligachev is an ascetic, a "Savonarola of communism." Both are workaholics, setting them apart from the elderly colleagues who can no longer fully carry out their duties. Gorbachev and Ligachev understand each other instantly and discuss important matters through notes, knowing all rooms are bugged.

Andropov also appointed Nikolai Ryzhkov, a fifty-four-year-old former director of the area's largest factory, the Uralmash plant, as Central Committee secretary for economics, placing him in Gorbachev's inner circle.

Is Gorbachev thinking about what comes after Chernenko? Does he dream of becoming General Secretary? If he does, he keeps it so quiet that it doesn't alarm the older members. At home, Gorbachev never discusses this, shielding Raisa from worries.

Nevertheless, Gorbachev is testing the waters. At least two accounts suggest he's sending confidants to build bridges with old Foreign Minister Andrei Gromyko.

First, at Gorbachev's request, his old friend Yevgeny Primakov, director of the Institute of Oriental Studies, speaks to Gromyko's son, Anatoly, head of the Institute of Africa. Anatoly admits that his father doesn't think highly of Gorbachev, viewing him as an "unserious politician." He favors another Andropov protégé, Heydar Aliyev. According to Gromyko Jr., his father often says Aliyev is a "decent man, an excellent organizer," but adds, "One Stalin was enough for us."

Negotiations continue through another Gorbachev confidant, Alexander Yakovlev, the head of the Institute of World Economy and International Relations and former Soviet ambassador to Canada. Yakovlev later recalls Gromyko Jr.'s words as follows:

"To avoid ambiguity, I'll tell you my own view. My father . . . is willing to support this idea [Gorbachev's candidacy]. . . . He's tired of the Foreign Ministry and would like a change of scenery. He has his eye on the Supreme Soviet."

This means Gromyko wants to lead the Presidium of the Supreme Soviet. Formally, the chairman of the Presidium is considered the highest-ranking official in the USSR, the head of state—Western media even sometimes translate the title as "president of the USSR." In reality, the General Secretary holds the true power. In the 1970s, Brezhnev realized that having a ceremonial head of state prevented him from negotiating equally with US presidents, so he combined the two roles. Andropov followed suit, and now Chernenko holds both positions. Gromyko proposes splitting the roles once more: he would become the nominal head of state, and Gorbachev the real one.

Yakovlev conveys this to Gorbachev. The latter listens, paces the room thoughtfully, then says, "Tell Andrei Andreyevich that I've always enjoyed working with him. I'll be happy to continue, whatever roles we may find ourselves in. And add that I keep my promises."

A DRAW IN MOSCOW

In September 1984, the final match for the World Chess Championship begins in Moscow. The reigning world champion, thirty-three-year-old Anatoly Karpov, faces off against twenty-one-year-old Garry Kasparov. The venue is the Column Hall of the House of the Unions in Moscow, a building typically used for solemn state funerals—for instance, it was here that Stalin's coffin was displayed for public mourning.

Karpov first became world champion at twenty-four—not much older than Kasparov is in 1984. But that was in 1975, during a period of détente when Soviet and American Soyuz and Apollo spacecraft were docking in space. The son of an engineer from the Chelyabinsk region and an exemplary Komsomol member, Karpov became General Secretary Brezhnev's favorite chess player. Congratulating him on his title, Brezhnev famously said, "You've taken the crown—hold on to it! After all, people fight for a crown! We wish you success—don't give it to anyone and all that stuff." This message was broadcast on Soviet television, and everyone understood: Karpov was the nation's champion; no other was needed.

Kasparov knows that the entire Soviet sports and bureaucratic establishment supports Karpov and is eager for his victory. Still, prodigy Kasparov isn't completely on his own—he's got a powerful patron: Heydar Aliyev, the former leader of Azerbaijan, now a Politburo member and deputy head of the Soviet government. Kasparov isn't Azerbaijani, but he was born in Baku; his mother is Armenian, and his father is Jewish.

When Kasparov was sixteen, in 1979, he won his first major international tournament, and he and his mother, Klara, were brought to meet Aliyev. Aliyev asked how he could help, and Klara requested that their family be given access to the Central Committee's special grocery store; in regular stores, nothing was available, while the special ones provided rare goods. Aliyev granted her request, and their family was also given an additional apartment in the same building. The following year, on Aliyev's orders, a full training base was established for the young chess player: Kasparov moved to an elite sanatorium on the shores of the Caspian Sea, where he would live for the next ten years.

It's hard to convey how popular chess is in the USSR in the 1980s— millions follow the Karpov-Kasparov rivalry. Chess matches are broadcast live on television and radio.

According to the rules, the winner is the first to reach six points. From the start, Kasparov is tense, losing several games in a row. After nine games, Karpov leads 4–0.

Kasparov is frustrated, struggling to manage his nerves. He listens on repeat to Vladimir Vysotsky's song "Slow Down, Horses," hoping to find some calm.

Nearly the entire Moscow intelligentsia is rooting for Kasparov. Later he explains that many see him as a symbol of change. He is part of the film and pop culture circles, dating a popular Soviet actress. His rival Karpov, meanwhile, doesn't even know these stars.

One evening around 7:00 p.m., the USSR's most popular pop singer, thirty-five-year-old Alla Pugacheva arrives at Kasparov's hotel. His mother, Klara, opens the door. Garry is already asleep, but the pop star insists on waking him. Concerned for her young friend, she comes to offer advice. "Stretch the game out at any cost," she urges. "Play for a draw. Make forty draws if you have to."

Indeed, the momentum shifts, and the game unfolds as Pugacheva advised. The two strongest chess players in the world engage in draw after draw, day by day. After an energetic start in September, October and November drag on tediously. A popular joke at the time: "Tomorrow's weather forecast: rain in Kyiv, snow in Leningrad, and a draw in Moscow."

Pugacheva's interest in chess is no coincidence. Just a year before, in 1983, ABBA's Benny Andersson and Björn Ulvaeus, along with British playwright Tim Rice, had offered her a starring role in their new musical, *Chess*. The plot is inspired by the iconic chess matches of previous decades: a Soviet and an American competing for the world title, with chess as an obvious metaphor for the Cold War. The Swedes know of Pugacheva and invite her to join the cast of the musical, destined to become a global hit. But she realizes she'll never be allowed to leave the USSR for that long. Pugacheva must choose between potential global fame and her family, which remains in the USSR. She later recalls crying for days, but in the end, she declines.

On November 23, Karpov scores another victory, bringing the score to 5–0. But on December 12, Kasparov wins his first game. The organizers are anxious, realizing the match could go on indefinitely. With each passing day, Karpov looks paler and more exhausted; he's just one step from victory, yet seems to have no strength left.

On December 20, seventy-six-year-old Defense Minister Dmitry Ustinov dies. This means that the Hall of Columns is needed for its traditional purpose—a grand funeral procession—so the chess match must find a new venue.

POLITICAL TOURISM

In the summer of 1984, Gorbachev makes his first official trip abroad. The leader of Italy's Communist Party, Enrico Berlinguer, has died, and tradition dictates that a high-ranking Soviet representative must attend the funeral. Gorbachev eagerly volunteers: the former Stavropol First Secretary had only been to Italy once before, with Raisa, as part of a tourist group, and he had loved it. The trip to Rome leaves a profound impression on Gorbachev. He is particularly struck by the sheer number of Italians who turn out to bid farewell to the communist leader—and, most of all, by how the atmosphere sharply contrasts with the official, artificial pomp of Soviet state funerals.

The West tries to establish contact with the new leaders of the post-Brezhnev USSR. Chernenko, of course, is also incapable of traveling anywhere. As a result, younger Politburo members who appear to have potential begin receiving cautious invitations to Europe and America.

British prime minister Margaret Thatcher debates between Gorbachev and Romanov, following the advice of her advisors, who insist that one of these two is most likely to rise to power. Ultimately, she chooses Gorbachev. He is invited as a member of the Presidium of the Supreme Soviet of the USSR, as part of a parliamentary delegation.

Meanwhile, US president Ronald Reagan also wants to glimpse the future leadership of the USSR: a parliamentary delegation headed by Ukrainian First Secretary Volodymyr Shcherbytsky is invited to Washington—a fresh Soviet face, a young and energetic representative who confidently holds his own in discussions with Reagan in the Oval Office.

Gorbachev flies to London in December 1984. For a more informal meeting, Margaret Thatcher hosts her guest from Moscow at Chequers, the countryside retreat of British prime ministers. Indeed, they manage to have a candid conversation. Neither touches much of the food, but they engage in lively dialogue, frequently interrupting each other: both Thatcher and Gorbachev love to talk and aren't particularly skilled at listening. Gorbachev, for example, passionately argues that all Soviet citizens are satisfied with their lives, while Thatcher counters: Why, then, does the Soviet government forbid them from traveling abroad?

"He's someone we can do business with. I even liked him," Thatcher writes to Ronald Reagan a few days after the meeting. "He is undoubtedly fully loyal to the Soviet system, but he is willing to listen, engage in genuine dialogue, and form his own opinions."

But what impresses her most is not the Central Committee secretary himself, but his wife.

"Raisa Gorbacheva is completely different, unlike anyone we associate with the Soviet system. She's confident, vibrant, and lively. Perhaps she slightly resembles a teacher in some ways. Her outfit was stunning—her excellent taste was evident. That day, she wore a beautifully tailored gray pinstripe suit. I remember looking at her with envy: I wanted a suit like that too. And within just a few minutes of conversation, it became clear that Raisa was a highly educated woman, capable of engaging effortlessly with the British ministers I had invited to Chequers."

It is during this visit that an amusing exchange takes place between the couple. "We are representatives of the working class," Gorbachev explains.

His wife unexpectedly interrupts, "Not really. You're a lawyer."

"Well, maybe you're right," he concedes. "Perhaps it's just a sociological term."

While in London, Gorbachev learns that Defense Minister Ustinov has died, meaning he must urgently return to Moscow for the funeral. In the Politburo, a reshuffle begins: Romanov is appointed head of the funeral commission, a role that carries significant weight under Kremlin traditions.

EXILED FROM THE HALL OF COLUMNS

Marshal Ustinov is laid to rest on Red Square, and once the farewell is over, the chess championship match between Garry Kasparov and Anatoly Karpov resumes in the Hall of Columns. Both chess federation officials and Central Committee members hope the match will end soon: Karpov leads 5–1 and needs only one more point to secure victory.

The match has racked up enormous costs; the players and their coaches have missed international tournaments, visas are expiring, and family issues are arising—who could have predicted that it would drag on for four months? Public interest is waning, and the sports committee suggests relocating the match to Moscow's southwest, at the Hotel Sport, which was built for the 1980 Olympics. Kasparov and Karpov write a joint letter to the Politburo, requesting that the venue remain the same. In private, Karpov promises to wrap things up within a month.

Around the same time, the musical *Chess* premieres triumphantly at London's Barbican Theatre, followed by shows in Hamburg, Amsterdam, and Stockholm—without Pugacheva. Someone brings her the record, and she listens to it, hoping the young rebel Kasparov will win, as if he could somehow avenge her missed opportunity to perform abroad.

The draws continue until January 30, when Kasparov secures another win. This causes a stir. Kasparov supporter singer Vakhtang Kikabidze quips, "I don't understand why they report one Soviet chess player's victory over another on TV with a face like a Politburo member just died."

The organizers announce that the next game will take place at the Hotel Sport. The relocation causes a weeklong break, but on February 8 Kasparov wins yet again. The score now stands at 5–3 in Karpov's favor, but the momentum has shifted toward Kasparov. The organizers call a time-out, and the young challenger is determined to fight on.

On February 15, an unexpected turn of events unfolds: President of the International Chess Federation (FIDE) Florencio Campomanes holds a press conference, announcing that the match will be terminated and a new championship will take place in September. Kasparov is furious. He rushes to the microphone, demanding that the match go on.

"In those few seconds it took me to move from the audience to the podium and protest this illegal decision, I made the most important choice of my life. That day, I openly challenged my opponents, and my struggle became public!" Kasparov would later recall.

Karpov, also present at the press conference, confirms he is willing to play. Campomanes sticks to his decision.

Kasparov is convinced that stopping the match is a conspiracy by Karpov's backers, who can't risk their favorite losing. Karpov's supporters claim that it was actually Politburo member Heydar Aliyev who pushed to end the game. But at that moment, the Politburo is engaged in a different kind of chess match entirely.

4

YOUNG CHAMPIONS

I remember vividly how, when I was a very small child, my greatest fear in the world was Ronald Reagan.

At the time, we lived in Africa—my father was a cryptographer for the General Staff, serving in the Soviet military mission in Angola. Our apartment was on the ninth floor of a building in the center of Luanda, and leaving it was strictly forbidden. In fact, we weren't even allowed below the second floor, where there was a fenced-off playground surrounded by metal mesh. That's where the wall of photographs was. One of them showed Gorbachev shaking hands with Reagan. Did I know who Reagan was? Not really. But what I heard on television was enough.

Whenever I went to the playground, I tried to run past that wall as quickly as possible, making absolutely sure not to look at the photo. To me, it seemed that pure evil lived inside that picture. I believed Reagan was the embodiment of the devil himself—and "devil" was the scariest word I knew when I was four years old.

I knew there were gunfights outside. I'd heard the story of a girl who was hit in the arm by a bullet while riding with her parents to a New Year's party. And I once overheard the adults talking about the family we had replaced in Luanda—they had been killed. To my young mind, it was obvious who was responsible: Reagan.

(Much later, I learned it had been a domestic tragedy: a Soviet officer, driven by jealousy, had shot his wife, her suspected lover, and then himself. Even the Angolan rebels had nothing to do with it.)

THE CONCLAVE

General Secretary Chernenko dies at the Central Clinical Hospital on March 10, 1985. The first person to be informed of his death is academician Yevgeny

Chazov, the chief physician of the Central Committee. Chazov knows that who he informs first will influence everything to come. In the Ottoman Empire, when a sultan died, each of his sons would race to the palace to claim the throne first—while the Politburo is not quite as dramatic, it's close.

Chazov first calls Mikhail Gorbachev, then KGB chairman Viktor Chebrikov.

It's the evening of March 10. Gorbachev quickly understands that he must act immediately. He schedules a Politburo meeting for 10:00 that night. Almost instantly. Gorbachev also asks Foreign Minister Gromyko to meet with him thirty minutes before the meeting. "We need to join forces," Gorbachev says. Gromyko agrees.

It's clear that only those in Moscow will be able to attend. As it happens, many key players are away: Ukrainian leader Volodymyr Shcherbytsky is in San Francisco, having just flown in from Washington; Central Committee Secretary Grigory Romanov is on vacation at the Lithuanian resort of Palanga.

Gorbachev's rivals scramble to return to Moscow, but none succeed. Romanov can't fly out of the Klaipeda airport and must drive to Vilnius to catch a flight to Moscow (later, actor Gennady Khazanov would recall hearing that Klaipeda's Soviet official had been instructed to leave the runway uncleared of snow to delay Romanov's flight as much as possible). Shcherbytsky, meanwhile, is routed through New York instead of directly to Moscow, so he, too, misses the crucial meeting.

Before the Politburo meeting begins, Gorbachev approaches the head of the Moscow Communist Party, Viktor Grishin, and, with an edge in his voice, asks if he wants to chair the funeral commission. It's a direct challenge—traditionally, the head of the funeral commission becomes the next General Secretary. Essentially, Gorbachev is asking his main rival: "Are you ready to fight me?" With Gorbachev in control of the meeting, Grishin is caught off guard. He reflexively declines, withdrawing himself from the running before the meeting even starts. Other Politburo members witness this exchange.

The meeting adjourns after that—officially, the Central Committee Plenum must select the General Secretary. Gorbachev suggests holding it the next day, with the Politburo meeting beforehand to finalize the recommendation.

The members leave, but Gorbachev remains at work late into the night. Alongside his longtime friend jurist Anatoly Lukyanov, he drafts the speech he'll deliver at the Plenum. Other members of his team—Yegor Ligachev, Nikolai Ryzhkov, and Alexander Yakovlev—stay too. Ligachev spends the night contacting regional party leaders, who are also Central Committee members and will vote at the Plenum. Having begun replacing old Brezhnev-era officials with younger ones during Andropov's tenure, Gorbachev and Ligachev have many supporters among the regional leaders, who feel indebted to Gorbachev. Ryzhkov, who oversees the government from the Central Committee, focuses on securing support from younger ministers.

In the morning, at the Politburo meeting, as agreed, Gromyko speaks first and proposes Gorbachev. The others chime in, praising the candidate. The vote is unanimous.

What to expect from the new, young General Secretary, no one yet knows. Chess player Garry Kasparov recalls that around the time of Gorbachev's election, he visits a friend and a filmmaker, Mikhail Kozakov. All of the guests talk of one thing: Will the new General Secretary bring change, or will everything stay the same? Young Kasparov predicts that change is inevitable. But the older guests disagree. Historian Natan Eidelman, then fifty-four, says, "I've lived a long life. Mark my words: they'll make some noise and then settle down."

THE BEAST IN A SKIRT

Meanwhile, Andrei Sakharov isn't focused on Gorbachev—he's far more concerned about his wife's health, fearing she'll have another heart attack. "If you die, I won't go on living," he tells her as he massages her feet. "What do you mean?" Elena Bonner asks. "Well, I'll end my own life," he replies calmly. They discuss the ethics of suicide, and Bonner brings the conversation to a close, saying, "Fine, I'll recognize your right, but you have to promise you won't act impulsively—wait at least six months." Sakharov falls silent, then says, "All right. But do you think it'll hurt any less by then?" Bonner smiles. "Of course it will."

On April 16, 1985, Andrei Sakharov begins a new hunger strike to demand permission for his wife to go abroad for heart surgery. They both prepare carefully for this hunger strike, buying a radio and planning which books he'll take if he's detained. Separation is almost unbearable for the couple; Sakharov says he feels at peace only when his wife's knees press against his stomach at night. On the third day of his hunger strike, Sakharov is taken to the hospital. "There were no more shouts when they tore us apart," Bonner recalls, "we handled it differently by then."

On April 23, the Central Committee holds a plenary session in Moscow, where Gorbachev is set to make his first speech in his new role. The General Secretary speaks energetically, without notes, which impresses the attendees. His tone is cautiously critical; he calls the previous era "stagnant" and emphasizes "acceleration"—the idea that working faster and better will fix everything. It's a vision similar to Andropov's.

For three months, Bonner gets no word from the hospital where Sakharov is held. On July 11, Sakharov ends his hunger strike. He is released hours later. "It's not a defeat," he tells his wife. "I'm just taking a break."

They return to their familiar routines—watching movies, walking by the river, picnicking. KGB agents secretly film them, later piecing together footage that British journalist and KGB informant Victor Louis sells to ABC. The film shows Sakharov's supposedly "comfortable" life in Gorky.

On July 25, Sakharov begins his next hunger strike. "They took him again; it became almost routine," Bonner says. On July 29, Sakharov writes his first letter to Gorbachev, promising to stop public protests if his wife is allowed to go abroad. Gorbachev reads the letter on August 10, forwarding it to Chebrikov with a request for review.

One day in August, Bonner is driving when the gear stick suddenly comes off in her hand. She safely pulls over and later goes to a mechanic, who doesn't say anything but slips her a note: "It was cut."

On August 29, the Politburo discusses Bonner's medical needs. "Sakharov is sixty-five now; Bonner is sixty-three. Sakharov's health is declining; he's undergoing oncology tests due to significant weight loss," Chebrikov begins. "He has lost his influence as a political figure. It may be appropriate to let Bonner go abroad for three months, as a humane gesture." However, Chebrikov insists that Sakharov cannot leave the country due to his knowledge of Soviet nuclear weapons development. "If Sakharov were given a lab, he could continue military research. Bonner influences his behavior," he adds. "So, this is what Zionism looks like," Gorbachev sighs.

Central Committee Secretary for Ideology Mikhail Zimyanin strongly objects: "Bonner has no sense of decency. She's a beast in a skirt, an agent of imperialism."

In Washington, D.C., Bonner's son, Alyosha, now married to Liza Alexeeva, begins a hunger strike. The family is desperate for news from Gorky. On September 11, both US congressional houses pass a resolution urging the USSR to free Sakharov and Bonner. These developments reach Sakharov and Bonner via radio, despite Soviet jamming efforts; Sakharov even has a radio in his hospital room.

On October 21, Bonner is summoned to the Gorky visa office and informed she may go to America. "You're leaving October 25 from Moscow," they say. "What? Not a chance!" Bonner replies. "I haven't seen my husband in months. Until I spend as much time with him as I need to be sure he's okay, I'm not going anywhere. I couldn't care less about your permission!"

The visa officer repeatedly retreats to make calls. In the end, Bonner leaves without submitting her documents, feeling victorious. The next day, Sakharov is brought home.*

Sakharov persuades his wife to take the October 25 departure. "Fine, November 25," she counters. They visit the visa office together. There's yelling, arguments, phone calls. "Mrs. Bonner, with this behavior, you may not be going anywhere," says an official. But eventually, all her demands are met. She declines the government-provided plane ticket, stating she'll reach Moscow on her own.

During the remaining month, Bonner prepares Sakharov for life alone, creating a simple cookbook for him with recipes for buckwheat, meat, soup, and borscht. She also buys nearly a hundred pairs of socks. On November 25, she arrives in Moscow to find their apartment on the Garden Ring in complete disarray: windows wide open, birds nesting inside.

WITHOUT A SCRIPT

In May 1985, a crowd gathers near the Moscow railway station in Leningrad. The reason is startling: Mikhail Gorbachev, the new General Secretary, has spontaneously decided to walk among the people, spending half an hour talking with Leningrad residents. "Stay close to the people, and we'll never let you down!" a woman shouts at him. "How much closer can I get?" Gorbachev responds with a laugh, prompting laughter from the crowd.

---

* Years later, Bonner will receive a letter from one of the nurses involved in Sakharov's force-feeding. The nurse will write of her deep respect for both Sakharov and Bonner and will thank fate for allowing her to meet such a remarkable man.

Several TV operators are recording the entire interaction. The resulting footage is stunning: the young, energetic General Secretary looks like a rock star surrounded by adoring fans.

After years of stiff, elderly leaders, here is a leader who talks to people like a real person. The footage is shown to his wife, Raisa, who is moved to tears. "Everyone needs to see this," she insists, and that very evening, the full version airs on the main news program, *Vremya*.

Soviet TV viewers' infatuation with Gorbachev, however, will be short-lived. For the first few months, his ability to speak "without a script" will seem like a miracle. But before long, the frail Brezhnev and Chernenko will be forgotten—and the new General Secretary will come to be seen as someone who simply talks too much: at length, with passion, but ultimately without clarity. Most viewers will dismiss his speeches as mere empty demagoguery.

Yet there is another problem with Gorbachev's speech—his strong southern accent. This is how people speak in Eastern Ukraine and southern Russia, but typically, it is associated with the uneducated; those who have received a higher education usually rid themselves of this dialect. In this regard, the Soviet Union is far from a tolerant country—standard Russian, as spoken in Leningrad and Moscow, is considered the norm, and any deviation from it is viewed as deeply embarrassing. That's why many are astonished that Gorbachev never even tried to shed his rural pronunciation.

Moreover, he frequently places the wrong stress on even the simplest words (and even more so on complex ones), sometimes even inventing his own, entirely nonexistent terms. This hardly creates the image of an intellectual—rather, he comes across as an overconfident provincial who enjoys speaking but does not always fully grasp what he is saying.

YOUNG POPE

Within his first months in power, a key word enters Gorbachev's vocabulary: "perestroika"—"restructuring." Everyone likes the sound of it, though no one quite knows what it means. Yet this word will soon become the slogan of his entire tenure and the symbol of all the changes to come in the USSR.

After assuming leadership, Gorbachev begins slowly replacing the old Brezhnev-era Politburo members, although he lacks many suitable candidates. In April 1985, he appoints the key allies who helped him come to power—all loyal Andropov men: Central Committee secretaries Yegor Ligachev and Nikolai Ryzhkov, and KGB chairman Viktor Chebrikov. Over the following months, he dismisses senior officials carefully and individually: in June, he retires Grigory Romanov, his recent rival; in September, he replaces Premier Nikolai Tikhonov with Nikolai Ryzhkov; and in December, he parts ways with Moscow boss Viktor Grishin. For his successor, Gorbachev lacks a personal ally and accepts Ligachev's recommendation of an energetic official from Sverdlovsk (now Yekaterinburg): Boris Yeltsin.

Ligachev, who oversaw the neighboring Tomsk region, believes Yeltsin is a highly effective manager—the kind of person needed for Gorbachev's "acceleration" campaign. However, Ryzhkov, also from Sverdlovsk and previously director of Uralmash, strongly disagrees. "You'll regret this decision," he warns, but Ligachev insists.

At that time, Yeltsin has led the Sverdlovsk region for eight years. In his memoir, he describes his sadness about leaving: he's spent his whole life in Sverdlovsk; he's fifty-four, with children and a granddaughter. He has no idea how radically his life will change in Moscow. He later writes that, like most Soviet people, he regards Muscovites with suspicion, seeing them as snobs and Moscow as a Potemkin village—a beautiful showcase for foreigners.

Becoming First Secretary of the Moscow City Committee, he fully grasps Gorbachev's expectations: "Fight the mafia, overhaul the personnel, and dismantle Grishin's team," he will write in his memoir.

However, Gorbachev's most challenging Politburo member is Foreign Minister Andrei Gromyko. On one hand, Gorbachev feels indebted, as Gromyko supported him in his bid for power. On the other hand, Gorbachev disapproves of Gromyko's old-school Stalinist approach, characterized by an unwavering "Mr. Nyet" stance on negotiations. While Gromyko believes in talking only from a position of strength, Gorbachev wants to pursue diplomacy. Gromyko, in turn, grows increasingly frustrated, confiding to his son that the new General Secretary starts too many initiatives without finishing any.

In June, Gorbachev fulfills a promise: the Supreme Soviet appoints Gromyko as chairman, making him the ceremonial head of state. And he appoints Georgian party leader Eduard Shevardnadze, who has no diplomatic experience, as foreign minister. Gorbachev has known Shevardnadze since their youth; they simultaneously headed the Komsomol organizations in their respective regions.

While appointing an inexperienced Georgian is bold, Shevardnadze is hardly an outsider. He's a longtime party apparatchik and a Politburo member candidate, with thirteen years as Georgia's leader. Gorbachev isn't yet ready to bring in true outsiders.

Gorbachev has no advisors from his pre–General Secretary days—no allies apart from his wife, Raisa. Moreover, he has no real ideological allies; the Soviet system is built on obedience, not personal convictions. The pathway to power is designed for those who excel at loyalty and compliance, not intellectual curiosity. Independent thought is seen as a liability; indeed, anyone with real principles would struggle to endure endless speeches praising the General Secretary, the party, and the greatness of Lenin. Successful party bureaucrats are experts in shutting off critical thinking, seamlessly agreeing with—and even applauding—whatever nonsense the elderly leaders say from the podium.

Throughout his career, Gorbachev excelled at playing this game. Only upon reaching the top does he realize that a General Secretary is expected to have his own opinion on everything.

He draws inspiration from a few sources. One is Vladimir Lenin. Gorbachev believes the USSR failed to build true communism because Lenin's teachings were distorted and forgotten. A return to "pure Leninism" will, he thinks, set things right. This makes Gorbachev unique; while Soviet communists regularly cite Lenin, no one seriously reads him anymore. Gorbachev, however, dives into Lenin's complete works. Raisa's friend Lidia Budyka recalls visiting the Gorbachevs and seeing Lenin's volumes, marked with tabs and notes, on their table. Shocked, she asks if Gorbachev is truly reading them. He answers himself: "You know, Lidia, you should read Lenin's correspondence with Kautsky. It's better than any detective story." In his public speeches, he emphasizes that he's not reforming the Soviet system but rather restoring Lenin's original vision.

Another source is Gorbachev's own experience, and it's a bit unusual. He spent most of his life in Stavropol, climbing the career ladder. He doesn't have any close friends—no one from his old team followed him to Moscow. His only real advisor and confidante is his wife. They have a daily ritual: every evening after work, they take a walk together and Gorbachev tells her all about the political issues he's dealing with.

Once he becomes General Secretary, Gorbachev starts looking for people he can work with comfortably—that's how Anatoly Chernyaev ends up by his side. Chernyaev had been with the Communist Party's International Department since 1961, writing speeches for Soviet leaders and managing relations with foreign communist parties. He was already fed up with much of his work, finding it mostly pointless. So when he hears about Gorbachev's rise to power, he's genuinely thrilled. He hopes it'll bring a real change from the endless, empty quoting of Marxist-Leninist classics to something that feels like real life. And as he gets to know Gorbachev better, Chernyaev makes a surprising discovery: unlike most of his colleagues and predecessors, Gorbachev seems to get that the "hostile 'imperialist world'" vilified by Soviet propaganda is actually just a complex web of different nations and societies, "clearly not preparing to attack or invade the Soviet Union."

Chernyaev also notices something unusual about Gorbachev, maybe a trait he picked up from his philosopher wife: an "aversion to violence." Later one of Gorbachev's acquaintances would put it like this: "He knew his wife wouldn't go to bed with him if his hands were stained with blood."

"THE HAPPIEST DAY OF YOUR LIFE IS OVER"

In May 1985, feeling wronged and suspecting that victory had been stolen from him, Garry Kasparov takes an unprecedented step for a Soviet chess player: he gives an interview to the German magazine *Der Spiegel* without consulting any Soviet authorities. In the interview, he criticizes the Soviet Chess Federation and FIDE, and asserts that he no longer considers Anatoly Karpov to be the world champion. He also expresses a firm belief that although the title match is scheduled for September, Karpov and his patrons will do everything possible to sabotage it.

Soviet sports officials are outraged. A special meeting of the Sports Committee is set for August 9 to discuss Kasparov's "anti-state behavior." Realizing trouble is imminent, Kasparov calls Heydar Aliyev, but the Politburo member's office reassures him that while the situation is complicated, things will soon change.

Around this time, General Secretary Mikhail Gorbachev is gradually reshaping his team. Alexander Yakovlev, former Soviet ambassador to Canada, is appointed head of state propaganda, also overseeing sports. As Yakovlev settles into his office on Staraya Square, he comes across a file labeled "Kasparov." Inside, he finds that a decision has already been made: Kasparov is to be disqualified for behavior "disgracing the Soviet Chess Federation and Soviet sports as a whole." Yakovlev, however, disagrees with the prior decision and takes the file directly to Gorbachev. "Maybe we should let him play? Just let him focus on chess?" he suggests. "Let him play chess," Gorbachev agrees.

The world championship match is set to begin in September. In late August, Kasparov is advised to meet with Yakovlev, to whom he writes a letter expressing frustration at the federation's favoritism toward Karpov and the manipulation he perceives. Yakovlev invites Kasparov for a walk on Red Square. "Good letter." Yakovlev smiles. "Did you write it yourself?" "Yes, I did!" Kasparov replies. "A bit heavy on adjectives," Yakovlev jokes.

Kasparov once again laments the obstacles he faces, but Yakovlev interrupts, "Listen, just go play. The world chess champion is decided not on Staraya Square, but at the chessboard." Reassured, Kasparov hurries back to his mother: "Mom, they let me return to Karpov."

On September 3, the final match begins anew in Moscow's Tchaikovsky Concert Hall. Kasparov wins the first game, loses the next two, then recovers and takes the lead. Under the new rules, they're scheduled to play twenty-four games. The last one takes place on November 9, with Kasparov claiming victory. The final score is 13–11 in Kasparov's favor, making the twenty-two-year-old the youngest world champion in chess history.

The prolonged thriller that captivated the Soviet Union and the world for over a year has concluded. The thirty-four-year-old "Brezhnevite" Anatoly Karpov is defeated; the wunderkind from Baku has triumphed. Celebrations ensue, with Moscow's cultural elite offering their congratulations. Rona Petrosian, widow of the recently deceased world champion Tigran Petrosian, remarks, "I feel sorry for you, young man, because the happiest day of your life is over."

THE MINERAL SECRETARY

Newly appointed General Secretary Mikhail Gorbachev is eager to make a strong start, but he lacks a clear plan. He is largely aligned with Yuri Andropov's recent approach: restore order and everything will fall into place.

In March 1985, Politburo member and now the country's second-in-command Yegor Ligachev presents an idea to quickly improve the situation. He proposes that the Soviet Union's main issue is that people drink too much. Tackling alcoholism, he argues, would produce swift, visible results.

Ligachev is partly right. By the late 1970s, drinking has become almost a religion in the USSR. It is a way to escape the meaninglessness of the present and avoid facing reality. Belief in communism has long faded, yet everyone is expected to pretend otherwise. "It was marathon drinking," rock musician Boris Grebenshchikov recalls, describing his lifestyle at the time. "I saved up money all week, bought a case of wine called 'Bear's Blood,' and on Friday, we'd head to Vitya Tsoi's place and get stuck there for three days."

Gorbachev and the Politburo agree with Ligachev's proposal. Gorbachev's wife, Raisa, strongly supports the campaign, as her brother struggles with alcoholism.

Liquor and beer production is drastically cut, and vineyards in southern regions like Georgia, Moldova, Crimea, and Kuban are destroyed.* Stores authorized to sell vodka and wine implement limited hours, often from 2:00 p.m.to 7:00 p.m. or even as short as 2:00 p.m. to 4:00 p.m. A popular poem of the time goes:

At five, the rooster crows,
at eight—Pugacheva.
The store's closed until two,
the key is with Gorbachev.

Drinking on the job is now banned, restaurants and cafés stop serving alcohol, and public drunkenness can lead to fines or even job loss. Soviet censors joins the sobriety campaign, forbidding films, books, or plays that feature drinking.

The only opponents of the "dry law" are economists in the Council of Ministers. They quickly calculate that alcohol sales are a critical revenue source. In recent years, alcohol has accounted for up to 10 percent of the national budget. Any restrictions, they warn, will severely impact the economy. Gorbachev and Ligachev, however, deem these concerns "immoral," insisting it's unacceptable to profit from people's drinking.

---

* At the time, Moldavia—now called Moldova—was one of the fifteen republics of the USSR, with a population roughly equal to that of Kentucky and an area comparable to Maryland.

Statistically, the anti-alcohol campaign appears effective: birthrates rise, mortality rates decline, and the average life expectancy climbs to seventy years.

But there are unintended consequences. First, there's a boom in home brewing. By 1985, sugar is in short supply across the country as people turn to home distilling. Second, the alcohol shortage drives people to consume substances like cologne and windshield cleaner. Another popular substitute is Moment glue, which becomes a substance of choice for Soviet teenagers to sniff.

Finally, the most significant outcome of the "dry law" is the unprecedented wave of resentment it generates toward Gorbachev. Following a series of lifeless predecessors, Gorbachev—a young, energetic figure—enjoys a tremendous reserve of public goodwill, and people want to like him. But the first thing he does in office is impose a "prohibition," a deeply unpopular move that fails to address the core societal issues. If people drink to escape despair, banning alcohol may prevent them from drinking, but their despair remains.

Gorbachev will later recall that the first person to frankly tell him the "dry law" was a mistake was his mother. After becoming General Secretary, he visits her in Privolnoye, a village in the Stavropol region. She prepares a meal of borscht, homemade dumplings, and mineral water. "Not even a bottle of wine, Mother?" he teases. She replies, "You know, Misha, someone decided people shouldn't do that in this country. And I want to tell you it's a bad idea. At weddings, people curse you. On birthdays, they curse you. I'm not putting anything out, because tomorrow people will say, 'He's allowed, his mother is allowed, but we're not.'"

Thus, Gorbachev earns his first and mildest nickname from the public: the Mineral Secretary. The nicknames to follow will be far harsher.

FORGET EVERYTHING

After his conversation with the chief doctor, Grisha Yavlinsky decides he will fight. He demands medical boards, second opinions from other hospitals. He is taken to different clinics—always accompanied by his attending physician. The examinations are brief, and the conclusion is always the same: "Everything is correct. Lung removal is necessary."

Meanwhile, he is constantly moved from one ward to another—a deliberate tactic of psychological pressure. He hears the stories of his fellow patients, mostly ex-convicts, who tell him that just recently, on his floor, patients killed a nurse.

Then he is transferred to the oncology ward. Every three or four days, someone in his room dies. His wife is told: "We didn't want to scare you before, but now we have to say it—he has cancer."

At some point, a former professor from his university comes to visit him. He tells her the whole story of his illness. She isn't particularly surprised and says she'll try to help—her husband is the head of a district party committee in Moscow.

About a week later, Yavlinsky is summoned by the chief doctor, who hands him his hospital discharge papers, his passport, and the three rubles he had on him when he was admitted.

"That's it. Now forget everything, I'm warning you," the doctor says, repeating almost the exact words that a KGB officer had told him years earlier after Brezhnev's death.

Yavlinsky steps out of the office and opens the documents: They state that the diagnosis was not confirmed. The only condition found was mild varicose veins. He doesn't argue—he simply leaves and rushes home.

He returns to work at the State Committee for Labor.

A few months later, an acquaintance brings him a copy of *Literaturnaya Gazeta*. Taking up an entire spread is the story of a young man in Kazakhstan who was treated for tuberculosis he never had. The medications left him partly paralyzed. Eventually, they discharged him—so he took his father's hunting rifle, returned to the hospital, and shot the doctor.

"So it wasn't just a one-off," Yavlinsky realizes. "This was how they erased people—cutting them off so completely that even their old friends would be too afraid to stay in touch. No trial, no verdict—if the wrong person took a disliking to you, that was it. You were done."

But he chooses not to investigate what happened to him. He prefers to forget that year of his life. Besides, work begins to consume him—the government starts drafting new economic reforms, first *On Cooperatives*, then *On Enterprises*.

Yavlinsky frequently visits Gosplan, the state agency responsible for Soviet economic planning. On the first floor, he sees a bas-relief of Lenin with an inscription: "We are moving toward communism—inevitably, inexorably."

He immediately recalls the slogan "Communism is inevitable" that he once saw across from a dingy liquor kiosk in Leninsk-Kuznetsky.

"So that's where they got this quote! Very wise!" The economist laughs.

SOUP FROM ANDY WARHOL

Upon returning to America, Joanna Fields keeps her promise to Boris Greben-shchikov. She buys a guitar for him. Soon after, she finds another opportunity to join a tour group headed to the Soviet Union. BG is stunned—he thought she was joking. Joanna's second trip to Leningrad coincides with a major festival at the Leningrad Rock Club, where all the top Soviet rock bands are performing. "I was so thrilled that even if Lenin himself had appeared, I wouldn't have left," she recalls.

As Joanna exits the venue, she is briefly stopped by volunteer patrol members (whom she mistakes for KGB officers). They attempt to ask her questions, but Joanna repeats, "I don't speak Russian," until they eventually let her go.

Also unexpectedly attending the festival is Alla Pugacheva. Though she sometimes faces issues with the authorities, Pugacheva is an official performer, contracted with the State Concert Agency. The rock musicians largely ignore her—she's a pop singer, performing what they see as lowbrow material. Pugacheva, however, is drawn to experimentation and takes an interest in Aquarium's guitarist Sasha Lyapin, inviting him to join her band. He declines with a smile.

After the concert, all the musicians—Grebenshchikov, Tsoi, and others—flock to Joanna, an American bringing records and instruments. She's far more exciting for them than Pugacheva. During this encounter, she meets Kino's guitarist Yuri Kasparyan, and a romance sparks, though she's set to leave for America the next day.

Not long after, Joanna returns to Leningrad with new gifts. She knows her rocker friends often hang out with underground artists at Timur Novikov's gallery, where she brings gifts from Andy Warhol himself—several portraits of Marilyn Monroe and a few autographed cans of Campbell's soup. The musicians are thrilled, jokingly calling her Santa Claus. But when she visits the next day, she finds the soup cans empty. The musicians didn't see Warhol's soup as a prized artifact to keep but found eating it to be the truest homage to his art.

Joanna is both amused and bewildered. She often gets into ideological discussions with her Russian friends. They envy her freedom to travel at will, while she insists that semiunderground musicians in Leningrad are freer than she is. "In the States, the American Dream is lost in endless hours in front of the TV with microwaved dinners," she muses. "But in the USSR, people have to invent their own entertainment."

When the Leningrad rockers say, "We want to be as free as you," she replies, "Americans pay a high price for their freedom—working hard to pay off mortgages, student loans, and pension contributions. Access to capital and the 'opportunities' that supposedly come with it force Americans to plan far ahead. In the pursuit of a 'golden sunset' like cowboys they no longer are, they miss the moments when life is actually lived. In the Soviet Union, you can't take out a loan, so there's no need to plan or save. Everything happens as it will—food, drugs, laughter, fights, love."

Joanna flies back to California, while her Soviet friends keep trying to perform across the country. BG, for instance, heads to Novosibirsk for an underground show. After he leaves, the police raid the apartment, arresting everyone there. Tsoi holds a similar concert in Kyiv. A knock at the door, and an officer arrives with two witnesses, announcing, "Everyone stay where you are. Passport check. Tsoi—come with us!"

All the money collected for the concert is confiscated. Tsoi spends the night in a cell before being sent back to Leningrad the next day. Soon after, the Leningrad Rock Club receives a letter demanding action against the "nonlabor activities." In compliance, the club suspends Kino for six months.

BRUCE LEE

About a month after Kino is expelled from the rock club, Maryana and Vitya have a son, Sasha. They need money, so Tsoi tries to make a living through underground concerts. He quits his job at the boiler room and looks for work he can combine with music. First, he registers as a lifeguard at a boat station; then he takes a job as a bathhouse cleaner, spraying down the rooms with a fire hose.

Vitya is acutely aware that he's not like everyone else. For starters, he's Korean, which sets him apart from other Leningrad rockers and all their Western idols. If BG resembles David Bowie, Tsoi doesn't look like anyone

166 THE DARK SIDE OF THE EARTH

at all. When asked about his favorite Western bands, he always gives vague and peculiar answers: he doesn't listen to popular Western rock bands.

At some point, BG jokingly says Tsoi should be the "Red Bruce Lee," and the idea profoundly resonates with Vitya. He truly wants to be like Bruce Lee. The legendary actor and martial artist died in 1973 but remains the only global star of Asian descent. More than that, Bruce Lee isn't just an artist—he is a work of art himself, a cultural icon, a pioneer of a new lifestyle and way of thinking. This is precisely what Vitya aspires to.

After one concert, responding to questions from the audience, Tsoi says, "Music itself doesn't really interest me. I'm interested in music as a social phenomenon. And the only music like that is rock music—the only music that is truly mass, truly of the people."

This is the key difference between Tsoi and Grebenshchikov: how each of them sees himself. Grebenshchikov wants to be a musician—more precisely, a brilliant musician. Tsoi, however, wants to be a people's hero.

Good morning, the last hero,
Good morning to you and to those like you.

These are the opening lines of the song that begins the album *The Head of Kamchatka*, one of Tsoi's autobiographical works.

PROVINCIAL DRESDEN

On April 28, 1985, Lyudmila (Lyuda) Putina is cleaning her rented apartment in Leningrad. Her husband is away in Moscow, completing additional training at the Higher School of the KGB in preparation for an overseas assignment. She spends the entire day tidying up and doing laundry, preparing their home for the baby she's about to give birth to. That evening, feeling that her time has come, she steps outside, hails a cab, and heads to the hospital. At half past two in the morning, she gives birth to a daughter.

Lyudmila wants to name her Natasha, but her husband calls from Moscow, declaring that the baby's name will be Maria (Masha).

In Moscow, Putin is given another choice: he can either undergo another two more years of training, after which he might be eligible for a position in West Germany, or he can head to East Germany immediately. He decides not to wait. A position in West Germany would undoubtedly be more prestigious, with the allure of becoming a true spy—a childhood dream for him. But he's eager to go abroad as soon as possible.

The assignment he's given, however, is far from glamorous espionage. Officially, Putin is listed as a translator at the Soviet-German Friendship House in Dresden. In reality, his job is to monitor Soviet citizens visiting East Germany. Everyone knows that Dresden is a provincial backwater, and this job offers little in the way of career advancement. However, it does allow Putin and his family to experience the modest but comfortable lifestyle available in East Germany.

The Putins are allocated a two-room apartment on the outskirts of Dresden, where their second daughter, Katya, will be born. Personal cars are not provided to junior officers, so Putin shares a car with his neighbor and colleague, Sergei Chemezov.*

For the Soviet officers in Dresden, a favorite pastime is enjoying Radeberger beer. In these circles, Putin earns the cutesy nickname Uti-Puti.

Lyudmila will later recall that the social atmosphere in East Germany is markedly different from that of the Soviet Union; the dictatorship is much stricter: "We arrived when perestroika was already beginning in the USSR. But in East Germany, they still earnestly believed in the bright future of communism."

Putin is also quite surprised: "I thought I was going to an Eastern European country, to the heart of Europe. By then, it was already the late 1980s. But as I interacted with the Stasi officers, I realized that both they and the GDR were living in a state that the Soviet Union had experienced many years earlier. It was a rigidly totalitarian country, modeled on our own system, but frozen 30 years in the past. The tragedy was that many people genuinely believed in all those communist ideals. At the time, I thought: if any changes begin at home, how will they affect the fate of these people?"

OIL OR LIFE

On September 13, 1985, Saudi Arabian oil minister Ahmed Zaki Yamani announces that his country will no longer reduce oil production and, in fact, will increase it. This decision has a profound impact on the Soviet and global economies.

---

* Chemezov will later head Russia's defense industry when Putin becomes president.

Since 1980, oil prices have steadily declined. Members of the Organization of the Petroleum Exporting Countries (OPEC) had tried to counter this by agreeing on quotas and reducing production, but these measures were ineffective. Not all oil-producing nations were OPEC members, and the Soviet Union, for one, refused to reduce its output. Instead, to prevent a drop in revenue, the USSR ramped up production to the point that, by the early 1980s, it had become the world's largest oil producer.

Frustrated with the USSR's behavior, other oil producers also began quietly increasing production, violating OPEC's rules. By the summer of 1985, Saudi Arabia, as OPEC's production leader, found itself the only member strictly adhering to the quotas. In September 1985, Yamani convinces Saudi King Fahd that the quotas are ineffective in stopping the price decline and should be abandoned.

For Saudi Arabia, the USSR is not only an ideological adversary due to Afghanistan but also an economic competitor. The repercussions of Yamani's decision are catastrophic for the Soviet economy. Since the early 1970s, the USSR has depended on oil revenue, with agriculture in disarray and unable to feed the population. Grain had to be imported from the West, purchased with oil money. Gorbachev, once the party's agricultural secretary, knows the situation well—he even visited Canada to understand why their grain production far exceeded that of the USSR, to the point that they were exporting it. In 1984, the USSR's grain purchases from the United States and Canada peaked at 26.8 million tons.

Oil revenue funds more than just food imports. It finances consumer goods, which are of such low quality domestically that they are virtually unsellable.

But most importantly, oil revenue is crucial for the military. The costs of military operations skyrocketed with the Afghan war, and after Ronald Reagan announced plans to place anti-missile weapons in space, the USSR's Defense Ministry panicked, feeling compelled to keep up with Reagan's "Star Wars" program. Under Marshal Ustinov, the USSR devised a plan to mobilize all available resources for a dramatic increase in missiles and warheads, aiming to overwhelm any potential US defense systems. Soviet designers also extended the range of medium-range missiles, enabling them to reach not just Alaska but also California.

"By the depth of our militarization," former international affairs secretary Valentin Falin would later recall, "the Soviet economy had no equal among major nations. . . . We were engaged in an arms race not against the United States, but against ourselves. . . . A tank cost one less rural school, a bomber meant an unbuilt hospital, a strategic missile system cost a lost university, and a Typhoon-class submarine meant Moscow's annual housing budget."

The USSR produces over one hundred missile systems per year to outpace the Americans. In the end, Reagan's "Star Wars" program will turn out to be a bluff—it will never actually be launched. But in 1985, neither Gorbachev nor the Soviet generals know this yet. They demand ever more funding for rearmament—and continue to receive it.

TALKING TO A SACK OF POTATOES

As the new General Secretary, Gorbachev aims to initiate change, even if his plans for domestic reform are still vague. In foreign policy, however, his vision is clear: end the Cold War and foster cooperation with the West. This approach shocks the Politburo from the outset. At Chernenko's funeral, Gorbachev meets only with prominent Western leaders—US vice president George Bush, British prime minister Margaret Thatcher, French president François Mitterrand, and German chancellor Helmut Kohl.

The greatest international challenge facing Gorbachev is America's "Star Wars" program. He assembles a special advisory team, including Roald Sagdeev, head of the Institute for Space Research, to devise a strategy to counter Reagan's plans for deploying space-based weapons.

According to Sagdeev, Soviet leaders fall into two camps on this issue: the military-industrial complex advocates matching the Americans with a similar "Star Wars" system and preparing for war in space, while others—including Marshal Sergei Akhromeyev, the Chief of the General Staff—oppose an escalation. For Gorbachev, securing an American withdrawal from "Star Wars" becomes a top priority.

In August, Gorbachev gives an interview to *Time* magazine. Initially, he responds to questions in writing, but he soon warms to the idea of a live conversation. He speaks with four *Time* journalists for over two hours, focusing on the need to abandon "Star Wars." Moreover, he cracks jokes, like the story of a former Soviet finance minister who would constantly fall asleep during government meetings. Whenever someone woke him up, he'd answer any question with, "No money, there's no money," regardless of what he was actually asked. "I hope the American administration won't negotiate in the same way," Gorbachev says with a smile.

On November 3, 1985, US secretary of state George Shultz arrives in Moscow. During his meeting with Gorbachev, he unexpectedly begins talking about the future of the planet, urging him that in the new "information age" the Soviet Union "will hopelessly lag behind the rest of the world unless it changes its economic and political system." He explains that closed societies won't be able to "take advantage of the information age," meaning the Soviet system will inevitably have to transform. Surprisingly, Gorbachev isn't offended. Instead, he winks at Shultz, saying, "You ought to head up Gosplan here in Moscow. . . . You've clearly got more ideas than they do over there!"

In Washington, there is a deep-seated bias against the USSR—just as there is in the USSR against the United States. A vast cadre of Sovietologists, closely monitoring the power shifts in Moscow, views Gorbachev with immense distrust. Their reports consistently portray him as a typical product of the Soviet system, bent on deceiving the Americans. The most prominent figure in this group is Robert Gates, the deputy director of the CIA. From the very beginning of Gorbachev's rise to prominence, Gates paints him in the bleakest terms. In 1985, when Gorbachev had just become General Secretary, Gates warned in a report that he was a protégé of Andropov and Suslov, noting: "These heavyweights wouldn't have taken a weakling under their wing."

In November, the new Soviet leader meets with the president of the United States in Geneva. Gorbachev knows that Reagan is a professional actor. On one hand, he expects some trickery from the American, but on the other, he tries to pick up a few moves from his counterpart. Reagan, too, is preparing. It's important for him to look his best—the Soviet leader is twenty years younger, after all. So the American president arrives in Geneva a day early to beat jet lag, reset his internal clock, and be in peak form by the start of negotiations.

On the morning of November 19, Gorbachev arrives at Villa Château Fleur d'Eau by Lake Geneva. Reagan steps onto the porch to greet him, despite the below-freezing temperature, in just a suit—no overcoat. "You're dressed light. Don't catch a cold, or I won't have anyone to negotiate with," jokes Gorbachev. (Of course, Reagan dressed this way on purpose—to show his youth and vigor.)

They talk for a long time, first without advisors, then with them. But the conversation is going nowhere. Gorbachev is visibly irritated, as his advisor Roald Sagdeev recalls: "It was like talking to a sack of potatoes," Gorbachev complains. "He doesn't hear a word I'm saying. He's stuck in the notes his team prepared for him. A real dinosaur." Gorbachev notes that Reagan seems to have cue cards with quotes from Khrushchev. "Shall we print you cards with quotes from various American presidents too?" suggest Gorbachev's aides.

Then things go from bad to worse. After lunch, the leaders begin discussing "Star Wars." Their positions are worlds apart. But at one point, Reagan suggests that they step out of the advisor-packed room and take a stroll on the lawn toward a small lakeside pavilion. As they walk, Gorbachev tries to change the subject, mentioning that he's seen *Kings Row*—a classic 1942 American film and the most famous in which a young Reagan starred. Reagan is flattered and launches into his favorite topic, proposing they eliminate offensive weapons, at least by 50 percent. Gorbachev immediately agrees and counters by asking Reagan to abandon "Star Wars." Reagan insists, however, that the program is defensive, not offensive. Gorbachev is exasperated: "Do you really take us for fools?" Over dinner, Reagan toasts, saying that if aliens ever decided to attack Earth, perhaps by hopping on Halley's Comet, "then this disaster would unite all the nations on Earth"—in which case, the "Star Wars" program would save everyone.

The next day, they meet again, and this time Gorbachev walks onto the porch in just a suit, no coat—but again, the same issues persist. On a personal level, the two leaders genuinely like each other: Gorbachev laughs at Reagan's jokes, and the American president agrees that things are much easier without advisors. They talk about two more planned meetings: in the United States in 1986 and in the USSR in 1987. But politically, the dialogue is a complete failure. Because of the "Star Wars" issue, they can't reach any agreements. Gorbachev's insistent calls to abandon the program and increase trade make Reagan more determined to stand firm on both points.

Returning home to California, Reagan sends Gorbachev a warm, handwritten letter, urging him not to worry about "Star Wars," advising him to withdraw troops from Afghanistan soon, and inviting him to Washington in June 1986. Gorbachev, however, though pleased by the letter, pretends not to be moved by Reagan's outreach. He waits a month to reply, focusing only on his own arguments against "Star Wars" and leaving Reagan's invitation to Washington entirely unacknowledged.

THE WORMWOOD STAR

The mention of Halley's Comet during Reagan and Gorbachev's Geneva talks captures an especially timely subject: the comet, which passes near Earth roughly every seventy-five years, is set to make another close approach in February 1986. It had become both the best-documented and most infamous comet, often associated with major global upheavals, like the Norman conquest of England (1066), Genghis Khan's westward campaigns (1222), the beginning of Tamerlane's invasion (1378), the fall of the Byzantium Empire to the Turks (1456) and many more.

By the end of April 1986, attention shifts to another legendary celestial body—the "Wormwood Star." It appears in the New Testament's Book of Revelation, or Apocalypse, describing a star that falls from the sky before the end of the world, turning Earth's waters bitter.

The image of the Wormwood Star was popular in medieval art, often depicted by Renaissance artists like Albrecht Dürer, who portrayed it as a star crashing onto a rectangular building. Interestingly, in Ukrainian, "wormwood" is translated as *"chernobyl."* Dürer's rectangular building bears an uncanny resemblance to a modern nuclear power plant—the Chernobyl Nuclear Power Plant, located near the border between two Soviet Republics, Ukraine and Byelorussia.

By early 1986, Chernobyl represents the pride of Soviet nuclear energy. Four reactors are operational, with a fifth and sixth under construction. Since its commissioning, Chernobyl has already seen thirty-two incidents of varying severity, all kept secret. To minimize radiation exposure, authorities in the nearby town of Pripyat discreetly re-lay asphalt roads at night after each incident. Built in 1970, Pripyat is a young city with a carefully designed infrastructure: apartment buildings, supermarkets, schools, movie theaters, pools, and even a yacht club. With an average age of twenty-six, Pripyat's residents are young professionals eager to work at Chernobyl.

Pripyat was designed by Maria Protsenko, a female architect. She has an extensive development plan for the city stretching to 2005. Her name at birth was Mu Lan—she was born in China in 1946 and lived there until she was six. When her parents separated, she and her mother moved to Kazakhstan, where she attended university, married, and built a fantastic career under her new name. Her last completed project in Pripyat was the amusement park with a huge Ferris wheel, scheduled to open just after May Day in 1986.

Many look forward to the May holidays in Pripyat—no one more than Viktor Bryukhanov, the director of the power plant. At fifty, he has overseen the plant for sixteen years. When he arrived, there was no city, no plant—nothing. Viktor Bryukhanov built the power plant from scratch, launched four energy units, and his superiors are pleased with his work. Many in Pripyat already know that after the holidays, Bryukhanov will be awarded the title "Hero of Socialist Labor" and transferred to a prominent position in Moscow.

April 25, Friday. On this day, routine tests are scheduled at the plant: a shutdown of the fourth reactor. Technically, these tests should have been completed before the plant's commissioning in December 1983. But Bryukhanov postponed them to meet the year-end schedule and report that all targets were met on time.

The test ends in disaster. Around 1:25 a.m., the fourth reactor explodes.

It's happening . . . war with America has begun, thinks one engineer, feeling the shock wave. But the idea that the reactor is fully destroyed is too horrifying to accept.

Bryukhanov is called immediately and rushes from Pripyat to the plant. *I'll end up in prison*, he thinks, seeing the inferno. But even he can't yet believe the worst has happened. At 3:00 a.m., Bryukhanov reports to Moscow and Kyiv, stating that the radiation levels are "being evaluated." The dosimeters at the plant can't even measure the radiation; they max out at their highest setting. The reality—that radiation is tens of thousands of times above safe levels—is too shocking for anyone to accept.

By 8:00 a.m. on Saturday, April 26, Soviet prime minister Nikolai Ryzhkov is informed. Gorbachev learns a few hours later, though he's assured that the situation is under control and the reactor is cooling. Ryzhkov assigns a government commission, headed by his deputy Boris Shcherbina, to handle the incident. "Our primary objective," says the Soviet energy minister, "is to repair the damaged unit and restore it to the grid as soon as possible."

In Pripyat, city officials decide that life should continue as usual. People go to work, children attend school, and cafés and stores remain open as residents stock up for the holidays. The city is soon cordoned off by police—no one can leave without special permits, and all vehicles are turned back.

Maria Protsenko, the chief architect, is instructed to prepare an evacuation plan for the city—just in case. She calculates the number of buses needed. She also spends her days drawing new maps of Pripyat for the disaster response teams, as copy machines in the USSR are restricted to prevent the unauthorized duplication of banned literature. So Protsenko, knowing Pripyat better than anyone, painstakingly drafts map after map by hand.

The plane from Moscow carrying Deputy Prime Minister Boris Shcherbina lands in Kyiv at 7:00 p.m. on Saturday. "So, have you soiled yourself yet?" he asks Ukraine's minister of energy, Vitali Sklyarov. "Not quite yet, but it's looking that way," Sklyarov replies. When someone proposes evacuating the residents, Shcherbina snaps, "Why are you panicking?"

The Soviet vice-premier, disregarding any safety protocols, wears neither respirator nor protective gear, setting an example that other officials follow. Around midnight, now into Sunday, a full day after the explosion, Gorbachev calls Shcherbina, who reports that the situation is complicated but downplays the catastrophe, hiding the true extent of the disaster from the General Secretary. Sklyarov tries to protest.

"You're a coward!" Shcherbina yells at him, "How do you plan to evacuate all these people? We'll disgrace ourselves in front of the entire world!"

But by 2:00 a.m., Shcherbina changes his stance and calls Moscow, asking for permission to evacuate.

At 1:10 p.m. on Sunday, the radio in Pripyat, silent since the explosion, suddenly crackles to life. The voice of an announcer declares a temporary evacuation. Residents are told not to bring pets.

Maria Protsenko, overseeing the evacuation, boards each bus to instruct drivers on which neighborhood they'll be transporting.

Everyone believes they're being evacuated for just three days. Many hope to go to Kyiv, but they're dropped off in nearby villages, where families are placed with local residents. By 5:00 p.m. on Sunday, April 27, the evacuation is complete. Only Protsenko, a few power plant employees, and cleanup workers remain in Pripyat.

Finishing her tasks, Protsenko returns to her office, noticing a sore throat, headache, and a strange burning sensation on her ankles. Looking out the window, she spots a woman with a suitcase walking down the street. Confused, Protsenko learns that the city authorities overlooked the railway station. Trains are still stopping, letting off passengers. The woman with the suitcase, having left Pripyat to visit relatives days earlier, returned home unaware of the disaster—only to find her city turned into a ghost town.

MAY DAY

On Monday, April 28, at 10:30 a.m., the Politburo gathers with Gorbachev to discuss how to handle the Chernobyl disaster. They must decide whether or not to acknowledge the accident. Only three years ago, these officials decided to conceal the downing of a foreign aircraft, but Gorbachev's stance has changed. "We need to make a statement as soon as possible. No more delay," he urges. By this point, scientists in Sweden, Denmark, and Finland are already sounding alarms over rising radiation levels.

As Politburo members debate, Heydar Aliyev argues that they must inform Europe, stating, "The disaster is too vast to hide." Yegor Ligachev counters, "What exactly do you want to reveal?" Gorbachev remains silent; the eldest Politburo member, the cautious Andrei Gromyko, summarizes: "The statement should be worded to avoid undue alarm and panic."

That evening, the anchor of *Vremya*, the USSR's main news program, reads a brief announcement. It is the twenty-first item in the broadcast, aired near the end, with no details.

The next morning, Gorbachev calls another meeting. Ukrainian leader Volodymyr Shcherbytsky reports that panic is spreading across Ukraine. Once again, they debate the extent of transparency. "The more honest we are, the better," says Gorbachev. Former US ambassador Anatoly Dobrynin suspects that photos of the exploded reactor are likely already on Reagan's desk—denial would be foolish.

The Politburo refrains from making an outright decision to conceal the truth but, by inertia, continues withholding information. That evening, *Vremya* reports two deaths (accurate as of then) and mentions Pripyat's evacuation. Meanwhile, Western media outlets extensively cover the catastrophe. The *New York Post* runs a headline: "2000 DEAD IN NUCLEAR NIGHTMARE," echoed by the *Daily Mail*'s "2000 Dead in Atomic Horror."

American officials believe their tabloids over Soviet statements. An NBC source from the Pentagon claims satellite images reveal severe destruction at the Chernobyl plant, making reports of only two deaths seem implausible. Even Secretary of State George Shultz, who recently lectured Gorbachev on the value of transparency, tells journalists the Soviet announcement is absurd. By week's end, the *New York Post*'s anonymous sources claim the death toll has reached fifteen thousand, with bodies supposedly buried in nuclear waste pits.

This enrages Soviet officials. The KGB labels the Western coverage a coordinated campaign to defame the Soviet regime. With May Day celebrations approaching, Soviet authorities prepare to show the West that all is well in the USSR. Ignoring scientists' pleas, government commission head Shcherbina forbids the evacuation of residents within a ten-kilometer radius of the plant.

On April 30, wind shifts carry radioactive emissions toward Kyiv, raising radiation levels in the city hundreds of times above the norm. Reports reach Shcherbytsky, the Ukrainian leader, but he doesn't grasp the KGB report's radiation figures, writing on the document: "What does this mean?"

Soviet officials approach radiation hazards irrationally, some trusting in myths, or, like Shcherbina, displaying deliberate indifference. Moscow insists that canceling the May 1 celebrations would be a sign of weakness—on the contrary, they should proceed with the parade to demonstrate resilience. When Ukrainian officials express concerns, Moscow scolds them for cowardice.

A May Day parade is scheduled in Kyiv, where thousands are to march along Khreshchatyk, the main street, as Ukrainian leaders watch from the stands. On the eve of May 1, officials debate how to proceed. Shcherbytsky, a typical Brezhnev-era functionary, follows orders, even those not explicitly given. He decides to halve the number of participants, reducing each district's contribution from four thousand people to two thousand. He also instructs Kyiv and Ukrainian leaders to attend with their families, including children and grandchildren, to reassure Kyivans of their safety.

The parade begins at 10:00 a.m. as planned. Years later, a story emerges suggesting Shcherbytsky tried to cancel the event at the last moment, warning, "We can't hold a parade on Khreshchatyk; it's a low-lying area where radiation accumulates!" Supposedly, Gorbachev responded, "I'll bury you if you don't hold it!" This account—recounted by Shcherbytsky's wife and Kyiv's mayor—is dubious. In the days leading up to the demonstration, Shcherbytsky remained steadfast. He insisted on holding the celebration and gave clear instructions to his subordinates.

As a seasoned apparatchik, Shcherbytsky has long known that he would be "buried" if he disappointed Moscow. So any imagined dialogue about the May Day parade is more likely held with an imaginary Brezhnev in his mind than with the real Gorbachev. The current General Secretary, of course, knows about the planned celebration on Khreshchatyk, but in his indecision, he remains silent—it's hard to imagine him threatening reprisals against a party giant like Shcherbytsky.

Years later, Nikolai Ryzhkov will refute the notion that Gorbachev forced Shcherbytsky to send people into the streets. "That's all nonsense," Ryzhkov will say. "Despite my reservations about Gorbachev, he would never have ordered that."

According to Ryzhkov, Kyiv didn't even ask Moscow about the May Day parade.

Only on May 14, for the first time since the accident, does Gorbachev appear on television, addressing the Chernobyl disaster. His delayed speech contains a few main points: First, he provides Soviet citizens with a brief summary of the past weeks. Gorbachev's central message: all actions taken to address the consequences have been correct.

Then Gorbachev condemns the Western press: "Governments, political figures, and media outlets in some NATO countries, especially the United States, have launched an outrageous anti-Soviet campaign. . . . In short, we are facing a true mountain of lies—the most shameless and malevolent . . . while deflecting criticism of the United States' behavior on the world stage, their militaristic policies." Gorbachev finishes by addressing Reagan: he is ready to meet in any European capital—or, perhaps, in Hiroshima—to negotiate a nuclear test ban.

THE END OF SUMMER VACATION

In the summer of 1986, Viktor Tsoi and his band are invited to Kyiv to shoot a film.

A film school student, Sergei Lysenko, wants to make his graduation project using Tsoi's music, with him and other musicians in the lead roles. By then, everyone knows about the Chernobyl disaster, so the musicians are a little wary of traveling to Ukraine's capital. But they go anyway. The result is less a film and more a series of four Kino music videos edited together. And strange videos they are—at one point, Tsoi lies fully clothed on an operating table while his bandmates play doctors dissecting him.

The shoot in Kyiv feels surreal—there are no children anywhere (they are evacuated), and everyone seems to be living under a shadow of apocalypse. "When people tell you there's no need to worry, you know you're screwed. When they say to stay calm, that's when you realize it's time to panic," recalls Tsoi's costar, actor Alexei Kovzhun.

The filming process doesn't bring anyone much joy. Tsoi doesn't enjoy "pretending to be someone else, transforming into other characters." He wants to "express himself." Frustrated, he argues with the director, and the band returns to Leningrad. Before they leave, they're advised to throw away the clothes they wore in Kyiv.

Sergei Lysenko ultimately edits the footage into a film titled *The End of Summer Vacation*, but he fails to defend it as his thesis project. The university rector, upon seeing the musicians in their all-black attire, exclaims, "Fascists!" and demands the film reels be destroyed immediately.

Joanna Fields, the American friend of the Russian rockers, learns about the Chernobyl disaster from the news. She knows Tsoi, her lover Kasparyan, and the band are in Kyiv and begins to panic. She flies to the USSR with terrible fears: What if her friends have mutated, become lethargic or unrecognizable? But when she sees them, they appear unchanged.

"We checked ourselves with a Geiger counter when we got back from Kyiv—the radiation levels were elevated," Tsoi tells Joanna during their first meeting after the trip. "So, did you throw out your clothes?" she asks. "Of course not," the musicians reply calmly. They're far from wealthy enough to discard perfectly good clothing.

It's during this trip to Kyiv that Tsoi writes the prophetic song "A Quiet Night," with the following lyrics:

I waited for this time, and now it has come.
Those who were silent have ceased to be silent.

Indeed, after Chernobyl, the silence ends.

5

UNINVITED FREEDOM

When I was six, my parents sent me to Moscow. I often got sick, and there was no primary school in Luanda, but it was time for me to start first grade. My mother, father, and elder sister stayed in Angola, while my grandmother took charge of raising me.

The most important activity during this period of my life was reading Ogonyok *magazine. My grandmother and her friend our neighbor Rosa Borisovna shared a subscription—so after they finished the latest issue, it was passed on to me.*

The most fascinating part, of course, was looking at the photos. That's how Stalin, Trotsky, Bukharin, Beria, Molotov, Voroshilov, and Kaganovich became the main characters of my childhood. Every week, Ogonyok *published another investigation into Stalin's repressions: it was like a true crime series, and I loved it.*

In first grade, naturally, we read books about Lenin—about how he loved children, how he brought electricity to villages, how, as a little boy, he stole a plum from his mother and was punished, and how, while in prison, he made inkpots out of breadcrumbs and wrote letters with milk. But not a single story mentioned Stalin or Beria. This outraged me and felt like proof that all the most important things were being hidden from children.

The Moscow district where we lived used to be called Kirovsky in Soviet times, named after Bolshevik leader Sergei Kirov. In the 1920s and 1930s, he led Leningrad, until his assassination in 1934. Officially, it was claimed that conspirators—enemies of the people—were behind his death. Kirov's assassination became the excuse for starting the Great Terror.

But at school, we only heard heroic stories. One day, our teacher invited some older students to give a presentation on Kirov so we'd learn the history of our district. Their report didn't mention Stalin, the murder, the repressions, or the show trials—they had simply copied their material from regular text-books, not from Ogonyok *magazine.*

I was so indignant that I decided to stage the first rebellion of my life. Over-coming fear, shame, and timidity, I raised my hand and, almost in a whisper, said something like: "But in Anatoly Rybakov's book Children of the Arbat, *it says Stalin killed Kirov."*

My teacher was a simple woman; she had probably never read the perestroika-era press and believed that history should be a source of pride, not shame. She looked at me with a mix of horror and disdain and said something like, "All right, Professor, no need to lecture us."

To me, the word "Professor" felt incredibly insulting—and apparently, my classmates thought so too. They teased me for weeks afterward, calling me Professor.

"YOU MAY BE FREE"

In May 1986, a *Komsomolskaya Pravda* journalist visits one of Ukraine's most renowned writers, Vitaly Korotich. He writes poetry in Ukrainian and edits a literary magazine, *Vsesvit*, but the correspondent is here to talk about Chernobyl.

In fact, Korotich is not a dissident at all. In the past, he denounced Ukrainian "bourgeois nationalists" and wrote that Solzhenitsyn was a traitor and a deserter—just as expected of an official Soviet writer.

But now he doesn't mince words, saying what Kyiv's intelligentsia has been whispering for days: the suppression of information about Chernobyl was a crime against people's right to know. This is a bold stance—most establishment writers of the time are echoing official lines like, "Humans can triumph over the atom," "No need for panic!," and so on.

Korotich isn't worried about speaking out; he feels certain that *Komsomolskaya Pravda* would never dare publish such an interview. Yet, a few days later, he receives a call at home from Alexander Yakovlev, head of the Central Committee's Propaganda Department. Korotich is floored—it's like getting a call from on high. Yakovlev's tone is sly as he asks if Korotich would mind if this interview was shown to Gorbachev. Korotich, naturally, doesn't dare object. Within a week, he's summoned to Moscow.

Chernobyl has profoundly shifted Gorbachev's view of the country's status quo. He himself has come to realize just how deadly the absence of information can be. He never made the call to hide the truth about Chernobyl; he never insisted on disinforming the public—but everyone is so used to operating this way, the machinery of state propaganda runs so automatically. Everyone simply acts according to what they think "should be done." Officials and journalists alike have been trained to anticipate what their superiors would want, adapting information to match these assumptions. After Chernobyl, Gorbachev reaches a stark conclusion: this cannot go on. From Chernobyl onward, his vocabulary changes. Where he once spoke only of "acceleration" (*uskorenie*) and perestroika, a new word unexpectedly emerges: "glasnost"—the freedom to speak openly.

The true father of glasnost is, of course, Alexander Yakovlev. He is the only one in Gorbachev's inner circle who openly protests the misinformation and cover-up of the Chernobyl disaster, constantly urging the General Secretary to confront the truth. And when Gorbachev asks where to find people with a different mindset, Yakovlev happens to come across an interview with Korotich—a seasoned editor in chief unafraid of harsh truths.

Korotich arrives at Yakovlev's office, and Yakovlev offers him the position of editor in chief of *Ogonyok*, the USSR's most popular illustrated weekly. Korotich says he'll need to consult his family. Yakovlev insists this is unnecessary. "Did you consult your family before accepting the post of Central Committee secretary?" Korotich asks. "Of course not!" Yakovlev replies.

The journalist returns to Kyiv only to be told that his move to Moscow is already a done deal. "This is a party order," the local communist official declares. "Even if you persuade me you're ill, I'll personally escort you by ambulance to Moscow's Staraya Square, to the Central Committee building." It turns out that the very next day Korotich is expected by Politburo member Yegor Ligachev, the country's second-in-command—meaning there's no time to delay.

Korotich boards the overnight train to Moscow, heading straight from the Kyivsky station to Staraya Square. Ligachev is a straightforward man; he speaks nothing like Yakovlev. "Whether you want it or not, you're going." Ligachev adds that if Korotich listens to him, he won't come to regret it.

Suddenly, Ligachev glances at the wall clock and, like the White Rabbit in *Alice in Wonderland*, exclaims, "We're out of time! We'll talk more later. Come with me." He grabs Korotich by the arm, strides toward a side door, throws it open, and ushers him inside. The room is filled with Politburo members.

With Gorbachev away, Ligachev presides. He moves to the central chair at the head of the table and, without inviting Korotich to sit, announces, "Comrades, I'd like to introduce Korotich. You should all know him. There's a proposal, approved by Mikhail Sergeyevich, to appoint him as editor in chief of *Ogonyok*. No objections? You may be free," Ligachev concludes.

"Free, huh? That's a bit of a stretch," Korotich jokes. He leaves the room and tries calling *Vsesvit*, his office back in Kyiv. They tell him he's no longer on the staff—his personnel file has been sent to Moscow.

In the coming months, Ukraine's First Secretary, Volodymyr Shcherbytsky, will joke as he watches his compatriot's work: "Moscow gave us Chernobyl; we gave them Korotich."

This marks the beginning of a rather rapid liberation of the press in the USSR. First comes *Ogonyok*, followed by several other bold publications. Soon after, everyone begins writing whatever they please. For Soviet society, this will be an absolute shock—comparable to the global reaction in the twenty-first century following the rise of social media. A flood of opinions, an endless stream of unverified facts and gossip, a torrent of contradictory versions—and, as a result, the devaluation of the media's significance.

THE LIBERAL PEASANT

Alexander Yakovlev's biography is unusual, almost unthinkable, for the Soviet Union. Born in 1923 in a small village in the Yaroslavl region, he fought in the war, was severely wounded, and limped for the rest of his life. After studying at the Yaroslavl Pedagogical Institute, he ended up as a party instructor at the Central Committee. In 1957, Yakovlev was present at the 20th Congress of the Communist Party, where he heard Khrushchev deliver his now-famous secret speech condemning Stalin's personality cult. He was stunned and would later call his reaction "the wounded feeling of a robbed soul."

One result of Khrushchev's short-lived "thaw" was a temporary improvement in U.S.-Soviet relations. In 1959, Khrushchev became the first Soviet leader to make an official visit to the United States, and just before that, the two superpowers agreed for the first time on a student exchange program. In 1958, among the very first Soviet graduate students to head to New York's Columbia University was thirty-five-year-old Alexander Yakovlev. This education—almost unfathomable for a Soviet citizen—set him on an equally improbable career trajectory. By 1965, he was deputy head of the Central Committee's Propaganda Department; by 1970, he was acting head.

In August 1968, Suslov sent him to Prague to handle propaganda work. The first things Yakovlev saw upon landing were effigies of hanged Soviet soldiers. He had to live for several days in the embassy's attic, from which he coordinated the publication of pro-Soviet newspapers exposing the "counter-revolutionary nature" of the Prague Spring.

At the time, Yakovlev behaved like any devout communist ideologue. In 1972, he penned a scandalous article, "Against Anti-historicism," criticizing Russian nationalists. For this, he was exiled to Canada—as ambassador.

Yakovlev's position was double-edged. On one hand, he became close friends with Canadian prime minister Pierre Trudeau. On the other, he sometimes felt like an outsider among his own people. In 1976, the legendary hockey series between Canada and the Soviet Union took place. Ambassador Yakovlev attended every game, sitting next to the Canadian prime minister. But soon he accidentally learned that his image had been banned from Soviet television; editors meticulously edited him out.

A pivotal encounter for Yakovlev occurred on May 16, 1983, when Mikhail Gorbachev—then a modest Politburo member under General Secretary Andropov—arrived in Canada. The trip's primary goal was clear: Soviet agriculture was in crisis, and Canada was a major grain supplier.

Gorbachev arrived for a weeklong stay (he wanted more, but Andropov held him back). Ambassador Yakovlev prepared an intensive program for him. Gorbachev visited parliament, watching as Prime Minister Trudeau answered to the MPs. Stunned, Gorbachev watched the opposition openly criticize the head of government—something he had never witnessed. In astonishment, he called it "a circus."

But the shocks kept coming. Gorbachev was taken to an ordinary supermarket, then a Heinz ketchup factory, a winery, and finally a farm. Seeing its operation firsthand, he was floored by its efficiency: two thousand hectares run by four people, two of whom were the owners—a husband and wife. A former combine driver himself, Gorbachev couldn't believe it and asked three times to confirm. At the end of the trip, the delegation visited a farm owned by Canada's minister of agriculture. While the other guests stayed indoors, Gorbachev and Yakovlev strolled into the fields. Suddenly, the Politburo member began to say things that made the ambassador uncomfortable; this distinguished guest from Moscow started to criticize the Soviet economy.

Soon after, Gorbachev invited Yakovlev to return to Moscow as director of the Institute of World Economy and International Relations—the Central Committee's key think tank and intellectual hub. This post was Yakovlev's launching pad.

In Moscow, Yakovlev was perhaps the only one of Gorbachev's appointees whom Gorbachev had handpicked as a future advisor even before he assumed power. Yakovlev is a visionary with an ideology, someone who uses his influence not merely to wield it, but to reshape the country around him.

During his first year in office, Gorbachev, without Yakovlev, was a man adrift, unsure of where to direct his charisma and power. With Yakovlev by his side, he becomes a different Gorbachev. Yakovlev provides answers to the questions that had plagued the not-so-educated party worker for years. He becomes Gorbachev's university, except with a twist: Yakovlev's humanistic views completely align with those of Raisa Gorbacheva, a graduate of the philosophy school.

This new phase in Gorbachev's life begins after Chernobyl. Shocked by the inhumanity of the Soviet system, Gorbachev starts to listen more closely to those urging him toward liberal and democratic reforms—because he now senses the injustice and wrongness of it all. After Chernobyl, Alexander Yakovlev, an intellectual peasant, former Columbia student, and man who had spent a decade in Canada, becomes the Soviet Union's new chief ideologue.

Yet Gorbachev can't fully trust him. For some reason, he assigns oversight of state ideology not to one person, but to two: Yakovlev and Ligachev. This will soon lead to serious conflict within the leadership.

A STAR IN CHERNOBYL

In early May, two people enter Yakovlev's reception office on Staraya Square: a man and a woman. The secretaries are in shock—it's none other than Alla Pugacheva, the most famous singer in the USSR. Accompanying her is a young music critic, Artemy Troitsky, whom no one recognizes. Pugacheva asks for an urgent meeting with the Central Committee secretary. Naturally, Yakovlev is ready to meet her immediately. She is such a massive star that back in the seventies there was a joke: future history textbooks would say that Brezhnev was just a minor political figure of the Pugacheva era.

A few days earlier, Troitsky had come to Pugacheva with an idea of organizing a charity rock festival to help victims of the Chernobyl disaster. She loved the idea, but they both knew they needed approval from high-ranking officials. At the city party committee, now led by Boris Yeltsin, they were turned down. So, from there, they headed straight to Staraya Square—taking the metro, no less.

In Yakovlev's office, Troitsky eagerly explains that charity rock concerts are very popular in the West. He mentions that just last year, in July 1985, Bob Geldof organized the monumental Live Aid concert to raise money for Ethiopian famine victims. Michael Jackson and Lionel Richie had done something similar, recording "We Are the World" to aid Africa.

Having spent ten years in Canada, Alexander Yakovlev is perhaps the only member of the Central Committee who knows who Michael Jackson is and can grasp what Troitsky is talking about. "Splendid. It's an excellent initiative," Yakovlev says right away. "Organize the concert however you see fit. You have our full support." Pugacheva explains that they already have a plan—the concert should be held in the Olympiysky Stadium, Moscow's largest indoor arena, built for the 1980 Olympics.

Yakovlev has only one request: it shouldn't look like a "feast in a time of plague." He assigns Pugacheva and Troitsky a personal assistant to deal with any lower-ranking bureaucrats who might oppose the idea.

Some officials start advising Yakovlev against the concert. "She just wants more fame," they say. "So what?" the Central Committee secretary counters. "She's not doing this to make money for herself. Artists are supposed to seek fame—it's their profession."

Preparations begin. The concert is named Account 904—the number to which people are encouraged to send donations for Chernobyl victims. Pugacheva personally selects the performers.

By the concert day, May 30, thirty thousand tickets have been sold, a sellout. Just hours before the show, a delegation from the Ministry of Culture arrives: three people, two men in gray suits and a woman. They claim that not all performers have been approved by the authorities, so some simply won't be allowed onstage.

Gathering his composure, Troitsky replies, "Go talk to Gorbachev and Yakovlev; they'll explain everything. Your opinion here doesn't matter." Ministry officials, who until recently could cancel any unsanctioned event with ease, sputter, "Just so you know, we're against this! You're doing it at your own risk"—but it's clear they can't stop it.

The concert is broadcast on Soviet and French television. Not only is this the first large-scale rock concert in Soviet history, but it also marks a breakthrough in Soviet civil society. Up to this point, the state had a hand in everything, leaving no space untouched. And now it turns out that a grass-roots initiative is possible—that you can organize a massive event without officials, inspectors, or censors, without the bosses. But to make it happen, Pugacheva's influence is essential.

A few months later, in September 1986, party officials reach out to Pugacheva with a request of their own: to travel to the Chernobyl exclusion zone and perform in the temporary town set up for the liquidators. The situation is dire, and it's becoming harder to persuade people to take on these deadly assignments—so officials feel compelled to heed the liquidators' wishes. And, of course, every Soviet citizen dreams of seeing a Pugacheva concert.

Before the trip, she's advised not to take flowers or touch anything. Nine thousand people attend the concert—nearly a third of the Moscow audience. Nearly all of them bring flowers, and of course, Pugacheva cannot refuse them. At one point, she even invites a young liquidator onstage to dance with her. She's thirty-seven, and most of the audience are draftees, eighteen to twenty years old. Yet she remains an unquestioned sex symbol.

"I realized that the country had truly changed the moment Pugacheva went to Chernobyl," journalist Sasha Lyubimov would later recall. In his words, until that moment, it was evident that the authorities didn't care about people; there was no public opinion—everything was controlled. But sending a huge pop star to Chernobyl seemed like genuine socialism with a human face.

Years later, Gorbachev, congratulating Pugacheva on her birthday, would write to her: "We were learning what freedom was, but you didn't have to learn. You were already an example of a free person—and a brave one. I'll never forget how you took your band and went to Chernobyl. . . ."

THE COMMISSARS CATTANI

On July 30, 1986, Soviet television makes history by airing a foreign TV series—*La Piovra (The Octopus)*, an Italian criminal drama. In this gripping series, Inspector Corrado Cattani arrives in a small town dominated by the Mafia and, undeterred, takes them on alone. As the story unfolds, it becomes clear that the Mafia has connections to increasingly powerful figures. Fighting a lone battle, the inspector refuses to give up. The show becomes a massive hit in the Soviet Union, resonating deeply with audiences. Many viewers are convinced that a similar mafia exists within the USSR and yearn for heroes like Cattani to emerge in their own cities.

It is through *La Piovra* that Soviet citizens first encounter the word "Mafia." Until the late 1980s, the term "corruption" wasn't widely used in Russian. Yet, despite this linguistic gap, the public was certain that the country's ills stemmed from rampant theft. The nineteenth-century historian Nikolay Karamzin famously summarized Russia's state of affairs with one word: *kradut*—"they steal." Most Soviet citizens live in poverty and are convinced that systemic theft is to blame.

Anti-corruption campaigns are rare in the USSR, but when they occur, they captivate the public. The reputation of being crusaders against corruption had once boosted the careers of figures like Heydar Aliyev and Eduard Shevardnadze. Aliyev, until 1969, led Azerbaijan's KGB, while Shevardnadze, until 1972, was head of Georgia's Ministry of Internal Affairs. From these positions, they rose to lead their republics, launching thorough cleanups of the local elites at Moscow's command by targeting their predecessors' entourages.

A new wave of anti-corruption fervor swept through the USSR under Yuri Andropov, who sent a team led by Gdlyan to investigate corruption in Uzbekistan. But before 1986, these investigators saw themselves as parts of the system, dutifully carrying out orders. With the advent of glasnost, however, their sense of purpose began to shift. They soon began to see themselves not merely as agents of the state but as heroes of the people.

In 1986, however, Gdlyan and his deputy Ivanov are still loyal servants of the Prosecutor General's Office. Having watched *La Piovra* and noticed the parallels between their work and Cattani's, Gdlyan reacts as a dutiful Soviet citizen would: he realizes the moment is right to draw the attention of the higher-ups—and to win their support. More daringly, he writes directly to Gorbachev—a bold move in itself.

An Andropov-style anti-corruption crusade fits well with Gorbachev's vision of perestroika—or, at least, what he thinks it should look like, as his ideas for the movement are still evolving. Gdlyan feels empowered. Now he sees himself not merely as a prosecutor but as perestroika's special agent.

The crusade intensifies. In 1986, Uzbekistan's minister of cotton processing is sentenced to death, a sentence carried out in 1987. Gdlyan's team broadens its scope, setting its sights on Uzbekistan's new leader, Rashidov's successor Inomjon Usmonxo'jayev. But arresting and interrogating him would require Politburo authorization, and the Kremlin hesitates to take things that far.

"NO SEX HERE"

Gorbachev does not push for rapid change because he sees how many in power disagree with his ideas. Nobody openly criticizes him, but rumors circulate at Staraya Square that Gorbachev is receiving an increasing number of anonymous letters from military personnel, allegedly threatening to "deal with him as they did with Khrushchev." It is clear to everyone that two factions exist within the government, each holding sincerely opposite views on the state of the country and possible future developments.

In early 1986, Gorbachev tells the French newspaper *L'Humanité* that there are no political prisoners in the USSR, "nor any persecution of citizens for their beliefs"—a statement based on a report prepared by the KGB. In response, Sakharov writes to him from Gorky with a detailed account explaining that while the term "political prisoner" does not exist in Soviet law, there are several legal articles used to target dissenters: "dissemination of knowingly false slander tarnishing the Soviet social and state order," "anti-Soviet agitation and propaganda," and so forth. He also details the cases of prisoners of conscience he knows about. Strangely enough, this letter reaches Gorbachev, who then orders an investigation.

Many in the Politburo fail to understand why they should release "enemies"; Gromyko protests the loudest. Nevertheless, Gorbachev insists on sending a few people from Sakharov's list abroad, swapping them for Soviet spies arrested in the West.

As Alexander Yakovlev recalls, any criticism from the West is met with hostility in the Politburo—as slander that must be rebutted: "The greater the pressure, the sharper our reaction. 'Oh, is that how you want it? Trying to force us? We'll show you!'"

Nevertheless, everyday anti-Americanism in the USSR is waning. In 1986, thanks to Yakovlev's initiative, a new format appears on television: televised bridges, talk shows involving Soviet and American audiences. These programs are cohosted by Phil Donahue, already a popular American TV personality, and Soviet propagandist Vladimir Pozner.

By the late eighties, Donahue is an American icon. He essentially invented the talk show genre, initiating multiple revolutions in American attitudes. For example, in 1968, he became the first TV host to interview an openly gay man on air, shocking a conservative audience but helping to normalize the issue.

Pozner, meanwhile, is largely unknown in the USSR. However, throughout the previous decade, he regularly appeared on American television, serving as a spokesperson for Soviet propaganda. For instance, in 1979, he justified the Soviet invasion of Afghanistan, and in 1983, he defended the Soviet military's shooting down of a South Korean airliner. Pozner speaks fluent English, having spent his childhood in the United States; his father was a US citizen and Soviet agent who moved to the USSR in the 1950s, during the height of McCarthyism. In the eighties, Pozner becomes an agent of change, promoting a more favorable attitude toward the former ideological enemy, the United States.

The most legendary of these televised bridges, hosted by Donahue and Pozner, takes place on June 28, 1986. It is a conversation between women in studios in Leningrad and Boston. At one point, an elderly American participant humorously asks, "Our TV advertising is all about sex. Do you have such ads?" "There is no sex here, and we are categorically opposed to it," a Soviet woman named Lyudmila Ivanova replies firmly. The studio erupts in laughter, and another audience member shouts, "We have sex; we just don't have advertising!"

The phrase "there's no sex here" quickly becomes iconic, symbolizing much about Soviet life. First, it underscores the state's perceived right to control citizens' private lives. The party indeed acts as a kind of church, condemning divorce and marital infidelity. Any citizen can report family issues to the party organization, which will then intervene. It is well known that extramarital affairs can ruin one's career. This does not mean that Soviet citizens are celibate—only that they have become accustomed to treating sex as an entirely taboo topic.

The restrictions are even stricter in art: depictions of nudity or even hints of sexual relations are nearly forbidden. Even kisses in Soviet films are rare. A classic example from the Brezhnev era tells of Marshal Ustinov, who, upon seeing a reproduction of a painting featuring a nude woman in a magazine, insisted, "That's pornography!" Despite explanations that it was a classic piece hanging in the Tretyakov Gallery, he demanded the editor in chief be fired.

The absurdity of "there is no sex here" resonates with the audience because it perfectly captures Soviet propaganda: it denies the obvious, exemplifies hypocrisy, and is something nobody believes and everyone finds embarrassing to hear.

RED WAVE

Throughout 1986, Joanna Fields travels back and forth between Los Angeles and Leningrad—not only because she's fallen for Yuri, the guitarist of Kino, and not only because she's enchanted by Russian rock and her new circle of Soviet musician friends. She's crafted a bold plan: to release an album in America featuring the best underground bands from the USSR.

Joanna realizes that most Americans can't fathom the existence of rock music in Russia; for them, the Soviet Union is just nuclear bombs and aging communist leaders—not a place of young, talented rock stars. "I'm pretty sure I can get us a record deal. I just feel that people need to be inspired by you guys," she assures Grebenshchikov. She doesn't have to persuade anyone for long—everyone is on board with her daring venture.

Understanding the risks Grebenshchikov, Tsoi, and others face if the album is released in America, Joanna immediately proposes a cover story: "If shit is going to hit the Siberian fan, blame it all on me," she says, claiming she'll insist she smuggled the recordings out without consulting the musicians.

They devise a special code to use in phone conversations in order to keep the KGB agents who are listening in the dark. Grebenshchikov goes by the code name Jagger, while Joanna dubs herself Stingray—a moniker under which she will enter Russian cultural history.

Before long, this twenty-five-year-old American "tourist" starts drawing serious KGB attention. Surveillance intensifies, and Grebenshchikov and his friends are repeatedly questioned about their ties to Joanna. "I'm happy to explain everything myself," she offers, but the KGB refuses. "You scared them," Grebenshchikov, now her go-between, tells her.

On her next visit, he mentions that two sociology professors want to interview her about life in the USSR. His expression says it all—they're no professors, but agents. She agrees to meet.

The interview takes place in a suite at the Hotel Europe, where a banquet table overflows with food. Joanna, accustomed to her Russian friends' modest lives, is taken aback. "I felt like I had walked onto a movie set from the czarist era."

"Have you ever met with any Russian emigrants in the States?" the "professor" asks. "Have any contacted you? Does anybody else in the States ask you about your Russian travels?" Joanna replies that she only wishes good for everyone, calling her work "musical diplomacy" to promote understanding between nations.

Meanwhile, the FBI takes an interest in her, suspecting she might be a Soviet recruit. "I appreciate your interest in me, but nothing has changed, and I'm still going to Russia because of their rock music," she tells an agent.

The authorities remain unconvinced. "In theory, we cannot rule out that Fields is already cooperating with the Soviets," states her FBI dossier, which she will read years later. "She may not have access to sensitive information, but her parents and stepfather are politically influential."

Finally, in June 1986, the album *Red Wave* is released in the United States, albeit in a limited edition, yet covered by the Western press. Joanna "Stingray" Fields is suddenly a star; everyone wants an interview with her, calling her the Armand Hammer of the new generation. Joanna is over the moon—she even sends copies of *Red Wave* to both Ronald Reagan and Mikhail Gorbachev.

"Why are these bands' records being released in the US and not here?" Gorbachev reportedly asks when he is shown the *Red Wave* album Joanna produced. Unwittingly, he has just triggered massive troubles for many people, but that's how the bureaucratic machine works. The boss is displeased, which means his subordinates must act.

ROCK STAR OF REYKJAVÍK

Almost a year has passed since Gorbachev and Reagan first met in Geneva. Now, in August 1986, the Soviet General Secretary makes an unexpected move. He writes to Washington, proposing a brief meeting—even just for one day—in Reykjavík, roughly halfway between Moscow and Washington.

Reagan agrees, despite knowing that a breakthrough is unlikely. But Gorbachev has promised that this meeting will lay the groundwork for his upcoming visit to Washington, where they will sign the historic agreements.

Before leaving, Gorbachev unveils his strategy to the Politburo: he will offer Reagan a series of extraordinary concessions in exchange for scrapping the "Star Wars" program. If Reagan refuses, Gorbachev plans to expose him at the final press conference as a fraud and a warmonger. The Politburo members, naturally, do not challenge the General Secretary. The "Star Wars" program is a serious matter. Among the Soviet leadership, there's a widespread belief that the Americans aim to deploy hydrogen bombs in space, with everything else as mere pretext. And so, the two leaders meet in Reykjavík. The Soviet leader then begins listing his concessions—on the sole condition that Reagan agrees to confine "Star Wars" research to laboratory walls for the next ten years.

The American delegation is stunned. "Everyone was surprised," Secretary of State George Shultz will later recall, "he was laying gifts at our feet." But Reagan is reluctant to accept. He tells Gorbachev he is willing to promise—on his honor—that "Star Wars" will not be directed against the USSR. "Believe it or not," the American president insists.

Gorbachev loses his temper. He says, "If Reagan thinks he can outsmart me, then we should just end these negotiations." Reagan, in response, practically invites the USSR to join the Strategic Defense Initiative—so Gorbachev can be absolutely sure that "Star Wars" isn't aimed at the Russians.

The American delegation is on the verge of a collective heart attack. No one expected Reagan to make such an offer, and they're all silently praying that Gorbachev will turn it down. But Gorbachev doesn't even realize what Reagan is actually proposing. "Thank Gorbachev for shutting down Reagan's ridiculous idea," the president's advisors would later say, according to Roald Sagdeev, Gorbachev's advisor.

The next day brings another bombshell. Secretary of State Shultz asks Gorbachev: Is the USSR really ready to eliminate all nuclear weapons within ten years? "We can do that. We can eliminate them," Gorbachev replies with full confidence. "Well, then let's do it," Shultz shoots back.

This, of course, is a historic moment. The leaders of the USSR and the

USA have just agreed to destroy their entire nuclear arsenals by 1996. Sure, they're not the only nuclear players on the block—China, India, the United Kingdom, France, Israel, and even South Africa are in the game—but the sheer weight of the two superpowers is so massive that they could likely convince (or strong-arm) the others to follow suit.

But the euphoria in the room lasts only a few minutes. Suddenly, both leaders remember the elephant in the room: the pesky "Star Wars" program. Reagan warns that if he abandons the project, the American right wing will "kick his brains out." Gorbachev, channeling his inner motivational speaker, tries to talk Reagan into it: "You're three steps away from becoming a great President. If we overcome this together, none of your critics would open their mouths and the whole world would cheer."

Reagan stays firm. Gorbachev counters that he "can't go back to Moscow" if he allows tests of new space weapons. "They'll call me a fool and not a leader."

The talks collapse. "I still feel we can find a deal," Reagan says as they part ways. "I don't think you wanted a deal," Gorbachev snaps back. Reagan's advisors suggest extending the talks by another day, but he refuses. Later US ambassador Jack Matlock will theorize that Reagan, missing Nancy's calming presence, felt off his game and was eager to head home.

Reagan skips the final press conference and flies straight back to Washington. Gorbachev, on the other hand, is itching to meet the press—after all, he had planned to roast Reagan in front of the world if things went south.

"He was very angry," recalls Ambassador Dobrynin, who shares the car ride to the press center with Gorbachev. "He was eager to denounce Reagan at his press conference."

Gorbachev strides into the massive press hall, where more than a thousand journalists wait in silence. Raisa sits in the front row, her presence unmistakable. In his memoir, Gorbachev will later write that it was the silence that struck him most. "It was as if they represented the whole human race, waiting for their fate to be decided. And I understood what had happened at Reykjavík and how I had to act."

And then, in a move no one sees coming, he spins the failure as a breakthrough. Gorbachev describes the negotiations as an unprecedented success. For the first time in history, the USSR and the USA came so close to an agreement. Never mind that they didn't actually sign anything. "For all its drama, Reykjavík wasn't a defeat but a breakthrough," Gorbachev proclaims with the audacity of someone who knows how to work a crowd.

The hall erupts in applause. In the front row, Raisa wipes away tears of joy.

It's Gorbachev's first taste of international triumph. For the first time in his life, he feels like a rock star. In Reykjavík, he might not have out-maneuvered Reagan at the negotiating table, but he stole the show—and the headlines.

Back in Moscow, he slips back into his usual role as General Secretary of the Communist Party. At the Politburo meeting, he wastes no time tearing into Reagan: "Extraordinarily primitive, troglodyte, and intellectually feeble, he couldn't even look me in the eye at the end."

Then he reassures his colleagues with the confidence of a man who knows how to play the long game: "There's no need for haste. Time is working for us."

A DEAL WITH POWER

The Reykjavík Summit is the biggest story in the USSR. Suddenly, the United States isn't the enemy anymore. In the fall of 1986, Joanna Stingray is back in the Soviet Union, seeing the changes unfold before her eyes. She is print-ing black-and-white T-shirts with slogans in Russian and English: "Save the World" and "Спасем мир."

"Let's all wear these shirts at tomorrow's concert and dedicate the whole thing to peace," Tsoi suggests after getting his shirt. "And you, Jo, you have to get onstage with us and sing one of your songs in English."

Not long ago, just talking to foreigners was frowned upon, and sharing a stage with them? The symbolism here is impossible to miss: in this moment, Viktor Tsoi and Joanna Stingray are practically channeling John Lennon and Yoko Ono, who sang "Give Peace a Chance" fifteen years ago. And it's only been a year and a half since Michael Jackson and friends belted out "We Are the World." Saving the world isn't embarrassing anymore—it's trendy and noble. It's no longer seen as silly, and it hasn't yet crossed into cliché.

Viktor Tsoi is far from being a political poet. In the summer of 1986, shortly after his memorable trip to Kyiv, he writes the song "I Want Change." However, it doesn't gain much popularity at first. "I wrote it a long time ago, back when no one was talking about perestroika, and I didn't mean any kind of perestroika at all," Tsoi will explain in an interview. Yet when asked by a correspondent from an underground rock magazine what makes him protest, the typically laconic Tsoi responds simply, "Everything!"

The fact that *Red Wave* makes its way to Gorbachev causes a massive stir among Soviet cultural officials. Representatives from the state label Melodiya track down Boris Grebenshchikov to tell him they've decided to release his album.

But, of course, it's never that simple. Soon all the rockers whose songs are featured on *Red Wave* start getting phone calls with a two-part proposal. Part one: sign a letter accusing Joanna Stingray of stealing your songs and releasing them without your consent. Since the *Red Wave* cover describes the bands as "underground rock groups," Soviet officials now need to prove the opposite—that these bands are actually mainstream and successful. And Joanna? According to the officials, she's just a sneaky American trying to slander Soviet reality and smear the socialist state. Part two: rockers will be allowed to hold legal concerts, release albums through Melodiya, and tour across the country.

On the surface, it seems harmless. This is exactly what Joanna and her friends had planned from the beginning—she had always said they could pin everything on her. But the musicians react differently. Tsoi refuses, but Grebenshchikov agrees. Joanna doesn't take it personally. She decides to play along with the game the Soviet officials have cooked up. She walks into the Soviet Copyright Society herself and signs a paper admitting guilt. She even pays the state a fine to cover "moral and material damages."

Soon fame crashes down on them like an avalanche. Boris and his band, Aquarium, are offered performances at Leningrad's biggest venues. His songs—and soon Tsoi's—start playing on the radio. Yesterday's underground musicians are suddenly invited onto Soviet television. It's exactly what Gorbachev wanted—rock music is now officially allowed not just in America, but in the USSR too.

"They were happier, giggling like little boys with new bicycles to ride," Joanna will later write in her book about this magical period.

VAGRANT, STOKER, AND A MOVIE STAR

The forty-two-year-old film director Sergei Solovyov senses change in the air. His art-house films have already won several awards at international festivals, but he's eager for his new movie to resonate with young audiences—and he has no idea how to make that happen.

Solovyov has no idea what the younger generation likes. He needs a guide to this unfamiliar world. That's how he meets Boris Grebenshchikov. Someone gives him BG's phone number, explaining that he's the most popular young musician in the USSR.

The two arrange to meet at the Ostankino TV center. "How will I recognize you?" Solovyov asks, clueless that BG is already a legend. "Well, I'm a skinny blond guy." Boris chuckles. "And I'm a chubby, graying, bearded brunette," the director quips.

Soon after their meeting, Solovyov shows BG a script titled *Hello, Boy Bananan*, about a rebellious young misfit. He offers Boris the lead role, but Grebenshchikov declines, saying he's too old—already thirty-three. However, BG is ready to compose the soundtrack and contribute a few of his songs. And he agrees to help and recommends twenty-year-old artist Sergei "Afrika" Bugaev for the role.

The young blond known as Afrika moved to Leningrad from Novorossiysk a few years ago, fell in with the rock scene, and charmed everyone. Grebenshchikov recalls that at a New Year's party, Afrika spent the entire night naked with a glass jar on his dick—just for laughs. Later he started playing drums in various bands and got into contemporary art.

For Afrika, the opportunity is a lifeline. He has no official job (being an underground artist and musician doesn't count), which, under Soviet law, makes him a parasite. Working on a film, especially with Solovyov, is a perfect way to escape unwanted attention from the authorities. But Afrika has one condition: he wants his friends to be in the film as well.

He takes Solovyov to a Kino concert. The director has already heard a little about the band—but the concert exceeds all expectations. "When Vitya Tsoi takes the stage, I am completely blown away," Solovyov later recalls. After the performance, they are introduced, and Solovyov tells Tsoi that he very much wants to end his film with the song "I Want Change."

Tsoi, naturally, agrees, not even fully understanding what the film is about. He also dreams of being a movie star—just like his idol, Bruce Lee. "It's hard to feel like a star while working as a stoker," he says at that time.

The filming is set to begin in January 1987, and Afrika is counting the days—terrified that the police might arrest him for vagrancy before then.

A CALL FROM MOSCOW

Elena Bonner returns to Gorky in June 1986 after a long tour abroad. Before leaving the USSR, she promised the KGB she wouldn't talk to journalists or make political statements. In reality, she met with Margaret Thatcher and spoke at American universities. "If reporters showed up at these events in Berkeley or Columbia, well, that's not my problem," she would later explain. "I've always believed you don't have to be honest with the KGB. They lie to the whole world with a straight face."

On December 15, at 10:00 p.m., Sakharov and Bonner are watching television when there's a knock at the door. Three men enter. "Two are clearly KGB, and the third looks like a regular worker," Bonner describes. "We're installing a phone for you," one of them announces.

Sakharov and Bonner are baffled. What could this mean? As they leave, one of the KGB agents cryptically says, "You'll get a call tomorrow morning." Bonner checks the phone, but there's no dial tone.

The next morning, the phone comes to life. They wait for the call. By 3:00 p.m., Sakharov grows impatient. "No one's going to call. I'm going out for bread so we'll have fresh bread for dinner." And just as he's heading to the door, the phone rings.

"A call from Mikhail Sergeyevich [Gorbachev]," a woman's voice announces.

Outside the apartment, there's a commotion—loud chatter and laughter. It's the policeman stationed at their door, chatting with his girlfriends. Bonner flings the door open and yells, "Quiet! Gorbachev is calling!"

"You'll have the opportunity to return to Moscow. Get back to your patriotic work," Gorbachev begins. "The decree of the Presidium of the Supreme Soviet will be revoked. A decision regarding Elena Bon*ner* has also been made." He mispronounces her last name, placing the stress on the final syllable.

Sakharov thanks him and immediately starts talking about the release of prisoners of conscience. "Yes, I received your letter at the beginning of the year," Gorbachev replies. "Many have been freed, and conditions for others have improved. But the list includes very different kinds of people."

"All those convicted under these charges were sentenced unlawfully and unjustly. They must be freed!" Sakharov insists passionately.

"I cannot agree with you," Gorbachev counters. Hearing the resistance in Gorbachev's tone, and fearing he might outright refuse to free any political prisoners, Sakharov decides to end the call. "Thank you again, and good-bye," he says, hanging up.

About an hour and a half later, Sakharov recovers from the emotional whirlwind. "We still need bread for dinner. I'll go get it now," he says. Opening the door, he notices that the policeman, along with his desk and chair, has vanished. The security post was removed the moment the call came through from Moscow.

By evening, the phone in their Gorky apartment doesn't stop ringing. "Life was so much better without a phone," Sakharov jokes.

On December 23, 1986, at 7:30 a.m., the train carrying Sakharov and Bonner pulls into Moscow's Yaroslavsky station. A massive crowd awaits them—friends, admirers, and foreign journalists.

RAINBOW NIGHT

In December 1986, Joanna Stingray arrives in Leningrad from America with incredible news: she's managed to secure a deal with CBS Records to release an English-language album by Boris Grebenshchikov. It's an unbelievable breakthrough.

But the news in the Soviet Union isn't so pleasant. Her friends show her the latest issue of *Ogonyok* magazine—it contains a scathing article criticizing the *Red Wave* album. The article quotes Grebenshchikov's letter to the Soviet Copyright Society, where he denounces "citizen Stingray." Together they discuss how to respond. "It's strange," a friend muses. "The editor of the magazine, Vitaly Korotich, is supposedly very into Gorbachev's glasnost."

"I want to meet him. Let me try to explain *Red Wave*," Joanna proposes. "I'll go with you," Boris announces. However, they decide to head to Moscow after the New Year's celebrations—no one works in the USSR during the holidays anyway.

On December 31, 1986, Joanna and her noisy group of rockers celebrate the New Year—and the new life that has arrived for them. They are now true stars.

The party starts at the Swedish consulate. Joanna has brought rainbow wigs as gifts for her friends, and artists Afrika and Timur Novikov immediately put them on. Afrika, who loves dressing like a drag queen as part of his signature provocations, fully embraces the look.*

Sexuality is a curious topic within this crowd. None of Leningrad's rockers openly identify as gay, but that doesn't stop some of them from engaging in same-sex relationships. In the early 1980s, homosexuality, even outside of the USSR, remains a partially taboo subject. John Lennon, shortly before his death, admitted in an interview that he'd had "almost a love affair" with Beatles manager Brian Epstein. Elton John came out in 1976, but Freddie Mercury never publicly discussed his sexual orientation.

In the USSR, however, homosexuality is still a crime.

But on that rainbow-colored New Year's Eve in 1986, no one is thinking about such things. "It was such a beautiful moment in time, the culmination of all of my work with these bands and these guys as we crested the ladder of success and slid into celebration. It was bright, it was promising, and it was unspoiled by the malignant suspicions and lies of Soviet magazines, publishing companies, and government. It was Russia at its finest, full of love, light, and warmth," Joanna would later write.

Of all her star-studded friends, Joanna is most drawn to Yuri Kasparyan, the guitarist of Kino. Soon after the New Year, Joanna and Yuri visit the registry office to apply for their marriage license. Their wedding date is set for April 6. Joanna is horrified—why so long? But she eventually sees the silver lining. "I still see it as a genius idea with which Americans could benefit," she convinces herself, explaining that the wait gives couples time to think through their choice and the consequences.

On January 13, Joanna and Boris head to Moscow to meet Vitaly Korotich. Joanna explains *Red Wave* to the editor, sharing its success in the United States and the news of Grebenshchikov's upcoming English-language album. "Evidently, rock music remains the universal language of communication of youth the world over," Boris chimes in.

---

* Years later, people like Kino drummer Gustav Guryanov, artists Timur Novikov, and even Sergei "Afrika" would talk openly about their homosexuality. But by the twenty-first century, Afrika would fiercely deny it, transforming into a staunch conservative and a trusted ally of Vladimir Putin. Some, including journalist Artemy Troitsky, speculate that the KGB might have gotten their hooks into him in the 1980s.

"Joanna, what you did was a wonderful project, and I would like to officially apologize for the negative article," Korotich says warmly as they finish the meeting.

But just a few days later, *Komsomolskaya Pravda* publishes another scathing article titled "Red Wave on Murky Waters." This is a clear sign that the authorities are displeased. But the young rockers don't know how to read the signs.

For the next few months, Joanna returns to California, overwhelmed with emotion as she and her family prepare for the wedding. The plans are grand. The ceremony is to take place at the Peter and Paul Fortress in Leningrad (now a museum, formerly a prison), and NBC plans to send a film crew to cover the event.

Three weeks before the wedding, Joanna gets a call from her travel agency— the one that usually organizes her trips to Leningrad. "We were supposed to get the thirty visas today for the trip, but unfortunately we only received twenty-nine," the agent says apologetically. "Joanna, your visa has been declined."

At first, Joanna doesn't believe it. Then she cries and tries every possible avenue. She writes to Vitaly Korotich, Soviet TV host Vladimir Pozner, American billionaire Armand Hammer, senators, and congressmen. Nothing works. No one responds. She's ignored.

The wedding is ruined. Soviet officials, who believed Gorbachev was angry at the American woman who released an album of Soviet rockers, are satisfied. They've punished the troublemaker.

ASSA

Afrika is luckier—no one catches him, and he calmly flies to Crimea, where Sergei Solovyov is filming his movie, ultimately titled *Assa*.

According to the film's plot, in the final scene the main character— a rebellious musician performing in a restaurant, played by Afrika—is killed. Another takes his place—this role is played by Viktor Tsoi. Without even listening to the tedious instructions about what he can and cannot do, Tsoi heads straight to the stage and begins singing his song "I Want Change":

"Our hearts demand change,
Our eyes demand change,
In our laughter, in our tears, in the pulse of our veins—
Change, we're waiting for change."

As the final shots roll, the camera pulls back—Tsoi is no longer singing in a restaurant but on a massive open-air stadium stage, with a huge crowd of fans hanging on his every word. The freedom-loving hero is dead, but director Solovyov hints that thousands like him will rise to take his place.

In January 1987, Tsoi arrives in Crimea to film his scene in the restaurant. It's the first time in his life he sees the sea. And it's where he meets a woman named Natasha.

Natasha Razlogova is six years older than Vitya—he's twenty-four, and she's thirty—and she comes from a completely different world. Her father is a diplomat, and her older brother is a well-known film critic. She belongs to the Moscow bohemian elite; he's part of the Leningrad underground. She's a linguist, fluent in two languages, but got bored and decided to work in film—so now she's an assistant director, even though the job is far beneath her intellectual level. Natasha has been married and has a son, but her marriage fell apart.

"I was introduced to her when I visited MosFilm Studios, and we became friendly when I saw her again in Yalta for the filming of *Assa*," Tsoi will later tell Joanna Stingray. "I told her I had a son and a formal marriage that is part of my business. I was very serious, but I was smitten."

"He was so nice! That's all I thought. We were from two different worlds with no real reason to communicate further," Natasha will recall in a conversation with Joanna later.

Tsoi has only two scenes in the film, so once it's shot, he returns to Leningrad. Natasha stays in Yalta.

But Viktor can't stop thinking about her. He manages to get her hotel phone number from someone on the film crew, calls her, and says he wants to see her. "Well, you can always come to Yalta," she replies. She assumes he's a rock star and a trip to Crimea for a date would be nothing to him. But he's still working as a stoker and barely has any money.

"If Solovyov organizes another trip for Kino, then I'll definitely come," Tsoi answers. That's where the conversation ends.

He keeps calling her every day, and eventually, he does make his way back to Yalta. It's during this visit that their romance begins: Natasha even moves into Viktor's room.

Then they part ways again: she returns to Moscow, and he goes back to his family in Leningrad.

GHOSTS OF POWER

At the start of 1987, the corruption investigation led by Gdlyan and Ivanov finally lands its biggest name: Yuri Churbanov, son-in-law of the late General Secretary Leonid Brezhnev and husband of Brezhnev's daughter, Galina. On January 14, Churbanov is arrested on corruption charges and simultaneously expelled from the Communist Party.

When Churbanov married Galina Brezhneva, he was just a modest police officer. Thanks to his advantageous marriage, by the age of forty-three he had risen to the position of First Deputy Minister of Internal Affairs under Nikolai Shchelokov. His boss Shchelokov didn't live to face trial, taking his own life instead, in 1984, a year after the suicide of his wife. Churbanov would later claim that he, too, was encouraged to consider suicide as the "most honorable way out," but he refused.

Initially, Churbanov denies any wrongdoing. But, as he recounts, the head of the KGB, Viktor Chebrikov, visits him in the detention center.

"Yuri, you know the rules. And you understand that the Politburo's approval was necessary for your arrest. And as you know, the Politburo doesn't make mistakes," the KGB chief tells him.

In February 1987, Churbanov admits to taking bribes from a wide range of former Uzbek officials, including the current leader of the republic, Usmonxo'jayev—the very man who succeeded Rashidov and is now actively dismantling his predecessor's legacy.

It's hard to say how voluntary this letter was. Later Churbanov will claim that all his confessions were made under pressure from investigators. He alleges that Gdlyan and Ivanov threatened him with execution if he didn't admit to what they wanted. The truth is probably somewhere in between: Soviet investigators were not exactly known for respecting human rights, and Churbanov was far from innocent. Like many in his position, he likely never considered the showering of lavish gifts on him during official trips to be acts of corruption. As the son-in-law of the General Secretary, he had grown accustomed to a life of luxury and didn't see it as criminal. On the contrary, he believed he was being unjustly punished by enemies of the late Brezhnev.

During the investigation, Churbanov admits to receiving a gold-embroidered robe and skullcap, a coffee set, and a bribe of 90,000 rubles while in Uzbekistan. However, at trial, he retracts these confessions and insists on his innocence.

In September 1987, investigators raid Galina Brezhneva's home. Her property is cataloged and confiscated. The event seems surreal. Yet the story appears in *Ogonyok* and *Moscow News*, symbols of glasnost. Soviet citizens read the reports, barely able to believe their eyes.

The Brezhnev family's story becomes a tragic one, but it's a significant chapter in Russian history. During the raids, Galina drinks heavily. She had struggled with alcohol before, but in her father's lifetime she shone at high-society events, living a luxurious lifestyle. Now she drinks alone, forgotten by nearly everyone.

In December 1988, Churbanov is sentenced to twelve years in a labor camp, with confiscation of property. In 1990, Galina will successfully appeal the confiscation, proving in court that the seized items—her father's gifts—were unrelated to her husband's crimes. She will regain a dacha, a bank account, antique furniture, chandeliers, a collection of weapons and animal trophies, and even a confiscated Mercedes.

That same year, while Churbanov is still in prison, Galina will divorce him.

This family drama has no immediate impact on the political developments of the late 1980s and early 1990s in the USSR. But a decade later, the ghosts of Galina Brezhneva and Yuri Churbanov will return to haunt the Kremlin. As ailing Boris Yeltsin will prepare to leave the presidency, his daughter Tatyana Dyachenko and future son-in-law Valentin Yumashev will be determined not to repeat the fate of Brezhnev's family. Their fear will be justified: the Prosecutor General's Office will even open a criminal case involving Yeltsin's relatives. Tatyana and Valentin will go to great lengths to retain control of the situation. They support bringing Vladimir Putin to power—a successor with similarities to former KGB chief Viktor Chebrikov—after receiving assurances of immunity.[*]

THE HYDRA OF GLOBAL FREEMASONRY AND ZIONISM

In 1987, Boris Yeltsin's political career is just beginning. At this point, he is merely the First Secretary of the Moscow party organization.

---

[*] Galina Brezhneva will never learn of Tatyana Dyachenko's efforts to avoid her fate. She will die on June 30, 1998. Yuri Churbanov, released from prison, will outlive both his ex-wife and Boris Yeltsin, passing away in 2013.

On May 6, 1987, the first protest demonstration of perestroika-era Moscow takes place on Manezhnaya Square. It is organized by the so-called Historical and Patriotic Association Pamyat (Memory), a nationalist group that at the time is barely known.

The official reason for the protest is to defend old Moscow and its historical landmarks, which are allegedly being destroyed. The leaders of Pamyat are particularly outraged by the construction of a memorial on Poklonnaya Hill dedicated to those who died in the Great Patriotic War. They claim that the site holds unique archaeological artifacts that must not be destroyed. According to them, the construction is a conspiracy by Jewish architects who hate Moscow and want to erase its historical value.

The slogans unfurled by Pamyat activists in central Moscow are a strange mix. They support perestroika but oppose its so-called enemies, with banners reading: "Down with the Saboteurs of Perestroika!," "Stop Construction on Poklonnaya Hill!," "We Demand a Meeting with Gorbachev and Yeltsin!"

Their true goal, however, is political recognition. Pamyat becomes the first nationalist organization—in the United States, it would be called a white supremacy group—to openly enter the political arena, taking advantage of the newly declared policies of glasnost and free speech.

"They tell us there's no enemy, but there is—both external and internal," explains Dmitry Vasilyev, the leader of Pamyat, a stout, bald forty-one-year-old man, during the protest.

The activists wave black, yellow, and white banners—the colors of the Russian Empire's nineteenth-century flag, which was later adopted by monarchist and fascist Russian émigrés in the mid-twentieth century. Now Pamyat resurrects these imperial symbols.

Over a thousand people attend this unauthorized demonstration—an extraordinary number for 1987. The police do nothing. They neither disperse the protesters nor order them to leave. Instead, their demands are quickly relayed to Boris Yeltsin, head of the city. According to his own memoir, Yeltsin agrees to meet with the protesters.

Yeltsin doesn't seem to fully understand who these people are and hardly argues with them. In fact, he even expresses sympathy: "There's a lot of speculation around you; many people criticize you unfairly."

The meeting turns into a Q and A session. When Pamyat asks for help with their official registration, Yeltsin responds, "We'll need to think about that."

The conversation shifts to classic xenophobic grievances, such as the influx of nonresidents into Moscow, which Pamyat insists must be stopped. Yeltsin doesn't argue. Instead, he confirms that, on average, 2 million visitors enter Moscow daily in winter, rising to 3 million in summer. He laments that food shortages occur because the state planning system doesn't account for these visitors' needs. Moscow is overcrowded, he says, leading to issues with schools, stores, and transport. To address this, Yeltsin promises that out-of-towners—then referred to as *limitchiki*—will no longer be hired in Moscow.

Encouraged by Yeltsin's pliability, Vasilyev launches into his favorite conspiracy theories. He claims that a secret society exists in the USSR, working to destroy traditional culture, "Americanize" Soviet citizens, and intentionally exacerbate socioeconomic problems. These conspirators, he alleges, have infiltrated "the bureaucracy—this hydra of global Freemasonry, Zionism, and imperialism."

Even here, Yeltsin doesn't push back. He nods seriously, acknowledging that the bureaucratic apparatus—"deep state" in American terms—inherited from the Brezhnev era indeed hinders perestroika, though he assures them that Moscow's party apparatus has been renewed by 40 percent in the past year.

Following this meeting, Pamyat becomes the talk of the entire country. Dmitry Vasilyev emerges as the USSR's first public, noncommunist politician. Major international newspapers, including the *New York Times*, the *Washington Post*, and the *Guardian*, write about Pamyat as the first opposition political organization in the USSR.

What is known about Vasilyev and Pamyat? At their meetings, Vasilyev reads aloud from *The Protocols of the Elders of Zion*, a notorious forgery created by the tsarist secret police at the turn of the twentieth century. He believes in its authenticity without question. One of his favorite passages claims that Jewish Freemasons plan to construct underground tunnels in all capitals to enable them to blow up government buildings. "When I read the protocols, I looked at the map of the Moscow Metro with horror," Vasilyev would say. "All the key junction stations are located under government buildings." And indeed, he adds, the Moscow Metro was started by a Jew—Lazar Kaganovich, Stalin's former right-hand man.

As Pamyat gains notoriety, rumors of impending Jewish pogroms spread across Moscow. These rumors echo events from the early twentieth century, when pogroms broke out in the Russian Empire shortly after the publication of the *Protocols*.

Dmitry Vasilyev, a trained actor, graduated from the Moscow Art Theatre School and even played a minor role as Pyotr Stolypin in the film *Lev Tolstoy*. Stolypin, who was often vilified in Soviet textbooks as a reactionary and enemy of the revolution, is Vasilyev's ideal politician.[*]

DANGEROUS JERKS

In April 1987, the Secretary of the Central Committee for Ideology, Alexander Yakovlev, summons his subordinates. He informs them that during the Reykjavík Summit, General Secretary Gorbachev promised Ronald Reagan that the Soviet Union would stop jamming Western radio stations. This means they now need to develop a new approach to engaging with audiences—one that would provide a worthy alternative to foreign media.

"How do we protect our youth from the corrupting influence of Western radio propaganda?" Yakovlev allegedly asks, before proposing the creation of a new youth-oriented weekly TV program designed to compete with the *enemy voices*.

About a month later, on May 28, 1987, after lunch, twenty-four-year-old journalist Sasha Lyubimov steps out of the office for a smoke. He works at Soviet international radio, broadcasting to foreign countries, and is a staffer in the Danish section. Joining him at the window on the eighth-floor stairwell of the State Broadcasting Committee building in central Moscow is his friend Oleg Vakulovsky, who works in the Swedish section.

From their smoking spot, they have a clear view of St. Basil's Cathedral and the Kremlin towers. Lyubimov gazes out the window and suddenly notices a small airplane approaching the Kremlin. He doesn't think much of it—after all, Moscow is hosting yet another international peace conference. The participants, a mix of leftists and hippies from Europe and America, are staying nearby at the Rossiya Hotel, just across from the Kremlin. Sasha assumes the little plane is part of the entertainment for the conference guests.

---

[*] It would have been unthinkable in the late 1980s, but in 2012 a statue of Stolypin would be erected in front of the Russian government building—at the initiative of Vladimir Putin.

He's already itching to go home, but there are still a couple of hours left in the workday. He knows that if he writes a short piece, he'll earn a fee. The pay structure at international broadcasting is simple: three rubles for a news item, seven for a commentary. A news story with a short interview? That's five rubles—a quick win. Sasha and Oleg realize this is their chance. One of them stays at the office while the other heads out to find out what the deal is with the plane landing in Red Square.

An hour and a half later, they both release a story about an aviation enthusiast from West Germany flying to Moscow to support perestroika. They earn their five rubles each and head off to celebrate with drinks. The next day, they're hauled in for a meeting with the top brass.

It turns out that the pilot, eighteen-year-old Mathias Rust from Germany, isn't a peace conference participant. He's an adventurous teenager who took it upon himself to fly to Moscow. His intentions, admittedly, are noble: he was upset by the failed Reykjavík Summit between Gorbachev and Reagan and decided to bridge East and West himself.

Rust rented a small Cessna from his flying club. First, he flew to Reykjavík, where the summit had taken place. "I felt a connection with the spirit of the place," he would later say. "I was filled with emotions and disappointment over the summit's failure and my inability to be there last autumn. That motivated me to continue."

A few days later, he reached Helsinki and told the air traffic controller he was heading to Stockholm. Instead, he turned off his transponder, dropped his altitude, and headed for the Soviet border. Along the way, he could have—should have—been shot down.

But first, his plane was mistaken for a Soviet Yak-12. Then he slipped past the air defense system around Moscow, which happened to be down for maintenance that day. Finally, no one dared shoot down the plane without explicit orders—everyone remembered the tragedy of the Korean airliner and the strict prohibition against attacking civilian targets that followed. In the end, the teenager reached Moscow, circled Red Square twice, and landed near St. Basil's Cathedral.

When he emerged from the plane, people ran toward him—not to arrest him, but to ask for autographs. A journalist even managed to snag an interview before Rust was arrested, about an hour after landing. That same day, Soviet international broadcasting aired the news—in Swedish and Danish. Thus, the USSR itself, purely by accident, became the first to inform the world that a strange aviation enthusiast from West Germany had flown to the Kremlin unimpeded.

The following morning, Sasha and Oleg sit red-faced, trying to explain themselves to their superiors. They decide to stick to the truth: they were smoking, saw an opportunity to earn a quick five rubles, and wanted to grab drinks after work. . . .

Later, Lyubimov will recall: "The head of the State Broadcasting Committee looked at us with such despair, his eyes practically screaming: 'Under Stalin, people like you would have been jailed. The dissidents who protested in 1968? Sent to asylums. Solzhenitsyn? Exiled. And yet it won't be dissidents or intellectuals who bring us down—it'll be jerks like you. The problem isn't the smart ones—it's the fools who, damn it, just wanted to earn five rubles.'"

But Sasha knows he's not risking anything. He's part of the golden youth—his father is a high-ranking KGB officer, a former staff member of the Soviet embassy in London who was expelled as a spy. Sasha graduated from the most prestigious university in the USSR, MGIMO. He got into international broadcasting thanks to his father's connections—and it's unlikely he'll be fired.

On the day Mathias Rust lands near the Kremlin, Gorbachev is in East Berlin, attending a Warsaw Pact summit with the Soviet military leadership. Upon hearing the news from Moscow, he tells the Soviet minister of defense, "If I were you, I'd resign immediately."

The sight of a Cessna on Red Square gives Gorbachev the perfect excuse to clean house at the Ministry of Defense. The aging generals and marshals were largely hostile to disarmament talks and negotiations with the Americans. As a result, Gorbachev doesn't just fire the minister of defense and the head of air defense but also about three hundred senior military officials.

"Let everyone—here and in the West—know where the power lies: in the political leadership, in the Politburo," Gorbachev's aide Anatoly Chernyaev writes in his diary. "Now the alarmists claiming the military opposes Gorbachev and is about to overthrow him will finally shut up."

Gorbachev's most trusted man in the Ministry of Defense is Chief of the General Staff, Marshal Akhromeyev, a key participant in all negotiations with the Americans. By all logic, he should be the next defense minister. But just days before the scandal, he and Gorbachev had a major falling-out.

That April, during talks with US secretary of state George Shultz, Gorbachev makes unprecedented concessions in his push to secure an agreement with the Americans. One of them is his offer to eliminate the Soviet SS-23 short-range missiles—despite Akhromeyev's pleas not to. When the marshal learns of this only after the fact, he rushes to Gorbachev, urging him to reconsider and retract the offer, arguing that the SS-23 is a brand-new, state-of-the-art system.

Gorbachev erupts. "Are you suggesting that I, the General Secretary, am incompetent in military affairs? That I'm now changing my position and withdrawing my word just because Soviet generals told me to?" he shouts at the aging marshal.

The fallout is immediate. Instead of the experienced Akhromeyev, Gorbachev appoints the youngest of the top military officials—sixty-two-year-old Dmitry Yazov—as the new defense minister.

In September 1987, Rust will be sentenced to four years in prison, but he will be released a year later under amnesty and sent back home.

As for Sasha Lyubimov, he faces no punishment. In fact, quite the opposite happens. Around this time, the State Broadcasting Committee is considering creating a new youth program, just as Yakovlev had requested. The head of the department, Eduard Sagalaev, spots the two young men walking down the hallway, looking utterly thrilled to have avoided dismissal or even a reprimand. "Let's take these two," he says, pointing them out.

A few months later, Lyubimov and two other Soviet international radio employees—Vlad Listyev and Dima Zakharov—become the first hosts of the legendary program *Vzglyad* (The View). Three young men discussing the news live on air and showing video reports might not sound groundbreaking, but in the Soviet Union, it is a sensation. For the first time, viewers see a real, unscripted conversation—not a carefully preapproved script vetted by censors.

PEASANT VERSUS ANTI-SEMITISM

On June 4, 1987, Politburo member Alexander Yakovlev walks into Gorbachev's aide Anatoly Chernyaev's office and shows him a flyer distributed by the nationalist group Pamyat, titled *Stop Yakovlev!*

The flyer is long-winded, but its message boils down to this: 1987 could be as catastrophic as 1941, because "bourgeois media are triumphantly proclaiming that Yakovlev will finally sideline Yegor Ligachev and become the second-most powerful person in the state." The author of the flyer (Pamyat's leader Dmitry Vasilyev) continues: "This will mean a one-sided democratization, a game played with only one goal. It will mean complete freedom for cosmopolitans and the silencing of patriots. It will mean that the filthy stream of musical narcotics, pornography, and sadism flooding us will grow stronger!"

Vasilyev goes on to accuse Yakovlev of trying to restore diplomatic ties with Israel and rehabilitate "Trotsky the Freemason." He concludes with a dramatic call to action: now the top priority is to "*stop Yakovlev!*"

Yakovlev is deeply upset. According to Chernyaev, "he is almost in tears, talking about how hard this is for him." Yakovlev is convinced that Pamyat is a KGB creation and that "this scum has the direct backing of Ligachev."

Chernyaev advises Yakovlev to shrug it off, not to take it seriously, and, above all, not to show the flyer to Gorbachev. But Yakovlev has already done just that. "You think this is about you? No, it's about me," Gorbachev reportedly responded.

"I'm a Russian peasant from Yaroslavl," Yakovlev tells Chernyaev with a characteristic rural accent, "but I am biologically repelled by, nauseated by, anti-Semitism and all forms of nationalism. Leaving aside the state interest, if we provoke Russian chauvinism now, it will unleash a wave of nationalism from the periphery that will rip this 'empire' apart."

The rift between the two Politburo ideologues—Yakovlev and Ligachev—is widening and becoming increasingly evident. It shows up in small battles: Yakovlev pushes for something to be permitted; Ligachev pushes to ban it. Gorbachev is forced to act as arbiter. One telling example is the debate over Anatoly Rybakov's novel *Children of the Arbat*, in which Stalin is depicted as a cold-blooded and calculating murderer. Ligachev is vehemently against its publication, but Gorbachev ultimately gives it the green light.

Gorbachev believes that he's educating the Politburo on how to be more democratic. Of course, he doesn't fully realize that he has no hope of reeducating the seasoned party bureaucrats. In the early years of perestroika, they behave exactly as they were trained—never contradicting their superiors. But their core beliefs remain unchanged.

THE FIRST "FIRST LADY"

While relations between Ronald Reagan and Mikhail Gorbachev gradually improve, Nancy Reagan can't stand Raisa Gorbacheva. To her, Raisa is unbearably arrogant and far too talkative.

In her memoir, Nancy writes about their first meeting: "From the moment we met, she talked and talked and talked—so much that I could barely get a word in, edgewise or otherwise. Perhaps it was insecurity on her part, but . . . my fundamental impression was that she never stopped talking."

Raisa's manners often surprise even Soviet officials. Alexander Yakovlev recalls one such incident: On a flight back to Moscow after an international trip, Raisa suddenly asks for wine, raises her glass, and says, "Let's drink to our cause, to loyalty to Mikhail Sergeyevich. Swear you will always be faithful to him!" The room falls into awkward silence. Gorbachev remains quiet, and Raisa presses on. Yakovlev tries to change the subject—he has no intention of swearing loyalty, even as a joke.

Gorbachev's aide on international affairs, Anatoly Chernyaev, also frequently notes Raisa's overbearing nature in his diary. For example, she scolds him for not organizing her personal itinerary with enough care, despite the fact that Chernyaev—de facto national security advisor—has far more pressing political responsibilities and isn't in charge of her leisure time. He also grumbles about Gorbachev's decision to build two luxurious seaside residences, one in Crimea and another in Abkhazia. He never dares criticize his boss, even in his thoughts, so he blames Raisa's bourgeois tastes instead.

But Nancy Reagan's prejudice or Kremlin officials' complaints pale in comparison to how Raisa is received by Soviet citizens. This is where things get dramatic—nobody likes her.

The main reason? They've never seen anything like her before. They don't even know what a First Lady is supposed to be. The wives of Brezhnev and other leaders never appeared in public, so Raisa Gorbacheva is breaking new ground.

What's the role of women in the Soviet Union? On paper, they have equal rights and can take on the hardest jobs—laying asphalt, working construction, and unloading freight cars. But in leadership? Almost unheard of. By 1987, only one woman in Soviet history has ever been a member of the Politburo: former minister of culture Yekaterina Furtseva, and popular rumor attributes her position to a romantic relationship with Nikita Khrushchev. Feminism? Even the most educated people treat it as a joke.

Women who dare to voice their opinions publicly often earn a bad reputation in the USSR. Elena Bonner is branded a "beast in a skirt" by a Politburo member; Andrei Sakharov, who loves his outspoken wife, is widely seen as henpecked for "allowing" her to behave that way.

Raisa Gorbacheva faces a similar fate, even though she speaks publicly only rarely. But her appearance is enough to draw ire: she dresses too stylishly, too independently, "not like one of us." Offensive jokes about her circulate endlessly.

Sometimes she gives people ammunition. In September 1987, during a three-day visit to the bleak port city of Murmansk, Raisa accompanies her husband. It's already cold there, and for the first two days, she's seen on television in a gray coat and a white fur hat. But on the third day, it gets a bit chillier, and she appears in a different coat and a black fur hat. Soviet viewers are outraged. "Two coats? Maybe that's normal for Paris, but not for Murmansk, where people eat meat once a month!" they fume.

Her husband works hard to shield her from such criticism. Still, according to press secretary Andrei Grachev, Raisa closely follows what the international press writes about her and is deeply hurt by misunderstandings, shallow judgments, and outright lies. Yet she remains the consummate "top student," meticulously preparing for her husband's visits, unafraid to engage with journalists, and always taking the initiative in conversations.

"MY NAME IS KAPLAN"

On August 24, 1987, the USSR's most famous singer, Alla Pugacheva, arrives in Leningrad. She's set to perform a joint concert with German rock musician Udo Lindenberg as part of their Rock for a Nuclear-Free World by 2000 tour.

Pugacheva is perhaps the only Soviet pop singer who's invited to perform abroad. She's far from an underground artist, yet she constantly challenges societal norms. Loved by millions, she also has countless detractors. It's clear she irritates both the party leadership and the KGB.

On August 24, she runs into one of those detractors. At the reception desk of the Pribaltiyskaya Hotel, she's told that her favorite suite, the one she always stays in, is occupied. Her manager swears the room was booked in advance, but it's no use, Pugacheva insists, snapping that "prostitutes in this hotel are treated better than artists."

The hotel's head administrator dismisses Pugacheva's demands as "the whims of a diva" and threatens to "put her in her place." The singer loses her temper as well. Eventually, she's placed in another room, but that evening a police officer shows up, asking her to give a statement about the incident.

There's little doubt the hotel, frequented by foreigners, is under tight KGB surveillance. It's equally clear the secret service protects the currency-earning prostitutes working there. The hotel staffer who picked a fight with Pugacheva must have connections—her confidence suggests she's not just an ordinary employee, but probably an agent herself.

By August 26, *Leningradskaya Pravda* publishes a letter from a reader under the headline "Clashing with a Star." The author is none other than the hotel administrator who refused Pugacheva her room. She details the singer's alleged rude behavior.

That's just the beginning. Soon articles about the incident appear in every Soviet newspaper. Some outlets publish letters from outraged readers demanding Pugacheva be stripped of her titles and awards, banned from traveling abroad, and even calling for her tongue to be cut out or her mouth sealed with tar. The underlying accusation, though never stated outright, is clear: Pugacheva performs abroad too often and has started acting like a spoiled Western pop star.

Alla Pugacheva always had problems with the authorities. Many officials hated her. The head of State Television, Sergei Lapin, after seeing her onstage for the first time, demanded that she never appear on-screen again—because, as he crudely put it, "She touches the microphone like she's about to give it a blow job."

Pugacheva has one serious problem that irritates the authorities—she is a woman. A completely free and independent woman. That's not how things are done in the Soviet Union.

Sure, there are plenty of popular female singers in the USSR. They sing about the motherland, love, happiness, nature—everything they're expected to sing about. But only Pugacheva sings about deep emotions and pain: loneliness, struggle, independence. She sings about what hurts—not just for herself, but for everyone. She is the voice of all Soviet women—and men too, for that matter. Because they also often feel longing, suffering, frustration, the urge to rebel, or to tell everyone to go to hell—but no one in the Soviet Union says these things out loud. No one except Alla Pugacheva.

People also constantly see political subtext in her songs. In 1987, she sings "Hey, You Up There," supposedly directed at noisy neighbors keeping her awake. But every Soviet citizen believes she is really addressing the country's frustrating leadership.

Though the KGB may have sparked the scandal, it's unlikely to be a coordinated campaign. Instead, Soviet media, still navigating the newfound glasnost, are discovering it's far safer to expose celebrities than criticize officials. Pop stars with existing KGB issues are especially easy targets. Besides, the USSR has never had a tabloid press before—this is its first baby step. Journalists quickly realize how much the public craves gossip about celebrities' lives.

In early September, Central Committee Secretary for Ideology Alexander Yakovlev notices the flood of articles about Pugacheva and decides to step in. "I don't care if she cursed or even fought someone—this kind of witch hunt is unacceptable," he will later recall. Following classic Soviet protocol, Yakovlev orders a few articles to be written in her defense.

For the first few weeks of the scandal, Pugacheva stays holed up in her Moscow apartment, convinced that she is canceled and her career is over. In September, she leaves for concerts in West Germany and Switzerland, even considering not returning to the USSR. But eventually, she comes back.

In the following months, articles about Pugacheva continue to proliferate. One Moscow newspaper publishes a particularly striking claim: that Pugacheva is actually Jewish and her real name is Alla Borukhovna Pevzner. In a country where anti-Semitism is on the rise and groups like Pamyat are gaining traction, the insinuation is unmistakable.

Pugacheva responds immediately. She calls the newspaper and asks to speak to the author of the piece. "You've got it wrong. My name isn't Pevzner—it's Kaplan. And next time, I won't miss." It's a dangerously edgy joke for the Soviet Union. Pevzner and Kaplan are stereotypical Jewish surnames, but Fanny Kaplan is a historical figure every Soviet citizen knows. She was the woman who attempted to assassinate Lenin in 1918 but missed. For a pop star like Alla Pugacheva to troll a Soviet journalist by comparing herself to Lenin's would-be assassin—and adding that she won't miss next time—suggests she sees herself as nothing less than an enemy of the Soviet state.

NEEDLE

Viktor Tsoi and Natasha Razlogova continue their long-distance romance over the phone until the summer of 1987, when Natasha leaves Moscow for a dacha in Latvia, where there is no phone. At that point, Tsoi decides he can no longer live without her.

"He came to me and said, 'You know, I'm in love . . . ,'" his wife, Maryana, would later recall. "Thank God he had the courage not to hide his relationship with Natasha and confessed everything right away. I know what love is; he didn't need to prove anything to me. I told him, 'Fine, then pack your suitcase.' So we parted quietly. . . ."

Tsoi leaves Maryana and, somehow, finds Natasha's dacha on the Baltic Sea. After that, he begins living between two cities: he continues working as a stoker in Leningrad but tries to visit Natasha in Moscow as often as he can.

In the summer of 1987, Tsoi's longtime acquaintance director Rashid Nugmanov, a former student of Solovyov, invites him to play the lead role in his new film.

Nugmanov is from Soviet Kazakhstan. Officially, the USSR has no racism, but despite Tsoi's musical popularity, it's hard to imagine any director from Moscow or Leningrad casting him as a lead because of his Asian appearance. In Kazakhstan, however, Tsoi doesn't stand out as a stranger.

The film is called *Needle*. It opens with Kino's song "A Star Called the Sun." Tsoi's character fights against a drug cartel and tries to save his girlfriend from addiction. He takes her to the shores of the drying Aral Sea—a body of water that was once full but has turned into a lifeless desert due to Soviet-era environmental mismanagement. The sight of the characters wandering through a desert that was recently a sea becomes a powerful metaphor for the state of the USSR.

In the final scene, set in a snowy Almaty, a gangster stabs Tsoi's character in the stomach. He struggles to walk along a snow-covered path, leaving a trail of blood behind him. In the background, his song "Blood Type" plays.

Tsoi loves the film. "We don't have real heroes in cinema. No supermen, no gods who can do everything—fly through the streets, defeat everyone. Young people need a hero. Maybe I'm not cut out for the role of a hero, but since there's no one else right now, I want to start. I want young people to have their own heroes. They look at Arnold Schwarzenegger, at Bruce Lee, but they're not ours," he says in an interview.

Tsoi's mother disapproves of the changes in his life—his breakup with Maryana and his romance in Moscow. He asks her to send him a coat from Leningrad to Almaty, and she slips a note into the pocket. After reading it, Viktor stops speaking to his mother for an entire year.

MUSIC RING

"Hi, Joanna, it's Kenny. How are you? I'm so sorry for your visa problem," begins Kenny Schaffer, the producer Joanna Stingray had enlisted to work on Boris Grebenshchikov's English-language album.

"Thanks. It's been hard, but we just keep trying to fix it."

"You know, I had a great meeting in Moscow about our Boris project. I'm afraid your visa problem could affect it. I hate to say this, but I think for Boris's sake you should step away from the project," she recalls the exchange in her memoir.

Joanna doesn't fight it. She keeps writing to politicians and searching for a way back into the USSR.

By the summer of 1987, friends tell her about a new loophole: tourists arriving in Leningrad by cruise ship from Finland can stay in the USSR for seven hours without a visa. Seven hours is better than nothing, she decides. In August, Joanna Fields officially changes her last name to Stingray in her passport and books a ticket on the ferry from Helsinki to Leningrad. Accompanying her are NBC journalists still following her personal drama.

The gamble pays off. She gets through the border, meets Yuri, and they even manage to file a new marriage application. This time, the date is set for November.

The story of the canceled wedding grows so big that during diplomatic talks US secretary of state George Shultz asks Eduard Shevardnadze about it. Shortly afterward, Joanna finally receives a Soviet visa, ending her separation from Yuri.

Back in Los Angeles, she begins preparing for the wedding again when, out of the blue, David Bowie calls—her Leningrad friends' idol, especially Grebenshchikov's. Bowie wants to turn her story into a movie and even plans to play Boris himself. *This is it*, Joanna thinks. *Now I can die happy.*

Bowie offers Joanna $35,000 for the rights to her life story. She knows it's not much. But on the other hand, it's David Bowie. The catch: she'd have to give up full control of her story. Joanna hesitates for a long time. Ultimately, she returns to Leningrad, where her friends and fiancé are waiting. She never responds to Bowie's offer.

She doesn't become a star in America. But that doesn't matter—because she's becoming a star in the USSR.

In November Joanna and Yuri finally head to the registry office. This time, they get married. Leningrad's rock scene throws a massive celebration.

During the wedding concert, Joanna hears "Blood Type" by Kino for the first time. She's convinced it's a protest song against the war in Afghanistan. The audience is wild for Viktor Tsoi. Years later, watching a recording of that concert, Joanna reflects on the moment: "I could see what I refer to as the changing of the guard. Boris will always be the godfather of Russian rock 'n' roll, and his place in history is hammered in granite, but on this night, Viktor became the most adored and famous Russian rocker of that time."

FEBRUARY WON'T COME

In 1987, Sakharov travels abroad for the first time since his release—this time without Bonner. The trip is organized by the Soviet state-owned Charity Foundation, which needs Sakharov as a fundraiser; his name opens Western donors' wallets. Before his departure, Alexsander Yakovlev even bets a case of cognac with a fellow Politburo member on whether Sakharov will return or stay in the West. Yakovlev, of course, wins the bet.

From Vermont, Alexander Solzhenitsyn closely monitors Sakharov's activities. On one hand, he writes that he is happy for Sakharov and approves of his political demands. On the other, he is baffled by American journalists who repeatedly ask whether he plans to return to Russia. "They don't understand the difference between Sakharov and me," he writes. "Sakharov is needed by this system. He has great merits before it, and he doesn't reject it entirely. I, on the other hand, cut them down to their Leninist roots. It's either this system or my books."

Still, Solzhenitsyn begins to warm to perestroika. He sees it as a way to avoid a repeat of the February Revolution of 1917: "Thank God, it seems to be proceeding gradually, evolutionarily. I'm happy with this path: no revolution, no total collapse. There won't be another February, which I feared so much."

"I WAS ALWAYS THE BOSS"

Moscow nationalists from the Pamyat society weren't demanding a meeting with Yeltsin by chance. In 1987, the new leader of Moscow was becoming a rising political star—a living symbol of perestroika.

Yeltsin tries to emulate Mikhail Gorbachev at every turn, striving to follow the General Secretary's example. When Gorbachev mingles with the public, Yeltsin does the same. Yeltsin even rides to work on a trolleybus in full view of journalists, showcasing his democratic image. Gorbachev criticizes the Brezhnev-era stagnation and removes "stagnation-era" officials; Yeltsin does this too, but more aggressively. He also champions the fight against corruption, accelerating personnel changes in the Moscow apparatus at an unprecedented pace.

In his zeal to be the "perfect student," Yeltsin often overdoes it, irritating many of his colleagues. Members of the Politburo dismiss his trolleybus rides as "cheap populism." Meanwhile, Moscow city officials complain about Yeltsin's heavy-handed management style. Rumors circulate that a dismissed party official committed suicide shortly after an intense meeting with him.

(Later, Yeltsin will deny this in his memoir, insisting that the official took his life months after their conversation, not immediately afterward.)

The one most annoyed by Yeltsin's behavior is his former patron, Yegor Ligachev, the second-most powerful man in the party. Complaints about Yeltsin's leadership flow directly to Ligachev.

Those close to Yeltsin note how much it infuriates him to be treated as a subordinate. Yeltsin, accustomed to being in charge, resents being anyone's second. As he describes his career trajectory: "I was always the boss. Whether it was a foreman or the head of a department, but never a deputy."

In September, while Gorbachev is on vacation in Abkhazia, Ligachev takes charge of the Politburo sessions. He launches yet another tirade against Yeltsin, even forming a Central Committee commission to investigate Moscow's administration—a clear declaration of war. Yeltsin decides to go all in.

On September 12, 1987, Yeltsin writes a deeply emotional letter to Gorbachev. He refuses to accept Ligachev's reprimands and accuses him of obstructing his work and orchestrating a "coordinated smear campaign." Yeltsin critiques Ligachev's style: "His methods, especially now, are unfit (though I don't wish to dismiss his positive qualities). In general, Yegor Kuzmich lacks structure and professionalism."

Yeltsin ends the letter by offering his resignation, clearly hoping Gorbachev will intervene on his behalf.

According to Yeltsin, when Gorbachev returns from vacation he calls Yeltsin and says vaguely, "Let's discuss this later." In Gorbachev's own account, he was more specific: "Wait, Boris, don't rush. Let's deal with it after the seventieth anniversary of the October Revolution."

(Gorbachev's version seems less convincing—he may have meant it, but it's doubtful he had the time to make such personal appeals.)

KILLED WITH WORDS

October 1987: The Central Committee Plenum is meant to be a grand celebration of the seventieth anniversary of the revolution—a milestone of immense significance in the USSR.

Yeltsin feels that if Gorbachev is ignoring him, it's time to force a choice: either him or Ligachev.

Gorbachev is delivering his celebratory address, while Yeltsin agonizes over whether to take the podium or not. Gorbachev finishes; no discussion follows. Ligachev, presiding over the session, is already closing the meeting. But Gorbachev notices Yeltsin's raised hand and invites him to speak.

Yeltsin essentially repeats what he had written in his recent letter to Gorbachev, though in softer terms. He begins with criticism of Ligachev, then complains that perestroika is stalling: "At first, there was tremendous enthusiasm . . . then people's faith began to falter, and that worries us greatly." He goes on to criticize unnamed members of the Politburo for excessive flattery toward Gorbachev. Finally, he proposes stepping down from his position.

Perhaps he still hopes that Gorbachev will side with him. But it is his main adversary, Ligachev, who responds. For much longer than Yeltsin's speech, Ligachev lambastes him:

"He wanted to impose his negative agenda. You claim that the people have gained nothing real. That's irresponsible and must be condemned."

Gorbachev is equally displeased with Yeltsin's performance. He was in a festive mood, and Yeltsin's outburst spoils the day. He invites others to share their thoughts. And then it begins. Central Committee members, sensing the General Secretary's mood, line up to denounce Yeltsin.

It's worth explaining why Yeltsin's actions are seen as so egregious, considering that he hasn't said anything particularly oppositional. In the Communist Party of the Soviet Union, there is an inviolable rule, established by Stalin: the party must remain united; the minority must submit to the majority. A split in the ranks is the ultimate taboo. Public criticism within the party is unthinkable. Yeltsin broke this sacred rule, challenging party unity.

Even though such collective denunciations seem outdated, the attendees are mostly older officials who remember earlier eras. All of them rush to take part in condemning Yeltsin.

Even the liberal Yakovlev toes the expected line: "It was neither bold nor principled. It was a political mistake and a moral failure. And it's immoral to place personal ambitions above the party's interests. Yeltsin confused the country's great cause with petty grievances and ambitions."

Shevardnadze concludes: "In these circumstances, Yeltsin's speech is a betrayal."

Gorbachev is furious—so much so that he takes it out on US secretary of state George Shultz, who happens to be visiting Moscow the same day. Talks meant to finalize the date of Gorbachev's visit to the United States are derailed when Gorbachev lashes out at Shultz over minor grievances, accusing the American administration of continuing to distrust the USSR, and refuses to commit to a date for the trip. Even Gorbachev's inner circle is shocked by his outburst, failing to grasp that Shultz is merely an unwitting target for the General Secretary's pent-up anger.

A few days later, on November 7, during the Revolution Day parade, Yeltsin stands on the Mausoleum tribune alongside the other Politburo members, as if nothing had happened.

But then comes the mysterious day of November 9. According to Yeltsin's memoir, he falls gravely ill. He writes that he suffers a heart attack and is taken to the hospital.

Gorbachev has a different version. He later will claim that on November 9 he was informed that Yeltsin was found in his office, bloodied, as if he had attempted to stage a suicide with scissors.

Regardless of the circumstances, Gorbachev decides it's time to dismiss the head of Moscow. Yeltsin maintains that he never considered suicide, though he admits to being in a state of deep depression, plagued by excruciating headaches: "I was ready to climb the walls, barely holding back screams. It was pure torment. Often, I felt I was on the verge of breaking."

On November 11, Yeltsin is still in the hospital when Gorbachev calls him, insisting he attend a meeting of the Moscow city party committee, where he will be officially removed from his position. Gorbachev knows Yeltsin is unwell, but he doesn't believe it—he suspects Yeltsin is faking.

"I can't come; I'm bedridden; the doctors won't even let me get up," Yeltsin protests.

"That's all right," Gorbachev replies cheerfully. "The doctors will help."

It's a moment Yeltsin will never forgive: "No matter how much Gorbachev disliked me, what he did was inhuman, immoral. I never expected this from him. Why was he in such a rush? Did he think I'd change my mind? Or did he believe that in my weakened state, I'd be easier to crush? Did he want to finish me off physically? Such cruelty is impossible to comprehend."

Yeltsin, heavily medicated, is taken to the city party committee meeting. There, in front of the Politburo, his former subordinates—one after another—publicly disown him, denouncing him as an awful person and a terrible leader.

Ironically, as Moscow's chief, Yeltsin often dismissed his own subordinates in a similar fashion, subjecting them to grueling hours of public rebukes. But now, drugged and exhausted, he remains silent. "How else can you describe it when a person is killed with words? It truly felt like a real execution . . . ," he will write later, dramatically recounting the meeting in his memoir.

THE FAKE SPEECH

In February, after Yeltsin is removed from the Politburo, Gorbachev calls him in the hospital and offers him the position of minister of construction. But he ends the conversation with a warning: "Keep in mind, I won't let you back into politics!"

"I agreed because, at that moment, I didn't care about anything," Yeltsin would later recall. "What was left in my chest where my heart used to be? Nothing but ashes. Everything inside and out was burned to the ground."

Yeltsin's memoir, published three years later when his career is at its peak, is filled with lofty reflections on his suffering and struggles. But in the winter of 1988, what matters more than the real Yeltsin is his mythical double. Yeltsin, the folklore hero, begins to live a life of his own, separate from reality.

Soviet newspapers report Yeltsin's dismissal in dry, bureaucratic terms, but rumors spread like wildfire. By a strange coincidence, the day after the scandalous meeting the popular youth program *Vzglyad* airs a new music video by Alla Pugacheva. The song contains the following lyrics:

Beat, beat, beat your own so that others are afraid,
So they don't stand out, so they don't push ahead.

This is Pugacheva's first appearance on television since the scandal at the Pribaltiyskaya Hotel, and the clip is, of course, her response to the controversy. But many viewers interpret the song in an entirely new context—it seems like a direct reaction to Yeltsin's dismissal.

As *Vzglyad* host Lyubimov would later recall, the next day officials at every level rushed to the TV center to investigate: How did the creators of *Vzglyad* know about Yeltsin's firing in advance? And how did Pugacheva manage to write a song about it so quickly?

No one believes it was a coincidence. The political scandal takes on a life of its own.

A group of politically active students even stages a coordinated protest: some stand with picket signs near metro stations, while others march to the public reception office of the Moscow party committee, demanding the publication of Yeltsin's October speech at the Central Committee Plenum.

No one knows what really happened to the former Moscow party secretary, so speculation runs rampant. Enter Mikhail Poltoranin, editor in chief of the *Moscow Pravda* newspaper and one of Yeltsin's close allies. Fearing he'll be fired next, Poltoranin decides to help his embattled boss—and himself—by creating a myth.

Poltoranin wasn't at the plenum and, like everyone else, doesn't know why Yeltsin was punished. But with rumors swirling, he concocts a speech Yeltsin supposedly delivered, casting him as a fearless truth teller. The speech bears no resemblance to reality; Poltoranin doesn't consult Yeltsin at all. Instead, he crafts a heroic narrative that aligns with the frustrations of ordinary citizens.

In the USSR, spin doctors don't exist because there are no public politics. Yet Poltoranin becomes, in essence, the country's first one. He taps into the public's anger about key issues—food shortages, bureaucratic privilege, the war in Afghanistan—and weaves them into a speech supposedly delivered by Yeltsin.

"Mythical Yeltsin" says, "It's hard to explain to a factory worker why, in the seventieth year of Soviet power, he has to stand in line for hours just to buy sausages with more starch than meat, while your, comrades', festive tables are full of caviar, and other delicacies."

This fictional Yeltsin calls for the withdrawal of troops from Afghanistan, accuses the bureaucracy of stalling perestroika by sinking every good intention "into the swamp of red tape," and even directly confronts the hated Politburo hard-liner: "Don't shout at me, Comrade Ligachev, and don't lecture me. No, I'm not a boy—I have principles."

But the most scandalous—and utterly fabricated—line is a jab at the unpopular First Lady: "I must ask the Politburo to spare me from the petty oversight of Raisa Maksimovna, from her near-daily calls and scoldings." Poltoranin includes this because he senses the public's dislike for Raisa. To fully connect with "the people," he had to mention her. In reality, Raisa Gorbacheva never meddled in Yeltsin's work. Poltoranin invents not only a mythical Yeltsin but also a mythical Raisa.

This fabricated speech will play a pivotal role in Soviet history. These words, never uttered by Yeltsin, transform him into a superstar, the leader of the opposition, and a beloved figure. At the same time, the supposed "revelations" about Raisa Gorbacheva, who is accused of overstepping her bounds, cement her as a public villain. These false personas will take root in millions of minds, shaping the behavior of the real Yeltsin and the real Mikhail Gorbachev and Raisa Gorbacheva—and influencing the course of events to come.

RETURN TO POLITICS

After his dismissal from the Politburo, Yeltsin describes feeling surrounded by a vacuum. Nearly all of his former friends stop speaking to him. It's a strange holdover from Stalin's era—while the USSR no longer punishes people for associating with "enemies of the people," and Yeltsin himself is far from an enemy, still holding a ministerial position, the old habit persists.

This becomes a pivotal moment in Yeltsin's life. Those who abandoned him at this point cease to exist for him, while those who stood by him or offered support become his closest allies. For instance, one of his three former bodyguards, Alexander Korzhakov, doesn't leave his side. Officially,

Yeltsin, as a minister, no longer qualifies for state protection. Yet Korzhakov continues visiting him and even loses his job in the KGB as a result.

Another key relationship begins with an interview for the magazine *Ogonyok*. When Yeltsin receives a call from the country's most popular weekly publication, he's thrilled—it's a chance to defend himself publicly. He readily agrees to the interview. However, weeks later, the journalist calls back to apologize: the editor in chief, Vitaly Korotich, showed the piece to Central Committee overseer Alexander Yakovlev, who banned its publication.

Yeltsin is disheartened, while *Ogonyok* staffers are outraged—they thought glasnost meant they could write about anything. Valentin Yumashev, then editor of the magazine's letters section, later recalls: "I felt embarrassed and ashamed for Yeltsin. We were the flagship publication of perestroika, preaching glasnost to everyone else, but we chickened out ourselves." Right there in Korotich's office, using a government phone line, Yumashev calls the State Construction Committee, asks for Yeltsin, and proposes making a documentary about him.

In the USSR, securing film stock for such a project is no small feat. Fortunately, Yumashev has connections: "At the time, the Central Studio for Documentary Films (CSDIF) really liked me—I had several projects in production simultaneously: about teenagers, underground music, the first hippies, informal youth movements. I suggested to my colleagues on one of these projects that we scrap the approved film and secretly use our limited film stock on Yeltsin. We had no idea what would happen to him—whether the party machine would grind him into dust or if he'd prevail."

The team starts filming a documentary about life after power—how Yeltsin, the truth teller, became a political pariah. One of their key ideas is to follow Yeltsin to a regular district clinic. As the mayor of Moscow, Yeltsin had access to elite Central Committee medical facilities, and even as a minister, he still enjoys privileges. But with public outrage over party officials' perks running high, Yeltsin decides to visit the nearest, most ordinary clinic instead. Yumashev and the camera crew tag along.

Later, in his memoir, Yeltsin will recount: "When the receptionist, an older woman, was recording my details—address, age, place of work—and asked about my position, I replied, 'Minister.' She nearly dropped her pen. Then she said, 'In all my years, this is the first time a living minister has registered at a district clinic.'" (It's worth noting that Yumashev would later ghostwrite this memoir for Yeltsin.)

During filming, Yeltsin grows fond of the young journalist. This friendship will shape the course of Russian history: nine years later, Yumashev becomes head of Yeltsin's presidential administration and plays a pivotal role in selecting Vladimir Putin as Yeltsin's successor.

"MOSCOW NIGHTS" IN WASHINGTON

After snapping at US secretary of state George Shultz in the aftermath of Yeltsin's rebellion, Gorbachev quickly regains his composure and sends Reagan a letter, agreeing to visit Washington in early December. The timing is opportune: the two nations have finally reached an agreement on a substantive treaty to eliminate intermediate-range and shorter-range missiles. Following two fruitless summits, both leaders are eager to show tangible progress.

In Washington, things aren't smooth sailing either. Soviet experts continue to warn against trusting Gorbachev. Robert Gates, the CIA's deputy director and a recognized Soviet specialist, submits a report to Director William Webster and Vice President George Bush, arguing that Soviet reforms are merely "breathing space" before resuming the "further increase in Soviet military power and political influence."

In December 1987, Gorbachev arrives in Washington for the first time. Everything he encounters leaves a deep impression on him, and he seems to have finally learned how to handle Reagan's quirks. When the US president rambles about aliens potentially attacking Earth and how the Strategic Defense Initiative could save humanity, Gorbachev lets it slide. He no longer bristles when Reagan repeats the Russian proverb "Trust, but verify" for the umpteenth time on camera, instead smiling and noting, "You repeat that at every meeting." And when Reagan tells a tired joke about an American and a Russian debating freedom—"In our country, anyone can criticize Reagan!" "So what? In our country, anyone can criticize Reagan too!"—Gorbachev laughs heartily, pretending to hear it for the first time.

But these moments are trivial compared to what Gorbachev considers the historic significance of his visit. He feels he is breaking through barriers and relishes the attention of the Western press and public. At home, he had felt universally adored only during his first year in power—before the anti-alcohol campaign began. In America, however, it seems like everyone genuinely loves him. A parade of American celebrities come to meet him: from Henry Kissinger and Robert De Niro to Yoko Ono and Meryl Streep. Among them is forty-one-year-old entrepreneur Donald Trump.

It is becoming increasingly clear that while Gorbachev is adored by Western intellectuals, he is far less admired at home. Chernyaev frequently laments in his diaries that the Soviet intelligentsia is petty and foolish, unable to grasp the true greatness of Gorbachev that the West so clearly sees.

There are many explanations for this, including the fact that in the West Gorbachev is always heard through a translator, which makes him sound like a refined intellectual. Russian audiences, however, hear his awkward speech firsthand, complete with mispronunciations and misplaced stresses. Gorbachev is aware of this shortcoming but refuses to correct it.

This time in Washington Gorbachev performs his signature move: stopping his motorcade mid-street to greet the public. The crowd welcomes him like a savior, and this impromptu interaction makes him an hour and a half late for his next meeting with Reagan at the White House. "I thought you'd gone home," Reagan jokes when Gorbachev finally arrives.

The defining moment for Gorbachev comes at a White House dinner, attended by stars from politics and Hollywood. As the evening winds down, American pianist Van Cliburn begins to play "Moscow Nights," one of Gorbachev's favorite songs from his youth. Overwhelmed, Gorbachev starts singing along. Raisa joins in. The rest of the Soviet delegation, taking the cue from their leader, also begins to sing. The surreal scene unfolds: a dozen Soviet guests in the White House serenading the room with a tender Russian ballad about love, accompanied by an American pianist, as the US president listens with delight.

Shortly afterward, *Time* magazine names Gorbachev Person of the Year. Not long ago, Yuri Andropov had held a similar title—but as a figurehead of impending nuclear war. Gorbachev, by contrast, is celebrated positively. "Perhaps Gorbachev's most obvious accomplishment is that he has reinvented the idea of a Soviet leader," writes *Time*. The magazine calls previous Soviet leaders "gargoyles in fur hats," while Gorbachev seems human.

Time acknowledges that the Cold War is far from over, the USSR remains a dictatorship, and many political prisoners are still behind bars, but it emphasizes the visible progress. The magazine publishes a lengthy profile titled "The Education of Mikhail Sergeyevich Gorbachev," alongside a piece about his wife: "The Rise and Rise of Raisa Gorbachev."

Back home, Gorbachev's global fame and diplomatic success don't excite everyone. Just six months earlier, he had publicly dismissed over a dozen generals to assert his authority. Now many in the military are unhappy with the Intermediate-Range Nuclear Forces Treaty. Marshal Akhromeyev will even resign as Chief of the General Staff in protest, but Gorbachev, who respects him, asks him to stay on as a military advisor.

Some fear the West will gain access to sensitive Soviet military secrets, such as the "poor conditions and weak internal discipline" within the Armed Forces. But the main concern is that the treaty undermines the strategic balance between the USSR and the United States.

A TICKET TO NEW YORK

In December 1987, Boris Grebenshchikov arrives in Moscow with one goal: to fulfill his dream of visiting America. He needs an exit visa, and the Ministry of Culture is supposed to give him the green light. In the morning, he shows up at the ministry, but they tell him the documents aren't ready yet and ask him to come back later in the day. At 5:30 p.m., he returns, only to be told to "wait."

By 6:00 p.m., the ministry is set to close, and just one minute before that, they hand him his passport. It's empty—there's no visa. He's been denied permission to travel.

At first, Boris can't believe everything has fallen apart. It seemed so real. Joanna Stingray had introduced him to American music producer Kenny Schaffer, a man who had worked with Jimi Hendrix, Bob Marley, and Alice Cooper. Schaffer had been obsessed with the idea of discovering a Russian musician, teaching them to sing in English, and turning them into an American superstar. Then Joanna came along and told him she'd found the perfect person—someone who didn't even need lessons, as he already sang in English: Boris Grebenshchikov.

Schaffer flew to the USSR, met Boris, and decided he was "the one." He secured permission for Grebenshchikov to perform in the United States, even buying him a plane ticket to New York. All that remained was to visit the Ministry of Culture and pick up the passport. That's where it all fell apart.

Crushed and defeated, Boris boards a train back to Leningrad. Once home, he heads straight to Viktor Tsoi's place, where the two drink themselves into oblivion.

Meanwhile, in Moscow, some of Boris's fans are scrambling to save the situation. Viktor Khrolenko, an up-and-coming Soviet-American entrepreneur, remembers that he has a special gift in his suitcase. It's from Jacqueline Kennedy, intended for Anatoly Dobrynin, the former Soviet ambassador to the United States and now the Central Committee secretary for international affairs. Khrolenko heads to Staraya Square to deliver the gift. The mention of Jacqueline Kennedy's name opens every door. During his conversation with Dobrynin, Khrolenko mentions that a young musician, Boris Grebenshchikov, has been denied permission to travel to the United States. Dobrynin, who could override the Ministry of Culture with a single phone call, takes note.

A few hours later, Grebenshchikov's mother starts calling all his friends. "Boris, don't unpack your suitcase! You need to get back to Moscow immediately!" she yells. "Moscow? What for? It's over," mutters a hungover Boris. "Khrolenko called," his mother patiently explains. "You're booked on the first Sunday flight from Sheremetyevo to New York."

After spending a few days in New York, Boris flies to Los Angeles, where Joanna meets him.

There, Boris has an experience reminiscent of Vladimir Vysotsky's visit to West Berlin years earlier. He steps into a supermarket and is utterly overwhelmed. Wandering among rows of fresh fruits and vegetables, he freezes, unable to choose between twelve types of apples. The sheer variety of coffee leaves him in a state of shock. "I'd never seen him so disoriented," Joanna Stingray later recalls.

Things get even more surreal when he goes to an eye doctor. Yes, there's medicine in the USSR, but Boris never trusted the system and didn't want to waste time booking appointments. In the United States, he's promptly prescribed glasses. "So this is what the world really looks like!" he exclaims, marveling at the clarity.

Boris signs a contract, stays in America, and begins working on a new album. For the first time, he feels like he's exactly where he's meant to be.

PIRATES AND PATRIOTS

Viktor Tsoi rings in the New Year of 1988 in Kazakhstan, having just wrapped filming for *Needle*. He is full of plans—Kino has recently finished recording their new album, *Blood Type*, and he's thrilled with it. He wants Joanna's help to release it in America, delaying its Soviet release until later.

While walking through Almaty, Tsoi stops at a kiosk and suddenly notices something shocking: the new Kino album is on sale. It's prominently displayed with a sign reading: "Bestseller." Confused, Tsoi can't figure out how this could have happened—he hasn't authorized its release.

"It's total piracy. We finished recording the album, and literally the next day I flew to Almaty. I walked around the city and saw it at the kiosks: *Kino, 1988, Blood Type*," he says, bewildered, in an interview. "Then I flew back to Leningrad—and it's at every corner, in every stall. . . ."

It turns out that the owner of the recording studio where Kino made the album was so impressed with the material that he decided not to wait. He gave the cassette to some acquaintances in retail. Moreover, he believed he was acting as a patriot—the audience in the Soviet Union, he thought, deserved to hear Tsoi's new songs before anyone in America.

This is the second time something like this has happened to Tsoi. In 1987, after the release of *Red Wave*, the Soviet state record label Melodiya produced a Kino record on orders from above, without asking the band's permission. Now it's happening again: Tsoi's songs are being listened to across the country, topping all unofficial charts. But Tsoi receives no money from it—all the profits go to pirates or the state, neither of which has any intention of sharing.

Despite this, Tsoi begins a new chapter in his life. He quits his job at the boiler room and moves to Moscow. Yet even now, he doesn't have his own apartment—he lives with Natasha's relatives.

He tours to earn a living, but he has to perform solo. Guitarist Yuri Kasparyan has gone to California with Joanna, and Tsoi is waiting for his return to resume full concerts with Kino.

In March 1988, *Assa* is released in theaters, seemingly solidifying Tsoi's status as a star. But things aren't so simple. While Grebenshchikov is now fully recognized and legitimate, Tsoi remains in a gray zone. He's occasionally mentioned in the press—one article from the spring of 1988 dubs him the "Don Quixote of the Boiler Room."

After solo concerts, Tsoi often agrees to answer audience questions. He openly discusses his conflict with the record label and frequently positions himself in opposition to traditional Soviet culture. "Their poetic language, their imagery, their symbols—it all sounds fake now. And the fact that they keep singing this stuff today, without noticing the falsehood, creates mistrust and rejection," he says after a performance in Tallinn. "I don't understand how anyone can listen to songs about how wonderful everything is here—about love, friendship, and so on. Few believe it. And they're right not to. . . . You see, we've been lied to about all of it."

After one concert, someone asks him, "Viktor, do you believe in perestroika?"

"For now, yes," he replies. "Things are better now than they were before. But I'm not sure it'll last."

TROUBLED HISTORY

In October 1987, Gorbachev forces Politburo member Heydar Aliyev into retirement. A former leader of Azerbaijan, Aliyev had maintained full control over the republic even after moving to Moscow. At just sixty-four, he is younger than Ligachev, but for Gorbachev, he is an old rival—once a powerful favorite of Andropov. The new General Secretary continues his purge of the political elite.

Gorbachev has no intention of stopping there—he needs to remove all the old leaders of Azerbaijan and Armenia and replace them with loyal figures who will implement perestroika. But a radical shake-up requires justification— proof that the previous leadership has failed. Therefore, the authorities in Moscow watch from the sidelines and do not intervene.

In December 1987, a group of Karabakh Armenians submits a petition to the Central Committee, requesting that Nagorno-Karabakh be transferred to Armenia. The appeal gathers over seventy thousand signatures. The logic aligns with perestroika—if activists from the nationalist Pamyat society can march through Red Square and meet with Moscow's First Secretary, then Armenians, too, have the right to voice their demands. However, Nagorno-Karabakh is not ethnically homogenous—about a quarter of its population is Azerbaijani.

The history of the peoples of the South Caucasus is ancient and tangled. Nagorno-Karabakh, known until the nineteenth century as the Karabakh Khanate, was once part of the Iranian Empire before being conquered by the Russian Empire. After the formation of the USSR, it became the Nagorno-Karabakh Autonomous Region within the Azerbaijani SSR. While Armenians make up roughly three-quarters of the population, both Armenians and Azerbaijanis claim the land as their own.

Events escalate rapidly. On February 13, 1988, a rally takes place in Stepanakert, the capital of Nagorno-Karabakh. Its organizers distribute banners reading: "Lenin—Party—Gorbachev" to give the police no pretext to intervene.

For many in Azerbaijan, this comes as a shock. But by February 19, 1988, a countermarch is organized in Baku, with demonstrators carrying banners declaring that Karabakh must remain part of Azerbaijan.

Armenian and Azerbaijani media start publishing more articles on the once-taboo topic. Prominent cultural figures weigh in, and soon the issue is being debated everywhere. Tensions rise.

In Yerevan, Armenia's capital, the Karabakh Committee is formed— effectively the first public opposition organization in the USSR. Members of the committee organize an enormous, multiday rally in Yerevan's main square—by the end of the month, the number of participants reaches 1 million.

On February 20, something occurs that is unimaginable within Soviet political logic. Nagorno-Karabakh's parliament makes an official appeal to the parliaments of Azerbaijan and Armenia, requesting that the territory be transferred from one Soviet republic to another. Never before in Soviet history has an official body openly defied the system. Yet here, a regional council challenges it, demanding a change to the borders of Soviet republics. Azerbaijani legislators leave the hall in protest—their votes wouldn't change anything anyway.

On February 22, the first armed clash takes place, and two Azerbaijanis are killed. The Soviet authorities try to suppress the information to prevent further escalation.

Meanwhile, a flow of Azerbaijani refugees begins streaming from Armenia into Azerbaijan. They are settled in two villages near Sumgait, a city north of Baku.

THE POGROM IN A SOVIET CITY

Sumgait is far from being a prosperous Soviet city. It is populated mainly by workers crammed into overcrowded dormitories. The food supply is poor, hospitals and schools are inadequate, and the city's ecology is disastrous— Sumgait is home to several chemical plants. Child mortality is so high that the city even has a dedicated children's cemetery. The average age of residents is just twenty-five, and one in five people in Sumgait has a criminal record.

On February 26, 1988, a crowd gathers in Lenin Square in Sumgait. Refugees from Armenia are telling horrific stories about how members of their family were killed. One of them claims Azerbaijani women in Armenia had their breasts cut off (all of it fiction).

That same day, February 26, on Yerevan's main square, a million people gathered. Among them is Levon Ter-Petrosyan, a forty-three-year-old doctor of sciences and Middle East scholar. He stands in the crowd, chanting with everyone else, "Karabakh! Karabakh!" At the rally, Armenian writers who had traveled to Moscow and met with Gorbachev take the stage: "We've found some understanding in Moscow. Don't interfere right now; they're taking the matter seriously. Please, go home; let's see how the events unfold." This is how Ter-Petrosyan recalls their words. After this, the rally ends, and the protesters disperse.

On the same day, television broadcasts a statement from the USSR's Chief Military Prosecutor. For the first time, he comments on the recent clashes. In the USSR, such things are usually hidden, but glasnost has arrived, and Gorbachev is calling for openness. Or perhaps the prosecutor is simply trying to calm the million-strong crowd in Yerevan. He says that blood has been spilled in Nagorno-Karabakh, but there are no Armenian victims—only two Azerbaijanis have been killed.

This news immediately reaches Azerbaijan. Everyone in the USSR knows: if the authorities admit to *two dead*, it likely means there are dozens, if not hundreds.

On February 28, around five thousand people gather in Sumgait's main square. Every speech ends with the chant "Death to Armenians!" The crowd includes refugees, criminals, and unidentified agitators. "The smell of weed in the square was just like it is now in New York's Washington Square," journalist Dmitry Muratov, a future Nobel laureate, would later recall.

A local Communist Party leader climbs onto the podium. He's visibly overwhelmed but tries to calm the crowd, promising that Nagorno-Karabakh will *definitely* remain part of Azerbaijan. Someone hands him an Azerbaijani flag, and he ends up leading a march through the city. The tail end of the column quickly breaks up into small groups—and in the center of Sumgait, the pogrom begins. Terrifying, insane.

Such pogroms had happened before in the Caucasus—several times throughout the twentieth century. The city of Shusha in Nagorno-Karabakh, for example, had been burned to the ground two times.[*]

The most famous pogrom in Russian history happened in 1903 in Kishinev, now Moldova. Back then, Russians killed Jews. Here, Azerbaijanis are killing Armenians, but the descriptions are eerily identical. People break into their neighbors' homes, drag them into the streets, beat them savagely—many to death—rape women, and set bodies on fire. One chilling detail connects the pogroms of the Russian Empire in 1903 with those in the USSR in 1988: the police do not intervene.

It seems as though Gorbachev has decided to give local leaders the chance to prove their own incompetence—so that he can later dismiss them. No one could have foreseen where this would lead.

VICTIMS AND CONSEQUENCES

According to official data from the USSR Prosecutor General's Office, twenty-six Armenians and six Azerbaijanis were killed that day, with more than a hundred people severely injured. But rumors immediately begin to spread that the actual number of deaths is well over a hundred. Journalist Dmitry Muratov would later recall seeing an overflowing morgue at a nearby military base.

World chess champion Garry Kasparov, an Armenian from Baku, is also in shock over what has happened. He goes to speak with Yevgeny Primakov, one of Gorbachev's advisors.

"A terrible tragedy—so many people have died, I know; people have told me," Kasparov begins. Primakov cuts him off: "Twenty-six people died."

Kasparov insists: "What do you mean, twenty-six? For God's sake, I'm from there; I know—there were far more victims."

"Are you a party member?" Primakov asks. "How can you not believe *Pravda*? It says twenty-six people died."

During the pogrom, the deputy head of the USSR KGB, Filipp Bobkov, is already in Baku—and soon arrives in Sumgait. Later this fact fuels

---

[*] The third time would come in 1992.

contradictory rumors: Was the KGB secretly the organizer of the unrest? However, no convincing evidence emerges that the pogrom was deliberately orchestrated from Moscow. On February 29, 1988, the Politburo discusses what happened. The USSR leadership is even more confused than they were after the Chernobyl explosion.

Defense Minister Dmitry Yazov demands the imposition of martial law. Gorbachev hesitates: "We need to consider that people don't yet know what happened in Sumgait. Otherwise, this could snowball."

A mass exodus of Armenians begins from other Azerbaijani cities as well, including Baku, which has the largest Armenian community in Azerbaijan.

As a result of the pogrom, Gorbachev, unsurprisingly, dismisses the previous leaders of both republics—Armenia and Azerbaijan—and replaces them with longtime acquaintances. For example, Abdurrahman Vezirov, the former head of the Azerbaijani Komsomol and currently the Soviet ambassador to Pakistan, is appointed as the new leader of Azerbaijan. His appointment is met with enthusiasm by the family of Baku native Garry Kasparov—the world chess champion's uncle is married to the new First Secretary's sister. However, not everyone in the republic shares this joy—Vezirov has a poor command of the Azerbaijani language.

6

FULL STOP

My grandmother had an incredibly hard life. She was born the same year as Gorbachev and Yeltsin, in a small village. She was ten years old when the war began. Her family had six children. When her father went off to the front, her mother wept: "How will I feed them all?" "Why feed us? We can get full all by ourselves," one of the little ones said. Two of them died during the war—from hunger or typhus.

Father, of course, never came back—he was killed in the very first month.

At twelve, my grandmother left home for the district center to study, work, and send money to her mother. "When I finished school, my waist was so small I could easily wrap my palms around it and make them meet," she used to say.

She never joined the Communist Party, because she was sharp-tongued and irreverent toward authority. Once, on a train, a fellow passenger—a Komsomol district secretary, a big shot at the time—tried to flirt with her. But she was principled and proud and told him immediately that she wasn't interested. He persisted, and she warned him that if he didn't leave her alone, he'd regret it. "What can you possibly do to me?" he laughed. "Anything," my future grandmother replied, and, with a swift motion, snatched his cap off his head and threw it out the train window.

Clothing was incredibly expensive back then, and losing a cap was a major misfortune. The young man quickly realized she was completely crazy and moved to the next compartment. She was, of course, taking a huge risk—the young Komsomol official could have easily gotten her fired or even caused her far more serious problems.

My grandmother was very proud of this story and recounted it with laughter— just as she did other tales of boldly fending off anyone who dared to approach her romantically. Her alcoholic husband, my grandfather, who beat her for years and died of cirrhosis of the liver, was likely the only man in her life.

She was an independent, self-made woman. But she had a hypertrophied sense of honor and pride. She always spoke the truth, never asked anyone for anything—"because it's shameful"—and often said she'd happily "hang all the communists by their feet." Later, she just as passionately came to despise the democrats.

In her old age, the idea of imaginary mass executions of government leaders who didn't care about the people became her favorite topic. She could vividly and at length describe how she'd blow up the Kremlin, shoot Gorbachev, and tear the hair out of "his whore Raisa."

Like any pensioner, she watched television constantly—and hated almost everyone on it. She believed Alla Pugacheva—"that slut Pugachikha"—ought to be tarred and feathered. And as for the "whores who betrayed the motherland and fled to the West," like Rostropovich and Vishnevskaya, they should never be allowed back into the country—"let them starve to death."

To me, to all our relatives, friends, and even strangers, she was always a kind, gentle, and loving person—yet somehow she always spoke only of pride and hatred.

"I CANNOT COMPROMISE MY PRINCIPLES"

On March 13, 1988, the newspaper *Soviet Russia* publishes a letter written by Nina Andreeva, a chemistry lecturer from the Leningrad Technological Institute: "I Cannot Compromise My Principles." Soviet newspapers often publish readers' letters, but this one becomes, perhaps, the most legendary publication in the entire history of Soviet media.

The next day, Yegor Ligachev, the Second Secretary of the CPSU Central Committee, gathers the entire party leadership. The situation is unprecedented: Gorbachev is absent, having left on an official visit to Yugoslavia. Even Alexander Yakovlev, also responsible for ideology, is not in Moscow—he's in Mongolia. Ligachev proudly shows everyone Andreeva's text, praises it, and calls for adherence to her line in future work. The state news agency, TASS, releases a "clarification," stating that Andreeva's letter should and must be reprinted in regional publications.

So what does the chemistry lecturer write about? Today her text could be summarized as "Make the Soviet Union Great Again."

Andreeva begins with history: she is vehemently opposed to the criticism of Stalin and Soviet achievements. She wants to take pride in Soviet history, not be ashamed of it: "The formula of the 'cult of personality' is being forcibly applied to industrialization, collectivization, and the cultural revolution—processes that elevated our country to the ranks of the world's great powers. All of this is being questioned. It has reached the point where 'Stalinists' (and anyone can be labeled as such, if desired) are being forced to repent. . . ." Repentance, for Andreeva, is completely unacceptable.

Curiously, she enlists Winston Churchill as an ally, claiming he once wrote about Stalin: "He inherited Russia with a wooden plow and left it armed with nuclear weapons." Churchill, of course, never wrote any such thing, but from this moment, the phrase becomes a favorite mantra among "Russian patriots." Following Andreeva's lead, they will repeatedly attribute the quote to Churchill.

Finally, Andreeva observes that Soviet society is divided: on one side are the liberals; on the other, the "defenders of tradition." Andreeva seems reluctant to formally align herself with either camp, but she clearly sympathizes with the second group—and she openly despises the first.

Andreeva accuses liberals of prioritizing the "self-worth of the individual" over proletarian collectivism. Here's how she mocks their humanism: "At a time when millions of people on our planet are dying from hunger, epidemics, and the military adventures of imperialism, they are demanding the development of a 'legal code for the protection of animal rights.'"

According to Andreeva, it is the liberals who falsify history: "They try to convince us that the country's past consists of nothing but mistakes and crimes, while remaining silent about its greatest achievements, both past and present."

Describing the second camp, she mentions the people who idealize patriarchal Russia—in other words, nationalists (though Andreeva avoids using that word): "The 'traditionalists' have undeniable merits in exposing corruption, in fairly addressing environmental issues, fighting alcoholism, protecting historical monuments, and countering the dominance of mass culture, which they rightly view as consumerist psychosis," she writes. (This description clearly alludes to the Pamyat society.)

It is obvious that this text is a continuation of an old ideological battle: liberals versus the alliance of nationalists and communists. However, while this struggle had previously been sensed only by a few within the party apparatus, now it is being written about in a national newspaper.

The liberal public is horrified. Even the tone and subtext of official reports make it clear that a tectonic shift has occurred. Yesterday's course toward democratization is over. Vitaly Korotich will later recall that, after reading Andreeva's letter, "I realized they would arrest me soon and started packing my things."

And while Korotich's fears may still be premature, changes in television happen immediately. The youth program *Vzglyad*, which Ligachev disapproved of, is shut down. One of its hosts, twenty-five-year-old Sasha Lyubimov, realizes it's time to return to his previous job at Soviet international broadcasting in the Danish language. He even feels a sense of relief—the job pays much better and is far less stressful. No pressure from the authorities, no risks.

Then Gorbachev returns to Moscow. On March 23, a congress of collective farm workers takes place in the Kremlin. During a break between sessions, members of the Politburo are drinking tea in the presidium room. One of them, sixty-two-year-old Vitaly Vorotnikov, starts berating *Ogonyok*, saying, "Something has to be done about the press." Ligachev chimes in: "The press has started biting back. . . . Look at that article in *Soviet Russia*. An excellent article. That's our party line."

The other Politburo members begin nodding in agreement: "Yes! A real, proper article. That's exactly what we need. Things have gotten completely out of hand. . . ." Everyone seems to be fed up with "fake news media."

"I skimmed it briefly before leaving for Yugoslavia," Gorbachev begins. "I read it more carefully after I came back—"

Gorbachev is interrupted: "It's a solid article. . . ."

"Well, I have a different opinion . . . ," Gorbachev suddenly declares.

"*What on earth?!*" Vorotnikov blurts out, unable to hide his surprise. The room freezes. A silent scene.

"What do you mean, 'What on earth?'" Gorbachev sweeps his gaze over his stunned colleagues. "I smell a split here. The article is against perestroika. . . . I have never objected to anyone expressing their views—whatever they may be—in the press, in letters, in articles. But I've learned that this article has been turned into a directive. Party organizations are already discussing it as an official guideline. Counterarguments to this article have been banned from publication. . . . That's a whole other matter. I don't cling to my seat. But while I'm here, while I hold this chair, I will defend the idea of perestroika."

Gorbachev clearly understands that the overwhelming majority of the Politburo leans conservative. He instructs his ally Yakovlev to prepare a report explaining why "I Cannot Compromise My Principles" is a harmful and hostile text.

The Politburo meets the next day. Gorbachev opens by stating that he does not believe Andreeva wrote the text herself—surely, she must have powerful backers. Surprisingly, the Stalinists, who hold an overwhelming majority, don't put up a fight. On the contrary, they fall over themselves to distance themselves from their views. The fear of the boss outweighs everything else.

Gorbachev gives the floor to Ligachev. Ligachev admits that the editor of *Soviet Russia* came to him, showed him the letter, and yes, he liked it: "But that's all. I had no further involvement." Ligachev assures everyone that the Politburo remains united—"not superficially, but truly united." The only thing he allows himself is a small complaint about the emboldened press, saying they "blacken Soviet history, advocate for a multiparty system, and anyway, that word 'Stalinism' was planted on us by the West."

Vitaly Vorotnikov, who blurted out, "*What on earth?!*" the day before, stammers out his apologies as best he can.

Then Yakovlev takes the floor. Drawing on his extensive party experience, he launches into a full-blown attack on Nina Andreeva from Leninist positions: "The entire meaning of the article—in spirit, in tone, in every one of its points—is against Gorbachev. This is a manifesto of anti-perestroika." Yakovlev's speech drags on until evening.

Everyone agrees, though some take the opportunity to gripe about journalists. Defense Minister Dmitry Yazov, for instance, cannot understand why newspapers glorify the late singer Vladimir Vysotsky instead of soldiers fighting in Afghanistan: "Vysotsky . . . What heroic feat did he accomplish?"

In the end, the Politburo unanimously—as always—decides to publicly condemn Andreeva's article and to publish a scathing response in *Pravda*. Ryzhkov hints that Ligachev should be removed from overseeing ideology. But Gorbachev feels he's already won and sees no reason to crush the Second Secretary.

However, mid-level executives are still unsure who has truly won. The controversial youth program *Vzglyad*, originally conceived by Yakovlev, is brought back on air—but with a new set of more moderate hosts to avoid provoking Ligachev.

HAMLET GORBACHEV

At the beginning of 1988, as war is on the verge of breaking out between two Soviet republics—Armenia and Azerbaijan—one man stands apart, deliberately ignoring the rising tide of mutual hatred. That man is Sergei Parajanov, the unrecognized genius of Soviet cinema. An Armenian, Parajanov is in Baku, filming in Azerbaijani, adapting an old Turkic folk tale, *Aşıq Qərib*. His indifference to politics frustrates many, but he brushes off criticism with his trademark phrase: "I will take revenge on their hatred with my love."

Unexpectedly, an outcast banned from living in Moscow, Kyiv, and Yerevan finds himself famous. His new film, *Ashik Kerib*, is invited to the Rotterdam Film Festival, and the Soviet authorities grant him permission to travel abroad. He is sixty-four years old, and this is his first trip outside the USSR. Due to bad weather, he is stranded in Tbilisi for three days, unable to fly out. But he refuses to leave the airport, fearing he might miss his flight. Friends bring him food and administer his insulin injections right there—he developed diabetes while in prison.

The airport is overcrowded, and Parajanov has brought several enormous bags filled with gifts: Kurdish skirts, bundles of Oriental shawls, huge sacks packed with Georgian tea. "Who are you planning to give all this to?" he is asked upon arrival. "I'll find someone. Worst case, I'll just throw it into the crowd," he replies seriously.

In Rotterdam, he suddenly feels like a star. Journalists line up to interview him. To one of them, he claims he spent fifteen years in the Gulag. "Sergei, isn't six years enough for you? Where did you get that number?" asks his friend documentary filmmaker Vasily Katanyan. "From wherever I needed to!" Parajanov grumbles.

A new life begins. Offers to direct come from Italy, Germany, and the United States—Parajanov is in high demand everywhere. In November 1988, he is nominated for the European Film Academy Award for "Best Director"— but loses to Wim Wenders, who wins the award for his film *Wings of Desire* (*Der Himmel über Berlin*).

Naturally, Parajanov is often asked about perestroika. "I welcome it, if only because I got to see Gorbachev. Look at him closely—he's the perfect actor to play Hamlet. And instead of Elsinore, they could use the Kremlin as the set!" he says in an interview with the French newspaper *Libération*.

TWO ENVOYS FROM MOSCOW

In the month following the Sumgait pogrom, the situation in both Armenia and Azerbaijan escalates further. Gorbachev is outraged. In his view, all of this is the work of enemies of perestroika.

He believes he is moving the country along the path of reform while local nationalists are destroying his efforts. His aide Anatoly Chernyaev will later write in his diary that only two topics absolutely drive Gorbachev into a rage: Nagorno-Karabakh and Yeltsin.

The Politburo debates what to do about the Armenian opposition. Proposals include introducing additional censorship in Armenia, disconnecting phone lines between Armenia and other countries, banning foreign journalists from visiting the region, and even arresting activists from the Karabakh Committee.

However, Gorbachev worries that arrests could turn them into heroes. At the same time, he talks about the need for greater openness and the involvement of "healthy forces" in public discussions—a well-worn Soviet cliché. In the USSR, "healthy forces" always refers to puppet organizations acting under the strict control of the Kremlin and the KGB.

Meanwhile, the popularity of the Karabakh Committee grows beyond Armenia's borders. Moscow's perestroika-era media, such as *Ogonyok* magazine, though late to the story, actively cover the events in Sumgait. The sympathies of the Moscow intelligentsia clearly lean toward the Armenians. On March 21, Andrei Sakharov writes a letter in support of the demands of the Armenians of Nagorno-Karabakh.

Elena Bonner and Andrei Sakharov take the news from the region very much to heart. Friends from Armenia send them thirty death certificates of victims from the Sumgait pogrom. Bonner binds them into a small booklet, which she carries with her everywhere.

Elena Bonner has a close personal connection to Armenia: her stepfather, Gevork Alikhanyan, was the first leader of the republic after Soviet power was established. In 1938, he was executed.

In March 1988, Sakharov (without Bonner) is invited to a meeting between Moscow's intelligentsia and Gorbachev. When the discussion turns to Karabakh, Gorbachev declares that the authorities "were three hours late." Sakharov jumps up, rushes to the presidium table, and, waving the death certificates from Sumgait, shouts, *"You weren't three hours late—you were three days late! You must admit it!"*

Gorbachev sends two Politburo members—two sworn ideological rivals—to introduce new First Secretaries to Azerbaijan and Armenia. Yegor Ligachev heads to Baku, while Alexander Yakovlev goes to Yerevan.

The fact that Gorbachev, in a critical moment, cannot choose between the conservative Ligachev and the liberal Yakovlev is a defining trait of his leadership. In the Politburo, they still share the powerful position of chief ideologist—despite their recent clash over Nina Andreeva. Entrusting the two of them to handle the Caucasus problem together makes the whole situation even more absurd.

Ligachev is a staunch defender of the status quo, a traditionalist. His natural instinct is to resist any kind of change. So, in Baku, he declares that there will be no changes and that the borders of the Soviet republics will remain exactly as they are.

Yakovlev is a herald of change. He doesn't believe the Soviet system is optimal and is convinced that reforms are necessary and people's demands must be heard. In Yerevan, he insists that only careful, gradual progress can lead to the desired outcome. He persuades the Armenian leadership to abandon their demands for the immediate transfer of Nagorno-Karabakh but promises that changes may be possible in the future. Yakovlev even addresses a rally in the Armenian capital.

In other words, both envoys from Moscow say what they believe is right and what their audiences in Baku and Yerevan want to hear. Yet their messages directly contradict each other. Ligachev and Yakovlev, clearly distrustful of each other, make no effort to coordinate their actions—they don't even communicate, reporting solely to Gorbachev.

After the negotiations, Yakovlev contacts Gorbachev to report on his successes. But as soon as Yakovlev hangs up, the phone rings again. *"You lied to us! We don't believe you!"* shouts one of the Armenian activists. The media has just reported on Ligachev's promises in Baku—that Nagorno-Karabakh will forever remain part of Azerbaijan.

Changes occur within the leadership of the Karabakh Committee. Previously, the key figures were natives of Nagorno-Karabakh itself. Now a pan-Armenian Karabakh Committee emerges, led by prominent intellectuals from Yerevan.

The new leader of the committee is forty-three-year-old Levon Ter-Petrosyan, a Middle Eastern studies scholar specializing in ancient Semitic languages. His father was one of the founders of the Syrian Communist Party and moved to the USSR with his family in the 1940s. Ter-Petrosyan is not a radical. However, he is neither a member of the Communist Party nor reverent when it comes to speaking about the "indestructible Soviet Union."

Thus, unexpectedly, Armenia becomes the first Soviet republic where a powerful opposition movement arises. However, at this stage, they cannot yet imagine fighting for independence—the idea simply doesn't cross their minds.

CROOKS AND THIEVES

In an effort to emulate Lenin, Gorbachev finally sets out to reform the Soviet economy using the same model that had worked in the USSR during the 1920s. Back then, in Lenin's final years, the government introduced the so-called New Economic Policy (NEP), which, despite its commitment to communism, allowed small-scale private businesses—cooperatives—to operate legally. Stalin eventually put an end to this policy, but Gorbachev now plans to revive it, permitting small-scale private entrepreneurship. However, the overall economy is still meant to remain the same—centrally planned and fully controlled by the state.

On May 26, 1988, the Supreme Soviet passes what is perhaps the most consequential law of perestroika—the Law on Cooperatives.

Everything goes wrong almost immediately, perhaps due to deeply ingrained psychology. For the previous sixty-five years, the Soviet state had taught that any form of entrepreneurship was a crime. The criminal code even contained an article for *speculation*—the act of making a profit. If the Soviet Union had a shadow economy before this law, now a significant part of the economy simply slips further into the shadows.

All state enterprises are required to trade at government-set prices. A state-owned factory producing underwear, for example, is obliged to sell its goods for one ruble per pair. But now, the factory director can open his own cooperative and sell all the factory's underwear to it. The cooperative might paint a small flower on the underwear—or not—and then sell it in a cooperative shop for ten rubles. People will still buy them, because there are no other options available. The state gets its one ruble, while the other nine go straight into the factory director's pocket—now a proud *cooperator*.

Worse still, not all cooperatives are created equal. Cooperatives founded by KGB officials could have virtually unlimited privileges, including the right to trade in precious metals. Young members of the Komsomol also establish their own cooperatives, enjoying privileges like easy access to office space and fast-track permits. Many of them trade in computers—a highly lucrative business since the USSR produces none of its own. This is how many future oligarchs begin their business careers.*

Ordinary Soviet citizens, however, face far greater obstacles: constant inspections, struggles to secure premises, the challenge of installing a phone line, and the need to convince the police they aren't breaking any laws.

Still, the old belief held by both the authorities and society—that all entrepreneurs are crooks—remains firmly in place. The only difference now is that communist morality no longer forbids such practices, and the regulatory agencies can be *persuaded*.

The Law on Cooperatives marks the beginning of a uniquely Soviet form of capitalist ideology: its adherents believe that all business is inherently criminal and there's nothing wrong with that—it's simply how life works, as long as you don't get caught. In this system of values, nothing is taboo; corruption isn't a vice but a natural law. This cynical world view would go on to define the future ideology of Putin's capitalist Russia.

THE TRUTH IN WHISKEY

In New York, Boris Grebenshchikov and his producer Kenny Schaffer meet with Walter Yetnikoff, the head of CBS Records. At the time, Yetnikoff is one of the most powerful figures in the American music industry, having led the label since 1975 and been instrumental in the success of artists like Michael Jackson, Barbra Streisand, and Billy Joel.

One famous story highlights Yetnikoff's influence: in 1983, when MTV refused to air the "Billie Jean" music video, claiming that music by Black artists didn't fit the channel's rock-oriented concept, Yetnikoff threatened

---

* Mikhail Khodorkovsky, Mikhail Fridman, and other well-known Russian entrepreneurs of the 1990s began their careers by trading computers.

to pull all CBS artists from the network. MTV relented, and the incident revolutionized pop music.

A year later, at the 1984 Grammy Awards, Michael Jackson invited Yetnikoff onstage to share his spotlight, calling him "the best record company president in the world."

Now this legendary figure is sitting across from Grebenshchikov. Yetnikoff has a personal reason to show interest in the first Soviet artist to make it to the United States: his parents were emigrants from Odessa, though Yetnikoff himself was born in New York. However, as BG would later recall, their initial conversation is about neither Russian roots nor music. Instead, Yetnikoff offers BG a glass of whiskey—and Boris casually remarks that Glenmorangie, the label head's choice, is not as good as Macallan.

"You know your whiskey?" Yetnikoff responds, astonished. According to BG, this offhand comment seals the deal. Yetnikoff turns to producer Kenny Schaffer and says, "Well, bring me the contract." Schaffer asks if Yetnikoff wants to hear any tracks first or learn more about the Russian musician's background. Yetnikoff allegedly replies, "A man who knows his whiskey is good enough for me."

Grebenshchikov later fulfills a dream by meeting his idol, David Bowie. Joanna jokingly asks someone to pinch her when she sees them together. However, by then, BG has another fascination: the Eurythmics. He's particularly eager to work with their singer and songwriter David Stewart. Armed with a CBS Records contract and Yetnikoff's blessing, BG can afford to indulge his ambitions. A quick phone call, and Stewart agrees to produce the album of this previously unknown Russian musician. The album will be titled *Radio Silence.*

"WE LOST AFGHANISTAN"

By April 1988, the Soviet Union is finally on the verge of withdrawing troops from Afghanistan. Several rounds of negotiations take place in Geneva, Switzerland. Formally, the talks are between Afghanistan and Pakistan, with the USSR and the United States as mere observers. But it's clear to everyone that the real agreement is between the two superpowers—after all, this is their proxy war. The Soviet Union agrees to withdraw its troops, and the Americans agree to stop providing military aid to the mujahideen.

The final agreement in Geneva is set to be signed on April 14. Before that, Gorbachev decides to meet personally with Afghan president Najibullah, who had replaced Karmal, to maintain diplomatic propriety.

In Politburo meetings, while discussing the ongoing war, Gorbachev repeatedly mutters his mantra: "We can't just flee Afghanistan." But in his view, the withdrawal of Soviet troops is not a shameful retreat; it is the honorable conclusion of a senseless military adventure. He often emphasizes that the Geneva agreements provide the Soviet Union with legal justification for its actions—unlike the Americans, who had no such legal cover when they withdrew from Vietnam.

Initially, the Afghan leader takes the news stoically, assuring Gorbachev that he can hold on to power even without Soviet troops. But then he repeatedly changes his position. He begs Gorbachev not to take away his "operational mastermind"—Moscow political advisor Viktor Polyanichko—and proposes unrealistic projects, like having the USSR, India, and Afghanistan jointly declare war on Pakistan. But Gorbachev has already mentally turned the page on this chapter of history. In a few months he will acknowledge that Najibullah will not remain in power without Soviet troops.

On one hand, the decision to withdraw the troops is a consensus within the Soviet leadership. On the other, many in the military struggle with a single question: *What, then, were we fighting for?*

At one point, even after the Geneva Accords are signed, Foreign Minister Shevardnadze joins the military in their demands, suggesting to the Politburo that they leave behind at least ten to fifteen thousand troops. But Gorbachev is unyielding: he gives the minister a brutal dressing-down in front of the rest of the Politburo.

"I consider Shevardnadze's hawkish chatter irresponsible," the General Secretary scolds. "And I hear talk like this: 'We lost Afghanistan.' As if we ever 'had' it. They compare losses—too much or too little—with the Great Patriotic War. Shameful logic! Every life matters! Isn't it enough that thirteen thousand died and forty-three thousand were wounded? Over a million people have lived through this nightmare. And I'm not even mentioning the economy: six billion rubles a year we're sinking into this. From every perspective—human and economic—we must get out of there. And really, think about it, who are we even fighting there?"

GOLD AND OGONYOK

In April 1988, a unique exhibition opens in the building of the Prosecutor General's Office: treasures confiscated from officials in Uzbekistan are put on display. The tour for the prosecutor general and journalists is led by Telman Gdlyan himself. This, perhaps, is his finest hour. The report on the exhibition airs on the *Vremya* news program; then every Soviet media outlet covers it. Gdlyan becomes one of the most popular figures in the USSR; everyone knows his name. Newspapers gush with praise, repeating that Gdlyan has returned 8 million rubles to the state.

In early June 1988, investigators Gdlyan and Ivanov visit *Ogonyok* editor in chief Vitaly Korotich—"because you're the most free-thinking editor," as they tell him. They begin complaining that their investigation into the mafia within the leadership of Uzbekistan has stalled—they are being blocked by forces in Moscow—and they ask him to publish an article titled "Confrontation."

The text reads more like a political manifesto than an article by Soviet legal officials. The two Soviet Commissar Cattanis see themselves as people's avengers and speak far more boldly than any state officials dare. Gdlyan and Ivanov hint that corrupt officials are far more widespread in the USSR than it seems. And the ones obstructing the investigation are precisely the Moscow patrons of the Uzbek embezzlers. They don't name these figures yet but promise to reveal their identities soon.

Normally, Korotich clears publications like this with his patron Yakovlev. But here, he realizes that the ideologue of perestroika might get cold feet, so it's better not to ask. "I waved my hand and said, 'Let come what may,' and sent it to print," Korotich recalls. "By that time, the censors had grown sloppy—there was no need to get approval from the Central Committee."

The article comes out on June 26, just one day before the start of the 19th All-Union Communist Party Conference.

GORBACHEV'S REVOLUTION

In his first two years at the helm, Gorbachev becomes convinced that the system he inherited is dysfunctional and must be reformed. Yet both he and his closest advisors, like the jurist Anatoly Lukyanov, remain steadfast communists. In his spare time, Gorbachev diligently rereads Lenin—he genuinely believes that salvation lies in returning to a *purer* Leninist communism. However, Gorbachev reads Lenin quite selectively: he seems to overlook the Bolshevik leader's more brutal and bloodthirsty passages, while carefully noting down all the humanitarian and democratic ideas.

This leads him to a clear conclusion: Stalin perverted Lenin's teachings, which is why repressions, the Gulag, and dictatorship became possible. But this, Gorbachev believes, can be corrected: the USSR can become a democratic country simply by adhering to Lenin's *true* directives.

Gorbachev's main anchor is the slogan of the 1917 October Revolution: "All power to the Soviets." Back in 1917, the "Soviets" (meaning "councils" in Russian) were self-appointed, unofficial bodies that acted as a counter-balance to the Provisional Government and ultimately destabilized the bourgeois-democratic republic in Russia. For Lenin, "All power to the Soviets" was a cover; once he seized power, he immediately abandoned the slogan and established a dictatorship. However, even in the first constitution adopted by the Bolsheviks in 1918, it was stated that power in the country belonged to the Soviets, which would periodically convene at a congress—declared the highest governing body.

So Gorbachev adopts an early Soviet-specific model of government as his foundation. He believes the only way to change anything in the country is to invoke Lenin. And he sincerely believes it will work.

At his request, over several months, the jurist Anatoly Lukyanov drafts new articles for the constitution, fundamentally transforming the USSR's political system. The essence of this reform is to introduce nationwide elections, giving voters a real influence over power.

Technically, elections already exist in the Soviet Union, but they're bizarre. Ballots always feature just one name, chosen by the party leadership. Then, on the appointed day, voters show up at polling stations and "vote"—which means checking off a box next to that one and only name. This doesn't bother anyone—generations have grown up with no memory that elections could be competitive. In the USSR, these elections serve a different function: they are a kind of national holiday, a ceremonial act performed collectively. Everyone understands that it's just a ritual, but the majority still participate.

Gorbachev's recipe is to make elections competitive. He has no intention of dismantling the system; on the contrary, he believes this will strengthen it. At the first stage, he assumes, the heads of local councils will still be the

First Secretaries of local Communist Party cells. And if voters are dissatisfied with them, they'll elect someone else. This way, old First Secretaries, lacking public support, will be replaced by new ones. Gorbachev imagines this as a way to quietly refresh the party elite, replacing its aging members with younger supporters of perestroika. He has no doubt that these new politicians will be his like-minded allies. And he is certain that they will all be communists—the idea that active politicians might emerge outside the Communist Party simply does not cross his mind.

Gorbachev's entourage enthusiastically supports his reform. To implement it, the legislation needs to be changed quickly. By established custom, the Communist Party must give its blessing to any significant change. To do this, he decides to convene a party conference.

Discussing the new system with his aides, Gorbachev admits that it's time to move away from collective leadership—the old men in the Politburo are simply too unreliable. He needs to take charge himself, which means replacing the aging Gromyko as chairman of the Presidium of the Supreme Soviet. His inner circle agrees: there's no other option; all hopes rest on Gorbachev.

AN ENVELOPE OF COMPROMISING MATERIAL

Gorbachev opens the nineteenth party conference and boldly announces his plan for a "radical reform of the political system."

Any dissident would envy the courage with which Gorbachev describes Soviet reality: "democratic principles in words but authoritarianism in practice," "empty talk about democratic institutions and a deficit of criticism and glasnost." If anyone else had said this, they would immediately face criminal charges for "anti-Soviet agitation and propaganda." But Gorbachev is the supreme leader—they applaud him just as fervently as they once applauded Brezhnev.

There's no disagreement in the hall about Lenin's principle of "all power to the Soviets"—everyone remembers the slogan from school, though no one actually understands what it means. What unsettles many is another of Gorbachev's proposals: limiting officials to "two five-year terms, with a third only in exceptional cases." A heated debate ensues.

However, the truly revolutionary feature of this party conference is that it is broadcast live on television. For the first time, Soviet citizens witness unexpected moments of political struggle—something completely unheard of.

On the first day of the conference, the main topic of discussion is Gdlyan and Ivanov's article in *Ogonyok*. The investigators state directly that four high-ranking delegates at the conference are suspected of corruption. The party bosses are thrown into a panic—everyone wonders *What if it's me?*

On the second day, *Ogonyok*'s editor in chief, Vitaly Korotich, is called to account. Knowing he will have to take the stand and defend himself, Korotich calls Gdlyan: "You've dragged me into this mess. I trusted you, and I still do, but I need evidence."

Just minutes before the session begins, an official Volga car pulls up to the gates of the Kremlin. Ivanov steps out and hands Korotich a large envelope made of thick paper, sealed with wax and stamped "Top Secret." The label reads: "To M.S. Gorbachev. To be opened personally."

Gorbachev summons Korotich to the podium.

"Are there delegates among the suspects?" someone shouts from the hall.

"I can't name names, and in this case, I wouldn't want to," Korotich replies meaningfully. "There is the presumption of innocence. But I'm handing the Soviet Prosecutor's report to Mikhail Sergeyevich Gorbachev."

And in front of the entire country—as the conference is being broadcast live—Korotich hands the sealed, wax-stamped envelope to the General Secretary.

"Come on, come on," Gorbachev urges him impatiently.

A few days later, Korotich calls Gorbachev via the government line to ask what he plans to do with the documents.

"You know, don't rock the boat!" the General Secretary replies.

Meanwhile, the events at the conference spark a wave of rumors. Across the country, people speculate about what was in the envelope—most assume it contained damning kompromat on members of the Politburo. Gdlyan, who had been likened to Inspector Cattani from *La Piovra*, now increasingly draws comparisons to Captain Zheglov, the hero of the Soviet film *The Meeting Place Cannot Be Changed*, played by Vladimir Vysotsky. In the film's finale, Zheglov arrests the gang leader—a criminal nicknamed Gorbaty (the Hunchback). The popular joke now is that Gdlyan-Zheglov will also, in the end, have to take down the leader—"Gorbaty-Gorbachev."

A few months later, Korotich learns from Gdlyan that the envelope didn't contain information on heavyweights from Moscow—as *Ogonyok*'s readers had eagerly expected—but rather on four party officials from Uzbekistan, including Rashidov's successor, former republic head Inomjon

Usmonxoʻjayev. "The mountain gave birth to a mouse," bold perestroika journalists would comment.

Amid the scandal over the envelope, the essence of the party conference goes almost unnoticed. Editor in chief of *Izvestia*, Ivan Laptev, later will recall an episode from the conference: "'My God!'—one party secretary says to another as they leave the hall—'It only just hit me what we voted for half an hour ago!'" This, of course, is the exception rather than the rule. Most delegates clearly do not understand what they approved—not during the conference, not immediately afterward, nor even six months later. As a result, they will be genuinely surprised and outraged when the reforms begin to be implemented.

POLITICAL REHABILITATION

Delegates have little time to read through long documents, of course, because before them unfolds a real political spectacle. The second and even bigger scandal of the party conference is the return of Boris Yeltsin—a near-mythical figure who has been the talk of the country for the past six months.

Yeltsin, too, is one of the conference delegates—and he is desperate to speak. He devises an interesting strategy. At that moment, one of the most pressing topics in Soviet society is Stalin's repressions and the rehabilitation of victims who were executed or perished in the Gulag. Yeltsin reasons that since enough time has passed since his expulsion from the Politburo—more than six months—and since he has committed no actual crime, he too can demand rehabilitation. But not posthumously—he seeks rehabilitation while still alive.

However, the list of speakers is already packed, and Yeltsin's name is not included. Moreover, Gorbachev has made it clear that he will not let him back into politics. So the former head of Moscow prepares to storm the podium. On the final day of the debates, Yeltsin descends from the balcony and enters the main hall. Later he will express surprise that the KGB agents let him into the parterre so easily. Holding his red delegate's badge high, he walks purposefully down the central aisle toward the podium—locking eyes with the presiding Gorbachev.

"When I got to the middle of the vast hall, everyone understood. The Presidium, too. The speaker fell silent. A deadly, chilling hush settled over the room. . . . Each step echoed in my soul. I felt the breath of more than five thousand people, their eyes locked on me from every direction," he writes in his memoir.

This is Yeltsin's first public speech as a politician. Until now, he has been defined not by his own words but by the mythical Yeltsin invented by journalist Mikhail Poltoranin. This is also the debut of Yeltsin the opposition figure—a test of whether he can live up to the myth that has surrounded him for the past six months.

First, he complains about being persecuted, mentioning that *Ogonyok* refused to publish his interview. Then he recounts the story of his dismissal: "I was gravely ill, bedridden, unable to stand, with no strength or possibility to rise. . . . They pumped me full of medicine. . . . I was seated there, but I couldn't feel anything, let alone speak properly. . . ."

He follows up by commenting on Gorbachev's political reforms, criticizing them for not being democratic enough: "Elections must be universal, direct, and secret, including for secretaries, the General Secretary. . . . Introduce clear age limits for these bodies, including the Politburo, at sixty-five."

This is obvious populism—and a direct challenge to Gorbachev. Until now, everyone believed the head of the USSR was the country's leading democrat. But here comes Yeltsin. And that's not all—Yeltsin proceeds to unleash ruthless criticism against the nation's leadership.

He targets the Politburo members who remained silent for years: "Now it turns out only Brezhnev is to blame for stagnation. But where were those who have been in the Politburo for ten, fifteen, even twenty years? Why did they push forward the sick Chernenko?" It's clear that this is a personal attack on Gorbachev.

He denounces the lavish lifestyles of the party elite: "They're building luxurious mansions, dachas, and sanatoriums on such a scale that it's embarrassing." Finally, he uses the hottest buzzword of the season—"mafia": "The rot is likely deeper than anyone imagines, and I know for certain—the mafia exists in Moscow."

He closes with a request for "political rehabilitation while alive" because "freedom of criticism" and "tolerance for opponents" are now permitted.

Yeltsin steps down from the podium to applause. Everyone understands: this is a declaration of war. The disgraced man has returned, and his real speech is far harsher and more dangerous than the fictional version written by Poltoranin.

"BORIS, YOU'RE WRONG"

A recess is announced—after which no more speeches are scheduled, and voting on the final documents is set to begin. But after the break, Ligachev takes the stage. His task is clear: he must strike back at Yeltsin.

Yeltsin later writes in his memoir that the Politburo had prepared for such a scenario—but it's obvious they hadn't. Judging by how clumsy and unpolished Ligachev's speech is, it's clear he threw together his notes during the break. He has no strategy—he simply relies on his commanding authority.

"We cannot remain silent because Communist Yeltsin has taken the wrong path," Ligachev begins his assault.

He then compares his own life's achievements to Yeltsin's, since both were recently regional First Secretaries. Ligachev boasts that, under his skillful leadership, Tomsk Oblast was able to provide for itself, while under Yeltsin, Sverdlovsk Oblast fell into crisis: "And you, Boris, put your region on ration cards!"

But Yeltsin is not Ligachev's only target. Without naming names, it's clear he is also attacking recently outspoken figures like Korotich and his protector, Yakovlev.

"How can we accept that certain media portray Soviet people as slaves, supposedly fed only lies and demagoguery? Some newspaper editors have misunderstood glasnost as a license for recklessness. They use their papers to settle personal scores and promote unworthy individuals."

Yeltsin, in his memoir, paints Ligachev's speech as a highly dramatic moment:

I sat motionless, looking down at the podium from the balcony. It felt as though I might lose consciousness from it all. Seeing my state, some of the guys on duty rushed to me, took me to a doctor who gave me an injection so I could endure and sit through the end of the conference. I returned, but it was both a physical and moral ordeal; everything inside me was burning, my vision was swimming. . . . I felt that they were satisfied, they had beaten me, they had won. At that moment, I fell into a kind of apathy.

It's unclear how truthful Yeltsin's account of his physical suffering is. However, in the very next paragraph, he (or his ghostwriter, journalist Valentin Yumashev) offers a sharp political analysis of Ligachev's speech:

He pinned all sorts of labels on me, spun every kind of lie about me. Despite his desperate efforts, it was petty, vulgar, and uncultured. I think that after this speech, his political career essentially ended. He dealt himself such a devastating blow that he could never recover. From then on, he could provoke only nervous laughter from many people, and there was nowhere for him to go.

The public clash between Yeltsin and Ligachev is essentially the first televised debate in Soviet and Russian history—and Yeltsin wins unequivocally. Ligachev comes off as poorly spoken and overly self-assured.

According to Chernyaev, Gorbachev had not originally planned to address Yeltsin in his closing remarks—the speech had been prepared in advance. But then Raisa Gorbacheva entered the break room. Furious over Yeltsin's words, she demanded, "This cannot be left unanswered!" Her emotions leave a strong impression on Gorbachev. In his concluding remarks, he tears into Yeltsin, effectively aligning himself with Ligachev.

IN ANTICIPATION OF A CONSPIRACY

As Gorbachev prepares for the party conference and revolutionary changes to the legislation, he occasionally tries to imagine a scenario in which everything falls apart. Yet his imagination conjures only one outcome: conservatives rebel, organize a conspiracy against him, attempt to overthrow him—but the people remain on his side.

In April 1988, he even shares an anecdote with his inner circle. Allegedly, a traffic police officer stops his son-in-law, a doctor at Moscow's First City Hospital, and starts pressing him for answers about the General Secretary's whereabouts. "Where's Mikhail Sergeyevich? Don't play coy—just tell me. We know. His motorcade hasn't entered the city in three days! Rumors are spreading that he's been ousted. . . . If it's true, say so. People are fired up; they're saying if he's been removed, we'll take to the streets with weapons!" the officer supposedly tells him.

In reality, Gorbachev had been absent for three days due to a medical checkup. Whether the story is true or a loyalty test remains unclear, but at the time, Gorbachev frequently talks about a potential conspiracy and his removal. He even uses this line of thought to intimidate the Politburo, occasionally declaring that he "doesn't cling to his seat" and is ready to leave at any moment—but "as long as I'm General Secretary, I will defend the ideals of perestroika." Strangely, this argument always works; the party bosses lose their resolve entirely.

Nevertheless, after Nina Andreeva's article, Gorbachev decides it's time to radically reform the party apparatus. Yet he knows he can't simply fire the entire senior generation—there are too many of them, and there's no one to replace them. Instead, he opts for restructuring: dramatically downsizing the apparatus, eliminating redundant departments with overlapping functions, and retiring as many Brezhnev-era career climbers as possible. All the conservatives obediently resign "of their own accord." No one has yet learned how to argue with the boss.

It proves difficult, however, to dismiss those who have been with him since the beginning and helped him rise to power, such as Ligachev. Gorbachev devises a reshuffle: Ligachev and Yakovlev are no longer in charge of ideology. The former becomes overseer of agriculture, while the latter takes on international relations. This is meant to strip them of opportunities to clash. At the same time, Gorbachev "promotes" KGB chief Viktor Chebrikov by making him a Central Committee secretary.

On one hand, Chebrikov, like Ligachev, has been a long-standing ally. On the other, his values are clearly different: he still considers Sakharov and Solzhenitsyn traitors, resists releasing political prisoners, and praised Nina Andreeva's article. Moving him from the KGB to Staraya Square is effectively retirement, and everyone knows it.

But who will replace Chebrikov? Gorbachev and Yakovlev select his successor together—and they deem Vladimir Kryuchkov, the head of foreign intelligence and a former assistant to Andropov, to be the perfect candidate. To the architects of perestroika, Kryuchkov seems well educated and pro-Western.

He also accompanied Gorbachev on his earlier visit to the United States. During a working dinner with CIA deputy director Robert Gates and National Security Advisor Colin Powell, Kryuchkov had reportedly surprised them. When offered a glass of Johnnie Walker Red Label, Kryuchkov smiled and said he drinks only Chivas Regal.

POPULAR FRONTS

By the summer of 1988, opposition movements are emerging across the Soviet Union. Until now, Armenia had been the only republic with a functioning opposition group. But now the Estonian Popular Front is established, followed by the Movement for Perestroika in Lithuania—soon to be known by its Lithuanian name, Sąjūdis. Similar Popular Fronts soon appear in Latvia, Moscow, and Leningrad.

The method of creation is strikingly similar to the Armenian scenario. In each case, respected intellectuals—writers and academics—take the lead. They form public organizations under slogans like "For Perestroika" and "For Gorbachev." Headquarters are typically set up in the offices of the republican Union of Writers or Academies of Sciences.

It is clear that much of this process is orchestrated. These organizations are being created with the assistance and direct involvement of the KGB. This is part of Gorbachev's plan: he wants grassroots organizations in support of perestroika to emerge across the country. He needs them as a counterbalance to the conservatives in the Politburo and as a broad base of public support for the next time another "Nina Andreeva letter" surfaces.

Vladimir Kryuchkov, head of the KGB, reports enthusiastically to Gorbachev that the Soviet population is overwhelmingly in favor of perestroika. As a result, Kryuchkov is tasked with creating a network of organizations to support the reforms across the Union. Naturally, he starts with the most politically active and mature regions: the Baltic republics, Moscow, and Leningrad.

The founders of these organizations are, of course, representatives of the local creative intelligentsia. Some of them, both in the Baltic states and in Moscow, are KGB informants or, at the very least, report their activities to the agency. However, it doesn't take long before these organizations spiral out of control. The KGB remains aware of what is being discussed in the Popular Fronts, but it cannot contain their momentum.

In the Baltic states, the ideas of freedom and independence enjoy overwhelming popularity. The political culture of Estonia, Latvia, and Lithuania differs dramatically from that of the rest of the USSR. From 1918 to 1940, all three republics were independent democratic states. According to Soviet history textbooks, however, revolutions took place in all three countries in 1940, after which they supposedly joined the Soviet state voluntarily. This is the official version, and questioning it is strictly forbidden.

In Latvia, on June 2, 1988, a congress of the creative unions takes place—an event permitted by the authorities, attended by the head of the republic, Boris Pugo. Seventy-year-old journalist and professor at the Academy of Arts Mavriks Vulfsons takes the floor. To everyone's astonishment, he declares that the entire Soviet version of history is a lie: there were no revolutions in the Baltic states in 1940; they were simply occupied by Stalin as part of his deal with Hitler. The audience is in shock.

After the session, First Secretary Pugo approaches Vulfsons and tells him, "You've just killed Soviet Latvia."

This is one of the Soviet Union's greatest unspoken truths: in 1939, Stalin made a secret agreement with Hitler—known to history as the Molotov-Ribbentrop Pact—to divide Eastern Europe between them. On September 1, in accordance with this pact, the Third Reich attacked Poland, marking the start of World War II. Soon after, the Soviet Union occupied the three Baltic republics. Acknowledging this fact would render the annexation of the Baltic republics to the USSR illegal and imply they could legitimately restore their independence. The Kremlin continues to deny the existence of any secret protocols attached to the Molotov-Ribbentrop Pact that determined the fate of the Baltic states.

After World War II, the Red Army "liberated" Estonia and Latvia (as described in Soviet textbooks) and incorporated them as Soviet republics. But in all three Baltic republics, underground guerrilla groups continued fighting against the Red Army; they were called Forest Brothers.

Actress Ingeborga Dapkūnaitė describes it as a painful and still recent past for many Lithuanian families. Her grandmother, for example, ran a village canteen in the late 1940s. During the day, she served communists; at night, the Forest Brothers came to her for food. One day, a regular customer, an NKVD officer, warned her that lists had already been drawn up for Lithuanians to be deported to Siberia—and her family was on it. As a favor, he crossed their names off.

Not long after, all the villagers were summoned to the main square. There, on the ground in front of the church, lay the naked bodies of the Forest Brothers. The dead were the sons and brothers of the villagers.

Years later, when Ingeborga Dapkūnaitė's father joined the Communist Party, his mother wept. That was the day she told him this story for the first time.

The West never recognized the Soviet occupation of the Baltic countries, and even in the late 1980s, many residents of these Soviet republics still remember life during independence. In addition, they feel supported by the West, which continues to deny the legitimacy of the Soviet annexation.

On June 24, 1988, the first large rally organized by Sąjūdis takes place in the Lithuanian capital of Vilnius. Around twenty thousand people gather. The authorities approve the demonstration, framing it as a send-off for delegates traveling to the party conference in Moscow.

Musicologist Vytautas Landsbergis speaks at the rally, telling the Secretary of the Lithuanian Communist Party that he and his comrades are not the true representatives of the republic, as they were not elected by the people. However, he says, if they defend the interests of the people, they may earn the right to represent them. Secretary Algirdas Brazauskas decides to respond. He addresses the crowd and promises to proclaim Lithuanian the official state language and to halt the construction of the Lithuanian nuclear power plant.

The most striking effect of the Popular Front's activity, however, can be seen in Latvia, where the organization takes a stand against the construction of a metro system in Riga. The population of the Latvian capital is nearing 1 million, and according to Soviet norms, cities with populations exceeding one million are required to build metro systems. Plans for the first line's stations are already finalized, but activists from the Popular Front organize multiple mass protests. Their argument is clear: construction will bring an influx of migrant workers from Russia, further increasing the proportion of Russian speakers in Latvia and diminishing the percentage of ethnic Latvians. The protests succeed, and the Riga metro project is never implemented.

THE SINGING REVOLUTION

In August 1988, Alexander Yakovlev, acting on Gorbachev's orders, visits Latvia and Lithuania. Demonstrations are already underway in both republics. The most liberal member of the Politburo meets with the local intelligentsia and concludes that the process cannot be suppressed, so it might be worth trying to lead it.

The reality is that most residents of these republics favor independence— albeit "within the USSR." This idea contains a certain contradiction, but it represents the limit of the boldest aspirations of Soviet citizens in the summer of 1988.

Yuri Gagarin, the first man in space (1961), was the Soviet Elvis. At first, the whole world admired him—but, over time, he grew weary of his fame, and the light in his eyes began to fade.

Mikhail and Raisa Gorbachev were almost the model Soviet couple. He rose steadily through the ranks of the Komsomol (the Communist Youth League) and then the Communist Party, while she had to wait for the chance to defend her dissertation and find work.

Soviet leader Leonid Brezhnev and U.S. president Richard Nixon initiated the so-called détente because they shared a common trait—not ideology, but a mixture of hedonism and cynicism that outweighed any desire to start a nuclear war.

ABOVE: Aleksandr Solzhenitsyn dreamed for many years of winning the Nobel Prize in Literature so he could attend the ceremony and use the world stage to tell the truth about the Soviet Gulag. But under the influence of his wife, Natalia "Alya" Svetlova, he changed his mind and decided it was better to stay in Russia at any cost.

RIGHT: The unrecognized genius of Soviet cinema, Sergei Parajanov, was unable to realize most of his artistic visions, and so he turned nearly every moment of his life into a theatrical performance.

Andrei Sakharov and his wife, Yelena Bonner, spent nearly ten years in exile in Gorky, but they remembered those years as the happiest of their lives—because they loved each other.

American Joanna Fields began her work in musical diplomacy after meeting Boris Grebenshchikov, a legend of underground Soviet rock and roll. She would become famous under the pseudonym Stingray.

The entire world followed the rivalry between two Soviet chess grand masters, Garry Kasparov (left) and Anatoly Karpov (right), seen here at the opening of the World Chess Championship match in London, with Prime Minister Margaret Thatcher.

ABOVE: Despite the catastrophe at the Chernobyl nuclear power plant in April 1986, the authorities of the Ukrainian SSR did everything possible to ensure that the May Day parade went ahead as planned, even though it posed a deadly risk to all participants.

BELOW: Soviet pop star Alla Pugacheva was a sex symbol and a legend for generations of Soviet citizens, who joked that, next to her, even Leonid Brezhnev seemed like a minor political figure of the Pugacheva era.

In 1988, Mikhail Gorbachev flew to New York to attend the United Nations General Assembly, where he met with outgoing U.S. president Ronald Reagan and vice president George H. W. Bush, who would soon be elected president. It was these three men who brought the Cold War to an end.

ABOVE: In 1988, investigators Telman Gdlyan (second from left) and Nikolai Ivanov (first left) organized an exhibition of gold and stacks of cash confiscated in Uzbekistan, inviting Soviet television to showcase their fight against corruption.

LEFT: The massive demonstrations in early 1988 demanding the unification of Nagorno-Karabakh with Armenia marked the beginning of a protracted conflict between Armenia and Azerbaijan.

When Lithuanian actress Ingeborga Dapkūnaitė (left) first read the script for the film *Intergirl*, about the lives of Soviet sex workers, she immediately knew it would be a blockbuster.

14

15

ABOVE: In 1989, the first opposition democratic faction in the Soviet parliament, called the Interregional Deputies Group, was created. Its cochairs, from left to right, were Yuri Afanasyev, Boris Yeltsin, Andrei Sakharov, and Gavriil Popov.

RIGHT: Upon learning that the Berlin Wall had fallen, in November 1989, cellist Mstislav Rostropovich, who had been stripped of his Soviet citizenship, urgently flew from Paris to Berlin. He arrived at the wall's ruins and began playing Bach's suites.

16

ABOVE: In September 1989, Boris Yeltsin made his first trip to the United States and, like so many Soviet citizens before him, he was most shocked by the abundance of goods in American supermarkets.

LEFT: Anatoly Sobchak was one of the most popular pro-democracy politicians during the collapse of the Soviet Union. Everywhere he went, he was followed by his indispensable aide, KGB officer Vladimir Putin.

Underground Soviet rocker Viktor Tsoi dreamed of becoming a Red Bruce Lee—and his dream came true. In 1989, he was named the most popular actor in the USSR.

After writing a sharply critical analysis of the Soviet economy, the young economist Grigory Yavlinsky received the following comment from his boss: "Now you'll either become very famous or go to prison. Prepare for both."

During the August 1991 coup against Mikhail Gorbachev, cellist Mstislav Rostropovich spent the night inside the besieged Russian White House. A guard named Yura was assigned to protect him, though he didn't know how to fire a gun. Yura's instructions were simple: in case of danger, shout, "Don't shoot! Rostropovich is here!"

Upon returning to Moscow, Yakovlev proposes to the Politburo the idea of transforming the USSR into a confederation, granting Lithuania, Latvia, and Estonia special status. This is, of course, a revolutionary proposal—and the others do not understand it at all.

On September 11, 1988, three hundred thousand people gather at the Song Festival Grounds in Tallinn—more than a third of the republic's population. Although people are simply singing, the event is unmistakably political.

Soon, in Lithuania, during the founding congress of Sajūdis, the Communist Party First Secretary, Brazauskas, clearly vying for popular support, makes a significant decision: to hand over Vilnius Cathedral back to the Catholic Church. Until then, as in the rest of the USSR, celebrating any religious holidays—including Christmas—had been forbidden.

Actress Ingeborga Dapkūnaitė will recall how teachers in schools would deliberately ask children on December 25 what gifts they had received. It was a trap—children had to pretend that Christmas wasn't celebrated, that there were no gifts, and everything was reserved for the officially sanctioned "secular" New Year. Once, as a schoolgirl, Dapkūnaitė fell into this trap and confessed to her teacher. Her parents were summoned to the school, and her father, a diplomat, was threatened with expulsion from the party. But now that is all in the past: from 1988 onward, celebrating Christmas is allowed. The actress recalls that on that Christmas night, she and her family climb the hill in the center of Vilnius—and see festive candles glowing in every window.

THE GRANDSON OF THE RED COMMANDER

In November, the KGB reports that the situation in the Baltic republics is out of control, and the Politburo sends there three of its members. This time, it's not Yakovlev, but moderate conservatives. All three are horrified. They report back to Moscow that protesters confronted them with signs: "Russians, go home!," "Down with Moscow's dictatorship!," and "Immediate exit from the Union!"

Former KGB chief Chebrikov tells his colleagues that he attended a beauty contest in Estonia. During the swimsuit round, one of the participants is asked: What would she say to Chebrikov if she met him on the street? "Leave us alone!" she answers. The members of the Politburo are stunned—both by the audacity of the girl and by the fact that in Estonia, of all places, there is—horror of horrors—a beauty contest where participants walk onstage, even worse, in bikinis.

Around this time, the newspaper *Soviet Latvia* publishes an article sharply criticizing the Popular Front and accusing its activists of nationalism. This is quite unexpected because, until now, the media avoided criticizing the Popular Front—everyone knows these organizations were established at Gorbachev's initiative and under the KGB's patronage. Even more surprising than the tone of the article is its author's surname—Alksnis.

In the early years of the USSR, there was a well-known man with that name. Yakov Alksnis was one of the first Soviet military commanders, who actively participated in the Civil War on the Bolshevik side and served as head of the Red Army Air Force. But when Stalin launched the Great Terror in 1937, Alksnis himself ended up in the defendant's seat. Under torture, he confessed to being a Latvian spy. In 1938, he was executed.

Yakov Alksnis's family was exiled to Siberia, where his grandson, Viktor, was born. Viktor's first language, naturally, was Russian. However, after Yakov Alksnis's posthumous rehabilitation in 1957, the family returned to Latvia. Like his grandfather, Viktor became a military man; by 1988, he was a lieutenant colonel in the Soviet army.*

After writing the article, as Viktor Alksnis recalls, he wakes up famous. His surname was already well-known—rehabilitated posthumously, the Red commander Yakov Alksnis had become a national hero in Soviet Latvia. A street in Riga, a military school, and even a steamship were named after him. So when Viktor Alksnis publishes a scathing article against the Popular Front, everyone takes notice—and everyone understands exactly what kind of family the author comes from.

---

* This story is not uncommon for the Baltic republics. Russified Latvians and Estonians often rise to high positions—such as former first secretaries Boris Pugo and Karl Vaino. Like Viktor Alksnis, they grew up in Siberia, speak their native languages with difficulty, and have a reputation as agents of Russification. However, their careers unfold differently. The younger Latvian leader, Pugo, was a diligent and efficient subordinate. Gorbachev noticed that Pugo was unpopular in Latvia due to his poor command of the Latvian language and brought him to Moscow for a promotion. Karl Vaino, on the other hand, resisted perestroika, leading Gorbachev to send him into retirement. His family moved to Moscow, and his grandson, Anton Vaino, would later become chief of staff to President Vladimir Putin.

Soon a colleague—a colonel from the counterintelligence unit of the Baltic Military District—invites him for a conversation.

"Viktor, you did the right thing by speaking out about this issue. The situation is very alarming. The KGB of the Latvian SSR has effectively ceased to exist, splitting along national lines: there is the Russian half and the Latvian half. The same thing has happened to the prosecutor's office and the Central Committee of the Latvian Communist Party," Alksnis recalls the officer telling him. "In every state structure, there is now a split, and Latvians have overwhelmingly joined the People's Front."

For this reason, the officer explains, a decision has been made to create a counterweight to the Popular Front—the so-called Latvian Interfront. Since the KGB is no longer trusted, this mission has been assigned to the counter-intelligence division of the Baltic Military District. Alksnis, as a rising star in Latvian politics and a trusted Soviet officer, is invited to join the Interfront. Naturally, he complies.

"WHY ARE YOU TRYING TO SCARE ME, YEGOR?"

At the end of September 1988, *Literaturnaya Gazeta* publishes an article by Arkady Vaksberg titled "Thunderous Applause." It tells the story of an honest Azerbaijani prosecutor who tried to fight corruption in the republic during Heydar Aliyev's rule—only to lose his job and be exiled from Azerbaijan. The publication causes an uproar—everyone assumes that another high-profile purge, like the one in Uzbekistan, is imminent.

The article is clearly intended as a warning to Aliyev's team, which remains powerful in Azerbaijan, signaling that they should not interfere with the new republic leader, Gorbachev's ally Vezirov.

On November 17, 1988, a massive rally gathers in Lenin Square in Baku. A tent city appears in the square. According to one of the founders of the Popular Front of Azerbaijan, Arabist scholar Zardusht Alizadeh, "Within a week, the square is supplied with firewood for bonfires, tents, and provisions, which are distributed for free." Up to half a million people gather daily. Later Alizadeh will speculate that the rally is provoked by officials close to former First Secretary Heydar Aliyev as part of a scheme to oust the current head of the republic, Vezirov.

One of the rally's demands is either to grant autonomy to Azerbaijanis living in Armenia or to revoke the autonomy of Armenians in Karabakh.

In response, Armenia begins a large-scale deportation of Azerbaijanis from its territories—over the next few months, approximately two hundred thousand people will be expelled.

First Secretary Vezirov is too afraid to assume responsibility, so the initiative is taken over by the new Second Secretary of the republic, Viktor Polyanichko. Not long ago, he was assigned as Moscow's overseer to Afghan leader Najibullah, but now he has been transferred to Azerbaijan. The Politburo has essentially given up on Afghanistan; the situation in the Caucasus seems far more urgent and dangerous to the Kremlin. Polyanichko relies on tried-and-true methods. Over the following months, he will fight to keep Azerbaijan within the USSR, as if trying to succeed where he failed in Afghanistan.

On November 23, Polyanichko imposes martial law and a curfew in Baku. The square is blockaded. Gradually, the number of demonstrators and those camping out in the square dwindles.

On November 25, the Politburo discusses the situation in Azerbaijan. According to Chernyaev, the KGB reports that "they're burning tanks, military trucks, and have killed three Russian soldiers. In Baku, they march with green flags and portraits of Khomeini, demanding a Sumgait-style massacre of Armenians everywhere." (This is clearly an exaggeration.)

Ligachev begins: "We need to assert power, restore order, and show everyone! How much longer can we tolerate this?" Gorbachev initially responds with irony but then explodes: "Why do you keep scaring me, Yegor?! Why do you keep shoving this in my face—saying this is what your perestroika has led to! But I was and remain for perestroika. And I'm not afraid of what's unfolding!"

On the night of December 5, the rally in Baku is forcibly dispersed. Around a thousand people are arrested.

Baku-born Garry Kasparov is in Paris at the time, participating in an exhibition tournament while closely following news from the USSR. One day, he is introduced to Miloš Forman, the director who left Czechoslovakia after the crushing of the Prague Spring. They have lunch together, discussing Gorbachev, perestroika, and glasnost.

Kasparov insists that the changes underway are irreversible. But Forman is deeply skeptical: "You're just too young to understand—this is all temporary. Maybe it's a thaw, but everything will go back to the way it was."

Kasparov holds his ground.: "No, I can feel it happening."

"All right." The Hollywood director laughs. "Then tell me—how exactly will it happen?"

"I don't know. . . . One day, you wake up, open the window—and they're just gone."

"SPITEFUL, BUT TALENTED"

The issues in the Baltic republics and the Caucasus do not occupy all of the Politburo's working hours: on November 3, they discuss literature. The question is raised about whether to reinstate Solzhenitsyn's Soviet citizenship. However, former KGB head Chebrikov is adamantly against it: after all, "he's a traitor to the homeland," he insists.

This discussion is not coincidental. Throughout the year, Moscow's major literary journals have been debating whether Solzhenitsyn should be published. *Novy Mir* proposes to print his Nobel lecture in December and, starting in January 1989, *The Gulag Archipelago*. Moreover, the October issue of the journal comes out with a cover announcement—a single line: no specifics, just a vague promise that an unnamed work by Solzhenitsyn will soon be published.

The editor in chief of *Novy Mir*, Sergei Zalygin, is summoned to the Central Committee. Moreover, he is ordered to stop the entire print run and strip and replace the covers bearing the subversive announcement. However, something incredible happens—the printing press workers protest. They deliberate about where to complain—and write to Memorial; it is a public organization dedicated to commemorating the victims of Stalinist repressions, with Sakharov serving as one of its cochairs.

A public campaign in support of Solzhenitsyn begins—led by the very Moscow intelligentsia who had supported him and written letters defending him when he lived in the USSR, and whom he had so harshly criticized and labeled the "smug intellectuals" after moving to the United States.

Meanwhile, another group writes a counter-letter, urging the authorities not to publish him under any circumstances—arguing that Solzhenitsyn is a monarchist, a nationalist, and an enemy of democracy.

More and more articles link Solzhenitsyn to the Pamyat society. Naturally, such speculation outrages the writer: "Some say, 'When Solzhenitsyn returns, he will lead Pamyat—and this will result in a dictatorship of Russian chauvinism in the USSR.'"

Similar opinions are voiced in the West. Historian Richard Pipes, an advisor to Reagan on Russian affairs, speaks at Harvard, warning that if Gorbachev is not supported, "the reactionary movement of Solzhenitsyn will prevail."

Some of Solzhenitsyn's writings, however, leave a powerful impression on Gorbachev. He admits to Chernyaev that he has read the chapter "Lenin in Zurich" from *The Red Wheel*, Solzhenitsyn's saga about the 1917 revolution. "It's a powerful piece. Spiteful, but talented," Gorbachev says with admiration. What strikes him most is Solzhenitsyn's claim that Lenin had "only one-quarter Russian blood." Intrigued, Gorbachev requests all archival records on Lenin's ancestry and, upon receiving them, locks the files away in a safe. "This kind of thing really hits people hard," Gorbachev tells Chernyaev, echoing Solzenitsyn's thesis that Lenin's forebears included Jews, Swedes, and Kalmyks.

In early December, Sakharov calls Solzhenitsyn at home—their first conversation in fourteen years. Solzhenitsyn recounts the exchange as follows:

"To set the record straight. I'm deeply offended by how you portrayed Elena Georgievna [Bonner] in *The Calf* [Solzhenitsyn's memoir]. She is an entirely different person," the academic allegedly says. "I would like to believe that," the writer sighs in response. At that moment, Solzhenitsyn claims, he wants to shower Sakharov with reproaches—criticizing him for condemning his *Letter to the Soviet Leaders* "without reading it carefully," which, according to Solzhenitsyn, undermined his position in the West—to the advantage of the KGB and the glee of New York liberals.

But instead, Solzhenitsyn inquires about Sakharov's health. "For my age—satisfactory," the academic replies, then bids farewell. Yet, a minute later, Sakharov calls back—he had forgotten the reason for his call: to congratulate Solzhenitsyn on his seventieth birthday.

According to Solzhenitsyn, he sits afterward with a heavy feeling—he would have liked to clear the air. But it will never happen—this is their last conversation in life.

In early December 1988, Sakharov and Bonner—traveling abroad for the first time since their return from exile in Gorky—go to Paris. President François Mitterrand has invited them to celebrations marking the fortieth anniversary of the Universal Declaration of Human Rights. They are provided with a limousine and six bodyguards. Yet Bonner and Sakharov employ all their Gorky-honed skills to escape the security detail; they manage to slip away, walking quietly through the city and sitting in a café.

MORE THAN A TRIUMPH

Gorbachev's plans are ambitious. While the Baku protests are being dispersed, he is finalizing preparations for his trip to the UN General Assembly. Both he and his aides approach the event with utmost seriousness—Gorbachev's speech must be a triumph. A year earlier, the General Secretary had been named Man of the Year; now he seeks to cement that success.

Months prior, he begins a Politburo session unexpectedly: "They're asking why we need such a massive army. People have been worried about this for a long time. If we make public the scale of our spending, all of our new thinking and new foreign policy will go to hell," the General Secretary sums up. The prime minister agrees: unless military spending is reduced, "there can be no talk of improving living standards."

Gorbachev gets to the main point: at the UN, he plans to announce a unilateral reduction of the Soviet military—an incredibly powerful move. The entire Politburo agrees. The plan is for Gorbachev to also speak at the United Nations about the impending release of all political prisoners, the right of Soviet citizens to freely emigrate, debt forgiveness for Third World countries, and the reduction of the Soviet military presence in Eastern Europe.

Gorbachev's speech at the United Nations really is a resounding success. "No one expected this," his aide Chernyaev recounts in his diary. "The hall sat perfectly still for an hour. Then it erupted in ovations. They wouldn't let MS [Gorbachev] leave, he had to keep standing and bowing as if he were onstage. . . . This was more than a sensation . . . a triumph that won't fade." Chernyaev is no sycophant—this is genuinely how he and the rest of Gorbachev's team feel.

But Gorbachev won't get to savor this triumph for long. As he leaves the General Assembly Hall and gets into the car, he is connected to Prime Minister Ryzhkov.

Ryzhkov delivers the news: a catastrophic earthquake has struck Armenia.

THE EARTHQUAKE

It occurs on December 7, 1988, at 11:41 a.m., near the Armenian town of Spitak, which is effectively wiped off the map. In a matter of seconds, according to official figures, 24,817 people die.

Most residential buildings are destroyed, burying thousands of people alive beneath the rubble. In the aftermath, conspiracy theories gain popularity in Armenia, suggesting that the earthquake was caused by the use of some kind of secret weapon aimed at destabilizing the republic.

Levon Ter-Petrosyan will recall that, early that morning, he is shaving in his apartment in Yerevan when he feels a very strong jolt. He knows that during an earthquake, one should stand in a doorway—and that's where the second tremor hits him. The eight-story building sways. Ter-Petrosyan goes down to the courtyard and sees it filled with small children and their grandmothers—everyone, terrified, has run outside.

Ter-Petrosyan drives to the writers' union building, the office of the Karabakh Committee. On the very first day, they organize the collection of clothes, medicine, and food for the victims—people bring their belongings here from all over Yerevan: "We sent our guys out into the streets; they stopped public buses, asked passengers to get off, and drove the buses to the Writers' Union. We loaded them with supplies and sent them out. And all the drivers complied."

On the second day after the tragedy, Soviet prime minister Nikolai Ryzhkov flies to Spitak. Initially, he plans to stay for three days—but in the end, he remains for two months. He effectively stops performing his duties as head of the government and instead coordinates rescue and debris clearance efforts. According to him, nearly the only structure left standing in Spitak is the open-air stadium. That's where they gather the coffins of the dead. Very quickly, the coffins fill the stadium's bowl—they begin stacking them in layers, but more and more keep arriving.

Mikhail Gorbachev is still in New York, but he decides to cut his visit short and fly to Armenia. Even before his departure, representatives of various countries offer their help. In the end, this becomes the most extensive cooperation between the USSR and the West since the end of World War II.

The United States sends several planes with doctors and equipment to Armenia. Businessman Armand Hammer flies to Armenia, bringing $1 million in aid. Among the volunteers is Jeb Bush, son of the US president-elect.

The Armenian diaspora around the world becomes particularly active. French singer of Armenian descent Charles Aznavour creates the charitable foundation Aznavour pour l'Arménie and within a few days records the song "Pour Toi, Arménie." Another musical project to aid the victims,

Rock Aid Armenia, emerges in the United States, featuring musicians from Deep Purple, Pink Floyd, Queen, and other bands.

Kino also takes action to help those affected. They perform several benefit concerts, including their first-ever show abroad—a charity concert in Copenhagen. Viktor Tsoi says:

"What struck me most was the earthquake in Armenia. It showed that we can't go on living like this anymore. This is the breaking point, a call to fix what can still be saved. Otherwise . . . I don't know what might happen."

The earthquake completely changes the political landscape of Armenia. Significant power in the republic shifts to the hands of the Karabakh Committee: while local authorities cannot take a step without coordinating with Moscow, the Karabakh Committee efficiently organizes rescue operations and aid efforts on the ground. Before long, this will greatly irritate Soviet officials.

"When the Soviet Union began collecting money from around the world to eliminate the consequences of the earthquake, we said that we didn't trust the USSR and insisted that in Europe, those funds be accumulated by our French singer, the Armenian Charles Aznavour, or in the United States by our governor of California [Courken George Deukmejian, Jr.], also an Armenian. "Then Moscow got scared that we were starting to accumulate funds outside the Soviet Union," Vazgen Manukyan, a member of the Karabakh Committee, would later reflect.

On the fourth day after the earthquake, Gorbachev arrives in Armenia—his only trip to the Caucasus during his tenure as head of the Soviet Union. Together with Raisa he witnesses the destruction—and cannot recover from the shock. They had never seen anything more horrifying.

Nevertheless, even in Spitak, people repeatedly ask the General Secretary about Karabakh. This irritates Gorbachev greatly. Years later, he will recall hearing insults directed at Raisa: the earthquake victims openly express their accumulated hostility toward her.

From Spitak, Gorbachev travels to Yerevan, and there, as tradition dictates, he heads to the central square to speak with the people in front of TV cameras. "We will not leave you alone with this tragedy; we will help you," he says. "And Karabakh?" a young man in the crowd asks. Gorbachev begins to lose his temper: "Listen, I thought you wouldn't bring up the Karabakh issue again at a moment of national disaster." Gorbachev hopes the crowd will side with him—but almost everyone in the square is focused on Karabakh. He realizes that he has failed to win the sympathy of the people—instead, they are all against him.

He vents his frustration in a televised interview for Armenian television. He claims that the Karabakh issue is being exploited by "dishonest people, demagogues, adventurists, corrupt individuals, and blackshirts"(a term for fascists). Whom does Gorbachev target with such monstrous epithets? Of course, the members of the Karabakh Committee.

On December 10, the building of the Writers' Union of Armenia is surrounded by troops. A man in a trench coat walks inside.

"Are you Ter-Petrosyan?" he asks. "Send the people home. Clear everyone out of here."

The leader of the Karabakh Committee does not understand who he is talking to. "Listen, these are your Soviet people. Go talk to these people yourself."

The visitor becomes angry: "Did you not understand me?"

"I understood you. But it's you who don't understand me right now," Ter-Petrosyan replies. "You are a Soviet military officer. And these are the Soviet people. Talk to your people; explain the situation. Maybe they'll listen to you."

"Well, Ter-Petrosyan, I'll deal with you later," the man snaps, and runs out of the office. Twenty minutes later, armed soldiers appear and arrest all the members of the Karabakh Committee. They inform Ter-Petrosyan that the unintroduced guest was the military commandant of Yerevan, General Albert Makashov.

The detainees are transferred to Moscow and held at Matrosskaya Tishina prison. Ter-Petrosyan spends a month in solitary confinement.

Meanwhile, upon returning to Moscow, Gorbachev falls ill, stays home, and does not go to work at the Kremlin for over a week. According to Chernyaev, it is during this winter, shaken by what she saw in Armenia, that Raisa Gorbacheva asks him, "Maybe it's time to resign and write memoirs?"

"YOUR DEMOCRACY WILL DIE"

Sakharov closely follows the news from Armenia. Together with fellow scholars from the Institute of Oriental Studies, he tries to devise a plan to resolve the Karabakh crisis. Sakharov compiles their ideas into an action program: to hold referendums in every populated area of Armenia and Azerbaijan to determine the proper placement of the border. He also adds the demand to immediately release the members of the Karabakh Committee.

With this plan, Sakharov goes to Alexander Yakovlev. The Politburo member quickly reads the text and says it is very interesting but completely unrealistic. He counters with a suggestion: Why doesn't Sakharov go to Baku and Yerevan himself to assess the situation on the ground?

After discussing Armenia, Sakharov changes the topic and asks about the new electoral law passed at the summer party conference. "Why the rush?" the academician asks, suggesting that the amendments should be refined and adopted via a nationwide referendum. "We don't have time for a referendum. If we don't act quickly, we'll be crushed!" Yakovlev answers firmly. He promises, however, that the system will be revised in the future: eventually, there will be a bicameral parliament and direct presidential elections.

The day after the conversation at Staraya Square, Sakharov assembles a delegation to travel to the Caucasus.

The first stop is Baku. They are received at the Academy of Sciences. One by one, local academics and writers claim that the Nagorno-Karabakh issue does not exist—it was invented. No one wants to listen to Sakharov's proposals or discuss a referendum.

The Moscow delegation is then taken to speak with Azerbaijani refugees. "The speakers were undoubtedly pre-selected," Sakharov later writes. "I remember a young woman screaming about how Armenians had hacked children to pieces, ending with a triumphant cry: 'Allah punished them!' (referring to the earthquake). . . . Overall, despite the clearly staged nature of many accounts, we were left with the undeniable impression of a large, mass tragedy affecting countless people."

The last meeting in Baku is with the head of Azerbaijan, Vezirov. He assures the guests from Moscow that there are no problems, that everything is already being resolved, and that mistakes are being corrected. "Right now, the Armenians are experiencing a great national tragedy," Bonner starts, "Eastern people are famous for their generosity and nobility. So take a magnanimous step—give them Nagorno-Karabakh as a gift to a friend in need. The whole world will be impressed, and this act will be remembered for generations!" The First Secretary's expression changes: "Land is not given as a gift. It is conquered."

After the meetings in Baku, Sakharov and his companions fly to Armenia. The program there is the same: meetings at the academy, visits to refugees, and discussions with the First Secretary. However, the mood in Armenia is far more tragic, as people are shaken by the earthquake. Still, no one wants to hear about compromises or referendums—they demand that Nagorno-Karabakh be theirs entirely.

Many people also demand the release of the Karabakh Committee members, but the authorities insist that they are extremists and enemies of the people.

From Yerevan, Sakharov and the rest of the delegation fly to Karabakh. There, they meet Arkady Volsky, the temporary administrator sent from Moscow. He tells them that the main issue is tackling the local mafia: "The mafia is international," he explains. "They easily find common ground," and adds that the underground economy's capital in Azerbaijan is 10 billion rubles, while in Armenia it's 14 billion.

Some locals tell Sakharov that part of the problem is that Armenians supposedly want to cut down a sacred relic grove for Azerbaijanis and build a harmful chemical plant on its site. The delegation goes to check and discovers that the grove has long since disappeared and the site is now occupied by luxury dachas belonging to Baku's elite.

"All these years, top officials spent their vacations here. This was their 'protected grove'—one they are ready to defend to the death (though not their own, of course)," Sakharov writes.

The most harrowing part of the trip turns out to be their visit to Spitak, the earthquake-devastated town. Upon arrival, Sakharov sees burly men fighting over humanitarian aid, throwing away unwanted baby food into the snow, and loading the rest into trucks to take it somewhere. "They're holding back because of you. There are usually real fights," the helicopter pilot explains. "There are no lists of who survived or what people need. The authorities are either confused or have fled—and they're stealing more than anyone else."

Returning to Moscow, Sakharov calls Yakovlev and offers his help in organizing the distribution of aid, saying he is ready to return to Armenia. But the authorities decide not to turn to him for help anymore.

A month later, Azerbaijani scholar and politician Zardusht Alizadeh arrives in Moscow for the conference organized by Sakharov. He and his associates are in the process of creating a democratic opposition party in Baku, so he hopes to learn from the experience of his Russian counterparts.

However, his dialogue with the Moscow dissidents immediately goes awry. For example, they adopt a statement demanding the release of the Karabakh Committee members from custody. Alizadeh expresses his point of view: he believes the Karabakh Committee should be condemned because their actions have caused immense suffering to Azerbaijanis. In his speech, he cites Dostoevsky, saying that no noble cause is worth the tears of a child. One of the participants is outraged: "How dare you Azerbaijanis talk about children's tears after Sumgait?" "Do you really believe the entire Azerbaijani people participated in the Sumgait pogrom?" Alizadeh asks in response.

Chairing the session, Sakharov asks Garry Kasparov, who is present at the conference, what he thinks about the Karabakh Committee. Kasparov supports the guest from Azerbaijan: "When they started their movement, they gave no thought to the fate of the Armenians in Baku. Baku is a cosmopolitan city where people live without regard to nationality."

After the session, at the metro station, Zardusht Alizadeh runs into academician Viktor Palm, one of the founders of the Estonian Popular Front. They begin walking along the platform, and the Estonian politician advises his young Azerbaijani colleague to avoid violence, warning that it only serves the authorities—who are unmatched when it comes to provocation. He tells him that the Soviet Union is doomed, but the authorities may trigger bloody wars to justify imposing order through military force.

As they part ways, already inside the metro car, the chemist gives him a final warning: "Do everything you can to avoid being dragged into an armed confrontation. Otherwise, you will lose your freedom. Your democracy will die."

7

SEASICK ALONG THE WAY

One New Year's Eve, when I was eight, I prepared a festive concert as a gift for my grandmother and Rosa Borisovna. I wrote two songs on current political topics and performed them before the holiday dinner.

The first song (a reworking of a poem by the Russian poet Nikolay Nekrasov that we had studied in school) literally described the events of the past year:

Not the wind howling through the forest,
Not streams rushing down from the hills,
But Boris discussing with Yegor,
Which way to go with their wills. . . .
Two congresses meet in our land,
Gorbachev watches from on high,
He picks Lukyanov to take a stand,
And suddenly, Sakharov dies,
As Boris is thrown from the bridge nearby. . . .

It was an undeniable success—both my grandmother and Rosa Borisovna were delighted. Their political views were polar opposites, a mix of Elena Bonner and Nina Andreeva. My grandmother combined the temperament of Sakharov's widow with the world view of the "I Cannot Compromise My Principles" manifesto, while Rosa Borisovna was extremely liberal but highly diplomatic.

Despite their differences, they both loved me, nurtured my political awareness, and encouraged my creativity. Emboldened by their enthusiasm, I decided to perform the second song, about which I'd initially had doubts:

Look around, here and there, tam-tam-ta-dam,
It's all ours, everywhere, tam-tam-ta-dam.
The radiation, the AIDS, tam-tam-ta-dam,
And the eternal shortages, tam-tam-ta-dam.

Of course, I didn't know what AIDS was, though it was constantly mentioned on TV. The word was short and fit well into the song's rhythm. The second verse focused entirely on AIDS:

AIDS rages on, it sings, it bites,
It robs our days, it haunts our nights,
No peace, no joy, no dreams alive,
And perestroika hits year five!

Both my grandmother and Rosa Borisovna laughed heartily, but I sensed that my grandmother was looking at me with disapproval, as if I'd done something terribly inappropriate and shameful. Things got worse when Rosa Borisovna advised me not to sing the song in front of my parents: "Otherwise, they'll think I taught you this."

They didn't explain what had upset them, of course. Rosa Borisovna quickly changed the subject, launching into a discussion of the Jewish pogroms she was convinced were imminent. She was genuinely afraid of them and frequently discussed with my grandmother how she would hide her "when it starts."

THE NEW PRESIDENT

On January 20, 1989, the inauguration of the new US president, George Bush, takes place in Washington. "We will continue the new closeness with the Soviet Union," he says in his speech. "One might say that our new relationship in part reflects the triumph of hope and strength over experience. But hope is good and so is strength. And vigilance."

These words are highly symbolic, because in the new administration, vigilance immediately takes precedence over hope. Bush's new foreign policy team believes that Reagan had been too naive, and that Secretary of State Shultz, in particular, had made unnecessary concessions. The key specialist on the USSR in the new administration is Robert Gates, now Deputy National Security Advisor, who is known for his distrust of Gorbachev. His boss, General Brent Scowcroft, largely shares these suspicions. He believes that perestroika is merely a cover operation, that the veterans of the Politburo remain strong, simply waiting for the system to be refreshed, and "they are unlikely to be mistaken."

Bush, who had recently engaged so cordially with Gorbachev during his visit to the United Nations, avoids meeting him and instead sends the General Secretary a letter delivered personally by Henry Kissinger. In the letter, Bush warns that he will need some time to develop his new foreign policy.

Gorbachev, who initially maintained some distance in his relations with Reagan, writes Bush a surprisingly candid reply—as if addressing an old friend: "I lead a strange country. I am trying to guide my people in a direction they do not understand, and many do not want to go in this direction. When I became general secretary, I thought that by now Perestroika would already be complete. In reality, economic reform has only just begun."

In a dispatch sent to Washington in February 1989, US ambassador Jack Matlock puts it even more starkly: "It can be said that the Soviet Union has effectively declared its bankruptcy, and there is no going back."

Bush does not respond to Gorbachev's openness—and this deeply wounds the General Secretary. Foreign policy is Gorbachev's strong suit, his only refuge, and he has grown accustomed to being popular around the world. But now the new US president does not reciprocate, and to make matters worse, KGB chief Vladimir Kryuchkov constantly reports that this is no accident. According to him, the CIA has created a special group with the goal of discrediting perestroika and Gorbachev personally. This group, Kryuchkov claims, is led by Gorbachev's longtime critic Robert Gates.

THE MASTER AND THE AYATOLLAH

On February 15, 1989, a historic moment arrives: the last Soviet soldier departs Afghanistan, marking the USSR's official completion of its troop withdrawal. This war began ten years ago and soon came to be seen by Muslims around the world as religious: a jihad against the atheist Soviet empire.

But exactly one day before this, another event occurs that symbolizes the start of a new religious war: between the Islamic world and the West. On

February 14, 1989, Iran's spiritual leader, Imam Khomeini, issues a fatwa calling for the killing of anyone involved in the publication of the novel *The Satanic Verses* by British writer Salman Rushdie.

Rushdie is an emigrant, but not from Iran. He was born into a Muslim family in Bombay, back when it was still part of the British Empire. In 1961, Rushdie, then fourteen, moved to England. He studied at Cambridge and later worked as a copywriter at the advertising agency Ogilvy.

In 1981, Rushdie gained worldwide fame—and the Booker Prize—for his novel *Midnight's Children*. However, he is not just a writer; he is a committed provocateur. He believes that a writer must be an antagonist to the state. In *Midnight's Children*, he insults Indian prime minister Indira Gandhi, while his next novel ridicules former and current Pakistani leaders.

He is a highly politicized writer with a reputation for being anti-Western: he supports the Islamic Revolution in Iran, criticizes American foreign policy, calls the United States "a bandit posing as sheriff," and refers to Margaret Thatcher as "Mrs. Torture."

Rushdie has a favorite Russian writer, but it is not Alexsander Solzhenitsyn. Instead, it is the far less well-known Mikhail Bulgakov, author of one of Russia's most beloved novels, *The Master and Margarita*. Under the influence of this book, Rushdie writes *The Satanic Verses*, something he himself acknowledges repeatedly—it is essentially a modern retelling of *The Master and Margarita*.

The action in Bulgakov's novel takes place in his contemporary 1930s Moscow, where the devil makes an appearance, as well as in first-century Jerusalem, shortly before the crucifixion of Jesus Christ. Rushdie's novel also exists in two timelines: in contemporary London, where the devil and an angel arrive, and in seventh-century Mecca, at the moment of the Prophet Muhammad's revelations. For both authors, the devil is not the ultimate evil; far more terrifying is the surrounding reality of Moscow and London.

Bulgakov's novel was never published during his lifetime, and the author died shortly after completing it.

Rushdie chose a problematic source of inspiration—something that becomes clear immediately after the publication of *The Satanic Verses*. The book is published in the United Kingdom in September 1988 and is immediately banned in India, then in Bangladesh, Sudan, South Africa, Sri Lanka, Malaysia, and Brunei. In February 1989, the book is released in the United States. On February 12, in the Pakistani capital of Islamabad, a demonstration of one hundred thousand protesters takes place. The demonstrators attack the American Cultural Center and seize the office of American Express. Six people are killed.

Two days later, Ayatollah Khomeini issues his fatwa: "I inform all brave Muslims of the world that the author of *The Satanic Verses*, a text written against Islam, the Prophet, and the Quran, as well as all editors and publishers aware of its content, are sentenced to death. I call on all Muslims, wherever they may be, to kill them immediately so that no one will dare insult the faith of Muslims again." The Iranian government offers $2 million for Rushdie's head. For the next nine years, the writer lives under the protection of British police.

The Ayatollah likely never read the book—he simply reacts to the news. But it is a cunning populist move. Iran is in international isolation, having recently suffered a de facto defeat in its war with Iraq, which was supported by the West. With this statement, Khomeini signals his readiness to lead the entire radical Islamic world. But more importantly, he marks a shift within the Islamic world itself. Just yesterday, Muslims around the globe united against godless communists; now they are outraged by Western blasphemers.

Salman Rushdie is supported by intellectuals worldwide—except for Solzhenitsyn, of course. As a believer, Solzhenitsyn prefers to remain silent. Nevertheless, Rushdie becomes, in the eyes of Western society, the new Solzhenitsyn—a creator fighting for freedom and therefore risking his life. In the years to come, he becomes the most prominent voice expressing Western fears about the Islamic world—much like Solzhenitsyn once personified opposition to communism.

Khomeini's fatwa completely eclipses, for the rest of the world, the Soviet withdrawal from Afghanistan. The passage of the last regiment across the border via the "Friendship Bridge" is shown only on Soviet television. Meanwhile, the *New York Times* publishes a surprised article questioning why authorities and society in the Soviet Union remain so indifferent to Salman Rushdie—no one speaks out in his defense.

Ogonyok editor in chief Vitaly Korotich compares Khomeini to Stalin, adding: "We live in times when no one wants to ruin relations with another country over a book that no one in the USSR has even read."

INTERGIRL

In January 1989, director Pyotr Todorovsky's film *Intergirl* (*Interdevochka*) hits Soviet theaters, marking yet another revolution in the USSR—this time, a sexual one. The movie tells the story of Leningrad sex workers (specifically those serving foreign clients), known as "currency prostitutes."

Under Soviet law, any dealings with foreign currency are a crime, and prostitution is an unimaginable taboo. Most Soviet viewers had no idea such a profession even existed in their country, let alone that it could be the subject of a film. Despite this, the movie is far from erotic—there's no explicit sex, and only one actress briefly bares her chest.

One of the prostitutes is played by twenty-five-year-old Lithuanian actress Ingeborga Dapkūnaitė. "When I read the script, I immediately knew this would be explosive. And that's exactly what happened—it became Russia's *Pretty Woman*, with all the Soviet nuances, of course," she recalls.

The film shocks Soviet audiences on every level. Just three years earlier, a Leningrad woman declared on television that "there is no sex" in the USSR. Two years ago, Alla Pugacheva complained that prostitutes in Leningrad's Pribaltiyskaya Hotel "were treated better than the artists." And now everything has come together—the film about sex workers is shot in that very hotel.

What defines the fate of *Intergirl* is its creators' decision to form a cooperative and purchase several copies of the film, allowing them to organize their own screenings. In the USSR, movie ticket prices are fixed—fifty kopeks at any theater. However, if an actor appears at the screening, it can be declared a "concert," and tickets can be sold at ten times the price—five rubles each.

Dapkūnaitė recalls being offered a promotional tour for the film, with a promise of 7,000 rubles for ten days. At the time, her salary at the Vilnius State Theatre is just 150 rubles per month.

"You can pick any city in the USSR," the producer offers.

"What's your farthest city?" she asks out of curiosity.

The farthest cities turn out to be Ulan-Ude, the capital of Buryatia, an autonomous republic in the Russian Federation, and Tselinograd in Kazakhstan (the future capital, Astana). Dapkūnaitė goes to both.

"I'd never seen such success," she recalls. "In Ulan-Ude, we had ten screenings a day, the theaters were packed, and people even brought stepladders to sit on in the aisles. In Tselinograd, there were fewer screenings, but the halls held up to five thousand people."

With part of her earnings, Dapkūnaitė buys her grandmother a house outside Vilnius. That house would later save her family—when food shortages hit in the 1990s, her relatives would survive on vegetables and fruit grown in her grandmother's garden.

THE RED HUNDRED

In the winter of 1989, the USSR begins its parliamentary election campaign—these are the first competitive elections in many decades. However, the rules for these elections, devised by Gorbachev and his team, are very peculiar. On the one hand, alternative elections take place across the country in territorial districts. On the other hand, registering as a candidate is not easy—each aspiring parliamentarian must be approved by a "voters' assembly," giving local party authorities tremendous opportunities for manipulation.

Moreover, alongside the elected legislators, there are many seats reserved for public organizations: trade unions, writers' and filmmakers' unions, the Academy of Sciences, and so forth. Finally, a full one hundred seats are allocated to the Communist Party—a quota that becomes known as the "Red Hundred."

The rules provoke a storm of outrage in many quarters (for example, in the Baltic republics and Azerbaijan). It's remarkable: just yesterday elections seemed impossible, but today, thanks to Gorbachev's boldness, they are being held. Yet almost no one is grateful to the General Secretary—his reforms seem inconsistent and half-hearted. The elections are not 100 percent free, given the quota reserved for the party elite. Moreover, on the ground, regional officials do everything they can to interfere in the election process: removing undesirable candidates and favoring their own. However, they cannot do this overtly—Gorbachev would clearly not approve of such manipulations. As a result, local authorities try to use administrative resources as discreetly as possible, and almost every time this leads to a scandal, with regional officials backing down. This is a unique moment in history: an authoritarian system is afraid to reveal its authoritarian nature and instead wants to appear democratic—all because the leader himself wants to see it that way.

KINO AND DISNEYLAND

In February 1989, Viktor Tsoi and Yuri Kasparyan fly to America for the first time. At the Los Angeles airport, they are met by Joanna, who rents a white limousine with champagne for the occasion. As they drive through the city, they lean out of the windows, singing. Their first long-awaited stop is a guitar shop.

They stay in Joanna's parents' beach house in Malibu, stroll along the shore, and watch surfers in Venice. According to Joanna, Vitya clearly enjoys being in a place where no one recognizes him and no one asks for his auto-graph. *The Needle* has become a box office hit, and Tsoi has been named Actor of the Year by *Soviet Screen* magazine—essentially making him the Soviet Bruce Lee, just as he had hoped.

But right now something else excites him even more—he, Yuri, and Joanna are heading to Disneyland. "Dream does come true," Vitya says with a childlike smile. They had talked so many times about his dream of visiting Disneyland, always convinced it was impossible and would never happen. He leaves Joanna one of their photos from the park as a keepsake, inscribing it: "The happiest place on Earth."

The Kino musicians return home to a completely different reality. They now have a producer—a new, trendy, and largely unfamiliar word in the USSR. Their concert director calls himself that as he organizes their tours. They no longer have any trouble securing venues for performances. They have recorded a new album, *A Star Called the Sun*.

In interviews, Tsoi describes his band's genre as pop music: "I make pop music. It should encompass everything—it should make people laugh when needed and make them think when needed. The only thing music shouldn't do is call people to storm the Winter Palace," he says, alluding to the 1917 Russian Revolution.

REPRESENTATIVE SAKHAROV

In March 1989, elections for the Congress of People's Deputies begin in the USSR. Initially, Sakharov does not plan to run—he is convinced that he will simply not be allowed to participate. His wife, too, is against it: "There will be one Sakharov, and two and a half thousand of these parlia-mentarians. What will you do with that crowd?"

But the pressure is immense: people, including colleagues from the institute, keep coming to their home, insisting that Sakharov must be their representative. Eventually, Sakharov agrees to participate—and loses.

The Academy of Sciences is supposed to elect twenty-five representatives, but none of the most prominent scientists are among them, including Sakharov. The issue lies in the voting rules: Sakharov is nominated by sixty institutes but blocked by the governing body of the academy. This leads to mass outrage.

Activist Lev Ponomarev arranges a meeting at the House of Cinema, where an initiative group called Memorial plans to nominate Sakharov as a candidate from Moscow—an alternative way to enter the congress. He recalls leaving the Belorusskaya metro station and immediately encountering a massive line. "I asked, 'What are you standing for?' 'To get into the House of Cinema, to nominate Sakharov.' I thought, 'Holy shit,'" Ponomarev says, realizing it would not be easy to push through the crowd to the very event he had organized.

Sakharov, too, is astonished at the crowd's size: "These are people awakened from their passive slumber by the hopes of perestroika—workers, employees, the broadest segment of the intelligentsia. They recognized me and greeted me enthusiastically." That day, according to Sakharov, he receives "a moral mandate for parliamentary activity."

However, the decisive moment comes on February 2. A rally gathers outside the Academy of Sciences, where participants demand that the leadership annul the previous vote and hold a fairer election. The academy gives in to the demands—another vote is held, and the most popular scientists finally win. Sakharov becomes a parliamentarian representing the academy.

"There was euphoria all around—and they disarmed me," Elena Bonner will later recall. "The mistake of my life was to accept that Andrei would become a parliamentarian."

YELTSIN'S TRIUMPH

While Sakharov never planned to become a politician, for Yeltsin these elections represent a unique opportunity. Yeltsin is nominated in two hundred districts—but the system requires a candidate's inclusion on the ballot to be approved by a voters' assembly, which in practice is usually controlled by officials.

Yeltsin considers it most prestigious to run in Electoral District No. 1—all of Moscow. There are ten other candidates and the voters' assembly is instructed to eliminate all contenders except two: the director of an automobile factory, Yevgeny Brakov, and the cosmonaut Georgy Grechko.

All the other candidates, including Yeltsin, deliver their speeches, trying to win over the assembly—but it is clear that no one dares defy the authorities' instructions. Then, at the last moment, something unexpected happens. Cosmonaut Grechko asks for the floor and withdraws his candidacy, calling on the assembly to vote for Yeltsin.

This changes everything. The initial plan is now invalid, and the assembly members are free to vote for whomever they choose. Yeltsin is officially nominated.

Yeltsin triumphs, winning 89 percent of the vote, with a turnout of 83 percent. This marks the beginning of a new chapter not only in his life but in all of Russian politics. Yeltsin is no longer a persecuted folk hero—he is now, officially, the most popular politician in the country.

A BET FOR A BOTTLE OF COGNAC

The fiercest battle between the authorities and the opposition takes place in Leningrad. Democratic activists form the "Elections-89" coalition and compile a unified list of candidates. In response, the authorities use every trick in the book to ensure that none of these activists can get on the ballot. For instance, one politician isn't issued a pass to the factory where the voters' assembly is being held. In response, the "Elections-89" club begins supporting unknown candidates who have managed to register. One such dark horse is Anatoly Sobchak, a professor at Leningrad University.

Sobchak is a complete unknown in the city. He isn't a scholar of renown, a dissident, or a public figure—just a professor of civil law at Leningrad University. Naturally, the idea of participating in the elections doesn't even cross his mind. He attends the faculty meeting out of curiosity. The start of the meeting is sobering, as the chair announces a long-standing tradition: Vasilyevsky Island, where the university is located, is always represented in Soviet governing bodies by a worker from a local factory. He proposes that they waste no time, vote to support the next worker candidate, and go home.

But this time, the university staff digs in their heels. They refuse to back an unknown worker and insist on nominating their own candidates. The chair has no choice but to comply.

One of the younger professors nominates Sobchak, who treats it as a joke—an opportunity to practice his oratory skills. In his campaign speech, he talks about the rule of law and the primacy of universal human values. Unexpectedly, he advances to the next round. Another speech follows, and the university assembly votes for him.

But Professor Sobchak still doesn't take the process seriously—until a party official corners him in the corridor.

"Why are you doing this? You must understand that you have no chance. The representative will be a worker from the Baltic Shipyard."

At that moment, Sobchak, according to his own recollections, suddenly retorts:

"Let's make a bet. A bottle of cognac."

At the district meeting, Sobchak arrives with a prepared speech. By lottery, he is set to speak last. Sobchak's turn comes at around half past eleven at night. He climbs onto the stage and realizes that if he starts reading it, the voters will fall asleep on the spot. Then he recalls Martin Luther King and his "I Have a Dream" speech. Sobchak, as he puts it, "calls upon the shadow of the great American civil rights leader."

"I dream of a time when there will be no district voters' assemblies or preselections of candidates; when voters won't crowd behind closed doors guarded by police patrols; a time when corrupt and incompetent ministers will stop turning our lives into absurdity. . . . I dream of a time when our state will become a nation of laws. . . ."

The assembly supports him, and his name is included on the ballot. Unexpectedly, he finds himself a politician. On his way home, he hails a taxi—the driver turns out to be his former student, moonlighting as a cabbie.

"Why do you need this?" the driver questions his professor on the way. "It's all just a game. All of it is lies. Even if you break yourself, you still won't overthrow this system. If you're just bored with your life as a professor and want to play, I get it. If you're serious, I pity you. Because the system is unshakable, and professors won't bring it down."

Nevertheless, Sobchak takes it seriously. Every day, he stands with a megaphone near Vasileostrovskaya metro station, addressing citizens hurrying to work. Soon people grow used to his speeches—the entrance to the station turns into a sort of Speakers' Corner, as in Hyde Park. His students help him by driving around the city and putting up campaign posters.*

But the decisive moment comes during the televised debates: Sobchak outshines his opponent with his eloquence and wins, earning 76 percent of the vote.

The real surprise in Leningrad lies elsewhere: in every constituency across the city, candidates supported by the Communist Party lose. Not a single party official is elected as a representative.

ENTRENCHING SHOVELS

On March 18, 1989, another interethnic conflict erupts in the USSR. In Abkhazia, in the village of Lykhny, tens of thousands of people gather for what they call a *"people's assembly of Abkhazians."* They draft a letter to Moscow, requesting that the status of their republic be elevated. Abkhazia is an autonomous republic within Soviet Georgia, but the assembly's participants demand that Abkhazia become a full-fledged Soviet republic, on par with Georgia or Russia. This marks the second case—after Nagorno-Karabakh—where Caucasian peoples demand changes to internal Soviet borders.

As the Abkhazians demand a revision of the existing Soviet arrangements, protests begin among Georgians living in Abkhazia. On April 4, a solidarity demonstration starts in Tbilisi, in front of the Georgian government building.

The leaders of the protesters are Georgia's two most famous dissidents: fifty-year-old Zviad Gamsakhurdia and forty-nine-year-old Merab Kostava.

Gamsakhurdia is the son of a classic Georgian writer and a writer himself; he translated *Romeo and Juliet*, *King Lear*, and other works by Shakespeare, as well as Oscar Wilde and Jonathan Swift, into Georgian. Kostava is a music teacher. Zviad and Merab were classmates, but the defining cause of their lives has been their fight against Soviet power. They were first arrested by the KGB while still schoolboys.

Both men were founders of the Georgian Helsinki Group and cooperated with Amnesty International. They were routinely arrested, sent to prisons and psychiatric hospitals. For example, in 1977, they were once again accused of anti-Soviet activity. Gamsakhurdia, under KGB pressure, agreed to a

---

* One of them is twenty-three-year-old Dmitry Medvedev, the future president of Russia.

public recantation. His statement was recorded and broadcast on Georgian television. In exchange, he received a lenient sentence of two years in exile. Kostava, however, refused to repent and spent the next ten years in prison, only to be released in 1987 thanks to Sakharov's efforts.

By 1989, both men are recognized leaders of the Georgian national movement. "Merab Kostava was remarkably generous; Gamsakhurdia was not. Kostava was ready to forgive even his jailers. He was an extraordinary man. They both sacrificed everything in life. When Kostava was in the prison, his son committed suicide; he was accepted nowhere—neither to any university nor for any job. Zviad, on the other hand, was tormented his entire life, constantly under surveillance," recalls one of their closest allies, Akaki Asatiani. He is thirty-five at the time and also joins the April 1989 demonstration in central Tbilisi.

"Gamsakhurdia and I led the people. One column came from the stadium, while another joined near the Tbilisi Philharmonic. Tens of thousands gathered," Asatiani recounts. "The issue at hand was to overturn the decision of the Abkhazians. But at some point, the leaders realized that Moscow couldn't care less about Abkhazia. If we demanded independence, that would have a greater impact."

The slogans raised by the protesters are shockingly radical: "Occupation troops, get out of Georgia!" "Abolish the Abkhaz Republic!" "We demand full independence for Georgia!" "No to the Russian Communist Empire!" Until the spring of 1989, nothing like this had been seen anywhere, not even in the Baltic republics.

"One of my grandfathers was shot in 1937; the other was arrested and perished in the camps. My grandmothers raised me to hate the Soviet regime with a burning passion," Asatiani recalls of his mindset at the time. "In every sport, I always rooted against the USSR. The only exceptions were the ice hockey players—they were genuinely good, and somehow different. And I supported the cosmonauts, too—after all, they were people in space. But as for the rest of the Russians, I hated them with a deep, burning hatred."

A few young people declare a hunger strike and set up a tent camp in the square. The Georgian leadership reacts nervously. First Secretary Jumber Patiashvili initially assures Moscow that everything is under control, but on the third day, he starts to panic, calls Moscow, and asks for troops to be sent to Tbilisi.

"Patiashvili didn't grasp the situation. He was a rather petty man. If Shevardnadze had been in his place, he would have figured things out immediately. And the rest of them? Complete nonentities—where did they even find these people? Were they deliberately picking individuals without initiative?" Asatiani reflects. However, he also admits that the protest leaders were struggling too: "The process spiraled out of control; the crowd had taken charge, and it was impossible to manage."

On the fourth day, troops appear in the city. Tanks demonstratively roll past the protesters along Rustaveli Avenue, and combat helicopters fly over the city center at extremely low altitudes. Many Tbilisi residents expect the military to open fire at any moment. To prevent violence, citizens begin flooding the square—first the families of the hunger strikers, then many prominent Georgian intellectuals.

At the same time, a group of women gathers outside First Secretary Patiashvili's residence. They demand that he come out and promise the authorities will not use weapons to disperse the protest. But Patiashvili does not appear, and the women head to the square to join the demonstrators.

"There were many women right in the thick of it, and they wouldn't leave," Asatiani recalls. "I'm generally a calm person. The leaders asked me to try and convince the women to go home. I walked around saying, 'Come on, go home. Nothing will happen.' 'Well, if nothing will happen,' the women replied, 'then we'll stay.' Then I tried scaring them, saying something might happen. 'Even more reason to stay,' they said."

Around 4:00 a.m., the army begins dispersing the crowd.

"To be honest, we brought it on ourselves after the first blow. The soldiers didn't know how to disperse protests. The fight was brutal, really . . . ," Asatiani recounts. "About a hundred soldiers were injured or wounded—people were throwing stones at them. I was breaking trees in the First School garden, for instance. We tore boards off the park benches. Of course, we didn't have weapons, but we took some from the soldiers. There were karate fighters and rugby players on my flank. . . ." By morning, reports spread that the soldiers had been armed with entrenching shovels and had beaten women with them.

The next day—April 10, a Monday—is the day election results are announced across the country. In Leningrad, Anatoly Sobchak wakes up early and turns on the radio. He already knows he has won—he had been told the night before. Expecting to hear news about the election results, he instead hears about what happened the previous day in Tbilisi, the capital of Soviet Georgia.

Nineteen people were killed there, sixteen of them women. Sobchak has no idea yet that soon he will be tasked with investigating this case and determining who gave the order to disperse the protest.

The bloodshed in Tbilisi comes as a shock to everyone, starkly contrasting with Gorbachev's usual rhetoric about nonviolent solutions to problems. The public begins to question: Was this decision really made without Gorbachev's knowledge? Or did he know everything?

"If, before April 9, anyone in Georgia still had doubts—about whether Gamsakhurdia was a radical or not, whether he would succeed or fail—after April 9, those doubts were gone. It became a universal sentiment: only separation from the Soviet Union. The doubts ended on April 9," says Asatiani.

LENIN AND POKER

In the fall of 1988, the original trio of *Vzglyad* hosts, including Sasha Lyubimov, are unexpectedly brought back on air. The young journalists themselves are surprised by the decision—but it only strengthens their resolve.

"We came back, and we were pissed off," Lyubimov would recall. "Before, we were careful. We didn't have any real political content—just some music and human-interest stories. But now, we had a real edge. If this Party is so weak, then we might as well fuck it."

After the tragedy in Tbilisi, Sasha Lyubimov travels to Georgia to film a report. But TV executives refuse to air it—it's too bold.

Instead, *Vzglyad* invites a star guest to the studio: the renowned theater and film director Mark Zakharov. The plan is for him to discuss his creative projects, but things quickly go off script. First, he expresses condolences to "our Georgian brothers and sisters" and calls for a moment of silence on air. Then he shifts the conversation entirely—suggesting that Lenin's body should be removed from the Mausoleum and given a proper burial.

Zakharov is not attacking Lenin himself. On the contrary, he argues that turning the founder of the Soviet state into a mummy was Stalin's crime, a violation of Lenin's will and that of his family. Zakharov condemns it as immoral: "We have no right to deny a human body a proper burial—we must not act like pagans."

But for Zakharov, this historical discussion is directly connected to the present. "To me, Lenin's genius lies in his politics. He was a brilliant politician—one that we need now, for our perestroika. His decisiveness, bold course changes, extraordinary connection with the people, remarkable self-criticism, ability to acknowledge his mistakes . . . ," Zakharov says, listing what are clearly his hopes for Gorbachev.

Nothing more scandalous had ever been said on Soviet television. The idea of removing Lenin from the Mausoleum is tantamount to sacrilege for any Soviet citizen. And yet the man who dares to say it—Mark Zakharov—is not only a legendary and beloved filmmaker but also a newly elected parliamentarian. As a result, the communist leadership does not direct its fury at him but at *Vzglyad* and its hosts—especially Vladimir Mukusev, who is anchoring this episode.

"Raisa Maksimovna told me how Gorbachev watched *Vzglyad*," Mukusev will later recall. "He hated us—his face would turn red with anger, and he would throw his slippers at the TV. He could have shut us down with a single phone call, but he didn't. Why? Because he understood that to carry out his massive reforms, he needed strong television, strong media."

A few days after the broadcast, a new Communist Party plenum begins. Lyubimov later recalls opening *Pravda* and reading excerpts from the speeches delivered at the plenum—only to realize that nearly a third of the speakers were talking about *Vzglyad*. "These TV guys have gotten out of control—it's time to rein them in," they said.

"I knew this was a moment of truth. And as a seasoned poker player and con artist with my Tbilisi story in my back pocket, I, of course, had to use it," Lyubimov will later say.

The *Vzglyad* team debates their next move and decides to raise the stakes. Since Gorbachev himself hasn't commented yet, they take a gamble. One week after Zakharov's speech, they air the Tbilisi footage.

Vzglyad's popularity breaks all records. The program's director, Anatoly Lysenko, tells hosts:

"You need to understand one thing—you are more popular than Leo Tolstoy. Tolstoy was read by ten million people. And you? A hundred million see you every week, whether they want to or not."

THE CHINESE SALON OF DEMOCRACY

On April 15, at 7:56 a.m., in one of Beijing's hospitals, seventy-three-year-old Hu Yaobang, the former General Secretary of the Chinese Communist Party, dies. He lost his position as the party leader two years ago for supporting the demands of students protesting against corruption. At the time, however, China's real leader, Deng Xiaoping, decided otherwise—Hu Yaobang lost his position, though he retained a seat on the Politburo.

News of the reformist ex–General Secretary's death is announced during the evening broadcasts. Many students consider Hu Yaobang to have been their advocate. On April 17, they march to Tiananmen Square to lay wreaths at the base of the Monument to the People's Heroes in Hu Yaobang's memory. Officially, this violates the rules for mass demonstrations adopted in 1986, but no one interferes with the students. Many arrive at the square after dark and realize their action will go unnoticed—by morning, the wreaths will likely be removed. They decide to stay overnight.

That night, on Tiananmen Square, they draft their grievances against the authorities—articulated in the "Seven-Point Petition" of the students of Peking University. With this document, their action effectively transforms into a political protest. The primary demands include: rehabilitating Hu Yaobang, permitting independent media and freedom of speech, publishing income declarations of senior officials and their families, allowing demonstrations in Beijing, and increasing state spending on education.

It would be a mistake to see this as a student movement for democracy—the students' main demands are quite different. For the past ten years, China has been undergoing economic reforms initiated by Deng Xiaoping, making the country increasingly capitalist. Inflation is rising, and corruption is spreading. Many aspects of the new economic policies frustrate the students, but for many, the protest is primarily against the social injustice that has resulted from these market reforms.

In the morning, Wang Dan, a history student and head of the Peking University's so-called salon of democracy, hands the handwritten petition to one of the guards of the Great Hall of the People—the Chinese parliament. Receiving a signed acknowledgment, he returns to his dormitory to catch up on sleep.

Not all students think this is enough—several groups try to deliver the petition to other senior officials, most often mentioning Premier Li Peng, whom they see as the main opponent of reforms. However, they are unsuccessful, as security refuses to allow the students access to government residences.

On April 19, Wang Dan holds a traditional "salon of democracy," but this time not in a lecture hall, as before, but outside. Around three thousand people gather, and they decide to create the country's first independent student union.

That evening, another group of students heads toward the government residence. Once again, there's a standoff with security. Among the students, twenty-one-year-old Wu'er Kaixi (Uerkesh Dawlet) stands out—a student at Beijing Normal University's Faculty of Education and a Uighur by ethnicity. He is the only one who dares to give his name and address to the guards, after which many begin to see him as a leader of the movement.

A convoy of several dozen buses arrives at the scene. Police urge the students to return to their campuses. When the students refuse, they are herded onto the buses and taken to the dormitories of Peking University, where they are released. Such a soft approach to the students is encouraged by sixty-nine-year-old General Secretary Zhao Ziyang, a proponent of economic and political liberalization—essentially, China's Gorbachev. He believes that the Politburo cannot monopolize the right to pay respects to Hu Yaobang.

On April 22, the official funeral ceremony begins in Tiananmen Square. The students sing the national anthem of the PRC in unison and bow their heads silently during the moment of silence. The hearse carrying Hu Yaobang's body departs, but most of the students remain. They once again try to hand over the "Seven-Point Petition" to government representatives. Three students approach the closed doors of the Great Hall of the People and kneel, but no one comes out to meet them.

That day, Liu Xiaobo, formerly a literary critic and now a lecturer at Columbia University (and future Nobel laureate), is sitting in his New York apartment watching the news. The student demonstration strikes him so deeply that he decides to immediately return home to China—something historic is happening.

On April 23, convinced that the student movement has ended, Zhao Ziyang leaves Beijing for an official visit to Pyongyang. Premier Li Peng assumes his duties.

However, nothing ends. The next day, a professor's speech is broadcast via loudspeakers at Peking University, calling for "seizing all illegal incomes from corrupt officials and speculators and using the money for education." The idea resonates strongly with the students. On April 24, they announce an indefinite strike and stop attending classes.

Meanwhile, in Zhao's absence, the Politburo meets, calling the student movement an "organized and carefully planned political conspiracy." They decide to report the situation to Deng Xiaoping the next day. Formally, he is only the chairman of the Central Military Commission, but he is widely regarded as the highest authority. He agrees and pushes for a crackdown on "anti-party, anti-government turmoil." The first step: a hardline editorial in *People's Daily*, published on April 26:

> This is a planned conspiracy and turmoil. Its essence is the
> overthrow of the leadership of the Communist Party and the
> socialist system. If we tolerate this turmoil, the country will
> descend into chaos.

Liu Xiaobo is in Tokyo during a layover, preparing to board his flight to Beijing, when he learns of the *People's Daily* editorial. Horrified by the rhetoric, he realizes the student movement is doomed and that traveling to Beijing is dangerous. But just as his flight is called, Liu Xiaobo shrugs and decides to take his chances and fly to China.

The *People's Daily* editorial shocks and outrages the students—they don't recognize their movement in its portrayal. The next day, nearly two hundred thousand people march through Tiananmen Square. Soldiers are present but do not intervene.

On April 30, the liberal General Secretary Zhao Ziyang returns to Beijing and launches a scathing critique of his conservative colleagues. At first glance, something similar had happened recently in the USSR when Ligachev published Nina Andreeva's letter during Gorbachev's absence, only for Gorbachev to return and reverse course.

On May 1, Zhao convenes the Politburo and explains that the April 26 editorial has worsened the situation. The public's sympathies are with the students, so the authorities must tone down their repressive rhetoric and engage in dialogue with the students—essentially fulfilling their demands. On May 3, Chinese television broadcasts Zhao Ziyang's meeting with delegates from the Asian Development Bank. He states that the students' concerns about corruption are justified and describes the movement as inherently patriotic.

The next day, China marks the anniversary of the May Fourth Movement of 1919, which also began in Tiananmen Square. Seventy years later, one hundred thousand people gather there again. Police presence is minimal. After Zhao's statement, many believe the movement has succeeded. Most universities, except Peking (Wang Dan's school) and Beijing Normal (Wu'er Kaixi's), announce an end to the strike and a return to classes.

"GORBACHEV WILL FAIL"

The unrest in China has not yet become the world's top story—attention remains focused on the democratic elections in the USSR. However, reactions to the elections are mixed. On April 28, CNN airs an interview with US defense secretary Dick Cheney, marking the most scathing comment about perestroika to date.

"If I had to guess today, I would guess that he would ultimately fail," Cheney says about Gorbachev. "That is to say that he will not be able to reform the Soviet economy to turn it into an efficient, modern society. And when that happens, he's likely to be replaced by somebody who will be far more hostile than he's been in terms of his attitude towards the West."

Two days later, White House chief of staff John Sununu clarifies that this is not the president's view, and Bush himself states, "We want perestroika to succeed."

Just a week later, on May 10, the new US secretary of state, James Baker, arrives in Moscow. Soviet foreign minister Eduard Shevardnadze invites him home and speaks candidly over dinner—something unheard of in previous years. He opens up about the inefficiency of the Soviet economy, the black market, and pervasive corruption. According to Baker's recollections, Shevardnadze also admits that when Gorbachev first came to power "none of his team understood what was happening with the economy."

The next day brings an even more awkward moment. Baker meets with Gorbachev in the Kremlin for a one-on-one conversation and confesses that there are people in America who believe that if perestroika fails, the Soviet Union will grow weaker, and the United States will benefit from this. However, Baker assures him that the Bush administration does not share this view.

Afterward, they join their delegations, and Baker introduces his entourage. The first to be named is Robert Gates—a man Gorbachev has already heard plenty about. "From what I understand, the White House has created a special unit tasked with discrediting Gorbachev. I've been told you're in charge of it, Mr. Gates," the General Secretary says without hiding his irritation. Turning back to Baker, he adds, "Perhaps if we find a way to solve our problems, Mr. Gates will be out of a job."

Curiously, at nearly the same time, the *Washington Post* publishes an article titled "Why Bob Gates Is the Eeyore of Sovietology: Bush Needs More than Nay-Saying on Gorbachev."

Overall, Gorbachev's team finds the new secretary of state deeply underwhelming. "The American position is clear: the USSR has no way out; the collapse is underway. The Secretary of State came with nothing to offer," writes Anatoly Chernyaev in his diary. "Socialism is disappearing in Eastern Europe. . . . Communist parties in Western Europe are crumbling. . . . The economy is disintegrating; ideology, as such, no longer exists; the federation-empire is unraveling."

However, it's clear that Chernyaev writes this in a moment of emotional turmoil. Most of his diary entries from 1989 are far calmer. Gorbachev, for his part, does not share his closest aide's pessimism.

THE SOVIET WATERGATE

By late 1988, former Uzbek leader Inomjon Usmonxo'jayev begins testifying to investigators Gdlyan and Ivanov, claiming that he personally delivered suitcases of money to none other than Yegor Ligachev. The Prosecutor General's Office is stunned.

The allegations against Ligachev seem impossible. A staunch communist, a dogmatist, and an ascetic, he is a party fanatic—many things, but certainly not corrupt. It is well known that he moved to Moscow from Siberia with nothing more than a single suitcase.

Soon Usmonxo'jayev will retract his testimony and even write Ligachev a letter of apology, admitting he had falsely accused him under pressure. According to him, Gdlyan threatened to arrest his family and have him executed. "Soon after, coming to my senses just a few days later, I retracted my false testimony about bribing you and others," he will write.

But Gdlyan remains convinced that he is close to exposing the leader of the Soviet mafia.

In early March, Gdlyan easily wins the election and becomes a parliamentarian. At this moment, the authorities recognize the real threat he poses.

On March 24, 1989, the Central Committee establishes a special commission led by Boris Pugo, the former First Secretary of Latvia, tasked with investigating whether Gdlyan's team violated laws during their work in Uzbekistan. Unsurprisingly, Pugo uncovers numerous violations. Party leadership begins a slow campaign against Gdlyan, seemingly hoping he will get the message and back off.

On May 14, by-elections take place in Leningrad, where the city's party leadership suffered a scandalous defeat a month earlier. Over thirty candidates run, but it quickly becomes apparent that the front-runner is Nikolai Ivanov, Gdlyan's deputy.

Ivanov is not a Leningrader, but he is a star of national stature. The democratic opposition, including Andrei Sakharov, throws its support not behind Ivanov, but behind dissident Marina Salye. They even distribute leaflets against Ivanov: Leningrad's intelligentsia views people from the security apparatus with distrust and hostility, Ivanov included. For dissidents, this is a clear dividing line: *they* are the ones imprisoned, while Ivanov is among those who do the imprisoning.

However, Sakharov's endorsement does not change the overall picture: Ivanov remains a national hero and the clear favorite of the people. The turning point comes on May 12 during televised debates broadcast live across the country. At the start of the program, candidate Nikolai Ivanov, responding to the moderator's question about the root causes of the nation's troubles, states that the Soviet mafia has protectors in the Kremlin. But before he can elaborate, his allotted time runs out. Ivanov promises to name names when it's his turn to speak again, allowing his opponents to have their say. The entire country holds its breath, waiting to hear the names of the key villains.

But then, the clock strikes 9:00 p.m.—the time when *Vremya*, the evening news program, airs throughout the USSR. The debates are cut off. An hour later, the program resumes—but the broadcast to Moscow is not restored, as the capital's TV authorities decide to show a feature film instead. Viewers are furious.

When Ivanov finally gets his turn again, he claims that the name of Yegor Ligachev—the second-most powerful figure in the USSR—"surfaces" in the corruption investigation materials. Ligachev, however, is an easy target—widely seen as a reactionary and Yeltsin's enemy, he has no real supporters.

Muscovites call their friends in Leningrad, anxiously asking, "Who did Ivanov name?" The following day, the entire country is abuzz, discussing how the investigator accused Ligachev on live television, while the party mafia allegedly tried to cut him off the air and hide the truth.

This is tantamount to a declaration of war. The next day, *Pravda* publishes a statement from the Presidium of the Supreme Soviet, accusing Gdlyan and Ivanov of slander and violating investigative secrecy. The popular newspaper *Moscow News* soon dubs the scandal "Our Domestic Watergate."

On May 14, Ivanov triumphantly wins the election in Leningrad with 61 percent of the vote. The next day, a furious Ligachev appeals to the prosecutor's office, calling the accusations slander and a political provocation.

In his memoir, Ivanov writes that upon his returning to Moscow, his superiors at the prosecutor's office demand that he immediately surrender his personal firearm and allow an inspection of his office safe—but he refuses. According to Ivanov, he and Gdlyan are openly surveilled by KGB operatives, though authorities stop short of firing them.

A series of rallies is held in support of Gdlyan and Ivanov. One of them takes place on May 20 in Moscow, next to Luzhniki Stadium, organized by Memorial and the Moscow Popular Front. This event, positioned as a meeting between opposition parliamentarians and their voters, becomes the largest protest in Moscow in the entire history of the Soviet Union—one hundred thousand people attend. On the same stage stand the new stars of politics: Gdlyan, Ivanov, Yeltsin, and Sakharov. One of the speakers proposes that Yeltsin be elected chairman of the Supreme Soviet of the USSR and Gdlyan appointed the country's prosecutor general. The crowd erupts in applause.

"AN ATTEMPTED LEGAL COUP"

On May 24, 1989, *Literaturnaya Gazeta* publishes an exposé by writer and human rights advocate Olga Chaikovskaya titled "The Myth." She accuses Gdlyan and Ivanov of torturing people during their investigation, holding innocent individuals in detention for months, if not years, destroying thousands of lives—and possibly being responsible for deaths.

"One weekly [*Moscow News*] published an article about Gdlyan, in which it was mentioned how one of Rashidov's closest associates, Gaipov, was arrested. His mansion was surrounded, the investigators entered, and *sat down to drink tea*. Excuse me, '*sat down to drink tea*'? Who sat down? Prosecutor's Office staff. A strange procedural action, isn't it? Nevertheless, they sat down for tea, and meanwhile, Rashidov's confidant went into the next room and stabbed himself to death. 'When Telman Khorenovich [Gdlyan] rushed into the bedroom, Gaipov had already managed to inflict thirteen(!) stab wounds on himself.' Just how focused did you have to be on drinking tea to not notice that?" Chaikovskaya remarks sarcastically.

Throughout the article, she cites interrogation records and letters from the accused—but this is far from an impartial journalistic investigation. Emotions run high.

"There are those who believe that corruption must be fought by any means necessary, even unlawful ones (a dangerous idea—fascism rose to power precisely under the banner of extrajudicial crackdowns on crime and corruption). But even here, something doesn't add up. Gdlyan wasn't truly fighting corruption," Chaikovskaya fumes.

Accusing Gdlyan of using the investigation as self-promotion to advance his career, Chaikovskaya delivers her verdict: "What we are witnessing, essentially, is an attempted legal coup—a bid to restore the practice of extrajudicial reprisals."

Olga Chaikovskaya had been known since the 1960s for defending prisoners and advocating for their rights. She had supported Solzhenitsyn and Sakharov—her journalistic reputation is impeccable. She is a genuine human rights defender, a rarity in the Soviet Union, and not a propagandist serving the regime. Still, *Literaturnaya Gazeta* is a servile, state-controlled publication that is often used to go after political opponents.

"In [Gdlyan's] hands was a powerful lever—prison. If a person denied guilt, they simply stopped interrogating them for months. Defendants told the court about the appalling conditions of detention in Uzbekistan: many persistently described some kind of basements," Chaikovskaya writes. " 'It was hell,' they said, 'pure hell, and we would agree to anything just to escape it!' "

Her exposé convinces few. The authority of the media is already undermined, and the investigation gets lost in a flurry of scandalous publications that society isn't used to.

The very next day after publication—on May 25—the USSR Prosecutor General's Office opens a case against Gdlyan and Ivanov for "violating socialist legality." For Soviet citizens, the message is clear: the government has begun persecuting truth-seeking investigators.

Many Soviet citizens genuinely believe that the mafia cannot be fought with kid gloves; all methods are justified.

BEIJING AWAITS GORBACHEV

Gorbachev's visit to Beijing is scheduled for May 15—an event of historic importance, given that relations between the two countries had been frozen for so many years. A decade earlier, Deng Xiaoping had prepared for nuclear war with the USSR. Now, however, Chinese leaders are panicking—the student unrest feels like a disgrace.

They are terrified of "losing face" in front of their guest from Moscow, especially since the situation in the Soviet Union seems far more stable: recent protests in Georgia were suppressed by the army, and no mass demonstrations of this scale exist in Moscow. The question arises: Should they cancel the traditional welcoming ceremony for the high-profile guest in Tiananmen Square? Gorbachev is so popular worldwide that they are desperate to make a good impression on him.

But the students are also thinking about Gorbachev's visit. The leader of perestroika is immensely popular among them—they see his arrival as the perfect opportunity to pressure the Chinese authorities, who would hesitate to disperse a protest in front of their guest from Moscow.

Three days before Gorbachev's visit, students gather in Tiananmen Square and decide to stage a major action. Wang Dan proposes a hunger strike, but the majority votes against it. Instead, they write an open letter to Gorbachev, signed by more than three thousand people:

> You have led the Soviet people in carrying out the greatest, deepest, and most comprehensive restructuring of society in the entire history of the USSR. In the process of *Perestroika*, you have shown incredible courage and wisdom.

And then an unexpected speech comes from twenty-three-year-old psychology student Chai Ling: "The government has lied to us, ignored us.

All we want is for the government to open a dialogue with us and say that we are not traitors. We, the children, are ready to die. We, the children, are ready to sacrifice our lives for the truth."

She breaks down in tears and calls for a hunger strike.

Her speech moves many people, and by the next day, about a hundred students begin fasting in Tiananmen Square. The Chinese students likely know nothing about the recent hunger strike in Tbilisi and its tragic outcome. But most of them are confident that this action will conclude before Gorbachev's visit, believing that the Chinese authorities will make concessions.

Having flown in from New York, the professor Liu Xiaobo comes to the square—he will soon join the hunger strike.

The next morning, a high-ranking official comes to the fasting students. He urges them to end their protest and submit their demands through him, guaranteeing that they will be considered at the highest level. Chai Ling, seen as the leader of the hunger strikers, is absent from the meeting, and the proposal is rejected. As a result, the authorities decide that organizing the ceremonial welcome on Tiananmen Square, as required by protocol, is impossible.

The news that Gorbachev will not come to the square and that the authorities will not yield is a major shock for the students. The only opportunity to open a dialogue with the government before Gorbachev's arrival is lost.

"CONCEPTS OF A BYGONE ERA"

As planned, Gorbachev arrives in Beijing on May 15. That evening, an official banquet is held in his honor at the Great Hall of the People—right on the edge of Tiananmen Square. It feels like a scene from classic literature: inside the palace, the leaders feast, while outside, in the cold, ordinary people sit, hoping to be heard, yet the former ignore them.

The number of hunger strikers grows rapidly. By evening, there are nearly two thousand.

On the second day, Gorbachev meets with Deng Xiaoping. "Now we can officially declare that Sino-Soviet relations have been normalized," announces Deng. Gorbachev smiles, and then the Chinese leader suddenly says, "I want to say a few words about Marxism and Leninism."

"For me, this was quite unexpected. We had been discussing changes in today's world and our relations with China, and then suddenly there was this turn," Gorbachev will later recall.

Deng Xiaoping reflects on his earlier debates with Suslov and essentially explains why he is reforming China's economy in a way that defies Marxist doctrine:

"Since the birth of Marxism, more than a hundred years have passed. Major changes have taken place in the world, creating new conditions in different countries. Even Marx could not have answered all the questions that arose after his death. . . . Those who cannot adapt Marxism-Leninism to new conditions are not true communists."

Deng Xiaoping then suggests revisiting the issues that once existed between China and the USSR and begins to lecture Gorbachev on Chinese history, recounting which powers caused his country the greatest harm.

He starts with Portugal and Britain, the first to occupy Chinese territories and establish concessions, then moves on to Japan and tsarist Russia. He points out that Russia gained over 1.5 million square kilometers of Chinese territory through unequal treaties and after the October Revolution, in 1929, the Soviet Union seized islands near Khabarovsk. The Soviet Union also helped create the independent Mongolian state—Deng Xiaoping refers to it as "Outer Mongolia" and considers it another territory stolen from China.

According to him, in the 1950s the primary threat came from the United States, while in the 1960s it was once again from the USSR. He recalls his last visit to Moscow in 1960:

"If you're interested, you can review the official records of the negotiations, particularly my speech. . . . Its main theme was that the Soviet Union misunderstood China's place in the world. . . . The essence of all the problems was that we were in an unequal position, subject to mistreatment and oppression."

Gorbachev listens carefully and responds that the past cannot be changed: "If we were to pursue the restoration of past borders based on historical claims about which people lived on which lands, we would, in essence, have to redraw the entire world map. That would lead to a global conflict! The principle of the inviolability of borders brings stability to the world and preserves it."

Deng Xiaoping appears to agree: "Let the wind blow these issues away. After our meeting, we will no longer return to this topic."

But overall, Gorbachev is shocked by the encounter. He feels that Deng Xiaoping "operates with concepts and terms characteristic of a bygone era"—as he will later write in his memoir.

In 1990, Deng Xiaoping's son will say in an interview, "My father thinks Gorbachev is an idiot."

"DEMOCRACY IS OUR SHARED DREAM"

Gorbachev's visit to Beijing is covered by numerous foreign journalists. Many of them also visit Tiananmen Square, where the hunger-striking students remain. The protesters display banners, some even in Russian, reading: "Democracy Is Our Shared Dream."

The demonstrators are, of course, hoping that Gorbachev will meet with them and show support—perhaps by visiting the square or speaking at Peking University. But naturally, he has no intention of doing so. About a year earlier, when Ronald Reagan visited Moscow, Gorbachev was deeply offended by the American president's desire to meet with Soviet dissidents. For Gorbachev, the very idea is unacceptable—he has come to Beijing as an invited guest of the government, and in his world view meeting with the opposition would simply be inappropriate.

Gorbachev's interpreter, Pavel Palazhchenko, will add that even at the Soviet embassy there was a stark generational divide among diplomats: "The older generation considered the students 'agents of America,' while the younger ones sympathized with them." One member of the delegation decides to visit the square to see it firsthand and returns saying, "The kids are charming, but they're so incoherent. They just keep repeating the word 'corruption' over and over."

The final day of Gorbachev's visit coincides with the peak of the protests. Residents of Beijing flood toward Tiananmen Square, and by some estimates, their numbers reach a million. There are now around two thousand hunger strikers, and fainting spells begin to occur among them. Several leaders, including Wu'er Kaixi, are taken to the hospital.

The city is paralyzed by a transportation collapse. The Soviet delegation is forced to travel to the airport via side streets, avoiding the major thoroughfares, all of which are jammed with people. On the way to the airport,

Igor Rogachev, a deputy foreign minister, notices banners through the car window that read: "Down with Deng Xiaoping." "That's a mistake," he tells Gorbachev's interpreter, Palazhchenko. "This could end badly."

Singapore's prime minister, Lee Kuan Yew, feels the same way when watching TV coverage of the events in Beijing: "I had a sense that this demonstration would end in tears. In the history of China, no emperor who has been mocked has ever continued to rule."

GORBACHEV AND SPACE

After returning from China, Gorbachev calls Yeltsin and suggests they meet. They discuss a range of issues at length, but the main question on the General Secretary's mind is what Yeltsin's plans are—what he intends to do next. Gorbachev wants to mend their relationship.

"The congress will decide everything," replies the newly minted opposition figure. Gorbachev dislikes this answer, convinced Yeltsin is hiding something. The General Secretary presses further: Perhaps Yeltsin would like to work in the Council of Ministers? But Yeltsin repeats, "The congress will decide everything." Irritated, Gorbachev sees that Yeltsin refuses to engage and has effectively rejected his olive branch.

On the eve of the congress, Gorbachev gathers the newly elected parliamentarians and delivers a welcoming speech. Representative from Sverdlovsk Gennady Burbulis, a staunch supporter of Yeltsin, harbors a secret hope: to speak with Gorbachev one-on-one and explain that the General Secretary has many supporters—true, committed democrats—and that these are the people he should rely on, not the Central Committee apparatchiks. He views this gathering as the perfect opportunity. But as usual, Gorbachev is verbose, and his speech drags on for two or three hours. Burbulis sits on pins and needles, waiting for his moment to rush over to Gorbachev as soon as the speech ends.

Finally, the speech concludes. Burbulis dashes toward Gorbachev, managing only to say, "Mikhail Sergeyevich, just a minute, please . . . ," when suddenly, from behind the General Secretary, the first woman in space, Valentina Tereshkova, appears. She begins pushing the insistent Ural delegate aside: "What do you want from Mikhail Sergeyevich? Can't you see that he's tense, that he's exhausted?" While they bicker, Gorbachev slips away.

"FIGHT TO THE LAST PERSON!"

The night after Gorbachev's departure, several student protest leaders, including Wang Dan and Wu'er Kaixi, are brought inside the Great Hall of the People. Soon after, Premier Li Peng arrives.

Li begins to speak, but Wu'er Kaixi, dressed in hospital pajamas, sharply interrupts, "The students have demands that must be met. Otherwise, they will not leave the square!" The conversation quickly devolves into a heated and rather crude exchange. The students refuse to call this meeting the "dialogue" they have long demanded. Remarkably, footage of this meeting is broadcast on television worldwide. "In these televised debates, the students defeated Li Peng by a landslide," observes one viewer, Singapore's prime minister, Lee Kuan Yew.

Li Peng and the conservatives are deeply frustrated, believing they have done all they could. That night, a meeting of China's top leadership takes place—leaders argue through the night about what to do. At dawn, before the sun rises, General Secretary Zhao Ziyang appears on Tiananmen Square with his entourage. He looks disoriented. Clearly opposed to the use of force, Zhao finds himself in the minority. His appearance on the square is a last-ditch effort to prevent a bloody outcome.

He enters one of the buses where hunger strikers are sleeping, shakes everyone's hands, and asks how they are. He pleads with them to end the protest, but when asked what the authorities will do in response, he offers no clear answers.

After Zhao Ziyang's unexpected visit, rumors spread through the square that the government has decided to impose martial law and that a crackdown is imminent.

The next day, under the weight of the previous night's events, Chai Ling and other leaders announce the end of the hunger strike. Many participants leave Tiananmen Square, though several thousand remain for a "sit-in protest."

That evening, Li Peng formally announces the imposition of martial law and orders troops into the capital. Zhao Ziyang is removed from power.

The following morning, tanks roll into the city. Surprisingly, their progress is severely hindered by resistance from ordinary residents. Thousands of citizens pour into the streets to block the military's advance. They fraternize with soldiers, bringing them food, water, and cigarettes—preventing them from moving forward. The troops are ordered not to use force.

On the square, however, protesters still fear an imminent bloody assault. Rumors circulate that the army will soon break through the human blockade of citizens and launch a massacre on the square.

Late on the night of May 22, Wu'er Kaixi returns to the square from the hospital, visibly agitated and behaving erratically. Grabbing a microphone, he shouts that everyone must flee the square immediately and seek refuge in foreign embassies. Mid-speech, he collapses in a faint. Most of the crowd dismisses him as having lost his mind and do not take his warning seriously.

The army remains stationary, however, and both students and residents begin to believe the danger has passed. Demonstrations on Tiananmen Square resume. By this point, tens of thousands of activists from outside Beijing have converged on the city. With nowhere else to go, these outsiders now form the bulk of the protesters on the square.

On May 24, the troops unexpectedly turn around and leave. Euphoria sweeps the square, and the "Hunger Strike Headquarters" is renamed the "Tiananmen Square Defense Headquarters." Chai Ling is elected its leader: "I will defend the republic and Tiananmen Square with my young life. Heads may fall, blood may spill, but we will not abandon the square. We will fight to the last person!"

Wang Dan delivers a declaration dramatically titled "The Final Battle Between Light and Darkness": "We have nowhere to retreat, and we will occupy Tiananmen Square until Li Peng's regime falls." A tent city is erected, which people jokingly begin calling the Tiananmen's People's Republic.

THE CONGRESS GOES LIVE

On May 25, the First Congress of People's Deputies opens in the Kremlin. In essence, this is the first (at least partially) democratically elected group of representatives in Russia since the Bolsheviks dissolved the Constituent Assembly in 1917.

But even more significant is Gorbachev's decision to allow all congress sessions to be broadcast live on television. He could not have foreseen that this congress would erupt into genuine political debate, holding the entire country glued to their televisions and radios for two weeks.

On the eve of the congress, at a meeting of democratic deputies, Sakharov rises to explain that their strategy can only be this: "We must break onto the podium and tell the truth by any means possible—not addressing those in the hall, but those watching on television. If we can hold on for even a week, we will have a different country," as recalled by the young parliamentarian Sergei Stankevich.

"For a time, the legislators eclipsed TV stars, soccer players, opera tenors, and fashion designers," Anatoly Sobchak would later write. "In the inner sanctum of Kremlin power, words were spoken for which, only yesterday, you would have been sent to a labor camp or psychiatric hospital."

By law, the first session is chaired by the head of the Central Election Commission, who is supposed to formally announce the election results. But he presides weakly, stalling and shuffling through papers. Suddenly, a Latvian legislator rushes to the microphone and proposes a moment of silence to honor the victims of the Tbilisi events on April 9. The entire hall stands. After the minute of silence, the same Latvian continues, demanding to know, "Who gave the order to beat peaceful demonstrators in Tbilisi on April 9, 1989?"

This symbolic start sets the tone for what follows—everything strays from Gorbachev's script. Seeing that the head of the Central Election Commission cannot manage the proceedings, Gorbachev takes the initiative and starts running the session himself to stick to the approved plan. MPs immediately call this a violation of the law, but Gorbachev smiles and replies, "Is someone bothered by my undemocratic nature?"

The events in Tbilisi—and the broader question of the legitimacy of using violence—become the central topic of the congress. Many parliamentarians demand an investigation, while the Georgian delegation openly protests against the presence of General Igor Rodionov, the commander of the military operation in Tbilisi, who is also a congress member and seated in the hall.

The general takes the podium and not only refrains from apologizing but passionately defends his actions. He insists that he did everything correctly because at the rally he dispersed "vile calls for physical violence against communists were made day and night, and anti-Russian and nationalist sentiments were being incited." The hall gives him a standing ovation.

For the first time, Gorbachev publicly addresses the tragedy. First, he agrees to establish an independent parliamentary commission to investigate the Tbilisi crackdown. This is unprecedented: the USSR has never had a functioning parliament, let alone an independent parliamentary investigation not controlled by the state.

He also absolves himself of any responsibility, claiming that he returned from London to Moscow only on Saturday, April 8—the night before the tragedy. However, it soon emerges that Gorbachev actually returned a day earlier, on Friday, April 7. This means he either intentionally or unintentionally misled the congress, making the question of whether he was aware of the impending violent crackdown even more urgent.

CURTAIN-RAISER

At the very start of the first session, Gorbachev gives the floor to Sakharov. The academician calls for a complete overhaul of the agenda and proposes a fundamental transformation of the political system—declaring the congress the sole legitimate governing body and adopting a special decree on power. In his view, a revolution is already underway and must be officially recognized. Everyone understands that this is an attempt to strip the Communist Party of the power it has held for seventy-two years.

This is the legendary academician's first appearance on Soviet television. The whole country knows his name—but until this moment, no one has seen what he looks like: the sixty-nine-year-old scholar looks older than his age—tall and thin, he speaks in a high-pitched voice and has a lisp.

In his first address, Sakharov protests against automatically confirming Gorbachev as chairman: "There must always be a process: first, discussion, then candidates presenting their platforms, and only after that elections. We will disgrace ourselves before our entire nation if we act otherwise." At the same time, he admits that he sees "no one else capable of leading our country" apart from Gorbachev but emphasizes that his support is "conditional" and insists that any election must be competitive.

Sakharov's idea—that elections without discussion are a disgrace—unexpectedly resonates with the Lithuanian delegation. Vytautas Landsbergis, the leader of Sąjūdis, declares that the deputies "do not have the right to elect people who are practically unknown, to vote 'in the dark.'" The Lithuanian delegation refuses to participate in the Supreme Soviet elections altogether. Attempts to change their stance fail, and Lithuania effectively separates itself from the rest of the Soviet republics, refusing to engage in the election country's permanent parliament.

Another scandal erupts when a representative from Latvia, Colonel Viktor Alksnis—grandson of the famous Red Army commander—turns against his own delegation. From the congress podium, Alksnis declares that the elections in Latvia were undemocratic because the electoral districts were deliberately manipulated. This practice, known as gerrymandering in American politics, led to underrepresentation of Russian-speaking urban voters, he claims. Rural districts, populated predominantly by ethnic Latvians, had far fewer voters but the same number of representatives.

Alksnis demands that the elections be annulled and held again. His shocking demand is met with silence—everyone simply ignores it. The congress is already underway, and canceling it to rerun the elections is unthinkable.

THE END OF THE GODDESS OF DEMOCRACY

Meanwhile, the standoff at Tiananmen Square in Beijing continues, and tensions among the protest leaders—particularly between Wu'er Kaixi and Chai Ling—escalate.

On May 27, the protesters debate how long they should remain on the square—they can't live there forever. Two primary views emerge: disperse by May 30 or hold out until June 20, when the National People's Congress convenes, to push for Li Peng's resignation.

Most favor leaving by May 30. Liu Xiaobo, the future Nobel Peace Prize laureate, calls for the election of a charismatic leader, like Lech Wałesa in Poland, who can lead the movement once the protesters return home. He nominates Wu'er Kaixi (who, naturally, agrees). However, Chai Ling vehemently opposes this.

She declares that she will not leave the square on May 30 but will continue the struggle at least until June 20. The plan to disperse in an organized fashion collapses. The next day, Chai Ling gives an interview to the BBC:

"The students keep asking me: What should we do next? I am sad that I cannot tell them that all that lies ahead of us is bloodshed. . . . I believe that only when blood flows like a river on Tiananmen Square will the people of China understand what is happening and unite.

"I hope I can survive. I also hope that the next revolution begins immediately after that. When it happens, I will return to the struggle. As long as I am alive, my goal will be to overthrow this inhumane government and build a new government—a government of people's freedom," she says.

On May 30, students from the Central Academy of Fine Arts erect the *Goddess of Democracy* statue on the square—positioned directly across from the Gate of Heavenly Peace, with Mao Zedong's portrait. Tens of thousands of people gather at the square, taking photographs around the statue.

On June 1, troops again begin converging toward the center of Beijing, but few pay attention this time. On June 2, rock musician Hou Dejian gives an impromptu concert on the square, drawing around one hundred thousand listeners.

On June 3, Premier Li Peng holds a meeting with several Politburo members, Beijing officials, and military commanders. They decide that the army will begin clearing the square that very night at 9:00 p.m. and complete the operation by 6:00 a.m. the next day. Moreover, the troops are authorized "to use all available means to remove any obstacles to completing the assigned task."

Around 180,000 soldiers are mobilized to "suppress the counterrevolutionary rebellion." However, resistance emerges—not from students, but mainly from Beijing workers. Vehicles stall, and barricades made of overturned cars and buses appear along the troops' route. At 10:00 p.m., the order is given to open fire.

The protest leaders on the square are unsure how to respond. Chai Ling is in tears, while Wu'er Kaixi suffers another seizure and is taken to the hospital. Confusion and panic reign on Tiananmen Square.

The army reaches the square around 1:30 a.m. Loudspeakers urge the students to disperse. Around 3:00 a.m., Liu Xiaobo and several other professors attempt to lead the protesters away, but many initially refuse, citing their decision to "stay in the square until the last person is killed." However, they eventually agree and withdraw in an orderly fashion to their dormitories. By 5:00 a.m., military vehicles destroy the tent city and the *Goddess of Democracy*.

Only five confirmed deaths on the square are known, but the total number of casualties across the city remains unknown to this day, with estimates ranging from three hundred to three thousand people.

By June 5, the clashes come to an end, with one exception—the iconic Tank Man, a lone individual who attempts to block a column of tanks and is captured on film by an American cameraman. He stands in front of the tanks for several minutes before disappearing. It is very likely that he was not harmed and survived.

The West issues a measured condemnation of the events, while the Soviet leadership expresses support for the Chinese government. Although glasnost has been in full swing in the Soviet Union for some time, the media shows almost no interest in the situation in China. This is what *Izvestia* says the next day: "The Student Self-Government Association was distributing knives and sickles to the population and calling for the overthrow of the government. An emergency announcement classifies the events as a counterrevolutionary rebellion."

On June 9, Deng Xiaoping makes his first public appearance, meeting with soldiers who took part in clearing the square. The meeting symbolizes the conclusion of the military operation.

To this day, the Tiananmen Square events remain a taboo subject in China. In literature, they are usually referred to as the "6-4 Incident," referencing the date, June 4.

AN INSULT TO THE HONOR OF THE SOLDIERS

At the very moment when fighting begins between the army and protesters in Beijing, a confrontation unfolds in the Kremlin—at the congress session. Taking the podium is thirty-one-year-old Sergei Chervonopisky, a veteran of the Afghan war, former commandant of the Kabul airport, who lost both legs after stepping on a mine.

He reads an address to Gorbachev on behalf of the soldiers who fought in Afghanistan:

"On what grounds, or at whose behest, did Member of the USSR Congress of People's Deputies Sakharov give an interview to journalists from the Canadian newspaper *Ottawa Citizen* claiming that Soviet pilots in Afghanistan fired on their own surrounded Soviet soldiers to prevent them from being taken prisoner? We are deeply outraged by this irresponsible, provocative outburst from the well-known academic and regard his baseless accusations as a deliberate attack on the honor of the Soviet Armed Forces. . . . We perceive this as an insult to the honor, dignity, and memory of those sons of the motherland who fulfilled its orders to the very end. . . ."

At the conclusion of his speech, Chervonopisky proclaims the slogan: "State, Motherland, Communism."

"The entire hall stands up, applauding him for five minutes, it's just incredible; at a moment like that, staying in your seat is psychologically almost impossible," recalls Arkady Murashov, one of the democratic representatives. "But we sit."

Sakharov immediately heads to the podium to respond:

"I never intended to insult the Soviet army—" The hall erupts, drowning him out. A pattern has emerged at the congress: speakers are often "shouted down," their words smothered by applause or jeers. But Sakharov presses on: "I have deep respect for the Soviet army, for the Soviet soldier who defended our homeland during the Great Patriotic War. But when it comes to the Afghan war . . . That war in Afghanistan was a criminal adventure, undertaken by parties unknown, and no one has been held responsible for this enormous crime against the motherland. This crime cost the lives of almost a million Afghans; an entire nation was subject to a war of annihilation, a million people perished. . . ."

Sakharov stammers; speaking is visibly difficult for him. From the hall, crude remarks are hurled. Presiding chairman Lukyanov stands but hesitates to interrupt the academic. Sakharov, his voice breaking but unwavering, continues:

"This weighs on us as a terrible sin, a terrible reproach. We must wash off this shame, which lies upon our leadership. . . . I spoke out against the introduction of Soviet troops into Afghanistan, and for that, I was exiled to Gorky." (The hall erupts in noise.) "And I am proud of that; I am proud of my exile to Gorky as an honor that I earned."

He further explains that in his interview with Canadian journalists he relied on information about secret orders from Soviet commanders to eliminate their own soldiers "to prevent their capture."

"This matter is under investigation. And until it is clarified, no one has the right to accuse me of lying," he says in a soft, quiet voice, yet with firm resolve. "I will not apologize to the entire Soviet army—I have not insulted it. I criticized those who issued the criminal order to send Soviet troops into Afghanistan."

What follows is a frenzy. One after another, members of congress take the podium to denounce Sakharov as a traitor. During the congress, Yuri Afanasyev, a historian and rector of the Institute of History and Archives, had coined the phrase "an aggressively obedient majority"—and it is this majority that now directs its fiercest rage at Sakharov. The attack on the academic is the congress's most dramatic episode, a clear sign of the deep divide in Soviet society. For most in the hall, and likely for most across the country, to admit guilt—or even state culpability—is unthinkable, too humiliating, too painful.

"Comrade academic!" yells a teacher from the Tashkent region. "With one act, you have erased all your achievements. You have insulted the entire army, the entire people, all our fallen who gave their lives. I express the people's contempt for you. You should be ashamed!"

The hall erupts in applause.

After the session ends, Elena Bonner waits for her husband at the Kremlin entrance.

"Shall we go home? I'll whip something up," she offers. "And besides, you can skip the evening session."

He objects: "Why? Did I steal something?" He firmly insists that he will attend the congress that evening. They go together to the Rossiya Hotel for lunch. Other representatives avoid them like the plague. Later he will say, "I felt completely morally invincible."

For Sakharov, this is only the beginning. From this moment on, he begins receiving an overwhelming number of letters: "The vast majority of them abusive . . . ," he will note with his characteristic irony.

ADOPTED SON OF PARIS

Levon Ter-Petrosyan, along with his cellmates, like all Soviet citizens, are glued to the radio, listening to the broadcast from the Kremlin. Suddenly, one of the parliamentarians asks, "When will you release the members of the Karabakh Committee?"

"Soon, soon. They'll be free very soon," replies the presiding chairman, Anatoly Lukyanov. Ter-Petrosyan's cellmates begin congratulating him.

A colossal international campaign had already been underway in support of the Karabakh Committee. Supported by the Armenian diaspora worldwide, the movement garnered significant attention. A group of Nobel laureates signed a letter advocating for their release. Eleven French cities "adopted" each of the eleven arrested committee members, holding regular rallies to secure their freedom. For example, Paris—and Mayor Jacques Chirac personally—took responsibility for Ter-Petrosyan.

Indeed, the day after Lukyanov's statement, all members of the committee are placed on a plane and flown to Armenia. A hero's welcome awaits them, so to prevent this spectacle, they are kept in their cells for an extra day. Nevertheless, they are celebrated as heroes—each one lifted onto the shoulders of the cheering crowds.

During his imprisonment, Ter-Petrosyan lost a significant amount of weight: before, he weighed 172 pounds, but upon his release, he is down to 137. He is immediately sent to a hospital for examination, where doctors discover a spinal tumor—something he had never been aware of. He is urgently flown to France for surgery, where he is already widely known as a prisoner of conscience. Jacques Chirac personally greets him upon his arrival, and François Mitterrand's administration covers the medical expenses.

"Turns out, Gorbachev saved me by locking me up," Ter-Petrosyan jokes. "If he hadn't, I would've had six months to live."

On November 2, 1989, the congress of the Pan-Armenian National Movement, which had grown out of the Karabakh Committee, declares that its primary goal is achieving independence.

THE SILENCED MICROPHONE

The final day of the congress. There's only a short time left before the sessions conclude when Gorbachev announces that Academician Sakharov insists on speaking and is asking for fifteen minutes. The hall erupts in anger. Member of congress Sergei Stankevich recalls sitting next to the cosmonaut Valentina Tereshkova, who keeps muttering insults about Sakharov.

Gorbachev, with a hint of mockery, notes that Sakharov has already spoken seven times at the congress (in fact, he had addressed the floor forty-five times). The hall shouts, *"No!,"* demanding that Sakharov not be given the floor. But the General Secretary proposes a compromise: "Let's ask Andrei Dmitriyevich to keep it within five minutes."

"As it happens, comrades," Sakharov begins in his creaky voice, "it doesn't always work that way. I haven't yet spoken conceptually. I must say that my position is somewhat exceptional, and I am aware of this responsibility. Therefore, I will speak as I have prepared to speak."

With these words begins perhaps the most legendary speech in Soviet history—one in which he would propose his plan for radical political reform.

Sakharov starts by criticizing both the congress and Gorbachev: "The concentration of such power in the hands of one individual is extremely dangerous, even if this person is the initiator of perestroika. . . . Someday, it will be someone else."

He goes on to state that the country is heading toward an economic catastrophe, a tragic escalation of interethnic tensions, and a general crisis of public trust in the leadership. Sakharov is only finishing the introductory part of his speech when Gorbachev warns him, "One minute."

At this point, the academician announces that he has drafted a "Decree on Power," which he proposed back on the first day of the congress, and begins to read it aloud.

He calls for the abolition of Article 6 of the constitution, which enshrines the Communist Party's leading role. He demands that all senior officials of the state—including the head of government, the prosecutor general, the head of the KGB, and the head of state television—be elected by the congress: "The functions of the KGB will be limited to ensuring the international security of the USSR."

"You really need to wrap up, Andrei Dmitriyevich. You've already used two speaking times," Gorbachev interrupts. "I'm finishing. I'm skipping the arguments. I'm leaving out a lot," Sakharov says hurriedly.

Gorbachev is visibly indecisive—he sees the hatred with which the majority of members are looking at Sakharov. It's clear they don't understand why the General Secretary is tolerating him at the podium.

"That's it. Your time is up. Forgive me. That's it," Gorbachev says, flustered.

"I insist . . . ," Sakharov responds—but he is no longer heard. Gorbachev has turned off his microphone.

"That's enough, Comrade Sakharov. Comrade Sakharov, do you respect the congress? Good. That's it," Gorbachev coaxes. Sakharov continues speaking into the dead microphone for several minutes, but no one can hear him.

"Take your speech, please! I ask you to sit down." Gorbachev grows bolder, granting the floor to another member in the hall.

"Why must we listen to Comrade Sakharov right now? Why is he allowed to address the people of the Soviet Union from this congress podium? Isn't he taking on too much?" a member demands. Applause follows.

Later, Sakharov will write that it was precisely at the moment when Gorbachev turned off his microphone that "in an instant, I gained immense support from millions of people, a popularity I had never known in our country." Watching the congress on television in Vermont,

Solzhenitsyn agrees: "During the congress, Sakharov claimed his role as the de facto head of the opposition. He raised many vital issues, had to shout over the noise of the hall, and endured angry jeers and censure. And this popularity persisted through the last months of his life . . . the people visibly saw their persecuted defender."

TWO MEN BEFORE AN EMPTY HALL

At home, Elena Bonner is watching the final congress session on television with journalist Yuri Rost. Both are smoking—she sits directly in front of the television, while he stands on the balcony.

"Could you meet Andryusha [Sakharov]? I'm not feeling too well," Bonner asks after the congress adjourns. The photographer heads to Red Square and waits near St. Basil's Cathedral for hours as members pass by—Sakharov is nowhere to be seen. Rost begins to genuinely worry. Then, much later than everyone else, the academician finally appears.

Sakharov doesn't explain his delay to Rost—but years later, Gorbachev will reveal the story.

After the congress ends, Gorbachev stays late in his Kremlin office, working. Just as he's about to leave, his aides inform him:

"Mikhail Sergeyevich, someone's waiting for you."

"Who's waiting?"

"Sakharov."

"Why didn't you tell me earlier?"

"Well, he said, 'It's fine; let him finish. I'll wait.'"

Gorbachev heads back to the hall, where, at the corner of the stage near the curtain, Sakharov is sitting with a cup of tea, patiently waiting.

"Andrei Dmitriyevich, what's this? Are you planning to spend the night here?" Gorbachev jokes in surprise.

"No, I need to meet with you. It's a very serious matter," Sakharov replies.

Gorbachev grabs a chair, sits next to him, and together they sit on the stage, facing the vast, dark, empty Kremlin Palace hall.

"So, what are your impressions of the congress?" Gorbachev asks. Sakharov begins to share. According to Gorbachev's recollections, Sakharov says, "Yes, you see how conservative this hall is. . . ."

"True," Gorbachev agrees. "But imagine this: this is the first congress of its kind, and all this is happening before the eyes of the entire country, the whole world! It's incredible, really. We're caught up in it, and we don't even fully grasp what's happening. . . ."

"I'm worried about the conservatives. . . ." Sakharov chooses his words carefully. "It's clear they're unhappy with what's unfolding at the congress. They might force you, so the speak, to abandon your course. There are rumors that the right wing has some compromising material on you."

"Well then," Gorbachev says. "Go get a good night's sleep. I've never taken bribes, and I'm sure I never will."

"And we parted on good terms," Gorbachev will recount many years later.

On the way home, Rost asks Sakharov for his impressions. "Our clever leader is in a very difficult position. And after the congress, the situation hasn't become clear or cloudless. That's one side of the danger. The other lies in the political system itself, which allows for such immense personal power," he says of Gorbachev. "I must say, he proved himself to be an excellent conductor of the assembly. To some extent, he achieved the voting results he desired."

But the most important outcome, in Sakharov's view, is "the awakening of political consciousness among millions. It turned out that the people are not at all passive internally. They simply had no outlet for their energy. Once such a platform emerged, real political activity followed."

A NEW FEBRUARY

Within Gorbachev's inner circle, however, the mood is far grimmer. His closest aide, Anatoly Chernyaev fears a coup.

"The Politburo might confront MS: Where have you led us all? Isn't it time for you to step aside? And this crowd (the intellectuals)—we can rein them in without you," he reflects in his diary during the congress. "Both the gray masses and the intellectuals reject MS's domestic, especially economic, policies. The former—because of empty store shelves and co-op prices; the latter—because of incompetence."

The situation in the country reminds him of the Provisional Government period between the February and October Revolutions of 1917. He compares Sakharov and other opposition figures to the Mensheviks, the democratic party of the early twentieth century: "They revel in their intellectual superiority—both over the gray masses and over the authorities, including Gorbachev. They flaunt it arrogantly. And I think they will lose, just like their predecessors did in 1917. . . . But who will play the role of the Bolsheviks?"

Watching the congress unfold on television in Vermont, Solzhenitsyn draws a similar parallel:

"It's terrifying to watch these unfolding events. What can I do? I just want to warn Gorbachev: 'Don't forge when you don't know how to stitch.' This is all so familiar to me from February Seventeen! The endless elation of society. The intoxicating fog of hope. And this recklessness of expression. How much ecstatic, long-awaited euphoria! . . ."

He writes that he had rushed to complete "March Seventeen," part of his epic *The Red Wheel*, as a warning: "In the explosion of your joy, just don't repeat February's folly! Don't lose yourselves in this wild frenzy!"

Yet he laments that although his book had been broadcast on Radio Liberty, it had no impact on Soviet citizens: "Now people are preoccupied with something else: they are witnessing the course of today's Russian history. So, all my efforts went off the rails, in vain. March Seventeen arrived too late for this new February."

WIZARDS ON-SCREEN

In the summer of 1989, Defense Minister Dmitry Yazov receives a report stating that the US military has a special unit called Stargate dedicated to studying paranormal phenomena. Yazov, a committed communist and atheist, doesn't particularly believe in supernatural forces. But, as Marshal Ustinov once said, "The Americans aren't fools," so perhaps the Soviets need something similar.

More importantly, Yazov has a longtime friend with a deep fascination for UFOs and extraterrestrials—General Mikhail Moiseyev, the head of the Soviet General Staff. Yazov tasks Moiseyev with investigating the matter thoroughly.

Moiseyev takes the assignment seriously, establishing a Military Unit 10003, specifically tasked with researching the supernatural. Before long, Soviet military officials coin a new term: psywar—not psychological warfare, but psychic. They cannot comprehend why the Soviet Union is losing ground to the United States without direct conflict, and they arrive at a simple conclusion: the Americans must be using something magical.

Soon the Ministry of Defense is flooded with psychics, magicians, and sorcerers, all eager to "help the motherland." Huge sums are funneled into these experiments—just in the first year, 5 million rubles (roughly half a million dollars at the real exchange rate at the time) are allocated from the Defense Ministry's budget only for the unit's "philosophical research."

Paranormal phenomena begin to captivate the entire USSR. Many people, having lost their footing and faith in the future, seek explanations for their shaken world view. After the Congress of People's Deputies, state television executives discuss a pressing issue: society is too agitated, and it needs to be calmed. That responsibility falls to two psychics, who are given airtime to "heal" the population from the screen.

One of them is fifty-four-year-old Allan Chumak, a former sports journalist turned healer. Every morning, he appears on television, silently staring into the camera with an intense gaze and waving his hands. Millions of viewers gather around their screens with their families. Chumak also instructs them to place glass jars of water near their televisions, claiming to charge the water with positive energy. He is gray-haired and gentle, which leads viewers to see him as a "white magician."

But the true star of Soviet television becomes fifty-year-old psychotherapist Anatoly Kashpirovsky. His shows air during prime time, filling entire halls. He waves his hands dramatically while shouting commands. Audience members in the studio fall into trances, sway from side to side, and roll their heads. Millions of viewers believe Kashpirovsky can cure them of all their illnesses. Chumak's counterpart, dark-haired and aggressive, quickly earns a reputation as a "black magician"—and that makes him far more popular than Chumak.

In a country that, until recently, had preached materialism and categorically rejected anything otherworldly, the atmosphere of collective madness spreads with astonishing speed.

THE LAST CONFESSION

In June 1989, Sergei Parajanov starts filming his new movie—titled *Confession*. He says it will be an autobiographical film. Yet it is a strange one:

according to the script, the protagonist—Parajanov himself—dies in childhood at the very beginning of the film.

The shooting begins with a scene of a funeral. That evening, Parajanov's health takes a turn for the worse—he starts coughing up blood. He is diagnosed with lung cancer and undergoes surgery.

While in the hospital, he comes across a magazine featuring a lengthy article about Vladimir Mayakovsky. To his shock, he finds a passage claiming that Mayakovsky's muse, Lilya Brik, in her old age, had been hopelessly in love with Parajanov—and, tormented by unrequited love, had taken her own life.

Outraged, he writes a letter to the editors: "Lilya Yuryevna—the most remarkable of all the women fate ever brought into my life—was never in love with me. To explain her death as 'unrequited love' is not only an immoral rumor but a posthumous humiliation." His letter, however, is never published.

This is a typical case for Parajanov—most of the scripts he wrote ended up in the trash, and the films he envisioned were never made. He could never be certain that his ideas would reach a mass audience, so he turned every moment of his life into a performance, a theatrical spectacle. And even now, as he is a globally recognized star, a magazine with the fitting title *Theater* casually ignores him.

Parajanov's condition keeps worsening. French president François Mitterrand offers him treatment in Paris. But he hesitates for a long time—more out of superstition than anything else. A few years earlier, his close friend Andrei Tarkovsky had died of cancer in that very city. "They didn't save Andrei; they won't save me either," he says.

In his final days, he often reminisces about his late friends—among them, Vladimir Vysotsky:

"You all know him as a loudmouth, a brawler. But he was nothing like that. He was a profoundly deep person. He had a genius for silence. His silence was genius. . . . And he died like a genius—right on time. That's a rare gift, to leave at the right moment. . . . Just like Gagarin, by the way."

THE INTERREGIONAL DEPUTIES GROUP

In one of the final days of the congress, democratic-leaning parliamentarians decide to organize something resembling an opposition faction within the congress. Initially, it is a gathering of the Moscow representatives who participated in the first rally at Luzhniki, but soon delegates from across the country join in.

One of the key organizers, economist Gavriil Popov, recalls how challenging this was—because the two obvious opposition leaders, Sakharov and Yeltsin, were completely incompatible personalities. When it becomes clear that many parliamentarians' political views are widely divergent, even polar opposites, Sakharov proposes:

"Let's not search for positive common ground. That takes years. Instead, let's focus on what unites us in opposition. We are all against the Communist Party's power," Popov later writes. "Based on this, we united everyone— monarchists, anarchists, leftist communists, social democrats. . . ."

From the congress podium, Popov announces the creation of the faction—a word that terrifies many communists. For them, unity is sacred, and the word "faction" has been a slur ever since Trotsky's time. It is named the Interregional Deputies Group. The group includes only 388 out of 2,250 congress members. However, they are highly visible.

Shortly after the congress, the group holds its first conference. The democrats decide that they will have no single leader and instead elect five cochairs: Sakharov, Yeltsin, Popov, historian Yuri Afanasyev, and Estonian chemist Viktor Palm. The group's coordinating council includes the rising stars of Soviet democratic politics: Gdlyan, Sobchak, Burbulis.

"We are resolute opponents of all dictatorships," Popov declares at the conference. "We don't need a dictatorship of Gorbachev; we don't need a dictatorship of Ligachev. But we are also against a dictatorship of Afanasyev, Yeltsin, or Popov. We didn't start perestroika just to end up with yet another dictatorship—whether democratic or conservative."

NATIONAL BOLSHEVIKS IN THE CAUCASUS

In June, another conflict begins to brew in the Caucasus—this time between Georgians and the Azerbaijani population living in Georgia. A group of activists from the Azerbaijani Popular Front travels to mediate. Zardusht Alizadeh later recalls that much of the rising tension is fueled by the hardline nationalist rhetoric of Zviad Gamsakhurdia.

Gamsakhurdia declares that the "nomadic Turkic settlers" who remained in Georgia must leave after the collapse of the USSR and relocate to

Azerbaijan. When asked when exactly these Turks arrived in Georgian lands, he responds, "During the reign of Shah Abbas," referring to the ruler of the Iranian Empire in the late sixteenth and early seventeenth centuries. The legendary Georgian dissident Merab Kostava takes a far more moderate stance—his authority helps to ease tensions.

The Azerbaijani Popular Front activists return home, where leadership elections for their organization are set to take place in July. Although the Front was originally founded as a strictly democratic movement, the leading candidate for its leadership is now the nationalist Abulfaz Aliyev—who could be called Azerbaijan's Gamsakhurdia.

Abulfaz Aliyev is one of the most well-known Azerbaijani dissidents. He was arrested in 1975 when the republic was led by his namesake, Heydar Aliyev, and was accused of anti-Soviet agitation—the same charge that had been brought against Gamsakhurdia and Kostava in Georgia during the same years. However, his fate turned out to be far less tragic. He was not forced to make a public confession on television, as Gamsakhurdia had been, nor did he spend ten years in prison, like Kostava. By 1976, he was released, and more than that—he was reinstated at the Academy of Sciences, allowed to advance in his career, and by 1980 he had become head of a department. This fact would later fuel suspicions that Abulfaz had been recruited by the KGB and, throughout his political career, remained an ally of his fellow Nakhchivan native Heydar Aliyev.

Abulfaz Aliyev wins the election for the leadership of the Popular Front, although cofounder of the organization Zardusht Alizadeh openly calls the result fraudulent. Over the next year, the organization grows increasingly nationalist and authoritarian. As Alizadeh later says, "the National Bolsheviks" take over the movement.

Abulfaz Aliyev insists that all Azerbaijani citizens are Turks, that the Azerbaijani language does not exist—it is merely a Soviet invention by Stalin. He dreams of reuniting the "divided nation," referring to the Azerbaijani province in Iran.

By late summer of 1989, the Popular Front organizes a series of strikes across the republic and blocks the railway, which serves as a crucial connection between Armenia and the rest of the Soviet Union. The activists insist that Nagorno-Karabakh must be returned to Baku's control. As a result, both Armenia and Azerbaijan are virtually paralyzed.

In Baku, many believe that Moscow is favoring the Armenians, despite the fact that the members of the Karabakh Committee have just been released from prison. One of the more popular explanations for this supposed favoritism is a conspiracy theory that the Armenian diaspora bribed the Gorbachevs with an enormous sum—or, more specifically, that Armenian Americans gifted Raisa Gorbacheva diamonds, which is why she is allegedly lobbying for Nagorno-Karabakh to be handed over to Armenia.

The blockade of transportation routes proves to be a powerful lever of influence. On September 25, under pressure from the Popular Front, the Supreme Soviet of Azerbaijan adopts a sovereignty law declaring the supremacy of local laws over union laws.

A similar process is unfolding in neighboring Georgia. A conflict is brewing between the radical opposition, led by Zviad Gamsakhurdia, and some of the most prominent figures of Georgian cultural life.

In July, the founding congress of Georgia's own Popular Front takes place in Tbilisi. One of its participants is Merab Mamardashvili—once a university classmate of Raisa Gorbacheva, and now a globally renowned philosopher. He fiercely criticizes the nationalists:

"Truth is greater than the motherland. Because sometimes we consider something to be in the interests of our country when, in reality, it is not. Georgia cannot be a fetish. Christianity does not recognize idols or fetishes at all."

The hall erupts in outrage. Mamardashvili is nearly shouted off the stage. "How dare you!" people scream at him.

The session of the Popular Front makes one thing clear—Gamsakhurdia's popularity and that of his supporters are growing, while the voices of his critics are fading.

On October 13, an event occurs that seems to shift the course of Georgia's political trajectory even further. On a mountain road, Merab Kostava—human rights activist and close ally of both Gamsakhurdia and Sakharov—dies in a car accident. The crash, for many, appears suspicious, and as in all such cases, fingers immediately point to the KGB.

"I don't think it was an accident," Akaki Asatiani will later say. "A very strange story. The most important thing is that it happened at a moment when everything immediately changed without Merab. If he had lived, the movement wouldn't have split. He was the unifying force, the one person no one could argue with."

THE BALTIC WAY

August 1989 marks fifty years since the signing of the Molotov-Ribbentrop Pact, the secret deal between Hitler and Stalin. This anniversary holds not only symbolic but also practical significance.

The Soviet authorities deny that any secret protocols were attached to the agreement, which would have outlined the Soviet occupation of Latvia, Lithuania, and Estonia. However, if such protocols are proven to have existed, it would mean that the incorporation of Latvia, Lithuania, and Estonia into the USSR was illegitimate, and all laws enacted and enforced in the Baltic republics since 1940 would be subject to annulment.

At the congress, Gorbachev addresses the matter, claiming that no originals of the documents exist, that the situation is murky, but that it must be investigated. A commission is formed, with Alexander Yakovlev appointed as chairman.

As the fiftieth anniversary of the Molotov-Ribbentrop Pact approaches, on August 15 *Pravda* publishes an article claiming that the residents of the Baltic republics have fallen under the influence of extremists and succumbed to hysteria, acting on "narrow nationalist interests" instead of the "greater interests of the entire Soviet Union." On August 18, in the same *Pravda*, an interview with Yakovlev appears. Tasked by the congress to investigate the secret protocols, he acknowledges the existence of the deal between Stalin and Hitler, condemns it, but insists that the Molotov-Ribbentrop Pact had no bearing on the Baltic states' incorporation into the USSR. He reaffirms the official Soviet version: revolutions occurred in the three countries, and their governments voluntarily requested admission into the Soviet Union.

Five days later, on the fiftieth anniversary of the pact, a striking demonstration takes place across all three republics. On August 23, nearly 2 million residents of Estonia, Latvia, and Lithuania form a human chain spanning six hundred kilometers, connecting Tallinn, Riga, and Vilnius. A small "crop duster" plane flies above, dropping flowers on the demonstrators. It is a vivid testament to the fact that the citizens have not succumbed to hysteria or extremist influence.

Yakovlev would remain preoccupied with the issue for more than half a year—the commission's report would only be completed in December 1989. Years later, Yakovlev would discover that all this time, the original secret protocols had been sitting in Gorbachev's safe.

"Why deceive everyone for no reason?" Yakovlev would later wonder in his memoir. "I cannot grasp the logic of his thinking. I don't want to believe it was simple carelessness." However, Yakovlev is not certain whether Gorbachev himself ever saw these documents—it is possible that his chief of staff, Valery Boldin, simply chose not to show them to him.

Starting in 1989, Gorbachev's dependence on the people who bring him documents steadily increases. He is short on time, exhausted, and increasingly relies on those he considers trustworthy sources of information. There are only two such people: his chief of staff, Valery Boldin, and the head of the KGB, Vladimir Kryuchkov.

RADIO SILENCE

Grebenshchikov finishes recording his first English-language album, *Radio Silence*, and his label launches a promotional campaign. American media outlets begin interviewing him, and a highly complimentary segment airs on NBC. In it, BG shares his impressions of American culture, mentioning that he watches MTV closely. He criticizes the overuse of sexualized female imagery: "I see sex but no love."

Later, *Interview* magazine publishes an interview in which BG makes a bold statement: "America is no different from the Soviet Union. People are the same. Maybe the architecture varies, but not by much. Sometimes I can't even tell where I am—Moscow, Leningrad, or New York. As long as people's communication and thoughts are similar, everything remains the same."

However, his most controversial appearance is on *The Late Show with David Letterman* on July 14, 1989. BG performs the title track from *Radio Silence* and then joins Letterman for an interview.

"Do the Russians know you're here?" Letterman asks.

"No, it's a secret," Grebenshchikov quips.

"Are you making a lot of money?" Letterman presses.

"Nope," BG replies with a smile.

"Because here in the United States and in other places, rock 'n' roll people who are successful make huge sums of money."

"Isn't it why rock 'n' roll here is so boring?" the musician shoots back.

The audience gasps audibly.

"Well . . ." Letterman sizes up his guest.

"But it is!" BG insists.

"Friends all over the world," Letterman says, turning to the audience, "all part of that perestroika [that] we're hearing this."

In 1989, the most popular rock bands at the moment are Aerosmith, R.E.M., Bon Jovi, Guns N' Roses, and Metallica. The audience clearly disagrees with the lofty Russian's critique of American music.

BG embarks on a US tour. "We played in clubs—of all kinds, from decent ones to places that looked like mid-sized cafeterias," he will later recall. "People would drink, snack . . . Tables, a small dance floor in front of the stage. Honestly, it was all so dull that I don't even want to talk about it."

In September, *Rolling Stone* publishes a feature titled "Is This Boris Good Enough?" The piece is glowing, calling him the "Russian Bob Dylan," a born rock star, and a "religious fanatic whose rock 'n' roll religion is built on joy."

"I've experienced joy for thirty years," BG says in the article. "Even in the darkest days of my life, some observer inside me would ask, 'Ah, now you're truly in despair. Do you like it?' And I'd answer, 'Yes!'"

The journalist naturally asks about Gorbachev. BG's response: "We didn't trust them before, we don't trust them now, and we won't trust them in the future. I mean, who wants to trust them?"

"TWICE AS FREE"

"Yeltsin's political career is over," Gorbachev's circle confidently believes following the congress, where the former head of Moscow was not particularly prominent. "Yeltsin, I think, is done for," writes Chernyaev in his diary. "His idiocy became more apparent both at the rallies and at the Congress. And those who created the myth and took advantage of this idiocy may have realized that you can't ride far on him when real work and responsibility are required."

But Chernyaev is mistaking his hopes for reality. In truth, Yeltsin's popularity continues to grow. By the summer, he is invited to the United States to deliver lectures at several American universities, with promises of meetings with US officials. However, the trip turns out to be fraught with challenges.

On September 9, upon arriving in New York, Yeltsin is immediately displeased that no official representatives are waiting to greet him at the airport. His irritation with his aides deepens when he sees the itinerary. "Is this what you've planned for me?! Nothing but speeches and interviews! Ten a day! You think I'm some kind of Alla Pugacheva?"—recalls his accompanying journalist from *Komsomolskaya Pravda*, Pavel Voshchanov. "Cut half of it out! Do you hear me?"

To smooth over Yeltsin's mood, his aides suggest he have a drink. Within days, several American newspapers publish reports about the Moscow guest, describing him as a demagogue, a populist, and, most notably, a heavy drinker.

"For some inexplicable reason, alcohol always seemed to be within his reach, no matter where we went. At every visit, the conversation invariably began with, 'Mr. Yeltsin, would you like something to drink?' If this was hospitality, it certainly wasn't without a hint of malice," recalls Pavel Voshchanov in his memoir. Yeltsin's aides spend much of the trip discussing whether the Americans are deliberately trying to get him drunk because they all support Gorbachev.

The program is, indeed, exhausting. Yeltsin has to talk constantly, and many of his interlocutors are less than impressed. For one thing, some don't understand what is so wrong with Gorbachev and why Yeltsin criticizes him so harshly.

However, Yeltsin makes a few political statements that shock American journalists and land on the front pages. He declares that Gorbachev has less than a year left, perhaps just six months. He hints the Baltic republics might be granted independence. Finally, he claims that 48 million people in the USSR live below the poverty line.

The lighter part of the program does leave an impression on Yeltsin. He takes a helicopter flight around the Statue of Liberty. Sitting beside him is an NPR journalist, who tries to ask him questions. Yeltsin stares silently out the window and, at the end of the flight, declares, "I circled the Statue of Liberty twice and became twice as free!"

When Alla Pugacheva is asked to comment on these words during a broadcast of *Vzglyad*, she responds that she has always been free and never needed to fly around the Statue of Liberty.

One of the most awkward events is a short speech Yeltsin gives to journalists at Johns Hopkins University. By Voshchanov's account, Yeltsin had been drinking all night and answers questions from journalists while hungover. At the time, his team is unaware that the press conference is being filmed and that this footage will later cause an uproar.

The next day, on September 12, the *Washington Post* publishes an article titled "Yeltsin's Smashing Day: Boris' Boozy Bear Hug for the Capitalists." The piece is utterly scathing:

That he could stand up, let alone be engaging and sound urgent, seemed a little miraculous. It wasn't just the two hours' sleep he was going on. It was the amount of Tennessee sipping whiskey he had knocked back overnight. Vodka, okay. But Jack Daniel's black label in the land of the free? Yes, and a quart and a half of it too. This has been confirmed by those who saw the bottles. They weren't chambermaids, either. They were high officials of Johns Hopkins University. Boris N. Yeltsin, Soviet politician of the people, imbiber nonpareil, radical legislator and member of the Supreme Soviet, nyetter within the system, came swaying and galumphing and bassooning and mugging and hugging and doom-warning through the greater Baltimore-Washington corridor yesterday.

However, Yeltsin never sees this article, so it doesn't upset him.

The pivotal moment of the trip comes in Washington, where Yeltsin is taken to the White House for a meeting with National Security Advisor Brent Scowcroft. It's already known that President George Bush will casually drop by the meeting. On the way, Yeltsin digs in his heels: "What, a security advisor? I'm not meeting with any advisor! That's not my level! Is a meeting with the president planned? If not, turn the car around!"

They barely manage to persuade him. At the entrance to the White House, a young NSC Soviet expert, Condoleezza Rice, meets him—and the scene repeats itself, as Yeltsin's aide Lev Sukhanov later recounts. "Is the president going to meet with me?" Yeltsin demands threateningly. "I won't take another step if I'm not guaranteed a meeting with the president!" "Mr. Yeltsin, if you don't wish to speak with the president's National Security Advisor, you are free to return to your hotel," Condoleezza Rice replies with a polite smile. Yeltsin consents to the meeting with Scowcroft.

Finally, Brent Scowcroft greets Yeltsin with these lines: "Mr. Yeltsin, what exactly are you here for? What do you want?" Yeltsin does not show any embarrassment: "I'm interested in visiting your great country and getting to know your hardworking people." And at that moment, President Bush walks into the room.

According to his assistant Sukhanov, noticing that he and the president are the same height, Yeltsin says to him, "We're a match for each other." The interpreter prefers not to translate this line. Bush immediately apologizes for having little time—he has to record a televised address on drug issues—and asks Yeltsin, "What is your opinion on the events in the USSR?" Yeltsin then speaks at length and in detail, criticizing Gorbachev and handing Bush his ten-point reform plan. Exactly twelve minutes later, Bush stands up, apologizes, and, saying, "Give my regards to Mikhail Gorbachev," bids farewell. Soon after, Vice President Dan Quayle enters the room. Following his visit to the White House, Yeltsin also meets with Secretary of State James Baker. Despite the critical press coverage, he is treated like a political superstar.

PRAVDA AND DRINKING

Yeltsin returns to Moscow, and the next day, on September 19, *Pravda* reprints an article from the Italian newspaper *La Repubblica*. It claims that throughout his trip, Yeltsin behaved disgracefully, drank excessively, slandered his homeland, and demanded exorbitant fees. The text includes details that could only come from someone in his inner circle. It seems likely that one of Yeltsin's companions was working for the KGB.

However, much of the article appears to be unsubstantiated. Before the trip Yeltsin promised he would use the fees earned from his US lectures to buy a million disposable syringes—practically unavailable in the USSR—because the media frequently report on HIV infections among patients. Yet the Italian journalist claims that no syringes will materialize because Yeltsin has already spent the money: "He bought new clothes and shoes, entire boxes of white shirts, videocassettes of the three films *Rambo*, *ET*, and *Star Wars*, and two VCRs. He raced through supermarkets with the same energy that propelled him into Soviet history in the 1980s. 'Put it on the tab, put it on the tab,' Yeltsin ordered the company's accountant as he dashed between the counters, who dutifully noted every expense. Let the HIV-infected in Russia not delude themselves with hope."

The *Pravda* article becomes the main topic of discussion in the country. Public sympathy, of course, is on Yeltsin's side: everyone knows he enjoys a drink, but the smear campaign launched by the main state newspaper disgusts them.

Representatives Gdlyan and Ivanov even organize a rally in the Moscow suburb of Zelenograd—in support of Yeltsin and themselves against attacks from the Soviet government.

On October 1, Central Television airs a long segment about Yeltsin's trip to the United States, the centerpiece of which is the recording of his speech at Johns Hopkins University. Yeltsin does nothing particularly disgraceful: he simply gestures a lot and sometimes stretches out his words. In other words, it is clear that he is a little drunk (despite the fact that it was a morning event).

Here's how Yeltsin explains the situation in his memoir:

In America, my schedule was insane, plus the time zone changes, fatigue, and lack of sleep—all of it built up to such an extent that one night, to get some good rest, I took a couple of sleeping pills and immediately passed out. . . . At six in the morning, they were already trying to wake me up. . . . On top of that, special editors did a tricky montage of the videotape: slowing down the image by fractions of a second where needed, or stretching the words. This is what the video engineers at Ostankino told me.

THE FALL FROM THE BRIDGE

Soviet citizens had not yet finished discussing Yeltsin's American tour when another adventure befell him. On September 29, 1989, at 11:10 p.m., member of the Supreme Soviet Boris Yeltsin, soaking wet, arrives at the police post of the government residence.

This is the strangest story of Yeltsin's life—what happened to him that day remains unclear to this day. According to his version, he was on his way to visit his friend's dacha and dismissed his chauffeur because he wanted to take a walk. Suddenly, unknown assailants attacked him, put a sack over his head, shoved him into a car, and then threw him off a bridge into the Moscow River. However, he managed to escape, get out of the river, remove the sack, and, still wet, seek help from the police.

As Yeltsin's aide Lev Sukhanov recounts in his memoir, the policemen warm Yeltsin with tea and dry his clothes. Soon his wife, daughter, son-in-law, and loyal bodyguard Alexander Korzhakov arrive and take him home.

Yeltsin then calls Interior Minister Vadim Bakatin and asks him to "let the case of the attack slide." In other words, it's clear to everyone that Yeltsin made up the story about the kidnapping and the fall from the bridge, and he asks for the investigation to be dropped.

Nevertheless, rumors spread, many perestroika newspapers write about the incident, and Yeltsin himself gives comments, hinting that it was a KGB provocation and an assassination attempt.

On October 16, during a session of the Supreme Soviet, Gorbachev suddenly raises the issue of "the so-called attack on Comrade Boris Nikolayevich Yeltsin": "Many legislators have personally approached me, and the interviews Comrade Yeltsin has given to several newspapers demand clarification."

Gorbachev summons to the podium Interior Minister Bakatin, who reports on the investigation: Despite Yeltsin's request to keep the incident under wraps, the police officers had nevertheless informed their superiors. Yeltsin's driver was questioned, and he insisted that he had not dropped Yeltsin off early but had driven him directly to his friend's home, where the passenger got out holding two bouquets of flowers. Furthermore, according to Bakatin, Yeltsin's version did not hold water: falling from the bridge he specified and surviving was impossible, as the bridge was fifty feet high, while the river's depth was only about five feet.

Yeltsin is called to the podium as well, where he awkwardly admits that "there was no attack on me, I did not file any written statements, did not contact anyone, and I have no complaints against the Interior Ministry."

Gorbachev quips ironically that Yeltsin must have been joking. To finish him off, the transcript of the session is published in *Izvestia*. But it's pointless—this absurdity only works to Yeltsin's advantage and to Gorbachev's detriment.

Just a few days later, Yeltsin says at a rally, "The KGB called a special meeting to issue instructions to spread rumors that Yeltsin got drunk somewhere, that he went off carousing with women. They've completely crossed the line. . . . Their rage knows no bounds—it's turned into open persecution to smear and discredit a parliamentarian who's long been, shall we say, a thorn in their side."

This is Yeltsin's astonishing quality—nothing can damage his reputation. Whatever he does only seems to boost his popularity.

THE GDR ANNIVERSARY

At the beginning of October, Gorbachev has to travel to East Germany for the celebration of the German Democratic Republic's fortieth anniversary. He has no desire to go—he finds GDR leader Erich Honecker irritating, and the news from the region is grim. Massive protests have erupted in Leipzig and Dresden, crowds of East German refugees are fleeing to the West, and European media are openly speculating about the possibility of German reunification. Some even anticipate that Berliners might storm the Berlin Wall in Gorbachev's presence.

Gorbachev's aide Chernyaev, who has spent his entire career managing relations with foreign communist parties, reflects in his diary: "What we are witnessing is the total dismantling of socialism as a global phenomenon. And perhaps this is inevitable, and a good thing. For this is about the unity of humanity based on common sense. And this process was started by a simple guy from Stavropol."

However, upon arrival, Gorbachev immediately feels triumphant. As Honecker greets him, tens of thousands of people chant, "Gorby! Gorby!"—nobody pays attention to the GDR leader.

That evening, a torchlit parade takes place on Unter den Linden, the main street of East Berlin. Gorbachev will describe the scene this way: "The orchestras play, drums pound, searchlights sweep the skies, torches flicker, and above all—tens of thousands of young faces." All participants have been carefully selected by the Communist Party, yet as they march past the podium where Gorbachev, Honecker, and other Eastern Bloc leaders are standing, they chant: "Perestroika!" and "Gorbachev! Help us!"

Honecker, Gorbachev recalls, "looked as if he were in a trance."

The next day, Gorbachev meets with the GDR Politburo and, in the presence of his subordinates, begins lecturing Honecker, telling him that his party is falling behind the times and must adapt or face certain doom. "Those who are late in politics are punished harshly by life," Gorbachev says sternly. But Honecker has no intention of tolerating such rebukes. He retorts by recounting his recent visit to the USSR, where he saw empty store shelves devoid of even soap and matches. "They've ruined their own country, yet they come here to teach us," he whispers quietly.

Everyone understands that the Soviet leader has effectively given his blessing for Honecker's overthrow. Two weeks later, on October 18, 1989, the

Politburo of the East German Communist Party removes the elderly leader from power, and Honecker's deputy Egon Krenz takes his place.

SAKHAROV'S CONSTITUTION

In August 1989, Sakharov and Bonner visit Stanford and Berkeley, then stay with friends in the south of France: the hosts and Bonner swim in the pool while he, never approaching the water, sits nearby on a lounge chair, writing his version of a constitution.

One evening, they visit Monte Carlo. Sakharov quickly loses twenty-five francs and asks his wife for more money. He plays again and again—but never wins anything. They leave, but Sakharov is very upset and keeps pushing to return to Monte Carlo for just one more day, claiming he has done all the necessary calculations and devised a scheme to win big. But they don't have time.

Sakharov returns to Moscow and dives back into his opposition work. At one point, his aide Lev Ponomarev suggests that he create his own party as an alternative to the Communist Party of the Soviet Union. "Lev, what party? I'm already old. Do it without me!" Sakharov says, laughing. Ponomarev indeed begins shifting focus to the creation of a new, unregistered party based on the Interregional Deputies Group. It will soon be called Democratic Russia.

In October, Sakharov hands Gorbachev his draft of a constitution for a new state, which he calls the Union of Soviet Republics of Europe and Asia.

Even many of his allies immediately call the project utopian. Article 2 states: "The goal of the people of the Union of Soviet Republics of Europe and Asia and its governing bodies is a happy, meaningful life, material and spiritual freedom, well-being, peace, and security for the country's citizens and for all people on Earth, regardless of their race, nationality, gender, age, or social status."

The state described by Sakharov has many differences from the USSR. Each union republic is maximally autonomous—the central government handles only defense, foreign policy, and interregional transportation. In this Union, the death penalty is banned, and security services are forbidden from operating domestically; they can only engage in foreign intelligence. Finally, Sakharov's constitution prohibits expansionism and messianism.

"The borders between republics are inviolable for the first 10 years after the Constituent Congress," writes Sakharov, trying to resolve interethnic conflicts this way.

The capital of the state is not to be Moscow. Russia is just one of the republics, but all its autonomous regions are separated, and it is further "divided into four economic zones": European Russia, the Urals, Western Siberia, and Eastern Siberia. Each zone has full economic independence.

This state has an unmistakably socialist inclination—one article stipulates that "no one should live in poverty."

THE WALL AND THE CELLO

After Honecker's resignation, the protests in East Germany continue—it's clear that it's too late to start a perestroika in the German Democratic Republic. The Krenz government doesn't know what to do, but it agrees to adopt new border-crossing rules, allowing citizens to "emigrate permanently" from East Germany. In effect, the Berlin Wall becomes pointless. However, it's not that simple—the new rules still require a passport and a visa.

On November 9, a member of the GDR Politburo, Günter Schabowski, goes to give a press conference. Egon Krenz hands him the new rules, asking him to mention them in his discussion with journalists. But the press conference starts almost immediately after the Politburo meeting ends, so Schabowski doesn't have time to prepare.

He tries to avoid the topic of border crossings, but at the very end of the press conference, a journalist asks about it.

Schabowski replies, "The new rules for those leaving the country have not yet been finalized; this is only a draft of a future document. As far as I know, today it was decided . . . that every citizen of the German Democratic Republic . . . will be able to leave the GDR . . . through any border checkpoint."

"When will the law come into effect? . . . Without a passport?" someone asks.

The rules are supposed to be published the next day, but Schabowski doesn't know this. He puts on his glasses, flips through his papers, and improvises: "You see, comrades, I was told today that this document . . . only appeared today."

"When does the law come into force?"

"The order comes into effect, to my knowledge, immediately—right now," Schabowski extemporizes.

The room explodes; journalists shout questions in unison.

"I'm being very careful with my words because I'm not fully informed on this issue. I received this information just before coming here," the official says honestly, unaware of what he's just done.

"What will happen to the Berlin Wall now?"

"I've been informed that it's already seven p.m. That was the last question. Thank you for your understanding," Schabowski says, and rushes off, ending the press conference.

A few hours later, around 11:45 p.m. local time, residents of East Berlin surround the border guards. Overwhelmed, the guards open the gates, and a flood of people flows into West Berlin.

In Moscow, it's already 1:45 a.m. Gorbachev is asleep. His advisors decide not to wake him; the information coming from Berlin is too contradictory.

At that moment, the cellist Slava Rostropovich is at home in Paris, watching the BBC's live broadcast from Berlin. "I watched, drank, and cried," he will recall.

"I think Gorbachev's secret dream was to wake up one morning and find out that the Wall had disappeared on its own. Essentially, that's exactly what happened," Gorbachev's press secretary, Andrei Grachev, will later write. In the morning, when Gorbachev is informed of the news, he says the Germans did the right thing. "The fall of the Wall wasn't a surprise, and by that time, it was already clear to everyone," he will later recall.

"The Berlin Wall. . . . This is what Gorbachev has done!" writes his aide Chernyaev in his diary. "Indeed, he turned out to be great, because he sensed the footsteps of history and helped it move in its natural direction."

On the morning of November 10, Rostropovich is overflowing with emotion and begins calling his friends. He dials Antoine Riboud, the head of Danone. Riboud is in the middle of a board meeting, and because Rostropovich doesn't speak French very well, the businessman initially can't understand what the musician wants from him: *"Airplane, Wall, urgently!"* Rostropovich shouts. In the end, Riboud drops everything, takes his plane, and they fly to Berlin. A taxi takes them to the Checkpoint Charlie border crossing. Someone from a neighboring house brings out a chair—Rostropovich sits down and starts playing Bach's suites.

Soon TV journalists arrive—and these images will become one of the symbols of those days: the musician, stripped of his Soviet citizenship, playing the cello at the site of the former Berlin Wall checkpoint.

MOSCOW IS SILENT

The scene looks very different in Dresden, gripped by anti-communist demonstrations. It is there, in the KGB residency, that Vladimir Putin is still working.

His wife, Lyudmila, will recall receiving the news of the Berlin Wall's destruction with horror, as a personal tragedy: "When the Berlin Wall fell, and it became clear this was the end, there was this terrible feeling that the country that had almost become your own no longer existed."

Putin himself is very busy at the time: he and his colleagues must burn all the documents, all the evidence. "We destroyed everything, all our contacts, all our agent networks. I personally burned a massive number of materials. We burned so much that the stove burst. We burned day and night. Everything most valuable was sent back to Moscow," he will recount.

He will admit that the scariest moment comes when demonstrators in Dresden begin storming the local Stasi office: "We were afraid they would come for us next.

"I watched from the crowd as it happened. People broke into the Ministry of State Security building. Some woman was shouting: '*Look for the entrance under the Elbe! They're holding prisoners there, waist-deep in water!*' Prisoners? Why under the Elbe? There was a space like a detention center, but of course, not under the Elbe," he will explain. "I understood those people. They were tired of the Stasi's control, especially since it was absolute. Society was completely terrified. They saw a monster in the Stasi."

Putin will claim that at one point a crowd begins to gather around the KGB residency as well. According to him, he steps outside and asks the assembled people what they want, clarifying that this is the residency of a Soviet military organization. Someone in the crowd shouts back, "Then why do you have cars with German license plates in the yard? What are you even doing here?" He explains that under the agreement, they are allowed to use German plates. "And who are you, anyway?" someone yells. Putin replies that he is a translator and quickly retreats into the building. He calls the headquarters of the military group, only to hear: "We can't do anything without orders from Moscow." And Moscow is silent. That phrase becomes Putin's most haunting memory: "Moscow is silent." A decade later, he will describe it this way: "It felt to me then like the country no longer existed. It became clear that the Union was sick. And it was a terminal, incurable illness called paralysis. Paralysis of power."

EVERYTHING FALLS APART

In Moscow, there is virtually no reaction to the fall of the Berlin Wall— there isn't even an emergency meeting of the Politburo to discuss what has happened. Everything around them is collapsing, and the German Democratic Republic is just one small piece of the puzzle. They simply cannot keep up.

The day after the fall of the Berlin Wall, the Politburo of Bulgaria's Communist Party convenes in Sofia and decides to remove General Secretary Todor Zhivkov from power. Zhivkov is the oldest leader among the Eastern Bloc countries—seventy-eight years old and having ruled Bulgaria for thirty-five years. He also twice requested that Bulgaria be admitted into the USSR—and was twice denied.

The decisive Politburo meeting will later be broadcast on national television, shocking viewers and giving the sense that Zhivkov simply cannot comprehend what is happening to him.

On November 10, Gorbachev and Kohl speak on the phone, and the chancellor assures him that he does not want an exodus of East Germans or a destabilization of the German Democratic Republic. Indeed, within the first week after the fall of the Wall, around 9 million East Germans—nearly the majority of the country's population—visit the Federal Republic of Germany, and almost all return home. They do not want to move; they want to unite.

Surprisingly, Gorbachev still believes that the German Democratic Republic will continue to exist—especially since all Western leaders reassure him that they oppose German reunification. Margaret Thatcher had told him this quite bluntly during their meeting in London in September—at that time, the Berlin Wall had not yet fallen, but everyone understood where events were heading. François Mitterrand says the same thing to him over the phone after the Wall has fallen.

But on November 28, Kohl presents his ten-point reunification plan to the Bundestag.

Gorbachev is in shock. On December 5, when West German foreign minister Hans-Dietrich Genscher arrives in Moscow, the General Secretary shouts at him. The conversation, as Chernyaev notes, goes "far beyond the usual norms for communication between statesmen of this rank." Gorbachev feels that Kohl has deceived him: "He apparently believes his music is playing now—the tune of a march—and he has started marching to it himself." "Even Hitler wouldn't have dared to do such a thing," adds Shevardnadze.

"GET RID OF THIS SCUM"

The whole world is celebrating the peaceful transfer of power in Eastern Europe, while at the far edge of that Europe, in Soviet Georgia, events are unfolding that make violence increasingly likely.

Jaba Ioseliani, the godfather of the Soviet underworld, realizes once again that it is time for a career change. He has already been a gangster, then a theater scholar, then the creator of an underground business empire—now he understands that he must enter public politics. In August 1989, he gathers a group of young men with criminal pasts at Tbilisi's Dinamo Stadium. Until now, they had followed him as the undisputed king of the criminal world. But now they declare themselves an armed unit called the Mkhedrioni—which translates from Georgian as "horsemen." In medieval times, *mkhedrioni* were Georgian knights who fought against the Ottoman and Iranian armies. The new "horsemen" proclaim their mission: to fight for Georgia's independence from the Soviet Union.

However, the former gangster Ioseliani quickly finds himself with powerful patrons in the security services. Thanks to his connections in the Ministry of Internal Affairs, he secures official registration for his armed group, giving it the legal status of an NGO. That a mafia leader has allies in the Ministry of Internal Affairs is hardly surprising—after all, it was Jaba Ioseliani who, back in 1982, first suggested that organized crime across the Soviet Union establish contacts with the authorities.

Surprisingly, Jaba Ioseliani harbors a deep personal hatred for opposition leader Zviad Gamsakhurdia. He claims everywhere that after his arrest in 1977, Gamsakhurdia repented, betrayed his comrade Kostava, and sold out to the KGB. According to Ioseliani, they must "get rid of this scum before he destroys the entire nation."

EVERYONE'S SEASICK

Eduard Shevardnadze, the former leader of Georgia, is far removed from what is happening in his homeland. He is busy trying to manage Soviet-American relations. The first summit between Gorbachev and Bush is scheduled to take place in Malta—a neutral country in the Mediterranean Sea, and, as Condoleezza Rice will later complain, the worst possible location for a meeting in December.

Gorbachev arrives in high spirits. Prior to the summit, he visits Italy, where he is received not merely like a rock star—he is the new Beatles. "A deafening roar: 'Gorby! Gorby!' The police were trampled. The security guards were having heart attacks. At one point women broke through to Gorbachev: hysterical and in tears, they flung themselves at the car windows, were pushed back, and broke free again," writes Chernyaev. Naturally, it is Gorbachev—and not Bush—who feels in control of the situation. At the same time, the two sides are in drastically unequal positions. "In plain view, apart from the past and the fear of returning to totalitarianism, we have nothing yet," Chernyaev writes on the eve of the summit.

Initially, Bush wants the negotiations to take place on warships, as Roosevelt and Churchill once did at the onset of World War II. However, a fierce storm breaks out at sea, leaving half the participants suffering from seasickness. The only usable location is the Soviet cruise liner *Maxim Gorky*, moored in the harbor and rocking slightly less than the warships.

It's an ironic scene: the two leaders meet to mark the end of the Cold War—a cause for celebration—but everyone is sick.

No documents are signed at the summit—what agreements could be reached in such weather?—but it becomes legendary nonetheless, as both leaders declare that the Cold War is over. For Gorbachev, it is inevitable; he is a prisoner of his own image as a peacemaker, beloved by the world.

However, this is the first summit where Gorbachev's entourage is visibly dissatisfied with their boss. Marshal Akhromeyev, no longer Chief of the General Staff but still a member of the delegation, sets the tone. He states that Gorbachev has shown weakness—that he should have taken a much tougher stance against German reunification.

Still, the two leaders clearly establish a sense of trust in each other. "The world will be a better place if perestroika succeeds," Bush says, promising to provide support, such as repealing the Jackson-Vanik Amendment, enacted in 1975 to restrict US-Soviet trade because the USSR had refused to allow Jewish emigration.* For the first time, the Soviet and American leaders hold a joint press conference. An American journalist asks, "So, are you now friends?"

"We are partners," Gorbachev replies.

Later, several legends will arise around the Malta summit in Russia. An amusing story suggests that before negotiations began, Gorbachev and Bush decided to stage a sort of gladiatorial match: a wrestling bout between their bodyguards. Who won remains unknown.

While Bush and Gorbachev negotiate in Malta, spontaneous transformations continue across Eastern Europe. On December 3, Gustav Husak, the president of Czechoslovakia who came to power in 1968 following Brezhnev's decision to suppress the Prague Spring, resigns. Yet another formerly pro-Soviet regime ceases to exist. The leader of the Prague Spring, Alexander Dubček, is elected head of parliament, and the writer and dissident Václav Havel becomes president. Mikhail Gorbachev's old friend Zdeněk Mlynář can finally return to his homeland from exile.

Filmmaker Miloš Forman calls Garry Kasparov: "Hi, you know, you were right. I opened the window today—and they're gone."

Exactly a year has passed since they had lunch in Paris, when Forman insisted that all of this was temporary and that the thaw would soon end.

GREBENSHCHIKOV'S RETURN

While in the United States, Grebenshchikov follows news from the USSR through CNN and American newspapers, sensing that something catastrophic is happening back home. Though he is far removed from politics and pays no attention to the Congress of People's Deputies or its aftermath, he increasingly feels the urge to return—not because, like Liu Xiaobo, he wants to be in his homeland during a historic moment, but because he feels out of place in America. He says he's bored and doesn't fit into the cultural environment.

After finishing his tour, he returns to the USSR, and his homecoming is a major event. For most Soviet citizens, traveling abroad remains a distant

---

* The Jackson–Vanik Amendment would be repealed for Russia only in 2012—and immediately replaced by the Magnitsky Act.

dream, and few have the chance to leave the country. Many dream of emigrating, seeing "abroad," and especially America, as a utopia. Leaving for America is seen as a one-way journey—no one came back. Grebenshchikov's decision to return is nothing short of extraordinary.

"When I was in the States, watching events here on TV and in newspapers, I thought, that's it—civil war, too dangerous to even step outside, mafias shooting at each other. But when I got back, I realized that, yes, all of that exists, but so does nighttime Leningrad under the moon, and it hasn't gone anywhere. You can see your time and your country as something God-given, or you can see it as a stage for political, financial, or other spectacles. I chose the first," he reflects on his return.

He also echoes an idea first articulated in the nineteenth century by Russian philosopher Pyotr Chaadayev, who once wrote that Russia serves as an example to other countries of how *not* to live:

"I see Russia as a simplified model chosen by God to serve as an experimental testing ground," BG declares. "It's the sturdiest country in the world—no other could survive what we've endured."

In Chaadayev's time, such words led to him being officially declared insane. Yet Soviet journalists are thrilled by Grebenshchikov's observations.

Despite his constant critiques of America in every interview, BG mentions plans to return there to record another album. He admits it's challenging to overcome the internal conflicts within Aquarium, but he hopes to continue working with the band as well. He even shares a working title for a potential new album: *Everyday Life in a Civil War.*

The changes in the USSR during his year-and-a-half absence leave him stunned. "When I was in Moscow, I realized that if tonight, for instance, the Pamyat society decided to stage an attack to destroy the magazine *Ogonyok,* no one would pay attention to it. And if they did, many would probably breathe a sigh of relief."

BLIND SOLDIER

The Second Congress of People's Deputies is scheduled to open on December 12. Members of the Interregional Deputy Group meet daily to discuss their shared strategy. Sakharov is the group's unquestioned moral leader, but his proposal seems too radical to everyone. He believes they must demand that the congress repeal Article 6 of the constitution, which enshrines the leading role of the Communist Party. If the congress refuses, he says, they should call for a general strike.

According to legislator Sergei Stankevich, the idea of a general strike terrifies everyone. Parliamentarians argue that such an action would strike a blow against Gorbachev, playing into the hands of the conservative faction within the Politburo. They fear that the conservatives would overthrow Gorbachev and put an end to perestroika. Despite the majority voting against his proposal, Sakharov insists that he will present his call for a strike at the congress—not on behalf of the faction, but in a personal capacity.

But shortly before the opening of the congress, an odd incident happens to Sakharov. His wife, Elena Bonner, is not in Moscow—she is traveling to America to visit their children—so he is home alone, preparing for the congress. One day, he calls journalist Yuri Rost and asks him to come over for an important matter. Rost arrives immediately. Sakharov treats him to fresh almond cookies—a rare delicacy in Soviet times.

"Where did you get such luxurious cookies?" Rost smiles.

"I bought them at the Kremlin. Now I'm a bribed parliamentarian," Sakharov jokes.

Then he reveals the real reason he invited Rost. A veteran of the Afghan war is supposed to visit him—someone who personally witnessed an incident where Soviet soldiers were executed by their own commanders to prevent them from surrendering. It is precisely for discussing this episode in interviews with foreign journalists that Sakharov was viciously attacked during the first congress.

Sakharov and Rost talk late into the night, but the veteran never shows up. Instead, he arrives the next day, when Sakharov is home alone.

The soldier claims he had been blinded by a war injury. Sakharov questions him at length and even lets him stay the night. The next morning, after saying good-bye to his visitor, he replays their conversation in his mind and comes to a troubling conclusion—the man was lying. He didn't seem blind at all and, quite possibly, has never even been to Afghanistan.

PROPHET'S DEATH

On December 12, the congress opens. It is scheduled to last for twelve days. On the very first day, a clash occurs between Sakharov and Gorbachev. The academic proposes repealing all articles of the USSR constitution that contradict perestroika, clearly referring to the infamous Article 6.

"No, I don't think this will work. We'll leave this as is," Gorbachev replies irritably.

"As for Article Six, I'll pass on the telegrams I've received . . . ," Sakharov insists.

"Come see me, I'll give you three folders with a thousand of those telegrams," the General Secretary retorts.

"I have sixty thousand. I would give them to you."

"Let's not pressure each other by manipulating public opinion. We don't need to do that. Please," Gorbachev concludes.

On December 14, Sakharov returns from the Kremlin. "I'm very tired today, Lyusenka," he tells Bonner after lunch. "I'll go lie down for a bit. Wake me in a couple of hours, and we'll get back to work."

Late that evening, Bonner finds him dead on the floor of his study. A heart attack. "You lied to me!" she cries. "You promised me three more years!" Sakharov had always believed he would live as long as his father—seventy-two years—but he passed away at sixty-eight.

No one close to Sakharov questions the natural cause of his death. The only exception will be Anatoly Sobchak.

"I do not believe in the naturalness of Sakharov's death—it was too sudden and far too convenient for his political opponents," Sobchak will write in an article published only after his own death.* "A nationwide strike was scheduled for late December, which greatly worried the authorities, and Sakharov was one of the initiators and inspirers of that action. Incidentally, after Sakharov's death, this strike went virtually unnoticed. . . . Naturally, Sakharov's death significantly weakened the position of the democratic forces, which the ruling elite quickly exploited."

However, there is no doubt that Sakharov was very unwell, and none of

---

* Sobchak himself, incidentally, will die ten years later, like Sakharov, of a heart attack under far more suspicious circumstances.

his close friends or family had any suspicions. Just like the recent death of Kostava in Georgia, Sakharov's death altered the course of events.

"WHY ARE YOU SHOOTING US?"

It is during these very days, while Moscow buries Sakharov, that unrest begins in Romania—the most totalitarian state in the Eastern Bloc. This regime has the most horrific reputation: dictator Nicolae Ceaușescu has driven his country to destitution while simultaneously constructing an absolute North Korean–style totalitarianism.

It all begins on December 16 in the city of Timisoara, when authorities attempt to evict a Hungarian bishop from his home. Neighbors surround the house in a protective ring, trying to defend him. The protests quickly grow, and Ceaușescu orders the army to disperse the demonstrators. Defense Minister Vasile Milea refuses to open fire, and his deputy, Victor Stănculescu, takes command.

On December 17, the protests are suppressed. The true number of casualties is unknown, though rumors suggest tens of thousands.

Ceaușescu does not take the situation seriously—on December 18, he leaves for a working visit to Iran, leaving his wife in charge. This is standard practice for Romania: Elena Ceaușescu holds the position of deputy prime minister, and propaganda hails her as the "Mother of the Nation." However, by the twentieth, he is forced to return. He orders the self-defense units to assemble and be ready for action—handpicked proletarians who, if necessary, will help suppress the protests.

On December 21, Ceaușescu addresses a rally in Bucharest from the balcony of his residence. Right in the middle of his speech, people in the crowd begin shouting: "Down with him!," "Rat!," and "Timisoara!" Ceaușescu tries to calm the crowd, but security insists that he and his wife leave the balcony.

The city erupts in turmoil, with tanks on the streets. On the following day, December 22, the couple, along with a few close aides, evacuates Bucharest by helicopter—taking off directly from the roof of the Central Committee building.

It is announced that the minister of defense has committed suicide—though a legend will soon arise that Ceaușescu had ordered him to disperse the crowd, to which he allegedly replied, "I will not shoot at the people," and he was subsequently shot. At that moment, the deputy minister of defense, Stănculescu, who had recently suppressed the uprising in Timisoara, decides Ceaușescu's time is over and stops obeying him. He arrests the dictator's brother and closes Romanian air space, threatening to shoot down Ceaușescu's helicopter. The pilot lands the couple near the town of Târgoviște. They flag down a passing car and order the driver to keep going. However, upon their reaching Târgoviște, workers from a local factory greet the car with a hail of stones. Later that evening, they are detained by the military.

Yet the clashes continue. The events in Romania are completely unlike the transitions of power in other Eastern European countries: in Poland, Hungary, Czechoslovakia, Bulgaria, and the German Democratic Republic, the former communist leaders step down peacefully without clinging to their seats. Romania is the first country where the revolution is accompanied by bloodshed, and the confrontation does not cease even after Ceaușescu is overthrown.

In Moscow, the Second Congress of People's Deputies is still underway. Each session begins with Gorbachev reading the latest reports on the situation in Romania—typically, there is no accurate information, and for several days he keeps telling the legislators that Ceaușescu's whereabouts remain unknown. Parliamentarians ask him why the USSR is not acting, but he simply shrugs: the Western press is dramatizing the situation, and what is really happening remains unclear.

Gorbachev's head is spinning these days. Amid the congress, the Lithuanian Communist Party declares its separation from the Communist Party of the Soviet Union, and the United States begins its invasion of Panama. Meanwhile, the congress is preoccupied with two of the most important topics of recent years: the case of investigators Gdlyan and Ivanov, and the parliamentary investigation into the events in Tbilisi on April 9.

On December 23, investigator Nikolai Ivanov, Gdlyan's partner, declares, "They may physically destroy us, but they will never bring us to our knees before the mafia and its patrons. . . . I am absolutely convinced that the time will soon come when we will hold our own Honeckers, our Ceaușescus, our Zhivkovs accountable, and finally evaluate those fathers of stagnation who have driven our country into crisis."

The Romanian Revolution concludes the day after the congress ends in Moscow. On December 25, in the city of Târgoviște, where Nicolae and Elena Ceaușescu have been held in a military garrison for three days, a very strange trial begins. It is extremely brief, resembling more of a staged production, with no defense attorneys present. The deposed dictator insists it's all a sham and rejects the accusations.

"The sham is what you have done for twenty-five years," the judge retorts.

Nicolae and Elena Ceauşescu are sentenced to death. They are told they have ten days to appeal but are immediately taken to be executed. When Ceauşescu realizes he is about to be shot, he begins shouting, "Death to the traitors!" and then breaks into "The Internationale."

"Why are you shooting us? I was your mother!" cries Elena Ceauşescu.

The soldiers reply, "What kind of mother are you if you killed our children!"

Ceauşescu does not manage to finish singing "The Internationale." He and his wife are executed by firing squad. Their bodies are left on display for several days at the Steaua Stadium in Bucharest. It will later become known that the orchestrator of this trial was the same deputy minister of defense, Stănculescu, who had only recently overseen the massacre in Timisoara.

LITHUANIA AND PANAMA

At the same time, the most pressing conflict in the USSR is unfolding between Moscow's leadership and Lithuania. Vytautas Landsbergis, the leader of Sąjūdis, will later recall that he arrives in Moscow for the congress but insists everywhere that Lithuania is a neighboring country. He refuses to participate as a member of the congress, declaring that he no longer considers himself a citizen of the USSR. Soviet leaders look at him as though he has lost his mind.

"You must understand that your Red Army is not our army, and it will have to leave," says the Sąjūdis leader to Minister of Defense Yazov. "He turned crimson at such an insult," Landsbergis remembers.

The First Secretary of the Lithuanian Communist Party, Algirdas Brazaus-kas, seeing the overwhelming popularity of Sąjūdis and the idea of independence, and realizing that opposing the process is futile, devises a plan to try to lead it instead. He calls an extraordinary congress of the Lithuanian Communist Party, scheduling it for December 19–20—days when Gorbachev will be occupied with his own congress.

Brazauskas leaves Moscow and announces in Vilnius that the Lithuanian Communist Party must separate from the Communist Party of the Soviet Union. A significant portion of Lithuanian communists are either already members of Sąjūdis or sympathize with it, so they vote in favor of Brazauskas's proposal. However, there is a group of staunch supporters of Moscow. As a result, the party splits into two unequal parts.

The actress Ingeborga Dapkūnaitė recalls being deeply struck by the split within the Communist Party:

"I had known Landsbergis for a long time because he was my teacher at the conservatory. Everyone loved him, and his political stance didn't surprise anyone. But the transformation of Brazauskas—that was shocking. If even the communists were starting to push for independence, it gave people hope. Brazauskas was willing to give up the comfort of his position of power because he sensed the spirit of the times—that, of course, amazed everyone."

Gorbachev reacts to this much like he does to the news from Romania: he declares it "a grievous fact for all the communists of the country" but says that since there are no official documents yet, it's too early to draw conclusions.

That very same day, President George Bush announces the launch of "Operation Just Cause"—the military invasion of Panama. For the first time since the start of perestroika, the Americans begin a military operation; just over two weeks have passed since the Malta summit. The invasion plan had been approved by Secretary of Defense Dick Cheney, of course, well before Malta, but Gorbachev had not been given any prior warning.

Panama, admittedly, is a deeply problematic country. It is ruled by Manuel Noriega—one of the most cartoonish villains in modern history. Throughout his political career, he managed to simultaneously cooperate with the CIA, the KGB, the Medellín drug cartel, Pablo Escobar, and Fidel Castro's Cuban regime. At the beginning of 1989, presidential elections were held in Panama, but Noriega, as the army commander, annulled the results and installed his own puppet as the nominal head of state.

On November 10, Noriega gives an interview to Soviet journalists, offering to normalize relations with Washington "on the basis of respect for freedom, sovereignty, and noninterference in Panama's internal affairs." Then, on December 15, he declares that his country was in a state of war with the United States. On December 20, George Bush sends in twenty-six thousand troops to depose Noriega.

Gorbachev, of course, has no intention of defending the Panamanian dictator and drug baron. However, the situation deeply contradicts his world view: just six months earlier, he had declared an end to the Brezhnev

Doctrine, promising not to interfere in the internal affairs of neighboring states. As a result, revolutions erupted across Eastern Europe, and a civil war had begun in Romania just days before. Meanwhile, the United States appears to be moving in the opposite direction.

The Soviet Foreign Ministry issues an official condemnation of the operation in Panama. "The Americans couldn't have done anything better for our military-industrial complex than commit an act of aggression in Panama," comments Gorbachev's advisor Georgy Arbatov in the *Washington Post*.

The invasion of Panama, incidentally, will mark the first US military operation undertaken under the banner of defending democracy.

THE SOBCHAK COMMISSION

Back at the first congress in June, a parliamentary commission was formed to investigate the causes of the crackdown on the Tbilisi rally. The commission includes many notable figures, but its head is a relatively unknown lawyer from Leningrad, Anatoly Sobchak.

The Sobchak Commission achieves the unprecedented: first, they travel to Tbilisi and question all the witnesses from that night. They also carefully listen to Georgian opposition leaders.

During a discussion with the commission, Zviad Gamsakhurdia, as MP Stankevich recalls, declares the slogan "Georgia for Georgians." Sobchak gently asks, "What about the representatives of other peoples living in Georgia: Russians, Armenians, Abkhazians?" Gamsakhurdia replies, "They will have a choice: either become Georgians or leave." Sobchak responds, "I realized we now have two tasks. First, we must tell the full truth about what happened on April 9. And second, we must ensure that you never come to power."

The commission members then return to Moscow, and Sobchak insists on questioning two Politburo members: Second Secretary Yegor Ligachev and former KGB head Viktor Chebrikov. They evade the summons, but Sobchak repeatedly calls Gorbachev, threatening that if they don't appear, the commission will report to the congress that it couldn't complete its work.

In the end, the commission manages to reconstruct the events. Here is how the events of April look according to the parliamentary group's findings:

At the moment when the rally in Tbilisi was gathering, Gorbachev was indeed in London. In the General Secretary's absence, on April 7, Ligachev held an extended Politburo. By that time, the Georgian First Secretary had already called Moscow several times, demanding troops. Ultimately, the Politburo, led by Ligachev, sanctioned the deployment of military forces to the Georgian capital—though he later insisted that clear instructions were given to use force only as a last resort. Late that evening, Gorbachev and Shevardnadze returned from London.

The next day, April 8, Ligachev left for a previously planned vacation. Meanwhile, in Tbilisi, a meeting of the local party leadership took place. When the generals from Moscow entered the hall, the Georgian communists gave them a standing ovation. The Georgian party leadership demanded that the military put an end to the rally. The operation was led by General Igor Rodionov, commander of the Caucasus Military District. He decided that units of internal troops and paratroopers would enter the square when the crowd was at its thinnest—at 4:00 a.m.—and simply clear everyone off the square.

But then everything went off plan. In the morning, the military discovered that there were not two hundred people on the square, as they had estimated, but ten thousand. Rodionov, however, did not cancel the order.

At the congress, General Rodionov claimed that extremists among the protesters were planning to seize government buildings. The Sobchak Commission declared that there was no evidence of this—the rally had been peaceful.

Sobchak concluded the report on the commission's findings and then read out a note received from Ligachev. He claimed he bore no responsibility for what happened, as he had been on vacation. Sobchak, smiling ironically, commented on this position, "If a political or state leader makes a decision, then they bear responsibility for the consequences of that decision, regardless of where they learn about these consequences—whether on vacation or in their office."

Following Sobchak's report, the congress officially condemned the use of violence against the demonstrators. However, no one would be held accountable.

8

HEAD-ON COLLISION

My mom came back from Angola six months before my dad's assignment ended. While she was away, he fell in love with his boss's wife. When he arrived in Moscow, he almost immediately told my mom he was in love with another woman and that they needed to divorce.

Everyone in the family reacted differently. "He's never setting foot in this house again!" raged my grandmother. "We won't take a penny from him. We'll live on buckwheat if we have to, but we don't need anything from that scoundrel. And the kids? He's not seeing them either!"

Mom was in a daze. One night, she suddenly got ready, grabbed me, and we headed out—I didn't realize at first that we were following my dad, watching him head to his mistress. Why? I had no idea. And honestly, I didn't really care. I don't even remember if we followed him all the way to her apartment, if Mom confronted him at the door, or if we turned back halfway and went home.

I was completely absorbed in my imaginary world—it was far more interesting to me than my parents' problems. I hadn't seen much of my dad over the years anyway. Back when we lived in Angola, he used to come home from work for lunch and then put me down for a nap. I was five, and they believed kids absolutely had to nap after lunch. I never wanted to, of course. Dad, with military efficiency, tried to make me fall asleep quickly. He had this idea that to sleep, you shouldn't move. So if I moved a hand, he'd hit it. If I moved a foot, he'd hit that.

The news that Dad wouldn't be living with us anymore felt like a relief to me. I felt bad for Mom and Grandma—they were clearly devastated—but I couldn't understand why they were so upset.

LUKYANOV DOCTRINE

On December 23, 1989, as the Romanian revolution still rages, Viktor Alksnis, the leader of the Union group, takes the floor at the congress.

He begins with a warning: "Comrades, I once again draw your attention to the fact that the Baltic republics are on the path to leaving the USSR!" He elaborates on his thoughts in an unexpectedly conciliatory tone: "No one is going to frighten them with tanks, machine guns, or rifles—that is, suppress their right to self-determination." Instead, he proposes drafting a law to regulate the republics' exit from the USSR. According to the lieutenant colonel's idea, this law must spell out all the conditions, such as what financial compensation a republic must pay to the union budget.

"Uzbek women and children picked cotton in poisoned fields, and it was practically sent to Latvia for a pittance, where it was processed at our textile factories. These textile enterprises were built on the backs of these children. It turns out that we, in many ways, lived off these Uzbek women and children," he muses. He certainly isn't worried about Uzbekistan wanting to leave the Union—his priority is preventing Latvia's departure.

Following this speech, Alksnis is invited to meet Anatoly Lukyanov, Gorbachev's deputy.

Alksnis explains that since Lenin's time, the Soviet constitution has contained a clause stating that any republic can leave the USSR, but "there's no procedure for exit—no clarity on the fate of Union property, the army stationed in that territory, or the people who do not belong to the titular nationality of that republic." Lukyanov agrees.

Alksnis continues. In Latvia, for example, "fifty-two percent are Latvians and forty-eight percent are so-called Russian-speaking residents. And in Riga, Russians constitute sixty percent. Why not include a provision in the law stating that exit from the USSR is only possible via a referendum, where the results are tallied separately by regions and territories?" If so, he argues, Latvia could leave—"but without Riga and the entire eastern part, where the majority are Russians."

"What an interesting idea!" Lukyanov approves. Alksnis reminds him that regions with a predominantly Russian population exist in every republic: in Estonia, it's the northeast; in Lithuania, it's the Polish-speaking regions around Vilnius, and so on.

Lukyanov proposes that Alksnis join the working group tasked with drafting such a law—nicknamed "On the Non-Exit of a Union Republic from the USSR" by the legislator himself. A few months later, the Supreme Soviet passes the law almost unanimously.

Thus begins the collaboration between Alksnis and Lukyanov. By 1990, the Union members expand on this idea: they decide that separatism across the USSR must be countered with counter-separatism—fighting fire with fire. "How are large fires extinguished? By setting a counterfire," they argue. In their view, regions that wish to remain in the USSR should be carved out from Union republics that are seeking independence. They begin recruiting parliamentarians from Abkhazia and South Ossetia, the autonomous republics within the Georgian SSR.

"Lukyanov was our spiritual father. The Ministry of Defense and the KGB also provided their support," Alksnis will remember. This tactic of combating separatism would later be dubbed the "Lukyanov Doctrine"—although Lukyanov himself, of course, never officially developed it.

"I NEED A DRINK"

On December 25, the same day the Ceaușescus are executed in Romania, Gorbachev convenes a Central Committee plenum to decide what to do about the breakaway Lithuanian communists.

He assures everyone that "the current party and state leadership will not allow the disintegration of the Union state" but then makes an unexpected proposal: not to annul the decision of the Lithuanian party but to send the General Secretary—himself, Gorbachev—to Lithuania to persuade the local Communist Party "with all due respect to the Lithuanian people." Many members of the plenum insist that it's time to use force; otherwise, the USSR will fall apart. "I don't want to get my hands dirty with blood," Gorbachev replies.

On January 11, Gorbachev and Raisa arrive in Vilnius. In the square in front of the cathedral, he sees a banner: "Lenin recognized Lithuania, Stalin took its independence—what about Gorbachev?" It's a clever move, of course—Gorbachev wants to be seen as Lenin, not Stalin.

At the next meeting, Gorbachev sees an elderly worker holding a sign: "Full independence for Lithuania."

"Who told you to make that sign?" Gorbachev asks indignantly.

"No one. I made it myself."

"What do you mean by 'full independence'?" the General Secretary presses, hoping to embarrass his interlocutor.

"I mean our status in the 1920s, when Lenin recognized Lithuania's sovereignty, because no nation has the right to rule over another."

"In our large family, Lithuania has become a developed country," Gorbachev insists. "How can we be exploiters when Russia sells you cotton, oil, and raw materials—and not for hard currency?"

But he fails to shake the worker. "Lithuania had its own hard currency before the war. You took it from us in 1940. And do you know how many Lithuanians were sent to Siberia in the 1940s and how many died?"

"I don't want to talk to this man anymore." Gorbachev turns away. "If Lithuanians have such ideas and slogans, they are in for hard times. I don't want to talk to you anymore."

Raisa tries to calm her husband, but he sharply snaps at her, "Shut up."

For three days, Gorbachev speaks to various audiences, insisting that Lithuania receives more from the Union than it contributes to other republics. The most difficult meeting proves to be with Lithuanian intellectuals.

"If Lithuania leaves the Union, it will be relegated to the sidelines of history," the General Secretary threatens. "This is not the time to cut ties. . . . You criticize yesterday's day, yesterday's politics, yesterday's concepts. . . ." They bluntly reply that today he is in power, but tomorrow someone else, some marshal perhaps, will take his place.

At the end of the meeting, Gorbachev—perhaps for the first time—realizes that he may truly fail to convince anyone: "So, you really want to leave?" And the hall responds in unison: "Yes!"

Afterward, the three of them—Gorbachev, Lithuanian First Secretary Brazauskas, and Raisa—sit silently in the car. Eventually, the General Secretary speaks, seemingly to no one: "What happened to them?" And, without pause: "I need a drink."

Around this time, reflecting on the disastrous trip to Vilnius, Minister of Defense Yazov reportedly says, "If one republic leaves, Gorbachev is finished. But if he uses force to stop it, he's finished too."

POGROM NUMBER TWO

The dramatic events in Romania leave a profound impression on Abdurrahman Vezirov, the First Secretary of Azerbaijan. He is terrified and seriously fears he may soon share Ceaușescu's fate—especially since protesters in Lenin Square in Baku have mockingly altered his name to the Armenian-sounding "Veziryan" and parade his effigy through the streets dressed in women's clothes.

On December 25, the day the Ceaușescus are executed in Romania, Abdurrahman Vezirov, in a panic, demands that Moscow must urgently send troops.

In reality, he controls very little at this point—key decisions in Azerbaijan are made by Viktor Polyanichko, the Second Secretary and former de facto viceroy in Afghanistan.

He knows that Moscow will never agree to the use of force in Azerbaijan as long as democratic opposition leads the rallies. Radicals, however—especially Islamist ones—are another matter. Preparations proceed on two fronts: KGB head Kryuchkov consistently feeds Gorbachev alarming reports that protesters in Baku are parading portraits of Khomeini and that Soviet Azerbaijan is on the brink of an Islamic revolution. Meanwhile, on the ground, Polyanichko fuels divisions within the People's Front and encourages its most radical activists.

More radical figures increasingly gain access to national television. By December 1989, the "radicals" fully control the People's Front. In other words, it is the same thing that is happening in Georgia at the very same time.

According to the recollections of Zardusht Alizadeh, the leader of the Popular Front, Abulfaz Aliyev, gives the order on December 31 to destroy the state border with Iran. His subordinates hesitate, fearing that border guards might open fire. "Don't be afraid of anything; tear it down!" he tells them.

And indeed, on December 31, crowds dismantle the border fences with Iran and set fire to the guard towers. Effectively, the border between the USSR and Iran ceases to exist. This mirrors the recent events in Berlin: in both places, one people, artificially divided by politicians, are now reuniting. On both sides of the border live Azerbaijanis who speak the same language and share the same Shiite Muslim faith—on one side lies the Iranian province of Iranian Azerbaijan, and on the other, the Azerbaijan SSR. Yet these scenes remain absent from the global media. And Slava Rostropovich, a native of Baku and intimately familiar with Azerbaijan, does not fly here to play his cello.

On January 6, 1990, a split occurs within the Popular Front in Baku. "I fear violence, bloodshed, and defeat," warns one of the Front's founders, Zardusht Alizadeh. "On the path to freedom, alongside democracy, blood is also necessary!" responds the leader, Abulfaz Aliyev.

As a result, a group of the Popular Front's founders, led by Alizadeh, exit the organization, "leaving it in the hands of KGB agents and the mafia," as he will later write in his memoir. Meanwhile, the remaining members of the Front continue staging mass rallies in Lenin Square. Several thousand more troops from the USSR's Ministry of Internal Affairs are sent to Baku.

Garry Kasparov returns to his hometown of Baku. He has long lived in Moscow, but he still has many friends and relatives in Azerbaijan—including, for example, his grandmother. Or the First Secretary of the Republican Communist Party, Vezirov. However, Kasparov does not stay in Baku itself but in the nearby resort area of Zagulba, on the Caspian Sea coast, at a retreat center that had been allocated to him years earlier by former Azerbaijani leader Heydar Aliyev.

"I came to figure things out. To understand how to get everyone out. But at the time, I thought it would only be a temporary measure," the world chess champion will later recall.

On January 12, Viktor Polyanichko meets with the People's Front leaders—but only with its most radical factions. They discuss forming a "National Defense Council" to protect the republic from Armenian "invasion." There is little doubt that Polyanichko is stoking tensions to justify declaring martial law. Following the negotiations, two radical opposition activists appear on television. Ostensibly tasked with calming the public, they declare that Baku is overrun with homeless refugees while thousands of Armenians still live in comfort.

The next day, on January 13, anti-Armenian pogroms erupt in Baku. The crowd had gathered for a rally at Lenin Square, chanting slogans with a refrain: "Long live Baku without Armenians!" By evening, groups leave the square and begin attacking Armenians. A repeat of Sumgait unfolds—only on a far larger and more horrifying scale. In Baku's Armenian quarter, mass killings begin: people are thrown off balconies, beaten to death, burned alive. Up to one hundred people are killed—the exact number remains unknown.

"What is a pogrom in a city of a million people?" Kasparov reflects. "You need a precise list of addresses to know where to go. Moreover, the pogroms in

Baku are happening district by district—first one, then the next. Everything is highly systematic. That requires centralized coordination."

Thousands of terrified Armenians seek refuge in the massive Shafag movie theater, guarded by military forces. Later they will be escorted to the seaport, loaded onto ferries, and transported across the Caspian Sea to Soviet Turkmenistan. There, in the port city of Krasnovodsk, they will be put on planes to be flown to Yerevan.

All this time, the USSR's internal troops stationed in Baku do not intervene—this is a familiar pattern: pogroms often occur in plain view of indifferent police forces.

Kasparov later recalls that two local policemen were assigned to guard him at the retreat in Zagulba: "I remember sitting there at night, listening to reports about what was happening in the city, and hearing that buses full of rioters were heading our way."

"What will you do?" Kasparov asks a policeman.

"What can I do? I have a family. You understand what will happen if they get here," the guard replies.

"But you have weapons!"

"Listen, we respect you," the officer offers. "Here's what we'll do—you hit me over the head, take my weapon, and do whatever you want!"

It is clear that the only real option is to leave as quickly as possible.

Kasparov's friends in Moscow pool their money to charter a Tu-134 from the government fleet—a flight that costs them around $15,000. The plane arrives in Baku, but it has only sixty-eight seats.

"My grandmother was seventy-seven years old at the time," Kasparov recalls. "I told her we had to go. Of course, she didn't want to—everyone was buried there, her husband, the whole family. . . . 'Grandma,' I said, 'we have to. We'll come back, I promise.' She knew I was lying. . . . Everyone was leaving. But even I didn't fully grasp the scale of what was happening."

Many Baku Armenians come to Zagulba, hoping Kasparov can evacuate them. "But what could I do? I had only fifteen seats left on the plane. I walked into the hall and said, 'I can take some of you to Moscow. That's all I can promise.'"

That night, in total darkness, they drive to the airport. They manage to bypass the terminal and go straight onto the tarmac. "It was an evacuation in the dark. Scarier than the movie *Argo*," the champion will later recall.

BLACK JANUARY

It is only on January 14 that a delegation from Moscow arrives in Baku, led by Yevgeny Primakov. An Arabist scholar and longtime advisor to Gorbachev, he has obvious ties to the KGB. He knows the Caucasus well—he grew up in Tbilisi, spoke Armenian and Georgian as a child, and attended a military school in Baku.

Moscow decides to impose a state of emergency in Nagorno-Karabakh, but not in Baku itself. In the city, barricades made of trucks and concrete blocks are erected. On January 17, an uninterrupted rally begins in front of the Central Committee building of the Communist Party. Protesters set up gallows in the square—clearly a symbol of revolution.

On January 19, a massive rally demands the resignation of the republican leadership. Simultaneously, the Supreme Soviet of the Nakhchivan Autonomous Republic adopts a resolution to secede from the USSR and declare independence—the furthest any part of the Union has gone so far. Everyone knows that Nakhchivan is the birthplace of the republic's former leader Heydar Aliyev, and his influence there is immense.

The situation becomes so threatening that the Politburo dispatches security officials: Defense Minister Yazov and Interior Minister Bakatin. While sending them off, Kryuchkov urges them to show firmness and overcome the "Tbilisi syndrome."

But before signing the decree authorizing the use of force, Gorbachev calls Heydar Aliyev—his former rival for power and Andropov's favorite, whom Gorbachev himself had forced into retirement from the Politburo just two years earlier. At that moment, Aliyev is at a health retreat near Moscow, monitored by the KGB. The General Secretary demands that Aliyev "remove his people from the streets," but the former head of the republic, of course, denies any involvement in the events.

On the evening of January 19, the TV station in Baku is blown up. Future Nobel Laureate journalist Dmitry Muratov, who is in the city, tells that the attack is carried out by Alpha Group operatives who have flown into Baku on the personal aircraft of KGB chairman Kryuchkov. This explosion news proves decisive for Gorbachev. He finally authorizes military intervention. Beginning at midnight on January 20, a state of emergency is declared in the city—but no one knows this yet, since TV broadcasts have been cut.

Shortly after midnight, troops leave their barracks, and tanks begin to move toward the city center. They advance as if they are conquering an enemy city—even the deployment of troops in Beijing after two months of protests in Tiananmen Square the previous year was carried out far more carefully. Tanks roll over barricades, crushing cars and even ambulances in their path. A bus filled with civilians is fired upon. Soldiers shoot at fleeing people, and finish off the wounded.

That night, 130 people are killed, and hundreds more are injured. There are casualties among the military as well—at least twenty-one soldiers die.

The army takes control of the city. But by January 20, all of Baku comes out to bury the victims of the previous night's atrocities. After the brutal violence, Soviet power in Azerbaijan is no longer viable—now it is clear to everyone that the republic is under Soviet occupation. Thousands of communists burn their party membership cards. Not long ago, this would have been considered sacrilege. The leader of the Popular Front, Abulfaz Aliyev, changes his surname—he is now Abulfaz Elchibey, meaning "people's messenger." Many follow his example, renouncing their Russified surnames.

In Moscow, Heydar Aliyev, the former Politburo member and Azerbaijani First Secretary, holds a press conference and condemns the military actions in Baku. This essentially marks the restart of his political career.

First Secretary Vezirov leaves Baku suffering a nervous breakdown. Gorbachev, too, changes after these events. "Hair gone white, a gray face, some kind of emotional breakdown, a soul in crisis," is how Raisa will later describe her husband.

AMERICAN FASHION

On January 31, on Pushkin Square in Moscow, where dissidents often held unauthorized protests, a different kind of gathering takes place. The first McDonald's in the USSR opens its doors. The demand is so overwhelming that a mile-long line forms. For months, enormous lines will form daily.

The location chosen for the first American fast-food restaurant is already legendary—until now, it was home to the iconic Lira café, a favorite spot for Moscow's rock 'n' roll crowd. But no one mourns the closure of the famous Lira or its replacement with a fast-food restaurant. Everything American is incredibly fashionable. Previously, American jeans, cigarettes, and chewing gum were available only to the bohemian crowd, but now everyone wants them.

The entire country is watching American movies. Up until this point, Soviet television only showed domestic films, and the occasional foreign movie might slip through from the Eastern Bloc, India, Italy, or France. But in the late 1980s, VCRs make their way into the USSR, and Soviet citizens suddenly have the chance to watch what they want. At first, the obsession is with action films—*The Terminator* becomes a cultural turning point for multiple generations. Then, of course, comes erotica. For the USSR, where there was "no sex" just a few years prior, this is nothing short of a revolution.

America is no longer feared; on the contrary, everyone now wants the USSR to be just like America.

This fascination with everything American highlights one obvious reality: the Soviet economy is completely dysfunctional, and no one knows how to reform it. "We have no grain, no foreign currency; the situation is hopeless," Prime Minister Nikolai Ryzhkov admits at a February Politburo meeting. Just months earlier, he had fought to avoid being dismissed—but for what purpose no one can say.

One of the main problems is that all Soviet leaders were raised on the ideas of Marxism-Leninism. They are mentally incapable of abandoning these ideas—even Gorbachev. On the one hand, he speaks everywhere about "new thinking," but when it comes to rethinking the economy, he cannot begin. His aides try to insert references to private property into all his speeches, but he stubbornly crosses them out. As for private ownership of land, Gorbachev— once the party's overseer of agriculture—flatly says he will never agree to it.

YAKOVLEV VERSUS THE PARTY

At the end of January, Alexander Yakovlev comes to Gorbachev with a new plan. Urgent action is needed, he says—it's time to get rid of the Communist Party. Azerbaijan, Lithuania, the state of the economy—all signs point to the fact that people are at their breaking point. The only move left is to sacrifice the Communist Party of the Soviet Union, and specifically the Politburo.

Yakovlev proposes a bold maneuver: intercept the proposal Sakharov presented at the last congress—to repeal Article 6 of the constitution, which enshrines the "leading and guiding role" of the Communist Party. "Let the congress elect you president," Yakovlev suggests to Gorbachev.

In this way, the entire Politburo of the party would be automatically dismissed, but Gorbachev would continue to rule—not as General Secretary, but as president. In addition, Gorbachev would free himself from the constant obligation to attend the Supreme Soviet. The summer before, the "aggressively obedient majority" had seemed loyal, but by the winter of 1990, they had become an obstacle: a deeply conservative body increasingly hostile to Gorbachev's reforms and resistant to any changes.

At the same time, Yakovlev urges Gorbachev to take direct responsibility for the situation: to appear on television and lay out his program of action: "Land to the peasants, factories to the workers, genuine independence for the republics—not a union state, but a union of states, multi-party politics, and a real end to the CPSU monopoly. Take large loans from the West, implement military reform, withdraw troops from Eastern Europe, abolish ministries, and radically reduce the bureaucracy."

Another of Yakovlev's proposals is to dismiss Ryzhkov: "With a prime minister who thinks like a factory director, and a Gosplan trained under the methodology of the military-industrial complex, no reform can be achieved."

When Yakovlev recounts his conversation with the General Secretary to Chernyaev, the latter clarifies, "In other words, we're talking about a coup d'etat."

"Yes," Yakovlev agrees. "There's no time to lose."

But Gorbachev says neither yes nor no to Yakovlev; instead, he asks him to draft a proposal for this political reform.

THE RALLY NEXT TO THE KREMLIN

Local elections are scheduled across the entire country for the spring of 1990: parliaments of all the Union republics and city councils are to be elected. If just a year earlier no political organizations existed in the USSR, now there are many, with a key anti-communist force present in almost every region.

Lev Ponomarev, a former physicist turned political activist who worked with Sakharov and cofounded the Democratic Russia movement, decides that a preelection rally must be held in Moscow. Unlike previous protests, which took place on the outskirts—next to Luzhniki Stadium—he insists on holding this one in the very center, on Manezhnaya Square, right by the Kremlin walls. The Moscow authorities reply that he needs permission from Gorbachev himself. Soon he is told that Lukyanov is willing to meet him. Together with several colleagues, Ponomarev goes to the Kremlin.

"Lukyanov spends a long, long time explaining to us that Yeltsin is trash—literally—that we're making a mistake by backing Yeltsin, that he'll betray us. We waste so much time listening, nodding along because what else can we do? I don't argue with him. What matters is getting his signature," Ponomarev recalls. "And in the end—yes, he signs off on the rally at Manezhnaya Square, gives us some kind of official paper."

On February 4, 1990, the first massive, officially sanctioned rally in Soviet history takes place. Its main slogan is the abolition of Article 6 of the constitution, which enshrines the Communist Party's leading role. It also feels like a tribute to Sakharov.

"We were all blown away by how many people came," Ponomarev says. "And the authorities were just as blown away." About three hundred thousand people gather on the square, an unthinkable crowd—no May Day demonstration had ever drawn so many.

Korotich speaks first, delivering what he later calls lofty rhetoric: "Fear is dead! The cruel system has had its backbone removed. It wobbles like jelly, and they're scrambling to prop it up with a new fear. But we have already become the main force in our country. . . ." He watches the enormous crowd sway on the frosty Manezhnaya Square.

Next to him stands economist Gavriil Popov, who is running for the Moscow City Council and hopes to become its leader. He reflects, "God forbid someone slips a bomb into one of the trash bins on Manezhnaya Square. One explosion, one push, and the crowd, catching the scent of blood—as in 1917—will blindly surge forward."

"Long live the peaceful February Revolution of 1990!" cries Yuri Afanasyev, historian and the man who coined the phrase "aggressively obedient majority" at the congress last year. But the true star of the rally, of course, is Yeltsin.

The rally is led by Ponomarev and Afanasyev. They intentionally manipulate the speaker list a little—for example, pushing Telman Gdlyan to the sidelines because none of the democrats trust him. "Gdlyan always gave the same speech: 'This is the last time we'll meet a rally because they're breaking us up, they're destroying us, they won't let us gather again.' That was his tune," Ponomarev recalls.

At the end of the rally, Ponomarev announces the next rally on Manezhnaya Square, a week before the elections. The very next day, the CPSU Central Committee Plenum is held, where Gorbachev presents Yakovlev's program: abolishing Article 6 and introducing the post of president. The previous day's rally plays right into his hands.

However, most members of the Central Committee are, of course, terrified. They speak out against the General Secretary's proposal to abolish Article 6, spend hours condemning the "so-called democrats," and demand an end to the discrediting of the party and socialism. Then, following party discipline, they vote unanimously in favor of Gorbachev's proposal. Only one person abstains—Yeltsin. Now, in early March, a congress is scheduled to convene, where a new president of the USSR will be elected.

THE FEBRUARY REVOLUTION

Meanwhile, the democrats prepare for the promised new rally. But this time, things aren't so simple: after seeing such a massive crowd, the authorities are no longer willing to let them gather near the Kremlin. "I understand that it was a firm 'no,'" Ponomarev recounts. "They said, 'Anywhere on the Garden Ring, fine—but inside the Garden Ring, absolutely not.'"

The rally's organizing committee experiences its first major conflict. Ponomarev suggests accepting the Garden Ring. Suddenly, one of the activists, Lev Shemaev, a member of the Committee to Defend Gdlyan and Ivanov, removes his shoes, climbs onto the table, and begins yelling in full rally mode, *"Why are we listening to this Ponomarev? We need to march on Manezhnaya!"*

The meeting is held in a basement room with low ceilings, so Shemaev nearly bumps his head. The other participants start to waver. They murmur that perhaps Ponomarev is a KGB agent—after all, he recently went to the Kremlin to meet with Lukyanov, and who knows what he agreed to. The pressure grows to reject the authorities' demands and hold an unsanctioned rally on Manezhnaya Square.

"There are these key moments in a country's history that go unnoticed," Ponomarev reflects. "I'm certain this was one of them, one hundred percent. If the organizing committee had voted to march on Manezhnaya, that would have been it. That would have been a perfect excuse to break up the protest, and the military and the KGB would have prevailed. They would have given us our own Tiananmen."

But the organizing committee narrowly votes to agree to hold the rally at the Garden Ring, on February 25. A similar democratic rally is scheduled for Leningrad. The date is highly symbolic—the anniversary of the February Revolution, marking seventy-three years since the abdication of Tsar Nicholas II.

If no one expected much from the previous rally, it's now clear what kind of protest potential the capital has. Panic spreads through the city. Some claim that a million people will turn up for the demonstration, while others are convinced the crowd will storm the Kremlin. The KGB circulates rumors that activists from the Pamyat society are planning pogroms against Jews. On the wave of this chatter, organizers of the Leningrad rally even announce its cancellation.

Gorbachev himself is extremely nervous. "Our opponents have united against us. And we're still playing nice. We need to hit them in the face. The TV monopoly has been seized by these people—both politically and morally, scum. People without morals," he says at a Politburo meeting.

The day before the rally, internal troops enter Moscow—suddenly, words about a "February revolution" no longer sound like a joke. Prime Minister Ryzhkov appears on television, urging citizens to stay home.

Here's what Gorbachev's aide Chernyaev writes in his diary on the day of the rally:

> They've whipped up panic in recent days—probably the security services and "the apparatus" themselves. The entire Jewish population is expecting pogroms and fleeing abroad by the tens of thousands each month.
>
> The Moscow demonstration is under the slogans "for new representatives" and "down with the Kremlin mafia." They even wanted to form a living ring around the Kremlin. MS [Gorbachev] didn't react for a long time, but then he understood the danger, and it began: a statement from the government, mobilization of services, 17,000 internal troops, mobile security service for elite buildings. On the Arbat, leaflets appeared with photos of the building in Plotnikov Lane, listing the apartments where Politburo members live.

Despite the panic, Chernyaev himself goes to the rally—he lives nearby. He is sure that many participants carrying banners are "clearly paid." (Of course he's wrong.) He feels deeply hurt for Gorbachev, whom one speaker calls a "setting star, whose light is still visible somewhere in the West."

> Not a single kind word about MS. . . . The entire event's underlying message is the liquidation of the "existing order" and replacing those in power. The analogy writes itself: Nicholas II. He granted freedom but wanted it to be used at his discretion. The result—an uprising.

The rally's leader, Yuri Afanasyev, declares that 500,000 people have shown up. Chernyaev thinks there are no more than 100,000. The next day, the same argument flares up at a Politburo meeting. KGB head Kryuchkov claims there were no more than 70–100,000, while Minister of Internal Affairs Bakatin insists on 230–300,000.

Ryzhkov and Kryuchkov argue that "a huge victory has been achieved over 'these people,' and we need to keep pressing on. Finally, the people felt that we have power."

But Bakatin interrupts:

"What victory?! We scared the people. Many didn't come out because of fear. That's why they didn't gather a million, but they could have. Intimidation gave us order, but that's not politics. In a month, or on May 1, they'll bring out a million. And they'll march on the Kremlin, as they promised. What will we do then? Shoot them? Beat them with batons? Send in armored personnel carriers?! What kind of commission will the Supreme Soviet have to form then? This is a mass phenomenon, fueled by widespread discontent, and it cannot be underestimated. What's needed is politics—and at its core, dialogue. We need a 'round table.' If I don't understand something, then I shouldn't hold this position. But I don't agree with what the Politburo members are saying here."

Unexpectedly, the minister of internal affairs turns out to be the main liberal within the government. Everyone else is against him—most of all, Gorbachev. He insists:

"They're all scum! Political frauds! The direction these people are taking is clear: when you don't have political arguments, just slander and lie. No trust for them! No round tables! They want to destroy everything so that power will fall into the dust and all that's left will be for someone to pick it up!"

On March 3, Gorbachev turns fifty-nine. He is still a relatively young politician—though, for context, Nicholas II was ten years younger at the time of his execution. Yet it's unlikely that the General Secretary associates himself with the former tsar. If anyone could haunt him like a ghost, it would be the recently executed Nicolae Ceaușescu. Just two months ago, Gorbachev considered the Romanian dictator his antithesis, mocking him as a "prehistoric despot," while viewing himself as a European intellectual. But now, seeing the massive rallies in Moscow and reading the vitriolic statements of those who hate him, Gorbachev might well begin to feel a little of what Ceaușescu experienced in his final days.

Gorbachev is deeply shaken by the loss of popular affection. Until now, the KGB had carefully supplied him with nothing but praise and glowing reports. But now everything has changed. The slogans outside the Kremlin walls, the biting press coverage—all are stark evidence of this shift. Gorbachev increasingly tells those close to him that he has done all he could and it's time for him to step down. Raisa, who feels the sting of public hatred toward her even more acutely, passionately agrees.

RUSSIAN RESENTMENT

In March 1990, new elections are held across the USSR, including the Russian Federation, other republics, and major cities.

This time, Boris Yeltsin runs for a seat in the Russian Soviet Federative Socialist Republic Parliament (RSFSR) representing his native Sverdlovsk region. He openly declares his intention to fight for the position of its chairman—the top political office in Russia. His right-hand man, Gennady Burbulis, recalls that by this point, he and Yeltsin had already devised a new strategy: they realized that achieving anything at the Union level was impossible—"the Congress of People's Deputies of the USSR had turned into a swamp," dominated by Gorbachev and Lukyanov. So the decision is made to shift the political battle to the RSFSR level. They are no idealists. For them, it is a pragmatic move in the struggle for power.

Surprisingly, Yeltsin's chief rival, Yegor Ligachev, reaches the same conclusion, albeit for entirely different reasons. The Second Secretary of the

Central Committee is also dissatisfied with the congress—but because of its "rampant democracy," its excess of freedom and lack of order. Ligachev remains an unwavering believer in communism, confident that local party organizations will support him. Ideologically, Ligachev increasingly aligns himself with the so-called Russian Party. His opponent, the journalist Vitaly Korotich, paints this picture of Ligachev's circle:

> One of the most powerful political mafias began to form around him—sociologists call it tribalism. Ligachev's entourage consisted of conspicuously "Russian" people, as if dressed straight out of folk tales, minus the bast shoes and padded coats. These folks loved to loudly pontificate about Siberia, Russia's unique path, and the need to resist Western traps. For Ligachev's supporters, the West was a monolithic, insidiously evil force scheming to invade the innocent Russian soul and tear it to shreds.

Ligachev and his supporters feel genuinely aggrieved by the republics' push for independence. They frequently claim that the Russian people liberated half the world from fascism, built factories and plants across all the Soviet Union, and that other nations of the USSR owe an immeasurable debt to the Russians. The separatism of the Baltic republics, particularly any references to "Russian occupation," deeply offends Ligachev—to him, it is an act of betrayal, a vile ingratitude he simply cannot comprehend. How dare they fail to appreciate all the good Russians have done for them?

This is, of course, a textbook colonial mentality. Fifty years earlier, many British citizens were similarly baffled as to why India was not grateful for their presence, and thirty years before, the French could not fathom why Algeria failed to appreciate their "benevolence and care." Yet Ligachev considers himself a communist and an internationalist; the idea that he is a typical colonialist could never even cross his mind.

The resentment of Russian nationalists toward the "ungrateful colonies" was most clearly expressed during the First Congress of People's Deputies by one of the prominent Russian writers of the 1980s and a darling of the nationalist Pamyat society, Valentin Rasputin (no relation to the infamous mystic from the time of Tsar Nicholas II):

"Perhaps Russia should leave the Union, if you blame it for all your woes, and if its backwardness and clumsiness are such a burden on your progressive aspirations?"

At the time, in the summer of 1989, this was meant as a rhetorical question. Rasputin, of course, did not expect a positive answer. Quite the opposite—he assumed the republics would immediately come to their senses, apologize, and beg for Russia's forgiveness.

But a year later, it's clear that no one is rushing to apologize. Increasingly, Russian media begins to promote the idea that Russia is feeding the other fourteen Soviet republics at its own expense—that they are merely a burden. Russia, it is argued, needs to let them go quickly so that the Russian people can finally live well.

The unintentional author of this idea, Rasputin, is ideologically and politically much closer to Ligachev than to Yeltsin. But Ligachev and his allies cannot fully embrace this formula—the Soviet Union is far too precious to them. Yeltsin, however, begins to adopt this rhetoric. He is certainly no nationalist; this line simply suits his situational struggle against Gorbachev. It makes it easier to tell voters that all their problems stem from the federal center, from Moscow. By shedding the burden of the Union republics—and Gorbachev with them—Russia will breathe freely. This message would have been impossible to campaign on a year earlier in the Union parliament in Moscow, but it's perfect for the new campaign in Sverdlovsk.

A MAP PAINTED IN DIFFERENT COLORS

The idea that the Union's days are numbered does not terrify everyone. Arkady Murashov, a parliamentarian and coordinator of the Interregional Group, says that even before the 1990 elections, he knows the Communist Party had lost its grip and that opposition forces would win in many regions:

"In February 1990, I went to America for the first time and spoke in Phoenix, Arizona. I said, 'The Soviet Union is doomed. Soon, you'll see countries on the world map painted in different colors. Right now, it's all one red color—the Soviet Union—but soon, there will be many colors,'" he recalls. "By then, it was clear to me that the March elections for republican parliaments and local councils—like the Moscow City Council—were coming. We, the Interregional Group, had our finger on the pulse and knew what was happening in Georgia, Armenia, Ukraine—everywhere. It was completely obvious: What Soviet Union? Once they're elected, they'll all say, like the Balts, 'That's it, good-bye, folks!'"

By this time, the situation in the USSR is changing significantly. In September 1989, the People's Movement of Ukraine (Rukh) is founded—an equivalent of Sajūdis in Lithuania or the Popular Fronts in other republics. It brings together both established Soviet writers and dissidents like Vyacheslav Chornovil, who has spent more than a decade in prison for his anti-Soviet activities.

One of Rukh's first major actions is the "Reunion Chain." On January 21, 1990, around half a million people form a human chain stretching from Kyiv to Lviv to mark the anniversary of the unified Ukrainian People's Republic in 1919. Given the recent fall of the Berlin Wall, the peaceful revolutions in Czechoslovakia and Poland, and the bloody overthrow of Ceaușescu in Romania, this demonstration leaves a strong impression on many Ukrainian communists.

On March 7, Democratic Russia achieves a triumphant victory in the major Russian cities.

The leader of Moscow's democrats, economist Gavriil Popov, is elected the new head of the city. The first sessions of the new Moscow City Council begin with a scandal. Popov removes the bust of Lenin from the assembly hall, and the legislators abolish an old tradition: previously, Moscow City Council Representative Certificate No. 1 was always issued in Lenin's name. Popov decides to put an end to this strange idolatry.

In the Russian parliament, the democrats win far more seats than they did a year earlier in the Union parliament, but it is far from a majority. Democratic Russia will hold 465 seats, the communists 417, and the remaining 176 will waver between the two camps.

The hosts of *Vzglyad*, including Sasha Lyubimov, also become parliamentarians. He is an experienced political journalist, but at the same time, a privileged kid from an affluent Moscow family who has been abroad but has traveled little across Russia. His very first visit to the Kremlin as a parliamentarian leaves a deep impression: "I arrive late—because I was smoking outside. The Grand Kremlin Palace. Ceilings about fifty feet high. The hall is filled with the strong smell of onions and socks. That's Russia for you—a distinct stylistic feature. But the way they behave—it's a complete fucking disaster."

EVENING. RAIN. INDEPENDENCE

In Lithuania, elections take place in several rounds. Not all the results have been finalized yet, but it's already clear that Sąjūdis has achieved a convincing victory.

Many Lithuanian politicians argue that the first parliamentary session must be held as soon as possible—before the USSR Congress of People's Deputies scheduled for March 12. The expectation is that once Gorbachev is elected president of the USSR, he will gain additional powers and leverage to block Lithuania's independence. In reality, these arguments are dubious: Gorbachev already has vast powers, but he isn't using them.

Nevertheless, the Lithuanian parliamentarians decide to preempt him. They convene on March 10, not waiting for the second round of elections to conclude. Despite this, they have a quorum. The next day, they elect Sąjūdis leader Vytautas Landsbergis as the new chairman of the Supreme Soviet, defeating the First Secretary of the Lithuanian Communist Party, Brazauskas. Immediately afterward, they adopt several historic decisions—likely the most significant in Lithuania's history.

First, they vote for the Act of the Restoration of the State of Lithuania: 124 votes in favor, with 6 abstaining, and not a single vote against—meaning even the communists support the decision. They also annul the Soviet Lithuanian constitution and readopt the 1938 constitution, which had been in effect before the Soviet occupation. The country's prewar name, the Republic of Lithuania, and its historical coat of arms, are restored.

Thus, Lithuania takes the most radical step: abruptly and without any warning, it declares independence from the Soviet Union.

This comes as a surprise to everyone—even to some Sąjūdis legislators. Of course, they all strive for independence, but few thought it would happen so quickly, so abruptly, and so unexpectedly. No one, naturally, wanted to vote against it and risk going down in history as an enemy of their country's independence. But now everyone is in shock. It's dark outside, rain is pouring down, and only a few hundred people stand outside the parliament building—a far cry from the massive rallies for independence seen the previous summer.

THE FIRST PRESIDENT

On March 12, the Third Congress of People's Deputies convenes—an extraordinary session, therefore very short. It can largely be seen as Sakharov's congress because, just three months after the academician's death, Gorbachev has finally matured enough to repeal Article 6. On the other hand, it was Sakharov himself at the first congress who argued against concentrating all power in one pair of hands—even if those hands belonged to Gorbachev. The trade-off here is precisely that: the destruction of the party in exchange for the presidency.

According to legislator Murashov, the Interregional Group of Deputies experiences its first split: whether or not to support Gorbachev's candidacy for president. One faction, led by Yeltsin, insists that the elections must be conducted by universal vote. "In hindsight, it was probably demagoguery on our part," Murashov will reflect years later. "Because how could we even talk about nationwide elections? The Baltics certainly wouldn't participate, while the remaining 12 republics probably would, and Gorbachev would undoubtedly have had a 100% chance of winning. But he didn't go for it—probably because of the Baltic states." The other faction of the Interregionals, led by Anatoly Sobchak, supports endorsing Gorbachev.

In addition to the General Secretary, two other candidates are put forward: Prime Minister Ryzhkov and Minister of Internal Affairs Bakatin, but both withdraw their names. They are obvious stand-ins, meant to show there is no real alternative to Gorbachev.

Despite this, Gorbachev's inner circle remains nervous—he needs to secure two-thirds of the votes, and this is not guaranteed given the mood among both the democratic opposition and the conservative communists.

Nursultan Nazarbayev, the First Secretary of Kazakhstan, takes the podium. He proposes introducing a presidential system in the Union republics as well. It's clear this is a deal: regional leaders are ready to give Gorbachev the votes he needs, provided they, too, can call themselves presidents. Gorbachev doesn't like this but is forced to concede. "I won't hide it; this wasn't part of my plan. The creation of presidential posts in the union republics devalued much of what we hoped to achieve by strengthening central authority," he will later write in his memoir. But in the end, Gorbachev secures the required two-thirds.

On March 12, the inauguration of the first president of the USSR takes place. The entire hall rises to greet the first democratically elected—though not by popular vote—leader of the Soviet Union, except for one person. Telman Gdlyan defiantly remains seated.

THE BLOCKADE OF LITHUANIA

As soon as the congress concludes, all attention once again turns to Lithuania—it spoiled Gorbachev's celebration by declaring independence on the eve of his victory. Two months earlier, the autonomous republic within Azerbaijan—Nakhchivan, the birthplace of Heydar Aliyev—staged a similar demarche. But no one paid any attention then. That independence was crushed by tanks in Baku, and the Western press did not write a word about it. With Lithuania, things are different.

On the other hand, Sąjūdis members are convinced that the West will immediately recognize Lithuania's independence. Landsbergis had consulted with Stasys Lozoraitis, the son of the prewar Lithuanian ambassador to Washington and a leading figure in the Lithuanian-American community, who assured him that the United States was ready to recognize the new country. After all, the West had never de jure recognized the occupation of the Baltic states.

A group of Sąjūdis members also had flown to Moscow to meet with the sitting US ambassador, Jack Matlock. He told them not to count on international recognition for the time being. But they didn't believe him.

Now the whole world—and the entire Soviet Union—waits in bewilderment: What will happen next? No one expected Lithuania to attempt a midnight escape from the USSR.

Gorbachev, though now the president of the USSR, continues to convene the Politburo. He is so furious with the Lithuanians that he needs the old hawks, who always push him to use force. Generals from the General Staff, including Valentin Varennikov—the former commander of the Afghanistan operation—are invited to the meeting. (Incidentally, it was Varennikov who, in 1983, ordered the downing of the South Korean airliner.)

Varennikov presents his plan: to stage not Kabul '79 but rather Prague '68 in Vilnius. Declare a state of emergency, establish direct presidential rule, arrest the current Lithuanian leadership (referred to as "isolation" by Politburo members), and form a puppet government that will call on Moscow to send in troops—exactly the Czechoslovakian scenario.

The next day, Chernyaev takes Gorbachev aside for a talk: "This is a disaster. The death of your great cause. And all because of this imperial complex," he admonishes Gorbachev. "Oh, come on, Tolya, everything will be fine; it'll all go as it should!" Gorbachev doesn't even look up, continuing to shuffle through his papers.

Gorbachev's press secretary, Andrei Grachev, will recall that a week before Lithuania's independence, Brazauskas had visited Gorbachev. The latter waved him off: "Go wherever you want. But you're poor—you've got nothing of your own. How will you live without the rest of the Union? You'll come back with a begging bowl!"

In the end, Gorbachev doesn't send in the tanks but decides to impose an economic blockade on Lithuania—an embargo on the supply of petroleum products and many other goods, including medicines.

In response, Lithuania demands 500 million rubles from the USSR for damages caused during the Soviet period. "A ghost of Stalin haunts the Kremlin," Landsbergis declares vividly.

All of Moscow's actions have the opposite effect. If, after March 11, many Lithuanians had been shocked and bewildered by the hastily declared independence, now they increasingly rally behind Landsbergis and the decision of the Lithuanian Supreme Council.

The spring conscription into the Soviet army begins, and most young Lithuanians naturally boycott it. (This is also the case in Latvia, Estonia, Georgia, Armenia, and Western Ukraine—refusing to serve in the Soviet army becomes an increasingly popular stance.) But in Lithuania, Soviet military authorities suddenly resort to terroristic measures: they hunt down draft evaders and deserters, placing them in a psychiatric hospital in Vilnius as hostages.

Landsbergis will recall that his driver comes to him seeking advice about his son, who is currently serving in the Soviet army. On the one hand, if Lithuania is now independent, it feels wrong to serve in the army of another state. On the other hand, the son only has a few months left to serve—if he tries to escape now, he will be prosecuted as a deserter. "I advised that, if nothing was threatening him, he should finish his term without conflict with the military authorities," Landsbergis says.

THE MOST AMERICAN JOURNALIST OF THE USSR

In September 1989, the *New York Times* publishes an article about a new program on Leningrad television—it's called *600 Seconds*. It's merely a daily roundup of local city news, lasting precisely ten minutes. The idea sounds odd: Why would one of the world's largest media outlets be interested in mundane local news? Yet by that time, *600 Seconds* has become a phenomenon—not just another one of the many perestroika-era TV shows, but the most scandalous program in the USSR.

The *New York Times* article is titled "Hip, Hot and Hyper: Soviet TV Cuts Loose." The centerpiece of the piece is the show's host, Alexander Nevzorov. The paper compares him to Geraldo Rivera, the future Fox News anchor, who at the time is known as the creator of the controversial American talk show *Geraldo*. That show touches on almost all taboo topics: sex, drugs, violence, crime, Satanism; participants argue and fight—*Newsweek* dubs this genre trash TV.

Nevzorov's *600 Seconds* is also a kind of trash TV, though in the format of a short news bulletin. Each episode features piles of corpses, severed limbs, warehouses of rotting scarce goods, naked people, underage prostitutes—essentially everything that would shock even a twenty-first-century viewer. For the Soviet audience, it's nothing short of revolutionary—nothing like it has ever been shown on television, let alone in a news program.

Nevzorov has access to a police radio, so he's often the first to arrive at crime scenes. But sometimes he makes the visuals more vivid and dramatic—for instance, using ketchup to create the appearance of more blood.

"A corpse alone isn't a story," Nevzorov tells the newspaper *Arguments and Facts*. "We never aim to simply shock the audience, but we're also not afraid to show the grimmest details of life and death when there's a social phenomenon behind them."

Leningrad television broadcasts beyond the city, reaching the entire European part of the USSR. Nevzorov's show becomes the most popular program in the Soviet Union.

At the time, Nevzorov is just thirty-one years old. His biography is rather unusual—like Viktor Tsoi, he dodged the draft by spending time in a psychiatric hospital. He studied at the philology department of Leningrad University but didn't graduate. He sang in a church choir and even attended a seminary (which he also didn't finish). He worked as a stunt man in films, where he befriended members of the Leningrad KGB. Since the early 1980s, he's been working at Leningrad television.

Boris Grebenshchikov recalls knowing Nevzorov as a little boy—they once ended up at the same summer Young Pioneer camp: "He's five years younger than me, so he was in the youngest group at camp. All the old ladies, the nannies, the nurses, the cleaners—they absolutely adored him. They practically worshiped him because he was such a wonder child. And even then, he was outrageously spoiled."

CHURCH OFFICERS

In the spring of 1990, KGB chief Vladimir Kryuchkov visits Leningrad. His destination: the TV center, where he plans to have a confidential conversation with Alexander Nevzorov—or at least, that's what the *600 Seconds* host will claim.

"We sit on a bench in a small park opposite the TV studio on Chaplygina Street, 6," Nevzorov will recall. "Cats are yowling, drunks are sprawled around, and somewhere, presumably in a nearby block, someone is assaulting a woman—she is screaming her head off. And there we are, huddled up, sharing our plans for the future and building a friendship."

According to Nevzorov, Kryuchkov has a plan to save the Soviet Union. He understands that communist ideology has run its course and needs to be replaced. The best substitute, he believes, is religion.

"He has this illusion that the church wields real influence over the masses," Nevzorov recounts. "He thinks that if we work with the metropolitans, archbishops, and bishops, they would all rush to defend Soviet power, remembering all the good it had supposedly done for them. Ultimately, they would open their desk drawers, pull out their KGB officer epaulettes, which some had removed, but others had simply worn beneath their robes, and pledge loyalty. Kryuchkov believes the church had control over twenty to twenty-five million people who, under the influence of their religious leaders, would remain loyal and obedient."

The idea wasn't new. Alexander Solzhenitsyn first proposed it in his *Letter to the Soviet Leaders* in 1973. In 1987, writer Vladimir Voinovich published his satirical dystopian novel *Moscow 2042*, mocking Solzhenitsyn's ideas. The novel depicts a future Russia where the Communist Party merges with the KGB and adopts Orthodoxy as its new ideology. One character, Father Zvezdony, is a member of the new Politburo and the head of the church.

Ironically, Kryuchkov, who had spent years fighting both Solzhenitsyn and Voinovich in his official capacity, was now seriously attempting to bring their visions to life.

Kryuchkov supposedly confides in Nevzorov, admitting that he doesn't trust many people in the KGB. "He asked me to do some work with the priests," the journalist will recall. "I happened to be the lucky guy who had very clear, very lively connections on both sides—the KGB and the clergy. I knew them well; they were, in part, my world at the time."

Nevzorov is thrilled by the intrigue. "They start regularly bringing me priests for neutral conversations," he will recall. "I'd talk to them there and confirm my suspicion: there were simply no people in the church who weren't connected to the KGB."

However, by 1990, according to Nevzorov, the key figures in the church are people who have "gotten carried away with it all." "It was indeed impossible to become a bishop or archbishop without the KGB's permission. But by then, they had long since broken free of the KGB's leash and were running wild. The task was to figure out how to rein them back in."

One of Nevzorov's interlocutors is Metropolitan Alexei (Ridiger) of Leningrad—the future Patriarch of the Russian Church. "He himself has fairly solid ties to the KGB. But, to his credit, he is more level-headed than the others. He explains that the plan is unrealistic, that the church has no real influence over its parishioners, and that it is all a hollow game."

Indeed, according to Nevzorov, his work with the church hierarchy on Kryuchkov's instructions produces zero results: "They gave all the necessary assurances, we came up with some ideas together, but it eventually turned out they were completely powerless."

FROGS AND THE STINGRAY

In 1990, it feels as though the final barriers between Soviet artists and the West are breaking down. At the Sundance Film Festival, *Needle* is set to premiere, and Viktor Tsoi, Natasha Razlogova, Yuri Kasparyan, and Joanna Stingray all fly to Utah for the occasion. After the screening, the band Kino gives a small acoustic performance.

Although Tsoi sings in Russian, the performance leaves a deep impression on the audience. A Japanese company buys the distribution rights to *Needle* and invites Tsoi to Tokyo. Soon he and Joanna are on their way to Japan.

Tsoi, a great admirer of Japanese culture, is overjoyed. During dinner with Japanese star Keisuke Kuwata, Tsoi reflects, "It's so strange to be a huge star in your own country but completely unknown anywhere else in the world."

"There is a great tale in Japan about a frog born in a well," Kuwata replies. "The frog was very proud of the fact that he was the biggest creature in the well. As a result, he believed he was invincible, and one day he left the well and ended up in the ocean, only to realize that he was much smaller than he thought."

"We are much wiser than the frog. We know how small we are!" Tsoi laughs. "Joanna, she is not a frog. She is a Stingray."

Meanwhile, Boris Grebenshchikov realizes he won't become a star in America and moves on to London to record his next album. He tells everyone he prefers London to New York because it reminds him of Leningrad. Despite his ongoing contract with CBS Records, the lukewarm reception of his previous album has led to growing mutual dissatisfaction. BG wants Ray Cooper, a percussionist who worked with Elton John, the Rolling Stones, and Paul McCartney, to produce his new album, but the label doesn't approve.

Still, he pushes forward, working on an album tentatively titled *Radio London*.

Kino, on the other hand, embarks on a massive USSR tour organized by their new concert director, Yuri Aizenshpis. Many old friends look at Tsoi with open envy, and some claim he's truly changed—he now wears a wolf-fur coat and is often accompanied by bodyguards.

The band fills stadiums, achieving a level of popularity no Soviet rock group has ever seen. Joanna Stingray attends the tour's final concert. "The guys were shouting, the girls were sobbing uncontrollably, as if Christ himself had stepped onto the stage," she would later recount.

THE LAST MAY DAY

May 1 arrives—one of the Soviet Union's most significant holidays. The unshakable tradition includes a parade on Red Square, with members of the Politburo ascending the Mausoleum tribune to greet the passing columns of workers. The workers, in turn, are jubilant, often carrying portraits of the Politburo members. The leaders on the tribune smile and wave.

On May 1, 1990, everything goes awry. The first, official wave of demonstrators marches through Red Square as usual. But then another wave replaces it—these are the people who recently protested against Article 6, in support of Yeltsin and Gdlyan.

"Down with Gorbachev," "Down with the CPSU—the exploiter and robber of the people," "Down with socialism," "Down with the fascist red empire," "Freedom for Lithuania," "Lenin's Party, Get Off the Road!"—these are the slogans carried as demonstrators march through Red Square, staring at a stunned Politburo. For the first time, the party leaders and the people who hate them look one another directly in the eyes.

"Yegor, it's time to end this. Let's go . . . ," Gorbachev says to Ligachev. "Yes, it's time to end it," Ligachev will write in his memoir as he describes the scene.

The situation mirrors Ceaușescu's final rally—Gorbachev and the other members of the Politburo hurriedly descend from the tribune, followed by jeers, laughter, and whistles. "Shame! Scoundrels!" Red Square shouts. According to police estimates, there are about thirty thousand such demonstrators.

The offensive slogans make it into the televised broadcast, which is cut off only after the Politburo leaves the Mausoleum.

Gorbachev is furious—this is a personal insult. He blames the new head of Moscow, Gavriil Popov, directly for the incident. "Everything will continue like this if we let slander go unpunished," Ligachev insists, and Gorbachev agrees. The Politburo orders *Pravda* to condemn the demonstration.

THE NINA ANDREEVA COUP

Now that Gorbachev is president, he creates a new governing body to replace the no-longer-needed party Politburo: the Presidential Council. At last, he has an opportunity to rid himself of the old conservatives he has so long complained about and struggled against. But now Gorbachev's mood is one of deep resentment. The makeup of the Presidential Council is vivid proof of this. Of the former Politburo members, he retains only Yakovlev and appoints his aide Chernyaev. Yet, to their great surprise, he also appoints the nationalist writer Valentin Rasputin.

At one of the first sessions of the Presidential Council, Gorbachev loses his temper, shouting that the media has run wild and shows him no respect. He recounts how Raisa met with American Pamela Harriman, who was stunned by the Soviet people's ingratitude toward Gorbachev and their failure to understand the greatness of his mission. He concludes his tirade by declaring that the time has come to choose sides—including for everyone present.

Yakovlev leaves the meeting dejected—he is convinced that Gorbachev's final remark was directed at him. Gorbachev blames him for having unleashed the press. Yakovlev also tells Chernyaev that he is sure KGB head Kryuchkov is deliberately manipulating information to shape Gorbachev's mood to his advantage.

Both liberals in Gorbachev's inner circle watch with astonishment as the conservative opposition within the Communist Party of the Soviet Union visibly grows bolder. For example, an anti-perestroika rally takes place at the Krylya Sovetov Sports Palace. The legendary Nina Andreeva—the author of the infamous letter—speaks there, followed by Marshal Akhromeyev, Gorbachev's official advisor and former Chief of the General Staff. Yakovlev assures Chernyaev that both Andreeva and the Pamyat society led by Vasilyev are paid KGB agents. He even shows him a protocol from a party meeting at Lubyanka, the KGB headquarters: "This is the program for a Nina Andreeva coup, packaged in traditional phrases and promises to restore order!" Chernyaev exclaims in horror.

In March, Ligachev—not included in the Presidential Council but still a member of the Politburo—writes a letter to Gorbachev, urging him to immediately halt reforms: "Under the banner of democracy and glasnost, the ideological and moral foundations of society are being eroded. The destructive work of the opposition aligns with hostile forces from outside. Following Eastern Europe, their goal is to 'shake socialism' in the USSR and shift our country toward capitalist development. . . . The Party, the Fatherland are in danger—I would say, in extraordinary danger."

Gorbachev does not react at all, which surprises Ligachev the most. "Under Stalin, such a letter would have cost you your head. Under Khrushchev, you'd have been fired. Under Brezhnev, you'd have been sent as an ambassador to Africa. But under Gorbachev, it was simply ignored . . . ," he reflects.

In May, he writes an even more panicked letter to the president. Soon after, Gorbachev removes Ligachev from the Central Committee of the Communist Party, commenting on his decision with a dry remark: "Lately, he's been writing too many letters."

By the summer of 1990, Chernyaev raises the specter of a military coup in his diary. One of the potential organizers he names is General Makashov, the former commandant of Armenia. Back in 1988, under Gorbachev's orders, Makashov had arrested members of the Karabakh Committee—and now he would gladly arrest Gorbachev himself.

"YELTSIN MEANS WAR"

On April 1, a group of newly elected Russian legislators from Democratic Russia who support Boris Yeltsin gather in his office—Yeltsin is currently chairing the Committee on Construction in the USSR Supreme Soviet. Among them is electromechanical engineer Sergei Filatov, who had been nominated as a legislator by workers specifically "to support Yeltsin." At this meeting, the representatives need to strategize how to advance Yeltsin as chairman of the Russian Supreme Soviet.

"Boris Nikolayevich gave his programmatic speech, and our mood took a serious hit," Filatov recalls. "It was an absolutely illiterate speech, in the same old party style. Of course, the guys pounced on him and said, 'Boris Nikolayevich, you can't deliver this; you need to prepare properly.' He agreed."

Soon Gorbachev convenes a meeting with the newly elected Russian legislators. Initially, only those elected under the communist banner are invited—but since most Democratic Russia members are still technically communists, they insist on being included, and Gorbachev relents. However, Yeltsin himself is deliberately left off the guest list.

According to Filatov, Gorbachev asks, "We need to elect a chairman of the Supreme Soviet, who will also be the head of the Republic. Are there any suggestions?" "Immediately, a hand shoots up, and one of the representatives proposes Yeltsin. Without blinking, Gorbachev asks for other nominations. Ivan Polozkov, head of the Krasnodar region and a prominent hard-liner from Ligachev's camp—considered the epitome of obscurantism among the democrats—is put forward.

Gorbachev listens to all the proposals and ultimately advises against supporting Yeltsin. Filatov recalls Gorbachev saying, "Yeltsin means war."

Gorbachev cannot comprehend the phenomenon of Yeltsin's popularity. "Strange things are happening," he says at a Politburo meeting on April 20. "Yeltsin's behavior is incomprehensible. Both at home and abroad, he drinks himself into oblivion. Every Monday, his face is twice its usual size. He is inarticulate and proposes God knows what; he's like a broken record. Yet people keep repeating, 'He's one of us . . . ,' and forgive him everything."

On May 16, the Congress of People's Deputies of Russia convenes. In the first round of voting for the head of parliament, Yeltsin and Polozkov emerge as front-runners, receiving roughly equal support, though neither secures the required 50 percent. This is clearly an unexpected result for Gorbachev, who sincerely believes that Yeltsin is losing popularity. A second round is scheduled.

Arkady Murashov, a USSR legislator and coordinator of Democratic Russia, will later recount hearing all sorts of rumors about how parliamentarians are persuaded to vote for Yeltsin. For instance, some reports suggested that newly elected anti-communist leaders in Moscow may have offered apartments to out-of-town MPs, who were expected to relocate to the capital, in exchange for their support of Yeltsin.

In the second round, Yeltsin gains slightly more votes but still falls short of the threshold.

On May 23, Gorbachev himself appears before the Russian legislators to dissuade them from voting for Yeltsin. The result is the opposite of what he intended.

Before the third round, the General Secretary decides to replace his candidate: instead of Polozkov, the Communist nominee becomes Alexander Vlasov, a Politburo member and head of the Russian government. It is this third round that proves successful for Yeltsin. On May 29, he secures 534 votes—just 4 more than the required 50 percent.

Gorbachev learns of his rival's triumph while on a flight to the United States.

Following Yeltsin's election as chairman of the Supreme Soviet, the next issue arises: Should Russia, like the Baltic republics, adopt its own Declaration of Sovereignty? While the congress had been deeply divided during the leadership vote, there is near-unanimous support for sovereignty. From the podium, the argument is repeated that over 75 percent of the Soviet Union's industrial output is located in Russia, which means that Russia is essentially "feeding the entire country." If Russia becomes economically independent and stops subsidizing other republics, life will finally improve—this is a highly popular notion among the public.

It is worth noting that citizens of every Soviet republic believe that *they* are the ones subsidizing everyone else. All are convinced they contribute more than they receive and that Moscow exploits them.

Less than two weeks after Yeltsin's election, on June 12, the congress votes for the Declaration of Russian Sovereignty—an extraordinary moment of unity between the democrats and the Russian Party. It is, however, the first and last instance of such unanimity.

OPEN REBELLION

In early June 1990, Gorbachev is once again in Washington. The last time he visited the US president was in 1987, and back then it was Reagan. By now, the world has changed dramatically. So has Gorbachev himself and the dynamics within his team. Among the delegation is still the old marshal Akhromeyev, his military advisor. But whereas there was once mutual respect and trust between them, the former Chief of the General Staff now looks at the General Secretary with open suspicion.

The key moment of the negotiations is the discussion of the fate of a unified Germany. Gorbachev proposes that the new country could become an associate member of both NATO and the Warsaw Pact. Bush finds this highly unlikely. After lengthy discussions, Gorbachev changes his position: "The United States and the USSR are in favor of seeing a united Germany, with a final settlement leaving it up to where a united Germany can choose."

This statement horrifies not only Akhromeyev but also Shevardnadze. According to Bush's recollections, Akhromeyev, "his eyes flashing with anger," signals to other members of the delegation, and they begin whispering loudly to each other. "It was an unbelievable scene," Bush later notes. "None of us had ever seen anything like it before—virtually open rebellion against a Soviet leader."

Even American negotiators later will write that they do not understand why Gorbachev does not insist on keeping Germany neutral. Gorbachev himself will explain that he finds such deals unworthy—that he is committed to democracy and believes the German people have the right to determine their own future. But many of the president's advisors, especially Akhromeyev, are furious. From this moment on, murmurs of Gorbachev's betrayal begin. Being an honorable officer, Akhromeyev would never publicly insult his superior—but others will do so freely. Around the same time, news arrives from Moscow: at a farmers' congress, Yegor Ligachev calls Gorbachev a "traitor." It is a declaration of war from the conservative wing. Very soon, many media outlets will be flooded with conspiracy theories claiming that

Gorbachev sold out his homeland—or even that he is the Antichrist and the birthmark on his forehead is the devil's mark.

But as before, Gorbachev feels far more comfortable in America than he does at home—here, he is still a hero. However, due to the blockade of Lithuania, Congress does not invite him to speak at a joint session, so Gorbachev invites selected congressmen to the Soviet embassy instead, delivering his speech there. As they leave, some complain that it was much too long.

For the Soviet First Lady, this visit is far more pleasant than the previous ones. Raisa finds it much easier to connect with the new American First Lady than with Nancy Reagan. She even asks her, somewhat innocently, why she is so popular. "It's simple," Barbara Bush replies with a smile. "I threaten no one—I am old, white-headed and large, and I stay out of my husband's affairs."

"WELL, FUCK IT"

Back in 1989, Leningrad had already earned its reputation as the most democratic city in Russia, with the communists suffering a crushing defeat. By 1990, the democrats fully control the City Council—but its work is paralyzed. Two leaders of the Leningrad Popular Front—dissident Marina Salye and economist Pyotr Filippov—battle for control of the city, and for three months, no resolution is reached. By May, the exhausted deputies decide to bring in an outsider.

The ideal candidate is Anatoly Sobchak, the law professor turned political star of the Congress of People's Deputies of the USSR. Sobchak, however, is not initially interested in returning to his hometown, as he is deeply engaged in his work in the Soviet parliament. Nevertheless, yielding to the pleas of his fellow citizens, he agrees. At the end of May, he is elected chairman of the Leningrad City Council.

Almost immediately, Sobchak begins looking for a new assistant—until now, he hadn't needed to build his own team, but it has become necessary. According to a widely accepted version, he turns for advice to his former boss, the rector of Leningrad University, Stanislav Merkuryev. Merkuryev hands over his own assistant for international affairs—Vladimir Putin. Once upon a time, Putin had been Sobchak's student, and the professor allegedly even remembers him.

At that point, Putin had only recently returned from the German Democratic

Republic. In essence, the country he had been working on no longer existed, so Lieutenant Colonel Putin had nothing left to do. However, he isn't dismissed; he remains a full-time KGB officer while simultaneously working as Merkuryev's assistant at Leningrad University (obviously one of many). On the rector's recommendation, he approaches Sobchak for a job—because the city leader "is surrounded by all kinds of crooks" and lacks a proper team.

This scene is described in detail by Putin himself in the biographical book *First Person*. He recounts entering Sobchak's office in the Leningrad City Council, where Sobchak, allegedly acting on impulse, immediately says, "I'll talk to Merkuryev. Start on Monday. That's it. We'll sort everything out quickly and transfer you over."

Putin supposedly protests, "Anatoly Alexandrovich, I'd gladly do this. I find it interesting. I even *want* to do it. But there's one circumstance that might be an issue. I'm not just Merkuryev's assistant—I'm a career KGB officer."

According to Putin, Sobchak, caught off guard, thinks for a moment and then blurts out, "Well, fuck it!" Putin is stunned that the professor swears, but Sobchak continues, "I need an assistant. Honestly, I'm afraid to even step out into the reception area. I don't know who those people are out there."

Afterward, by Putin's account, he goes to his superiors at the KGB and informs them that the chairman of the Leningrad City Council, Sobchak, has offered him a job. "If that's impossible, I'm ready to resign," he tells them. "No, why? Go ahead and work there, no problem," they reply.

This scene raises a few questions, the main one being: Why would one of the most popular politicians in the USSR, just elected as the head of the country's second-largest city, see Putin and immediately want him to work for him? In the future, members of the Leningrad City Council would put forward theories that Professor Sobchak himself might have been an informant for the KGB in the past and Putin could have been his handler. However, this version would be promoted only by Sobchak's political opponents, who would never provide any evidence to support it.

RENOUNCE THE PAST

The time comes for the final showdown between two former friends: Gorbachev and Ligachev. A congress of the Communist Party convenes in Moscow. Gorbachev plans to deliver a decisive blow to his opponents, while his aides urge him to resign as General Secretary, remain only as president. But Gorbachev refuses: "You can't let this mangy dog off its leash. If I do, the whole machine will turn against me."

During the sessions, Gorbachev endures a great deal of rudeness. Here's how Yakovlev describes the congress:

> It was strikingly different from the others: turbulent, like a drunken man lost on his way home. He stumbles, gets up, crawls forward again, swearing incessantly the whole time.

Yet, in the end, it genuinely looks like Gorbachev has managed to out-smart all his enemies. He is reelected General Secretary—unopposed, as no one nominates an alternative candidate. The real struggle unfolds over the position of deputy general secretary: Ligachev is the main contender. But Gorbachev proposes electing Volodymyr Ivashko, the First Secretary of Ukraine, threatening that if Ligachev wins, he will resign. The congress delegates heed Gorbachev's warning.

After the meeting, the defeated Ligachev—as he would later recall—is suddenly approached by American historian Stephen Cohen, who speaks to him in Russian: "Yegor Kuzmich, allow me to shake your hand! You are brave; you are a very courageous person! You left with dignity!"

As he is leaving the Kremlin, he runs into Vitaly Korotich, whom he once appointed as the editor in chief of *Ogonyok*. "So, you say I'm a dying dinosaur? A mammoth? Have you ever thought about the fact that after the age of dinosaurs comes the age of rats? You'll regret us mammoths yet!" he snapped bitterly.

Still, despite his bureaucratic victory, Gorbachev does not look like a tri-umphant leader. "He is isolated," Chernyaev records in his diary. "Gone are the days when crowds swarmed him during breaks, asking questions. Now, he walks backstage alone, accompanied only by his bodyguard Volodya. He is pitiful. And it's terrible when the head of state inspires pity."

Among the congress delegates sits Yeltsin. He has a plan: at the very end of the congress, he will announce his resignation from the Communist Party. He intends to declare that he can no longer combine leading the republic with being a party member, as he now has obligations not only to the communists but to all the citizens of Russia.

The night before, Burbulis walks into Yeltsin's office and sees that his boss is visibly agitated.

Yeltsin starts complaining bitterly:

"How can I do this? I was nurtured by the party from childhood. Everything I have, everything I've been through, everything I've achieved, is tied to the Communist Party of the Soviet Union. And tomorrow, I must stand on that congress stage and publicly renounce my past!"

However, the next day, at the appointed hour, Yeltsin steps up to the podium, delivers his prepared speech, and then walks through the central aisle toward the door. Someone shouts, "Shame!" after him, but in this situation, it is Yeltsin who looks like the victor. His dramatic departure from the congress is broadcast on television, and the photographs appear in all the media. He is the first politician to spit in the face of the Communist Party. It is an enormously symbolic moment—a signal that the party no longer holds any power. Just a few years earlier, expulsion from the party was tantamount to death. This very same Yeltsin, after being removed from the Politburo, had been close to suicide. But now all that is in the past—you can leave the party, and nothing will happen to you.

TIME TO JUMP OFF THE TRAIN

Elections are also taking place in other Soviet republics. In Latvia and Estonia, the Popular Fronts win, but their margin is not overwhelming—many voters are frightened by what happened in Lithuania. Politicians in both republics hesitate to follow Vilnius's example; they leave the positions of Supreme Soviet chairmen to the communists and avoid pushing too hard for de facto independence, preferring to observe the outcome of the standoff between Gorbachev and Landsbergis.

Nonetheless, the central authorities are resolute.

"I'll crush them all!" Gorbachev shouts to his aide Georgy Shakhnazarov. But no sanctions are imposed against these republics.

In May, the commander of the Baltic Military District, Colonel General Fyodor Kuzmin, summons Lieutenant Colonel Alksnis and gleefully informs him:

"Viktor, we've finally managed to convince Gorbachev of the need to impose a state of emergency. The decree will be signed by the president and approved by the Supreme Soviet of the USSR, so no one will dare say this is an illegal action. It's planned for July 1990. I'm relaying a request from the leadership, including Gorbachev himself, that you head the Council of Ministers of the Latvian SSR."

Alksnis begins to refuse—he's a military man, knows nothing about economics. But the general insists:

"It has to be you, Viktor. You're a communist, you took an oath, so prepare yourself."

Alksnis begins preparing, time passes, but the imposition of the state of emergency is clearly delayed.

However, while the Baltic republics are under the close watch of both Western and Soviet media, the same developments on the Caucasus remain almost unnoticed. The Karabakh Committee, which has transformed into the Pan-Armenian National Movement (PANM), is the clear front-runner in the election race. Shortly before election day, one of its leaders, Vazgen Manukyan, writes an article titled "Time to Jump off the Train." In it, he outlines several scenarios for the Soviet Union's collapse: one possibility is akin to the mid-twentieth-century dissolution of the British Empire; another is the attempt at restoration, where a dictatorship might arise in Russia—in which case, he argues, it's even more important to keep a safe distance.

The PANM wins the elections, and its leader, Levon Ter-Petrosyan—who only a year ago was sitting in a Moscow detention center—becomes the chairman of the Armenian Supreme Soviet. Another former prisoner, Vazgen Manukyan, becomes prime minister.

The new leaders of the republic fly to Moscow—this time not in hand-cuffs, as they did previously—to meet with the Soviet authorities. The new Armenian leaders meet with Gorbachev's advisor Georgy Shakhnazarov, himself an Armenian. He spends a long time trying to convince them that they cannot separate from the USSR:

"The collapse of the Soviet Union is very dangerous. It's a global energy of destruction."

"Understood, we'll see," Ter-Petrosyan replies.

"400 DAYS"

Economist Grigory Yavlinsky is one of the youngest members of Ryzhkov's government. He heads the Consolidated Economic Department, which coordinates interactions among the various Soviet republics. Yavlinsky was brought into the government by his former university professor Leonid Abalkin, an academic and prominent economist, now the first deputy prime minister.

At the start of 1989, Ryzhkov sends Yavlinsky on a work trip to Japan. The young economist goes there and begins meticulously studying, day by day, as he later recounts, what transformations occurred in Japan after World War II and how the country achieved its economic miracle.

"I believed that the Soviet system would collapse within a year or a year and a half, but we still needed to achieve something while it lasted. That required implementing the right decisions within a specific chronological framework," he would later explain. From Japan, he returns with the concept of economic reforms need to be precisely laid out. He writes a program titled "400 Days."

At some point, his older colleague Professor Yevgeny Yasin, who heads the Council of Ministers' Commission for Economic Reform, calls him:

"Grisha, you know, Yeltsin is now speaking at the Congress of People's Deputies of Russia and talking about your program. Except he's calling it 'Five Hundred Days' instead of 'Four Hundred.' He says prices won't rise and everything will turn out great as a result. And the congress is giving him a standing ovation."

Yavlinsky is shocked—he and Yasin are trying to figure out how the program ended up with Yeltsin. "We need to tell him immediately that this is completely inaccurate. Let's go to the Kremlin!" he insists.

First, they track down Mikhail Bocharov, a well-known parliamentarian from Yeltsin's circle and the director of a brick factory, who is a contender for the post of head of the Russian government. Bocharov had discovered Yavlinsky's program, adjusted it slightly—changing four hundred days to five hundred—and brought it to Yeltsin.

"Why did you do this? You're deceiving him. This is completely untrue; prices will turn out very differently!" Yavlinsky shouts. Bocharov looks a bit embarrassed.

The next day, they all meet in Yeltsin's office. "Boris Nikolayevich, the problem is that none of what you told everyone follows from this program," Yavlinsky recalls saying. "But most importantly, this program has nothing to do with the RSFSR. It is addressed to the USSR leadership. Because in

Russia, there is no currency, no customs. The RSFSR has no economic tools. So, the program is aimed at the Union leadership."

Yeltsin frowns. "You know what? I'm not interested in that. Make it so that it works correctly," he insists.

"How am I supposed to do that?" Yavlinsky asks in bewilderment.

"I don't care. Sit down and do it," Yeltsin repeats.

And that's where the conversation ends.

"What does he mean, 'Sit down and do it'?" Yavlinsky asks.

The next day, Yeltsin begins forming the Russian government. He ultimately does not appoint the brick factory director Bocharov as prime minister, opting instead for a more experienced official—Soviet minister of aviation industry Ivan Silayev. At the same time, Yeltsin insists that Grigory Yavlinsky become deputy prime minister for economic reform.

Now Yavlinsky has to ask for permission from his current boss—Ryzhkov. There's a problem, though: the Soviet prime minister hates Yeltsin with all his soul, a grudge dating back to their days in Sverdlovsk. Yavlinsky cautiously tells him that he's been offered a position in the Russian government.

"How old are you?" Ryzhkov asks.

Yavlinsky replies that he is thirty-eight.

"Excellent," says Ryzhkov. "Great initiative. I wish you success."

From his boss's kind words, Yavlinsky concludes that Ryzhkov has absolutely no expectations for his appointment and doesn't believe any reforms are possible, or that anything will change.

Nevertheless, the newly minted deputy prime minister devises a way to implement his own program: he needs to convince Yeltsin to force Gorbachev to enact it.

"500 DAYS"

Yavlinsky tries to track down Russia's new leader but can't—Yeltsin has gone on vacation, and no one knows where. After some time, he finds out that Yeltsin has gone to Riga to meet with the leaders of the Baltic republics. Yavlinsky travels there, and the two take a long walk along the beach in Jūrmala. Yavlinsky persuades his new boss that they need to form a working group with Gorbachev to develop a joint economic reform plan for the USSR. Yeltsin agrees. He signs a letter addressed to Gorbachev, and Yavlinsky takes it back to Moscow.

When Gorbachev's economic advisor Nikolay Petrakov shows him Yavlinsky's proposal, the General Secretary doesn't pay much attention at first. But within minutes, he takes the paper again and reads it carefully. "*Where is this guy? Call him immediately!*" he yells.

Yavlinsky arrives with Yeltsin's letter to find Gorbachev, Petrakov, and Yakovlev in the office. The president of the USSR is wildly enthusiastic.

He still believes that he can find a way out of any hopeless situation—that, in the end, he will outmaneuver everyone and make the right move. And now the solution to the most complex problem—the economic crisis—has come to him in the form of a young economist from Lviv, who will design the reforms, sideline the useless Ryzhkov, and also reconcile him with Yeltsin. Gorbachev "looked joyfully excited, like a chess player who has found a successful continuation of what seemed to be a losing game," Petrakov will later write in his memoir.

It is decided to form a working group. From Gorbachev's side, his advisors academicians Stanislav Shatalin and Petrakov join, while Yeltsin is represented by Yavlinsky. They head to the government dacha in Sosenki, south of Moscow, where they begin developing a comprehensive set of reforms and the draft laws required to implement them. They work for a month and a half, tasked with finishing by September 1. Their plan calls for massive privatization, freeing prices from state control, integrating the Soviet economy into the global economic system, and transferring powers from Moscow to the republics.

Gorbachev and Yeltsin announce that they jointly support the "500 Days" program. This is an unbelievable moment: sworn enemies who despise each other suddenly shake hands in public and promise to carry out reforms together.

And only now do Ryzhkov and Abalkin find out about everything—and they are deeply offended. They declare that the "500 Days" program is reckless and will only worsen the crisis; the economy must be reformed slowly and gradually. They refuse to cooperate with the working group and, moreover, refuse to share any government documents. Abalkin's team starts preparing their counterproposals.

On July 30, Gorbachev goes on vacation to Crimea, accompanied by a swarm of officials who settle near his residence. One evening, Gorbachev and Raisa invite Chernyaev and Primakov over for the family dinner.

The conversation turns to Ryzhkov. Primakov insists that the prime minister needs to be dismissed. He is rallying the military-industrial complex around himself, openly taking anti-perestroika positions. "He is incapable of understanding the market, let alone implementing a market concept," Primakov argues, adding that Ryzhkov is also trying to undermine the reputation of the group writing the "500 Days" program. Chernyaev agrees.

"You're such kittens," Gorbachev says with a smile. "If I go and create another front of confrontation in a situation like this, we're done for. Ryzhkov and the Council of Ministers will become natural casualties of the inevitable march of the market economy. It'll happen just like it did with the party's power—and it'll happen this very year."

Primakov and Chernyaev nod, trusting that Gorbachev, of all people, surely knows best how to navigate these political intrigues.

MR. HUSSEIN

On June 28, the *Wall Street Journal* publishes an interview with Iraqi president Saddam Hussein. The journalist acknowledges that securing it was a rare stroke of luck, as this is "the first interview with an American newspaper in nearly six years for Mr. Hussein, who has a reputation for brutality." In the interview, Saddam predicts that a war in the Middle East could soon break out—blaming it on the Soviet Union's decision to allow Jews to emigrate en masse to Israel. According to him, Israel will now act far more aggressively toward the Palestinians, clearing territory for the newly arrived citizens.

While issuing threats of war, the Iraqi president is, in reality, asking for money. Iraq's economy is in ruins—the country has nothing left except its army.

By 1990, Saddam Hussein has ruled Iraq for over twenty years, with nearly unwavering support from the West. From 1980 to 1988, Iraq waged war against Iran—a conflict that erupted shortly after the Islamic Revolution in Tehran. The entire Western world stood behind Iraq. Ayatollah Khomeini's regime was widely seen as a threat to humanity, so the United States, the United Kingdom, France, and even the Soviet Union supplied Saddam with weapons to contain the spread of Iran's revolution.

The grueling and bloody war made Iraq's military the fourth largest in the world, but at the same time, it turned Iraq from a wealthy and prosperous country into an impoverished one. In 1980, Iraq had foreign currency reserves exceeding $35 billion. By 1988, it owed nearly $80 billion to foreign creditors, and the cost of rebuilding the country after the war was estimated at over $200 billion. Most of Iraq's debt was owed to its Arab neighbors, particularly Saudi Arabia and Kuwait. By 1990, the financial crisis in Iraq had reached a breaking point, and Saddam found himself in a desperate position. Since 1988, there had been four assassination attempts against him—signs of growing discontent within his own military.

Saddam's approach somewhat resembles Gorbachev's: the Soviet leader demands that the West support him with financial aid—otherwise, radicals like Ligachev might take over. Saddam, however, plays both roles himself—he is his own Gorbachev and his own Ligachev. He promises to be a reliable partner to the West if he receives financial assistance; if not, he threatens war.

The fundamental problem facing both Iraq and the USSR is the same: falling oil prices. By the spring of 1990, the price of oil has dropped to eighteen dollars per barrel. The main reason is OPEC's failure to adhere to production quotas, leading to overproduction, lower prices, and severe economic consequences for both Iraq and the Soviet Union. The primary culprits behind this oversupply are Kuwait and the United Arab Emirates (UAE), which have deliberately driven down oil prices to increase other nations' dependence on OPEC oil.

This infuriates Saddam Hussein. He believes that Iraq fought Iran on behalf of all the Arab states of the Persian Gulf, and therefore, they owe him—at the very least, they should forgive Iraq's past debts, and at most, they should provide new financial aid. Since Iraq is the only Arab country with a truly formidable military, Saddam sees military strength as his leverage to extract money from his neighbors. And so, he resorts to blackmail.

On July 17, Saddam Hussein, in a televised speech, sharply criticizes Kuwait and the UAE for exceeding the oil export limits set by OPEC. Saddam states that these countries "have stabbed Iraq in the back with a poisoned dagger." According to his calculations, this "treacherous blow" has cost Iraq $89 billion.

Many years later, during interrogations in 2003–2004, Saddam Hussein will insist that, beyond economic disputes, a decisive factor in the start of the Iraqi invasion was the insulting words of Kuwaiti Emir Jaber Al-Ahmad Al-Sabah, who allegedly told Iraq's foreign minister that he planned to bankrupt Iraq and turn "every Iraqi woman into a prostitute for ten dollars." By late July, Iraq begins deploying troops along the Kuwaiti border.

US president George Bush writes a conciliatory letter to Saddam Hussein, urging him to abandon military action. He also blocks a congressional resolution to impose sanctions on Iraq over human rights violations.

On August 2, the invasion begins. Iraq advances with one hundred thousand troops and nearly two thousand tanks, while the Kuwaiti army numbers around sixteen thousand soldiers. The resistance lasts for fourteen hours, with forty-two hundred Kuwaiti soldiers killed. The Iraqi army easily captures Kuwait City. Emir Jaber III, along with his family and ministers, flees to neighboring Saudi Arabia, while his brother dies in combat against Iraqi special forces.

Essentially, this is the first military conflict after the end of the Cold War. Within minutes of Iraq's attack on Kuwait, oil prices on global markets begin to rise. At the White House, officials are already developing a plan to immediately exclude Iraq and its newly occupied Kuwait from the world oil trade. It is now clear that this is not a localized conflict—this is a war that will affect the entire world. The United Nations passes a resolution condemning the invasion: the United States and the USSR vote the same way, marking a unique historical event.

This is the first sign that the end of the Cold War may not go as planned—that even after the ritual reconciliation between Gorbachev and Bush, the so-called "end of history" envisioned by State Department official Francis Fukuyama in his article written just a few months ago is far from reality.

Iraqi tanks continue advancing—toward the border between Kuwait and Saudi Arabia. Panic spreads in Riyadh, as everyone expects Saddam to move farther. "By seizing Kuwait, Saddam now controls 20% of the world's oil reserves," analyzes US secretary of defense Dick Cheney. "If he takes the Eastern Province of Saudi Arabia, he will control 45–50%."

In the first days of the war, Saudi King Fahd receives a letter from a member of a wealthy family with a large real estate business—Osama bin Laden. For years, bin Laden oversaw his family's operations in Pakistan and Afghanistan, but in reality, he coordinated fundraising for the jihad against the USSR. After the war in Afghanistan ended, he had little to do, but he reacts immediately to Iraq's invasion of Kuwait—he proposes that the king urgently mobilize Arab mujahideen who fought against the Soviet Union in Afghanistan. The king responds that he will certainly consider Osama bin Laden's proposal.

However, soon after, US secretary of defense Dick Cheney arrives in Riyadh and offers King Fahd the deployment of two hundred thousand American troops—to protect Saudi Arabia and its oil from Saddam.

BUS IN THE DITCH

After finishing his concert tour at the end of June, Tsoi wants to return to the quiet life he had before fame overwhelmed him. First, he and Natasha spend a week in Paris—a luxury unimaginable for a Soviet citizen but also a chance to walk the city unnoticed and undisturbed by strangers.

They then return and head to a small village in Latvia where Natasha's family usually spends their summer vacations. It is the same village where Viktor had found her two years earlier when she left Moscow for a vacation. This time, they stay there with their children: Natasha's eleven-year-old son, Zhenya, and Viktor's five-year-old son, Sasha.

In mid-August, Yuri Kasparyan arrives. Joanna has flown to Los Angeles alone, and the musicians of Kino are working on a new album. After a short stay, Kasparyan heads back to Leningrad.

On August 15, Viktor gets up early—around five in the morning—while everyone in the house is still asleep. He quietly gathers his fishing rods and heads to the lake. He usually returns by eleven or twelve, but this time, he is late. Natasha, familiar with his car's frequent breakdowns, assumes he might have been delayed on the road.

By 2:00 p.m., she begins to worry. She gets on her motorcycle and rides to the lake where Tsoi usually fishes. On the way, she notices a bus that has veered into a ditch. She passes it and hurries to the lake, hoping Vitya will already be home when she returns. But he isn't.

Viktor died while returning from fishing—his car collided head-on with the bus Natasha had seen in the ditch. He was twenty-eight years old.

The investigation concludes that he fell asleep at the wheel. Many fans refuse to believe this, suspecting instead that the accident was staged. However, Viktor was not an experienced driver. He had obtained his license just two months earlier, in June. With him already at the peak of his fame, it is easy to imagine that the driving examiners may not have been strict or thorough in testing his skills.

THE HONEYMOON

Two competing economic programs are ready, so Ryzhkov and Abalkin come to the dacha where Yavlinsky and his team are working. "We found ourselves in the camp of sworn enemies," Ryzhkov will write in his memoir, for whom abandoning the planned economy is utterly unacceptable. The conversation doesn't go well. As they part, the premier declares, "I will not bury the state with my own hands. Moreover, I will fight you gravediggers to my last breath."

On August 25, Gorbachev returns from vacation, and as per old Soviet tradition, all the country's top officials meet him at the airport. A scandal breaks out right on the tarmac. After the president leaves, Ryzhkov approaches a group of advisors to say good-bye and, "trembling with hatred," tells Petrakov, "Well, you'll go down in history!" "You already have," the president's advisor replies.

The next morning, Gorbachev meets with Yavlinsky's team. The young economists arrive at the Kremlin straight from their dacha, wearing short-sleeved shirts—an unheard-of audacity. But Gorbachev laughs along with them, like a lovestruck schoolboy. He's delighted by their proposals, and according to Petrakov, everyone feels as if they're walking on air.

Two days later, Ryzhkov with his team comes to see Gorbachev. He insists that Yavlinsky's plan will destroy socialism and the Soviet Union. "We must remove Yeltsin at all costs," demands Yuri Maslyukov, the head of Gosplan.

"Stop talking bullshit," Gorbachev interrupts.

Soon after, Gorbachev has a one-on-one meeting with Yeltsin—and they finally have a constructive conversation. They talk for five hours. "You know, we had a good man-to-man conversation," Gorbachev later tells Petrakov. "It's easier for me to find common ground with Boris than with many others who have only recently entered politics and think too highly of themselves. After all, Yeltsin and I went through the same school; we understand each other without words. Of course, at first, we aired our grievances. . . . But then we moved on to business, and I think it went well."

This could be a turning point in history. Gorbachev manages to overcome his personal resentment, and he is on the brink of beginning real economic reforms: definitively breaking with the conservatives and leading the reformist movement alongside Yeltsin. This is the honeymoon phase between Gorbachev and Yeltsin—something unimaginable just a short while ago.

MARIAH CAREY VERSUS RUSSIAN ROCK

In September 1990, Walter Yetnikoff, the longtime head of CBS Records and one of the most influential figures in the American music industry, announces his resignation. According to Boris Grebenshchikov, this event directly impacts his life.

What happens? At the end of the summer, Random House publishes *The Hit Men,* a controversial exposé by journalist Fredric Dannen about the inner workings of the recording industry. The book reveals unsavory details: payola schemes for airtime, secret deals, rampant drug use, and more. It doesn't just target Yetnikoff but also other music moguls. However, the owners of CBS Records take the revelations particularly hard.

Since 1988, CBS Records has been owned by Sony—a deal worth $2 billion that Yetnikoff himself had orchestrated. But now, according to Greben-shchikov, the Japanese owners believe that the book tarnishes their CEO's reputation, making it incompatible with their corporate standards.

Replacing the son of emigrants from Odessa is the son of Italian emigrants: Yetnikoff's former vice president, Tommy Mottola, takes over as head of the label. According to Grebenshchikov, Mottola has entirely different musical priorities—chiefly, making his girlfriend, Mariah Carey, a superstar. Greben-shchikov's contract is not renewed, and the second album he is working on in London never sees the light of day.

Of course, the problem may not be Mottola's tastes. Mariah Carey's debut album, released on June 12, 1990, tops the US Billboard 200 for eleven consecutive weeks and will be the best-selling album in the United States in 1991. It will sell approximately 15 million copies. In contrast, *Radio Silence* had no commercial success and did not make a significant impact on international charts.

Thus, Boris Grebenshchikov's American adventure ends. He becomes the first—and ultimately the last—rock musician from the Soviet Union to have a chance in the United States, and it comes to nothing.

THE CELEBRATION ENDS

On August 29, an expanded meeting of the Presidential Council begins, to which the heads of the Union republics, ministers, and members of the Supreme Soviet are invited—a guest list compiled by Gorbachev's secretary, Valery Boldin, who is himself a discrete opponent of the "500 Days" program.

"We sat for two days. Or rather—we fought," Ryzhkov will later write. The more the "500 Days" program is attacked, the weaker Gorbachev's resolve becomes. Yeltsin's team demands the Soviet premier's resignation. But Ryzhkov, according to Chernyaev, responds, "If someone leaves, then we all leave"—at this point looking directly at Gorbachev. "We all played a role in this collapse, we all brought it to blood, economic chaos, to where we are now. Why should I be the scapegoat?!"

The situation becomes even more muddled: the Russian parliament adopts the "500 Days" program, while the congress of Russia's Communist Party denounces it as "a betrayal of socialism and a surrender of the country to capitalism."

Meanwhile, Yavlinsky is invited to the joint session of the International Monetary Fund (IMF) and the World Bank. He presents his program—according to him, after the presentation, a Harvard professor, Hungarian economist Janos Kornai, approaches and tells him that it is "the best reform program in Eastern Europe."

The next day, Yavlinsky plans to take a walk around Washington—but he receives a call from Senator Bob Dole's office, saying that the latter wants to see him on Capitol Hill. Yavlinsky goes to meet him.

Their conversation lasts only a few minutes. Dole apologizes, saying he is in a hurry to attend a meeting. Yavlinsky starts to feel irritated: *What the hell did he drag me here for? I'd rather be walking around the city—I'm flying back tomorrow*, he thinks. But before parting, Dole says, "Three days ago, I was in Moscow and spoke with Boris Yeltsin. He asked me, 'This reform program—is it dangerous?' I told him that it's correct, but dangerous. What can you do, that's the nature of this restructuring. And Yeltsin replied, 'I won't implement it; I have presidential elections in the spring.' 'I just wanted to warn you,'" concludes Dole.

"That's when the celebration ended," Yavlinsky will recall.

Back home, the Supreme Soviet continues its scandal-ridden discussions of the "500 Days" program. Shatalin argues that the choice is not between socialism and capitalism but between "life and the grave." Gorbachev starts to retreat and proposes a compromise: he asks to develop something between the programs of Yavlinsky and Ryzhkov. Later Yeltsin will call it an attempt to "marry a hedgehog and a snake." Finally, the Supreme Soviet of the USSR rejects the "500 Days."

Gorbachev is so demoralized that he no longer even puts up a fight. "Life has hoisted this beautiful program into thin air," he tells Chernyaev, his voice weighed down by hopelessness.

HOW WE ARE TO REBUILD RUSSIA

Alexander Solzhenitsyn is deeply troubled that he cannot influence the events unfolding in Russia, though he finds solace in the thought that his predecessors—the great Russian writers of the early twentieth century—could not influence the Revolution of 1917 either: "What did Blok or Bunin achieve in 1917? Even if Leo Tolstoy had lived to see Seventeen—who would have listened to him in all that turmoil? . . . My place is to finish my work."

In August, Gorbachev signs yet another decree restoring Soviet citizenship to twenty-three cultural figures, including Joseph Brodsky and Alexander Solzhenitsyn with his wife. Not long after, Ivan Silaev, Yeltsin's head of the Russian government, publishes a letter in *Soviet Russia* inviting Solzhenitsyn to come to Russia as his personal guest. "It is impossible for me to be a guest or tourist on my native soil. . . . When I return to my homeland, it will be to live and die there . . . ," Solzhenitsyn responds.

At this time, he writes a massive article titled "How We Are to Rebuild Russia." *Komsomolskaya Pravda*, with its colossal circulation of 21 million copies per day, is eager to publish it. The article is published on September 18—as a separate pamphlet. It becomes a sensation, sparking widespread discussion. This marks the peak of Solzhenitsyn's fame in his homeland.

The essay's first thesis: "The Soviet Union will collapse anyway—and it must not be artificially held together."

"We have no strength for Empire!—and we do not need it. Let it fall from our shoulders!" writes Solzhenitsyn. But he immediately clarifies that Russia, Ukraine, Belarus, and Kazakhstan form a single whole and must remain united under a new name—"Rus'" or "the Russian Union."* All other eleven Soviet republics, however, can and must be let go—even if they resist.

Solzhenitsyn firmly positions himself as an anti-imperialist. He cites post-war Japan as an example, reminding readers that the country "was able to reconcile itself, relinquish its international mission and enticing political adventures—and immediately blossomed." He also recalls that Russian imperialists of the nineteenth century insisted that Poland and Finland were inseparable parts of Russia: "But who today would argue for that? Has Russia truly been impoverished by the separation of Poland and Finland?"

But that does not apply to Ukraine, Belarus, or Kazakhstan. "It is a recently invented falsehood that, since the 9th century, a distinct Ukrainian people has existed with its own non-Russian language . . . ," he asserts.

Solzhenitsyn acknowledges that if the USSR splits apart, Russia will need to repatriate many Russians—and he asks the practical question: How will this be funded?" His proposal: stop spending on foreign political influence and military needs:

How much longer will we supply and bolster the tyrannical regimes we ourselves planted in various corners of the Earth—these bottomless siphoners of our wealth? Cuba, Vietnam, Ethiopia, Angola, North Korea . . . Why do we need a globe-spanning military fleet? To conquer the planet? All of this already costs hundreds of billions a year. This must all be cut off—immediately. Even space exploration can wait.

Solzhenitsyn calls for the abolition of the KGB:

Their claims that they are especially needed now—for international intelligence—are transparent tricks. On the contrary, everyone can see the truth. Their sole purpose is to sustain themselves and suppress any movement among the people. This Cheka-KGB, with its bloody, 70-year history of atrocities, has neither justification nor the right to exist any longer.

---

* At the time, Byelorussia—now known as Belarus—was one of the fifteen republics of the USSR, slightly larger than Kansas in area and roughly equal to Michigan in population.

Finally, Solzhenitsyn clarifies that his values are not liberal. He emphasizes the importance of the traditional family:

I stand for the traditional family—so that women can return to the home, rather than having to work.

Solzhenitsyn's text makes a strong impression on many. Even Gorbachev's new press secretary, Vitaly Ignatenko, is impressed, telling the General Secretary, "History will remember him and you. Lenin will fade away, but the two of you will remain there."

Gorbachev is displeased and addresses Solzhenitsyn's article "How We Are to Rebuild Russia" at a session of the Supreme Soviet, saying the writer is living in the past and has revealed himself to be a monarchist. The reaction in Ukraine and Kazakhstan is particularly angry: Solzhenitsyn denied Ukrainians the right to exist as a nation, and he wrote that Kazakhs were a minority in their own republic, a claim that did not reflect reality. In Almaty, a protest even takes place—copies of *Komsomolskaya Pravda* are burned in the square.

The text sparks discussions beyond the USSR as well. The *New Republic* runs Solzhenitsyn's portrait on its cover, depicting him in a Lenin-style cap, comparing the article to Lenin's return to Russia in April 1917. Yet Solzhenitsyn is in no hurry to return himself. He will later write in his memoir that he simply doesn't know how to behave in the new circumstances, where he is no longer the sole truth teller and everyone can say whatever they want: "What am I supposed to do, jostle for space on the podium alongside Gavriil Popov and Telman Gdlyan?"

Yeltsin himself does not call Solzhenitsyn, but the text deeply resonates with him. According to his aide Galina Starovoitova, Yeltsin's advisor on nationalities, he becomes captivated by Solzhenitsyn's idea and begins quietly probing the leaders of Ukraine, Belarus, and Kazakhstan to see if they would be open to creating a new union of four republics. His counterparts are, at best, stunned by the proposal.

NOBEL PRIZE AND THE ROAD TO GOLGOTHA

On October 15, it is announced that the president of the USSR, Mikhail Gorbachev, is awarded the Nobel Peace Prize. The news does not bring any joy in the Soviet Union. By now, the president has almost no supporters left.

As early as September, his aide Chernyaev writes in his diary: "There is malice and hatred toward Gorbachev in the queues. Today in *Pravda* there's a selection of letters from workers, spitting venom at perestroika and at Gorbachev. Right next to them is praise for Stalin and Brezhnev. Yes, the road to Golgotha has begun."

For the president, this is no secret: the KGB now delivers him stacks of letters filled with curses, like this one: "Mr. Nobel Laureate, we congratulate you for driving your country into ruin, for earning this prize from global imperialism and Zionism, for betraying Lenin and October, for destroying Marxism-Leninism."

"Why does Kryuchkov gather all this and put it on your desk?" Chernyaev asks. "Do you think I haven't thought about that?" Gorbachev responds. And keeps reading.

The day after he is awarded the Nobel Prize, Gorbachev takes another hit. Yeltsin speaks at a session of the Russian Supreme Soviet, accusing him of breaking all their agreements on the "500 Days" program.

Yeltsin is not exaggerating: he says that the USSR government is sabotaging reforms (true), that Gorbachev "once again changes his mind under pressure from a sinking government" (also true), and that now Ryzhkov plans to resort to printing money, which is "a deception of the people," and that the USSR president's economic program is doomed to failure.

Gorbachev perceives Yeltsin's speech as a declaration of war (yes, again!). He convenes the Presidential Council—many haven't yet had the chance to read Yeltsin's address, but the atmosphere becomes increasingly hysterical. Chernyaev writes in his diary that the mood resembles a meeting of the Provisional Government in 1917, just before the Bolsheviks stormed the Winter Palace and overthrew it.

Lukyanov and Kryuchkov demand harsh measures. Ryzhkov begins shouting, "How much longer! The government is a whipping boy! No one listens to me. I, the head of the government, summon some official—he doesn't show up. Orders go unfulfilled. The country has lost control. The collapse is in full swing. All the media are against us!"

In the middle of the meeting, Gorbachev excuses himself—he has to meet with US defense secretary Dick Cheney, who has come to discuss the situation in Iraq. Leaving the room, he immediately changes his demeanor, once again becoming the confident global leader who just yesterday won the Nobel Prize.

But after his conversation with Cheney, he succumbs to emotions again and prepares to address the nation on television with a response to Yeltsin. Petrakov, Shatalin, and Chernyaev catch up to him in the hallway and try to dissuade him. "I've already decided; this cannot be let go," he fires back. "If I stay silent, what will the people say? That's cowardice, a trump card for Yeltsin. That paranoid is aiming for the presidential chair—he's nuts. We need to give him a good slap in the face."

Later, he decides not to appear himself and instead assigns Lukyanov to deliver the address. The honeymoon is over—from this point on, Gorbachev will regularly tell his aides that Yeltsin "is aiming for my seat."

THE BLACK COLONELS

On November 7, 1990, to mark the holiday, Defense Minister Yazov signs an order for the extraordinary promotion of two lieutenant colonels from the Union parliamentary group—Viktor Alksnis and Nikolai Petrushenko—to the rank of colonel, recognizing their work at the Congress of People's Deputies.

Yazov invites them to his office, where Petrushenko poses a question:

"Comrade Minister, we've been hammering Gorbachev, but we're short on material. After all, most of the real information about our defense capabilities and foreign policy remains classified. Could we get reliable data, say, on the outcomes of the disarmament talks?"

"That's classified information," Yazov replies, perplexed.

"But you understand—we need to bring down Gorbachev. To do that, we need facts. We're parliamentarians; we have our own sources of information. We won't say a word about getting this from the Ministry of Defense. We'll pin it on the Foreign Ministry or the CIA."

Yazov calls in an aide:

"These two hotshots are demanding data about our unilateral concessions to the Americans. . . ."

A week later, thick envelopes are delivered to Alksnis and Petrushenko, detailing all the concessions made by the Soviet Union over recent years.

The parliamentarians begin making regular speeches in the Supreme Soviet, full of exposés.

"It was a shock, of course!" Alksnis recalls. "It's one thing to accuse Gorbachev of failure—it's another to hit him with cold, hard facts. Naturally, we gave Shevardnadze hell."

Meanwhile, the state of emergency in the Baltic republics, anticipated by the military since summer, still hasn't been declared. Frustrated, Alksnis takes to the podium in the Supreme Soviet to demand harsher measures. He calls for a state of emergency in the USSR.

"That's when people started saying I was a 'Black Colonel,' that I'd soon be shooting parliamentarians or sending them to the Gulag on the southern shore of the Arctic Ocean." He chuckles.

In mid-November, Alksnis publicly declares that he's giving Gorbachev thirty days—otherwise, at the December Congress of People's Deputies, he'll raise the question of Gorbachev's resignation for "destroying the country."

Soon after, the Ministry of Defense leadership informs Alksnis that "the draft decree on the state of emergency is ready. If the Congress brings up the issue of Gorbachev's resignation, he'll just read out the decree and say: 'What resignation? This is an emergency. You can't change horses midstream. That's it—we're fighting to save the Union.'"

NO MORE DISSIDENT MENTALITY

In Georgia, elections were also scheduled for March, but the opposition boycotted them, forcing the authorities to postpone the vote to the fall. Most of the Georgian opposition believes that cooperation with the authorities is unacceptable—instead, they argue for creating their own alternative governing bodies, holding their own elections, and demanding the withdrawal of Soviet troops.

In September 1990, such alternative elections are held, completely bypassing the existing Soviet system of power. On one hand, it's a huge success: more than 50 percent of the population takes part in the three rounds of voting. But the opposition is divided—the most popular opposition leader, the nationalist Zviad Gamsakhurdia, strikes a deal with the authorities and agrees to participate in the Soviet elections scheduled for October.

"If we don't recognize Soviet authority and create our own parallel structures, what happens next? Nineteen people have already died; next time it will be one hundred and nineteen, then one thousand and nineteen. We must participate in the elections, no matter how much it offends the dissident mentality. And Gamsakhurdia agreed—he must have been thinking about this," reflects his right-hand man at the time, Akaki Asatiani.

"Zviad was in such form that he could visit ten to fifteen villages in a single day. There wasn't a single populated area in Georgia where he didn't give a speech," recalls Asatiani. "Grand rallies took place; people gathered in the tens of thousands."

A staunch opponent of Gamsakhurdia is the philosopher Merab Mamardashvili. In September 1990, shortly before the elections, he publishes an article titled "I Believe in Common Sense." The most striking and shocking words from this text read: "If my people choose Gamsakhurdia, then I will have to go against my own people in terms of my views and convictions. I do not want to believe this." He writes that "the language of pure national statehood, the language of leadership cults and racial purity," used by opposition leaders, will only ensure that "the existing totalitarian oppression" continues:

> Before it's too late, we must take each other's hands and go out
> into the streets. If Georgians refuse to protest, it means they have
> degenerated. For many, the only way out is to retreat into internal
> exile. I was invisible to the authorities before, and I am becoming
> invisible again. . . . I am not afraid of civil death. . . .
>
> I cannot comprehend how people from the human rights movement
> can turn violations of civil rights into a system. How can someone
> who considers themselves part of the Helsinki movement have not the
> slightest understanding of what human rights actually mean? . . ."

Almost 70 percent of voters take part in these elections—far more than in alternative elections. Gamsakhurdia's Round Table Party secures a decisive victory, winning 54 percent. Gamsakhurdia is elected chairman of the Supreme Council, effectively becoming the head of the republic.

For the philosopher Mamardashvili, as he himself wrote, the rise of nationalists to power means "civil death." And in November 1990, a month after the elections, he flies from Moscow to Tbilisi to continue his political struggle. Shortly before departure, at Moscow's Vnukovo Airport, he suddenly feels unwell—and dies of a heart attack.

GORBACHEV'S COUP

After Gorbachev fully reshuffled the Politburo in the summer of 1990, the balance of power within the leadership shifted completely. If previously the unofficial elder statesman of the Soviet Union's conservative camp had been Yegor Ligachev, now he is effectively sent into retirement—and the new leader of the conservatives becomes Anatoly Lukyanov, chairman of the Supreme Soviet and, like Ligachev once was, the second-most powerful figure in the country.

They are very different. Ligachev is a communist Savonarola, a fanatic and an ascetic, fervently devoted to communism. Lukyanov is a sophisticated political schemer, an experienced legalist, a long-game player. On the one hand, Ligachev's convictions were always clear to everyone—he never hid them. Lukyanov, on the other hand, never opens up to anyone; he tries to get along with everyone, wanting to appear as their ally. Gorbachev is completely convinced that Lukyanov is his loyal assistant, his right hand. But Lukyanov, now at the helm of the Supreme Soviet of the USSR, starts to see himself as a politician in his own right. His primary goal is to prevent the collapse of the Soviet Union.

Lukyanov's natural ally is KGB chief Kryuchkov. In the fall of 1990, Lukyanov and his allies set themselves a clear objective: to force Gorbachev to declare a state of emergency. The failure of the "500 Days" program and the beginning of the verbal war with Yeltsin are steps in the right direction—but not yet enough.

In mid-November, the Union parliamentary group, at Lukyanov's prompting, demands that Gorbachev appear before parliament and report on the state of affairs. The president agrees to deliver a keynote address. Even Chernyaev doesn't know what he's going to say: "Maybe he'll finally announce, 'I'm leaving.' That would probably be the right call. He could go to Oslo, collect his Nobel Prize, and live as a private citizen."

On November 16, Gorbachev gives his speech—and it is a failure. He talks for a long time, abstractly, and everyone piles on him with criticism: on one side, Union, and on the other, Yeltsin, sitting in the hall.

This turns out to be the last straw. Gorbachev spends the entire night writing a new speech and the next morning delivers it to the Supreme Soviet. It's his second attempt. This time, he speaks for twenty minutes and says exactly what the Politburo hawks want to hear. The Presidential Council is abolished, and in its place, a Security Council will be created. The old Council of Ministers will also be dissolved and replaced with a Cabinet of Ministers reporting directly to the president. In other words, he demands new powers for himself—and he gets them. The Supreme Soviet approves the president's proposal, believing he has finally matured into someone ready to rule with an iron fist. Everyone understands that the abolition of the Presidential Council means Yakovlev's resignation—he will be forced to leave, just like his enemy Ligachev before him.

The next day, the democratic newspaper *Moscow News* publishes an open letter to Gorbachev titled "The Country Is Tired of Waiting." Its authors also demand decisive action—but in a different sense. They want him to commit to reforms, resign as General Secretary, and dismiss the government.

"Political maneuvering has proven its futility. One can no longer evade responsibility for today's situation with incantations about socialist choice and communist perspectives. Either confirm your capacity for decisive action or step down," reads the letter. "Gorbachev was more upset by this than anything else during these days. He saw it as a personal betrayal," writes Chernyaev in his diary.

Essentially, these two days mark the end of perestroika. Gorbachev is so offended by the democrats that he sides with the conservatives.

"HIDDEN IN THE BUSHES"

On December 14, 1990, the Fourth Congress of People's Deputies begins, chaired by Anatoly Lukyanov. The very first speaker he calls up is Sazhi Umalatova, a Chechen woman. Umalatova belongs to the Union group, but until this moment, she is virtually unknown. She is a "professional parliamentarian"—since the age of eighteen, she has been consistently elected to various Soviet bodies as a representative of the Chechen-Ingush Autonomous Republic. In 1989, Gorbachev included her in the "Red Hundred" as the staunchest pro-Communist representative.

"I propose adding a vote of no confidence in the president of the USSR to the agenda. Please do not interrupt me. I will say unpleasant things," Umalatova stuns the hall. There has never been a precedent for impeachment in the Soviet Union. "Gorbachev no longer has any moral right to lead this country. . . . He has done everything he could. He has ruined the country, pitted nations against one another, and reduced a great power to begging with an outstretched hand. . . ."

Lukyanov calls for a roll-call vote to decide whether to include the impeachment proposal in the agenda. One thousand, two hundred, and ninety-two legislators (including Yeltsin, Sobchak, and many democrats as well as many Union members) vote against, while 423 (including Alksnis and Gdlyan) vote in favor. Nevertheless, a historic moment has occurred. "Lukyanov deliberately let her speak first, knowing what she would propose," writes Chernyaev in his diary.

This congress is markedly different from previous ones. The Lithuanian and Armenian delegations do not attend at all—empty seats mark their absence. During the congress, the delegations from Estonia and Moldova also leave the hall and head home.

On December 20, Foreign Minister Eduard Shevardnadze takes the floor. His entire speech is a polemic against the reactionaries—Alksnis, Petrushenko (whom he calls "young colonel-parliamentarians").

"Democrats, in the broadest sense of the word, have scattered, and reformers have hidden in the bushes. A dictatorship is coming—I state this with full responsibility. No one knows what kind of dictatorship it will be, or which dictator will come, or what kind of order will be imposed," Shevardnadze says dramatically. He then announces his resignation "in protest against the onset of dictatorship," while emphasizing that he remains a friend and ally of Gorbachev.

Everyone is shocked. The chairman announces a recess. Another announcement follows: buses are available for those who wish to visit the cemetery. As it has been a year since Sakharov's death, parliamentarians are invited to visit his grave.

The true recipient of Shevardnadze's words, of course, is Gorbachev himself—he is the reformer who had "hidden in the bushes." It is he who has elevated supporters of dictatorship.

After the recess, Lukyanov gives the floor to his protégé Alksnis. "Today we heard the word 'reactionaries,' and even 'scum' was mentioned. Well, here stands a 'reactionary'; here stands 'scum'—I accept these accusations. Yes, when an infant is thrown into a burning house, I am a reactionary. I am a 'hawk' when a pregnant woman is thrown from the ninth floor of a building.

I am a 'hawk' when the skin is ripped off an old man while he is still alive," Alksnis begins, as passionately as Shevardnadze had.

Without waiting for the session to end, Korotich heads to the cloakroom to retrieve his coat and runs into Yakovlev. "Come to my office, let's have some tea," the architect of perestroika invites him. They walk across the square— it's snowing. When they arrive at Yakovlev's office, the brass nameplate still reads: "Member of the Presidential Council A. N. Yakovlev."

"You're no longer a member of the council," Korotich will later recall saying. "By the way, how should I call you now? Give me your new phone numbers. . . ."

"Wait," Yakovlev replies, sinking heavily into a chair. "They'll drag us out to be shot and line us up against the same wall. I'll see you, and you'll see me."

Yakovlev, of course, is joking, but Korotich takes the grim possibility seriously. Recently, he received a fellowship at Columbia University in New York—his backup plan, should he be expelled from *Ogonyok*.

WITHOUT VZGLYAD

Eduard Shevardnadze's resignation is, without a doubt, the biggest news in the country. The journalists of *Vzglyad* want to immediately invite the now-former foreign minister for a live interview. When the head of state television, Leonid Kravchenko, hears about this, he consults Gorbachev. "You know, it's not the right time," the General Secretary instructs him. "He really let me down. . . ."

Sasha Lyubimov insists—if not Shevardnadze, then at least his closest aides from the Foreign Ministry, who have already agreed to appear. But Kravchenko refuses to back down and cancels the broadcast altogether. Not long ago, such interference would have been a major scandal: Alexander Yakovlev would have stepped in and likely complained directly to Gorbachev. But where is Yakovlev now?

The head of Central Television no longer feels the need to hide his intentions. Two weeks later, he signs an official order shutting down *Vzglyad* for good.

This is truly the end. The young heroes no longer have the will to fight. The hosts of *Vzglyad* are no longer the people they once were. By autumn of 1990, they decide to capitalize on their fame, creating their own production company to produce content and generate advertising revenue.

Their celebrity status is unmatched. Lyubimov later admits that, at first, it weighed heavily on him—until a rock musician friend explained how fame works: "You no longer belong to yourself. You visit their homes every week. You can't deny them the right to treat you as part of their lives, as their own property." Eventually, Lyubimov gets used to it—fame allows him to seduce any woman he desires.

Three of the eight hosts of *Vzglyad* are now members of the Russian parliament. They also plan to become businessmen and register a new company: VID (*Vzglyad* and Others). But when it comes time to distribute shares, the idols of millions turn on each other. Two hosts, Sasha Lyubimov and Vlad Listyev, receive 17 percent and 16 percent stakes respectively, with the remaining shares going to directors. The other hosts are left with nothing.

Even the relationship between Lyubimov and Listyev becomes strained. Lyubimov now calls himself the "head" of *Vzglyad*—though the other hosts refuse to recognize his authority. Nevertheless, he fights for control, even going so far as to devise a plan to "promote" Listyev out of the way by assigning him to a light entertainment show.

In October 1990, Soviet First Channel airs *Field of Wonders* for the first time, the Soviet version of *Wheel of Fortune*. It's hosted by Listyev, once considered the most serious of the *Vzglyad* hosts. The shift surprises many: He had been the face of the country's main political show, and now his guests guess words one letter at a time?

But soon *Field of Wonders* becomes the most popular program on television—and, crucially, the biggest earner of advertising revenue. Listyev quickly becomes so wealthy that he loses all sense of money's value. One day, planning to buy his wife some flowers, he purchases an entire kiosk's worth. Meanwhile, Lyubimov embarks on a nationwide tour, holding meet-and-greets, signing autographs, and basking in the glow of his fame—which, though fading, still lingers despite his absence from TV screens.

"WE'RE SCREWED"

The congress proceeds like clockwork, orchestrated by Lukyanov and his team. It approves the administrative reforms proposed by Gorbachev. The Presidential Council is dissolved: Yakovlev and Primakov find themselves unemployed. In its place, the Security Council is established—now the president's inner circle will consist of the heads of the security ministries.

The congress decides to hold a referendum in March on the preservation of the Soviet Union as a "renewed federation of equal sovereign republics"—Lukyanov's idea, intended to remove the dissolution of the USSR from the agenda.

The legislators approve Gorbachev's proposal to subordinate the Council of Ministers directly to him. On December 25, Nikolai Ryzhkov is rushed to the hospital with a heart attack. Only then does Gorbachev finally decide to dismiss the government, led by Ryzhkov.

"You can form a new Council of Ministers, but where will you find another people?" Ryzhkov reportedly says upon learning of his resignation. A remarkable display of self-importance from a man who clung to his position for years and effectively blocked any reforms, simply because he couldn't understand them—and, to top it all off, he blamed the people for everything that had happened.

Chernyaev writes in his diary that the president discusses candidates for the new prime minister and foreign minister with his advisors. For the post of foreign minister, both Chernyaev and Primakov propose Yakovlev.

"Not going to happen," Gorbachev replies curtly.

For the role of prime minister, Chernyaev recommends Anatoly Sobchak, who has gained valuable experience leading Leningrad. Gorbachev seems intrigued but ultimately chooses Valentin Pavlov, the Minister of Finance.

Finally, the congress must elect a vice president. Earlier rumors suggested Gorbachev might propose Shevardnadze or Yakovlev—but the political winds have shifted. The president of the USSR nominates Gennady Yanayev, a nondescript trade union official. On the first vote, the congress rejects him—but Gorbachev insists. On the second attempt, Yanayev is elected.

That day, Akaki Asatiani, the deputy head of the Georgian parliament, and Levon Ter-Petrosyan, the head of the Armenian parliament, are smoking outside the Kremlin Palace of Congresses. A man approaches them, asking for a cigarette. Asatiani gives him one, but the stranger's hands shake so badly he can't light it. The Georgian politician helps him light the cigarette and, as the man walks away, mutters:

"What the hell? Who let these bums in here?"

"Don't be rude," Ter-Petrosyan says. "That's not a bum; that's the future vice president of the Soviet Union."

"Seriously?" Asatiani's eyes widen. "Well, we're screwed."

"Screwed," Ter-Petrosyan agrees.

9

A VACATION AFTER THE WAR

In Soviet schools, there were two mandatory traditions: first graders were always inducted into the Oktyabryata (Young Octobrists), and fourth graders were made Young Pioneers. This usually happened on Lenin's birthday, April 22. For our class, it was scheduled for April 22, 1991, at the Lenin Museum on Red Square.

My school was in a remote and somewhat rough neighborhood on the outskirts of Moscow. It was a long ride to the center of the city. In previous years, the school arranged for a bus, but this time, we were taken by metro.

Among my classmates were a few troublemakers who hung out with older boys, shook down younger kids for money, and even sniffed toxic glue. Soviet superglue was the cheapest, most toxic drug for the most troubled teens. A few kids from my school will be found dead with glue bags over their heads. Technically, kids like that weren't supposed to be made Young Pioneers—we were constantly told that it was a great honor reserved for the best students. But in our case, they took everyone.

For me, there was a special draw to this event: after the scarf-tying ceremony, our entire class was to visit Lenin's Mausoleum and then the Kremlin Wall, where several Soviet leaders, including Stalin, Brezhnev, Andropov, and Chernenko, were buried alongside Soviet icons like Yuri Gagarin. This part fascinated me most, but my classmates couldn't have cared less.

In hindsight, it's clear that we were the last Young Pioneers of the Soviet Union. When we returned to school after summer break in September 1991, the teachers acted as if the Pioneer organization had never existed.

It was peak Soviet absurdity. Before that, they had dutifully played the role of loyal Soviet educators, feeding us orthodox lessons about Lenin, the party, communism, and the bright future ahead. They clearly didn't believe a word of it themselves, but they were all-in on indoctrinating us. Then, by the fall of '91, it was like someone flipped a switch. Suddenly, it was, "Kids, everything we told you before—that was obviously a lie. There's no communism, and you can forget about Lenin too. Now, the most important thing is God."

There's probably no better way to raise an entire generation of utterly cynical people. People who learn from childhood that the only way to avoid being deceived is to trust no one and believe in nothing.

PARATROOPERS IN VILNIUS

In January 1991, Vladislav Achalov, deputy minister of defense and commander of the Airborne Forces—who led military operations in Baku a year earlier—arrives in Riga, where the headquarters of the Baltic Military District is located. He holds a meeting, and according to Viktor Alksnis, "commanders at lower and mid-levels—colonels, division commanders, regimental commanders—all curse Gorbachev." After listening to them, Achalov says, "Then we will act on our own."

According to Viktor Alksnis, even though Mikhail Gorbachev does not dare to impose a state of emergency, "the mechanism is already set in motion": troops, special forces, and the Alpha Group are already being deployed to the Baltic republics. "The initiative has been taken up by local leaders. Commanders of military units, district command, the KGB, the Ministry of Defense," Alksnis explains. "People are eager for action because they have endured two years of this. The anti-army hysteria in the Baltics is brutal, and they are raring to restore order, to hit hard, and so on."

It is remarkable that people living in the same country, the USSR, seemingly shaped by the same cultural environment, perceive the world so differently. Many Russian-speaking residents of the Baltic states—especially the military—simply cannot and will not understand why Russians here are called occupiers. For them, this is an outrageous insult, persecution, and an expression of local nationalism. They refuse to hear anything about the Molotov-Ribbentrop Pact and call this digging up history. Throughout their lives, they have lived within the Soviet paradigm, believed in the "friendship of nations," and ignored the fact that this friendship was often built on violence. They do not want to part with this Soviet myth and are ready to fight for it because they understand that if they lose this myth, they will forever become occupiers and will likely be forced to leave the Baltics, where they have lived for decades, and where some of them were even born. They are fighting not on orders from Moscow—in fact, they are the main initiators of this fight.

In early January, a protest begins near the parliament building—it is clearly not spontaneous but pre-organized. Protesters try to break into the parliament building, but Lithuanian police disperse them using hot water from fire hoses. Landsbergis appears on television with an appeal: "Support your authorities; otherwise, you will have someone else's."

The protest at the parliament walls continues the next day, with slogans appearing: "Down with the parliament! Long live the USSR!"

And Moscow begins to act according to a scenario: almost exactly as it did in the same Lithuania in 1940 or in Czechoslovakia in 1968. First, on January 8, the Soviet television announces "numerous telegrams from residents of Lithuania urging the Union leadership to restore order in the republic." Then, on January 10, Gorbachev himself speaks, demanding "the immediate restoration of the USSR constitution and the annulment of previously adopted anti-constitutional acts."

All this time, the military is taking action—new units are arriving in Lithuania. On the morning of January 11, Soviet paratroopers start seizing buildings in the city. In central Vilnius, a tank crashes into a KAMAZ truck, and the driver is injured.

Landsbergis tries to call Gorbachev, but he is told that the president is having lunch and cannot come to the phone.

STORMING ON LIVE BROADCAST

On the night of January 12–13, three columns of Soviet armored vehicles—paratroopers and the Alpha Group—are moving through Vilnius: one is heading toward the parliament, another toward the television center, and a third is approaching the TV tower. Actress Ingeborga Dapkūnaitė is among the thousands of Vilnius residents who respond to Landsbergis's call and join the protests.

She will later recall the bitter cold in the city and the carefully planned schedule of shifts—everyone knows when and where they need to stand. The actors from her theater, for instance, are stationed near the parliament. Meanwhile, regular buses filled with people from remote villages and towns across Lithuania pour into the capital—the entire nation is determined to defend its independence. The mood is lively, even festive: people share thermoses of hot tea, warm food, and encouragement.

Around midnight, she leaves the parliament and heads home while her sister returns from the TV center. Together, they sit down to watch television.

On-air at that moment is host Eglė Bučelytė, who suddenly announces that the assault on the TV center has begun.

The studio has no windows, so Bučelytė can't see what's happening outside. She hears explosions and bursts of automatic gunfire but has no idea if the people gathered outside to defend the building against Soviet soldiers are still alive.

On the screen, Landsbergis delivers another address, recalling the "Forest Brothers"—Lithuanian guerrillas who continued fighting against the Soviet Union after World War II. "At that moment, I thought we, too, would have to hide in the forests and work underground," Bučelytė will later recount.

At some point, the studio phone rings. On live air, the host picks it up and informs viewers that Soviet soldiers have stormed the building. Moments later, the camera shows commandos calmly walking down a corridor. The studio door is locked, and paratroopers spend ten minutes hacking it down with an axe before the broadcast cuts off.

Bučelytė and the cameraman are led outside. One of the soldiers tells her that a Lithuanian policeman has shot a Soviet Alpha fighter.

Upon seeing these scenes, Ingeborga and her sister jump up, dress quickly, and rush to the TV center, where the crowd has grown significantly. Even in the middle of the night, buses from the regions continue to arrive. At that moment, no one knows about the casualties yet.

By morning, it will become clear that fourteen or fifteen people died during the assault on the TV tower—most from gunshot wounds, but some were crushed by military vehicles.

From a public perception standpoint, it's hard to think of anything more disastrous for Gorbachev than a live broadcast of the assault. By morning, the events in Lithuania dominate headlines worldwide. Gorbachev, Yazov, and Pugo all deny any involvement, insisting they knew nothing about it.

Landsbergis will later recount that he also tried to call Gorbachev that night but couldn't get through—the Soviet president, he says, was supposedly asleep.

"This botched operation to storm the TV tower happened because

Gorbachev chickened out and refused to sign the decree on a state of emergency. If he had, everything would have proceeded strictly by the book, and no one would have been able to accuse him of anything. The army and the KGB were ready to act. It would have been another Tiananmen Square, like in China, and the result would have been the same," muses Alksnis, clearly implying that the Chinese scenario is his ideal.

After the events, Gorbachev is cursed by everyone: the Lithuanians, the army, and Russian democrats alike.

TRIP TO TALLINN

Landsbergis finally gets through to Gorbachev the next day. The Lithuanian leader asks to allow doctors into the TV center to help the wounded. Gorbachev agrees. According to Landsbergis, the most significant result of this conversation is the assurance that there will not be another attack that night.

The events in Vilnius are an absolute shock for everyone in Moscow. Yeltsin urgently flies to Tallinn, Estonia, to meet with the heads of the parliaments of the Baltic republics. Together, they sign an appeal to the United Nations and the people of the USSR condemning military intervention in the affairs of sovereign republics—signed by Russia, Estonia, Latvia, and Lithuania. Landsbergis sends his approval by fax. "On January 13, Russia became a subject of international law for the first time," Burbulis will later say of the event.

After the agreement is signed, questions arise about how safe it is to return to Moscow and what consequences might follow the events and statements in Tallinn. Some suggest that Yeltsin's plane might be shot down on the way back, so he must avoid flying on the same aircraft he arrived on. "We decided to play a bit of cloak-and-dagger, leaving in cars, using different convoys. What were we afraid of? No one really knew," Burbulis recalls.

According to Landsbergis, Boris Yeltsin's departure back to Russia is organized by Dzhokhar Dudayev, at the time a Soviet aviation general serving in Tartu, Estonia. Dudayev, future leader of the Chechen separatists, provides Yeltsin with his car, in which the head of the Russian parliament drives from Tallinn to Leningrad.

Meanwhile, Yakovlev and Primakov try to persuade Gorbachev to go to Vilnius—to lay a wreath and speak at the local parliament. Gorbachev instructs them to write speeches for the visit by morning. They write the texts and place them on his desk. For the entire day, Gorbachev's press secretary, Ignatenko, chases the president to figure out his plan. But Gorbachev pretends as if no conversation about a trip to Lithuania ever took place. In the end, Ignatenko concludes that Gorbachev was not misinformed—he is merely pretending.

Chernyaev writes a resignation letter. It concludes with the words "Mikhail Sergeyevich! Ever since I began working 'with you,' I never imagined I would again experience the same agonizing shame for Soviet leadership's policies as I did under Brezhnev and Chernenko. Alas! It has happened." Chernyaev's secretary takes the letter, locks it in a safe, and keeps it there. A few days later, Chernyaev changes his mind, deciding that abandoning Gorbachev in such a difficult moment would be a betrayal.

DESERT STORM

Soviet generals, planning to "restore order" in Lithuania, assume the world won't notice—because all attention is on the impending operation in Iraq. Back in the fall of 1990, the UN Security Council issued an ultimatum to Saddam Hussein: he must withdraw his troops from Kuwait by January 15, 1991. Since August of the previous year, the United States has been steadily deploying troops to the Persian Gulf region.

The chief architect of this military campaign is US secretary of defense Dick Cheney. In his memoir, he writes that the chairman of the Joint Chiefs of Staff, Colin Powell, is far from enthusiastic about the prospect of military action—like many American officers, he is still haunted by the trauma of Vietnam: "Part of it was just Colin, the way he was attuned to public approval, but listening to him also made me think about how Vietnam had shaped the views of America's top generals. They had seen loss of public support for the Vietnam War undermine the war effort as well as damage the reputation of the military."

For Cheney, overcoming this psychological barrier is critical. He is determined to launch the operation at any cost—so much so that he even tries to convince President Bush not to bring the question of troop deployment before Congress. *What if Congress votes against it? The troops are already in position; there's no turning back.* He is equally skeptical of the negotiations led by Secretary of State James Baker. But in the end, everything plays out as Cheney wants—talks fail, and Congress votes in favor.

On his end, Gorbachev also attempts to show that his word still carries weight on the world stage—he sends Yevgeny Primakov, a longtime acquaintance of Saddam, to Baghdad. But by then, no one cares about his efforts—Cheney has already deployed nearly half a million troops to the Middle East, making any diplomatic mission pointless.

Soviet military officials closely watch the movement of American forces and operate under the principle of "Why can they do it, but we can't?" From their perspective, the operations in Lithuania and Iraq are almost identical. Saddam has violated international law; Landsbergis has broken Soviet laws—so force can and should be used against them.

On January 15, the UN Security Council's ultimatum expires. George Bush delivers a televised address announcing the start of the military operation—one of the most unusual war declarations by an American president. He can barely contain his smile, as if on the verge of laughter.

The next day, Operation Desert Storm begins. Almost immediately, Gorbachev tries to position himself as a mediator: "Hussein is politically discredited, his military potential is crippled, the threat of regional hegemony is neutralized—so why keep killing others and putting our own boys at risk?"—as Chernyaev later summarizes his proposal to Bush.

Meanwhile, KGB chief Kryuchkov warns Gorbachev that the Americans are on the verge of launching a nuclear strike on Iraq and insists he must issue a protest—to prevent catastrophe. Experts from the Foreign Ministry and the Central Committee strongly urge him to help Saddam "save face"—after all, he has been a Soviet ally for so long; abandoning him now would be disgraceful.

"FIERY CUP OF CIVIL WAR"

On January 15, a fourteen-minute documentary by the country's most popular TV journalist, Alexander Nevzorov, airs on Leningrad television. The film is titled *Ours*, and its main characters are the very paratroopers who stormed the Vilnius TV tower: "Unshaven, unwashed, bloodstained, with spit and stones flying at them, tracer bullets . . . but they stand their ground and do not retreat," Nevzorov begins the story with heavy pathos.

Nevzorov presents a completely unexpected version of the events of January 13. He claims that Soviet tanks fired only blanks, that the paratroopers approached the tower only after the shooting had begun, and that either the casualties were staged or provocateurs had pushed young women under the tanks. Perhaps, Nevzorov speculates, the casualties were not even real victims of the event but people who had died in car accidents elsewhere.

As for the soldiers who stormed the TV tower, Nevzorov insists that "they saved Lithuania from an indelible bloody shame, from the frenzy and national hysteria incited by the broadcasts, which provoked the people to madness." According to him, turning off the television was essential—otherwise, things would have turned out much worse.

What exactly would have been worse? Nevzorov does not hesitate to elaborate in vivid detail. He claims that Landsbergis had allegedly called for "the extermination of all non-Lithuanian residents." Supposedly, there was already a prepared plan for the mass executions of Russian families. "Lithuania has decided to drink the fiery cup of civil war and fratricide to the bitter end," Nevzorov declares repeatedly, with a voice full of anguish and under soul-wrenching music.

However, the story of the TV tower assault is just a small part of the film. Overall, Nevzorov flips the narrative inside out—his documentary focuses on an imminent assault on the Vilnius Police Academy, where forty-three police officers loyal to their Soviet oath have taken refuge (he implicitly acknowledges that all others now serve independent Lithuania).

The commander of this detachment, Boleslav Makutinovich, announces that the storming will begin at any moment: "Landsbergis has given the order not to take us alive."

The film includes dialogues that seem incredible for the documentary genre. For instance:

"And you plan to stand to the end? To death?" Nevzorov asks with a burning gaze.

"What else can we do?" Makutinovich answers dispassionately. "What would you advise me, Comrade Nevzorov?"

"Stand," the journalist heroically replies.

(As a sidenote, it must be mentioned that no assault on the police academy will ever occur, nor will there be any mass executions.)

Finally, the main villains revealed in the film—apart from the almost infernal Landsbergis—are the leaders of the USSR. Nevzorov does not name names but refers to them as "cowards and scoundrels" who "give orders to soldiers and then abandon them to face spit and bullets."

Nevzorov's film makes such an impression on Anatoly Lukyanov that the Supreme Soviet decides to broadcast it on the First Channel. The film airs twice—on January 16.

Ours is a shock to the entire Soviet TV audience. First, because such a perspective had never before been presented on television. On one side was state propaganda, dull and unconvincing—no viewer believed it, and probably not even the announcers themselves, except for dogmatic communists like Ligachev. On the other side were the new perestroika-era programs, symbolized by *Vzglyad*. The hosts of *Vzglyad* were young, intelligent democrats, advocating for freedom and against the Soviet empire and communism. And now, suddenly, a third perspective emerges: passionate and agenda driven, employing every propagandist trope and trick available. It glorifies the empire and calls for people to fight for it. Such a call had never before been heard in Soviet media.

It had been just over two weeks since *Vzglyad* was taken off the air—and now here comes its vibrant replacement.

Nevzorov could be called the Nina Andreeva of a new generation. It's notable that both are from Leningrad. They defend the same values but in completely different styles. And while Gorbachev and Yakovlev immediately rebuked Nina Andreeva three years ago, Nevzorov encounters no obstacles. On the contrary—his patrons in power are not offended at all by his calling Gorbachev, Yazov, and Pugo "cowards and scoundrels." Quite the opposite.

Clearly, Nevzorov's film airing on the First Channel is meant to shift public sentiment in the USSR—and to embolden those leaders still hesitant to spill blood.

At the same time, Nevzorov himself ascends to another league: after *Ours*, he gains direct access to those state leaders who share his position. He becomes a frequent guest in the Kremlin and other offices. "I could insistently say what I believed needed to be done. I could say it to Lukyanov, or Yazov, or Kryuchkov, or someone else," he later recalls.

Many years later, Nevzorov will look back on this period of his work with a critical eye, attributing it to his participation in an information war: "Later, I realized that there's probably no more shameful justification than 'I was following orders.' It means you've replaced your own understanding of good and evil, your own judgment, with the inadequate notions of some fool in a military cap. Now I understand just how repulsive the word 'order' is—not an excuse at all but something utterly vile. But back then, for me, the word still didn't sound so disgusting."

THE LARGEST PROTEST

Public sentiment, at least in Moscow, does not change; on the contrary—Nevzorov's film provokes a storm of outrage. On January 20, the first Sunday after the events in Vilnius, a rally in support of Lithuania gathers on Manezhnaya Square. It is possibly the largest protest in the history of the Russian capital—up to half a million people participate.

The protesters' placards read: "Today Lithuania—Tomorrow Russia. We won't allow it!," "Mikhail Sergeyevich Hussein," "Bloody Mikhail, Leave in Peace," "Yazov to Court!" Many also demand that the program *Vzglyad* be returned to the air and criticize Nevzorov: "We'll Go Blind Without Vzglyad," "Freedom to Vzglyad," "We won't trade Vzglyad for Nevzorov."

Journalist Sergei Semanov, known for his nationalist views and full support of Nevzorov, also attends the rally. The sheer size of the crowd is a blow to him. "I could not have expected so many people in this atmosphere of apathy," he writes in his diary. "And in the crowd—it's all Russians, no Caucasians or Jews to be seen. Yes, today I watched the heart of the Russian people firsthand."

Semanov notes, however, that "there are very few young people. I saw almost no students or high schoolers—mainly middle-aged and older folks, many women (no young ones at all), poorly dressed—at best, lower-middle class, but really, 'the common people,' 'the working class'. . . . It's worth thinking and discussing why this happens—after all, in the West, political demonstrations are full of youth, especially university students."

This is a fascinating phenomenon of perestroika. On the one hand, the current revolutionary romantics are people over forty, the Sixties Generation—those who once listened to Vysotsky and many of whom read Solzhenitsyn. They are the ones who can no longer endure the oppressive Soviet gloom. Many of them, like physicist Lev Ponomarev, believe that life can begin anew after forty. It is unsurprising that the rising stars of politics for these people are fifty-nine-year-old Yeltsin, fifty-three-year-old Sobchak, fifty-year-old Gdlyan, fifty-four-year-old Popov, and sixty-five-year-old Afanasyev. Against this backdrop, the thirty-eight-year-old Sergei Stankevich looks like a child.

Soviet youth, on the other hand, are apolitical. Tsoi and Grebenshchikov might sing about wanting change, but that's just part of the fashion. When Tsoi was asked in an interview whether he and Grebenshchikov planned to become Members of Parliament, he sneered: "Me and BG as parliamentarians? What nonsense. . . . Politics is all dirt and lies. . . . President Gorbachev is bad: I see no signs that our shitty lives are getting any better."

The young dissenters from *Vzglyad* are far from being fervent revolutionaries. None of them show up at the rally to denounce censorship. They are enjoying their image as rock stars and preparing to go on a tour across the country.

In reality, the last generation of Soviet citizens can no longer genuinely hate communism because they grew up during perestroika and their lives are filled with new joys that were impossible until recently: they have foreign jeans, videotapes with foreign films, trendy music, and other pleasures that were forbidden only yesterday—they don't want to waste time on boring political discussions.

LENIN IS THE MUSHROOM

Around the same days as the storming of the Vilnius TV tower and the airing of Nevzorov's film on First Channel, Leningrad television broadcasts a new episode of the popular show *The Fifth Wheel*. This program typically features the host interviewing a famous guest: previous guests included Boris Yeltsin and Anatoly Sobchak. This time, the host, Sergei Sholokhov, announces that his guest is "a well-known political figure and film actor, Sergei Kuryokhin, who has just returned from Mexico." In fact, Kuryokhin is a musician, a star of the Leningrad Rock Club, and a close friend of Grebenshchikov, Tsoi, and Joanna Stingray. He is also known for his provocations and hoaxes. This time Kuryokhin claims he will reveal the greatest secret of the October Revolution. Thus begins the greatest hoax in the history of Soviet television.

Kuryokhin begins by saying he was inspired by the works of Carlos Castaneda and that he supposedly stumbled across this phrase in a letter Lenin wrote to Plekhanov: "Yesterday I gorged myself on mushrooms and felt marvelous." Using scientific terminology and citing various (of course, fabricated) studies, he concludes that Lenin regularly consumed hallucinogenic mushrooms, specifically *Amanita muscaria*. He develops his theory further, claiming that "*Amanita muscaria* has its own consciousness, and when a person consumes a lot of mushrooms, their personality is gradually replaced, and they themselves become a mushroom." He dramatically concludes, "I want to say that Lenin was a mushroom and, moreover, he was a radio wave."

Kuryokhin then presents a diagram of Lenin's armored car, sliced open, and asserts that it resembles a fungal mycelium. The program's "experts" include the head of the Mushrooms for Peace international movement and Sergei "Afrika" Bugaev, who is introduced as the grandson of a drug dealer who allegedly supplied Lenin with hallucinogenic mushrooms.

Toward the end of the program, Sholokhov and Kuryokhin can no longer contain their laughter. The host struggles to finish his questions because he is choking with laughter. "Seryozha, we need to concentrate. Stop laughing," Kuryokhin says while laughing himself. They then close the program with serious faces: "The facts are irrefutable, but perhaps you have alternative facts," Sholokhov says.

Today all of this might be seen as an unremarkable prank. But on Soviet television, it looks completely different. A significant portion of the audience takes what they've seen seriously. The next day, a group of old communists goes to the Leningrad party committee to clarify whether Lenin was, in fact, a mushroom. A staff member of the committee, Galina Barinova, responds that he wasn't because "a mammal cannot be a plant." Some Soviet newspapers begin seriously debunking Kuryokhin's lie, with headlines like "We Will Not Allow Lenin's Name to Be Tarnished," "Blasphemy," and "Defend Lenin."

At first, even Alla Pugacheva believes this insane story. "I don't like being tricked, but here I was quite pleased. It was stunning. Kuryokhin just turned my life upside down back then," she later says in an interview.

PAVLOV'S MONEY

On the evening of January 22, the USSR's main news program broadcasts an announcement by the new prime minister, Valentin Pavlov. He declares a sudden monetary reform: in three days, all 50- and 100-ruble banknotes will become invalid. That is not all—bank deposits are frozen, and citizens can withdraw only 5,000 rubles.

This is undoubtedly the most insane measure taken by the Soviet government. If, up until this point, there were still people in the USSR who supported what the authorities were doing, now there are none left.

The idea of withdrawing large-denomination banknotes from circulation was not new—it had existed for a year already in the plans of Ryzhkov's government, where Pavlov had served as minister of finance. The intent was to regulate the amount of cash in circulation but, more importantly, to strike at the shadow economy. Like many Soviet economists, Pavlov believes that all of the USSR's problems stem from the black market and underground entrepreneurship.

In general, private business in the USSR had already been decriminalized in 1988 after the adoption of the Law on Cooperatives. Nonetheless, Pavlov remains convinced that the health of the economy is being undermined by secret millionaires.

Another conspiracy theory that the prime minister believes in—and not only him—is that some enemies from abroad, aiming to undermine the Soviet economy, have either flooded it with counterfeit money or, on the contrary, exported Soviet cash overseas. Moreover, Pavlov claims that smugglers have taken as much as 7 billion rubles abroad.

Since both shadow millionaires and foreign enemies obviously deal only in large-denomination bills, Prime Minister Pavlov decides to thwart their plans by confiscating large bills from everyone.

The old banknotes turn into pumpkins at the stroke of midnight that very day, and you have only three days to exchange them at the bank for shiny new ones. But no more than a thousand rubles—because, according to the government, no honest citizen could possibly have more than that.

The announcement is deliberately made in the evening so that no one has time to spend their money the same day: all banks and shops in the USSR are already closed. But clever citizens know that railway ticket offices work at night: the life hack of that evening is to exchange money by buying train tickets to all possible destinations—they can later be returned. However, such cunning individuals are few; the majority of citizens panic, rushing around and standing in massive lines at savings banks the next few days. Stories circulate about pensioners suffering heart attacks and dying while standing in line.

The particular cruelty of the situation lies in the fact that, in recent months, wages and pensions at many enterprises have been issued only in large-denomination bills—all of this is seen as deliberate mockery of ordinary people.

"For its surprise and speed, the reform resembles, if not a well-planned robbery, then at least a military operation, with the country's population playing the role of the enemy," jokes the newspaper *Kommersant* the following day.

What particularly undermines trust in the government is not only the reform itself but also the lies preceding it. Just two weeks earlier, the prime minister had appeared on television, promising that there would be no monetary reform. Nevertheless, after the reform, he proudly claims that he kept this secret from everyone—even his own wife.

TO ORGANIZE AN ASSASSINATION

After watching Nevzorov's report from Vilnius, parliamentarian Alksnis sends him a telegram on red government stationery: "Thank you for the truth, I'm impressed. Colonel Alksnis."

Shortly after, Nevzorov calls Alksnis in Moscow and invites him to come to Leningrad to take part in his program. *600 Seconds* is one of the most popular shows in the country, so the parliamentarian, of course, agrees.

Alksnis arrives at the VIP lounge of Sheremetyevo Airport, where the flight is slightly delayed, and suddenly he spots Anatoly Sobchak, "with some young man."

"Although Sobchak and I were at odds and constantly sparred in the Supreme Soviet, on a personal level our relationship was perfectly civil," Alksnis recalls. He sits down next to Sobchak, who immediately gives his assistant an order: "Vladimir Vladimirovich, go sort out my ticket, and bring us and Mr. Alksnis something to drink and snack on."

Soon the young man—who is, of course, Putin—returns with cognac and some snacks. When the boarding is announced, he insists to Alksnis, "Viktor Imantovich, you go along with Anatoly Alexandrovich. I'll carry all your things; that's my job."

"To be honest, he didn't leave any impression at all. I'd met assistants who were often much smarter than their bosses, but this one was like a gray spot," Alksnis will later recall.

They land in Leningrad, where Nevzorov meets Alksnis. At the sight of the journalist, Sobchak's expression changes visibly. The reason: starting in early 1991, Nevzorov's stance on the mayor had shifted dramatically—once his supporter, he now spared no effort in criticizing Sobchak.

Alksnis and Nevzorov head to the Leningrad TV studio. There, Nevzorov unexpectedly asks, "Viktor Imantovich, could you arrange an assassination attempt on me?"

The parliamentarian is confused—*is this a joke?*

"Well, let's imagine the situation: I come to Latvia," Nevzorov clarifies, "and then the Latvian People's Front organizes an assassination attempt on me. Could you arrange it?"

Alksnis, thrown off by this bizarre twist, promises instead to introduce Nevzorov to Cheslav Mlynnik, the commander of the Riga special police force (OMON).

On February 5, Nevzorov films a new episode of his patriotic series *Ours*—this time about the Riga OMON. The narrative closely mirrors the first part about Vilnius but with new protagonists.

"Moscow will betray you anyway," Nevzorov says bitterly in this episode.

"Even if Moscow betrays us, we're not leaving," Mlynnik responds stoically.

THE RUSSIAN ALBUM

In 1991, Grebenshchikov returns to the USSR. After two years of trying to become an international rock star—one album released in America and another that never saw the light of day in Britain—he gives up. "It's far more interesting for me to work where it works," he will later explain his decision.

The country he returns to is very different from the one he left. There are new idols, new rock stars—there's no longer an underground; everything is allowed. Tsoi is gone, the rock club no longer exists, and working with former members of Aquarium is no longer an option.

"For me, it was a joy not to play some program of Aquarium hits . . . ," he will later recall. "We were all uninterested. Everyone just didn't want to look at each other. And everyone was drinking monstrously. We broke up Aquarium, played the last concert, and split so that we'd never have to see each other again." He even says, "Since the Soviet Union has ceased to exist, Aquarium is no more either."

Of course, the USSR still legally exists.

Grebenshchikov assembles new musicians into a group called the BG Band and embarks on an endless tour across the Soviet Union—this time performing as part of a chamber ensemble in small clubs. He remains a legend, but not the kind that now fills stadiums.

Grebenshchikov's music also changes dramatically—after returning from the West, he writes a new album titled *The Russian Album*. It's folk, a return to an imaginary Russia, featuring folk instruments, pseudo-Russian vocabulary, invented Orthodox saints, and mythical monsters from Russian chronicles. Traumatized by his failed conquest of the West, BG retreats inward and creates an alternative universe—a mystical Rus'.

Alexander Solzhenitsyn became a devotee of Holy Rus' during his years in Vermont. For BG, two years in Los Angeles and London were enough to inspire the same turn.

LADDERS, HOOKS, AND ROPES

On March 17, 1991, a referendum on preserving the USSR is held in eight republics: Russia, Ukraine, Belarus, Azerbaijan, Kazakhstan, Uzbekistan, Kyrgyzstan, and Turkmenistan.* In all of these republics, more than 70 percent vote in favor, although the questions vary from one republic to another.

The question, formulated by Anatoly Lukyanov, draws smirks from many and is jokingly called "Do you want to be rich and healthy, or poor and sick?" It is worded so vaguely that answering "no" is nearly impossible: "Do you consider it necessary to preserve the Union of Soviet Socialist Republics as a renewed federation of equal sovereign republics, where the rights and freedoms of people of any nationality will be fully guaranteed?"

Having secured this victory, Gorbachev prepares to deliver another blow to Yeltsin: the Russian parliament, which just six months earlier had elected him as its chairman, is now ready to issue a vote of no confidence against him.

Yeltsin has only one way to fight back: to bring people into the streets. A massive rally in the center of Moscow—similar to February's pro-Lithuanian protest—could prove to everyone that Yeltsin remains popular. This time, however, the KGB once again spreads rumors that Yeltsin's supporters are

---

* At the time, Kyrgyzstan was one of the fifteen republics of the Soviet Union, with a population roughly equal to that of Colorado and a territory close in size to South Dakota. Turkmenistan was one of the fifteen republics of the Soviet Union, with a population roughly equal to that of Minnesota and a territory comparable to California.

preparing to storm the Kremlin. Allegedly, plans exist to surround it, with ladders, hooks, and ropes ready to scale the medieval walls. And Gorbachev believes it. He convenes the first meeting dedicated to the potential declaration of a state of emergency, issues a decree banning rallies in Moscow for nearly a month (from March 25 to April 15) and reassigns control of the city's police force. Now they answer not to Gavriil Popov but to the USSR's minister of internal affairs, Boris Pugo.

On March 27, troops are brought into Moscow. All approaches to the Kremlin are blocked—even Chernyaev's car is turned away, despite him showing his credentials as the president's aide. He is forced to walk from the Moskvoretsky Bridge on foot and take the metro home in the evening.

The presence of military forces in central Moscow makes a profound impression on the legislators. At the Russian Congress, parliamentarians warn that another Vilnius—or even a Tiananmen Square—could happen in Moscow.

Despite the ban on rallies, despite it being a weekday and military equipment on the streets, three parallel protests take place in different locations: on Mayakovsky Square, Pushkinskaya, and Arbat.

This day, March 28, 1991, can surely be considered a decisive historical moment that everyone has forgotten. Never before had the Soviet authorities come so close to switching to a forceful scenario. Any provocation in central Moscow could have led to unpredictable consequences: bloodshed, a state of emergency—Gorbachev was already prepared to agree to it all. There is no doubt that Vladimir Kryuchkov had all the levers necessary to activate this mechanism. Yet he does not give the order. Perhaps even he believes the reports his agency prepared for Gorbachev: that Yeltsin would soon be overthrown by the Russian deputies themselves, that the deployment of troops and Gorbachev's show of firmness were steps in the right direction, that everything was under control, and that all that remained was to squeeze the democrats a little harder.

However, the sight of troops on the streets and the grand scale of unauthorized rallies leave the legislators with the opposite impression. The Russian Congress refuses to dismiss Yeltsin and instead calls for presidential elections. Everyone disperses peacefully, and Gorbachev orders the withdrawal of troops from the capital. Supporters of the "strong hand" throw up their hands in despair—an unprecedented opportunity to establish the dictatorship Shevardnadze had recently predicted is lost.

RED WINE ON A WHITE SHIRT

On March 23, Boris Yeltsin arrives in Georgia—he meets with Zviad Gamsakhurdia at the Kazbegi ski resort. As Akaki Asatiani recalls, the president of Georgia has no interest in engaging with Soviet authorities and refuses any contact with Gorbachev, but he sees Yeltsin completely differently—as a partner and ally. The two leaders sign agreements guaranteeing the recognition of each other's borders and sovereignty.

The meeting is warm and friendly. Boris and Zviad drink Georgian wine and toast to each other and to their shared independence from the Soviet Union. During the dinner, however, an unfortunate incident occurs: Two large ceremonial drinking horns are brought in for the leaders, in keeping with Georgian tradition. But as Yeltsin lifts his horn, the metal tip suddenly falls off, and the wine spills directly onto his white shirt. Stunned, Yeltsin stands drenched in dark red liquid, resembling blood. Gamsakhurdia tries to smooth things over, handing him his own horn, while aides rush in with a fresh shirt. But later, in Tbilisi, many will recall this episode as an ill omen.

An unusual friendship develops between Yeltsin and Gamsakhurdia, rooted in their shared fondness for elaborate feasts. At one point, the Russian leader even invites his Georgian counterpart to Moscow, planning a grand gathering for friends and colleagues. He needs a toastmaster, and Gamsakhurdia agrees, traveling to the Russian capital to preside over the event for his new friend Boris.

But the relationship soon sours. Gamsakhurdia begins forging closer ties with the leaders of Russia's autonomous republics. Georgia officially recognizes the sovereignty of Tatarstan, and even stronger relations form between Gamsakhurdia and Dzhokhar Dudayev, the newly emerging leader of Chechnya.

Asatiani recalls that shortly before seizing power in Chechnya, Dudayev visits Tbilisi and meets with Gamsakhurdia.

Yeltsin finds all of this deeply unsettling. He begins to suspect the worst—that Gamsakhurdia has struck a deal with Gorbachev. It is no secret to the Russian president that the Soviet leadership—Gorbachev and Lukyanov in particular—is actively encouraging Russia's autonomous regions to seek greater independence as a way to rein in Yeltsin. Now he starts to believe that Georgia's overtures toward Chechnya and Tatarstan are part of a scheme to undermine him, with Gamsakhurdia playing along with the Kremlin. And this is something Yeltsin cannot forgive—not even from his favorite toastmaster.

Akaki Asatiani, Speaker of the Georgian Parliament, recalls a conversation with Yeltsin:

"Listen, you seem like a reasonable guy. Look, I could be interfering in Abkhazia and South Ossetia, but I'm not. So why are you stirring things up in Chechnya and Tatarstan? Is that fair? Explain that to Zviad, will you?"

VICE PRESIDENT BELONOGOV

Simultaneously with the referendum on preserving the Union, Yeltsin holds a referendum on introducing the post of president in Russia—and it proves to be a smart move. He remains incredibly popular among voters.

The next step is to figure out how the power system will work once Russia becomes a presidential republic. Naturally, a president must have a vice-president—everyone agrees on this because it mirrors the American system and aligns with Solzhenitsyn's vision outlined in "How to Rebuild Russia."

Yeltsin and Burbulis discuss who might fill the role of vice president. Gavriil Popov is eager for the position and is considered a candidate. Another suitable figure is Galina Starovoitova—everyone thinks that having a female vice president would be very progressive. Moreover, she was a close aide to Sakharov. However, as often happens, the person responsible for the choice chooses himself. Burbulis concludes that he is the ideal candidate for vice president. That's how he and Yeltsin agree to run together as a pair.

Yeltsin's team is quite large, and among them, there are very few of his countrymen—he doesn't surround himself with people from the Urals. Burbulis is one of the rare Sverdlovsk natives on his team, though they didn't work together during Yeltsin's time as regional head; they met in Moscow. Nevertheless, a few other Uralites in less prominent roles decide to offer their boss some sound advice.

Burbulis, they point out, isn't ethnically Russian, and his surname might alienate some voters. Sure, Yeltsin has the majority's support, and victory is almost guaranteed, but why take the risk? Why sacrifice extra percentage points when, on the contrary, you could pick a running mate who would attract even more voters?

They propose Alexander Rutskoy—a legendary military pilot whom the press heavily features in 1991. At forty-three, Rutskoy has a hero's story. He fought in Afghanistan, was shot down, ejected, and broke his spine upon impact. Doctors told him he would never walk again. Yet he recovered, returned to Afghanistan, was shot down again, and evaded capture for several days without food or water in the scorching forty-degree heat. Eventually, he was caught, and—so he tells Soviet journalists—spent days hanging from a rack while being tortured. His captors promised him a Canadian passport and $2 million, but Rutskoy refused to betray military secrets and was ultimately exchanged for a Pakistani prisoner. Rutskoy became a Hero of the Soviet Union and later ran for the USSR Congress of People's Deputies with the backing of the Pamyat society but lost. However, he subsequently became a Russian parliamentarian and began supporting Yeltsin, even founding a faction within the RSFSR Communist Party called Communists for Democracy—which the press jokingly nicknames Wolves for Vegetarianism.

From a political strategy perspective, Rutskoy is the ideal candidate for vice president—a perfect counterbalance to Burbulis, the forty-five-year-old boring intellectual, former lecturer on Marxism-Leninism.

Yeltsin delays the unpleasant conversation for as long as possible, even though Burbulis—who effectively runs the campaign—has already heard rumors about his replacement. Only on the eve of filing the official documents does Yeltsin summon him to his office. "Gennady Eduardovich, we had an agreement. . . . But now the situation is such that there are concerns your surname might cost us a few percentage points in the vote." Burbulis steps aside willingly, agreeing to continue his work as before.

At that moment, Burbulis recalls how his mother advised him, before entering university, to take her Russian surname—Belonogova—to avoid unnecessary problems in life. Back then, Gennady Burbulis proudly refused. Only in the spring of 1991 does he regret it for the first time.

CANDIDATE EIDELSTEIN

The Russian presidential election is scheduled for June 12—a date Yeltsin deliberately chooses to coincide with the first anniversary of the Declaration of Independence. Alongside him, five other candidates enter the race. The candidate backed by Gorbachev is former interior minister Vadim Bakatin, who was dismissed in December the previous year for excessive liberalism. The Soviet president believes Bakatin is a strong rival to Yeltsin and can at least make it to the second round.

The conservative communists nominate a candidate of their own: recent prime minister Nikolai Ryzhkov. An even more radical figure emerges in General Albert Makashov, an active-duty military officer and former commandant of Armenia, known for his role in suppressing the Karabakh Committee. He appeals to those yearning for a "strong hand." "Makashov embodied the collective image of all that Soviet and Russian imperial romanticism at the time," journalist Nevzorov will later describe him.

But the real discovery of the campaign is Vladimir Zhirinovsky, leader of the Liberal Democratic Party of the Soviet Union. Virtually unknown before this election, Zhirinovsky becomes a star in just a month. His father's last name was Eidelstein, but—unlike Burbulis—he had prudently changed it to his mother's surname. He openly positions himself as a Russian nationalist, with slogans like "I will defend the Russians!" Zhirinovsky is a phenomenon. Many journalists are convinced he's too crude, too vulgar, to ever be taken seriously. He acts like a walking caricature of a Russian imperialist.

Yeltsin's supporters have no doubt that Zhirinovsky is a KGB protégé. However, KGB deputy head Filipp Bobkov will later claim that the idea to create Zhirinovsky's party came from party officials:

The Central Committee of the CPSU suggested creating a pseudo-party, controlled by the KGB, to channel the interests and sentiments of certain social groups. I was categorically against it; it would have been pure provocation. At a plenum, I raised the question: why should the CPSU create a rival party for itself? Let the emergence of new parties happen naturally. But I didn't convince the plenum participants.

Candidates allegedly supported by the KGB also receive help from Nevzorov. On his *600 Seconds* program, Nevzorov runs very complimentary segments about both Makashov and Zhirinovsky. In an interview, Zhirinovsky promises not to give away "a single inch of Soviet land."

On June 10, just two days before the vote, a televised debate between the candidates takes place. All candidates attend, except for Yeltsin.

"We were the front-runners. What else was there to say, and to whom? Debates were a form of self-discreditation because the competitors were neither influential nor promising," Burbulis will later explain the decision. At that moment, no one on Yeltsin's team realizes they are setting a precedent—future incumbent presidents will follow this tradition of ignoring debates. Never in his life will Putin take part in any kind of debate.

Yeltsin's victory is essentially guaranteed, as there isn't a single candidate—except perhaps the intellectual policeman Bakatin—who appeals to a democratic audience. On the contrary, all Yeltsin's opponents are vying for support from the same imperial-patriotic camp.

Yeltsin wins in the first round, securing 57.3 percent of the vote. In second place is Ryzhkov with 16.9 percent, and sensationally, Zhirinovsky comes third with 7.8 percent. Yet those who dismiss his talk of national greatness as absurd are proven wrong.

From this moment on, Zhirinovsky will remain one of Russia's most famous politicians for the next thirty years, maintaining a reputation as a nationalist populist who supports the authorities and benefits from their generous financial backing. "In my opinion, he's like a circus clown, painted in all kinds of colors on the arena, but behind the mask is a smart man who watches what's happening with a certain sadness," reflects his longtime acquaintance Alksnis. "Plus, he's the first person in Russia to make money from politics, making himself rich by selling himself and selling politics."

Gorbachev's favored candidate, Vadim Bakatin, finishes last, receiving just 3.4 percent—a figure that can be seen as a reflection of the Soviet president's own popularity at that moment.

Having been elected by popular vote, Yeltsin naturally becomes far more legitimate than Gorbachev, who was never elected directly by the people. Those in Gorbachev's inner circle begin to notice that Yeltsin increasingly makes statements about the situation in the Union as a whole and in other republics—raising suspicions that he is developing ambitions to take Gorbachev's place. Naturally, Kryuchkov delivers fresh reports to the Soviet president, alleging that Yeltsin is scheming and has American backing. The situation worsens when, following his election, Yeltsin embarks on a visit to the United States, where he is received at the White House by George Bush.

Alongside the nationwide presidential elections, mayoral races are also held in Moscow and Leningrad. The incumbents in both cities, Gavriil Popov and Anatoly Sobchak, emerge victorious. At the same time, Sobchak holds a referendum on restoring the city's historical name—St. Petersburg.

THE ARCHITECT AT THE RUINS

On May 7, the newspaper *Soviet Russia* publishes an article titled "The Architect at the Ruins." Its author is Gennady Zyuganov, a little-known bureaucrat from the Communist Party's Propaganda Department.

The article takes the form of an open letter addressed to his former boss, Alexander Yakovlev. Zyuganov accuses the former Politburo member of coining labels like "Brezhnev's stagnation" and "command-administrative system," slandering the Soviet Union, and spreading "shameless historical lies." Furthermore, Zyuganov claims that in Lithuania, Georgia, Armenia, and Eastern Europe "red flags and banners reading 'Communists, forgive us, you were right' are appearing en masse at May Day rallies."

Thanks to this article, Zyuganov becomes famous—he is the first to challenge Yakovlev, a man despised within the Communist Party of the Soviet Union. Soon Zyuganov will become the permanent leader of the Communist Party of Russia, a position he will hold for thirty years.

Meanwhile, sixty-seven-year-old Alexander Yakovlev approaches fifty-five-year-old Vitaly Korotich with a new project: the creation of a new party that would unite all democratic forces. The editor in chief of *Ogonyok* likes the idea but declares he won't participate: he is utterly exhausted and convinced that the country is leaving the democratic phase of perestroika and teetering on the brink of an authoritarian turn. "Maybe," he says, "I'll accept one of the offers and go to teach at a Western university."

"And you've lost faith too," Yakovlev says sadly. "And you're leaving too."

"Not just leaving," Korotich replies. "I feel as though I'm dying as a politician. I no longer have the strength for the turn in fate you're proposing. I envy your optimism and zest for life, but the latest events are crushing me. I don't have the energy to run from rally to rally, to tear my shirt open on my chest—it's all become unbearable!"

"And it's unbearable for you too," Yakovlev echoes.

It's a very symbolic end to their relationship. The pragmatic Korotich steps aside, no longer willing to lead the country's most popular magazine. The idealist Yakovlev keeps fighting, even though he is now unemployed.

Soon Yakovlev will announce a new party called the Movement for Democratic Reforms, together with Gavriil Popov, Anatoly Sobchak, Eduard Shevardnadze, and other prominent democrats.

COUP ATTEMPT NO. 1

On June 17, Prime Minister Pavlov and three security ministers—Kryuchkov, Yazov, and Pugo—arrive at a session of the Supreme Soviet. Everything begins with a speech by the head of the government, who demands that parliament grant him additional powers, arguing that Gorbachev himself doesn't have enough time to manage everything.

After this, the session is closed to the press, and the head of the KGB takes the podium. Kryuchkov claims that as far back as 1977 Yuri Andropov sent a report to the Politburo stating that the CIA had infiltrated agents into the Soviet leadership to destroy the Soviet Union from within. According to Kryuchkov, he now has evidence that this was precisely what has happened. He allegedly informed Gorbachev about it, but the president brushed it off. Everyone present interprets this as a thinly veiled attack on Yakovlev.

Pugo complains that he is being prevented from creating an effective structure to combat crime. Yazov laments that the USSR has turned into a second-rate power. Essentially, this is an uprising of the highest state officials right under the president's nose.

"When they laid out all the facts, everyone's hair stood on end," Alksnis will recall. "We knew things were bad, but *this* bad . . . When the security chiefs are already saying: that's it, we're done, then it's time to immediately introduce a state of emergency. The speeches were like: enough, we've had it. And then Lukyanov played an inexplicable role. He was a supporter of the Union, supposed to fight for its preservation, but instead . . . He says, 'Comrades, let's not dramatize the situation. Yes, it's serious, but let me consult with Mikhail Sergeyevich, and we'll discuss it further with the ministers,' and so on. And he convinced everyone; the decision was postponed for a few days."

However, among those in attendance at the same meeting is Arkady Murashov, a member of the Interregional Deputies Group: "It was like a groan, the groan of people who *wanted* to do something but didn't know how or what. What could they do? Force the Ukrainian *parliament* to stop passing its laws? Or the Georgians? Or the Armenians? In Kazakhstan, Nazarbayev was already sitting there as a de facto head of state. What exactly were they proposing? Force? They didn't even *have* any force left."

At first, Gorbachev does not react to what's happening—and the next day, Yanayev announces to the Supreme Soviet that the president agrees with Pavlov's proposal.

On June 20, the American ambassador to Moscow, Jack Matlock, hosts a farewell dinner for a small circle of Russian politicians—he is set to finish his term in August and is saying good-bye to colleagues. Among the invited is Moscow's mayor, Gavriil Popov. However, Popov warns that he won't be able to attend the dinner but would like to speak briefly beforehand. Matlock agrees.

The conversation takes place in the Spaso House library. Waiting for the waiter to leave the room, Popov starts discussing something trivial, but at the same time, he takes a piece of paper and writes in large letters: "*A PLAN IS UNDERWAY TO REMOVE GORBACHEV. YOU MUST INFORM BORIS NIKOLAYEVICH.*" At the time, Yeltsin is in the United States and is soon scheduled to meet with President Bush.

"I WILL INFORM HIM. WHO IS BEHIND IT?" Matlock writes on the same sheet.

"PAVLOV, KRYUCHKOV, YAZOV, LUKYANOV," Popov writes back. Then he takes the sheet, tears it into pieces, and puts them in his pocket.

To keep up appearances, they talk for a few more minutes—to deceive the KGB officers listening in. Afterward, Popov leaves.

Matlock immediately relays this information to Secretary of State James Baker, National Security Advisor Brent Scowcroft, and the president. There are still about two hours left before Bush's meeting with Yeltsin.

Soon Matlock receives a call from the State Department conveying Bush's directive: he must go to the Kremlin immediately and warn Gorbachev.

"Even if our information had been more precise, I wouldn't have dared to name the conspirators to Gorbachev. How could one believe that the American ambassador is informing the head of a state—which until recently was an adversary—that the prime minister, the head of intelligence, the defense minister, and the chairman of parliament are plotting against him?" Matlock will later write in his memoir.

The ambassador calls Chernyaev and requests an urgent meeting with Gorbachev. Chernyaev invites Matlock to come to the Kremlin. That same morning, Gorbachev's aide receives a call from an acquaintance warning him that suspicious military movements have been spotted outside Moscow. Skeptical, the aide decides not to share this information with Gorbachev but still arranges the ambassador's urgent meeting with the president.

Matlock arrives and, in Chernyaev's presence, informs Gorbachev about the impending coup—without revealing his source.

Gorbachev laughs and assures them that everything is under control: "This is 1,000% impossible. But I appreciate George sharing his concerns," Chernyaev recounts Gorbachev's response.

That same night, Bush decides to call Gorbachev directly to warn him again. The KGB, however, doesn't put the call through—Gorbachev is out for a walk with his wife, and someone decides not to disturb him.

The next day, Gorbachev reprimands Kryuchkov for not connecting the call in time. Only after this does he call Bush back himself, and the US president tells him about the brewing coup. Later Matlock will express puzzlement in his memoir over why Bush, a former CIA director, openly discussed this over a line that the KGB was undoubtedly monitoring.

It is only after this that Gorbachev heads to the Supreme Soviet to strip the prime minister of his additional powers. His speech is unexpectedly forceful and persuasive, leaving his opponents stunned and powerless.

After the session, Gorbachev speaks with reporters while his rebellious ministers stand silently nearby. "The coup is over," the president declares with a broad smile. He takes no action against the mutinous ministers, remaining absolutely convinced that they pose no threat.

JEALOUSY AND MONEY

In June 1991, Gorbachev has another moment of international glory—he is invited to the G7 (Group of Seven) summit. But this time, it's no longer the triumph it once was. Everyone in the world is aware of Gorbachev's struggles at home, though abroad he is still treated like a superstar. At the same time, he occasionally has jealous outbursts when other leaders show attention to Yeltsin or the heads of other Soviet republics.

During the G7 summit, a particularly awkward scene unfolds between Gorbachev and Bush—the Soviet leader begins reproaching the American for the lack of US economic assistance to the Soviet Union: "Isn't it strange: a hundred billion dollars were scraped up to solve a regional conflict [referring to the Persian Gulf War]. Money can be found for other programs. But what we have here is a project to transform the Soviet Union, to give it a totally new quality, to bring it into the world economy so that it will not be a disruptive force and the source of threats." And he asks whether the United States has truly decided what kind of Soviet Union it wants to see.

The implication is clear: if there's no financial support, he might once again shift toward authoritarianism.

Chernyaev listens to Gorbachev's speech and fumes, "If it weren't for Bush, you wouldn't even be here at the G7. Why are you being so tactless and senseless?"

Bush is visibly irritated.

To top it all off, after the talks, Gorbachev is informed that Bush allegedly told his aides, "Gorbachev's tired and nervous, he's not in charge, not sure of himself, that's why he suspects me of being disloyal. It looks like its time to shift our attention to Yeltsin."

"I don't believe it. . . . This contradicts everything about Bush's behavior lately," Chernyaev insists. "Why are they feeding you this nonsense?!"

THE ART OF DRINKING

For several months, the heads of the republics and the president of the USSR argued while drafting a new Union Treaty, and finally, they are close to reaching their goal. On July 29, Yeltsin and Nazarbayev visit Gorbachev at his dacha in Novo-Ogaryovo. They drink together until three in the morning—a moment of maximum closeness when they manage to agree on everything.

Late-night drinking is not Gorbachev's usual style, but he understands that he must find common ground with Yeltsin—and Nazarbayev is the only one who can help facilitate this.

As Burbulis would later recount, the presidents of Russia and Kazakhstan had "exclusive relations"—every time Nazarbayev came to Moscow, it was tradition for them to have dinner and drink all night. "For us, this was always a challenge because Boris Nikolayevich welcomed his closest ally with an open heart," Burbulis admits. He regularly participates in these meetings and often wonders: Why does Yeltsin always get so drunk, while Nazarbayev seems unaffected? Burbulis finally asks Korzhakov, Yeltsin's head of security, to discreetly inquire with Nazarbayev's bodyguards about his secret.

It turns out that Nazarbayev would begin preparing for his trips to Moscow two or three days in advance, cleansing his esophagus and stomach: "There are classic techniques using oil and a specific diet that turns the stomach into a reservoir. Liquids don't enter the bloodstream as quickly. The key trick is to occasionally step away, induce vomiting, and clear the stomach.

This way, you can keep the conversation going," Burbulis recounts. "But Yeltsin? He never did that. Our guy was just an open-hearted Russian soul."

This time, the night of shared drinking proves remarkably productive. It is decided that the Union Treaty will be signed on August 20, with Russia, Kazakhstan, and Uzbekistan as the initial signatories. Belarus, Azerbaijan, and Tajikistan will join in September, and Turkmenistan, Kyrgyzstan, and Ukraine will follow in October.*

Furthermore, in August, the Union government is set to change. Nazarbayev will replace Pavlov as prime minister, and both Kryuchkov and Pugo will step down.

The three presidents are careful to speak in ways they believe will avoid surveillance—they step outside into the warm night air, away from potential listening devices. What they don't realize is that a listening device is hidden inside the drinks cart. The recording of their conversation will later be discovered in the office of Gorbachev's chief of staff, Valery Boldin. By morning, Pavlov, Kryuchkov, and Pugo are aware of the threat hanging over them—they are less than a month away from being dismissed.

The morning after the drinking session, Gorbachev complains to Chernyaev, "Oh, Tolya. Such petty, vulgar, provincial people. Both of them! You look at them and think, 'Who are we doing all this for? With whom?' I'd just drop it all. But I know I'll have to leave it to them in the end. I'm tired."

Fortunately, Gorbachev's vacation is just around the corner. On July 31, he hosts George Bush in Moscow, and they sign the historic Strategic Arms Reduction Treaty—START I.

CHICKEN KIEV

Even US president George Bush is convinced that the Soviet Union must be preserved. On August 1, after leaving Moscow, he travels to Kyiv to persuade the Ukrainian elite to support Soviet president Mikhail Gorbachev. From Bush's perspective, the collapse of the USSR poses the danger of nuclear weapons spreading across the globe. Moreover, he is used to dealing with Gorbachev as the head of the Soviet Union.

---

* At the time, Tajikistan was one of the fifteen republics of the Soviet Union, with a population roughly equal to that of Wisconsin and a territory slightly larger than Mississippi.

In Kyiv, George Bush addresses the parliament of what is still the Ukrainian SSR, warning that the Americans are against Ukraine's secession from the USSR:

> Some people have urged the United States to choose between supporting President Gorbachev and supporting independence-minded leaders throughout the U.S.S.R. I consider this a false choice. In fairness, President Gorbachev has achieved astonishing things, and his policies of glasnost, perestroika, and democratization point toward the goals of freedom, democracy, and economic liberty. . . .
>
> We will maintain the strongest possible relationship with the Soviet Government of President Gorbachev. But we also appreciate the new realities of life in the U.S.S.R. And therefore, as a federation ourselves, we want good relations—improved relations— with the Republics. . . .
>
> Yet freedom is not the same as independence. Americans will not support those who seek independence in order to replace a far-off tyranny with a local despotism. They will not aid those who promote a suicidal nationalism based upon ethnic hatred.

The speech triggers a scandal—Ukrainian advocates for independence criticize it vehemently, and a *New York Times* journalist derisively dubs it the "Chicken Kiev Speech."

Still, Bush's rhetoric is hardly surprising. Terms like "local despotism," "suicidal nationalism," and "ethnic hatred" are not mere exaggerations at the time—they are fairly accurate descriptions of what is unfolding in Yugoslavia.

The major international story of the summer of 1991 is not the attempts to reform the USSR but the surge of violence in the Balkans. On June 25, Slovenia and Croatia declare their independence from the Yugoslav federation. The European Community (the precursor to the European Union) urges them to slow down.

The nationalist-led government in Yugoslavia refuses to accept the country's dissolution and is determined to take a hard line. By June 27, the first war breaks out—against Slovenia. In just ten days, dozens of people are killed. The most famous native of this country, Melanija Knavs—the future

Melania Trump—is twenty-one years old and still living in Slovenia. She is studying at the University of Ljubljana but has already begun her modeling career and dreams of moving to Milan or Paris.

After failing to retain Slovenia, the Yugoslav army shifts its focus to Croatia, launching a war that will last four years.

Against the backdrop of Serbian leader Slobodan Milošević, Gorbachev appears almost ideal. This is why the dominant theme in global media throughout the summer of 1991 is the urgent need to prevent the USSR from disintegrating in the Yugoslav fashion.

However, not everyone in the US administration shares George Bush's "Chicken Kiev" approach. One key figure believes that the breakup of the Soviet Union should not be feared but rather encouraged—after all, if Gorbachev fails to hold on to power, he could easily be replaced by a general from the army or the KGB. It would be far easier for the United States to deal with fifteen newly independent states than a single, unpredictable USSR. That figure is Defense Secretary Dick Cheney.

SPA IN MOSCOW

On August 4, Gorbachev, along with Raisa, their daughter, son-in-law, grand-daughters, and Chernyaev, departs for his vacation in Crimea. As protocol dictates, the state's top leadership gather at the airport to see him off.

A popular myth persists, based on Anatoly Lukyanov's recollections. Supposedly, while walking across the tarmac to board the plane, Gorbachev turns around and says, "Well, go ahead and try." This phrase is interpreted as him tacitly blessing their plans to declare a state of emergency during his absence. However, this is clearly fiction—it contradicts all logic of the events. Everything that happened before and after makes it clear that Gorbachev neither wanted a state of emergency nor planned to delegate such authority in his absence.

On August 8, Kryuchkov meets with the head of the Moscow party committee, Yuri Prokofiev. They discuss that Gorbachev has lost authority, the people no longer support him, and it is therefore necessary to negotiate with Yeltsin.

"Force him to cooperate! Yeltsin is a coward. Ambitious, but a coward. That's what we need to bet on," Kryuchkov reflects. Prokofiev suggests playing on Yeltsin's hatred toward Gorbachev. They agree that Yazov must speak with the president of Russia and convince him: "Yeltsin isn't stupid and understands that there's an army standing behind the marshal."

On August 17, several Soviet leaders gather at ABC, a code name for a luxurious spa hotel in Moscow owned by the KGB. Kryuchkov plays the host, while the guests include two Central Committee secretaries—Oleg Shenin (responsible for personnel) and Oleg Baklanov (overseeing the military-industrial complex)—as well as Defense Minister Yazov, Prime Minister Pavlov, and the head of Gorbachev's office, Valery Boldin.

They start with a steam in the sauna before stepping outside for fresh air. A table is already set in a shaded gazebo. Yazov, Pavlov, and Shenin drink vodka, while Kryuchkov, Baklanov, and Boldin opt for whiskey.

Kryuchkov begins by stating that Pavlov will be dismissed after the twentieth. "I'm ready to resign right now!" the prime minister fires back defiantly, though he continues to complain that the country is on the brink of famine and that it's time to declare a state of emergency.

The head of the KGB explains that he has been regularly briefing Gorbachev, but the president "reacts inadequately." Kryuchkov proposes forming a Committee on the State of Emergency and offering Gorbachev the option to hand over power. If he refuses, they'll leave him in Crimea and announce he's unwell, with Yanayev stepping in as acting president.

When the vodka runs out, an officer is sent to fetch more.

They then discuss who will travel to Crimea. Yazov jokes that Boldin must go, as he is closest to Gorbachev. "When he sees you, the president will probably say, 'Et tu, Brute?'"

"If I must, I'll go," Boldin responds.

Yazov refuses to go himself, suggesting General Varennikov go in his place. The defense minister has several reasons to remain in Moscow. Chief among them, perhaps, is that his wife, Emma, had been in a serious car accident in May and had only recently emerged from a coma in August. He has no desire to leave his ailing wife. Later Yazov would name another reason: "It felt awkward to face the president with an ultimatum, looking like a traitor."

Yazov leaves first, while the others stay for dinner. Saying good-bye, the defense minister mutters aloud, "He could have signed the treaty and then gone on vacation. Everything would have been fine. . . ."

GUESTS FROM MOSCOW

At 4:30 p.m. on August 18, five cars drive onto the grounds of the presidential residence Zarya in Crimea. Normally, they wouldn't have been allowed in—after all, they arrived unannounced. But emerging from the first vehicles are KGB generals, who also happen to oversee the president's personal security. Seeing automatic weapons pointed at them, one of the KGB generals shouts, "Put those weapons down! What, do you want it to be like Romania here?!" The guards are confused—what does Romania have to do with anything? The visitors are let through. They enter Gorbachev's house and settle in the living room.

The head of Gorbachev's personal security informs the president that he has unexpected guests. Gorbachev is surprised—how can that be? He hasn't summoned anyone. He prepares to call Kryuchkov to ask what kind of surprise this is. But the phones don't work.

Gorbachev immediately understands what this likely means—only a coup. So he doesn't leave his office, instead mentally preparing for the confrontation. Then he calls to Raisa and warns her. She already knows—she saw the visitors pass by without greeting her.

Then he invites into his office the visitors, who have been loitering in the living room. They are two Central Committee secretaries—Baklanov and Shenin—along with the commander in chief of the Ground Forces, Varennikov, and the head of Gorbachev's staff, Boldin.

They had agreed that Shenin would start the conversation, but things quickly go off script. Gorbachev roars at them, cursing furiously. Baklanov responds, suggesting that the president must be tired, urging him to think about his health. He informs Gorbachev that the signing of the Union Treaty will not happen and that Yeltsin has already been arrested. Then he corrects himself: *he will be arrested* as soon as he returns to Moscow from Kazakhstan. Baklanov proposes that Gorbachev temporarily transfer his powers to Yanayev and agree to the introduction of a state of emergency.

"Mikhail Sergeyevich, you won't need to do anything. Stay here. We'll do all the dirty work for you," Baklanov concludes his brief introduction.

Gorbachev sharply replies that he won't sign anything.

"Resign!" demands General Varennikov. Gorbachev refuses, and the general launches into a passionate speech, accusing the president of violating the oath he swore on the constitution, enabling separatists, neglecting the military, and so on. He speaks so long that Gorbachev rudely interrupts him:

"I've heard all this before. Go back and report my position," Gorbachev instructs them, as if he were still their superior.

The visitors head toward the exit, but there they are blocked by Raisa. "What do you want here?" she asks.

"We are your friends." Baklanov smiles and tries to extend his hand. She ignores the gesture.

The gates are shut behind the visitors—no one is allowed to leave the residence. The president and his family remain locked in, cut off from the outside world.

"WE HAVE NO PLAN"

By 8:00 p.m., Kryuchkov summons everyone to the Kremlin—decisions about the formation of the State Committee on the State of Emergency (GKChP) must be finalized in Prime Minister Pavlov's office.

Both Pavlov and Yanayev are late. Both are slightly drunk. Yet when Yanayev finally arrives, it's the prime minister who jokingly scolds him: "Here we are discussing important matters, and the vice president is out gallivanting somewhere."

Kryuchkov leads the meeting but yields the chair to Lukyanov. The head of parliament is visibly agitated, demanding that his name be removed from the list of GKChP members. He insists that if Gorbachev is unwell, there must be a formal medical statement to prove it.

After 10:00 p.m., the delegation from Crimea arrives. They recount their conversation with Gorbachev. Everyone then turns to Yanayev—it is now up to him to declare a state of emergency.

"I will not sign this decree," says the vice president, lighting a new cigarette from the stub of the last one. "The president must return after he's had some rest, recovered, and come to his senses. Besides, I don't feel ready—neither morally nor professionally—to fulfill these duties."

Yanayev continues to resist, demanding that Lukyanov assume the president's duties instead. But Lukyanov pulls out the constitution and points to the clause showing that this responsibility falls to the vice president.

In the end, Yanayev is persuaded. He signs, followed by Pavlov, Kryuchkov, Pugo, Yazov, and Baklanov.

"What do you have? Give me the plan," Lukyanov demands angrily.

"We have no plan, Anatoly Ivanovich," says Yazov.

"But why not? We do have a plan," insists Kryuchkov.

He announces that a list has already been prepared of dozens of politicians to be arrested immediately. "We'll need a thousand!" Pavlov quips with a laugh.

Boldin starts feeling unwell and is taken to the hospital. Shortly after, Yazov heads to his dacha to be with his wife.

MORNING AT THE DACHA

Boris Yeltsin is supposed to fly to Moscow from Almaty in the afternoon of August 18, but Nursultan Nazarbayev invites him to stay for dinner. Given their "exclusive relationship," Yeltsin does not refuse. According to the memoir of his press secretary Voshchanov, Yeltsin swims, plays the domra, drinks heavily, and as a result, his plane departs from Almaty five hours late.

It's hard to say what role this dinner plays in world history—whether Yeltsin would actually have been arrested upon arrival in Moscow, as Baklanov expects. According to one version, the KGB has a plan to redirect Yeltsin's plane from Vnukovo to the Chkalovsky military airfield, where his security detail would be neutralized, and he himself would be sent to Zavidovo, the government dacha where Brezhnev loved to hunt, and locked up there. However, this plan is ultimately not carried out. Perhaps the KGB assumes that a drunk Yeltsin poses no immediate threat and that there will be time to arrest him in the morning.

But Yeltsin's press secretary Voshchanov describes the events differently. According to him, Yeltsin and Nazarbayev drink late into the night, after which the Russian president is loaded onto the plane and flown to Moscow. Meanwhile, Defense Minister Yazov is waiting for him at Vnukovo Airport. The decision has been made that Yazov will speak with the Russian president and persuade him not to resist the state of emergency. After waiting for more than an hour, Yazov leaves for home, following reports that Yeltsin's arrival is delayed indefinitely due to the Russian president's "ill health." Yazov understands perfectly well what this means and knows that talking to an "unwell Yeltsin" would be pointless.

Meanwhile, the president of Russia arrives at Moscow. His body is placed into a vehicle and transported from the airport to his dacha in the government compound Arkhangelskoye-2.

On August 19, Yeltsin's daughter wakes him up. On television, announcers are already reading statements about the introduction of a state of emergency. At this stage, it's already clear that nothing is going according to plan.

Throughout the morning, Yeltsin's wife calls his associates, and soon they all gather at his dacha. The Russian president, having heard the news, calls the leaders of Ukraine and Belarus. They are quite reserved, both saying they lack sufficient information to make any decisions. Yeltsin also calls Pavel Grachev, the commander of the Airborne Forces. They had recently met, had a few drinks together, and, Yeltsin believes, bonded. "Are you with us?" Yeltsin asks. Grachev, who days earlier had been tasked with developing plans to seize key buildings after the state of emergency was introduced, hesitates but replies, "With you!" He doesn't disclose his role in the coup to Yeltsin.

Soon, in Yeltsin's kitchen, his closest allies gather: Gennady Burbulis, Ivan Silayev, and even the mayor of St. Petersburg, Anatoly Sobchak, who happens to be in Moscow that day. They conclude that a coup d'etat has occurred and decide that negotiating with the conspirators is impossible. They draft an "Appeal to the People," calling on citizens to ignore the orders of the GKChP.

Then—fearing they might all be rounded up together—Russia's leaders disperse. Sobchak flies back to St. Petersburg, leaving Yeltsin his bodyguard. Yeltsin, Silayev, Burbulis, and the others, each in his own car, head to the Russian White House—the Russian parliament building in Moscow.

Here, a decisive moment occurs. Approaching the highway, they spot an ambush. Members of the Alpha Group—the same forces that stormed the Vilnius TV tower six months earlier and in 1979, seized Amin's palace in Kabul—are now stationed near Yeltsin's dacha, at the exit from Arkhangelskoye-2. However, the Russian officials speed past them—and the commandos don't stop them. For some reason, Kryuchkov has ordered them to keep an eye on Yeltsin rather than arrest him. Perhaps he still believes that an agreement can be reached with the Russian president.

One of the few people arrested that morning is parliamentarian Telman Gdlyan, who holds no power and has no political influence.

Since early morning, the head of the KGB and the minister of defense have been holding meetings with their subordinates. Yazov orders several military units to be brought into Moscow: two airborne divisions, one tank division, and one motorized rifle division.

Kryuchkov calls Yazov later in the morning:

"I can't find anyone: Pavlov, Yanayev, Baklanov—no one's here."

"Where could they have gone?" the defense minister wonders.

"They were drinking with Yanayev until morning," the KGB chief sighs.

YELTSIN ON THE TANK

Yeltsin arrives at the White House. His team begins to assess the situation: Burbulis heads the political headquarters, Rutskoy prepares for defense, and Russia's foreign minister, Andrei Kozyrev, starts calling diplomats. Soon they begin to gather to find out what is happening. On one side of the White House stand black cars with diplomatic license plates; on the other side, tanks are coming. Yet no one stops the foreigners from entering the building or from meeting with Yeltsin.

Before the meeting with the ambassadors, Yeltsin's aides remind him that he must call for Gorbachev's release. Yeltsin is not very pleased: "Why? People don't care about him. They support the president of Russia," he says irritably.

Around eleven o'clock, an aide runs in and, according to Burbulis's recollections, nearly shouts, "The tanks that came to surround us have stopped; some crews have opened their hatches and are talking with people." Yeltsin stands up and says resolutely, "I'm going out there."

Burbulis tries to dissuade him: there could be snipers on the rooftops, provocateurs in the crowd—it's a huge risk. Yeltsin suggests at least stepping out onto the balcony to assess the situation. After standing on the balcony for a couple of minutes and seeing the crowd gathered in the square, he decides: "That's it. Give me the text of the appeal—I'm going out there."

And so, he goes down, climbs onto a tank, and reads the appeal that had been written that morning at his dacha. Naturally, a crowd of journalists surrounds the White House—and now, the main news worldwide is not only the coup but also Yeltsin's resistance.

"This was a brilliant, I would even say instinctive, political move," Burbulis later assesses Yeltsin's action. "In this act, there was not only a chance for victory but victory itself. By noon, he had completely turned the situation around. From that moment on, we were receiving calls all day—we realized that something incredible had been accomplished."

Meanwhile, in the Kremlin, the first meeting of the GKChP begins—everyone is present except for Pavlov, who had been taken directly from his dacha to the hospital. They decide to immediately arrest Yeltsin, shut down all newspapers except the communist ones, and impose martial law in Moscow.

SOBCHAK CURSES

On the morning of August 19, journalist Alexander Nevzorov is feeling elated—he immediately heads to see General Viktor Samsonov, commander of the Leningrad Military District, and drags him to the TV station to record an announcement. "I powdered the bastard up, powdered him up, sat him in front of the camera, and said: come on, let's go, let's roll," he will recall years later. Samsonov announces that martial law has been declared in the city.

Meanwhile, the mayor of Leningrad, Anatoly Sobchak, is flying in from Moscow after the morning meeting at Yeltsin's dacha. His aide, Vladimir Putin, does not meet him at the airport—he is on vacation. Instead of heading to his office, Sobchak goes straight to the headquarters of the Leningrad Military District on Palace Square.

Bursting into General Samsonov's office, Sobchak finds all the city's top brass assembled there: the head of the KGB, the First Secretaries of the city and regional Communist Party committees. According to Sobchak, in that moment, he recalls every curse word he has ever heard in his life—and begins shouting at them, framing it all as a legal argument.

He demands to know if they understand the conditions under which a state of emergency can be declared.

"First, in the event of war. Is there a war? No! Second, in the case of natural disasters. Is there a natural disaster? No. Third, during an epizootic outbreak. Do we have an epizootic outbreak, for fuck's sake?"

No one in the room knows what "epizootic" means, but everyone shakes their heads no.

"Then the state of emergency has been declared illegally! This is a goddamn state crime!" he roars. "Do you want to be tried as state criminals in a new Nuremberg tribunal? Disperse the fuck out of here!"

The local officials, visibly rattled, begin to scatter. Left alone with General Samsonov, Sobchak softens his tone.

"I understand you're a military man, and you have your orders. I know you've already ordered the Pskov Airborne Division to enter the city. What matters to us is that there are no tanks in the streets and not a drop of blood spilled."

He extends his hand to Samsonov.

"Let's settle this man to man. No one knows who's going to win this. If your side prevails, you'll be the first to arrest me—I won't resist. And you'll get your next star for arresting Sobchak. If we win, I promise you won't face any punishment. I'll get you off the hook."

Samsonov agrees to stop the tanks on the outskirts of St. Petersburg.

BACK TO THE USSR

The main goal of the State Committee on the State of Emergency (GKChP) is to restore the old Soviet power vertical, eliminate separatist governments in the republics, and stop all discussions of independence. The first target is, of course, the Baltic republics, where Moscow's security forces already tried to impose a state of emergency six months earlier.

A state of emergency is declared in all three republics, military equipment appears on the streets, and soldiers seize local TV stations. At the same time, the authorities in all three republics call what has happened a coup and urge nonviolent resistance.

The most dramatic events unfold in Riga. "The Latvian SSR was the only republic where the GKChP actually succeeded," Alksnis will later recall, "at least for two days, on August 19–20. The Riga OMON takes power in the republic during those days, and not a single protest rally takes place, even though the Popular Front used to easily gather thousands of people."

This is the personal initiative of the OMON commander, Cheslav Mlynnik. He does not wait for orders from his superiors in the Ministry of Internal Affairs or the command of the Baltic Military District. Years later, he will proudly say that he could have become the dictator of Latvia.

On the night of August 20, Prime Minister Ivars Godmanis, expecting an assault, dismisses all his staff, including his security, and stays alone in his office—waiting. When the OMON arrive, he protests their actions but offers no resistance, leaving the building with his head held high.

A completely different approach is taken by another independence leader, known for his uncompromising stance toward the Kremlin—Zviad Gamsakhurdia.

One of Yazov's deputies arrives in Tbilisi with a specific demand: to disband the National Guard. The president of Georgia agrees and immediately signs an order to transform it into a police unit. Strangely, this former dissident—who for months behaved with maximum independence and never traveled to Moscow—shows complete loyalty to the GKChP.

However, the National Guard fighters headed by the president's former classmate Tengiz Kitovani refuse to obey the president's order—this marks the beginning of a serious conflict between them.

General Varennikov arrives at the office of Leonid Kravchuk, the Speaker of the Ukrainian Parliament, and demands that a state of emergency be declared in Ukraine. The latter doesn't argue but knows excessive bureaucracy will stall the process without consequences. He promises to bring Varennikov's proposal to the Supreme Soviet—after all, under the law, they're the ones who must approve a state of emergency. "And if you don't bring it up, we'll help you," Varennikov hisses threateningly.

But for that, Kravchuk explains, he needs documents: a medical report on Gorbachev's condition, written orders from Moscow, GKChP decrees. "Even Lenin, when he sent out his representatives, wrote out their credentials by hand, specifying what tasks they were authorized to handle."

Varennikov flies to Lviv to assess the situation. The GKChP expects unrest there—Western Ukraine is where pro-independence activists are most active. But the city is quiet.

CIAO, DARLING

On the day of the coup, Alla Pugacheva is in Odessa, on Ukraine's Black Sea coast. The night before, she had performed a concert. When she learns that the old Soviet Union is trying to claw its way back, she does something completely out of character—she goes to the people. Together with Mikhail Zhvanetsky, the beloved satirist and proud son of Odessa, she heads to the beach.

A huge crowd quickly gathers around the two celebrities, everyone eager to hear what the singer thinks of the latest news.

"They won't succeed. Their time is over," she says confidently.

"Alla Borisovna, what if we elect you president?" someone in the crowd shouts.

"Go ahead; I'm ready," Pugacheva replies with a smile.

"Will you manage?"

"Me?" She pauses for effect. "Of course."

The crowd around Pugacheva swells until it starts to feel like an impromptu rally.

"Since we're all gathered here, why not hold a protest march? But it would be better to go with a song. What should we sing?" she asks.

Someone suggests the once-popular Polish revolutionary song "Warszawianka":

Hostile winds blow over us,
Dark forces oppress us with spite,
Into a fateful battle, we march against our foes. . . .

But no one remembers the rest. So Pugacheva offers one of her own hits, "Ciao, Darling," a farewell to a tiresome husband. Everyone knows the lyrics by heart:

Ciao, ciao, Superman,
Ciao, ciao, Troubadour,
Ciao, suspicious, cold,
Forever dissatisfied, petty bore!

The whole beach sings in unison—a fittingly absurd farewell to the Soviet Union, though the sunbathers, caught in the moment, likely don't realize what exactly they're saying good-bye to.

Afterward, the singer suggests a collective swim, and together with hundreds of fans, she wades into the sea. Everyone is ecstatic, and no one fears breaking the ban on mass gatherings.

ADVICE FROM PINOCHET

During the day, fifty-nine-year-old Emma Yazova learns about the coup her husband is involved in from the TV news. She immediately calls a friend and asks for a ride to Moscow—she is still in a cast after her accident and cannot move on her own. They arrive at the Ministry of Defense, where Yazov meets his wife at the entrance. She is in tears, telling him this is a civil war and begging him to stop everything and call Gorbachev immediately.

"There's no connection," he replies.

At that moment, the GKChP press conference begins on television.

"What kind of people have you gotten involved with?" She cries even harder. "You used to laugh at them. Call Gorbachev!"

The press conference is indeed a bizarre improvisation. Sitting in a row are Yanayev, Baklanov, Pugo—but nearly all the questions are answered by Yanayev. His hands are trembling, and he keeps blowing his nose into a handkerchief.

The only real news he shares is that on August 27 a session of the Supreme Soviet will convene to legitimize the GKChP. In addition, he states that all media outlets will have to undergo a reregistration process.

A *Pravda* correspondent quotes Boris Yeltsin, who has called the state of emergency a "right-wing reactionary unconstitutional coup" and urged a general strike. Yanayev responds that he spoke with Yeltsin and is continuing to seek ways to cooperate with him, adding, "The long-suffering people cannot afford such luxuries as a general strike."

The boldest question comes from *Nezavisimaya Gazeta* journalist Tatyana Malkina:

"Do you realize that you carried out a coup last night, and which comparison do you think is more fitting—1917 or 1964?" (She is referring to the overthrow of Tsar Nicholas II and the removal of Khrushchev from power, respectively.)

"With all due respect, I must disagree," Yanayev replies, insisting that the GKChP is acting within constitutional norms and claiming that any historical parallels are dangerous.

The trolling continues with a correspondent from the Italian newspaper *Corriere della Sera*, who asks whether the GKChP consulted with General Pinochet, the infamous former dictator of Chile. Yanayev ignores the question.

A *Kommersant* correspondent asks whether an investigation will be launched into Gorbachev's actions. Yanayev responds that Gorbachev "deserves nothing but respect, not an investigation. He is not a state criminal but a man who did everything to set us on this democratic path."

The whole Soviet Union is watching the press conference, and everyone can see how pitiful and unsure the members of the GKChP look. But the most important viewer sits in the Ministry of Defense—Emma Yazova. She watches, crying, and pleads with her husband to come to his senses and stay away from these useless men.

EVENING AT THE DACHA

That evening, the mayor of St. Petersburg, Anatoly Sobchak, arrives at the city's TV center and at 8:00 p.m. appears on St. Petersburg television, denouncing the coup and calling its organizers a "bunch of irresponsible political hacks." He urges citizens to gather the following day for a rally at Palace Square.

Alexander Nevzorov sees the broadcast and immediately calls Anatoly Lukyanov in Moscow to share his thoughts. However, the chairman of the Supreme Soviet calmly reassures him that everything is under control. Nevzorov is livid: How can Lukyanov dismiss Sobchak's speech so lightly? He demands to know what Lukyanov plans to do next. "I'm thinking of heading to my dacha," Lukyanov replies.

"What are the GKChP members doing?" Nevzorov presses. Lukyanov responds that they're resting too.

Well, that's it—we're screwed, Nevzorov would later recall thinking.

Sobchak's speech isn't the only act of defiance against the GKChP's orders to control TV broadcasts. At 10:00 p.m., during the *Vremya* news program on the main channel, journalist Sergei Medvedev airs a report about the protest rally near the White House, including footage of Boris Yeltsin's now-iconic speech from atop a tank. This is a blatant sign that the top brass's directives are being ignored. Even on the first day, many fail to take the coup seriously, with acts of sabotage spreading. By airing this report, Central Television essentially legitimizes the rally at the White House. The next day, tens of thousands of people flood to the scene.

According to Nevzorov's version of events, he pitches an unconventional idea to the GKChP members on how to disperse the growing crowd near the White House—using movie special effects.

"I looked at the mood of the crowd," he later explains. "They were wonderful people, but these were all, essentially, intellectuals who had never smelled blood. Naturally, if they saw automatic gunfire erupt, with people next to them collapsing in pools of blood, their coats ripping open and guts spilling out—they would've panicked and run. So I asked for a few competent officers who could be rigged with movie-style fake blood. At the signal, the 'gunmen' would open fire, and protesters would see defenseless, unarmed people writhing and bleeding out right next to them. Of course, they would have scattered."

According to Nevzorov, the minister of defense, Yazov, finds the idea amusing.

"Oh yes, excellent plan, excellent plan—but where the hell are we going to get that stuff?" Yazov reportedly asks. Nevzorov assures him he can grab it from a film studio.

"First, we couldn't find a pyrotechnician. Then, there were no officers available. And finally, it turned out all the coup leaders had already left for their dachas," Nevzorov grumbles in frustration.

CHERNYAEV'S SWIM TRUNKS

"I declare that everything being said about the state of my health is a lie," Gorbachev says. "An unconstitutional coup has been carried out based on lies. . . . I have been deprived of all communication, all contact with the outside world. I'm under arrest, and no one is allowed to leave the premises of the dacha. . . ."

Gorbachev's speech is recorded on a home video camera by his son-in-law, Anatoly Virgansky. He and the president's daughter, Irina, have a few video-tapes lying around—they record the ousted president's address directly over an American erotic melodrama, *9½ Weeks*. Later they take apart the cassette, cut the tape into pieces with manicure scissors—they had filmed four takes—and start figuring out how to smuggle the president's message to the outside world.

Around this time, Gorbachev's aide Anatoly Chernyaev shares an idea with Raisa Gorbacheva. He's a strong swimmer, so he suggests making a break for it through the water—after all, the guards haven't banned detainees from swimming. "I could easily manage five, maybe even ten kilometers. Should I risk it?" he asks.

Raisa thinks it's an excellent idea: "I'll pack the tape into a small bundle and give it to you in the evening." Gorbachev chimes in, suggesting they hide the tape in his swim trunks.

Despite their isolation, the Gorbachevs have access to a radio—they can even pick up foreign stations. This means they know everything happening outside, including Yeltsin's rebellion and the rally near the White House in Moscow.

All of this fills them with extreme optimism—until they suddenly hear on the news that a group of doctors is about to be sent to Crimea to conduct a medical examination of Gorbachev and produce proof that he is ill and unfit to carry out his duties. This news makes Raisa feel faint—she believes that doctors from the KGB will soon arrive at the dacha and could do anything to a person: maim him, turn him into a disabled invalid. Her anxiety leads to a minor stroke.

As it turns out, her fears are unfounded—the GKChP has no intention of sending any doctors to Gorbachev. Kryuchkov simply instructs the Kremlin's physicians to fabricate a fake medical certificate stating Gorbachev's illness—forging documents quickly is much simpler than torturing the president.

ELIMINATING YELTSIN

On the morning of August 20, Kryuchkov decides that delaying Yeltsin's arrest is no longer an option—he must be captured and sent to Zavidovo. However, the president of Russia is no longer leaving the White House, meaning it will have to be taken by storm.

Meanwhile, in Moscow, near the White House, a massive rally is gathering—against the GKChP and in support of democracy. At the same time, an equally large demonstration begins in St. Petersburg, on Palace Square.

The city's mayor, Anatoly Sobchak, calls Vladimir Kryuchkov in the morning—but not to protest the actions of the GKChP. It's a personal matter—his deputy, Vladimir Putin, has submitted a resignation letter from the security services, and Sobchak is supposedly asking for the request to be expedited and signed. At least, that's how Putin will tell it later. It's rather surprising, though, that amid all this chaos, Sobchak and Kryuchkov are discussing Putin—even more so that Kryuchkov, dropping everything, signs the resignation as soon as the next day. Yet this is Putin's version of events.

Around midday, several generals gather in the office of USSR deputy defense minister Vladislav Achalov to develop a plan to storm the White House—they name it Operation Grom (Thunder). During the meeting, General Alexander Lebed arrives, visibly worried, reporting that there are too many people on the square and barricades are being built. Significant casualties are unavoidable.

By evening, at 8:00, the plan is discussed at the GKChP meeting. Everyone is in favor. In addition, Baklanov brings decrees introducing direct presidential rule in the Baltic republics, Moldova, Georgia, and several cities in Russia.

UNDER SIEGE

On the morning of August 19, cellist Slava Rostropovich wakes up at home in Paris, exhausted and shattered after a long concert tour. He turns on the news and doesn't immediately grasp what's happening. Switching to CNN, he sees the faces of the members of the GKChP. *If my homeland is dying, if the place where I was born is perishing, maybe this will be my grave too*, he will later recall thinking.

He packs a small bag, "thinking I won't come back." He doesn't take his cello. Telling his wife he has some business to attend to, he leaves without a word to anyone else and heads straight to Charles de Gaulle Airport. He's determined to fly to Moscow—much like Liu Xiaobo, who three years earlier flew from New York to Beijing after hearing about the protests in Tiananmen Square.

The problem is, Rostropovich doesn't have Soviet citizenship—he never updated his documents, despite Gorbachev's decree, since traveling the world with a Monaco passport is far more convenient. Moreover, he doesn't even have a Soviet visa. There's no guarantee he'll be let into Moscow.

Nevertheless, upon arriving at Sheremetyevo Airport, the musician strides confidently to passport control. He knows that a so-called Congress of Compatriots is scheduled to take place in Moscow around these days—a gathering of emigrants invited to return to their homeland. At the border, he declares that he's been invited to the congress, and that some misunderstanding must have prevented him from obtaining a visa in advance. Of course, they recognize him immediately—and issue a visa on the spot.

From the airport, Rostropovich doesn't head to the congress, but straight to the White House.

Russia's foreign minister, Andrei Kozyrev, stealthily makes his way through Sheremetyevo, navigating border checks with utmost discretion, and boards a flight to Paris—ready to form a government-in-exile if necessary. At the same time, Russian parliamentarian Galina Starovoitova, already in London, is tasked with meeting Margaret Thatcher to lay the groundwork for an exile government.

According to Gennady Burbulis, two key groups are operating inside the White House: the military defense group, led by Alexander Rutskoy, and the civilian intellectual group, headed by Burbulis. The head of Russia's KGB, General Viktor Ivanenko, spends three days tirelessly calling his colleagues, persuading and explaining to them, "Hold back, step aside, endure this for two or three days, and we'll overcome this threat. It's better for you not to take on this responsibility."

Later on August 20, Burbulis meets Yegor Gaidar. The well-known journalist and economic editor of *Pravda* arrives to show his moral support. The two men—Burbulis at forty-five, Gaidar at thirty-five—shake hands. Gaidar says, "Once this idiocy is over, let's sit down and discuss what can be done in this post-emergency situation—something useful and important." That same evening, Gaidar and a few friends leave the Communist Party.

For some reason, the arrested Gdlyan is released this evening—and even given a ride to the White House.

The entire White House prepares for a night assault. Rostropovich is assigned a bodyguard named Yura, who is given a machine gun. Yura, however, doesn't know how to shoot, so he is given the following instruction: if the assault begins, shout, "Don't shoot; Rostropovich is here!"

Yeltsin, together with Burbulis, bodyguard Korzhakov, Moscow mayor Popov, and press secretary Voshchanov, descends into the bomb shelter built beneath the building for use in the event of a nuclear war.

THE NIGHT ASSAULT

By evening, the mood shifts dramatically among troops, from the rank and file to their commanders. It becomes clear that the crowd outside the White House numbers between fifty thousand and one hundred thousand people—far more than General Lebed had seen earlier in the day. Many members of Alpha, the elite KGB unit, openly discuss the situation, and some announce they won't take part in the assault. Ultimately, Alpha commander Viktor Karpukhin informs Kryuchkov's deputy that he considers the storming of the White House "inexpedient."

Defense Minister Yazov speaks with air force commander Yevgeny Shaposhnikov.

"We need to find a way out of this situation," Shaposhnikov says.

"What way out?" asks Yazov.

"With dignity. We need to pull the troops out of Moscow," Shaposhnikov replies.

"And the GKChP?" Yazov presses.

"Declare it illegal and dissolve it."

One of the few who remains resolute is Interior Minister Boris Pugo. When his deputy, General Boris Gromov, tries to talk him out of the assault, Pugo smiles and says, "It's an order. And an order must be carried out."

Around midnight, a column of twenty BMPs moves toward the center to take control of the Garden Ring. When the convoy enters the tunnel under Kalinin Avenue, protesters, fearing an imminent assault on the White House, attempt to block it. In the ensuing panic and chaotic gunfire, three people are killed—Dmitry Komar, Ilya Krichevsky, and Vladimir Usov.

This becomes the turning point of the night—and arguably, the entire coup.

Around this time, Defense Minister Dmitry Yazov returns from the GKChP meeting. His deputy, Vladislav Achalov, briefs him on the situation in the city: the atmosphere around the Russian parliament building is tense, the number of defenders is growing, the first clashes have occurred, and there are casualties.

Yazov's psychological state is deteriorating: all his subordinates tell him that no one wants to take responsibility and the military will end up as scapegoats—just as had happened before in Tbilisi and Vilnius. None of the generals are keen on the idea of firing tank shells at Muscovites. His wife, Emma, is sobbing at home. She still begs him to come to his senses.

Yazov loosens his tie and orders Achalov, "Go to your office! Give the command: 'Stop!'"

Achalov calls Pavel Grachev, the commander of the Airborne Forces, and Boris Gromov, the commander of the Interior Forces, to inform them that Yazov has ordered the troops to stand down.

"I think that, of course, the days of August 19–21 were the best party in Moscow's history," recalls journalist Artemy Troitsky. "Honestly, I've never seen anything livelier in Moscow. It was exhilarating and inspiring. Three guys, unfortunately, died—that was a tragedy, but, well, accidents happen at parties sometimes. Overall, though, it was a celebration—people built barricades, lit fires, sang songs, and the enthusiasm was absolutely extraordinary. It was a holiday, a massive celebration, especially at night when attacks were expected and everyone naturally felt like heroes."

"I'M OUT OF THE GAME"

At around two in the morning, Yazov informs Kryuchkov that he has ordered the troops to stand down. Kryuchkov yells at him, but Yazov hangs up the phone and summons Achalov. "I'm not talking to him anymore," the frustrated defense minister declares, and sends Achalov, along with General Varennikov, to the GKChP meeting in his place.

"What, lost your nerve?" Baklanov greets them mockingly.

A long argument ensues over who is to blame for the failure. The KGB accuses the military of "not wanting to do anything and being incapable of anything." Baklanov lashes out at Kryuchkov for failing to cut off water, phones, and electricity to the White House and demands immediate action. "If we don't take them, they'll hang us," he says about the Russian leadership.

Kryuchkov agrees to cut off the White House's phone lines, but as for the electricity, he shrugs: "It's too late. Dawn is already breaking.

"We need to rethink everything," he concludes.

Around 4:00 a.m., Kryuchkov contacts Burbulis and asks him to arrange a meeting with Yeltsin. "I was very unsettled by Kryuchkov's behavior," Burbulis would later recall. "He persistently appealed to the idea that they just needed to meet, that he and Boris Nikolayevich could come to an agreement. He would explain everything to Yeltsin. Kryuchkov seemed to have some inner certainty that if he could just meet with Yeltsin face-to-face, he would explain it all." But Yeltsin refuses the meeting.

The President of Russia spends the night in the bunker, in the so-called reserve office. According to the recollections of press secretary Voshchanov, a lavish table is set there. They drink, once it becomes clear that the threat of an assault has passed, and everyone heads back upstairs—except for Moscow mayor Popov, who is unable to walk.

"Pashka, I got drunk like a pig!" he says to Voshchanov.

The security detail decides not to drag the mayor upstairs and leaves him to sleep in the bomb shelter.

"I'm out of the game," Yazov says to Kryuchkov over the phone in the morning. "The military collegium is gathering now to decide on withdrawing troops from Moscow. I'm not going to any more of your meetings!" With no other option, the committee members drive over to the Ministry of Defense themselves.

Baklanov, outraged, asks, "Why did we even start this in the first place?"

"We knew how to make a mess—now we need to own up to it," Yazov retorts.

Everyone begins shouting at one another. Yazov proposes flying to see Gorbachev. Moscow party secretary Prokofiev yells, "Give me a pistol; I'd rather shoot myself! . . ."

"They lacked audacity, decisiveness," Nevzorov later reflects on the GKChP members. "But they couldn't have it—these people had been hollowed out by the system. Yazov was afraid people would really throw themselves under the tanks by the dozens, like they did in China. In his mind, all he could see was Tiananmen Square. There was no Leon Trotsky there who could calmly shoot one of his dinner guests mid-conversation and then continue talking as they dragged the body out, leaving a trail of blood behind."

In the morning, Yeltsin's press secretary comes up from the bunker to his office and finds Rostropovich sitting there, drinking instant coffee.

"My dear boy! Don't be mad, I made myself at home," the musician says with a grin. So, is it victory? Victory, brother! We did it!"

"How about we have a little drink?" Voshchanov asks.

"For victory? Pour it, my good man!"

A CONCERT IN SIBERIA

Boris Grebenshchikov finds out about the coup in Moscow while on tour in Eastern Siberia. He and his band are preparing for a show in the city of Ust-Ilimsk when the radio broadcasts the news about the creation of the GKChP.

Ironically, Ust-Ilimsk holds a significant place in Russian history: it's the very location where Catherine II exiled Russia's most famous eighteenth-century dissident, the philosopher Alexander Radishchev. Finding themselves in such a historically symbolic place on the very day a dictatorship is being officially restored in Russia, Grebenshchikov and his band naturally joke that there's nowhere left for them to go—they've already arrived at their place of exile.

However, the BG Band continues their tour. Their next stop is Irkutsk, a regional center also well-known for its history of exiles. In the nineteenth century, the Decembrists—conspirators who planned to establish a constitutional monarchy in Russia after the death of Alexander I—served their sentences there.

According to Grebenshchikov, watching the political events in Moscow unfold from Siberia feels strangely detached. "We were listening to Siberian radio. Someone had a receiver. And the mood there was something like: 'Those people over in Moscow have completely lost their fucking minds.'"

At the start of their concert in Irkutsk, a man in a red tie tries to rush the stage.

"We nearly beat him up," Grebenshchikov would later recall. But the stranger starts yelling, "No, no, guys, you don't understand! I'm on your side! I'm against the KGB. Let's speak out together against the GKChP!"

Despite his apolitical stance, Grebenshchikov lets the man deliver a fiery speech in defense of democracy. At the end of his tirade, the speaker turns to the audience and asks, "So, are you ready to lie down in front of the tanks?"

"Yeah, yeah, we'll lie down; just get out of here and let us enjoy the concert," Grebenshchikov recalls the audience's reaction.

At the end of the concert, the same man reappears, this time shouting, "We won!"

"It took about three seconds to figure out who 'we' were." Grebenshchikov laughs. "But in the end, no one had to lie down in front of any tanks."

A RACE TO CRIMEA

After their final meeting, the GKChP members decide they need to go to Gorbachev. Yazov calls his wife to warn her that he has to fly to Crimea. She begs him not to leave without saying good-bye. He agrees and waits.

The flight is scheduled for 2:00 p.m., but she's nowhere to be seen. One p.m. One ten. One fifteen. Finally, she arrives—they hug for just a second, and he immediately gets into the car.

And promptly gets stuck in traffic—it's the Tamanskaya Division being withdrawn from Moscow. Everyone is stuck, including the minister.

At the airport, Kryuchkov is visibly nervous. Just a short while earlier, Russian prime minister Ivan Silayev had called to inform him that Yeltsin was sending his own delegation to retrieve Gorbachev. At that moment, Kryuchkov decided he had to reach Gorbachev first—at all costs.

At 2:15 p.m., Yazov arrives at the airfield, and the presidential plane, carrying GKChP members Yazov, Kryuchkov, and Baklanov, as well as Supreme Soviet chairman Lukyanov and Deputy General Secretary Ivashko, takes off from Moscow for Crimea.

Yeltsin's delegation—Vice President Rutskoy, Prime Minister Silayev, and Soviet presidential advisors Primakov and Bakatin—plans to depart at 4:00 p.m. However, before they even take off, they learn that Kryuchkov has deceived them, and the race begins. The second group tries to overtake the first, but this is, of course, impossible—after all, the presidential Il-62, carrying the first group, is significantly faster.

Yeltsin asks air force commander Shaposhnikov how the first plane can be delayed. Shaposhnikov replies that it could be shot down. "That is unacceptable," Yeltsin answers seriously.

Nevertheless, at 3:20 p.m., Lukyanov records in his diary that the plane receives a message claiming Yeltsin has ordered the destruction of the Il-62 carrying the GKChP members. "I believed it," Lukyanov would later say.

Even so, the presidential jet lands safely at the Belbek military airfield, and its passengers proceed to the Zarya residence. There, they encounter a new surprise. Gorbachev's personal security detail has revolted and refuses to take any further orders from their KGB superiors. The guards meet the visitors with machine guns and shouts of "Freeze!"

"What's the matter, guys? We're on the same side . . . ," the visitors plead.

"Freeze!" the guards repeat firmly.

Clearly, they have also been watching the news and now understand who has the upper hand. The arriving party is no longer "the bosses"—they are defeated plotters. The very guards who had acted as Gorbachev's jailers over the past few days have now become his defenders.

Gorbachev is informed of the guests' arrival, but he already knows from the news that Yeltsin's delegation is en route as well. He refuses to see the first group until the second one arrives. However, the second plane is initially denied landing permission at Belbek and circles the military airfield for a long time.

Rutskoy, Silayev, Primakov, and Bakatin arrive at Zarya after dark. Gorbachev meets with them immediately and suggests they stay the night. However, the group insists that they must leave for Moscow urgently—right away. He asks his family to pack their things, and only then decides to have a word with Lukyanov, his longtime friend, since their university days.

Gorbachev and his family fly back along with Rutskoy, Silayev, and the others. As a precaution, they take Kryuchkov with them as a hostage—just in case the plane is targeted. Kryuchkov, however, sits alone in the second cabin.

Both planes land in Moscow after midnight. Gorbachev is offered the chance to go to the White House and greet the people who secured the GKChP's defeat and his release from captivity. This moment could have been historic for Gorbachev—it might have defined his entire future, just as Yeltsin's speech on the tank defined his. But Gorbachev is exhausted, and more importantly, Raisa is in very poor health; she can't even make it down the steps of the plane without help. So he doesn't hesitate. He goes home with his family, refusing the laurels of victory in this three-day drama. The crowd waits for him outside the White House until 4:00 a.m.

The only triumphant figure of the failed coup will be Yeltsin.

ARRESTS AND SUICIDES

By the evening of August 21, Russian authorities begin considering launching criminal cases against the coup plotters. However, little hope is placed in the USSR's prosecutor general—after all, he had just been issuing arrest warrants for Yeltsin and his team. As a result, the RSFSR Prosecutor's Office steps in. In his memoir, Russian prosecutor Valentin Stepankov will write that on this evening, he calls Burbulis in the White House and offers to take the risk of initiating proceedings against the GKChP members and arresting them.

Kryuchkov and Yazov are arrested right at the airport as soon as they land. The KGB chief is deeply depressed and doesn't resist. Yazov, clearly prepared for this outcome, asks, "What am I supposed to do?" and, when told to proceed to the airport building, answers with a simple, "Understood!"*

The question arises: Where to take the arrested conspirators? Sending them to a regular detention center is out of the question since there's no guarantee of the staff's loyalty. The first idea is to lock them in the basement

---

* Vladimir Kryuchkov, like the other members of the GKChP, will be released from prison in 1993 on a promise not to leave the country, and will be amnestied in 1994. A trial of the GKChP will never take place. In 1998, he will become an advisor to Vladimir Putin, director of the Federal Security Services (FSB)—the successor agency to the Soviet KGB—and in 2000, he will be an honored guest at Putin's inauguration. Yazov will become an advisor to the Russian minister of defense. In 2020, Putin will award him the Order "For Merit to the Fatherland." Kryuchkov will die in 2007, Yazov in 2020.

of the White House. But in the end, it's decided to temporarily hold them at the Senezh retreat hotel outside Moscow—conditions there are worse than at Gorbachev's offical residence in Crimea, but it is still far from a prison.

The same night, two employees from the president's administration—who had not opposed the GKChP up to this point—took it upon themselves to "detain" Yanayev "in the name of democracy." The vice president complies and simply lies down to sleep on the couch in his office. Incidentally, it's a large office—once belonging to the head of Stalin's secret police Lavrenty Beria, where Beria himself had been arrested (and, according to one version, killed on the spot). Yanayev is arrested there the next morning.

On August 22, prosecutors spend the entire day searching for Interior Minister Boris Pugo. He's not at his dacha, but they eventually locate his residence and spend a long time ringing the doorbell. Pugo's elderly father-in-law finally opens the door. Inside, they discover that Boris Pugo and his wife, Valentina, have taken their own lives. Pugo leaves a note: "I committed a completely unexpected mistake for myself—one equivalent to a crime. . . ."

This isn't the only suicide in the aftermath of the coup—a wave of suicides follows that many will find strange. On the night of August 26, Nikolai Kruchina, the administrator of the Central Committee of the Communist Party of the Soviet Union and a man relatively close to Gorbachev, jumps out of a window. He leaves behind a note. It says, "I am neither a criminal nor a conspirator, but I am a coward."

A month and a half later, his predecessor in the same role, Georgy Pavlov, falls from the balcony of his own apartment. This will give rise to conspiracy theories about the lost "party's gold"—after all, the heads of administrative affairs had full knowledge of where the party's funds were transferred, and their sudden and unexpected deaths took that information to the grave with them.

But perhaps the most symbolic death is that of Marshal of the Soviet Union Sergei Akhromeyev, Gorbachev's advisor and former Chief of the General Staff.

On August 19, upon learning of the GKChP's creation, he cuts short his vacation in Sochi, where he had been staying with his wife and grand-daughter, and flies to Moscow. Donning his marshal's uniform, he goes to see Yanayev and offers his services. On August 20, Akhromeyev visits the

Ministry of Defense. Returning to the Kremlin, he tells his secretary that things look bleak and asks her to bring him a folding cot—he decides to spend the night at work.

On August 22, Akhromeyev writes a personal letter to Gorbachev. Then, on the morning of August 25, he tries to hang himself using a cord tied to the window frame—but the cord snaps. Afterward, he spends the day working, speaking to colleagues and secretaries. That evening, he tries again and succeeds. On his desk, they find six suicide notes. In one of them, he wrote: "I cannot live when my Motherland is dying, and everything I considered the meaning of my life is being destroyed. My age and the life I've lived give me the right to leave this world. I fought to the end."

IRON FELIX

August 22 is a historic day. Everyone in Moscow understands that the old life—frightening, unjust, impoverished, and unfree—has ended, and something new is about to begin. It's a day of triumph, but also a day when no one really knows what to do next.

In the morning, a rally gathers near the White House, filled with triumphant speeches by the victors. Boris Yeltsin speaks, along with Gavriil Popov, Alexander Yakovlev, and Eduard Shevardnadze—Gorbachev, however, does not show up. "Just a blatant mistake," Chernyaev writes in his diary. "He was busy drafting decrees on appointing new ministers instead. . . . Though, maybe this was 'agreed upon' with Yeltsin, who didn't want to share even a drop of his victorious glory with anyone."

From the White House, the crowd moves to Staraya Square, with calls to storm the headquarters of the Central Committee of the Communist Party of the Soviet Union. To prevent this, Moscow authorities decide to divert the crowd. A rumor spreads that the monument to Felix Dzerzhinsky is being dismantled over on Lubyanka Square.

At the time, this monument is perceived as the ultimate symbol of Soviet repression. Dzerzhinsky was the legendary founder of the Soviet secret police—first known as the Cheka, then the OGPU, NKVD, and later KGB. He was a Soviet saint, but even Soviet textbooks openly stated that he was ruthless toward enemies of the revolution and organized the Red Terror.

Dzerzhinsky died in 1926, before Stalin's repressions began, which meant his name was never taboo in the USSR. His crimes weren't denounced at the 20th Party Congress, and during the height of Khrushchev's Thaw in 1958, a statue of him, so called *Iron Felix*, was erected across from the KGB headquarters on Lubyanka Square. Like Lenin, Dzerzhinsky was a sacred figure, long revered as a "knight of the Revolution," a man with a "cool head and a fiery heart," and the undisputed idol of KGB officers.

With the failure of the GKChP coup, *Iron Felix* now stands as the perfect symbol to be toppled.

At first, demonstrators try to remove the Dzerzhinsky monument on their own. They attach a cable to a bus and attempt to drag it down. The police stand by and do not intervene. Some suggest that if the eleven-ton statue falls, it will certainly kill someone—it's hollow inside and could shatter into pieces.

Then Deputy Mayor of Moscow Sergei Stankevich climbs onto the bus and, through a loudspeaker, urges the crowd to wait. He assures them that city authorities will organize the dismantling of the monument.

The crowd waits, but the equipment doesn't arrive. Tension builds, and someone suggests storming the KGB headquarters itself. Inside the building, staff observe nervously as the crowd outside plots to bring down their idol. The doors are barricaded, and the officers are armed—but will they resist if the crowd storms the building?

Stankevich shouts into the megaphone, "Anyone calling for a storming of the building is a KGB agent! Detain them!"

Finally, after dark, the monument is carefully removed from its pedestal, loaded onto a platform, and taken to the new building of the Tretyakov Gallery.

Solzhenitsyn, with his entire family—his wife and sons—cannot tear himself away from the television as he watches CNN's broadcast from Moscow:

"When we saw on television how that cursed Dzerzhinsky was being hoisted by a crane—how could the heart of an old prisoner not tremble?! . . . ," he would write in his memoir. "I was waiting, I was calling with my heart—for the rebellious crowd to storm the Big Lubyanka! . . . They could have smashed it with no trouble, and with what enormous consequences. The entire course of this 'revolution' would have turned out differently and might have led to a swift cleansing—but our amoebic democrats talked the crowd out of it—and doomed themselves to keep the old KGB, the CPSU, and much else of that kind hanging over our heads. . . . It seemed to me (for a fleeting day): I had never experienced such a great day in my entire life."

A few days later, Russian foreign minister Andrei Kozyrev will ask Yeltsin if he regrets that the protesters, who were preparing to storm the building on Lubyanka, were stopped. Yeltsin is firm: "The KGB is the only functioning structure left from the old regime. Of course it was criminal, like all the others. But if we had destroyed it, we would have gotten total chaos," Yeltsin replies.

Yet years later, Kozyrev would deeply regret that the Lubyanka building had not been taken: "That was a magnificent crowd, all supporters of democracy. They wouldn't have lynched anyone. But those archives would have been opened. It was a unique chance—and, alas, it was lost."

The dismantling of the Dzerzhinsky monument is organized by thirty-three-year-old Vasily Shakhnovsky, who was recently an engineer, then became a local legislator, and now works as the chief of staff for the Moscow mayor's office. Later he will reflect that this was about the moment when a generational shift took place:

> The Sixties generation suddenly faded into the background. Given
> the complexity of the tasks ahead, no one was particularly eager
> to take charge. It was time to govern, and we had about two and
> a half people with real-life experience. So, either crooks or, in the
> best sense, madmen came to the forefront. And the idealists of the
> Sixties? They abandoned us.

Indeed, his boss, the mayor of Moscow, Gavriil Popov, one of the few sixtiers in power, will resign in a few months—and never return to politics again.

AWAY FROM THE CENTER

On August 23, Gorbachev and Yeltsin arrive together at the session of the Russian Supreme Soviet. This meeting reveals just how much everything has changed since the coup: all the former roles are now obsolete. Yeltsin is the victor; Gorbachev, the loser—though he does not yet realize it.

Taking the podium, Gorbachev distractedly waves some papers in front of the parliament and says:

"Boris Nikolayevich just gave me a brief summary of the cabinet meeting. . . . But I haven't read it yet."

"Well, read it then," Yeltsin says in a commanding tone.

And Gorbachev dutifully begins reading it aloud.

The humiliation does not end there. In Gorbachev's presence, right at the parliament session, Yeltsin signs a decree banning the Communist Party of Russia. Gorbachev weakly protests, saying that it is undemocratic. But Yeltsin insists that the party leadership was complicit in the coup.

The next day, Gorbachev resigns from his position as General Secretary of the Central Committee of the Communist Party of the Soviet Union and proposes that the entire Central Committee dissolve itself. This marks the avalanche-like collapse of the party: the remaining leaders of the Union republics who are still in the Politburo immediately withdraw, while the heads of Belarus, Tajikistan, and Turkmenistan announce the separation of their own Communist Parties from the Communist Party of the Soviet Union.

On August 24, Gorbachev dissolves the Soviet government because it had entirely participated in the coup—but he does not appoint a new one. Only the vacant positions in the security agencies are filled: Yevgeny Shaposhnikov becomes minister of defense, and Vadim Bakatin is appointed head of the KGB. Responsibility for managing the economy is handed over to Russian prime minister Ivan Silayev and his deputy—once again—Grigory Yavlinsky.

Yeltsin moves into the Kremlin—and now both men are working there, though in neighboring buildings. Yeltsin takes over the building previously occupied by the Supreme Soviet of the USSR and where Lukyanov had once worked.

On August 24, Yeltsin asks Foreign Minister Andrei Kozyrev what can be done to "solidify our leadership in foreign policy"—in other words, to make Western leaders finally forget about Gorbachev and turn toward Yeltsin. Kozyrev suggests that the strongest move would be to recognize the independence of the Baltic republics. And Yeltsin triumphantly declares, "In an hour, I expect representatives of the three Baltic republics in this office."

During the signing ceremony, a Latvian representative asks, "How will this affect Gorbachev's position?"

"If he has any brains, he'll immediately follow our example," Yeltsin sharply replies.

The rest of the USSR now struggles to figure out how best to proceed: Should they swear allegiance to Yeltsin, as he now seems to be running the country, or should they energetically cut ties with the center?

Leaders of the republics who supported the GKChP and obeyed its orders now find themselves in an awkward position. For example, Mikalay Dzyemyantsyey, the chairman of the Supreme Soviet of Belarus, announces his resignation as early as August 22.

The president of Georgia, Zviad Gamsakhurdia, declares that he never truly supported the GKChP—it was merely a tactical maneuver. His critics are quick to remind him of his similar behavior in 1977 when he recanted his dissident activities and received a suspended sentence.

On August 24, the Supreme Council of Ukraine holds its first session following the failed coup. Parliamentarian and Ukraine's oldest dissident, Levko Lukyanenko, who had fought for Ukraine's independence from the Soviet Union as early as the 1960s and was once sentenced to death for his efforts, brings a school notebook in which he has handwritten the "Declaration of Independence."

Parliament Speaker Kravchuk is afraid to put the act to a vote, but at the same time, he fears meeting Dzyemyantsyey's fate. Outside the parliament, a massive rally is raging. Many communists seriously fear that they might be lynched at any moment. "We'll vote for whatever you want; just don't hang us," member of the Rukh Yuriy Kostenko will later recall one of the legislators saying.

Another legislator from the Rukh, poet Dmytro Pavlychko, grabs Kravchuk and, in a grave tone, promises to strangle him if he doesn't start reading the "Declaration of Independence." And so, parliament votes overwhelmingly in favor of the act. A referendum on independence is scheduled for December 1.

Shortly thereafter, Moldova, which had opposed the GKChP from the very beginning, also declares its independence.

YELTSIN STRIKES AN IMPERIAL BLOW

On August 25, Pavel Voshchanov's phone rings—he's being connected to his boss, President Yeltsin, who, to the press secretary's surprise, has gone on vacation to Jūrmala, Latvia. From there, Yeltsin gives instructions: a statement must be made by the press secretary, but it should appear as though it comes from the president himself. In his memoir, Voshchanov describes the task Yeltsin sets for him: "The main goal is to intimidate our neighbors, who have started having delusions of grandeur, with territorial claims."

Voshchanov drafts the statement, obtains Yeltsin's approval, and two days later it is distributed to news agencies: "The RSFSR reserves the right to raise the issue of revising borders. This applies to all neighboring republics, except for the three Baltic states—Latvia, Lithuania, and Estonia," the text declares.

Afterward, he tries to contact Yeltsin again, but the president is unavailable. Nonetheless, the next day Voshchanov holds a press conference. He doesn't hide the fact that he was specifically referring to Ukraine and Kazakhstan, which Solzhenitsyn once suggested should be considered an inseparable part of Rus'. "If these republics join a union with Russia, then there's no problem," Voshchanov says. "But if they leave, we must be concerned about the population living there and remember that these lands were developed by Russians. Russia is unlikely to give them up so easily."

Afterward, Voshchanov gets into a heated exchange with two journalists representing Ukraine and Kazakhstan.

"Ukraine's place in the USSR is a legacy of communism. If Mr. Yeltsin is against its independence, then he was and remains a staunch communist!" the Ukrainian reporter begins. In response, Voshchanov snaps:

"Don't want to live in a union with Russia, and that union is a 'legacy of communism' for you? By all means, don't live in it! But in that case, return Crimea and Donbass to us! The fact that they're part of Ukraine now—that's nothing more than a legacy of communism! You received them by Khrushchev's decree with the approval of the Presidium of the CPSU Central Committee. . . . The communists handed you a territorial gift. Why are you rejecting that?!"

In the following days, massive protest rallies erupt in the Kazakh and Ukrainian capitals, Almaty and Kyiv. Russia's vice president, Alexander Rutskoy, visits both cities, condemns Voshchanov, and promises that Yeltsin will punish the press secretary.

Back in Moscow, Rutskoy comes to Voshchanov to share some whiskey. "Pashka, you're like a sapper dog for us: if you run across the minefield unscathed, we'll follow; if you blow up, we'll find another way," Rutskoy explains.

It's clear that after defeating the GKChP, Yeltsin no longer sees himself as merely the leader of one of the fifteen Soviet republics—he sees himself as the man who defeated and conquered the whole USSR. It's no coincidence that he hastily moves into the Kremlin and now shares it with Gorbachev; he is preparing to succeed Gorbachev as the head of the Soviet Union. In this new role, the parade of sovereignties he once welcomed no longer suits him. He's ready to let go of the Baltic states, but Ukraine and Kazakhstan must stay.

The first to protest is Sakharov's widow, Elena Bonner. On August 29, in a twist of irony, *Pravda* publishes her letter: "By making territorial claims against Russia's neighbors, [Yeltsin] has effectively taken a dangerous step backward. A 'Great Russia' means a new military-industrial complex, new totalitarian structures, and an attempt to reverse the 'locomotive of history.' All democratic forces who saved the country during those three days must now clearly define what we are creating: a powerful, militarized, bureaucratic Russia—'autocracy, Orthodoxy, and nationality'—or a free, democratic commonwealth of states."

Solzhenitsyn immediately joins the debate. He even considers publishing an open letter to Yeltsin, urging him not to recognize administrative borders between the republics as state borders and to retain the right to revise them. His wife dissuades him: "Shouting advice across the ocean would look tactless."

"Good Lord! What an angry uproar about 'Russian imperialism' arose—not just in the deeply interested United States, but even more so among Moscow's radical democrats of the Sakharov school," Solzhenitsyn will write in his memoir.

ECONOMISTS IN THE ALPS

In early September 1991, an economic conference takes place in the Austrian village of Alpbach, near Innsbruck. Among the attendees are several Soviet economists: Anatoly Chubais, Pyotr Aven, Alexander Shokhin. They discuss the latest developments in Moscow—Gorbachev has tasked Yavlinsky with trying to rescue the Soviet economy.

As they deliberate on possible solutions, they come to a conclusion: it is too late to reform the USSR. There is no point in trying anymore—it is time to act solely within Russia's framework. They even draft a collective statement, which later becomes known as the Alpbach Declaration.

"The supra-republican center is doomed to be weak. Therefore, it should not exist at all," they write. "This is not an ideological stance but a purely pragmatic conclusion."

It is rather symbolic that a century earlier, Russian liberals had begun gathering in the Alps to form a democratic opposition to Tsar Nicholas II. Later, nearby, in Zurich, Switzerland, Vladimir Lenin had lived until 1917, before embarking on his journey to Russia, where he would soon take power. This group of economists, too, will return from the Alps to Moscow to begin negotiations on forming Russia's new government.

Meanwhile, at that very moment, Grigory Yavlinsky, as the de facto leader of the Soviet government, is working on a plan to revive the Soviet Union. He believes that while the state can no longer exist in its previous form, it should be preserved as an economic union with a common customs space and a single currency. Gorbachev likes the idea.

CHECHEN REVOLUTION

Two weeks after the failed coup attempt in Moscow, another overthrow takes place—this time in Grozny, the capital of the Chechen Republic, an autonomous region within Russia.

On September 6, a session of the republic's Supreme Council is underway. The scenario closely resembles those in Ukraine and Belarus, where opposition figures accused the republican leadership of supporting the GKChP. But while in Kyiv, Rukh activist Dmytro Pavlychko had only verbally threatened to strangle Parliament Speaker Kravchuk, in Grozny, violence erupts. Around five in the evening, armed opposition supporters storm the building where the Supreme Council is meeting and begin beating legislators. The mayor of Grozny (formerly the city's Communist Party First Secretary) is thrown out of a third-floor window—he later dies in the hospital.

The previous leadership is declared overthrown, and power is seized by the so-called Executive Committee of the Congress of the Chechen People, led by Soviet army major general Dzhokhar Dudayev. At the same time, they take control of the television center and the radio broadcasting headquarters.

However, in Moscow, this is not seen as a coup. After all, the ousted Communist leadership had indeed supported the GKChP. Russian Parliament Speaker Ruslan Khasbulatov, himself a Chechen, had long harbored personal resentment toward the ousted First Secretary of the autonomous republic, Doku Zavgayev—at one point, he even suggested that Zavgayev should be "brought to Moscow in an iron cage." Even the violent death of

Grozny's mayor does not cause much shock—several communist officials in Moscow had also fallen from windows in recent days. In that sense, the events in Chechnya appear to be part of the trend.

The opposition, led by Dudayev, is seen as an ally—they had opposed the GKChP, and their actions have helped remove the old communists.

Khasbulatov assumes he will be able to govern the republic remotely from Moscow. During a visit to Grozny, he sets up a provisional governing council for Chechnya—then leaves. This body has no real power. Meanwhile, Dudayev's Executive Committee announces parliamentary and presidential elections for late October.

But in Moscow, no one is paying attention.

VACATION IN SOCHI

The celebration of victory over the GKChP has barely ended when Yeltsin disappears. He goes on vacation to Sochi and stops communicating.

A prosaic explanation for Yeltsin's absence—he is drinking. Many of his subordinates would later say this is classic Yeltsin: after winning and securing power, he simply sits back and basks in his triumph.

Meanwhile, Burbulis is trying to form a new government. Three groups are set up on the basis of the Russian government to develop economic reform programs. The first is headed by Grigory Yavlinsky, the second by Evgeny Saburov, and the third by Yegor Gaidar. This is the very same editor of the economics section of *Pravda*, and his closest friends are Anatoly Chubais and his circle—young economists who have just written the Alpbach Declaration.

Each group is assigned a cottage in the same Arkhangelskoye village. Burbulis monitors their work, as he's the one who needs to go to Sochi and report to Yeltsin on who should be appointed as head of government.

According to Burbulis, he prefers Gaidar's team: "I visited them more often, I paid more attention, and I was more biased toward this group." During one of their meetings, Burbulis asks, "Who are the people we could trust with all of this?" Gaidar answers without hesitation, "Only we can do this. No one but us will do it."

On September 24, Burbulis flies to Sochi to meet with Yeltsin, bringing with him Gaidar's program. Apart from economics, it contains a very clear political proposal based on the Alpbach Declaration: the Soviet Union is doomed; all of Gorbachev's attempts to revive it with the Union Treaty are in vain. Russia must develop independently as a sovereign state and base its economic development on that.

Burbulis realizes that it won't be easy to sell the thirty-five-year-old Gaidar to the sixty-year-old Yeltsin—an experienced party leader who is completely unaccustomed to working with young people. And indeed, when Yeltsin hears that the candidate is thirty-five years old, he is quite taken aback.

Then Burbulis comes up with a romantic explanation for why they should rely on Gaidar. Yes, he's a boy, but not just any boy—he's magical!

Burbulis understands that Yeltsin will probably be greatly impressed by the fact that Gaidar is the grandson of the famous writer Pavel Bazhov, who was born in the Urals. "We, Ural residents, are soaked in Bazhov's tales from childhood to old age, 'The Mistress of the Copper Mountain.' And, in general, for Yeltsin and for all of us Ural residents, this was some kind of spiritual, lyrical, maybe even magical connection." And through his father, Gaidar is the grandson of the Soviet writer Arkady Gaidar, the author of *Timur and His Squad*, which, according to Burbulis, is also very important, symbolizing "the revolutionary, romantic impulse to participate in great transformations."

These irrational arguments genuinely impress Yeltsin—he believes that the grandson of two famous writers is exactly what's needed.

THE LAST SOLDIER OF THE EMPIRE

After the defeat of the GKChP, battles erupt at every level. Yesterday's leaders are dismissed under the pretext of punishing GKChP supporters. A striking example is the drama at St. Petersburg television. First, the head of city broadcasting shuts down Nevzorov's program, *600 Seconds*. The journalist theatrically declares himself the last soldier of the empire, willing to fight till the end.

However, shortly afterward, St. Petersburg mayor Sobchak fires the head of city television (accusing him of being old-school communist) and reinstates Nevzorov, stating that "no one will lose their job in television except those who combine it with service in the KGB."

"He's being foolish," Nevzorov comments on Sobchak's statement, pointing out that the mayor's office employs at least eight KGB officers.

In late November, Nevzorov announces the creation of his own national liberation movement, "Ours." He holds a rally in the same small park where he had sat with Kryuchkov a year and a half earlier. "Every true Russian citizen secretly dreams of a GKChP because, in essence, the country has been seized by the enemy," he declares into the microphone, clarifying that the enemy is the Gorbachev-Yeltsin-Sobchak leadership.

Nevzorov also invites Alksnis to join his movement. Shortly after, *600 Seconds* is shut down again. However, no mass movement materializes, and Nevzorov's longtime friends in the KGB offer him no support.

"KGB officers, being smart people, were the first to bolt," Nevzorov reflects. "What's great about the KGB? It's that in tough times for the country, it's always the first to disappear. Police might still remain loyal to some kind of oath. But these guys? They left no trace in an instant. Even Vladimir Vladimirovich [Putin], when the Soviet Union was collapsing before his eyes, did nothing. I knew all the KGB officers who, at the time, were my timid like-minded allies—they wanted to jump off the Liteyny Bridge. Including some well-known figures."

Nevzorov claims that he, along with his loyal allies, Vilnius and Riga OMON commanders Boleslav Makutinovich and Cheslav Mlynnik, was ready to buy a truck—a KAMAZ full of sandbags—drive to Red Square, stack the bags in a circle, set up machine guns, and take up a defensive position. "And then it turned out it was just the three of us, damn it, and no one else."

EITHER DO IT OR DON'T SEEK FORGIVENESS

On September 2, an opposition rally gathers in the center of Tbilisi—this time against Zviad Gamsakhurdia. The president, himself a former dissident, sends the police to disperse the protest. The officers open fire—no one is killed, but several people are wounded. This shocks Georgia, perhaps no less than the crackdown on the April 9, 1989, demonstration. Parliament demands an open discussion of the events, but the authorities ban the live broadcast of the debates. In protest, forty-nine legislators—members of the ruling party—leave Gamsakhurdia's camp.

Among the staunch opponents of the new government are also former fighters of Tengiz Kitovani's National Guard. Moreover, they begin recruiting members of the disbanded paramilitary group the Mkhedrioni—in other words, gangsters loyal to the recently imprisoned crime boss Jaba Ioseliani. An astonishingly broad coalition forms against the celebrated national hero Gamsakhurdia: prominent figures of Georgia's cultural elite stand alongside underworld kingpins.

On September 23, Gamsakhurdia declares a state of emergency. In response, the rebellious National Guard effectively seizes the state television building— allegedly to protect journalists from censorship. Clashes erupt in the city between supporters and opponents of Gamsakhurdia, both sides armed— using weapons looted from Soviet military depots. Or perhaps not looted at all—many in Tbilisi believe Moscow is deliberately arming the opposition.

"Gamsakhurdia was lost," Parliament Speaker Akaki Asatiani will later say. "He dispersed a few protests, and then spent four hours in church praying, seeking forgiveness: 'Forgive me, Lord.' I believe that if you're a ruler, you either do it—or don't seek forgiveness."

Gamsakhurdia's circle shrinks further. In early November, Parliament Speaker Akaki Asatiani resigns, citing "health reasons": "I was actually a healthy man, but in those last two months, I developed angina. . . . I had no idea what that was. I said, 'I'll leave, just lie around at home. I can't take this anymore. That's it.'"

THE GHOST OF THE UNION TREATY

Gorbachev still clings to the hope of signing the Union Treaty, but by now, his only allies are the five presidents of the Central Asian republics: Kazakhstan, Kyrgyzstan, Tajikistan, Turkmenistan, and Uzbekistan. They remain the only leaders still committed to preserving the Union. The Kazakh leader, Nursultan Nazarbayev, is still willing to head the Soviet government, though he knows he is taking a great risk: if he leaves Almaty for Moscow, he will lose control over his republic, and if his career in Moscow fails, he will have no way back.

Another supporter of Gorbachev and the Union Treaty is Kyrgyzstan's president, Askar Akayev. In October 1990, at Gorbachev's request, he flies to Washington to meet with President Bush. Gorbachev instructs him to once again ask for financial aid for the Soviet Union. But to Akayev's surprise, the Americans treat him not as an envoy of Gorbachev, a regional leader within the Soviet Union, but as the president of an independent country. Bush receives him in the Oval Office—something Akayev never expected: "It was a clear signal that the Americans were already working toward the collapse of the USSR. Personally, I enjoyed the attention—but I remembered that I had been sent by Mikhail Sergeyevich to ask for loans. And only in Washington did I fully realize that they had already placed their bets on Yeltsin, and written off Gorbachev."

Bush asks Akayev to "send my regards to my friend Mikhail Gorbachev"—but promises no money.

Meanwhile, Yavlinsky finalizes the draft for an economic agreement. He later describes it as a blueprint for what would become the European Union (at that time, the EU does not yet exist). On October 18, Gorbachev, Yeltsin, and representatives of the five Central Asian republics, Belarus, and Armenia sign an agreement to create an Economic Community, which envisions a single currency and a common customs area.

On November 2, Gorbachev flies to Madrid for a Middle East peace conference. There, he once again asks Bush for money.

The American president tries to avoid that conversation: "Under our legislation, I must assure Congress that our borrowers are creditworthy." But Gorbachev interrupts him: "Ten to fifteen billion dollars is not such an enormous sum that we wouldn't be able to repay it!"

"That's exactly why I'm asking again: Do you think a return to a totalitarian regime is possible?" Bush suddenly asks.

Gorbachev insists that this is precisely why he urgently needs money—to prevent such a rollback. In the end, Bush promises Gorbachev $1.5 billion. After the talks, when the negotiators are leaving, Secretary of State James Baker leans over and whispers into the ear of Gorbachev's interpreter, Pavel Palazhchenko, "Take the one and a half billion—it's real cash; take it before we change our minds. Too little? But we can't offer more."

A few days later, Yeltsin finally forms the Russian government. Yegor Gaidar becomes deputy prime minister for the economy, Anatoly Chubais is appointed head of the State Property Committee, and several other authors of the Alpbach Declaration receive ministerial posts.

"Around 80 USSR ministries have been abolished. About 50,000 bureaucrats in Moscow alone are out on the street by November 15," writes Chernyaev in his diary.

Gorbachev clearly believes that the new treaty will be signed. In November, he asks Kyrgyzstan president Akayev to talk about the agricultural reform taking place in his republic. Akayev eagerly describes the process, and at one point, the Soviet president—who once operated a combine harvester—asks, "Listen, I want to come and see it for myself."

And he does—flying with Akayev to the Chu Valley to inspect how former unprofitable kolkhozes have been transformed into private farms. He is thrilled with what he sees and declares, "That's it; we need to make a decision. We need to spread your experiences to other republics, to other regions of the Soviet Union."

By this point, he has no real levers of power left—the Soviet government effectively no longer exists. Yet, full of enthusiasm, Gorbachev still dreams of continuing reforms.

CHECHEN INDEPENDENCE

On October 27, the Congress of the Chechen People, led by Dzhokhar Dudayev, follows through on its plan to hold elections for parliament and the presidency in the republic—an autonomous region within Russia. Years later, it remains unclear how representative these elections were.

Dudayev's opponents claim it is merely a staged event: in the center of Grozny, where a rally is taking place; a few ballot boxes are simply placed on the square, with no clarity on who is actually counting the votes. In six districts of the republic, elections do not take place at all. Nevertheless, the organizers announce that 72 percent of Chechnya's residents have voted, with 90 percent supporting Dudayev.

The "temporary council" appointed by Moscow calls the elections fraudulent and refuses to recognize them. Meanwhile, Georgian president Zviad Gamsakhurdia immediately congratulates Dudayev on his victory.

Dudayev's first decree proclaims Chechnya an independent state. By this point, Yeltsin has returned from vacation. His new Parliament Speaker, Chechen Ruslan Khasbulatov, realizes that the situation has slipped out of control and demands the immediate use of force to remove Dudayev from power. On November 7, Yeltsin signs a decree imposing a state of emergency in Chechnya. In response, Dudayev's supporters seize the buildings of the republican Ministry of Internal Affairs and the KGB. Chechen police officers begin to defect en masse to the side of the newly declared president.

The situation is paradoxical. De jure, the army and internal troops are still under Gorbachev's command—Yeltsin has no authority over them.

Meanwhile, the Soviet president had declared a state of emergency in Azerbaijan two years earlier but refrained from doing so in Lithuania a year ago. To him, violent clashes are a nightmare—he does not want any more blood on his hands.

When Gorbachev learns about Yeltsin's decree, he is outraged:

"What is he doing?! This would mean hundreds of deaths, if it starts! . . . All the factions and groups that were arguing and fighting among themselves there have now united against the Russians. The militants are already gathering women and children to put them in front of their ranks when the troops approach!"

The Soviet president consults with his security ministers—all of them oppose sending troops into Chechnya.

Gorbachev calls Yeltsin. "Within seconds, I realized that talking was pointless—he was completely wasted, barely coherent," he tells Chernyaev. Later he reprimands Vice President Alexander Rutskoy, whom Yeltsin had tasked with handling the Chechen crisis:

"Alexander, calm down. You're not on the front lines—encircle them from the mountains; blockade them; don't let a single Chechen through; arrest Dudayev; isolate the others. What are you thinking? Do you not see how this will end? . . . I have information—no one in Chechnya supports Yeltsin's decree. Everyone has united against you. Don't lose your mind."

Later, while discussing the situation with Yakovlev and Chernyaev, Gorbachev says:

"Here's what worries me. It seems like his entourage is deliberately keeping Yeltsin drunk. We could be facing a very serious turn of events. . . . They are turning him into a blind instrument."

The next day, despite Khasbulatov's insistence, the Russian parliament votes against declaring a state of emergency in Chechnya.

De facto, the republic begins to separate from Russia: it stops transferring oil revenues to Moscow's budget and starts seizing weapons from Soviet military garrisons stationed in the region. Ethnic Russians living in Chechnya begin to be driven out.*

---

* Boris Yeltsin will send troops into Chechnya in 1994. In 1996, Dzhokhar Dudayev will be killed. The war in the republic will resume in 1999, when Vladimir Putin becomes Russia's prime minister, and will continue into the first decade of the 2000s.

The "Chechen factor" becomes yet another source of growing tension between Yeltsin and Gorbachev—the Russian president is convinced that his opponents are continuing to wage war against him in the spirit of the "Lukyanov Doctrine," even though Lukyanov himself, along with Kryuchkov and Yazov, has long been sitting in prison.

THE LAST ATTEMPT

The new Union Treaty is set to be signed on November 25. It envisions a single armed force for the Union of Sovereign States (USS), a president and vice president, a federal government, and a common parliament, where each republic is represented by twenty members, except for Russia, which has fifty-two. The text of the treaty concludes with the statement: "For the states that sign this treaty, the 1922 Treaty on the Formation of the USSR is considered null and void."

However, on the eve of the scheduled signing, Yeltsin declares that if Ukraine does not sign the treaty, Russia will not sign it either. He is deeply concerned that the new state would be dominated by Muslim Central Asian republics—whose leaders, including Nazarbayev, remain aligned with Gorbachev. Yeltsin concludes that Russia will join the USS only together with Ukraine. His decision is influenced by Solzhenitsyn's long-standing argument that Russia should let go of the Asian republics, the advice of economic experts from the Gaidar and Chubais group—who believe it would be far easier to reform Russia's economy than to carry the crumbling Soviet Union—and, finally, his own personal rivalry with Gorbachev. Yeltsin has grown tired of their power struggle and wants to be rid of his former boss once and for all.

"This would radically shift the balance of power in the Union between Slavic and Islamic countries," Yeltsin admits in a conversation with George Bush. "We cannot allow a situation where Russia and Belarus have only two votes against the five votes of the Islamic nations."

Moreover, Yeltsin argues that Russia has "constantly been feeding the Central Asian republics," making any union with them more of a burden than a benefit. He is still unaware of the vast oil and gas reserves in Kazakhstan, Uzbekistan, and Turkmenistan—while most of these resources had been discovered in Soviet times, their full economic potential would not become evident for another decade.

In the end, the signing of the Union Treaty on November 25 falls apart—eight republican leaders gather at the Kremlin but conclude that the text needs further revision. Then, on December 1, Ukraine holds its independence referendum. More than 92 percent vote in favor, and Leonid Kravchuk wins the presidential election. Ukrainian dissident legend Vyacheslav Chornovil takes second place—but that's hardly surprising, as former communist Kravchuk adopts much of his platform. Both candidates try to present themselves as true Ukrainian nationalists.

Gorbachev calls Yeltsin, urging him to meet with Kravchuk and Nazarbayev to discuss next steps. According to Gorbachev, Yeltsin is already drunk:

"It's over anyway. Ukraine is independent."

"And you, Russia?" Gorbachev asks.

"What about me? I'm Russia. We'll manage. There's no future for the Union. . . . But what if we return to the idea of a 'Big Four' union: Russia plus Ukraine plus Belarus plus Kazakhstan?" Yeltsin muses.

Gorbachev is unimpressed. "And where does that leave me? If that's the plan, I'm out. I won't just drift around like shit in an ice hole. It's not about me. But understand this—without the Union, you will all collapse. You will destroy all the reforms. You need to make up your mind. Everything depends on the two of us now, more than ever."

"How could we possibly do it without you, Mikhail Sergeyevich!" Yeltsin laughs mockingly.

MOSCOW'S TSAR IS BACK

For Gorbachev, the idea of Ukraine's secession is unthinkable—even in theory. His wife, Raisa, is Ukrainian, and he himself is half-Ukrainian. He is convinced that all it takes is a little more pressure on the stubborn Kravchuk, the former Communist Party secretary for ideology, and everything will fall into place. Since Yeltsin refuses to join the USS without Ukraine, Gorbachev now tries to persuade Kravchuk—now the president of an independent Ukraine—to agree to some form of confederation and asks the Russian president to help convince him.

It is decided that Yeltsin will negotiate with his Ukrainian counterpart on neutral ground—in Belarus. The plan is simple: the Russian president and the head of the Belarusian parliament, Stanislav Shushkevich, both of whom are more favorably inclined toward the idea of a renewed union, will work together to persuade Kravchuk to make some concessions.

Yeltsin flies to Minsk on an official visit. First, he addresses the Byelorussian parliament, and then he lays flowers at the Tomb of the Unknown Soldier.

To the great surprise of his entire delegation, he tells the MPs that he found a document in the Kremlin archives, which is hundreds of years old, and that he plans to present it to the Belarusian parliament: "This is an edict from the Russian tsar. It confirms that Russia has harbored sincere fraternal feelings for Byelorussia for centuries."

He then pulls out the ancient document with the tsar's signature and tries to read it. The text is written in Old Slavonic, so many of the words are completely unintelligible—but Yeltsin does not give up and stubbornly tries to pronounce the tsar's letter. He is evidently expecting his grand gesture to be received with great enthusiasm, as Russian Minister of Foreign Affairs Kozyrev will later recount.

However, the MPs soon realize that the document speaks of the victory of Russian troops over the army of the Polish-Lithuanian Commonwealth, which once included the territory of present-day Belarus. Moreover, the tsar, celebrating his victory, promises to care for his new serfs and never give away their land again. The hall erupts in cries of indignation—Yeltsin, unknowingly, behaves as if he is the new Russian tsar, who has come to his subjects.

The Parliament Speaker, Shushkevich, struggles to calm down his colleagues. The broadcast of Yeltsin's speech is interrupted.

While Yeltsin is still in Minsk, Shushkevich heads to the legendary national park Belavezhskaya Pushcha—the location of the informal meeting with the president of Ukraine. Without waiting for Yeltsin, he proposes to Kravchuk, "Leonid Makarovich, let's go hunting."

In the middle of the forest, they spot a wild boar. Shushkevich tells Kravchuk: "Leonid Makarovich, shoot!" Kravchuk aims, but Shushkevich advises, "No, let's get closer." They move forward, but the boar gets scared and runs off. Kravchuk is very disappointed—the prey slips right from their hands. "A hunter must never listen to anyone. Never!" he tells himself.

Finally, Yeltsin arrives. According to Burbulis, the fourth person expected in the Belavezhskaya Pushcha is Nazarbayev, who is at that moment in Moscow negotiating with Gorbachev and keeping them all on edge, promising to arrive any minute. But he doesn't come.

The serious discussion about the future begins in the morning: six people sit down at the negotiating table, two from each country. Yeltsin is counting on Shushkevich's support, but after the incident in the parliament, the Belarusian Speaker doesn't back the conversation about a renewed union.

Yeltsin asks cautiously, "Would you agree to sign the Union Treaty if it includes the proposals of Ukraine and your own?"

"Boris Nikolayevich, I can't," answers Kravchuk. "Because the referendum has already been held, and the Ukrainian people voted for independence. If I answer positively now, it will mean I betrayed my people. I need to fly to Kyiv and tell them: you elected me, but I have not justified your trust. . . ." He concludes his explanation on a high note: "I don't even know where the Kremlin is; I don't even know who Gorbachev is. From December 1, 1991, for me, there is no Kremlin, no Gorbachev."

Then he asks Yeltsin a question: "If this were the case in Russia, who would you listen to—Gorbachev or your people?" "Of course, my people," Yeltsin answers grimly. "It's clear that without Ukraine, the Soviet Union won't exist. We need to think about which document we're going to work on now."

Gennady Burbulis proposes this wording for the document: "The USSR as a subject of international law and a geopolitical reality ceases to exist." The full text of the agreement is written by Gaidar, dictated by Kozyrev and other delegation members. They find the historical justification: in 1922, four republics created the USSR: the Russian Federation, Belarus, Ukraine, and the Transcaucasian Federation. The latter no longer exists, so the remaining three republics have the legal right to annul their previous decision.

The text is titled "Agreement on the Creation of the Commonwealth of States." They show it to the three leaders. Yeltsin, Kravchuk, and Shushkevich ask to add one word, to make it the "Commonwealth of Independent States." And they sign it.

Yeltsin asks Kravchuk, "What are we going to do with Crimea and the nuclear weapons?" Kravchuk replies: "Let's not resolve the issue with Crimea right now. First, let's create the Commonwealth, and then we'll deal with the borders."

According to the widow of Sobchak, Lyudmila Narusova, during the negotiations in the Belavezhskaya Pushcha, the mayor of St. Petersburg is on the phone with Burbulis, urging him not to give away Crimea: "Tell Yeltsin; remind him everything I told him about Crimea before signing and agreeing.

In 1954, Crimea was transferred to Ukraine illegally, in violation of all Soviet legal norms. Be sure to remind him, or there will be war." However, Burbulis will not recall such a conversation with Sobchak.

For everyone involved, what is happening in the Belavezhskaya Pushcha is a surprise. Neither Kravchuk nor Shushkevich had planned to destroy the Soviet Union—they just didn't know it was possible. The document they now face frightens them. No one knows what the consequences will be. No one rules out that they might be arrested as conspirators—they still suspect that the Soviet empire might have some unknown powerful force left.

Yeltsin immediately calls Soviet defense minister Shaposhnikov and informs him that he has been appointed commander in chief of the Armed Forces of the newly created Commonwealth by the three presidents. Shaposhnikov has no objections—this means the likelihood of the military taking power to preserve the USSR is small.

Everyone goes up to Yeltsin's room—he has the largest suite—to discuss who will explain things to Gorbachev. They assign this task to Shushkevich—after all, he's the host. Shushkevich can't get through to the Kremlin: "Gorbachev is busy and can't respond. He'll call you."

Meanwhile, Kozyrev manages to get through to George Bush so that Boris Yeltsin can inform him. At first, the White House can't believe that someone from a Belarusian village is calling about such an important matter. But eventually, Bush picks up the phone before Gorbachev does.

Shushkevich's conversation with Gorbachev begins strangely. "Tomorrow, all three of you, I'm expecting you in the morning. Kravchuk, Yeltsin, and Shushkevich," Gorbachev orders in his usual tone.

"Mikhail Sergeyevich, I can't. I have a session of the parliament tomorrow, and I must chair it," the Belarusian leader responds.

"What do you mean—you can't?" Gorbachev doesn't believe it. "I just can't," insists Shushkevich.

Then everyone goes down to dinner. During the meal, Yeltsin is informed that it may be dangerous to stay in the Belavezhskaya Pushcha—they've received intelligence that Gorbachev is planning to arrest the leaders of the three republics, and the residence is already surrounded by KGB special forces.

"Leonid Makarovich, I have information that we need to leave here quickly," Yeltsin tells Kravchuk. The Russian and Ukrainian delegations head to the airfield. When saying good-bye to Kravchuk, Yeltsin makes a characteristic hand gesture and says, "How we fucked Mishka," referring to Gorbachev. However, even after returning to Kyiv, Kravchuk fears arrest.

Gorbachev has absolutely no intention of arresting anyone. That night, he calls various people he considers his allies. For example, he calls the president of Kyrgyzstan, Akaev: "Askar, have you heard what your colleagues have done?" Akaev does not yet know the details and tries to reassure the Soviet president: "They've done something. . . ." Gorbachev starts asking himself questions: "I don't know; where is the center now? Where is my place?"

In the following days, the parliaments of the three republics ratify the Belovezha agreements. "We effectively and legally abolished the Soviet totalitarian empire on December 8, 1991. We passed its sentence," Burbulis will say many years later. "But the deep imperial poison, the imperial mentality, sometimes flickering, sometimes emerging as an uncontrollable wave of obscurantism—it will still break through."

EXILE FROM THE KREMLIN

Even in Minsk, while speaking before the Belarusian parliament, Yeltsin joked: "In the Kremlin right now, there's not only the office of the president of the Soviet Union, but also the office of the president of Russia, and who is the host and who is the guest there is a state secret."

After the ratification of the Belovezha Accords, he begins to increasingly assert himself as the true leader and becomes more determined in pushing out Soviet officials.

On December 17, Yeltsin signs the act transferring the property of the Supreme Soviet of the USSR to the Russian Federation. The former Soviet parliament isn't even formally dissolved—it simply loses its premises.

On December 19, a decree is prepared about the transfer of the president's property to the Russian authorities. In other words, they are about to begin removing furniture from under Gorbachev. However, he continues to sit in the Kremlin, even though he declares that he will resign if something amorphous is formed in place of the USSR, meaning he still doesn't believe the Belovezha Accords are serious.

On December 21, the leaders of eleven former Soviet republics gather in Almaty to sign another declaration establishing the Commonwealth of Independent States (CIS). "I suggested to my colleagues: honestly, we should at least invite Gorbachev, maybe even offer him the position of Secretary General of the CIS, at least temporarily, right?" President of Kyrgyzstan Askar Akaev will later recall. "They immediately rejected it. I was very upset."

The declaration specifically includes a clause stating that the position of president of the USSR is abolished.

"Gorbachev was simply crudely thrown out," writes Chernyaev in his diary. "Even Nicholas II was sent an 'authoritative delegation' from the Duma asking him to abdicate."

The next day, Gorbachev, Chernyaev, Yakovlev, and Shevardnadze gather together to write a farewell speech. The former foreign minister shares his predictions: "There will be a coup; there will be an explosion—massive and ruthless." Yakovlev says, "Yeltsin, God willing, will last until spring."

On December 23, Gorbachev, Yeltsin, and Yakovlev meet for six hours to discuss how the Soviet president will hand over affairs. Yakovlev plays the role of mediator, but even he can't smooth things over. Yeltsin is not inclined to be ceremonious—for example, he refuses to maintain Gorbachev's immunity. "If Gorbachev wants to admit something, he should do it now," he says harshly at a press conference.

On December 25, Gorbachev, in his Kremlin office, addresses the nation on live television, announcing his resignation. It's a live broadcast, and he asks the director, Kaleriya Kislova, "How will I know when to start?" "There's a camera in front of you; the operator will wave his hand." "Is it like diving into water?" Gorbachev smiles.

This is the same Kislova who ten years earlier directed the live broadcast of Brezhnev's ceremonial arrival in Baku—in the absence of Brezhnev, who had fallen asleep.

After his televised address, Kislova switches on the camera, which shows the red flag descending over the Kremlin. She then goes to say good-bye to Gorbachev. With her, two workers unscrew a large plaque that reads: "Gorbachev Mikhail Sergeevich, President of the USSR."

He stands in his office, takes off his tie, and says, "Raisa Maksimovna just called. The office staff came and told her that we have to leave the apartment within twenty-four hours."

In two days, at 8:30, Yeltsin enters the office—Gorbachev still hasn't packed his stuff and has an interview scheduled with Japanese journalists. But it's urgently moved to the next room.

For the next thirty years, Gorbachev would be regarded by his own people not as a statesman, but as a failure—seldom honored, rarely celebrated in the country he once led. "No one seems to grasp," reflects Nobel laureate and journalist Dmitry Muratov, a close friend of the former Soviet president, "that Gorbachev—together with Reagan, Shultz, Kissinger, and others—gave the world thirty years without war. Today, it's fashionable to say that war drives progress. But in truth, it was only because they ended the Cold War that the world could make the extraordinary technological leap we've witnessed in recent decades."

Indeed, after 1991, the United States and European nations nearly halved their military expenditures, redirecting vast resources toward science, medicine, and education. Mobile communication, breakthroughs in medical technology, the rise of artificial intelligence—all of it, in one way or another, grew out of the pause in global confrontation. As early as September 1991, George Bush called it the "peace dividend."

A Vacation After the War—that was the title of a film Vladimir Vysotsky once dreamed of making in Hollywood, though he never did. Gorbachev and his American partners made that dream real—not on-screen, but in history itself. And yet, as we now know, the vacation was not forever. It lasted only thirty years.

THE REVOLUTION DEVOURS ITS OWN CHILDREN

On December 26, units of the rebellious Georgian National Guard, led by Tengiz Kitovani, storm a detention center and free the notorious crime boss Jaba Ioseliani. Thus begins a strange partnership that Ioseliani himself would later describe as "an obscure sculptor and a very famous thief." From that moment on, Kitovani and Ioseliani jointly lead the insurgents fighting against President Zviad Gamsakhurdia.

They demand Gamsakhurdia's resignation, promising him and his remaining supporters safe passage out of the Supreme Council building on Rustaveli Avenue in Tbilisi. By the end of December, the Georgian president's authority no longer extends beyond the city center.

Gamsakhurdia refuses to step down—until January 6, when he is finally forced to concede and flee his post. He escapes to Armenia, while power in Georgia passes to the so-called Military Council, composed of just two men: Kitovani and Ioseliani.*

The former head of parliament, Akaki Asatiani, is convinced the coup plotters had backing from Moscow: "Shevardnadze didn't control them directly, of course, but he encouraged and incited them. And the man who actually carried out the operation to overthrow us was Burbulis—he coordinated the whole thing." Asatiani is convinced that the reason was Gamsakhurdia's support for the rebellious Chechen leader, Dudayev. According to Asatiani, during their last meeting, Yeltsin told him, "Tell Zviad about that mustached one," referring to Dudayev. "You understand? This is my final warning."

Years later, Gennady Burbulis would respond evasively when asked about his role in Gamsakhurdia's fall: "I don't remember anymore; I'd have to check the documents." Yet the influence of Moscow's "invisible hand" in Tbilisi—whether through Burbulis or Shevardnadze—should not be overstated. By late 1991 and into 1992, the new Russian officials weren't entirely sure they could control events even within their own borders.

The fact that an organized crime leader came to power in Georgia is deeply symbolic. Across the collapsing Soviet Union, gangsters turned out to be the best prepared for the state's disintegration. As the old government structures ceased functioning and Soviet security forces disbanded, criminals moved swiftly to fill the power vacuum in many places.

LIMBO

Lithuanian actress Ingeborga Dapkūnaitė is preparing to travel to America at the end of December. She has been invited to perform in the play *Slip of the Tongue* at Chicago's renowned Steppenwolf Theatre, where her costar will be none other than John Malkovich.

---

* Gamsakhurdia would flee Georgia, hide in Chechnya, attempt to return, and die under unclear circumstances in 1993. Kitovani and Ioseliani would invite Eduard Shevardnadze to lead Georgia. By 1995, both men would be arrested, while Shevardnadze—the once democratic Soviet foreign minister—would serve as president of Georgia until 2003, when he would be overthrown in the Rose Revolution.

At twenty-eight, it's her first role abroad—an opportunity so surreal it feels like a dream, an impossible fantasy come true.

The political situation around her is just as ridiculous. Her homeland, Lithuania, had declared independence almost a year ago, yet Ingeborga is still traveling on Soviet documents because the newly free Lithuania hasn't gotten around to printing passports. Even more absurd, the Soviet Union—technically dead but still kicking—keeps issuing exit visas, and those can only be stamped in Moscow. So a country could break away, get a pat on the back from places like Iceland, but to actually leave the USSR, you still had to ask Moscow bureaucrats for permission. For Ingeborga, like any good Soviet citizen, this isn't weird at all—it is just how life has always worked.

"For a few years, in 1990 and 1991, we lived as if in limbo—it's a Catholic concept, where the soul is stuck between heaven and hell, unable to move on. We too spent quite some time in that state of suspension," she will recall.

On December 29, she boards a train in Vilnius. Her Soviet passport holds two precious exit visas: one for Poland and one for the United States. She also has a Polish entry visa, and her American visa is supposed to be issued in Warsaw.

As she crosses the Belarusian-Polish border, a Soviet border guard checks her documents. He doesn't yet realize that it's no longer technically a Soviet border and is still following Soviet instructions to the letter.

Ingeborga cheerfully explains her plans: she'll go to Warsaw, get her visa, and then fly to America.

"Pack your things; get off the train; you're going nowhere. Come on, hurry up," the officer orders flatly.

She doesn't understand what's happening—and he doesn't see what's unclear. As a citizen of the USSR, Dapkūnaitė is required to obtain her US visa in Moscow—nowhere else. Those are the Soviet rules. It doesn't matter whether the Soviet Union exists or not; the rules haven't been canceled.

"Don't hold up the other passengers. Gather your things," the border guard snaps. The dead Soviet Union sinks its claws into her dream, determined to keep her from reaching America.

"I've changed my mind," Ingeborga says, her eyes full of tears. "I won't go to America. I'll just go to Warsaw—I have a Polish visa, right? I'll walk around for a bit and come back."

That, at least, isn't against the rules.

"Oh, I see," the guard sneers. He grabs her passport and viciously crosses out her US exit visa with a thick pencil, over and over.

The actress is devastated. She travels on to Poland in tears. Neither she nor the border guard realizes yet that Soviet exit visas are now meaningless—and their absence will trouble no one.

On the very last day of 1991, Dapkūnaitė receives her US visa in Warsaw, and on January 1, 1992, she flies to Chicago.

FORGOTTEN IN SPACE

Soviet cosmonaut Sergei Krikalev spends this New Year aboard the space station Mir. He left Earth on May 18, 1991—before the coup, before Yeltsin was elected president of Russia, before Freddie Mercury died in November, and before the end of the war in Iraq. Krikalev's hometown was still called Leningrad, not St. Petersburg. He launched from the Baikonur Cosmodrome in the Kazakh SSR, and the man who bid him farewell was Oleg Baklanov, then a space industry overseer in the Central Committee—not yet a member of the GKChP.

Krikalev blasted off into space thirty years after Yuri Gagarin's historic flight—he would end up spending nearly 4,200 times longer in orbit on this mission alone. Yet, unlike the first cosmonaut, Krikalev's face would remain unknown to most; he would never become a star.

According to the original plan, Krikalev was supposed to return in October 1991. But by summer, it became clear that the Soviet space program was in deep trouble. Funding was scarce, and one of the planned missions for the fall was canceled. In July, mission control asked Krikalev if he was willing to extend his stay in orbit—by another six months. The cosmonaut weighed his options and agreed.

"The strongest argument is economic because this allows us to save resources," Krikalev said from orbit. "It's tough for me—not great for my health. But the country is in such difficulty now that saving money has to be the top priority."

In reality, mission control faces a difficult dilemma: either risk the life and health of the cosmonaut or endanger the Mir station itself. If everyone returns to Earth, the uncrewed station will most likely be lost.

Life on Mir is far from easy. Space is cramped, the air reeks of sweat, and the constant hum of fans and pumps is loud enough to cause hearing loss. But Krikalev knows how to ignore it all. His favorite pastime is staring out the window, gazing at Earth for hours.

On October 2, a new group of cosmonauts arrived at Mir, and on October 10, they returned to Earth—leaving Krikalev. In total, he would spend 311 days and 20 hours in space. During that time, he would take another spacewalk, run an experiment testing a can of Coca-Cola in zero gravity, exercise daily to prevent muscle atrophy, and wonder what would happen to the Soviet space program now that the Soviet Union itself no longer existed.

His wife, Elena, works at mission control and occasionally speaks with her husband, left stranded in space. But she tries not to upset him with bad news—she doesn't tell him that his salary has become worthless or that her colleagues are planning a strike, which could put his return to Earth in jeopardy altogether.

Krikalev will return on March 25, 1992, to a different country—he will be the last citizen of the now-defunct Soviet Union. And he won't notice much of a difference. "Nothing much seems to have changed," he will say upon landing back on Earth.

What surprises him most isn't the new borders or the emergence of new states, but how the seasons change. "At first, the Earth was dark, and now it's white. Winter has come, and before that, it was summer. Now, it's beginning to bloom again. That's the most impressive change you can see from space."

COMMONWEALTH
OF INDEPENDENT STATES
1991 TO PRESENT

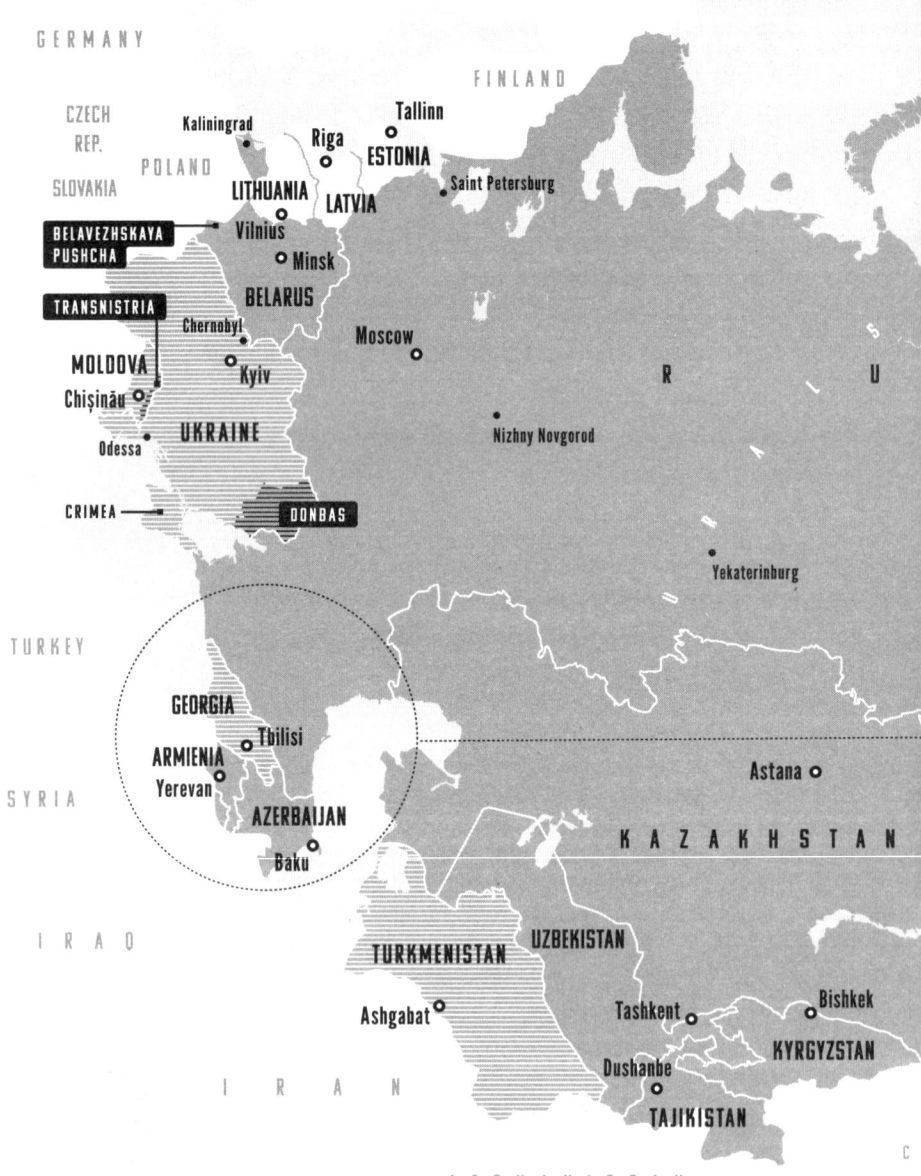

GERMANY

FINLAND

CZECH
REP.

Kaliningrad

Riga

Tallinn

POLAND

ESTONIA

Saint Petersburg

SLOVAKIA

LITHUANIA

LATVIA

BELAVEZHSKAYA
PUSHCHA

Vilnius

Minsk

BELARUS

Moscow

TRANSNISTRIA

Chernobyl

MOLDOVA

Kyiv

Chișinău

Nizhny Novgorod

Odessa

UKRAINE

CRIMEA

DONBAS

Yekaterinburg

TURKEY

GEORGIA

Tbilisi

ARMIENIA

Astana

Yerevan

SYRIA

AZERBAIJAN

KAZAKHSTAN

Baku

IRAQ

UZBEKISTAN

TURKMENISTAN

Bishkek

Ashgabat

Tashkent

KYRGYZSTAN

Dushanbe

IRAN

TAJIKISTAN

AFGHANISTAN

R   U

C

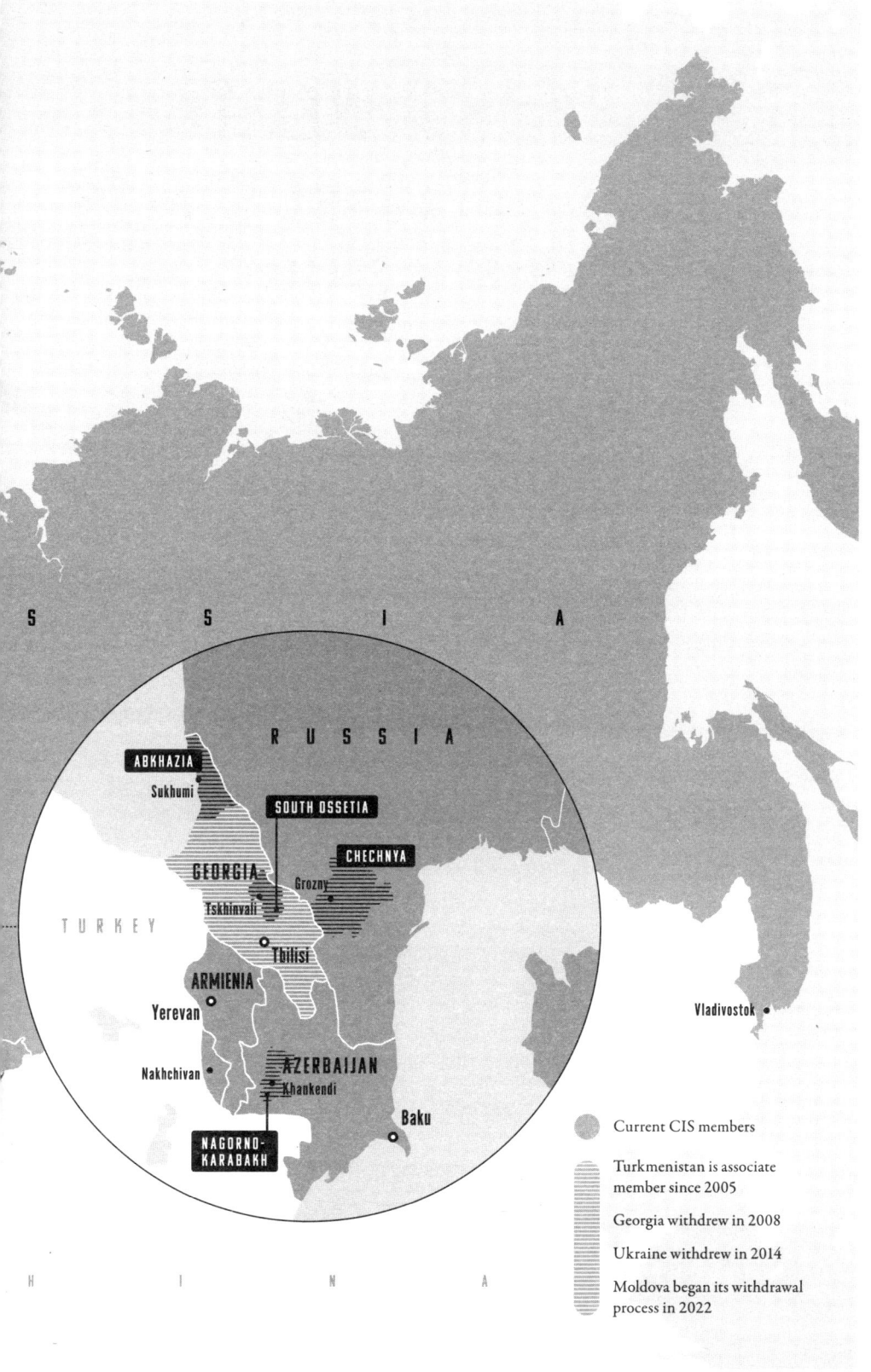

S   S   I   A

R U S S I A

ABKHAZIA
Sukhumi

SOUTH OSSETIA

CHECHNYA

GEORGIA   Grozny
Tskhinvali

Tbilisi

TURKEY

ARMENIA
Yerevan

Nakhchivan   AZERBAIJAN
Khankendi

Baku

NAGORNO-
KARABAKH

Vladivostok

H   I   N   A

Current CIS members

Turkmenistan is associate
member since 2005

Georgia withdrew in 2008

Ukraine withdrew in 2014

Moldova began its withdrawal
process in 2022

EPILOGUE

1

"In Russia, one must live a long life"—this phrase was often repeated by the Soviet dissidents. Many of them lived long enough to witness the collapse of the Soviet Union, the fall of the totalitarian system, and they were happy.

I remember their eyes and voices well in 1991—mostly, of course, I saw them on television.

Back then, they didn't inspire any sympathy in me. Victors are rarely likable. They sounded so self-assured, as if they had forgotten that any triumph lasts for just one fleeting, joyful moment.

Their moment of glory passed quickly. President Yeltsin soon dismissed the so-called young democrats, surrounded himself with former communists and KGB officers, and launched a war in Chechnya.

2

A lot of time has passed since then. I was nineteen when Vladimir Putin became president of Russia and restored the Soviet national anthem. I was twenty-four when he called the collapse of the USSR the greatest geopolitical catastrophe of the twentieth century.

I knew countless people crushed and hollowed out by the fall of the Soviet Union. They were impoverished; their world had collapsed.

My uncle, a People's Artist of the Turkmen SSR and soloist of the Ashgabat Opera, was forced to abandon all his possessions and flee with his family—just to survive. The former First Secretary of the Communist Party of Turkmenistan had turned into a mad dictator, banned opera, and repressed all the artists. Until the end of his life, my uncle made ends meet by singing in a church choir in a small town in Central Russia.

I know countless stories like his. It wasn't just the material foundations of many people's lives that were destroyed—everything they believed in, had been raised on, and lived for was annihilated.

In recent years, working as a journalist, I've consistently interviewed all kinds of people whose conscious lives and careers had peaked during the Soviet era. Many of them appeared to me as miserable old people whose lives had lost their meaning—shattered by the collapse of the empire they had devoted themselves to. And then, before my eyes, they started to change. It was as if they grew younger, spread their wings, their eyes filled with joy. Russia's occupation of Crimea, Putin's new foreign policy—these gave them confidence and hope that none of it had been in vain.

For example, in 2011, Oleg Baklanov, the former curator of the Soviet military-industrial complex and a GKChP member, wept in front of me as he remembered the lost chance of 1991. But by 2018, he was happy and proud. By then, his strongest feeling had become hatred toward America.

"An American sticks a finger up his ass and thinks he's winding up a gramophone," he said, quoting a crude Soviet children's rhyme and laughing heartily as he commented on US foreign policy.

Putin had no intention of restoring the Soviet Union. He had no need for the old Soviet ideology—no interest in a bright future, justice, freedom, or equality. Instead, he merged American capitalism with Russian nationalism.

The ideologists of the Prague Spring in 1968 dreamed of "socialism with a human face"—but Putin found a different formula: "capitalism without a human face." No human rights, no democracy—just cynicism and brutality.

Ironically, Nina Andreeva, an orthodox communist who refused to compromise her principles back in 1989, stuck to her beliefs even thirty years later. She lived in poverty until the end of her life and, as late as 2020, wrote another open letter—this time against Putin and his "criminal oligarchic regime."

Most Soviet dissidents never stayed silent—they opposed Putin and the reconstruction of an authoritarian system. Many of them had to witness the collapse of their ideals.

In 2010, Andrei Sakharov's widow, Elena Bonner, couldn't attend a protest against Putin on Moscow's Pushkin Square. She was living in Boston with her children and was seriously ill. But she sent a letter:

I am a Muscovite, a Jew of "Caucasian nationality." In 1941, I defended my country; in 1945, I cried with joy. In 1953, I protested against the "Doctors' Plot." From the spring of 1937, I waited for any news that my mother would return from the labor camp. And when she came back, rang the doorbell—I didn't recognize her, I mistook her for a beggar. And all these years in my dreams, I cried over my father, who was executed. And I wept for my grandmother, who took her last breath in besieged Leningrad.

And all my life, I felt guilty—that they arrested my mother, that I didn't recognize her when she came home. Guilty that my father was executed. Guilty that I didn't stay and die with my grandmother in the blockade of Leningrad. I was busy saving my motherland, you see! My motherland!

And now I have no strength left to save it. I don't even know how. Consider me there on Pushkin Square at the rally, saving the motherland once again—though my legs no longer carry me.

Among the losers of the Putin era were not only the former dissidents but also those pragmatic young reformers who had rallied around Yeltsin in the 1990s, hoping to reshape Russia.

In 2021, I found myself at a celebration organized by Gennady Burbulis to mark the thirtieth anniversary of Yeltsin's election as president. Almost all surviving members of Yeltsin's first reformist government were present. The gathering felt more like a clandestine meeting of aging members of a banned organization than a reunion of the nation's founding fathers. Burbulis gave a speech; they listened to recordings of sixties-era dissident ballads, drank vodka, ate cake—and dispersed with quiet sorrow.

Another group of losers was the younger generation—those who had grown up believing that "life, liberty, and the pursuit of happiness" were the true values. Many couldn't reconcile themselves with Putin's invasion of Ukraine and were forced to leave Russia.

Their peers—a generation of Ukrainians raised with the same values— were forced to fight and die for their country.

3

The people now in power in Russia are the last Soviet generation—those who absorbed Soviet culture but not Soviet faith. They admired the Cold War, viewed dissidents as traitors, and took pleasure in grandiose talk of their own greatness. Yet, at the same time, they always craved American jeans, cigarettes, and alcohol.

The psychological traumas they suffered during the collapse of the USSR continue to shape Russia's future. They carry their cynical disbelief in democracy and human rights like a banner.

And not just in Russia—perhaps such people hold power across the world today.

They boldly call tyranny "freedom" and election fraud "voting." They are convinced that democracy is obsolete. They speak of "conservatism," "traditional values," and "greatness," all the while knowing that the most comfortable stance is to believe in nothing at all.

In history, there is no final point—no happy ending, no tragic conclusion. Yesterday's victors may become tomorrow's losers. The bright side can one day turn dark, and then, just as suddenly, shift back again.

ACKNOWLEDGMENTS

I would like to dedicate this book to my mother and my grandmother. My grandmother passed away in 2008. My mother died in 2024.

I was unable to attend my mom's funeral because the Russian authorities sentenced me in absentia to eight and a half years in prison.

I would also like to thank the protagonists of this book—those whose stories and reflections helped me write it. I conducted more than three hundred interviews for this book, and I cannot name everyone, including some who must remain anonymous for their own safety. Sadly, many of them did not live to see it published.

Thank you for their stories to: Adam Michnik, Akakiy Asatiani, Albina Nazimova, Alexei Leonov, Alexander Nevzorov, Alla Gerber, Alla Pugacheva, Anatoly Chubais, Andrei Dunaev, Andrei Isaev, Andrei Kozyrev, Andrei Kurayev, Andrei Makarevich, Andrei Sharonov, Anastasia Kurekhina, Arkady Murashov, Artemy Troitsky, Askar Akayev, Azer Mursaliev, Boris Grebenshchikov, Dmitry Muratov, Garry Kasparov, Gennady Burbulis, Gennady Khazanov, Gennady Zyuganov, Georgy Yefimov, Grigory Yavlinsky, Ihor Yukhnovsky, Ingeborga Dapkūnaitė, Jack Matlock, Joanna Stingray, Konstantin Kagalovsky, Konstantin Zatulin, Kseniya Sobchak, Laima Vaikule, Lev Ponomarev, Levon Ter-Petrosyan, Leonid Boguslavsky, Leonid Kravchuk, Lyudmila Narusova, Mikhail Baryshnikov, Mikhail Borshchevsky, Mikhail Gorbachev, Natalya Dollezhal, Nikolai Travkin, Oleg Baklanov, Oleg Sysuyev, Olga Slobodskaya, Olga Starovoitova, Oles Doniy, Petr Aven, Petru Luscinski, Platon Borshchevsky, Roald Sagdeev, Ruslan Linkov, Sergei Baburin, Sergei Filatov, Sergei Krasavchenko, Sergei Stankevich, Stanislav Shushkevich, Stepan Khmara, Straub Talbott, Valery Todorovsky, Vasily Shakhnovsky,

Viktor Alksnis, Viktor Ivanenko, Viktor Khrolenko, Vitaly Korotich, Vitautas Landsbergis, Vladimir Posner, Vladimir Zhirinovsky, Veniamin Smekhov, Wolfgang Schäuble, Yevgenia Albats, Yelena Lukyanova, Yuliy Gusman, Yuri Feklistov, Yuri Rost, Zardusht Alizadeh, Zory Balayan, and many more.

I'm deeply thankful to all my colleagues who supported me in working on this book: Alina Saidasheva, Pavel Krasovitsky, Anna Afanasyeva, and Olga Terekhova—your help has been invaluable. I also want to thank those who asked me not to mention their names, as they or their families still live in Russia.

And I would like to thank my readers: at a time when books are being banned, removed from libraries, and even destroyed, being a reader is not always easy.

SOURCES

CHAPTER 1: UNFULFILLED HEROES

Author's interview with Mikhail Gorbachev.

Boesen, Kathrine. "Jerry Rubin and the Youth International Party." University of Copenhagen, 2011.

Bonner, Yelena. *Dochki-materi.* Moscow: Progress, 1994.

Bonner, Yelena. *Volnye zametki k rodoslovnoi Andreia Sakharova.* Moscow: Prava Cheloveka, 1996.

Chuprinin, Sergei. *Ottepel. Sobytiia. Mart 1953—avgust 1968 goda.* Moscow: Novoe literaturnoe obozrenie, 2020.

Deleuze, Gilles. "May '68 Didn't Happen." In Gilles Deleuze, *Two Regimes of Madness: Texts and Interviews 1975–1995.* Semiotext(e), 2007.

Dobrynin, Anatolii. *Sugubo doveritelno. Posol v Vashingtone pri shesti prezidentakh SShA* (1962–1986 gg.) Moscow: Mezhdunarodnye otnosheniia, 2019.

Farber, David. *Chicago '68.* Chicago: University of Chicago Press, 1988.

Forman, Miloš, and Jan Novak. *Turnaround: A Memoir.* New York: Villard Books, 1994.

Gorbacheva, Raisa. *Ia nadeius.* Moscow: Novosti, 1991.

Kamanin, N. P. *Skrytyi kosmos.* Vols. 1–4. Moscow: Infortekst-IF, 1996–1997.

Mlynář, Zdeněk. *Kholodom veet ot Kremlia.* New York: Problems of Eastern Europe, 1988.

Rost, Iurii. *Sakharov. "Kefir nado gret'": Istoriia liubvi, rasskazannaia Elenoĭ Bonner Iuriiu Rostu.* Moscow: Boslen, 2018.

Rubin, Jerry. *Do It!: Scenarios of the Revolution.* New York: Touchstone, 1970.

Sakharov, Andrei. *Razmyshlenia o progressive, mirnom sosushchestvovanii i intellektualnoi svobode.* Frankfurt: Posev, 1968.

Sakharov, Andrei. *Vospominaniia.* Moscow: Prava Cheloveka, 1996.

Solzhenitsyn, Aleksandr. *Arkhipelag Gulag.* Paris: YMCA-Press, 1973.

Solzhenitsyn, Aleksandr. *Bodalsia telenok s dubom: Ocherki literanurnoi zhisni.* Moscow: Soglasie, 1996.

Vaissié, Cécile. *Sartre et l'URSS. Le Joueur et les survivants.* Rennes: Presses universitaires de Rennes, 2023.

Voznesensky, Andrei. *Na virtualnom vetru.* Moscow: Vagrius, 1998.

"Vsia pravda o sudimostiakh Sergeia Paradzhanova." *Segodnia*, January 29, 2008. https://
web.archive.org/web/20171003125402/https://www.segodnya.ua/ukraine/vcja-pravda
-o-cudimoctjakh-cerheja-paradzhanova.html.

White House Press Secretary Telegram, John F. Kennedy to Nikita S. Khrushchev,
April 12, 1961, National Security Archive. https://nsarchive.gwu.edu/document
/20832-02.

Yevtushenko, Yevgeny. *Shestidesantnik: Memuarnaia proza*. Moscow: AST, 2006.

Yevtushenko, Yevgeny. *Volchii pasport*. Moscow: Vagrius, 1998.

CHAPTER 2: TIMELESSNESS AND VODKA

Afanaseva, Olga. *Mstislav Rostropovich. Liubov's violoncheliu v rukakh*. Moscow, 2015.

Aksiutin, Iu. V. "Kashchei razvitogo sotsializma." *Rossiya* 21, no. 2 (2010).

Author's interview with Alexei Leonov.

Author's interview with Natalia Dollezhal.

Author's interview with Filipp Bobkov.

Author's interview with Mikhail Baryshnikov.

Boguslavskii, S. "Kremlevskie tainy: Vverkh po lestnitse, vedushchei vniz." *Literaturnaya
Gazeta*, no. 4 (January 30, 1991).

Brzezinski, Zbigniew. *The Grand Chessboard: American Primacy and Its Geostrategic
Imperatives*. New York: Basic Books, 1997.

Brzezinski, Zbigniew. *Power and Principle: Memoirs of the National Security Adviser,
1977–1981*. New York: Farrar, Straus and Giroux, 1983.

"Bunny Goes Bugs: Rabbit Attacks President." *Washington Post*, August 30, 1979.

Carter, Jimmy. "Malaise" speech, July 15, 1979.

Dobrynin, Anatolii. *Sugubo doveritelno. Posol v Vashingtone pri shesti prezidentakh SShA*
(1962–1986 gg.). Moscow, 2019.

Gati, Charles (ed.). *Zbig: The Strategy and Statecraft of Zbigniew Brzezinski*. Johns Hopkins
University Press, 2013.

"General'nii pogrom." *Ukraïnskii visnik* 6 (March 1972). https://zubruc.eu/node/109870.

Gevorkian, Natalia, Andrei Kolesnikov, and Natalia Timakova. *Ot pervogo litsa: Razgovory s
Vladimirom Putinym*. Moscow, 2000.

Gorbacheva, Raisa. *Ia nadeius*. Moscow, 1991.

Grum-Grzhimailo, T. "Shtrikhi k portretu Mstislava Rostropovicha." *Kontinent*, no. 73 (1992).

"Ideinye pererozhdentsy," *Iszvestia*, March 16, 1978.

Katanian, Vasilii. *Paradzhanov. Tsena vechnogo prazdnika*. Moscow, 1994.

Khentova, S. M. *Rostropovich*. Saint Petersburg, 1993.

Kochetov, Vsevolod. "Chego zhe ty khochesh?" *Oktyabr*, no. 9–11 (1969).

Kuniaev, Stanislav. *Russkii dom*. Moscow, 2013.

Kuniaev, Stanislav. *Vospominaniia*. Moscow, 2012.

Medvedev, Roi, and Dmitrii Ermakov. *"Seryi kardinal." M. A. Suslov: politicheskii portret*.
Moscow, 1992.

Medvedev, Roy. *Okruzhenie Stalina*. Moscow, 2010.

"O bor'be KPSS za splochennost mezhdunarodnago kommunisticheskogo dvizheniia.
Doklad tovarishcha M. A. Suslova na Plenume TsK KPSS 14 fevralia 1964 goda."
Pravda, April 3, 1964.

Pantsov, Aleksandr. *Den Siaopin*. Moscow, 2014.

Sakharov, Andrei. *Vospominaniia*. Moscow, 1996.

Shatunovskii, I. "Chelovek v futliare." *Ogoniok*, no. 4 (1989).

Sidorov, Evgenii. "Zapiski iz-pod poly." *Znamia*, no. 2 (2008), no. 3 (2010), no. 12 (2010), no. 6 (2011).

Snegirev, Vladimir. *Aleksandr Yakovlev. Chuzhoi sredi svoikh. Partiinaya zhizn "arkhitektora perestroiki."* Moscow, 2023.

Solzhenitsyn, Aleksandr. *Bodalsia telenok s dubom: Ocherki literanurnoi zhisni.* Moscow, 1996.

Tarkovsky, Andrei. *Martirolog. Dnevniki*. Moscow, 2008.

Tumanov, Vadim. "Vse poteriat — i vnovnachats mechty . . ." Moscow, 2016.

"U.S. Foreign Policy in the Carter Years, 1977–1981: Highest-Level Memos to the President." National Security Archive. https://nsarchive.gwu.edu/briefing-book/dnsa/2023-12-14/us-foreign-policy-carter-years-1977-1981.

Vaïsse, Justin. *Zbigniew Brzezinski: America's Grand Strategist*. Harvard University Press, 2018.

Vishnevskaia, Galina. *Galina: istoriia zhizni*. Moscow, 1991.

Vlady, Marina. *Vladimir ili Prervannyi polet*. Moscow, 1989.

"V 1976 godu na Petrapavlovskoï kreposti ostavili 42-metrovuiu nadpis, Vy raspinaete svobodu, no dusha cheloveka ne znaet okov!" *Meduza*, November 28, 2022. https://meduza.io/feature/2022/11/28v-1976-godu-na-petrapavlovskoy-kreposti-ostavili-42-metrovuyu-nadpis-vy-raspinaete-svobodu-no-dusha-cheloveka-ne-znaet-okov.

V Politbiuro TsK KPSS . . . Po zapisiam Anatoliia Cherniaeva, Vadima Medvedeva, Georgiia Shakhnazarova (1985–1991). Moscow, 2008.

Wiener, Jon. *Gimme Some Truth: The John Lennon FBI Files*. Berkeley: University of California Press, 2000.

Wilson, Elizabeth. *Mstislav Rostropovich: Cellist, Teacher, Legend*. Faber & Faber, 2021.

Yakovlev, Aleksandr. *Omut pamiati*. Moscow, 2000.

Yakovlev, Aleksandr. "Protiv antiistorizma." *Literaturnaya Gazeta*, no. 46 (November 15, 1972).

CHAPTER 3: LAVISH FUNERALS

Author's interview with Artemy Troitsky.

Author's interview with Anastasia Kuryokhina.

Author's interview with Boris Grebenshchikov.

Author's interview with Garry Kasparov.

Author's interview with Gennady Khazanov.

Author's interview with Grigory Yavlinsky.

Author's interview with Joanna Stingray.

Author's interview with Yuli Gusman.

Blotskii, O. M. *Vladimir Putin*. Moscow, 2003.

Bonner, Yelena. *Postskriptum. Kniga o gorkovskoï ssylke*. Paris, 1988.

Elliott, Michael, and Yuri Zarakhovich. "Garry Kasparov: The Master's Next Move." *Time*, March 29, 2007. https://content.time.com/time/subscriber/article/0,33009,1604889,00.html.

Gdlyan, Telman, and Nikolai Ivanov. *Kremlevskoe delo*. Moscow, 1994.

Gevorkian, Natalia, Andrei Kolesnikov, and Natalia Timakova. *Ot pervogo litsa: Razgovory s Vladimirom Putinym*. Moscow, 2000.

Gik, E. "Garri: vunderkind i genii igry. Epilog." *Nauka i zhizn*, no. 2 (2006). https://www
.nkj.ru/archive/articles/4109/.

Kalgin, Vitalii. *Viktor Tsoi*. Moscow, 2015.

Kalgin, Vitalii. *Viktor Tsoi. Svoimi slovami. Kniga interviu. 1983–1990*. Moscow, 2003.

Kasparov, Garry. *Child of Change: An Autobiography*. Hutchinson, 1987.

Kasparov, Garry. *Unlimited Challenge: An Autobiography*. Grove Press, 1990.

Katanian, Vasilii. *Paradzhanov. Tsena vechnogo prazdnika*. Moscow, 1994.

Putin, Vladimir, Nataliya Gevorkyan, Natalya Timakova, and Andrei Kolesnikov. *First
Person: An Astonishingly Frank Self-Portrait by Russia's President*. PublicAffairs, 2000.

Rybin, Aleksei. *Tri kita: BG, Maik, Tsoi*. Saint Petersburg, 2013.

Sakharov, Andrei. *Vospominaniia*. Vol. 1. Moscow, 1996.

Schmemann, Serge. "Karpov and Kasparov Gird for Big Chess Match." *New York Times*,
September 3, 1985. https://www.nytimes.com/1985/09/03/nyregion/karpov-and
-kasparov-gird-for-big-chess-match.html.

Sheremet, Pavel. "U menia ne bylo inoï dorogi - ili tiurma, ili komsomol." *Kommersant*,
March 10, 2003. https://www.kommersant.ru/doc/370014.

Snegirev, Vladimir. *Aleksandr Yakovlev. Chuzhoi sredi svoikh. Partiinai zhizn "arkhitektora
perestroiki."* Moscow, 2023.

Solzhenitsyn, Aleksandr. "Ugodilo zernyshko promezh dvukh zhernovov: Ocherki
izgnaniia." *Novy Mir*, no. 9, 11 (1998); no. 2 (1999); no. 9, 12 (2000); no. 4 (2001);
no. 11 (2003).

Stingray, Joanna, and Madison Stingray. *Stingrei v Strane Chudes*. Moscow, 2019.

Stingray, Joanna, and Madison Stingray. *Stingrei v Zazerkale*. Moscow, 2019.

Tarkovsky, Andrei. *Martirolog. Dnevniki*. Moscow, 2008.

Troitskii, Artemii. *Istoriia sovetskogo roka*. Moscow, 1990.

Tsoi, Marianna. *Viktor Tsoi. Tochka otscheta*. Moscow, 1991.

Tsoi, Marianna, and Aleksandr Zhitinskii. *Viktor Tsoi. Stikhi, dokumenty, vospominaniia*.
Leningrad, 1991.

Vlady, Marina. *Vladimir ili Prervannyi polet*. Moscow, 1989.

Zhitinskii, Aleksandr. *Tsoi Forever*. Saint Petersburg, 2012.

CHAPTER 4: YOUNG CHAMPIONS

Author's interview with Garry Kasparov.

Author's interview with Grigory Yavlinsky.

Author's interview with Mikhail Gorbachev.

Chernyaev, Anatoly. *Sovmestnyi iskhod. Dnevnik dvukh èpokh. 1972–1991*. Moscow, 2008.

Church, George J. "The Rise and Rise of Raisa Gorbachev." *Time*, January 4, 1988. https://
time.com/archive/6711232/the-rise-and-rise-of-raisa-gorbachev/.

Falin, Valentin. *Bez skidok na obstoiatelstva. Politicheskie vospominaniia*. Moscow, 2016.

Falin, Valentin. *Konflikty v Kremle. Sumerki bogov po-russki*. Moscow, 1999.

Fisher, Max. "Robert Gates Was Wrong on the Most Important Issue He Ever Faced."
Washington Post, January 7, 2014. https://www.washingtonpost.com/news/worldviews
/wp/2014/01/07/robert-gates-was-wrong-on-the-most-important-issue-he-ever-faced/.

Gevorkian, Natalia, Andrei Kolesnikov, and Natalia Timakova. *Ot pervogo litsa: Razgovory s
Vladimirom Putinym*. Moscow, 2000.

Gorbachev, Mikhail. *Naedine s soboi*. Moscow, 2012.

Higginbotham, Adam. *Midnight in Chernobyl: The Untold Story of the World's Greatest Nuclear Disaster*. New York: Simon & Schuster, 2019.

Hoffman, David E. *The Dead Hand*. Doubleday, 2009.

"An Interview with Mikhail Gorbachev." *Time*, September 9, 1985.

Kalgin, Vitalii. *Viktor Tsoi*. Moscow, 2015.

Kalgin, Vitalii. *Viktor Tsoi. Svoimi slovami. Kniga interviu. 1983–1990*. Moscow, 2003.

Rybin, Aleksei. *Tri kita: BG, Maik, Tsoi*. Saint Petersburg, 2013.

Sakharov, Andrei. *Vospominaniia*. Moscow, 1996.

Solzhenitsyn, Aleksandr. "Ugodilo zernyshko promezh dvukh zhernovov: Ocherki izgnaniia." *Novy Mir*, no. 9, 11 (1998); no. 2 (1999); no. 9, 12 (2000); no. 4 (2001); no. 11 (2003).

Stingray, Joanna, and Madison Stingray. *Stingreĭ v Strane Chudes*. Moscow, 2019.

Stingray, Joanna, and Madison Stingray. *Stingrei v Zazerkale*. Moscow, 2019.

Taubman, William. *Gorbachev: His Life and Times*. W. W. Norton, 2017.

Troitskii, Artemii. *Istoriia sovetskogo roka*. Moscow, 1990.

Tsoi, Marianna. *Viktor Tsoi. Tochka otscheta*. Moscow, 1991.

Tsoi, Marianna, and Aleksandr Zhitinskii. *Viktor Tsoi. Stikhi, dokumenty, vospominaniia*. Leningrad, 1991.

Usol' tsev, Vladimir. *Sosluzhivets. Neizvestnye stranitsy zhizni Prezidenta*. Moscow, 2004.

V Politbiuro TsK KPSS . . . Po zapisiam Anatoliia Cherniaeva, Vadima Medvedeva, Georgiia Shakhnazarova (1985–1991). Moscow, 2008.

Zhitinskii, Aleksandr. *Tsoi Forever*. Saint Petersburg, 2012.

CHAPTER 5: UNINVITED FREEDOM

Author's interview with Alexander Lyubimov.

Author's interview with Alla Pugacheva.

Author's interview with Artemy Troitsky.

Author's interview with Boris Grebenshchikov.

Author's interview with Garry Kasparov.

Author's interview with Laima Vaikule.

Author's interview with Levon Ter-Petrosyan.

Author's interview with Roald Sagdeev.

Author's interview with Vazgen Manukyan.

Barabanov, Boris. *Assa. Kniga peremen*. Saint Petersburg, 2008.

Beliakov, Aleksei. *Alla Pugacheva. Zhizn i udivitel nye prikliucheniia velikoi pevitsy*. Moscow, 2019.

Bonner, Yelena. *Dochki-materi*. Moscow, 1994.

Bonner, Yelena. *Postskriptum. Kniga o gorkovskoi ssylke*. Paris, 1988.

Bonner, Yelena. *Volnye zametki k rodoslovnoi Andreia Sakharova*. Moscow, 1996.

Chernyaev, Anatoly. *Sovmestnyi iskhod. Dnevnik dvukh ėpokh. 1972–1991*. Moscow, 2008.

Dymerskaya-Tsigelman, L. "A Lecture in Moscow." *Jews and Jewish Topics in Soviet and East-European Publications*, no. 4 (Winter 1986–1987): 46–53.

Gates, Robert. Memorandum "Gorbachev's Gameplan." November 24, 1987. https://nsarchive.gwu.edu/document/22555-document-08-cia-deputy-director-robert-gates.

Gdlyan, Telman, and Evgenii Dodolev. *Mafiia vremen bezzakoniia.* Yerevan, 1991.

Gdlyan, Telman, and Evgenii Dodolev. *Piramida-1.* Moscow, 1990.

Gdlyan, Telman, and Nikolai Ivanov. *Kremlevskoe delo.* Moscow, 1994.

Gorbacheva, Raisa. *Ia nadeius.* Moscow, 1991.

Grachev, Andrei. *Dalshe bez menia . . . Ukhod Prezidenta.* Moscow, 1994.

Grachev, Andrei. *Gorbachev.* Moscow, 2001.

Grachev, Andrei. *Kremlevskaia khronika.* Moscow, 1994.

Grachev, Andrei. *Poslednii den SSSR. Svidetelstvo ochevidtsa. Vospominaniia pomoshchnika prezidenta Sovetskogo Soiuza.* Moscow, 2022.

Kalgin, Vitalii. *Viktor Tsoi.* Moscow, 2015.

Kalgin, Vitalii. *Viktor Tsoi. Svoimi slovami. Kniga interviu. 1983–1990.* Moscow, 2003.

Korey, William. *Russian Antisemitism, Pamyat, and the Demonology of Zionism.* Routledge, 1995.

Korguniuk, Iurii, and Sergei Zaslavskii. *Rossiiskaia mnogopartiïnost: stanovlenie, funktsionirovanie, razvitie.* Moscow, 1996.

Korotich, Vitalii. *Ot pervogo litsa.* Moscow, 2018.

Laqueur, Walter. *Black Hundred: The Rise of the Extreme Right in Russia.* New York, 1993.

Laruelle, Marlene. "The Iuzhinskii Circle: Far☒Right Metaphysics in the Soviet Underground and Its Legacy Today." *Russian Review* 74, no. 4 (2015): 563–80.

Ligachev, Egor. *Predosterezhenie.* Moscow, 1999.

Mikhailov, V. "Krasnaia volna na mutnoï vode." *Komsomolskaia pravda*, no. 18 (January 23, 1987).

Mitrokhin, Nikolai. *Russkaia partiia: Dvizhenie russkikh natsionalistov v SSSR, 1953–1985 gody.* Moscow, 2003.

Molotov, Igor. *Chernaia diuzhina. Obshchestvo smelykh.* Moscow, 2017.

Morrison, Donald. "Mikhail Gorbachev of the Soviet Union." *Time*, January 4, 1988. https://time.com/archive/6711213/mikhail-gorbachev-of-the-soviet-union/.

Poltoranin, Mikhail. *Vlast v trotilovom ėkvivalente: Iz tainikov igornogo Kremlia.* Moscow, 2010.

Pribylovskii, Vladimir. *Slovar novykh politicheskikh partii i organizatsii Rossii.* Moscow, 1993.

Reagan, Nancy, and William Novak. *My Turn: The Memoirs of Nancy Reagan.* New York: Random House, 1989.

Rost, Iurii. *Sakharov. "Kefir nado gret'": Istoriia liubvi, rasskazannaia Elenoï Bonner Iuriiu Rostu.* Moscow, 2018.

Rybin, Aleksei. *Trikita: BG, Maik, Tsoi.* Saint Petersburg, 2013.

Sakharov, Andrei. *Vospominaniia.* Moscow, 1996.

Shnirelman, Viktor. *Ariiskii mif v sovremennom mire.* Moscow, 2015.

Shultz, George P. *Turmoil and Triumph: My Years as Secretary of State.* New York: Charles Scribner's Sons, 1993.

Snegirev, Vladimir. *Aleksandr Yakovlev. Chuzhoi sredi svoikh. Partiinai zhizn "arkhitektora perestroiki."* Moscow, 2023.

Solzhenitsyn, Aleksandr. "Ugodilo zernyshko promezh dvukh zhernovov: Ocherki izgnaniia." *Novy Mir*, no. 9, 11 (1998); no. 2 (1999); no. 9, 12 (2000); no. 4 (2001); no. 11 (2003).

Stingray, Joanna, and Madison Stingray. *Stingrei v Strane Chudes.* Moscow, 2019.

Stingray, Joanna, and Madison Stingray. *Stingrei v Zazerkale.* Moscow, 2019.

Taubman, William. *Gorbachev: His Life and Times*. W. W. Norton, 2017.

Troitskii, Artemii. *Istoriia sovetskogo roka*. Moscow, 1990.

Troitsky, Artemy. *Back in the USSR: The True Story of Rock in Russia*. Boston and London: Faber and Faber, 1988.

Tsoi, Marianna. *Viktor Tsoi. Tochka otscheta*. Moscow, 1991.

Tsoi, Marianna, and Aleksandr Zhitinskii. *Viktor Tsoi. Stikhi, dokumenty, vospominaniia*. Leningrad, 1991.

Tupitsyna, Margarita, and Viktor Tupitsyn. "Beseda s Timurom i Afrikoi." RISK: Al'manakh, vol. 1. Moscow: ARGO-RISK, 1995. https://www.vavilon.ru/metatext /risk1/tupitsyn.html.

Verkhovskii, Aleksandr, and Vladimir Pribylovskii. *Natsional-patriocheskie organizatsii v Rossii. Istoriia, ideologiia, ekstremistskie tendentsii*. Moscow, 1996.

V Politbiuro TsK KPSS . . . Po zapisiam Anatoliia Cherniaeva, Vadima Medvedeva, Georgiia Shakhnazarova (1985–1991). Moscow, 2008.

Waal, Thomas de. *Black Garden: Armenia and Azerbaijan Through Peace and War*. New York and London: New York University Press, 2013.

Yakovlev, Aleksandr. *Omut pamiati*. Moscow, 2000.

Yeltsin, Boris. *Ispoved na zadannuiu temu*. Moscow, 2008.

Zhitinskii, Aleksandr. *Tsoi Forever*. Saint Petersburg, 2012.

CHAPTER 6: FULL STOP

Alizadeh, Zardusht, and Rasim Agaev. *The End of the Second Republic*. Moscow: Granitsa, 2006.

Author's interview with Boris Grebenshchikov.

Author's interview with Dmitri Muratov.

Author's interview with Garry Kasparov.

Author's interview with Levon Ter-Petrosyan.

Author's interview with Vazgen Manukyan.

Author's interview with Viktor Alksnis.

Author's interview with Vitaly Korotich.

Author's interview with Vytautas Landsbergis.

Chernyaev, Anatoly. *Sovmestnyi iskhod. Dnevnik dvukh èpokh. 1972–1991*. Moscow, 2008.

Drannikov, Valerii. "Nikolai Ryzhkov: eto byl dlia nas zhutkii urok." *Kommersant*, December 8, 1998. https://www.kommersant.ru/doc/15016.

Gdlyan, Telman, and Nikolai Ivanov. *Kremlevskoe delo*. Moscow, 1994.

Kalgin, Vitalii. *Viktor Tsoi. Svoimi slovami. Kniga interviu. 1983–1990*. Moscow, 2003.

Katanian, Vasilii. *Paradzhanov. Tsena vechnogo prazdnika*. Moscow, 1994.

Korotich, Vitalii. *Ot pervogo litsa*. Moscow, 2018.

Lieven, Anatol. *The Baltic Revolution: Estonia, Latvia, Lithuania and the Path to Independence*. Yale University Press, 1994.

Rykovtseva, Elena. "Volosatyi kulak." *Radio Svoboda*, June 25, 2014. https://www.svoboda .org/a/25423506.html.

Sakharov, Andrei. *Vospominaniia*. Moscow, 1996.

Snegirev, Vladimir. *Aleksandr Yakovlev. Chuzhoi sredi svoikh. Partiinai zhizn "arkhitektora perestroiki."* Moscow, 2023.

Solzhenitsyn, Aleksandr. "Ugodilo zernyshko promezh dvukh zhernovov: Ocherki izgnaniia." *Novy Mir*, no. 9, 11 (1998); no. 2 (1999); no. 9, 12 (2000); no. 4 (2001); no. 11 (2003).

Taubman, William. *Gorbachev: His Life and Times*. W. W. Norton, 2017.

Vaksberg, Arkady. "Burnye aplodismenty." *Literaturnaya Gazeta*, no. 38 (September 21, 1988).

V Politbiuro TsK KPSS . . . Po zapisiam Anatoliia Cherniaeva, Vadima Medvedeva, Georgiia Shakhnazarova (1985–1991). Moscow, 2008.

Waal, Thomas de. *Black Garden: Armenia and Azerbaijan Through Peace and War*. New York and London: New York University Press, 2013.

Yakovlev, Aleksandr. *Omut pamiati*. Moscow, 2000.

CHAPTER 7: SEASICK ALONG THE WAY

Aleksandrova, Mariia, Liubov Afonina, and Elena Bazhenova. *Istoriia Kitaia s drevneishikh vremen do nachala XXI veka. Tom 9: Reformy i modernizatsiia (1976–2009)*. Moscow, 2016.

Alizadeh, Zardusht, and Rasim Agaev. *The End of the Second Republic*. Moscow; Granitsa, 2006.

Author's interview with Akaki Asatiani.

Author's interview with Alexander Lyubimov.

Author's interview with Arkady Murashov.

Author's interview with Garry Kasparov.

Author's interview with Gennady Burbulis.

Author's interview with Ingeborga Dapkūnaitė.

Author's interview with Joanna Stingray.

Author's interview with Ksenia Sobchak.

Author's interview with Lev Ponomaryov.

Author's interview with Lyudmila Narusova.

Author's interview with Mikhail Gorbachev.

Author's interview with Sergei Stankevich.

Author's interview with Viktor Alksnis.

Author's interview with Vytautas Landsbergis.

Balasubramanian, Radha. "The Similarities Between Mikahil Bulgakov's *The Master and Margarita* and Salman Rushdie's *The Satanic Verses*." *International Fiction Review*, 1995.

Barmé, Geremie. "Confession, redemption, and death: Liu Xiaobo and the protest movement of 1989." In *The Broken Mirror: China after Tiananmen*, edited by George Hicks. Longman, 1990, 52–99.

Brown, Jeremy. *June Fourth: The Tiananmen Protests and Beijing Massacre of 1989*. Cambridge University Press, 2021.

Chaikovskaya, Olga. "Mif." *Literaturnaya Gazeta*, no. 21 (May 24, 1989).

Chernyaev, Anatoly. *Sovmestnyi iskhod. Dnevnik dvukh èpokh. 1972–1991*. Moscow, 2008.

Dobbs, Michael. "The Kremlin: 'A Sad Return to the Days of Gunboat Diplomacy.'" *Washington Post*, December 20, 1989. https://www.washingtonpost.com/archive/politics/1989/12/21/the-kremlin/d49649ca-bda5-4138-b24e-174ccd866270/.

Dodolev, Evgenii. *The Vzgliad. Bitly Perestroiki*. Moscow, 2011.

Galenovich, Iurii. *Chzhao Tszyian i reformy v Kitae*. Moscow, 2012.

Gdlyan, Telman, and Nikolai Ivanov. *Kremlevskoe delo*. Moscow, 1994.

Gevorkian, Natalia, Andrei Kolesnikov, and Natalia Timakova. *Ot pervogo litsa: Razgovory s Vladimirom Putinym*. Moscow, 2000.

Grebenshchikov, Boris. *Kratkii otchet o 16-ti godakh zvukozapisi*. 1997.

Grebenshchikov, Boris. *Zdes' tak zabavno*. Kharkiv, 1992.

Hendrickson, Paul. "Yeltsin's Smashing Day." *Washington Post*, September 12, 1989. https://www.washingtonpost.com/archive/lifestyle/1989/09/13/yeltsins-smashing-day/8c33cb83-3752-4ea8-af55-e9dd9e997225/.

Ignatius, David. "Why Bob Gates Is the Eeyore of Sovietology." *Washington Post*, May 27, 1989. https://www.washingtonpost.com/archive/opinions/1989/05/28/why-bob-gates-is-the-eeyore-of-sovietology/472befc3-a054-4301-a491-221dc4adf560/.

Kalgin, Vitalii. *Viktor Tsoi. Svoimi slovami. Kniga interviu. 1983–1990*. Moscow, 2003.

Keller, Bill. "Soviet Writers, and Government, Avoid Public Outcry on Rushdie." *New York Times*, February 24, 1989. https://www.nytimes.com/1989/02/24/world/soviet-writers-and-government-avoid-public-outcry-on-rushdie.html.

Ling, Chai. "Interview at Tiananmen Square with Chai Ling." *Asia for Educators*, Weatherhead East Asian Institute, Columbia University. https://afe.easia.columbia.edu/special/china_1950_chailing.htm.

Moore, Molly. "Cheney Predicts Gorbachev Will Fail, Be Replaced." *Washington Post*, April 28, 1989. https://www.washingtonpost.com/archive/politics/1989/04/29/cheney-predicts-gorbachev-will-fail-be-replaced/bf9e3626-8940-4eda-8afe-902bef92bd35/.

Pervyi Sezd narodnykh deputatov SSSR. Stenograficheskii Otchet. Moscow, 1989.

Putin, Vladimir, Nataliya Gevorkyan, Natalya Timakova, and Andrei Kolesnikov. *First Person: An Astonishingly Frank Self-Portrait by Russia's President*. PublicAffairs, 2000.

Rost, Iurii. *Sakharov. "Kefir nado gret'": Istoriia liubvi, rasskazannaia Elenoï Bonner Iuriiu Rostu*. Moscow, 2018.

Sakharov, Andrei. *Vospominaniia*. Moscow, 1996.

Schweisberg, David R. "China declares martial law." *UPI*, May 20, 1989. https://www.upi.com/Archives/1989/05/20/China-declares-martial-law/8922611640000/.

Sobchak, Anatoly. *Khozhdenie vo vlast*. Moscow, 1991.

Solzhenitsyn, Aleksandr. "Ugodilo zernyshko promezh dvukh zhernovov: Ocherki izgnaniia." *Novy Mir*, no. 9, 11 (1998); no. 2 (1999); no. 9, 12 (2000); no. 4 (2001); no. 11 (2003).

Southerland, Dan. "Liu Xiaobo: A Reporter Looks Back." *Radio Free Asia*, July 13, 2017. https://www.rfa.org/english/commentaries/liu-reporter-07132017165434.html.

Stingray, Joanna, and Madison Stingray. *Stingrei v Strane Chudes*. Moscow, 2019.

Stingray, Joanna, and Madison Stingray. *Stingrei v Zazerkale*. Moscow, 2019.

Sukhanov, Lev. *Kak Eltsin stal prezidentom. Zapiski pervogo pomoshchnika*. Moscow, 2011.

Taubman, William. *Gorbachev: His Life and Times*. W. W. Norton, 2017.

Voshchanov, Pavel. *Yeltsin kak navazhdenie. Zapiski politicheskogo prokhodimtsa*. Moscow, 2019.

Wheatley, Jonathan. *Georgia from National Awakening to Rose Revolution: Delayed Transition in the Former Soviet Union*. Routledge, 2016.

Yeltsin, Boris. *Ispoved na zadannuiu temu*. Moscow, 2008.

CHAPTER 8: HEAD-ON COLLISION

Alizadeh, Zardusht, and Rasim Agaev. *The End of the Second Republic.* Moscow: Granitsa, 2006.

Atkinson, Rick. *Crusade: The Untold Story of the Persian Gulf War.* Mariner Books, 1994.

Author's interview with Akaki Asatiani.

Author's interview with Albina Nazimova.

Author's interview with Alexander Lyubimov.

Author's interview with Alexander Nevzorov.

Author's interview with Arkady Murashov.

Author's interview with Askar Akayev.

Author's interview with Boris Grebenshchikov.

Author's interview with Elena Lukianova.

Author's interview with Garry Kasparov.

Author's interview with Gennady Burbulis.

Author's interview with Grigory Yavlinsky.

Author's interview with Jack F. Matlock Jr.

Author's interview with Levon Ter-Petrosyan.

Author's interview with Lev Ponomaryov.

Author's interview with Lyudmila Narusova.

Author's interview with Mikhail Borshchevskii.

Author's interview with Olga Starovoytova.

Author's interview with Platon Borshchevskii.

Author's interview with Ruslan Linkov.

Author's interview with Sergei Baburin.

Author's interview with Sergei Filatov.

Author's interview with Vazgen Manukyan.

Author's interview with Viktor Alksnis.

Author's interview with Vitaly Korotich.

Author's interview with Vytautas Landsbergis.

Balaghi, Shiva. *Saddam Hussein: A Biography.* Greenwich Press, 2008.

Chernyaev, Anatoly. *Sovmestnyi iskhod. Dnevnik dvukh ėpokh. 1972–1991.* Moscow, 2008.

Chetvertyi Sezd narodnykh deputatov SSSR, 17–27 dekabria 1990 g. Stenograficheskii otchet. Vols. 1–4. Moscow, 1991.

Dodolev, Evgenii. *The Vzgliad. Bitly Perestroiki.* Moscow, 2011.

Fabrikant, Geraldine. "Yetnikoff Stepping Down as Chief of CBS Records." *New York Times,* September 5, 1990. https://www.nytimes.com/1990/09/05/business/yetnikoff -stepping-down-as-chief-of-cbs-records.html.

Finlan, Alastair. *The Gulf War 1991.* Osprey, 2003.

Freedman, Lawrence, and Efraim Karsh. *The Gulf Conflict 1990–1991: Diplomacy and War in the New World Order.* Princeton, NJ: Princeton University Press, 1993.

Gevorkian, Natalia, Andrei Kolesnikov, and Natalia Timakova. *Ot pervogo litsa: Razgovory s Vladimirom Putinym.* Moscow, 2000.

Goldstein, Patrick. "New Book on Music Industry Is No Hit With the 'Hit Men.'" *Los Angeles Times,* August 5, 1990. https://www.latimes.com/archives/la-xpm-1990-08-05 -ca-55-story.html.

Gorbachev, Mikhail. *Naedine s soboi.* Moscow, 2012.

Grachev, Andrei. *Dalshe bez menia . . . Ukhod Prezidenta.* Moscow, 1994.

Grachev, Andrei. *Gorbachev.* Moscow, 2001.

Grachev, Andrei. *Kremlevskaia khronika.* Moscow, 1994.

Grachev, Andrei. *Poslednii den SSSR. Svidetelstvo ochevidtsa. Vospominaniia pomoshchnika prezidenta Sovetskogo Soiuza.* Moscow, 2022.

Grossman, Mark. *Encyclopedia of the Persian Gulf War.* ABC-CLIO, 1995.

Guseinov, Vagif. *Bolshe, chem odna zhizn.* Moscow, 2013.

Hiro, Dilip. *Desert Shield to Desert Storm: The Second Gulf War.* Routledge, 1992.

Hurst, Steven. *The United States and Iraq since 1979: Hegemony, Oil and War.* Edinburgh University Press, 2009.

Kalgin, Vitalii. *Viktor Tsoi.* Moscow, 2015.

Kalgin, Vitalii. *Viktor Tsoi. Svoimi slovami. Kniga interviu. 1983–1990.* Moscow, 2003.

Karsh, Efraim, and Inari Rautsi. *Saddam Hussein: A Political Biography.* Grove Press, 2002.

Keller, Bill. "Hip, Hot and Hyper: Soviet TV Cuts Loose." *New York Times,* September 7, 1989. http://nytimes.com/1989/09/07/arts/hip-hot-and-hyper-soviet-tv-cuts-loose.html.

Korotich, Vitalii. *Ot pervogo litsa.* Moscow, 2018.

Lieven, Anatol. *The Baltic Revolution: Estonia, Latvia, Lithuania and the Path to Independence.* Yale University Press, 1994.

Ligachev, Egor. *Predosterezhenie.* Moscow, 1999.

Lowry, Richard S. *The Gulf War Chronicles: A Military History of the First War with Iraq.* Lincoln, NE: iUniverse, 2008.

Lukyanov, Anatoly. *Perevorot mnimyi i nastoiashchii.* Moscow, 1993.

Mamardashvili, Merab. "Veriu v zdravyi smysl." *Molodezh Gruzii,* September 21, 1990. https://web.archive.org/web/20201022073329/https://mamardashvili.com/ru/merab-mamardashvili/publikacii-iz-arhiva/interview/veryu-v-zdravyj-smysl.

Matlock, Jack. *Autopsy on an Empire: The American Ambassador's Account of the Collapse of the Soviet Union.* New York, 1994.

Nevzorov, Alexander. *Pole chesti.* Saint Petersburg, 1995.

Putin, Vladimir, Nataliya Gevorkyan, Natalya Timakova, and Andrei Kolesnikov. *First Person: An Astonishingly Frank Self-Portrait by Russia's President.* PublicAffairs, 2000.

Remnick, David. *Lenin's Tomb: The Last Days of the Soviet Empire.* New York: Vintage Books, 1994.

Rybin, Aleksei. *Trikita: BG, Maik, Tsoi.* Saint Petersburg, 2013.

Semanov, S. "Dnevnik 1990 goda." *Novoe literaturnoe obozrenie,* no. 84 (2007).

Shaking Hands with Saddam Hussein: The U.S. Tilts Toward Iraq, 1980–1984. National Security Archive Electronic Briefing Book No. 82.

Simons, Geoff. *Iraq: From Sumer to Saddam,* second edition. New York: St. Martin's Press, 1996.

Solzhenitsyn, Aleksandr. *Kak nam obustroit Rossiiu: Posil'nye soobrazheniia.* Leningrad, 1990.

Stingray, Joanna, and Madison Stingray. *Stingrei v Strane Chudes.* Moscow, 2019.

Stingray, Joanna, and Madison Stingray. *Stingrei v Zazerkale.* Moscow, 2019.

"Strana ustala zhdat." *Moskovskie novosti*, November 18, 1990.

Taubman, William. *Gorbachev: His Life and Times*. W. W. Norton, 2017.

Troitskii, Artemii. *Istoriia sovetskogo roka*. Moscow, 1990.

Tsoi, Marianna. *Viktor Tsoi. Tochka otscheta*. Moscow, 1991.

Tsoi, Marianna, and Aleksandr Zhitinskii. *Viktor Tsoi. Stikhi, dokumenty, vospominaniia*. Leningrad, 1991.

Vneocherednoi tretii Sezd narodnykh deputatov SSSR, 12–15 marta 1990 g. Stenograficheskii otchet. Vols. 1–3. Moscow, 1990.

Vtoroĭ sezd narodnykh deputatov SSSR, 12-24 dekabria 1989 g. Stenograficheskiĭ otchet. Moscow, 1990.

Waal, Thomas de. *Black Garden: Armenia and Azerbaijan Through Peace and War*. New York and London: New York University Press, 2013.

Winship, Frederick M. "Yetnikoff Steps Down as CBS Records Chief." *Washington Post*, September 5, 1990. https://www.washingtonpost.com/archive/business/1990/09/06/yetnikoff-steps-down-as-cbs-records-chief/501a56a1-106a-4ac2-ab0a-3c13c7f8d58d/.

Zhitinskii, Aleksandr. *Tsoi Forever*. Saint Petersburg, 2012.

Zubok, Vladislav M. *Collapse: The Fall of the Soviet Union*. New Haven, CT: Yale University Press, 2021.

CHAPTER 9: A VACATION AFTER THE WAR

Atkinson, Rick. *Crusade: The Untold Story of the Persian Gulf War*. Mariner Books, 1994.

Author's interview with Akaki Asatiani.

Author's interview with Alexander Korzhakov.

Author's interview with Alexander Lyubimov.

Author's interview with Alexander Nevzorov.

Author's interview with Anatoly Chubais.

Author's interview with Andrei Dunayev.

Author's interview with Andrei Kozyrev.

Author's interview with Arkady Murashov.

Author's interview with Askar Akayev.

Author's interview with Boris Grebenshchikov.

Author's interview with Dmitri Muratov.

Author's interview with Elena Lukianova.

Author's interview with Gennady Burbulis.

Author's interview with Grigory Yavlinsky.

Author's interview with Ihor Yukhnovskyi.

Author's interview with Ingeborga Dapkūnaitė.

Author's interview with Yuri Feklistov.

Author's interview with Jack F. Matlock Jr.

Author's interview with Konstantin Kagalovsky.

Author's interview with Leonid Kravchuk.

Author's interview with Levon Ter-Petrosiyan.

Author's interview with Lev Ponomarev.

Author's interview with Lyudmila Narusova.

Author's interview with Mikhail Gorbachev.

Author's interview with Natalia Dollezhal.

Author's interview with Oleg Baklanov.

Author's interview with Olga Slobodskaya.

Author's interview with Pavel Grachev.

Author's interview with Petr Aven.

Author's interview with Petru Lucinschi.

Author's interview with Sergei Baburin.

Author's interview with Sergei Krasavchenko.

Author's interview with Sergei Stankevich.

Author's interview with Stanislav Shushkevich.

Author's interview with Stepan Khmara.

Author's interview with Vasily Shakhnovsky.

Author's interview with Viktor Alksnis.

Author's interview with Viktor Ivanenko.

Author's interview with Vladimir Zhirinovsky.

Author's interview with Vytautas Landsbergis.

Bakatin, Vadim. *Doroga v proshedshem vremeni.* Moscow, 1999.

Bakatin, Vadim. *Izbavlenie ot KGB.* Moscow, 1992.

Baker, James A. *The Politics of Diplomacy: Revolution, War, and Peace, 1989–1992.* New York: G. P. Putnam's Sons, 1995.

Balaghi, Shiva. *Saddam Hussein: A Biography.* Greenwich Press, 2008.

Barakhova, Alla. "Den banditizma, terrorizma i proizvola." *Kommersant*, September 6, 2001. https://www.kommersant.ru/doc/281761.

Beschloss, Michael, and Strobe Talbott. *At the Highest Levels: The Inside Story of the End of the Cold War.* New York: Little, Brown, 1993.

Bush, George H. W. Speech in Kyiv, August 1, 1991 (Chicken Kiev speech).

Bush, George H. W., and Brent Scowcroft. *A World Transformed.* Alfred A. Knopf, 1998.

Cheney, Dick. *In My Time: A Personal and Political Memoir.* New York: Threshold Editions, 2011.

Chernyaev, Anatoly. *Sovmestnyi iskhod. Dnevnik dvukh e pokh. 1972–1991.* Moscow, 2008.

Declassified CIA files, CIA Freedom of Information Act Electronic Reading Room.

Declassified Memoranda of Conversations between George H. W. Bush and Mikhail Gorbachev, James Baker and Mikhail Gorbachev, George H. W. Bush and Eduard Shevardnadze, James Baker and Eduard Shevardnadze, George H. W. Bush and Boris Yeltsin, George H. W. Bush and Leonid Kravchuk, George H. W. Bush and Stanislav Shushkevich, George H. W. Bush and Nursultan Nazarbayev.

Documents on U.S.-Soviet Relations published by Wilson Center Digital Archive.

Finlan, Alastair. *The Gulf War 1991.* Osprey, 2003.

Freedman, Lawrence, and Efraim Karsh. *The Gulf Conflict 1990–1991: Diplomacy and War in the New World Order.* Princeton, NJ: Princeton University Press, 1993.

Fukuyama, Francis. *The End of History and the Last Man.* Free Press, 1992.

Gaidar, Egor. *Dni porazhenii i pobed.* Moscow: Vagrius, 1997.

Gaidar, Egor. *Gibel imperii. Uroki dlia sovremennoi Rossii.* Moscow: ROSSPEN, 2006.

Gaidar, Egor. *Vlast i sobstvennost: Smuty i instituty. Gosudarstvo i yvoluliutsiia.* Saint Petersburg, 2009.

Gaidar, Egor, and Anatolii Chubais. *Razvilki noveishei istorii Rossii.* Saint Petersburg, 2011.

Garthoff, Raymond L. *The Great Transition: American-Soviet Relations and the End of the Cold War.* Brookings Institution Press, 1994.

Grachev, Andrei. *Dalshe bez menia . . . Ukhod Prezidenta.* Moscow, 1994.

Grachev, Andrei. *Gorbachev.* Moscow, 2001.

Grachev, Andrei. *Kremlevskaia khronika.* Moscow, 1994.

Grachev, Andrei. *Poslednii den SSSR. Svidetelstvo ochevidtsa. Vospominaniia pomoshchnika prezidenta Sovetskogo Soiuza.* Moscow, 2022.

Grossman, Mark. *Encyclopedia of the Persian Gulf War.* ABC-CLIO, 1995.

Hiro, Dilip. *Desert Shield to Desert Storm: The Second Gulf War.* Routledge, 1992.

Hurst, Steven. *The United States and Iraq Since 1979: Hegemony, Oil and War.* Edinburgh University Press, 2009.

Karsh, Efraim, and Inari Rautsi. *Saddam Hussein: A Political Biography.* Grove Press, 2002.

Khomenko, Sviatoslav. "Kak Leonid Kravchuk sporil s Gorbachevym, razvalil SSSR, a v kontse proslezilsia." BBC, December 8, 2021. https://www.bbc.com/russian /features-59492080.

Korotich, Vitalii. *Ot pervogo litsa.* Moscow, 2018.

"Lenin—grib." *Piatoe Koleso*, January 1991.

Lieven, Anatol. *The Baltic Revolution: Estonia, Latvia, Lithuania and the Path to Independence.* Yale University Press, 1994.

Ligachev, Egor. *Predosterezhenie.* Moscow, 1999.

Lowry, Richard S. *The Gulf War Chronicles: A Military History Of the First War with Iraq.* Lincoln, NE: iUniverse, 2008.

Lukyanov, Anatoly. *Avgust 91-go. Byl li zagovor?* Moscow, 2010.

Lukyanov, Anatoly. *Perevorot mnimyi i nastoiashchii.* Moscow, 1993.

Mandelbaum, Michael, and Strobe Talbott. *Reagan and Gorbachev.* New York: Vintage Books, 1987.

Matlock, Jack. *Autopsy on an Empire: The American Ambassador's Account of the Collapse of the Soviet Union.* New York, 1994.

Medvedev, Vadim. *V komande Gorbacheva: vzgliad iznutri.* Moscow, 1994.

Memorandum of Telephone Conversation between George H. W. Bush and Boris Yeltsin, November 30, 1991. https://bush41library.tamu.edu/files/memcons-telcons /1991-11-30--Yeltsin.pdf.

"Mikhail Gorbachev: za svoiu stranu otvechaem my, a ne Zapad." Interfax, December 24, 2021. https://www.interfax.ru/russia/812178.

Oberdorfer, Don. *From the Cold War to a New Era: The United States and the Soviet Union, 1983–1991.* Baltimore: Johns Hopkins University Press, 1998.

Palazhchenko, Pavel. *Professiia i vremia.* Zapiski perevodchika-diplomata. Moscow: *Novaya gazeta*, 2020.

Prokhanov, Alexander. *Slovo k narodu.* Moscow, 2013.

Remnick, David. *Lenin's Tomb: The Last Days of the Soviet Empire.* New York: Vintage Books, 1994.

Ryzhkov, Nikolai. *Desiatlet velikikh potriasenii.* Moscow, 1995.

Savranskaya, Svetlana, Thomas Blanton, and Vladislav Zubok (eds.). *Masterpieces of History: The Peaceful End of the Cold War in Europe, 1989.* Central European University Press, 2010.

Sell, Louis. *From Washington to Moscow: US-Soviet Relations and the Collapse of the USSR.* Durham, NC: Duke University Press, 2016.

Shaking Hands with Saddam Hussein: The U.S. Tilts Toward Iraq, 1980–1984. National Security Archive Electronic Briefing Book No. 82.

Shushkevich, Stanislav. *Moia zhizn. Krushenie i voskreshenie SSSR.* Moscow, 2012.

Simons, Geoff. *Iraq: From Sumer to Saddam*, second edition. New York: St. Martin's Press, 1996.

Snegirev, Vladimir. *Aleksandr Yakolev. Chuzhoi sredi svoikh. Partiinai zhizn "arkhitektora perestroiki."* Moscow, 2023.

Solomentsev, Mikhail. *Zachistka v Politibiuro. Kak Gorbachev ubiral vragov perestoiki.* Moscow 2011.

Solzhenitsyn, Aleksandr. *Kak nam obustroit Rossiiu: Posil'nye soobrazheniia.* Leningrad: Sovetskii pisatel, 1990.

Solzhenitsyn, Aleksandr. "Ugodilo zernyshko promezh dvukh zhernovov: Ocherki izgnaniia." *Novy Mir*, no. 9, 11 (1998); no. 2 (1999); no. 9, 12 (2000); no. 4 (2001); no. 11 (2003).

Stepankov, Valentin, and Evgenii Lisov. *Kremlevskiii zagovor. Versiia sledstviia.* Moscow, 1992.

Sukhanov, Lev. *Kak Eltsin stal prezidentom. Zapiski pervogo pomoshchnika.* Moscow, 2011.

Talbott, Strobe. *Endgame: The Inside Story of SALT II.* New York: Harper & Row, 1980.

Talbott, Strobe. *The Russia Hand: A Memoir of Presidential Diplomacy.* New York, 2003.

Talbott, Strobe. *The Russians and Reagan.* New York: Vintage Books, 1984.

"Tengiz Sigua: podderzhka GKChP stala rokovoi oshibkoĭ Zviada Gamsakhurdia." RIA Novosti, August 19, 2011. https://ria.ru/20110819/415754772.html.

Viets, Susan. *Picnic at the Iron Curtain: A Memoir. From the Fall of the Berlin Wall to Ukraine's Orange Revolution.* Delfryn Books, 2012.

Vorotnikov, Vitalii. *Khronika absurda. Otdelenie Rossie ot SSSR.* Moscow, 2011.

Voshchanov, Pavel. *Yeltsin kak navazhdenie. Zapiski politicheskogo prokhodimtsa.* Moscow, 2019.

Yakovlev, Aleksandr. *Omut pamiati.* Moscow, 2000.

Yazov, Dmitrii. *Marshal Sovestkogo Soiuza.* Moscow, 2010.

Zubok, Vladislav M. *Collapse: The Fall of the Soviet Union.* New Haven, CT: Yale University Press, 2021.

Zyuganov, Gennady. "Arkhitektor u razvalin." *Sovetskaia Rossiia*, May 7, 1991.

ILLUSTRATION AND MAP CREDITS

PHOTO INSERT

1. Picture Alliance / Valentin Mastyukov/TASS
2. No Credit
3. Corbis via Getty Images
4. Sophie Bassouls/Sygma via Getty Images
5. Yuri Mechitov
6. Yuri Rost
7. Joanna Stingray
8. Garry Kasparov's personal archive
9. Ukrinform
10. Alla Pugacheva's personal archive
11. Bettmann Archive via Getty Images
12. Fred Grinberg/RIA Novosti archive
13. Photolure News Agency
14. No Credit
15. No Credit
16. No Credit
17. Picture Alliance/AP Photo
18. Dmitri Lovetsky/Picture Alliance/AP Photo
19. No Credit
20. Grigory Yavlinsky's personal archive
21. Yuri Feklistov

MAPS

Maps on pages xii–xiii and 486–487 by Olga Terekhova

INDEX

ABOUT THE AUTHOR

Mikhail Zygar is a journalist, writer, and filmmaker, and the founding editor in chief of Russian news channel Dozhd, which provided an alternative to Kremlin-controlled federal TV channels by giving a platform to opposition voices. The recipient of an International Press Freedom Award, Zygar writes a weekly column for *Der Spiegel* and also writes for the *New York Times*, *Time* magazine, *Vanity Fair*, and *Foreign Affairs*. He is also the author of *All the Kremlin's Men*, *The Empire Must Die*, and *War and Punishment*. Currently a guest lecturer at Columbia University, he lives in New York with his husband.